Examining Emotional Fatigue and Social Indifference in the New Media Era

Ayten Bengisu Cansever Bayhan
https://orcid.org/0000-0002-1165-7273
Istanbul Gelisim University, Turkey

IGI Global
Scientific Publishing
Publishing Tomorrow's Research Today

Vice President of Editorial	Melissa Wagner
Director of Acquisitions	Mikaela Felty
Director of Book Development	Jocelynn Hessler
Production Manager	Mike Brehm
Cover Design	Jose Rosado

Published in the United States of America by
IGI Global Scientific Publishing
701 East Chocolate Avenue
Hershey, PA, 17033, USA
Tel: 717-533-8845 | Fax: 717-533-7115
Website: https://www.igi-global.com E-mail: cust@igi-global.com

Library of Congress Cataloging-in-Publication Data

LCCN: 2026004848 (CIP Data Pending)
ISBN13: 9798337383071
Isbn13Softcover: 9798337383088
EISBN13: 9798337383095

British Cataloguing in Publication Data
A Cataloguing in Publication record for this book is available from the British Library.

Table of Contents

Detailed Table of Contents

Digital burnout has emerged as a defining condition of contemporary platformed life, closely linked to the commodification of human attention. This chapter critically examines how digital platforms are designed to intensify cognitive load, fragment attention, and normalize exhaustion. Drawing on critical media theory, political economy, and cognitive psychology, it argues that burnout is a structural outcome of attention economies driven by algorithmic optimization and surveillance capitalism, rather than an individual failure of self-regulation. The concept of attention collapse is introduced to describe the erosion of sustained focus and emotional resilience under constant stimulation. By situating fatigue within broader socio-technical systems, the chapter highlights the implications for education and democratic participation, calling for attention to be reconceptualized as a shared social and ethical resource.

This book chapter examines social media within the context of digital labor regimes, focusing on how users—particularly influencers—strategically and performatively manage emotions. It argues that social media transforms individuals not only into content creators but also into digital emotional laborers who regulate emotions to sustain visibility and engagement. The concept of emotional labor is adapted to the digital context and analyzed through the commodification of emotions, algorithmic incentives, and the attention economy. Within platform capitalism, user interactions and emotional expressions are converted into economic value, while self-branding and authenticity performances shape influencer culture. The chapter further explores visibility labor and relational labor, addressing digital emotional fatigue and burnout, and demonstrates how emotions on social media have shifted from individual expression to a platform-regulated form of labor.

nature of internet memes as a form of digital communication, and commodity of affective economies.

As evidenced by a variety of AI-induced ethical predicaments, it is now imperative to reassess the ethical norms governing humans from a broadened perspective, integrating AI. In this extended S–O–R model, this paper investigates how exposure to AI leads to emotional exhaustion and antisocial behaviour. Employing a research approach that combines the use of Partial Least Squares Structural Equation Modelling (PLS-SEM) in analysing a sample of 412 subjects, further data will be obtained through thematic analysis about emotional anaesthesia. Research shows that the relationship between algorithmic stimuli and social indifference is mediated by emotional fatigue, and that the negative effects of its experiential nature are inevitably offset by the positive effects of this mediation on this behaviour, which is beneficial. This research thus demonstrates how emotional fatigue plays a determining role in helping people detach from certain stimuli by connecting it with affective relations in the era of algorithms.

The rapid growth of digital technologies has transformed the way individuals experience, express, and manage emotions. While social media platforms have enhanced connectivity and access to information, they have also created an environment of continuous emotional exposure and cognitive overload. This chapter explores the emerging phenomenon of digital emotional fatigue and its link with rising social indifference in the digital age. It argues that constant interaction with emotionally intense content ranging from global crises to personal narratives gradually leads to emotional exhaustion, desensitization, and reduced empathetic engagement. he chapter further examines the role of algorithm-driven systems in shaping emotional experiences by prioritizing engagement over well-being, often amplifying high-arousal content. It also highlights the growing importance of

In the contemporary digital media ecosystem, audiences are exposed to an unprecedented volume of news through 24-hour news cycles, social media platforms, and algorithm-driven information flows. While this constant connectivity increases access to information, it also contributes to emotional fatigue, psychological exhaustion, and growing social indifference among media consumers. This chapter examines how continuous exposure to crisis imagery, breaking news alerts, and repetitive narratives of conflict and disaster shapes the emotional well-being of contemporary audiences. Drawing on perspectives from media studies, psychology, and digital communication, it explores the concept of "screens of solitude," where individuals remain constantly connected yet experience emotional isolation and cognitive overload. The chapter also analyzes the roles of algorithmic amplification, doomscrolling, and mediated trauma in shaping audience responses to news consumption and discusses the need for responsible journalism and mindful media engagement.

Social media emotional labour, in which users consciously display, manage, and control their emotions in order to meet societal expectations and maintain their online presence, is an essential part of digital connection. Users, particularly professionals, influencers, and empathy, service workers, should foster optimism and engagement, as this chapter investigates how platforms like Facebook, Instagram, LinkedIn, and Twitter (X) impact emotional expression. From a sociological and psychological perspective, this chapter examines digital settings' surface and deep actions, with a focus on how constant exposure and connectivity heighten emotional needs. Various mental health issues, such as burnout, stress, emotional tiredness, and anxiety, are discussed as a result of emotional labour.

The essay discusses the rising likelihood of emotional burnout and social isolation resulting from the digital revolution, which transforms human interactions, work, and socializing. It explores the negative implications of prolonged engagement with social media and virtual communication on mental health and social cohesion, supported by recent psychological and human-computer interaction research. The paper proposes strategies to mitigate digital fatigue, including digital detox and mindful technology use, while also addressing the role of workplace and educational initiatives in maintaining social connections. It advocates for a comprehensive approach to promote well-being that harmonizes the benefits of digital connectivity with emotionally healthy practices and sustainable social engagement, highlighting the need for supportive digital experiences that foster both connection and health.

The explosion of digital media has led to greater public exposure to violent and misogynistic content, on social media, in the news, and throughout the entertainment system. This chapter examines the emotional fatigue as an important psychological nutrient related to overexposure to gender-biased and violent media representations. Drawing on theories of media effects, the theorisation of feminism in relation to the media, and different models of emotional exhaustion, the chapter investigates how continued exposure to the media stimuli of distress may result in emotional exhaustion, desensitisation, decreased empathy, and disengagement. It also has shown the mediation effect of emotional exhaustion in influencing public perceptions and attitude about gender-based violence in contemporary digital media environments.

Preface

We are living through what may prove to be one of the most consequential transformations in the history of human emotional life. Over the past two decades, digital media technologies — social platforms, algorithmic content delivery systems, always-on mobile devices, and the networked information environment they collectively constitute — have not merely changed how we communicate. They have changed how we feel, how we attend to one another, and how much of ourselves we are able to bring to the task of caring about the world beyond our immediate circumstances. This edited volume takes that transformation as its central subject.

Examining Emotional Fatigue and Social Indifference in the New Media Era brings together eighteen chapters by scholars working across media studies, communication theory, cognitive and clinical psychology, organizational behavior, cultural studies, and political communication. What unites them is a shared commitment to understanding a paradox that has come to define our moment: the more connected we become through digital technologies, the more emotionally depleted, desensitized, and socially withdrawn many of us seem to be. Emotional fatigue — the chronic depletion of the psychological capacity to feel, respond, and engage — and social indifference — the progressive withdrawal of moral and empathic concern from the lives of others — are not marginal phenomena. They are, the contributors to this volume argue collectively, structural outcomes of how digital media are designed, how platforms are organized, and how the attention economy operates.

The concept of digital burnout, once confined primarily to occupational psychology, has expanded dramatically in the digital era. It now describes a generalized condition that affects social life, civic engagement, intimate relationships, and political participation. Young people growing up within algorithmically curated media environments, professionals navigating always-on remote work cultures, content creators performing emotional labor for platform visibility, athletes managing public digital personas, and ordinary users scrolling through an unending feed of crises and outrages — all inhabit versions of the same emotionally exhausting landscape.

Understanding that landscape, its mechanisms, its human costs, and its possibilities for transformation, is what this volume sets out to do.

The urgency of this inquiry has only deepened in recent years. According to global surveys, a substantial and growing proportion of social media users report experiencing symptoms consistent with emotional fatigue and compassion burnout. The Reuters Institute Digital News Report consistently finds that more than four in ten global news consumers now deliberately avoid news because it negatively affects their mood. Rates of anxiety, depression, and social withdrawal among digitally intensive populations — particularly young people — have risen sharply in multiple countries across multiple demographic groups. Political apathy is increasing even as political content has never been more visible or more emotionally charged. The average user now spends more than two and a half hours per day on social media platforms, and yet reported feelings of loneliness, disconnection, and social meaninglessness have not declined in parallel with this expansion of connectivity.

Platform capitalism — the economic system organized around the extraction of value from human attention and behavioral data — has produced media environments that are, in the phrase of one contributor to this volume, burned out by design. Algorithmic systems prioritized to maximize engagement have discovered, empirically, that fear, outrage, moral indignation, and anxiety are more engaging than calm reflection. The result is an information environment in which the most emotionally exhausting content is systematically amplified, and in which the psychological consequences of this amplification — desensitization, withdrawal, cynicism, and fatigue — are treated not as a design failure but as a business opportunity: a new problem to be monetized through the sale of wellness applications, productivity tools, and digital detox programs.

These dynamics unfold differently across cultures, across generations, across professional contexts, and across the political economies of different regions of the world. A central contribution of this volume is its genuinely global perspective. Contributors bring empirical and theoretical perspectives from Turkey, India, Lebanon, the United Arab Emirates, Ireland, and beyond, situating the phenomenon of digital emotional fatigue within the diverse socio-cultural contexts in which it actually occurs. This comparative breadth allows the volume to move beyond the WEIRD — Western, Educated, Industrialized, Rich, Democratic — sample bias that has limited much existing research, and to develop more nuanced, culturally sensitive accounts of how digital exhaustion is experienced, expressed, and resisted.

This volume is addressed to a broad and interdisciplinary readership. Scholars and advanced students in media studies, communication, sociology, psychology, digital humanities, and cultural studies will find the theoretical contributions directly relevant to their own research agendas. Practitioners in organizational development, human resources, digital mental health, education, and public policy will find evidence-based frameworks that can inform their work with populations experiencing digital burnout. Educators at all levels will find the volume's analysis of attention collapse, algorithmic governance, and the emotional costs of digital media directly applicable to their pedagogical contexts.

Beyond the academy, this volume speaks to anyone who has felt the gap between the hyperconnectivity promised by digital platforms and the emotional reality of living within them. It is intended, ultimately, as a contribution not only to scholarship but to the broader public conversation about what kind of emotional and social life is possible, and worth working toward, in the new media era.

CHAPTER OVERVIEW

The volume opens with Chapter 1, Burned Out by Design: Digital Burnout and the Collapse of Attention in Platformed Life, which establishes the conceptual foundation for the entire collection. Drawing on critical media theory, political economy, and cognitive psychology, this chapter introduces the concept of attention collapse to describe the cumulative erosion of sustained focus and emotional resilience under conditions of constant platform-driven stimulation. The central argument — that burnout is a structural outcome of attention economies organized by algorithmic optimization and surveillance capitalism, rather than an individual failure of self-regulation — frames the analytical perspective that runs throughout the volume. The chapter situates digital burnout within the structural logics of platform capitalism and calls for attention to be reconceptualized as a shared social and ethical resource.

Chapter 2, Emotional Labor on Social Media: Visibility, Performance and Burnout in Digital Culture, extends the structural critique into the domain of digital emotional labor. Building on Hochschild's foundational work, the chapter examines how social media platforms have transformed emotional expression into a form of unpaid productive labor embedded within the visibility economy. Through a comprehensive analysis of platform capitalism, algorithmic pressure, and the gendered dimensions of digital emotional performance, the chapter demonstrates how users are systematically required to manage, perform, and commodify their feelings in order to achieve and maintain visibility — and how this requirement generates exhaustion, inauthenticity, and burnout.

Chapter 3, Affect Across Borders and the Creation of Transnational Affective Publics Through Mamdani's Social Media Campaign, offers the volume's first empirical case study. Drawing on qualitative content analysis of TikTok videos and comments produced by Turkish users in response to the New York City mayoral election of Zohran Mamdani, the chapter examines the formation of transnational affective publics through the lens of Papacharissi's affect theory. The analysis reveals how Turkish users engaged with a distant political event not as passive observers but as active meaning-makers, weaving local political memory and cultural accumulation into a shared affective flow. The chapter makes an important contribution to understanding how affect travels transnationally and how platform-mediated political engagement operates in contexts of widespread political apathy.

Chapter 4, Emotional Exhaustion Across Cultures in the Digital Age: A Cross-Cultural Analysis of Media-Induced Fatigue and Social Indifference, provides the theoretical and empirical grounding for the volume's cross-cultural ambitions. Drawing systematically on Hofstede's cultural dimensions framework and Hall's distinction between high- and low-context communication cultures, the chapter constructs a culturally moderated model of the pathway from media exposure to emotional exhaustion and social indifference. It formulates and defends a set of testable hypotheses regarding how individualism, uncertainty avoidance, and digital literacy moderate the relationship between social media use and its emotional consequences, and proposes a research agenda for genuine cross-cultural validation.

Chapter 5, Analyzing Digital Burnout Through the Lens of Attention Restoration Theory and Indian Psychological Frameworks, represents one of the volume's most original theoretical contributions. Integrating Kaplan and Kaplan's Attention Restoration Theory with Indian Knowledge Systems — specifically Yogic and Ayurvedic frameworks — the chapter constructs a cross-cultural theoretical synthesis of digital burnout that transcends the epistemological limitations of Western cognitive science alone. The chapter's central output is the Sustainable Attention Regulation Architecture (SARA), a four-layer sequential recovery model that maps the user's psychological descent from Rajasic hyper-engagement through cognitive collapse into Tamasic inertia, and proposes a culturally grounded pathway to cognitive sovereignty and affective restoration.

Chapter 6, Hypervisibility Leading to Indifference: Emotional Fatigue and the Politics of Affective Exhaustion, confronts what is perhaps the central paradox of the digital media environment: the fact that the unprecedented visibility of suffering generates not heightened moral engagement but its opposite. Drawing on affect theory, on Chouliaraki's concept of the spectatorship of suffering, and on Sontag's earlier reflections on the ethics of looking, the chapter theorizes the movement from hypervisibility through affective saturation to compassion fatigue and social indifference. Case illustrations from the Global South demonstrate concretely how cycles of visibility and exhaustion unfold within digitally mediated publics, and how algorithmic amplification shapes the uneven distribution of moral concern.

Chapter 7, Emotional Fatigue in the Age of Hyperconnectivity: Algorithmic Affects, Digital Burnout, and the Rise of Social Indifference, examines the mechanics of affective capitalism and algorithmic personalization in driving emotional exhaustion. The chapter analyzes how digital platforms engineer emotional arousal for commercial purposes, how the normalization of crisis as a constant feature of digital feeds produces compassion fatigue, and how coping mechanisms including memes, humor, irony, and selective disengagement function as both adaptive responses to emotional overload and as contributors to longer-term social indifference. The chapter includes a detailed analysis of political apathy and activism fatigue as downstream consequences of digital emotional exhaustion.

Chapter 8, Emotional Fatigue and Social Indifference Among Young Athletes in the Era of Digital Social Environment, brings the volume's analytical framework into contact with a specific and particularly vulnerable population: adolescent and young adult athletes navigating the intersection of elite athletic development and the digital social environment. The chapter analyzes the performance-visibility cycle, the psychological consequences of viral success and online criticism, the authenticity paradox in social media content creation, and the physiological correlates of emotional fatigue. Drawing on developmental psychology and sports science, it makes a compelling case for the unique vulnerability of this population and calls for sport organizations to develop psychosocial support systems adequate to the digital era.

Chapter 9, Emotional Fatigue in the New Media Era: Memes, Irony, and Digital Coping within Affective Capitalism, makes one of the collection's most theoretically provocative arguments: that the humor, dark irony, and performative detachment characteristic of digital culture are not simply expressions of indifference but sophisticated, if ultimately insufficient, responses to emotional overload within affective capitalism. The chapter examines how memes and ironic engagement function as coping strategies that allow users to acknowledge suffering and sustain social connection while maintaining a degree of protective emotional distance, and explores the longer-term consequences of this coping culture for democratic engagement and collective empathy.

Chapter 10, Scrolling into Numbness: Reframing Emotional Fatigue and Social Indifference in the Algorithmic Age, offers a comprehensive reframing of the relationship between algorithmic media consumption and the progressive numbing of emotional responsiveness. The chapter integrates media psychology, emotional labor theory, and digital sociology to analyze how the attention economy treats user emotions as raw material, how performative empathy differs from genuine moral engagement, and how the structural conditions of digital media produce social indifference not as a character failing but as a rational adaptation to an emotionally extractive environment.

Chapter 11, Scrolling Through Exhaustion: Emotional Fatigue and Social Indifference in the Digital Age: How Digital Life is Reshaping Human Emotions and Social Connection, provides a broad synthetic analysis of the multiple mechanisms — information overload, compassion fatigue, algorithmic personalization, emotional whiplash, and the normalization of crisis — through which digital media reshape the emotional lives of users. The chapter pays particular attention to the COVID-19 pandemic as a crucible in which these dynamics were intensified and made newly visible, and situates the discussion within a broader account of the structural conditions that make genuine emotional sustainability difficult to achieve.

Chapter 12, Scroll, React, Detach: Emotional Fatigue and the Rise of Social Indifference in Digital Media Consumption, examines virtual ecosystems as socio-psychological environments with their own distinctive emotional demands. The chapter analyzes how the architecture of digital platforms — infinite scroll, autoplay, constant notifications, and engagement-optimizing algorithms — produces a distinctive form of cognitive and emotional exhaustion characterized by simultaneous hyperconnectivity and social detachment. The chapter engages with well-being theories, social comparison dynamics, and the paradox of the connected yet alone experience to develop a nuanced account of digital social alienation.

Chapter 13, Digital Emotional Labor: Performing Emotions, Fatigue, and Social Indifference in Online Work Environments, examines the transformation of emotional labor in digitally mediated professional contexts. As remote and hybrid work have become the norm for a large and growing proportion of the global workforce, the chapter analyzes how text-based and video-mediated communication alter the modalities through which emotional labor is performed, the new forms of invisible emotional effort generated by digital work, and the organizational conditions that fail to recognize or support workers navigating chronic digital emotional exhaustion. The chapter calls for a significant reorientation of organizational research and practice to address the distinctive emotional demands of digital work.

Chapter 14, Screens of Solitude: News Cycles, Crisis Imagery, and Emotional Fatigue in Digital Media Audiences, focuses on the specific emotional dynamics of digital news consumption. The chapter analyzes how the contemporary news environment — characterized by media saturation, 24-hour crisis coverage, and algorithmic amplification of emotionally charged content — generates emotional fatigue and news avoidance. Drawing on framing theory, agenda-setting research, and media psychology, it examines the cumulative emotional burden of sustained exposure to crisis-based news and its consequences for political cognition, civic engagement, and the capacity for informed democratic deliberation.

Chapter 15, Understanding Emotional Labor on Social Media Platforms, revisits the theoretical foundations of emotional labor in the social media context, offering a careful analysis of how the structural features of platforms — variable reward schedules, engagement metrics, algorithmic visibility — transform emotional expression into a form of unpaid digital labor. The chapter pays particular attention to the concept of emotional labor as it operates for ordinary users rather than professional influencers, examining how the everyday emotional work of maintaining social relationships, managing online identity, and responding to algorithmic demands generates cumulative exhaustion across diverse user populations.

Chapter 16, Finding a Balance Between Being Connected and Well-Being: Overcoming Emotional Fatigue and Social Detachment in the Virtual World, takes an explicitly constructive orientation, examining the theoretical and practical conditions for achieving sustainable digital well-being. Drawing on psychological resilience research, digital well-being theory, and social detachment literature, the chapter analyzes the paradox of the connected yet alone experience and proposes frameworks for navigating virtual ecosystems in ways that preserve rather than deplete emotional resources. The chapter makes an important contribution to the practical literature on digital well-being, moving beyond individual-level self-care toward a more systemic account of the conditions for genuine balance.

Chapter 17, Exposure to Violent and Misogynistic Content with Reference to Emotional Fatigue in Recent Media, examines a specific and particularly troubling category of emotionally exhausting digital content: the increasingly routine exposure of social media users to violent and misogynistic material. Drawing on social learning theory, media psychology, and research on desensitization, the chapter analyzes how repeated exposure to content depicting gender-based violence and harassment generates emotional fatigue, shifts in affective responses, and progressive normalization. The chapter situates this analysis within the broader account of media saturation and its consequences for empathy, moral concern, and social attitudes toward gender-based harm.

Chapter 18, Well-Being Apps and the Commodification of Emotional Care: Psychological, Social, and Ethical Implications in the New Media Era, turns a critical eye on one of the most prevalent proposed solutions to digital emotional fatigue: the growing ecosystem of mental health and well-being applications. Drawing on critical platform studies, clinical psychology, and the sociology of care, the chapter analyzes how the commodification of emotional care through subscription-based digital wellness products transforms the meaning and practice of psychological support. The chapter examines the tensions between therapeutic intent and commercial logic in well-being app design, and raises important ethical questions about engagement-driven approaches to emotional health.

This volume makes several distinctive contributions to scholarship on digital media, emotional life, and social psychology that I believe will shape research and practice in this area for years to come.

First, the collection insists on the structural, rather than individual, nature of digital emotional fatigue. Against narratives that frame digital burnout as a personal failing — a problem of insufficient willpower, poor time management, or inadequate digital self-care — the contributors collectively demonstrate that emotional exhaustion is produced by the deliberate design of digital platforms, the economic imperatives of attention capitalism, and the social norms generated within algorithmically organized media environments. This reframing has significant implications not only for scholarly understanding but for public policy, platform regulation, and the design of interventions: if burnout is built into the system, it cannot be solved by telling individuals to put their phones down more often.

Second, the volume advances the conversation on cross-cultural variation in digital emotional fatigue in ways that go substantially beyond existing research. By bringing together perspectives from Turkey, India, Lebanon, and multiple other cultural contexts, and by engaging seriously with non-Western theoretical frameworks including Indian Knowledge Systems and collectivist social psychology, the collection demonstrates that the experience of digital exhaustion is culturally mediated in ways that have important consequences for how we theorize, measure, and address it. The SARA model proposed in Chapter 5 is perhaps the most ambitious expression of this cross-cultural ambition, but the comparative perspective runs throughout the volume.

Third, the collection advances our understanding of the relationship between digital emotional fatigue and democratic life. Several chapters demonstrate with particular force that the erosion of emotional capacity in digitally saturated environments has direct consequences for civic engagement, political participation, empathic concern, and the collective capacity for sustained attention to public issues. This connection between individual psychological depletion and collective democratic impoverishment is one of the most important and undertheorized dimensions of the digital media environment, and this volume makes a substantial contribution to its analysis.

Fourth, the volume opens important new conversations about coping, resistance, and the conditions for genuine emotional sustainability in digital life. Rather than concluding simply with a diagnosis of exhaustion, the collection includes chapters that take seriously the question of what emotionally sustainable digital participation might look like, what structural, platform-level, and policy changes would be required to make it possible, and what resources — psychological, cultural, and institutional — are available to support it.

Finally, the interdisciplinary breadth of the volume — bringing cognitive science, affect theory, platform studies, organizational psychology, political communication, cultural studies, and computational analysis into sustained dialogue — models an approach to digital media research that I believe the complexity of this phenomenon demands. No single discipline, no single methodology, no single theoretical tradition is adequate to the challenge of understanding what digital media are doing to human emotional life. This volume is offered in the conviction that the best scholarship on this question will be collaborative, interdisciplinary, and globally attentive — and that the stakes of getting it right are very high indeed.

Ayten Bengisu Cansever Bayhan
Istanbul Gelisim University, Türkiye

Acknowledgment

The completion of this edited volume represents the collective effort, generosity, and intellectual dedication of many individuals and institutions, and it is a privilege to express our gratitude to each of them here.

First and foremost, we extend our deepest appreciation to the chapter authors whose scholarship forms the heart of this book. Scholars from Turkey, India, Indonesia, Lebanon, the United Arab Emirates, Ireland, and beyond contributed their expertise, time, and intellectual energy to this project. Their willingness to engage with a subject as complex and consequential as digital emotional fatigue — and to do so with rigor, originality, and care — made this volume possible. We are grateful not only for the chapters they produced but for the collaborative spirit they brought to the review and revision process.

We are deeply thankful to the editorial and production team at IGI Global for their guidance, patience, and professionalism throughout the publication process. Their support at every stage — from initial proposal to final manuscript — was invaluable, and their commitment to advancing interdisciplinary scholarship continues to create important platforms for emerging and established researchers alike.

We owe a significant debt of gratitude to the peer reviewers who offered their time and expertise to evaluate the chapter submissions. Their constructive and thoughtful feedback strengthened every contribution in this volume, and the quality of the final work reflects their dedication to scholarly excellence.

Our sincere thanks go to our home institution, Istanbul Gelisim University, Faculty of Fine Arts, and the Department of Visual Communication Design, for providing the academic environment and institutional support that made this editorial work possible. The encouragement of our colleagues and the intellectual community we share have been a constant source of motivation.

We are grateful to the broader scholarly community working at the intersection of media studies, digital culture, psychology, and communication — the researchers, teachers, and practitioners whose ongoing work continues to illuminate how digital life shapes human experience. This volume stands on the shoulders of that community's cumulative inquiry.

Finally, we wish to acknowledge the many students, users, workers, and individuals whose daily experiences of digital exhaustion, social disconnection, and emotional overload gave this project its urgency and meaning. It is ultimately for them — and for a deeper understanding of the conditions they navigate — that this work was undertaken.

Ayten Bengisu Cansever Bayhan
Istanbul Gelisim University, Türkiye

Chapter 1
Burned Out by Design: Digital Burnout and the Collapse of Attention in Platformed Life

Ratan Sarkar
http://orcid.org/0009-0008-5480-0165
Tezpur University, India

ABSTRACT

Digital burnout has emerged as a defining condition of contemporary platformed life, closely linked to the commodification of human attention. This chapter critically examines how digital platforms are designed to intensify cognitive load, fragment attention, and normalize exhaustion. Drawing on critical media theory, political economy, and cognitive psychology, it argues that burnout is a structural outcome of attention economies driven by algorithmic optimization and surveillance capitalism, rather than an individual failure of self-regulation. The concept of attention collapse is introduced to describe the erosion of sustained focus and emotional resilience under constant stimulation. By situating fatigue within broader socio-technical systems, the chapter highlights the implications for education and democratic participation, calling for attention to be reconceptualized as a shared social and ethical resource.

INTRODUCTION

The contemporary digital environment is marked by an unprecedented intensity of informational flow, sensory stimulation, and affective demand. Social media platforms, mobile applications, and algorithmically curated content streams have become central infrastructures of everyday life, shaping how individuals perceive time, relate to others, and allocate attention. While these platforms promise connection, efficiency, and personalization, they simultaneously generate widespread

DOI: 10.4018/979-8-3373-8307-1.ch001

experiences of exhaustion, distraction, and emotional depletion. Digital burnout—once largely associated with occupational stress—has expanded into a generalized condition affecting social, educational, and political life (Han, 2015; Crary, 2013).

At the center of this transformation lies attention. Traditionally understood as a finite cognitive capacity, attention has become a primary site of economic extraction within the attention economy (Wu, 2016). Digital platforms do not merely compete for users' time but for continuous engagement, employing interface designs that maximize scrolling, clicking, and emotional response. Infinite feeds, push notifications, autoplay features, and algorithmic recommendation systems function together to fragment attention and discourage disengagement (Williams, 2018). As a result, users experience difficulty sustaining focus, heightened irritability, and a persistent sense of being perpetually "on."

This chapter introduces the concept of *attention collapse* to capture the cumulative breakdown of sustained attention under platformed conditions. Attention collapse refers not simply to momentary distraction but to a deeper erosion of cognitive endurance and affective stability. It manifests as chronic fatigue, reduced capacity for deep reading and critical thinking, and growing indifference toward social and political stimuli. Empirical research demonstrates that frequent interruptions significantly increase stress and cognitive strain (Mark et al., 2008), while the mere presence of smartphones reduces available cognitive capacity, even when devices are not actively used (Ward et al., 2017).

Dominant public narratives often individualize these symptoms, framing burnout as a failure of self-discipline, time management, or digital self-care. Such explanations obscure the structural dynamics of digital media systems. Critical media scholars emphasize that platforms are not neutral tools but socio-technical systems shaped by profit-driven imperatives (Terranova, 2004). The economic logic of surveillance capitalism depends on continuous data extraction, which in turn requires prolonged user engagement (Zuboff, 2019). Emotional arousal—whether outrage, fear, pleasure, or anxiety—becomes a central mechanism for sustaining attention (Schüll, 2012).

The consequences of digital burnout extend beyond individual well-being. In educational contexts, attention collapse undermines sustained reading, deep learning, and reflective pedagogy (Newport, 2016). In democratic contexts, diminished attention capacity weakens civic engagement, informed deliberation, and empathy, contributing to political apathy and affective polarization (Tufekci, 2015). Constant exposure to mediated crises—pandemics, climate disasters, and political conflict—further intensifies emotional fatigue, often producing disengagement rather than collective action (Crary, 2013).

By situating digital burnout within the structural logics of platform capitalism, this chapter moves beyond behavioral explanations toward a systemic critique of attention extraction. It advances the central argument that burnout is not a personal failure but a condition produced *by design*. Recognizing this shift is essential for rethinking responsibility, agency, and resistance in the new media era.

RATIONALE

The rationale for this chapter emerges from the widening gap between dominant discourses of digital well-being and the structural realities of platformed life. Popular narratives frequently frame digital burnout as a consequence of excessive screen time or poor self-regulation, promoting solutions such as digital detoxes, mindfulness applications, or productivity techniques (Rosen, 2012). While these strategies may provide temporary relief, they individualize responsibility and obscure the political and economic forces that make disengagement increasingly difficult.

Scholars of the attention economy argue that digital platforms are deliberately engineered to capture and retain attention through persuasive design techniques rooted in behavioral psychology (Wu, 2016). Features such as variable rewards, social validation metrics, and algorithmic personalization are not incidental but central to platform profitability (Schüll, 2012). These mechanisms systematically intensify cognitive load and emotional arousal, creating environments in which sustained attention becomes structurally difficult to maintain.

The concept of attention collapse provides a critical lens for understanding burnout as a cumulative and systemic condition. Unlike traditional models of distraction that assume a stable attentional baseline, attention collapse highlights how continuous interruption gradually weakens cognitive capacity itself (Mark et al., 2008). Over time, the ability to focus deeply, reflect critically, and engage emotionally is eroded, reshaping habits of thinking, learning, and feeling (Newport, 2016).

This analysis is particularly timely in the context of intensified digital dependency following the COVID-19 pandemic. Remote work, online education, and mediated sociality blurred boundaries between labor, leisure, and rest, normalizing constant connectivity while intensifying exhaustion (Crary, 2013). Under these conditions, burnout functions as a form of silent governance, disciplining users into compliance with platform rhythms rather than enabling autonomy (Han, 2015).

From an educational perspective, attention collapse poses profound challenges to pedagogy and learning. Sustained attention is foundational to comprehension, critical inquiry, and intellectual growth. When attention is fragmented, education risks becoming superficial and instrumentalized (Citton, 2017). Similarly, democratic participation depends on citizens' capacity to attend, deliberate, and empathize—capacities undermined by affective overload and algorithmic amplification (Tufekci, 2015).

By integrating insights from media studies, political economy, and cognitive science, this chapter addresses a critical gap in existing scholarship. It argues for shifting the analysis of burnout away from individualized self-care toward collective engagement with platform power and design.

OBJECTIVES

This chapter pursues the following five objectives:

1. To conceptualize digital burnout as a systemic outcome of platform capitalism rather than an individual psychological deficiency.
2. To develop the concept of attention collapse as an analytical framework for understanding the erosion of sustained attention in digitally saturated environments.
3. To examine how algorithmic design, surveillance practices, and affective economies contribute to chronic cognitive and emotional exhaustion.
4. To analyze the implications of digital burnout for education and democratic engagement, particularly in relation to learning, civic responsibility, and social empathy.
5. To contribute to interdisciplinary debates on emotional fatigue and social indifference in the new media era by foregrounding attention as a political, ethical, and collective concern.

LITERATURE AND THEORETICAL BACKGROUND

This chapter is grounded in an interdisciplinary theoretical framework that brings together critical media theory, political economy, and cognitive psychology to examine digital burnout as a structural condition of platformed life. Central to this framework is the concept of the attention economy, which conceptualizes human attention as a scarce and economically valuable resource (Huberman & Wu, 2008). As argued by scholars such as Tim Wu, contemporary digital platforms operate not merely as communication tools but as competitive systems designed to capture, retain, and monetize user attention. Within this paradigm, attention is transformed into a site of extraction, where user engagement generates data that can be commodified and reinvested into predictive and behavioral advertising models (Jingtong, 2023).

The analysis further draws on the theory of surveillance capitalism, which highlights how digital infrastructures systematically collect, analyze, and operationalize behavioral data for profit maximization. Shoshana Zuboff's work is particularly significant in demonstrating how user activity is continuously monitored and translated into predictive products (Bodle, 2016). This logic necessitates sustained engagement, making user attention a central target of algorithmic optimization. Consequently, platform architectures are designed to minimize disengagement and maximize interaction through personalized content delivery, thereby intensifying cognitive and emotional demands on users (Montalvo et al., 2021).

To understand how these structural conditions affect human cognition, the chapter incorporates insights from cognitive psychology, particularly research on attention, cognitive load, and task-switching (Edwards et al., 2017). Studies have shown that frequent interruptions and multitasking increase mental strain and reduce the capacity for sustained focus. This body of work supports the development of the concept of attention collapse, which extends beyond momentary distraction to describe the gradual erosion of cognitive endurance under conditions of continuous digital stimulation (Somani et al., 2025). Unlike traditional models that assume attention as a stable capacity, attention collapse foregrounds its vulnerability to systemic fragmentation.

Additionally, the chapter engages with theories of affective economies, which emphasize the role of emotions in sustaining engagement within digital environments. Platforms do not merely capture attention through information but through the circulation of affect—such as outrage, fear, pleasure, and validation—which intensifies user interaction (Wahl-Jorgensen, 2018). Drawing on this perspective, emotional responses are understood as integral to platform profitability, while also contributing to exhaustion and burnout.

Finally, the framework is informed by critical perspectives on platform capitalism, which situate digital media within broader socio-economic structures. Scholars such as Terranova and Srnicek argue that platforms function as intermediaries that extract value from user activity while shaping patterns of communication, labor, and social interaction (Allmer et al., 2015). This perspective enables the chapter to move beyond individualistic explanations of burnout and instead locate it within systemic processes of commodification, control, and governance.

Taken together, these theoretical strands provide a comprehensive lens for analyzing digital burnout not as a personal failure but as a condition produced at the intersection of technological design, economic imperatives, and cognitive limits. The concept of attention collapse emerges within this framework as a critical tool for understanding the deeper transformations of attention, emotion, and subjectivity in contemporary digital life.

METHODOLOGY

This chapter adopts a qualitative, critical-theoretical methodology based on the systematic analysis and synthesis of existing literature across multiple disciplines, including media studies, sociology, political economy, and cognitive psychology. Rather than generating primary empirical data, the study engages with secondary sources to construct a conceptual framework for understanding digital burnout and attention collapse within platformed environments.

The methodological approach is interpretive and analytical, focusing on identifying key theoretical insights and integrating them into a coherent argument about the structural nature of burnout. Foundational texts on the attention economy, surveillance capitalism, and platform design are examined alongside empirical studies on cognitive load, multitasking, and digital distraction. This interdisciplinary integration enables the chapter to bridge macro-level analyses of digital infrastructures with micro-level understandings of cognitive and emotional processes.

The chapter employs a critical lens, emphasizing the role of power, economic interests, and technological design in shaping user experience. By situating individual experiences of exhaustion within broader socio-technical systems, the methodology challenges reductionist explanations centered on personal behavior. The aim is not to test hypotheses but to develop a theoretically grounded interpretation of digital burnout as a systemic and structurally produced condition.

The Political Economy of Attention

The transformation of attention from a cognitive faculty into an economic resource marks one of the most significant shifts in contemporary digital capitalism. Traditionally understood as a finite psychological capacity that enables perception, comprehension, and reflection, attention has increasingly been reconfigured as a commodity within what is now widely described as the attention economy. In this framework, attention is no longer simply a condition of human cognition but a measurable, tradable, and monetizable asset. Digital platforms operate as infrastructures designed to capture, sustain, and exploit this resource, embedding attention at the core of their economic logic.

The emergence of the attention economy can be traced to broader transformations in media systems, particularly the shift from broadcast to interactive and, more recently, algorithmically driven environments. In earlier broadcast models, audiences were relatively passive recipients of content, and attention was aggregated and sold primarily through advertising slots based on estimated viewership. However, the rise of digital platforms fundamentally altered this arrangement. Interactive media enabled users not only to consume content but also to produce it, generating continuous streams of data about preferences, behaviors, and interactions. With the advent of algorithmic systems, this data is now processed in real time to optimize engagement, creating a feedback loop in which user activity continuously informs and reshapes the content environment (Mathieu & Vengerfeldt, 2020).

Within this context, scholars such as Tim Wu have argued that attention has become the primary currency of digital media systems, where the competition is not merely for time but for sustained and intensified engagement. Importantly, the value of attention is no longer determined solely by duration—how long users remain on a platform—but by the quality and intensity of their engagement (Bachmann & Siegert, 2021). Metrics such as clicks, shares, comments, and emotional reactions provide more granular indicators of user involvement, enabling platforms to refine their strategies for capturing attention. This shift reflects a broader move from quantity to intensity, where deeply engaged users are more valuable than passive viewers because they generate richer data and are more susceptible to targeted interventions (Heitmayer, 2024).

The monetization of attention operates through multiple interconnected mechanisms. Advertising remains a central revenue stream, but its functioning has become increasingly sophisticated. Rather than selling generalized audience access, platforms offer highly targeted advertising based on detailed user profiles derived from behavioral data. Every interaction—scrolling, liking, pausing, or skipping—contributes to the construction of these profiles, allowing advertisers to reach users with unprecedented precision (Sánchez-Muñoz et al., 2025). In this sense, users are not merely audiences but active participants in the production of value. Their attention is continuously harvested, analyzed, and converted into economic assets.

This process is further illuminated by the concept of surveillance capitalism, which emphasizes the centrality of data extraction in contemporary economic systems. As articulated by Shoshana Zuboff, surveillance capitalism operates by capturing "behavioral surplus"—data generated through user activity that exceeds what is necessary for service provision—and transforming it into predictive products (Medeiros et al., 2024). These products are then sold in markets that anticipate and influence future behavior. Within this framework, attention is not only captured but also shaped, as platforms use predictive analytics to design environments that maximize the likelihood of continued engagement.

The relationship between data extraction, prediction, and behavioral modification is crucial to understanding why constant engagement is structurally required. Digital platforms depend on continuous streams of data to refine their predictive models. The more users interact, the more data is generated; the more data is available, the more accurate and profitable the predictions become (Montag & Elhai, 2023). This creates a systemic imperative to keep users engaged at all times. Features such as infinite scrolling, autoplay, and real-time notifications are not incidental design choices but integral components of an economic system that relies on uninterrupted attention flows.

Algorithmic optimization plays a central role in sustaining this system. Machine learning models are trained to identify patterns in user behavior and to deliver content that is most likely to elicit engagement. This often involves prioritizing emotionally charged or sensational content, as such material tends to generate stronger reactions and longer interaction times (Milli et al., 2025). As a result, users are drawn into cycles of continuous stimulation, where the boundaries between voluntary engagement and compulsive use become increasingly blurred. The platform environment is thus structured to minimize friction and maximize immersion, reducing opportunities for disengagement and reflection (Domalewska, 2025).

From a political economy perspective, this configuration reveals how digital platforms function as extractive systems that transform everyday activities into sources of economic value. Users simultaneously occupy the roles of consumers, producers, and data sources, contributing to a system that commodifies not only their attention but also their behavior and affect. This dual role complicates traditional distinctions between production and consumption, highlighting the ways in which digital labor is embedded in routine interactions (Vercellone & Stasio, 2023). Even seemingly trivial actions—such as liking a post or watching a short video—participate in the generation of value within platform economies.

Crucially, the structural dependence on continuous engagement has significant implications for user well-being. The imperative to capture and retain attention leads to environments characterized by constant stimulation, interruption, and cognitive demand. Rather than being neutral spaces for communication, platforms are engineered to maximize usage, often at the expense of users' cognitive and emotional capacities (Montag & Elhai, 2023). In this context, digital burnout emerges not as an unintended consequence of excessive use but as a predictable outcome of systems designed to extract attention intensively and persistently.

This perspective challenges dominant narratives that frame burnout as a result of individual failure, such as poor time management or lack of self-control. While such explanations emphasize personal responsibility, they overlook the structural conditions that make disengagement difficult. The design of digital platforms actively discourages withdrawal by embedding users in continuous feedback loops of reward and stimulation (Domalewska, 2025). As a result, users are not simply choosing to spend more time online; they are operating within environments that are systematically optimized to capture and hold their attention.

Understanding attention as economic infrastructure also requires recognizing its broader social implications. The commodification of attention reshapes not only individual experiences but also collective patterns of communication, knowledge production, and social interaction. When attention is treated as a resource to be extracted and monetized, the conditions for sustained reflection, critical thinking, and meaningful engagement are undermined (Heitmayer, 2024). This has far-reaching consequences for education, culture, and democratic life, where the capacity to attend deeply and critically is essential.

In brief, the political economy of attention reveals that digital burnout is embedded within the fundamental logic of platform capitalism. Attention is not merely a psychological capacity but a central component of contemporary economic systems, subject to processes of commodification, extraction, and optimization. By tracing the historical shift from broadcast to algorithmic media and examining the mechanisms through which attention is monetized, it becomes clear that burnout is not the result of misuse but of overuse by design. Recognizing this structural dimension is essential for moving beyond individualistic explanations and toward a more critical understanding of the conditions that shape attention in the digital age.

Platform Architecture and the Engineering of Engagement

Digital platforms are not neutral environments for communication or information exchange; they are carefully engineered systems designed to capture, sustain, and intensify user engagement. At the core of this architecture lies what is commonly described as persuasive design—a set of techniques derived from behavioral psychology that aim to shape user behavior in predictable and profitable ways (Cemiloglu et al., 2021). These techniques are embedded within interface structures and algorithmic processes, creating environments that subtly guide attention, encourage repeated interaction, and minimize disengagement. Understanding how these systems operate is essential for explaining how digital burnout is produced not through excessive use alone, but through the very design of platform infrastructures.

One of the most influential mechanisms of persuasive design is the use of variable reward systems, often compared to the logic of gambling. Drawing on principles of operant conditioning, platforms deliver rewards—such as likes, comments, or new content—at unpredictable intervals. This variability increases the compulsion to check and recheck platforms, as users anticipate the possibility of reward without certainty (Hristova et al., 2020). Much like slot machines, which rely on intermittent reinforcement to sustain engagement, digital platforms create cycles of anticipation and gratification that keep users returning. These feedback loops are often associated with dopamine release, reinforcing habitual use and making disengagement psychologically difficult (Flayelle et al., 2023).

Closely related to this mechanism is the design of infinite scroll, which eliminates natural stopping points in content consumption. Unlike traditional media formats—such as books or newspapers—that provide clear boundaries, infinite scroll creates a seamless and continuous flow of information. Users are not required to make active decisions about whether to continue; instead, content automatically extends downward, encouraging prolonged engagement (Bhadouria et al., 2025). This design reduces cognitive friction and undermines users' ability to regulate their own consumption, contributing to extended periods of passive interaction that can lead to cognitive fatigue.

Similarly, autoplay features further erode opportunities for disengagement by automatically initiating the next piece of content without user input (Lukoff et al., 2021). Whether in video streaming platforms or social media feeds, autoplay removes the pause that might otherwise allow users to reflect or stop. By collapsing the interval between content units, platforms maintain a continuous stream of stimulation that sustains attention while gradually increasing cognitive load (Ernst & Schnauber, 2024). Over time, this uninterrupted flow contributes to a sense of temporal disorientation, where users lose track of how long they have been engaged.

Push notifications represent another critical element of persuasive design, functioning as external triggers that draw users back into platform environments (Wohllebe, 2020). These notifications are strategically timed and often personalized to maximize their effectiveness. They create a persistent sense of urgency, signaling that something important or rewarding may be occurring in the digital space. Even when ignored, notifications exert a cognitive presence, fragmenting attention and increasing mental strain (Fournier et al., 2025). The result is a condition of perpetual partial attention, where users are constantly oriented toward potential digital interactions, even when engaged in offline activities.

Beyond these interface features, algorithms play a central role in optimizing engagement by continuously analyzing user behavior and adapting content delivery accordingly. These systems are designed to maximize retention, ensuring that users remain on the platform for as long as possible. Through machine learning techniques, platforms identify patterns in user interactions and prioritize content that is most likely to sustain attention (Singh, 2025). This often involves amplifying emotionally charged material—such as sensational news, controversial opinions, or highly curated personal content—that generates strong reactions and encourages further interaction.

In addition to retention, algorithms are optimized for emotional arousal, recognizing that heightened emotional states are closely linked to increased engagement. Content that provokes outrage, anxiety, or excitement is more likely to be shared, commented on, and revisited. As a result, platform environments tend to become saturated with emotionally intense material, creating cycles of stimulation that can be both captivating and exhausting (Shin, 2024). This dynamic contributes to the normalization of emotional volatility, where users are repeatedly exposed to content that demands immediate affective responses.

A further consequence of algorithmic optimization is the promotion of compulsive checking behaviors. By continuously updating content feeds and delivering new information, platforms create the impression that there is always something new to see or respond to. This sense of ongoing novelty encourages users to check their devices frequently, often in brief but repeated intervals throughout the day (Lervik-Olsen et al., 2023). These micro-interactions, while individually insignificant, accumulate into patterns of fragmented attention that disrupt sustained focus and increase cognitive load.

Taken together, these design elements reveal how digital interfaces function as behavioral control systems. Rather than simply facilitating user choice, platforms actively shape the conditions under which choices are made. The architecture of engagement is structured to guide attention, influence behavior, and optimize interaction in ways that align with platform interests (Chen et al., 2024). This challenges the assumption that users are fully autonomous actors within digital environments, highlighting instead the ways in which behavior is subtly orchestrated through design.

This orchestration is further conceptualized through the notion of algorithmic governance, which refers to the use of automated systems to regulate and manage user behavior. Unlike traditional forms of governance, which rely on explicit rules and visible authority, algorithmic governance operates invisibly, embedding control within the infrastructure of the platform itself (Törnberg, 2023). Users are not directly instructed on how to behave; instead, their actions are shaped through the selective presentation of content, the timing of notifications, and the structure of interaction pathways. This form of governance is continuous and adaptive, responding in real time to user behavior while simultaneously influencing future actions.

An important dimension of this process is the personalization paradox. Platforms present themselves as offering individualized experiences, tailoring content to the preferences and interests of each user. This personalization creates a sense of relevance and intimacy, making interactions feel uniquely suited to the individual (Garcia-Rivadulla, 2016). However, this apparent individuality is produced through standardized algorithmic processes that operate at scale. The same underlying systems govern all users, even as they generate differentiated outputs. Thus, personalization functions as both a mechanism of engagement and a form of control, aligning user experience with platform objectives while obscuring the structural nature of that alignment (Langlois & Elmer, 2019).

The effectiveness of these systems is closely tied to the principle of frictionless design, which aims to remove barriers to interaction and make engagement as effortless as possible. While this may enhance usability, it also has unintended consequences for user well-being. By minimizing friction, platforms reduce opportunities for pause, reflection, and decision-making (Laschke, 2023). Actions such as scrolling, clicking, or watching become automatic, requiring minimal cognitive effort but accumulating significant mental strain over time. Paradoxically, the ease of interaction contributes to fatigue, as users remain engaged for longer periods without conscious awareness of their activity (Janáček & Balázová, 2024).

The elimination of stopping cues is central to this dynamic. In traditional media environments, physical or structural limits—such as the end of a page or a scheduled broadcast—provided natural points at which users could disengage. In contrast, digital platforms are designed to be continuous and open-ended, offering no clear indication of when to stop (Rixen et al., 2023). This absence of boundaries encourages prolonged engagement and makes it more difficult for users to regulate their own behavior. As a result, time spent on platforms often exceeds initial intentions, contributing to feelings of exhaustion and loss of control (Domalewska, 2025).

The comparison with gambling systems, as explored by Natasha Dow Schüll, provides a useful lens for understanding these dynamics. Just as gambling machines are designed to sustain play through variable rewards and immersive environments, digital platforms create conditions that encourage continuous interaction (Schüll, 2004). Both systems rely on psychological principles that exploit human tendencies toward anticipation, reward-seeking, and habit formation (Hans et al., 2024). Importantly, the goal is not to maximize satisfaction but to sustain engagement, even when that engagement becomes compulsive or detrimental.

In this light, digital burnout can be understood as a direct consequence of platform architecture. The continuous stimulation, fragmented attention, and emotional intensity produced by these systems place sustained demands on cognitive and affective resources (Ravindran et al., 2014). Over time, this leads to exhaustion, not because users are incapable of managing their behavior, but because the environment is structured to maximize engagement beyond sustainable limits. Burnout, therefore, is not an accidental byproduct but an inherent feature of systems designed to capture and hold attention indefinitely (Priego, 2024).

By foregrounding the role of design in shaping user experience, this analysis shifts the focus from individual responsibility to structural conditions. It highlights the need to critically examine the ways in which digital platforms engineer engagement and the implications of these practices for cognitive and emotional well-being. Understanding platform architecture as a system of intentional design is essential for recognizing that the pressures leading to burnout are embedded within the very foundations of contemporary digital life.

Cognitive Load, Fragmentation, and Attention Collapse

The intensification of digital engagement has produced not only new patterns of media consumption but also fundamental transformations in how attention itself operates. While attention has traditionally been understood as a stable cognitive capacity that can be directed, sustained, and regulated, contemporary digital environments increasingly destabilize this capacity. The result is not merely distraction in a conventional sense but a deeper, cumulative condition that this chapter conceptualizes as attention collapse (Serrano-Puche, 2017). This concept captures the progressive erosion of sustained attention under conditions of continuous stimulation, interruption, and cognitive overload characteristic of platformed life.

To understand this transformation, it is important to distinguish between related but analytically distinct terms such as attention, concentration, and cognitive endurance. Attention refers to the selective allocation of cognitive resources to specific stimuli, enabling perception and comprehension. Concentration involves the sustained maintenance of this focus over time, allowing for deeper processing and engagement (Alloway & Alloway, 2011). Cognitive endurance, in turn, denotes the capacity to maintain concentration across extended periods without significant decline in performance. In traditional settings, these capacities are assumed to be relatively stable, even if limited. However, digital environments systematically undermine all three by introducing constant interruptions, competing stimuli, and fragmented temporal structures.

Research in cognitive psychology has consistently demonstrated that frequent interruptions impose significant cognitive costs. Studies on task-switching show that shifting attention between activities reduces efficiency, increases error rates, and generates mental fatigue (Brumby et al., 2019). Even brief interruptions can disrupt cognitive flow, requiring time and effort to reorient to the original task. Over repeated cycles, this process accumulates into heightened stress and reduced overall productivity. Importantly, the effects of interruption are not limited to moments of distraction; they extend into the quality of cognitive engagement, weakening the ability to process information deeply and coherently (MOMOH et al., 2025).

Moreover, the mere presence of digital devices—even when not actively used—has been shown to reduce available cognitive capacity. The constant possibility of incoming notifications or new information creates a background condition of anticipatory attention, where part of the mind remains oriented toward potential digital stimuli (Hartanto et al., 2024). This state of divided attention limits the resources available for sustained focus, contributing to a sense of cognitive depletion. In this context, attention is no longer fully available for the task at hand but is continuously distributed across actual and potential demands.

It is within this broader cognitive landscape that the concept of attention collapse becomes analytically significant. Unlike traditional notions of distraction, which imply temporary deviations from an otherwise stable attentional baseline, attention collapse refers to the gradual weakening of the baseline itself (Alloway & Alloway, 2011). Under conditions of perpetual stimulation, the capacity for sustained attention is not simply interrupted but structurally degraded. Over time, individuals may find it increasingly difficult to engage in activities that require prolonged focus, such as deep reading, critical analysis, or reflective thinking. What emerges is not a momentary lapse but a persistent condition of attentional fragility.

A key mechanism driving attention collapse is the fragmentation of temporal experience. Digital platforms organize time into discrete, rapidly shifting units—notifications, posts, messages, and updates—each demanding immediate attention. This structure encourages a mode of engagement characterized by rapid switching rather than sustained immersion (Lorenz-Spreen et al., 2019). As users move quickly from one stimulus to another, attention becomes distributed across multiple inputs, preventing the consolidation of thought. The result is a form of cognitive fragmentation in which ideas are only partially processed and rarely integrated into coherent understanding.

This fragmentation is closely linked to the normalization of multitasking, which is often perceived as an efficient way to manage multiple demands but is, in practice, cognitively inefficient. Neuroscientific research indicates that the brain does not truly perform multiple tasks simultaneously but rather switches rapidly between them. Each switch incurs a cognitive cost, reducing overall efficiency and increasing mental strain (Fisher & Keene, 2020). Despite this, digital environments encourage multitasking by presenting multiple streams of information simultaneously—chat windows, notifications, media feeds—creating an illusion of productivity while undermining actual performance.

Another critical dimension of attention collapse is its impact on memory and comprehension. Sustained attention is essential for encoding information into long-term memory and for constructing meaningful connections between ideas. When attention is fragmented, information is processed superficially and often forgotten quickly (Drüppel et al., 2025). This has significant implications for learning and knowledge acquisition, as it limits the ability to engage with complex material and to develop critical understanding. Reading, for instance, shifts from a deep, immersive activity to a fragmented process of scanning and skimming, where comprehension is partial and transient.

Importantly, attention collapse is not experienced uniformly but accumulates over time as a result of repeated exposure to digitally mediated environments. Each instance of interruption, multitasking, or superficial engagement contributes incrementally to the weakening of attentional capacity (Loh & Kanai, 2016). This cumulative effect distinguishes attention collapse from temporary distraction, highlighting its structural and long-term nature. It is not simply that individuals are occasionally distracted, but that their capacity to sustain attention is progressively diminished.

The experiential dimension of attention collapse often manifests as a paradoxical combination of constant activity and reduced productivity. Individuals may spend extended periods engaged with digital media, yet feel that little meaningful work has been accomplished (Jacobs, 2025). This disconnect between effort and outcome contributes to feelings of frustration, fatigue, and cognitive overload. The sense of being perpetually "busy" without achieving depth or completion reflects the underlying fragmentation of attention and the erosion of cognitive endurance.

A further consequence of attention collapse is the decline of deep attention, a mode of engagement characterized by sustained focus, critical reflection, and immersive thinking. Deep attention is essential for complex intellectual tasks, creative work, and meaningful learning. However, in environments structured around rapid stimulation and continuous updates, deep attention becomes increasingly difficult to maintain. It is gradually replaced by shallow attention, which prioritizes speed, novelty, and surface-level engagement. This shift has profound implications not only for individual cognition but also for broader cultural and intellectual practices.

The question of whether attention collapse is reversible remains open and contested. On one hand, cognitive capacities are adaptable, and individuals may be able to retrain their attention through deliberate practices that prioritize focus and minimize distraction. On the other hand, the structural conditions of digital environments continue to exert pressure toward fragmentation, making sustained attention increasingly difficult to achieve (Alloway & Alloway, 2011). This tension underscores the importance of understanding attention collapse not merely as an individual challenge but as a systemic condition shaped by technological design and economic imperatives.

Ultimately, attention collapse represents a critical threshold in the transformation of cognitive life under digital capitalism. It signals a shift from episodic distraction to structural degradation, where the very capacity for sustained attention is compromised. By framing this condition in systemic terms, the concept moves beyond behavioral explanations and highlights the need to address the underlying architectures that produce and reinforce cognitive fragmentation. In doing so, it provides a foundation for analyzing the broader consequences of digital burnout and for rethinking the role of attention in contemporary society.

Affective Economies and Emotional Exhaustion

While the previous section examined the cognitive dimensions of attention collapse, it is equally important to understand the affective conditions through which digital platforms sustain engagement. Attention in contemporary digital environments is not captured solely through information but through emotion. Platforms operate within what can be described as affective economies, where emotions are not incidental responses but central mechanisms of value generation. In these economies, feelings such as outrage, anxiety, pleasure, and validation circulate, intensify, and accumulate, becoming key drivers of user interaction (Paasonen, 2016). This emotional dimension is critical to understanding digital burnout, as it reveals how continuous engagement is sustained through affective stimulation that ultimately leads to exhaustion.

Affective economies function by attaching emotional value to content and interactions, thereby increasing their capacity to capture and hold attention. Content that provokes strong emotional responses—whether positive or negative—is more likely to be engaged with, shared, and amplified. Digital platforms are structured to detect and prioritize such content, as emotional intensity correlates closely with engagement metrics. This creates a feedback loop in which emotionally charged material becomes more visible, further stimulating user responses and reinforcing the cycle of affective circulation (Paasonen, 2018).

Within this framework, users are not passive recipients of emotional content but active participants in its production and dissemination. Everyday practices such as posting updates, reacting to others' content, and curating personal profiles involve forms of affective labor. Users continuously manage impressions, express emotions, and respond to social cues, often in ways that align with platform logics of visibility and engagement (Denegri-Knott et al., 2023). This labor is not formally recognized as work, yet it requires sustained emotional investment and contributes directly to the generation of value within platform economies.

The demand for constant emotional engagement places significant strain on users, contributing to what can be described as emotional exhaustion. Unlike physical fatigue, which may be alleviated through rest, emotional exhaustion arises from prolonged exposure to affective stimuli and the continuous need to process, respond to, and manage emotions (Ragolane & Patel, 2025). Digital environments intensify this condition by presenting users with a relentless stream of emotionally charged content, ranging from personal updates and social interactions to global crises and political conflicts.

One of the defining features of contemporary digital life is the phenomenon of crisis saturation, where users are continuously exposed to news and representations of disasters, conflicts, and emergencies. While access to information can be empowering, the constant influx of distressing content can also overwhelm emotional capacities. The immediacy and frequency of such exposure create a sense of urgency that demands attention and response, yet the scale and persistence of crises often exceed individuals' ability to meaningfully engage. This mismatch between exposure and agency contributes to feelings of helplessness, fatigue, and eventual disengagement.

Paradoxically, the same mechanisms that initially stimulate emotional engagement can lead to affective numbing over time. As users are repeatedly exposed to intense emotional stimuli, their capacity to respond diminishes. What once elicited strong reactions may become normalized, leading to reduced sensitivity and a sense of indifference (Qi, 2025). This process is not indicative of a lack of empathy but rather a protective response to sustained emotional overload. However, the consequence is a weakening of emotional engagement with both personal and collective issues, contributing to a broader condition of social detachment.

The circulation of emotions within digital platforms is also shaped by algorithmic processes that prioritize certain affective states over others. Content that generates outrage, fear, or controversy tends to be more visible because it drives higher levels of interaction. This creates an environment in which negative emotions are disproportionately amplified, contributing to a heightened sense of tension and conflict (Milli et al., 2023). Users are drawn into cycles of reactive engagement, where emotional responses are continuously triggered and reinforced. Over time, this can lead to chronic stress and emotional depletion, as individuals struggle to manage the intensity and frequency of these experiences.

At the same time, platforms promote forms of positive affect, such as validation, approval, and social recognition, through mechanisms like likes, comments, and shares. These forms of feedback can provide moments of gratification and reinforce participation (Lindström et al., 2021). However, they also create dependencies on external validation, encouraging users to continuously seek affirmation through digital interactions. The pursuit of such validation can become a source of pressure, as individuals feel compelled to maintain visibility and engagement. This dynamic contributes to emotional instability, where feelings of satisfaction are contingent on fluctuating metrics of social approval (Voggenreiter et al., 2023).

The interplay between negative and positive affect creates a complex emotional landscape in which users oscillate between stimulation and exhaustion. Moments of excitement or validation are often followed by periods of fatigue or dissatisfaction, producing cycles of emotional highs and lows. These cycles are not random but are structured by platform design, which seeks to maximize engagement by sustaining emotional variability (Berger et al., 2021). While this variability can be engaging in the short term, it becomes draining over extended periods, contributing to the cumulative effects of digital burnout.

Importantly, emotional exhaustion is closely linked to the cognitive processes discussed in the previous section. As attention becomes fragmented and cognitive resources are depleted, the ability to regulate emotions is also compromised. Users may find it more difficult to process complex emotional experiences or to maintain stable affective states (Ravindran et al., 2013). This interconnection between cognitive and emotional dimensions reinforces the overall condition of burnout, where both mental and emotional capacities are strained.

Another significant aspect of affective economies is the blurring of boundaries between personal and public emotional expression. Digital platforms encourage users to share personal experiences and emotions in public or semi-public spaces, creating a continuous overlap between private life and mediated interaction. This visibility can intensify emotional experiences, as individuals become aware of being observed and evaluated by others (Fontefrancesco, 2023). The pressure to perform emotions in socially acceptable or engaging ways adds another layer of affective labor, further contributing to exhaustion.

The cumulative effect of these dynamics is a condition in which emotional engagement becomes both necessary and unsustainable. Users are required to remain emotionally responsive in order to participate in digital environments, yet the intensity and frequency of affective demands exceed sustainable limits (Steinert & Dennis, 2022). This contradiction lies at the heart of digital burnout, where the very mechanisms that sustain engagement also produce exhaustion.

Understanding digital burnout through the lens of affective economies shifts the focus from individual emotional regulation to the structural conditions that shape emotional experience. It highlights how platforms systematically organize and exploit affect, transforming emotions into resources for engagement and profit (Nielsen et al., 2025). In doing so, it reveals that emotional exhaustion is not simply a byproduct of excessive use but a consequence of environments designed to continuously stimulate and circulate affect.

In inference, the analysis of affective economies provides a crucial complement to the concept of attention collapse. While attention collapse captures the cognitive erosion associated with digital environments, affective economies illuminate the emotional processes that sustain and intensify engagement. Together, they offer a more comprehensive understanding of digital burnout as a condition that operates simultaneously at cognitive and emotional levels, produced through the interplay of platform design, algorithmic optimization, and the commodification of human experience.

Digital Burnout in Education

The transformation of attention and affect under platformed conditions has profound implications for education, where sustained attention, deep engagement, and reflective thinking are foundational to meaningful learning. As digital technologies become increasingly embedded in educational environments—through online learning platforms, digital resources, and hybrid pedagogies—the dynamics of attention collapse and emotional exhaustion begin to reshape not only how students learn but also how knowledge itself is produced and experienced (Barinkar & Zheng, 2025).

At the core of educational practice lies the capacity for sustained attention, which enables students to engage with complex texts, follow extended arguments, and develop critical understanding. However, in digitally saturated environments, this capacity is increasingly undermined by patterns of fragmented attention (Rider,

2021). Students accustomed to rapid, discontinuous streams of information often find it difficult to maintain focus on tasks that require prolonged concentration. Reading, for instance, shifts from a deep and immersive activity to a form of scanning, where engagement is intermittent and comprehension is partial. This transformation reflects not a decline in intellectual ability but a reconfiguration of attentional habits shaped by digital media (Ferreira, 2023).

The rise of online and platform-based education, particularly intensified during and after the COVID-19 pandemic, has further complicated these dynamics. While digital platforms have expanded access to education and enabled new forms of learning, they have also introduced conditions of continuous connectivity that blur the boundaries between study, leisure, and rest. Students are often required to navigate multiple digital interfaces simultaneously—video lectures, chat functions, notifications, and external resources—creating environments that encourage multitasking rather than focused engagement (Barinkar & Zheng, 2025). As discussed earlier, multitasking imposes cognitive costs that reduce efficiency and increase mental strain, ultimately contributing to fatigue and reduced learning outcomes.

This shift has significant consequences for comprehension and retention. Sustained attention is essential for encoding information into long-term memory and for building connections between ideas. When attention is fragmented, learning becomes superficial, with students retaining isolated pieces of information rather than developing integrated understanding (Rosen, 2017). This trend aligns with what has been described as the movement from deep learning to surface learning, where the emphasis shifts from critical inquiry and conceptual understanding to quick consumption and immediate output. Educational practices, in turn, may adapt to these conditions by prioritizing shorter, more interactive content formats, further reinforcing the cycle of fragmented attention (Rani et al., 2025).

Digital burnout also manifests in the form of screen fatigue, a condition characterized by mental exhaustion, reduced motivation, and diminished capacity to engage with academic tasks. Prolonged exposure to screens, combined with the cognitive demands of navigating digital environments, creates a sense of overload that can lead to disengagement. Students may experience difficulty concentrating, increased irritability, and a lack of motivation, all of which undermine the learning process (Nurani et al., 2022). Importantly, this fatigue is not solely the result of prolonged use but is intensified by the design of digital platforms, which encourage continuous interaction and limit opportunities for cognitive rest.

From a pedagogical perspective, these developments raise critical questions about the future of education in digitally mediated environments. If meaningful learning depends on sustained attention, how can it be achieved in contexts that systematically fragment that attention? The challenge is not merely to integrate technology into education but to critically examine how technological infrastructures shape cognitive and affective conditions of learning. Without such examination, there is a risk that education becomes increasingly instrumentalized, focusing on efficiency, output, and measurable performance at the expense of depth, reflection, and intellectual growth (Szűts, 2023).

Furthermore, the normalization of distraction within digital environments may lead to a redefinition of what counts as learning. Multitasking, rapid information processing, and constant connectivity are often framed as necessary skills for the digital age. However, this framing can obscure the cognitive costs associated with these practices and the ways in which they undermine deeper forms of engagement (Schuett, 2024). The question, then, is not simply whether students can adapt to these conditions, but whether such adaptation aligns with the broader goals of education as a space for critical thinking, creativity, and sustained inquiry.

In this context, digital burnout in education must be understood not as an individual failure to manage time or attention but as a structural condition produced by the intersection of platform design and pedagogical practice. Addressing this condition requires moving beyond strategies that focus solely on individual self-regulation and toward a more critical engagement with the systems that shape educational experience. By situating attention collapse within the broader context of platform capitalism, this analysis highlights the need to rethink the role of attention in education and to consider how learning environments can be structured to support, rather than undermine, sustained engagement.

Attention Collapse and Democratic Life

The implications of attention collapse extend beyond individual cognition and educational practice to the broader domain of democratic life. Democracy relies fundamentally on the capacity of citizens to attend—to engage with information, deliberate on issues, and participate in collective decision-making processes. Sustained attention enables individuals to follow complex arguments, evaluate evidence, and empathize with diverse perspectives (Ergas, 2016). However, in an attention economy characterized by fragmentation, emotional intensity, and continuous stimulation, these capacities are increasingly compromised.

Digital platforms have become central arenas for political communication, shaping how information is produced, circulated, and consumed. Algorithmic systems prioritize content that generates high levels of engagement, often amplifying material that is emotionally charged, sensational, or polarizing. As a result, political discourse is frequently structured around immediacy and intensity rather than depth and deliberation. Users are exposed to rapid streams of information that demand quick reactions rather than sustained reflection, contributing to a mode of engagement that is reactive rather than critical.

This environment fosters affective polarization, where political engagement is driven more by emotional responses than by reasoned analysis. Content that provokes outrage or fear is more likely to be shared and amplified, creating feedback loops that intensify division and reduce the space for nuanced discussion. At the same time, the constant influx of information—often conflicting or overwhelming—can lead to information fatigue, where individuals feel unable to process or make sense of what they encounter (Qureshi & Bhatt, 2024). This condition is closely linked to attention collapse, as fragmented attention limits the ability to engage deeply with political issues.

One of the paradoxical effects of this environment is that increased access to information does not necessarily lead to greater political engagement. Instead, it can produce disengagement and apathy, as individuals become overwhelmed by the volume and intensity of mediated content. The phenomenon of crisis fatigue, discussed in the previous section, is particularly relevant here (Shafique, 2024). Continuous exposure to political crises, social injustices, and global challenges can create a sense of helplessness, where individuals feel that their attention and concern do not translate into meaningful action. Over time, this can lead to withdrawal from political processes and a decline in civic participation.

At the same time, attention collapse creates conditions that make individuals more susceptible to manipulation and misinformation. When attention is fragmented and cognitive resources are limited, individuals are less able to critically evaluate information or to distinguish between credible and misleading sources (Ijaz et al., 2022). Algorithmic systems that prioritize engagement over accuracy can further exacerbate this problem by amplifying sensational or misleading content. In this context, the erosion of sustained attention becomes a vulnerability that can be exploited for political or economic purposes.

The role of algorithmic governance is particularly significant in shaping these dynamics. By determining what content is visible and how it is presented, algorithms influence not only what users see but also how they think and feel about political issues. This form of governance operates invisibly, embedding power within the infrastructure of digital platforms (Prodnik & Prodnik, 2025). Users may perceive their engagement as autonomous, yet it is structured by systems that prioritize certain types of content and interaction. This raises important questions about agency, control, and the distribution of power in digital environments.

The cumulative effect of these processes is a transformation of democratic participation itself. Citizens are increasingly positioned as reactive participants, responding to stimuli rather than engaging in sustained deliberation. Political engagement becomes episodic and emotionally driven, shaped by cycles of attention that are dictated by platform dynamics rather than by collective priorities (Gerbaudo,

2022). This shift challenges traditional models of democracy that assume informed, reflective, and engaged citizens are capable of sustained participation.

A critical question that emerges from this analysis is whether attention collapse leads primarily to apathy or to heightened susceptibility to manipulation. In practice, these outcomes are not mutually exclusive. On one hand, individuals may withdraw from political engagement due to fatigue and overload. On the other hand, those who remain engaged may do so in ways that are shaped by algorithmic amplification and emotional intensity, making them more vulnerable to polarization and misinformation (Gorski, 2022). Both outcomes represent challenges to democratic processes, as they undermine the conditions necessary for informed and collective decision-making.

Understanding attention collapse as a structural condition of digital environments highlights the need to rethink democracy in the context of the attention economy. If attention is a prerequisite for meaningful participation, then its erosion poses a fundamental challenge to democratic life (Michel & Gandon, 2024). Addressing this challenge requires not only improving media literacy or encouraging individual responsibility but also critically examining the systems that shape the distribution and quality of attention.

In brief, attention collapse represents a critical intersection between cognitive transformation and political consequence. By fragmenting attention and intensifying emotional engagement, digital platforms reshape the conditions under which democracy operates. The result is a form of participation that is both amplified and diminished—amplified in its immediacy and reach, yet diminished in its depth and sustainability. Recognizing this tension is essential for understanding the broader implications of digital burnout and for imagining new forms of engagement that can support democratic life in an era of platform capitalism.

Rethinking Attention: Ethical and Collective Perspectives

The preceding sections have demonstrated that digital burnout and attention collapse are not isolated psychological phenomena but systemic outcomes of platformed environments structured around the extraction and monetization of attention. If attention has been transformed into a central resource within digital capitalism, then its erosion raises not only cognitive and emotional concerns but also ethical and political questions (Michel & Gandon, 2024a). To move beyond descriptive analysis, it becomes necessary to rethink attention itself—not as a purely individual capacity to be managed or optimized, but as a shared social resource shaped by collective conditions and institutional arrangements.

Dominant responses to digital burnout tend to emphasize individual strategies of self-regulation, such as digital detoxes, mindfulness practices, or productivity techniques. While these approaches may offer temporary relief, they remain limited in scope because they treat burnout as a problem of personal behavior rather than structural design. By placing responsibility on individuals, such narratives obscure the ways in which digital environments are engineered to capture and sustain attention (Fish, 2017). The burden of adaptation is shifted onto users, who are expected to regulate themselves within systems explicitly designed to undermine such regulation. This framing not only depoliticizes the issue but also reinforces the very conditions that produce burnout.

Reframing attention as a collective and ethical concern requires a shift in perspective from individual management to structural critique. Attention is not simply a private resource that individuals can allocate at will; it is shaped by the environments in which individuals are embedded (Dika, 2022). Digital platforms organize the conditions of attention through interface design, algorithmic curation, and economic incentives, influencing what is visible, what is prioritized, and how users engage. As such, attention becomes a site of power, where competing interests—commercial, political, and social—intersect and contend.

From this perspective, the concept of attention justice becomes analytically significant. Attention justice refers to the equitable distribution and protection of attentional resources within society, recognizing that not all actors have equal capacity to capture or sustain attention. Large digital platforms possess disproportionate power to direct collective attention, shaping public discourse and individual experience alike (Belgroun et al., 2025). This concentration of power raises questions about whose voices are amplified, whose concerns are marginalized, and how attention is allocated across different issues and communities.

The ethical implications of attention extraction are particularly evident in the ways platforms prioritize engagement over well-being. Algorithmic systems are optimized to maximize interaction, often by amplifying emotionally charged or sensational content. While this may increase user activity, it also contributes to cognitive overload and emotional exhaustion (Voinea et al., 2024). The pursuit of engagement as an end in itself reflects a broader misalignment between platform objectives and user well-being, where the value of attention is measured in economic terms rather than in its contribution to meaningful experience or social good.

Rethinking attention also involves recognizing its role in enabling fundamental human and social capacities. Sustained attention underpins learning, creativity, empathy, and democratic participation. When attention is fragmented and depleted, these capacities are compromised, affecting not only individual well-being but also collective life. For instance, the ability to engage empathetically with others depends on the capacity to attend to their experiences in a sustained and reflective manner. Similarly, democratic deliberation requires the ability to focus on complex issues, evaluate competing arguments, and consider long-term consequences. The erosion of attention, therefore, has implications that extend far beyond personal productivity or mental health.

In this context, the question of ownership becomes central: who controls attention, and for whose benefit is it organized? In current platform economies, attention is effectively owned and managed by corporate entities that design and regulate digital environments. Users participate in these environments but have limited control over the conditions that shape their engagement (Schneider et al., 2025). This asymmetry highlights the need to consider alternative frameworks in which attention is treated not as a commodity to be exploited but as a common resource to be protected and cultivated.

Such a shift does not necessarily require immediate technical solutions but calls for a reorientation of how attention is conceptualized and valued. Instead of viewing attention as an individual asset to be optimized for efficiency, it can be understood as an ecological system that requires balance, sustainability, and care. Just as environmental resources are subject to overuse and depletion, attentional resources can be exhausted through continuous extraction. This ecological perspective emphasizes the importance of limits, boundaries, and restorative practices, not only at the individual level but also within the design of digital systems.

At the same time, it is important to recognize that attention is inherently relational. It is shaped by social interactions, cultural practices, and institutional contexts. The ways in which individuals attend to the world are influenced by the norms and structures that surround them. Therefore, addressing attention collapse requires collective engagement with the conditions that shape attention, including platform design, economic incentives, and regulatory frameworks. It is not sufficient to encourage individuals to "pay attention better" if the environments in which they operate are systematically structured to fragment and exploit their attention.

The concept of ethical platform design emerges as a critical area of reflection within this framework. While this chapter does not aim to propose prescriptive solutions, it is important to consider what it would mean for platforms to be designed in ways that support, rather than undermine, attentional well-being. This might involve rethinking metrics of success, moving away from engagement maximization toward more sustainable forms of interaction. It could also involve introducing friction or boundaries that encourage reflection and limit continuous consumption (Dennis, 2020). Such considerations point toward the possibility of alternative design paradigms that prioritize user well-being and social value over purely economic objectives.

Ultimately, the challenge of rethinking attention lies in recognizing its dual nature as both a personal capacity and a collective condition. Individuals experience attention subjectively, yet the structures that shape attention are external and systemic. Bridging this divide requires an approach that acknowledges the interplay between individual agency and structural constraint. It also requires a willingness to question the assumptions underlying current digital systems, particularly the idea that more engagement is inherently better.

In deduction, rethinking attention as a social, ethical, and political resource provides a necessary framework for understanding and addressing digital burnout. By moving beyond individualistic explanations and situating attention within broader structures of power and design, this perspective opens new avenues for critique and reflection. It highlights the need to consider not only how attention is used but also how it is organized, distributed, and valued within contemporary society. In doing so, it reinforces the central argument of this chapter: that digital burnout is not a failure of individuals but a condition produced by systems that prioritize extraction over sustainability. Recognizing this is a crucial step toward reimagining the role of attention in an era defined by its continuous capture and commodification.

CONCLUSION

Digital burnout and attention collapse are not incidental byproducts of contemporary media use but intrinsic features of platformed life. This chapter has demonstrated that the commodification of attention—driven by algorithmic governance and the logics of surveillance capitalism—systematically produces conditions of cognitive exhaustion and emotional fatigue. By reframing burnout as a condition produced through design rather than individual failure, the analysis challenges dominant narratives that attribute responsibility primarily to personal behavior or self-regulation.

Understanding attention as a social, ethical, and political resource opens critical pathways for rethinking both responsibility and resistance. The pressures of digital burnout cannot be addressed solely through individual coping strategies; they demand collective awareness and engagement with the structural systems that profit from continuous attention extraction. In a media environment characterized by emotional saturation, cognitive fragmentation, and growing social indifference, the question of attention becomes central to the future of learning, empathy, and democratic participation.

Reclaiming attention, therefore, is not merely a matter of personal discipline but a broader socio-political imperative. It requires reimagining the conditions under which attention is organized, valued, and sustained, and confronting the systemic forces that render exhaustion a normalized state of being in digital life.

Declarations

- Ethical compliance: Follows academic and ethical standards.
- Consent to participate/publication: Not applicable.

- Conflict of interest: None declared.
- Funding: No external funding.
- Data availability: Not applicable.
- Use of AI Tools: *Grammarly* and *Paperpal* (Premium) were used only for language refinement and readability improvement.

ACKNOWLEDGEMENTS

The author expresses sincere gratitude to colleagues and peers for their intellectual engagement and encouragement during the development of this chapter.

REFERENCES

Allmer, T., Sevignani, S., & Prodnik, J. A. (2015). Mapping approaches to user participation and digital labour: A critical perspective. In *Palgrave Macmillan UK eBooks* (pp. 153–171). DOI: 10.1057/9781137478573_9

Alloway, T., & Alloway, R. (2011). Attentional control and engagement with digital technology. *Nature Precedings*. DOI: 10.1038/npre.2011.5603.1

Bachmann, P., & Siegert, G. (2021). How to buy, sell, and trade attention: A sociology of (digital) attention markets. In *Digital attention markets* (pp. 147–157). DOI: 10.1007/978-3-030-61619-9_10

Barinkar, M. A., & Zheng, F. (2025). How digital platforms are changing the way students learn. *Preprints.org*. DOI: 10.20944/preprints202507.0332.v1

Belgroun, H., Michel, F., & Gandon, F. (2025). No such thing as free brain time: For a Pigouvian tax on attention capture. In *Proceedings of the AAAI/ACM Conference on AI Ethics and Society, 8*(1), 367–378. DOI: 10.1609/aies.v8i1.36555

Berger, J., Kim, Y. D., & Meyer, R. (2021). What makes content engaging? How emotional dynamics shape success. *The Journal of Consumer Research, 48*(2), 235–250. DOI: 10.1093/jcr/ucab010

Bhadouria, N., Macknight, S., Francis, A., & Yadav, A. (2025). The unblinking scroll: Exploring the perceptual and cognitive impacts of continuous reel scrolling. *International Journal of Multidisciplinary Research and Analysis, 8*(9). Advance online publication. DOI: 10.47191/ijmra/v8-i09-14

Bodle, R. (2016). A critical theory of advertising as surveillance: Algorithms, big data, and power. In *Advertising and surveillance* (pp. 148–162). DOI: 10.4324/9781315625768

Brumby, D. P., Janssen, C. P., & Mark, G. (2019). How do interruptions affect productivity? In *Apress eBooks* (pp. 85–107). DOI: 10.1007/978-1-4842-4221-6_9

Cemiloglu, D., Naiseh, M., Catania, M., Oinas-Kukkonen, H., & Ali, R. (2021). The fine line between persuasion and digital addiction. In *Lecture Notes in Computer Science* (pp. 289–307). DOI: 10.1007/978-3-030-79460-6_23

Chen, Y., Fu, Y., Chen, Z., Radesky, J., & Hiniker, A. (2024). The engagement-prolonging designs teens encounter on very large online platforms. *arXiv*. /arxiv.2411.12083DOI: 10.48550

Citton, Y. (2017). *The ecology of attention*. Polity Press.

Crary, J. (2013). *24/7: Late capitalism and the ends of sleep*. Verso.

De Medeiros, A. S., Glatzl, L. A., & Lifschitz, S. (2024). Surveillance capitalism revealed: Tracing the hidden world of web data collection. In *Proceedings* (pp. 388–397). DOI: 10.5753/sbbd_estendido.2024.244000

Denegri-Knott, J., Jenkins, R., Molesworth, M., & Grigore, G. (2023). Platformised possessions and relational labour. *Marketing Theory*, *24*(1), 23–44. DOI: 10.1177/14705931231201783

Dennis, M. J. (2020). Cultivating digital well-being and the rise of self-care apps. In *Philosophical Studies Series* (pp. 119–137). DOI: 10.1007/978-3-030-50585-1_6

Domalewska, D. (2025). Digital entrapment. *Kultura i Spoleczenstwo*, *69*(3), 151–171. DOI: 10.35757/KiS.2025.69.3.9

Drüppel, K., Dombrowski, J., & Trepte, S. (2025). Use it or lose it: The relationship between short-form video use and sustained attention. *OSF Preprints*. DOI: 10.31234/osf.io/qbxw4_v1

Edwards, D. J., Kaastra, L. T., Fisher, B., Chang, R., & Chen, M. (2017). Cognitive information theories of psychology and applications with visualization and HCI through crowdsourcing platforms. In *Lecture Notes in Computer Science* (pp. 139–153). DOI: 10.1007/978-3-319-66435-4_6

Ergas, O. (2016). Attention please: Positioning attention at the center of curriculum and pedagogy. *Journal of Curriculum Theorizing*, *31*(2). Advance online publication. DOI: 10.63997/jct.v31i2.581

Ernst, A., & Schnauber-Stockmann, A. (2024). Won't stop 'til you get enough? Determinants of disengaging from mobile media apps in daily life. *OSF Preprints*. DOI: 10.31219/osf.io/atk49

Ferreira, J. (2023). The challenge of hyperdistraction for design education. DOI: 10.21606/iasdr.2023.247

Fish, A. (2017). Technology retreats and the politics of social media. *TripleC*, *15*(1), 355–369. DOI: 10.31269/triplec.v15i1.807

Fisher, J. T., & Keene, J. R. (2020). Attention, working memory, and media multitasking. In *Cognitive perspectives on multitasking* (pp. 177–196). DOI: 10.4324/9781351235587-16

Flayelle, M., Brevers, D., King, D. L., Maurage, P., Perales, J. C., & Billieux, J. (2023). A taxonomy of technology design features that promote potentially addictive online behaviours. *Nature Reviews Psychology*, *2*(3), 136–150. DOI: 10.1038/s44159-023-00153-4

Fontefrancesco, M. F. (2023). Affective economy: A theoretical outline. *Encyclopedia*, *3*(3), 1020–1027. DOI: 10.3390/encyclopedia3030074

Fournier, H., Fournel, A., Osiurak, F., Koenig, O., Pâris, F., Gaujoux, V., & Ringeval, F. (2025). Attention hijacked: How social media notifications disrupt cognitive processing. *OSF Preprints*. DOI: 10.31234/osf.io/z4ruj_v1

Garcia-Rivadulla, S. (2016). Personalization vs. privacy. *IFLA Journal*, *42*(3), 227–238. DOI: 10.1177/0340035216662890

Gerbaudo, P. (2022). Theorizing reactive democracy. *Democratic Theory*, *9*(2), 120–138. DOI: 10.3167/dt.2022.090207

Gorski, L. C. (2022). Uninterested, disenchanted, or overwhelmed? An analysis of motives behind intentional and unintentional news avoidance. *Communications*, *48*(4), 563–587. DOI: 10.1515/commun-2021-0084

Han, B.-C. (2015). *The burnout society*. Stanford University Press.

Hans, A., Singh, N. T., Kumar, R., Kumar, A., & Choubey, A., & Suresh. (2024). The psychology behind addictive applications in technology. In *Proceedings of the conference* (pp. 669–672). DOI: 10.1109/IC2PCT60090.2024.10486603

Hartanto, A., Lua, V. Y. Q., Kasturiratna, K. T. A. S., Koh, P. S., Tng, G. Y. Q., Kaur, M., Quek, F. Y. X., Chia, J. L., & Majeed, N. M. (2024). The effect of mere presence of smartphone on cognitive functions: A four-level meta-analysis. *Technology, Mind, and Behavior*, *5*(1), 1–14. DOI: 10.1037/tmb0000123

Heitmayer, M. (2024). The second wave of attention economics: Attention as a universal symbolic currency on social media and beyond. *Interacting with Computers*, *37*(1), 18–29. DOI: 10.1093/iwc/iwae035

Hristova, D., Jovicic, S., Goebl, B., & Slunecko, T. (2020). The social media game: How gamification shapes our social media engagement. In *Social media and gamification* (pp. 63–94). DOI: 10.1201/9780429274596-8

Huberman, B. A., & Wu, F. (2008). The economics of attention: Maximizing user value in information-rich environments. *Advances in Complex Systems, 11*(4), 487–496. DOI: 10.1142/S0219525908001830

Ijaz, D., Araja, J., Walker, S., & Mahmoud, M. (2022). Understanding context collapse for social media users. In *Proceedings of the International Conference on Computational Science and Computational Intelligence* (pp. 807–812). DOI: 10.1109/CSCI58124.2022.00147

Jacobs, A. (2025). *Filter fatigue: Optimization, context erosion, and attention in digital systems. Zenodo.* DOI: 10.5281/zenodo.17425040

Janáček, E. M., & Balázová, L. J. (2024). Social fatigue and the virtual self in relation to excessive online self-presentation and its impact on real-life social interactions. *Studies in Psychological Science*, *2*(4), 1–8. DOI: 10.56397/SPS.2024.12.01

Jingtong, Z. (2023). The attention economy in the new media era: Challenges and recommendations. *International Business and Economics Studies*, *5*(3), 49–56. DOI: 10.22158/ibes.v5n3p49

Langlois, G., & Elmer, G. (2018). Impersonal subjectivation from platforms to infrastructures. *Media Culture & Society*, *41*(2), 236–251. DOI: 10.1177/0163443718818374

Laschke, M. (2023). Friction as a means of choice. *Proyecta56. Industrial Design Journal*, *3*(3). Advance online publication. DOI: 10.25267/P56-IDJ.2023.i3.08

Lervik-Olsen, L., Andreassen, T. W., & Fennis, B. M. (2023). When enough is not enough: Behavioral and motivational paths to compulsive social media consumption. *European Journal of Marketing*, *58*(2), 519–547. DOI: 10.1108/EJM-12-2022-0898

Lindström, B., Bellander, M., Schultner, D. T., Chang, A., Tobler, P. N., & Amodio, D. M. (2021). A computational reward learning account of social media engagement. *Nature Communications*, *12*(1), 1311. DOI: 10.1038/s41467-020-19607-x PMID: 33637702

Loh, K. K., & Kanai, R. (2015). How has the internet reshaped human cognition? *The Neuroscientist*, *22*(5), 506–520. DOI: 10.1177/1073858415595005 PMID: 26170005

Lorenz-Spreen, P., Mønsted, B. M., Hövel, P., & Lehmann, S. (2019). Accelerating dynamics of collective attention. *Nature Communications*, *10*(1), 1759. DOI: 10.1038/s41467-019-09311-w PMID: 30988286

Lukoff, K., Lyngs, U., Zade, H., Liao, J. V., Choi, J., Fan, K., Munson, S. A., & Hiniker, A. (2021). How the design of YouTube influences user sense of agency. In *Proceedings of the CHI Conference on Human Factors in Computing Systems*. DOI: 10.1145/3411764.3445467

Mark, G., Gudith, D., & Klocke, U. (2008). The cost of interrupted work: More speed and stress. In *Proceedings of the SIGCHI Conference on Human Factors in Computing Systems* (pp. 107–110). DOI: 10.1145/1357054.1357072

Mathieu, D., & Vengerfeldt, P. P. (2020). Data loop of media and audience. *MedieKultur: Journal of Media and Communication Research*, *36*(69), 116–138. DOI: 10.7146/mediekultur.v36i69.121178

Michel, F., & Gandon, F. (2024). Pay attention: A call to regulate the attention market and prevent algorithmic emotional governance. In *Proceedings of the AAAI/ACM Conference on AI Ethics and Society, 7*, 971–983. DOI: 10.1609/aies.v7i1.31696

Michel, F., & Gandon, F. (2024). Pay attention: A call to regulate the attention market and prevent algorithmic emotional governance. *arXiv*. /arxiv.2402.16670DOI: 10.48550

Milli, S., Carroll, M., Wang, Y., Pandey, S., Zhao, S., & Dragan, A. D. (2023). Engagement, user satisfaction, and the amplification of divisive content on social media. *arXiv*. /arxiv.2305.16941DOI: 10.48550

Milli, S., Carroll, M., Wang, Y., Pandey, S., Zhao, S., & Dragan, A. D. (2025). Engagement, user satisfaction, and the amplification of divisive content on social media. *PNAS Nexus*, *4*(3), pgaf062. Advance online publication. DOI: 10.1093/pnasnexus/pgaf062 PMID: 40070432

Momoh, E. Y., Adamu, M., & Isa, A. A. (2025). The effects of multitasking on cognitive performance and productivity: A comparative analysis. *Journal of Management Science and Entrepreneurship*. DOI: 10.70382/bejmse.v9i7.042

Montag, C., & Elhai, J. D. (2023). On social media design, (online-)time well spent and addictive behaviors in the age of surveillance capitalism. *Current Addiction Reports*, *10*(3), 610–616. DOI: 10.1007/s40429-023-00494-3

Montalvo, F. L., Miuccio, M., & Waldfogle, G. E. (2021). Ethical design of social technology. In *Advances in human and social aspects of technology* (pp. 20–47). DOI: 10.4018/978-1-7998-6453-0.ch002

Newport, C. (2016). *Deep work*. Grand Central Publishing.

Nielsen, L. Y., Krøjer, J., & Nielsen, M. L. (2025). The entanglement of emotional labour and digital work platforms. *MedieKultur: Journal of Media and Communication Research, 40*(78). Advance online publication. DOI: 10.7146/mk.v40i78.137268

Nurani, G. A., Nafis, R. Y., Ramadhani, A. N., Prastiwi, M., Hanif, N., & Ardianto, D. (2022). Online learning impacts on academic burnout: A literature review. *Journal of Digital Learning and Education, 2*(3), 150–158. DOI: 10.52562/jdle.v2i3.433

Paasonen, S. (2016). Fickle focus: Distraction, affect and the production of value in social media. *First Monday*. Advance online publication. DOI: 10.5210/fm.v21i10.6949

Paasonen, S. (2018). Affect, data, manipulation and price in social media. *Distinktion : Scandinavian Journal of Social Theory, 19*(2), 214–229. DOI: 10.1080/1600910X.2018.1475289

Priego, E. (2024). Finding equilibrium in a hyperconnected world: The struggle against burnout. DOI: 10.59350/9rxbb-45j13

Prodnik, J. A. (2025). *Power asymmetries in the algorithmic formation of public opinion*. Dialogues on Digital Society., DOI: 10.1177/29768640251385702

Qureshi, I., & Bhatt, B. (2024). Social media-induced polarisation. *Information Systems Journal, 34*(4), 1425–1431. DOI: 10.1111/isj.12525

Ragolane, M., & Patel, S. (2025). Too much, too fast: Understanding AI fatigue in the digital acceleration era. *International Journal of Arts, Humanities &. Social Science, 6*(8), 53–60. DOI: 10.56734/ijahss.v6n8a7

Rani, S., Pionera, M., Kuswandi, D., & Wedi, A. (2025). Optimization of instructional technology for attention span in the digital generation. *Pedagogika: Jurnal Pedagogika dan Dinamika Pendidikan, 13*(2), 383–393. DOI: 10.30598/pedagogikavol13issue2page383-393

Ravindran, T., Chua, A. Y. K., & Goh, D. H. (2013). Characteristics of social network fatigue. In *Proceedings of the International Conference on Information Technology: New Generations* (pp. 431–438). DOI: 10.1109/ITNG.2013.66

Ravindran, T., Chua, A. Y. K., & Goh, D. H. (2014). Antecedents and effects of social network fatigue. *Journal of the Association for Information Science and Technology, 65*(11), 2306–2320. DOI: 10.1002/asi.23122

Rider, S. (2021). Higher education: Learning how to pay attention. In *Debating higher education: Philosophical perspectives* (pp. 81–94). DOI: 10.1007/978-3-030-69628-3_6

Rixen, J. O., Meinhardt, L., Glöckler, M., Ziegenbein, M., Schlothauer, A., Colley, M., Rukzio, E., & Gugenheimer, J. (2023). The loop and reasons to break it: Investigating infinite scrolling behaviour in social media applications and reasons to stop. *Proceedings of the ACM on Human-Computer Interaction, 7*(MHCI), 1–22. DOI: 10.1145/3604275

Rosen, L. D. (2012). *iDisorder*. Palgrave Macmillan.

Rosen, L. D. (2017). The distracted student mind—Enhancing its focus and attention. *Phi Delta Kappan, 99*(2), 8–14. DOI: 10.1177/0031721717734183

Sánchez-Muñoz, M., Jiménez-González, G., & Nieves-Alegre, E. (2025). Challenges and opportunities in the attention economy in the digital age. In *ECORFAN eBooks* (pp. 85–99). DOI: 10.35429/H.2025.3.85.99

Schneider, N., Nabben, K., Tamari, R., & Zargham, M. (2025). Online governance surfaces and attention economies. *OSF Preprints*. DOI: 10.33767/osf.io/cdrmp_v1

Schuett, K. C. (2024). How do students and teachers respond to digital distraction in school? In *Digital education and learning* (pp. 85–94). DOI: 10.1007/978-3-031-53215-3_5

Schüll, N. D. (2004). Digital gambling: The coincidence of desire and design. *The Annals of the American Academy of Political and Social Science, 597*(1), 65–81. DOI: 10.1177/0002716204270435

Schüll, N. D. (2012). *Addiction by design*. Princeton University Press. DOI: 10.2307/j.ctt12f4d0

Serrano-Puche, J. (2016). Key features of digital media consumption: Implications of users' emotional dimension. In *Advances in intelligent systems and computing* (pp. 471–477). DOI: 10.1007/978-3-319-46068-0_62

Shafique, S. (2024). The impact of social media on political engagement: A double-edged sword. *Research Consortium Archive, 2*(3), 141–149. DOI: 10.62019/24s60j71

Shin, D. (2024). Misinformation, extremism, and conspiracies: Amplification and polarization by algorithms. In *Digital misinformation studies* (pp. 49–78). DOI: 10.1007/978-3-031-52569-8_3

Singh, R. (2025). The algorithm effect: How social media shapes your thinking. *International Journal of Advanced Research in Science. Tongxin Jishu, 529–531*, 529–531. Advance online publication. DOI: 10.48175/IJARSCT-28066

Somani, P. P., Iyer, V., Wani, P. S., & Tambuskar, D. P. (2025). Engagement in an age of distraction. In *IGI Global eBooks* (pp. 269–302). DOI: 10.4018/979-8-3693-8089-5.ch010

Steinert, S., & Dennis, M. J. (2022). Emotions and digital well-being: On social media's emotional affordances. *Philosophy & Technology*, *35*(2), 36. DOI: 10.1007/s13347-022-00530-6 PMID: 35450167

Szűts, Z. (2023). Learning in an attention-based economy and society. *Opus et Educatio*, *9*(4). Advance online publication. DOI: 10.3311/ope.530

Terranova, T. (2004). *Network culture*. Pluto Press. DOI: 10.2307/j.ctt183q5pq

Törnberg, P. (2023). Platforms as states: The rise of governance through data power. In *Bristol University Press eBooks* (pp. 42–58). DOI: 10.56687/9781529233551-006

Tufekci, Z. (2015). Algorithmic harms beyond Facebook and Google. *Colorado Technology Law Journal*, *13*, 203–218.

Vercellone, C., & Di Stasio, A. (2023). Free digital labor as a new form of exploitation: A critical analysis. *Science and Society*, *87*(3), 334–358. DOI: 10.1521/siso.2023.87.3.334

Voggenreiter, A., Brandt, S., Putterer, F., Frings, A., & Pfeffer, J. (2023). The role of likes: How online feedback impacts users' mental health. *arXiv*. /arxiv.2312.11914DOI: 10.48550

Voinea, C., Marin, L., & Vică, C. (2024). Digital slot machines: Social media platforms as attentional scaffolds. *Topoi*, *43*(3), 685–695. DOI: 10.1007/s11245-024-10031-0

Wahl-Jorgensen, K. (2018). The emotional architecture of social media. In *Emotions, media and politics* (pp. 77–93). DOI: 10.4324/9781315193434-6

Ward, A. F., Duke, K., Gneezy, A., & Bos, M. W. (2017). Brain drain: The mere presence of one's own smartphone reduces available cognitive capacity. *Journal of the Association for Consumer Research*, *2*(2), 140–154. DOI: 10.1086/691462

Watzl, S. (2022). The ethics of attention: An argument and a framework. In *The ethics of attention* (pp. 89–112). DOI: 10.4324/9781351202114-6

Williams, J. (2018). *Stand out of our light*. Cambridge University Press. DOI: 10.1017/9781108453004

Wohllebe, A. (2020). Consumer acceptance of app push notifications: Systematic review on the influence of frequency. *International Journal of Interactive Mobile Technologies, 14*(13), 36. DOI: 10.3991/ijim.v14i13.14563

Wu, T. (2016). *The attention merchants.* Knopf.

Zuboff, S. (2019). *The age of surveillance capitalism.* PublicAffairs.

Zulli, D., & Zulli, D. J. (2022). Extending the internet meme: Conceptualizing technological mimesis and imitation publics. *New Media & Society, 24*(8), 1876–1894. DOI: 10.1177/1461444820983603

Chapter 2
Emotional Labor on Social Media:
Visibility, Performance, and Burnout in Digital Culture

Buse Punar
http://orcid.org/0009-0007-9782-6157
Istanbul Arel University, Turkey

ABSTRACT

This book chapter examines social media within the context of digital labor regimes, focusing on how users—particularly influencers—strategically and performatively manage emotions. It argues that social media transforms individuals not only into content creators but also into digital emotional laborers who regulate emotions to sustain visibility and engagement. The concept of emotional labor is adapted to the digital context and analyzed through the commodification of emotions, algorithmic incentives, and the attention economy. Within platform capitalism, user interactions and emotional expressions are converted into economic value, while self-branding and authenticity performances shape influencer culture. The chapter further explores visibility labor and relational labor, addressing digital emotional fatigue and burnout, and demonstrates how emotions on social media have shifted from individual expression to a platform-regulated form of labor.

INTRODUCTION

The concept of emotional labor was introduced into the social sciences literature through Arlie Hochschild's seminal work *The Managed Heart* (1983) and was developed to explain the emotional performances that individuals—particularly

DOI: 10.4018/979-8-3373-8307-1.ch002

those employed in the service sector—are required to display as an integral part of their work (Hochschild, 1983; Yürür & Ünlü, 2011). Hochschild defines emotional labor as the process by which employees manage their feelings in accordance with organizational expectations and present them within prescribed frameworks, emphasizing that this form of labor is closely linked both to occupational discipline and to the commodification of emotions. In this respect, emotional labor has evolved into a comprehensive concept that extends beyond individual emotion regulation and points to a mode of work embedded within broader economic and social relations.

The processes of digitalization, the rise of social media platforms, and the emergence of the visibility economy have rendered emotional labor a defining dynamic not only in face-to-face service interactions but also within online environments. Social media has given rise to a new labor regime in which users continuously cultivate their visibility, personal brands, and digital networks of interaction (Fuchs, 2021). Within these platforms, whether as professional influencers or ordinary participants, users strategically manage their emotions in order to meet followers' expectations, sustain engagement, and conform to algorithmically defined criteria of visibility. Baym's (2015) conceptualization of "relational labor" further illustrates that these contemporary digital interaction structures rely on ongoing emotional work aimed at establishing and maintaining sustainable communicative relationships.

The functioning of social media platforms relies on technological and economic mechanisms that shape the visibility and circulation of emotions. Debates on platform capitalism (Fuchs, 2021; Srnicek, 2017) demonstrate that the emotional content produced by users has become one of the core resources of the digital economy. In particular, metric-based systems such as likes, comments, shares, and follower counts transform users' emotional expressions into quantifiable indicators, thereby converting them into economic value. According to Hearn and Schoenhoff's (2016) approach to the visibility economy, individuals in digital culture present themselves as "personal brands," the appeal of which is largely grounded in their emotional performances. Consequently, emotions on digital platforms function not merely as means of personal expression but emerge as central elements within processes of competition, self-promotion, and capital generation.

One of the key factors amplifying the visibility of emotional labor in digital environments is the decisive power of algorithms over content distribution. Algorithms tend to prioritize emotionally charged content, rendering it more visible and encouraging users to share content more frequently, more positively, and in ways that maximize engagement (Bishop, 2019). This dynamic implies that users are required to perform emotional labor not only for other users but also for the operational logic of the platform itself. McStay's (2018) concepts of "emotional artificial intelligence" and "empathic media" illustrate how emotions within this technological landscape become increasingly traceable, analyzable, and subject to modulation.

The gendered dimension of digital emotional labor also warrants particular attention. Duffy's (2017) work demonstrates that women content creators, in particular, are exposed more intensely to expectations of positivity, accessibility, attractiveness, and the provision of emotional support on social media. While digital platforms may create new opportunities for visibility, they simultaneously subject women to continuous surveillance, evaluation, and pressure to produce sustained emotional performances (Duffy, 2017; Gill & Orgad, 2015). For this reason, digital emotional labor is closely intertwined not only with economic and psychological processes but also with persistent gender-based inequalities (Hochschild, 1983; Ahmed, 2013).

Although emotional labor has traditionally been examined within face-to-face service work, contemporary digital culture requires a broader theoretical perspective that includes self-presentation, surveillance, emotional visibility, and digital labor exploitation. Erving Goffman's dramaturgical approach helps explain how social media users continuously perform identities before visible and invisible audiences, transforming digital platforms into permanent stages of emotional performance (Goffman, 1959). Similarly, Melissa Gregg highlights how digital labor dissolves the boundaries between work and private life, creating an "always-on" culture in which users remain constantly available, emotionally responsive, and visible (Gregg, 2013). David Lyon further strengthens this perspective by showing how surveillance has become normalized in everyday life, making self-monitoring and emotional regulation routine practices within social media environments (Lyon, 2018). In addition, Özgür Yılmaz emphasizes that users' online participation should not be understood merely as communication, but also as a form of unpaid digital labor that contributes to platform-based economic extraction (Yılmaz, 2021). Together, these perspectives expand emotional labor beyond interpersonal interaction and position it within the broader structures of platform capitalism, visibility economies, and digital exploitation.

The primary aim of this chapter is to examine how emotional labor emerges and is processed within social media environments accelerated by digitalization, the socio-technical dynamics through which it is shaped, and its multifaceted effects on users' experiences (Hochschild, 1983; Fuchs, 2021). The chapter explores the conceptual foundations of digital emotional labor, its historical development, its various forms, its relationship with algorithms, its gendered dynamics, and its broader implications within digital culture (Duffy, 2017; Bucher, 2018). In addition, it discusses how platform capitalism commodifies emotions and how users are positioned within this emerging digital regime of feelings (Srnicek, 2017; Illouz, 2007). Ultimately, the chapter demonstrates that emotions lie at the center of struggles for visibility, success, and engagement on social media, and that emotions are increasingly transformed into economic value, instruments of competition, and obligatory forms of performance (Hearn & Schoenhoff, 2016; Zuboff, 2019).

EMOTIONAL LABOR IN DIGITAL CULTURE

Arlie Hochschild introduced the concept of emotional labor to the scholarly literature through her influential work *The Managed Heart* (1983). According to Arlie Hochschild, the regulation of one's own emotions in order to display institutionally prescribed feelings during interactions with customers constitutes emotional labor within the service sector (Hochschild, 1983). In this context, employees discipline their emotional expressions in line with organizational expectations and direct them toward customers through predefined normative frameworks. The incorporation of emotions into institutional performance and their systematic production in exchange for wages render this practice conceptually identifiable as emotional labor. Over time, the concept has extended beyond the boundaries of the service sector and has been adapted to media, communication, and digital culture studies, offering a comprehensive analytical framework for understanding how emotions are organized and managed within online interactions, content production, and performative practices on digital platforms (Illouz, 2007; Sara Ahmed, 2013; Gregg, 2013).

Digital environments have given rise to a new visibility economy that requires individuals to position themselves as "brands" (Hearn & Schoenhoff, 2016). Within this economy, users acquire symbolic value through metrics such as likes, comments, shares, and follower counts, generating a form of digital social capital (Pierre Bourdieu, 1986; Duffy, 2017). As a result, social media has evolved from a space primarily dedicated to the circulation of information, images, or experiences into a performative arena in which emotional labor is continuously reproduced and commodified (Illouz, 2007; Fuchs, 2021). The need for users to develop emotion-management strategies in order to sustain visibility on platforms demonstrates how the emotional dimension of digital interaction is deeply intertwined with broader economic and cultural processes (Srnicek, 2017; Zuboff, 2019).

Within the digital ecosystem, emotional labor is not confined to content creators alone but extends into the everyday practices of ordinary users (Baym, 2015; Papacharissi, 2011). In order to align with the visibility logic of platform algorithms, individuals are often compelled to display emotions that are cheerful, motivating, optimistic, or socially acceptable (Bucher, 2018; Duffy, 2017). This situation calls for a rearticulation of Arlie Hochschild's distinction between surface acting and deep acting within digital contexts (Hochschild, 1983). For instance, when users share emotions they do not genuinely experience in an effort to construct a positive online identity, they engage in surface acting; when they actively regulate their internal emotional states to produce content that aligns with platform expectations, they move toward deep acting. In this way, the digital environment becomes a performative space of visibility in which emotions are strategically organized and managed (Goffman, 1959; Lyon, 2018).

This digitized form of emotional labor also reveals the presence of strong normative pressures behind what appear to be freely shared expressions (Gregg, 2013; Duffy, 2017). In order to avoid losing followers, maintain engagement rates, or sustain online relationships, users continually strive to remain "emotionally available," a condition that renders emotional burden ongoing and persistent (Baym, 2015; Papacharissi, 2011). As a result, digital emotional labor not only shapes individuals' online self-presentations but also generates a new field of tension between psychological well-being, social expectations, and platform capitalism (Fuchs, 2021; Srnicek, 2017; Zuboff, 2019).

DIGITAL LABOR AND PLATFORM CAPITALISM

With the widespread diffusion of digital technologies, new forms of work have emerged, transforming labor processes both spatially and functionally (Christian Fuchs, 2021; Nick Srnicek, 2017). Digital labor extends beyond traditional wage-based employment relations to encompass the often invisible activities produced by users in online environments, including content creation, data generation, interaction, and emotional performance (Fuchs, 2021; Tiziana Terranova, 2000). One of the most visible arenas in which debates on digital labor have intensified is the production practices of social media users. In this context, digital labor can be defined, in its simplest form, as the unpaid labor that social media users provide to platforms while simultaneously acting as both producers and consumers (Terranova, 2000; Yılmaz, 2021).

Through their everyday interactions, users generate content, create continuous data flows, and sustain levels of participation that enhance the economic value of platforms; however, this productivity often remains unrecognized and uncompensated (Fuchs, 2021; Terranova, 2000). Nevertheless, this definition alone does not fully capture the scope of digital labor. Özgür Yılmaz expands the concept by arguing that digital labor should encompass all forms of labor—both paid and unpaid—required for digital media to exist, be produced, circulated, and used (Yılmaz, 2021). This broader perspective demonstrates that digital labor is not limited to user activity alone but instead constitutes a multilayered labor regime, ranging from software developers and data center workers to content moderators and content creators (Srnicek, 2017; Fuchs, 2021). In this sense, digital labor represents a multidimensional and frequently invisible network of production that sustains the functioning of platform capitalism (Zuboff, 2019; Yılmaz, 2021).

At the center of debates on digital labor lies the invisibility of user labor (Fuchs, 2021; Tiziana Terranova, 2000). While spending time on social media platforms, users simultaneously produce content, generate data flows, and sustain continuous circulation that enhances the economic value of platforms. Yet this productivity is largely unrecognized, uncompensated, and not formally acknowledged as "labor" (Fuchs, 2021; Srnicek, 2017). Terranova's (2000) concept of "free labor" reveals that the digital labor users appear to perform voluntarily in fact constitutes one of the foundational pillars sustaining digital capitalism. The economic power of platforms rests on the transformation of users' interactions, emotions, preferences, and behaviors into aggregated data resources (Shoshana Zuboff, 2019). From this perspective, digital labor signifies a new production regime in which user activity is systematically exploited (Fuchs, 2021; Yılmaz, 2021).

The literature on platform capitalism situates this process within a broader economic framework. According to Nick Srnicek (2017), digital platforms operate through infrastructural business models that convert data derived from user interactions into economic value. These models rely on algorithmic designs that encourage users to spend more time on platforms, produce more content, and engage with greater emotional intensity (Srnicek, 2017; Taina Bucher, 2018). Platforms are therefore not technically neutral devices but systems that shape, regulate, and economically steer user behavior (Bucher, 2018; Shoshana Zuboff, 2019). In this sense, platform capitalism conceptualizes digital labor not merely as content production but as a multilayered labor regime operating through data generation, sustained interaction, and emotional intensity (Fuchs, 2021; Zuboff, 2019).

Within the social media economy, emotions have moved beyond the realm of personal experience to become a factor that directly shapes economic value (Eva Illouz, 2007; Sara Ahmed, 2013). The tendency of algorithms to prioritize content with high emotional intensity encourages users to strategically regulate their emotional performances (Taina Bucher, 2018; Shoshana Zuboff, 2019). For instance, posts that convey intense emotions such as anger, excitement, happiness, or surprise have been shown to generate higher levels of engagement (Bucher, 2018; Papacharissi, 2011). This dynamic places emotions at the center of data flows and renders digital emotional labor an integral component of the platform economy. The ways in which users make their emotions visible contribute simultaneously to the production of individual capital—such as followers, likes, and visibility—and to the economic returns of platforms themselves (Duffy, 2017; Hearn & Schoenhoff, 2016). In this sense, emotions begin to function as a form of "digital currency" within the social media economy.

Ultimately, digital labor, when intertwined with the operational logic of platform capitalism, transforms emotions into economic resources and user activity into an invisible mode of production (Christian Fuchs, 2021; Nick Srnicek, 2017). This process demonstrates that emotional labor is reproduced not only within interpersonal relations but also within a complex economic structure shaped by algorithms, data infrastructures, and corporate strategies (Shoshana Zuboff, 2019; Tiziana Terranova,

2000). From this perspective, the social media economy represents a new digital labor regime in which emotions are commodified, visibility acquires economic value, and user labor is systematically rendered invisible (Eva Illouz, 2007; Özgür Yılmaz, 2021).

TYPES OF DIGITAL EMOTIONAL LABOR

Digital emotional labor is a phenomenon that emerges in multilayered forms shaped by the interactional architecture of social media platforms, the functioning of the visibility economy, and the expectations users hold of one another (Liu, 2024). Recent literature suggests that this emotional labor produced in online environments can be analytically examined by conceptualizing it under distinct categories (Abidin, 2016; Baym, 2015; Duffy, 2017). When the structural dynamics of digital culture are taken into account, emotional labor appears not merely as a form of individual expression but as a practice closely intertwined with the economic logic of platforms, algorithmic preferences, and patterns of social interaction.Within this framework, digital emotional labor can be systematically addressed through four main types: influencer emotional labor, digital care labor, community management labor, and relational labor (Baym, 2015; Abidin, 2016; Duffy, 2017). Although these categories may appear analytically distinct, in practice they frequently intersect, overlap, and are simultaneously experienced depending on users' online positions and roles.

Table 1. Types of digital emotional labor

Type of Labor	Definition	Key Practices	Target Groups	Key References
Influencer Emotional Labor	The intensive management of emotions by content creators to build and sustain follower relationships, personal brand, and visibility.	Constant positivity performance, authenticity display, crisis framing as inspiration, follower responsiveness, lifestyle curation.	Professional influencers, YouTubers, Instagram content creators	Duffy (2017); Abidin (2016)
Digital Care Labor	Invisible emotional work performed in online communities to provide support, empathy, and solidarity.	Responding to messages, emotional guidance, peer support, solidarity building, mental health content creation.	Women users, mental health creators, activist communities, solidarity networks	Dobson (2020); Korn (2025); Duffy & Hund (2015)
Community Management Labor	Emotional regulation, moderation, and surveillance carried out to sustain the online identity of brands, institutions, or communities.	Negative comment management, crisis communication, conflict mediation, brand image sustainability, trend alignment.	Community managers, social media managers, brand representatives	Bishop (2019); Gregg (2013)
Relational Labor	Ongoing emotional, cognitive, and temporal effort invested in developing and sustaining digital relationships.	Regular interaction with followers, personal disclosure, empathy expression, community bonding, message responsiveness.	All social media users, influencers, ordinary participants	Baym (2015); Papacharissi (2011)

Note. Adapted from Baym (2015), Abidin (2016), Duffy (2017), Bishop (2019), Dobson (2020), and Korn (2025).

INFLUENCER EMOTIONAL LABOR

Influencers are content creators who generate social capital within digital culture by cultivating a sense of personal closeness, intimacy, and trust with their followers. This process requires an intensive form of emotional labor. Influencer emotional labor involves strategies such as maintaining a consistently positive demeanor, remaining emotionally available, responding sensitively to followers' demands, and organizing one's personal life in a performative manner (Duffy, 2017). This form of labor becomes particularly visible through practices including the performance of positive emotions (appearing constantly happy, energetic, and productive), the obligation to establish intimacy and authenticity, the commodification of personal life, emotionally sensitive crisis communication, and sustained visibility aimed at preventing follower loss. Abidin (2016) emphasizes that the sustainability of influencers' "micro-celebrity" status is fundamentally dependent on their emotional performances. For this reason, influencer emotional labor can be regarded as one of the forms of labor in which the dynamics of digital capitalism are most intensely manifested.

DIGITAL CARE LABOR

Digital care labor refers to the invisible forms of labor undertaken by users in online communities in order to provide support, offer emotional guidance, express empathy, or foster solidarity. This type of labor emerges particularly among mental health content creators, women users, solidarity networks, and activist communities (Dobson, 2020). Digital care labor shares important similarities with traditional forms of care work; however, within digital environments it becomes continuous, audience-driven, and often remains uncompensated (Korn, 2025).

The expectation that users remain constantly "available," respond to messages, provide support, and perform emotional regulation functions contributes to an increasing emotional burden and heightens the risk of burnout. For this reason, digital care labor is frequently regarded as a domain in which gender-based expectations—particularly those placed on women—are reproduced and reinforced within digital culture (Duffy, 2017).

COMMUNITY MANAGEMENT LABOR

Community management labor encompasses the practices of regulation, surveillance, moderation, and emotional balancing carried out to sustain the online identity of brands, institutions, or large-scale digital communities (Sophie Bishop, 2019). This form of labor involves processes with a high emotional load, including the management of negative comments, crisis communication, meeting follower expectations, emotionally mediating conflicts within the community, and maintaining brand image sustainability (Bishop, 2019; Duffy, 2017). Community managers perform not only technical functions but also act as agents of emotional regulation. Bishop (2019) conceptualizes this form of labor as emotional surveillance, emphasizing the continuous monitoring and management of affective dynamics within digital spaces. In order to ensure that the digital environment appears calm, motivating, and positive, community managers engage in intensive emotional work (Gregg, 2013; Lyon, 2018).

RELATIONAL LABOR

Relational labor, as defined by Baym (2015), refers to the ongoing emotional, cognitive, and temporal effort that users invest in developing and sustaining relationships on digital platforms. This form of labor includes processes such as maintaining regular communication with followers, responding to messages, producing intimacy through personal disclosures, and fostering a sense of connection among audiences. Baym (2015) emphasizes that relationships in digital culture are not sustained "naturally" or spontaneously but rather through systematic and continuous emotional work. For this reason, relational labor occupies a central role in the experiences of influencers, ordinary users, and community managers alike, functioning as a foundational mechanism through which digital relationships are maintained across diverse online positions.

ALGORITHMIC PRESSURE AND EMOTIONAL PERFORMANCE

Digital platforms operate as complex systems governed by invisible mechanisms that shape users' content production, emotional expressions, and online behaviors. At the center of these systems are algorithms, which function as key regulators determining which content is prioritized, which forms of emotional expression gain greater visibility, and which interaction practices users adopt within social media environments (Bucher, 2018; Gillespie, 2014). Although social media users may perceive their content production as freely chosen, the algorithmic logic of platforms profoundly structures efforts to achieve visibility and sustain engagement.

For this reason, digital emotional labor should be understood not merely as an outcome of individual emotional expression but as a compulsory form of performance guided and constrained by algorithmic pressure (Bucher, 2018; Shoshana Zuboff, 2019).

THE LOGIC OF ALGORITHMIC VISIBILITY

The algorithmic architecture of social media platforms demonstrates that the criteria governing visibility are not random but are instead designed in line with platforms' economic interests. Systems such as TikTok's *For You Page*, Instagram's *Explore* section, and YouTube's recommendation algorithms establish a data-driven visibility regime aimed at keeping users on the platform for longer periods of time. Within this regime, content characterized by high emotional intensity—such as happiness, surprise, nostalgia, empathy, anger, and dramatic self-disclosure—is more likely to be prioritized than other forms of content (Bucher, 2018; Fuchs, 2021; Van Dijck, 2013).

In what Bucher (2018) terms "algorithmic sensing," algorithms assess the emotional impact of content based on users' viewing durations, liking behaviors, or scrolling patterns and adjust visibility accordingly. As a result, emotions become one of the central determinants of digital circulation. The tendency of users to favor certain emotional themes or modes of expression in order to remain visible illustrates how algorithms have increasingly transformed into actors that govern emotional performance.

Algorithmic systems determine not only what kinds of content users are expected to produce but also how frequently they are required to engage in production. Platforms such as Instagram and TikTok reduce the visibility of posts from users who do not share content regularly, a dynamic that generates pressure—particularly for content creators—to remain "always online." As continuity becomes a behavior rewarded by algorithms, users increasingly feel compelled to produce content without interruption in order to sustain their online presence (Bishop, 2019).This pressure extends beyond production frequency to encompass emotional availability as well. Maintaining regular interaction with followers, responding to comments, sharing stories, and continuously monitoring current trends in order to generate new content become obligatory practices, especially for influencers. In this way, platforms exploit not only users' physical time but also their emotional energy.

TIKTOK, INSTAGRAM, AND YOUTUBE ALGORITHMS: MECHANISMS OF EMOTIONAL CONTENT

Each social media platform has developed its own algorithmic logic to steer user behavior and optimize content circulation; however, a shared core characteristic of these systems is their tendency to generate higher levels of engagement for content marked by high emotional intensity compared to other content types (Zhang, 2025). Research indicates that algorithms structurally reward content that captures attention, elicits affective responses, and keeps users on the platform for longer periods of time (Bucher, 2018; Gillespie, 2014). Within this context, emotional content ceases to function merely as a form of individual expression and instead becomes a value-producing mechanism situated at the center of the algorithmic visibility economy. Accordingly, users strategically adopt emotion-driven production practices in order to increase their visibility and sustain engagement, and in some cases orient themselves toward emotionally intensified performances demanded by platform algorithms (Duffy, 2017; Abidin, 2016).

Table 2. Platform algorithms and emotional content: A comparative overview

Platform	Algorithmic Logic	Rewarded Content Types	Emotional Pressure on Users	Psychological Consequences
TikTok (For You Page)	Micro-level emotional response measurement via viewing duration, replays, and engagement speed.	Short, high-impact videos: humorous, surprising, dramatic, or emotionally charged content.	Rapid emotional impact; constant novelty production; trend alignment; performative authenticity.	Emotional exhaustion from trend cycles; self-worth tied to virality; anxiety over irrelevance.
Instagram (Explore / Feed)	Relational proximity metrics: comments, DM responses, like frequency, and story interactions.	Positive, intimate, relationship-oriented aesthetics; lifestyle curation; visual positivity.	Aesthetic positivity norm; continuous availability; emotional alignment with audience expectations.	Performative happiness pressure; self-objectification; fear of follower loss.
YouTube (Recommendation Engine)	Watch time optimization; click-through rates; subscriber retention; emotional retention signals.	Emotionally intense, story-driven content; vulnerability disclosures; dramatic narratives.	Long-form emotional investment; sustained personal branding; crisis communication demands.	Burnout from sustained performance; emotional blurring of public/private identity.

Note. Compiled based on Bucher (2018), Duffy (2017), Abidin (2016), Gillespie (2014), and Van Dijck (2013).

The following sections elaborate on the platform-specific dynamics summarized in Table 2.

TikTok

TikTok's algorithm regulates content flows by measuring users' emotional responses at a micro level. As the emotional intensity of a video increases, users' viewing duration tends to lengthen; consequently, humorous, surprising, dramatic, or emotionally charged videos are more likely to be prioritized on the *For You Page*. This dynamic directs content creators toward producing short yet impactful content designed to elicit rapid and strong emotional reactions from viewers (Baumann, Arora, Rahwan & Czaplicka, 2025).

Instagram

Instagram's algorithm organizes content based on metrics that measure relational proximity, such as comments, direct message responses, and the frequency of likes. As a result, users feel compelled to share content that is more positive, more intimate, and more explicitly relationship-oriented in order to keep their connections active. Aesthetic positivity and emotional alignment thus become central instruments of visibility within the platform (Bucher, 2018).

YouTube

Across all three platforms, a shared core dynamic is the systematic privileging of emotionally intense content through higher levels of algorithmic visibility. The tendency of algorithms to foreground content that rapidly triggers affective responses and carries strong engagement potential positions emotional content as a primary determinant of digital circulation (Bucher, 2018; Van Dijck, 2013). This dynamic demonstrates that emotional labor within social media environments is not merely a peripheral element but a central component of the visibility economy. Consequently, users are compelled to strategically construct their emotional performances in order to gain visibility and sustain engagement on platforms, transforming digital emotional labor into a fundamental driver of algorithmic competition (Duffy, 2017; Abidin, 2016).

The rewarding of positive emotions on social media platforms generates sustained pressure on users to appear well, feel well, and make others feel well. This dynamic can be conceptualized as "performative happiness" (Illouz, 2007). As algorithms amplify positive content more widely, users are encouraged to suppress negative or ambivalent emotions and instead engage in a continuous performance of positive self-presentation.

Influencers are the most visible example of this pressure:

- appear energetic, productive, and motivating under all circumstances;
- frame even personal crises as "inspirational" narratives;
- maintain an aesthetically curated standard of living;
- assume responsibility for sustaining followers' morale.

This dynamic can be interpreted as the digital counterpart of Hochschild's (1983) distinction between surface acting and deep acting. The obligation to maintain constant positive performance creates a disjunction between users' genuine emotional states and the emotions demanded by platforms, a tension that, over time, may culminate in emotional exhaustion and burnout.

Platform algorithms seek to identify users' emotional dispositions by tracking the types of content to which they display heightened sensitivity. This process can be conceptualized as a form of "automated empathy." Algorithms analyze users' reactions to content by examining viewing duration, emotional expressions used in comments, emoji usage, and scrolling speed (Gillespie, 2014; Bucher, 2018; Kaye,

Chen & Zeng, 2021). Based on this analysis, platforms curate and deliver content with similar emotional tones to users. In doing so, algorithms reduce emotions to a form of "calculable behavioral pattern" (Van Dijck, 2013). However, behind this apparent form of empathy lie platforms' economic interests, as the primary objective is to keep users engaged for longer periods of time. At the same time, these "automated responses" prompt users themselves to engage in rapid, unreflective, and performative interactions in order to align with algorithmic demands. Users may increase their use of emojis, provide automatic responses to stories, or feel compelled to emotionally align with viral trends in pursuit of greater visibility. As a result, relational intimacy is increasingly displaced by automated emotional practices (Bishop, 2020).

In social media culture, "becoming a trend" has emerged as a significant marker of visibility and prestige (Annaki, Ouassou & Igamane, 2025). However, because trends shift at a rapid pace, users are compelled to continuously produce new content, experiment with new emotional themes, and adapt to the currents prioritized by algorithms. Within this cycle, three major emotional consequences become apparent:

- Emotional exhaustion: The persistent pressure to generate novel content depletes users' emotional energy (Gregg, 2013; Maslach & Leiter, 2016).
- Self-worth dependency: Metrics such as likes, comments, and view counts increasingly shape individuals' self-perceptions and sense of value (Vogel et al., 2014).
- Anxiety and feelings of inadequacy: Particularly among younger users, failure to keep up with trends is often interpreted as personal failure (Duffy, 2017).

Through these dynamics, the algorithmic trend cycle produces a performance regime in which individuals feel compelled to continuously reproduce and recalibrate their emotional selves (Erving Goffman, 1959; Taina Bucher, 2018; David Lyon, 2018).

IDENTITY, SELF-PRESENTATION, AND EMOTIONS ON SOCIAL MEDIA

Digital platforms have fundamentally transformed how individuals present their identities, define themselves, and manage their emotions. Social media has moved beyond being merely a tool for communication and has become a space in which individuals continuously position themselves, perform identities, and accumulate emotional capital (Hearn, 2010). Active participation on social media platforms serves as an indicator of the contemporary desire for visibility and for situating the self within the social sphere of digital culture. This transformation necessitates a reconsideration of classical sociological approaches to identity within a digital context (Papacharissi, 2011).

GOFFMAN'S DRAMATURGICAL APPROACH AND DIGITAL SELF-PERFORMANCE

Drawing on the metaphor of theater to analyze social interaction, Erving Goffman's dramaturgical approach provides a systematic account of how individuals present themselves within social contexts, framing self-presentation as a performative process shaped by situational expectations (Selimoğlu, 2025). Within this framework, individuals enact social roles in a manner comparable to actors performing on a stage, while social interactions are understood as distinct "scenes," each governed by specific norms and expectations (Goffman, 1959). This perspective operates with heightened visibility and intensity in digital culture. Social media platforms create interactional spaces in which users are positioned on a continuously accessible stage (Staab & Thiel, 2022).

The audience of this stage is expansive, heterogeneous, and often invisible, a condition that amplifies both the scope and the pressure of performance (Erving Goffman, 1959; Zizi Papacharissi, 2011). Moreover, because performances in digital environments are inherently archivable, they acquire a degree of permanence; self-presentation thus becomes not a momentary interaction but a representation that remains continuously accessible and open to evaluation (David Lyon, 2018; Shoshana Zuboff, 2019). Feedback loops such as likes, comments, and shares directly shape how these performances are received, encouraging users to align their behavior with audience expectations as well as algorithmic cues (Taina Bucher, 2018; Duffy, 2017). While carefully curating their online selves, users often feel compelled to maintain consistency between their online performances and their offline identities. This dynamic suggests that self-presentation functions not merely as a communicative strategy but as a form of self-discipline and emotional regulation (Goffman, 1959; Ahmed, 2013).

Baym (2015) and Marwick (2013) argue that Goffman's model—originally centered on face-to-face interaction—takes on sharper and more intensified performance strategies within social media contexts. In digital environments, audiences are not only observers but also active evaluators who, through algorithmic systems, contribute to rendering performances visible and consequential. As a result, users construct their identity presentations in ways that respond simultaneously to audience expectations and to algorithmic logics. In this process, Goffman's classical distinction between "front stage" and "back stage" becomes increasingly blurred. Private spheres are opened to public audiences, and everyday life itself is transformed into performance. Consequently, identity presentation comes to require continuous monitoring, regulation, and emotional management.

In digital culture, identity has become a permeable construct that can no longer be explained through rigid distinctions between online and offline domains (danah boyd, 2014; Nancy Baym, 2015). Boyd (2014) conceptualizes social media environments as "networked publics" and argues that these spaces shape identity construction through three core dynamics: persistence, replicability, and visibility. While these dynamics influence individuals' offline identities, they simultaneously compel them to align their offline selves with online performance. As a result, offline experiences are transformed into online displays, online performances generate expectations in individuals' everyday lives, and both domains continuously reference one another, producing what can be described as a hybrid identity (Baym, 2015; Zizi Papacharissi, 2011). As users carefully curate their online selves, they often feel pressured to render their offline selves consistent with these performances. This condition reveals that self-presentation functions not merely as a communicative strategy but as a mode of self-discipline and emotional regulation (Erving Goffman, 1959; David Lyon, 2018).

Within digital culture, identity increasingly takes the form of a brand. Hearn & Schoenhoff (2016) emphasize that individuals strategically mobilize emotional expressions on social media in order to construct a personal brand. In this process, emotions are transformed into value-producing resources that enhance individual visibility (Brooke Erin Duffy, 2017; Eva Illouz, 2007).

Emotional Branding involves several interrelated practices:

- Consistent emotional tone: Ensuring that each post reinforces the "brand identity" through a stable and recognizable emotional mood.
- Politics of positivity: The sustained effort to appear consistently strong, energetic, and motivating.
- Emotional availability: Establishing relationships of closeness, intimacy, and empathy with followers.
- Aestheticized emotions: Presenting emotions in visually curated and stylized forms (Zhang, 2022).

This process points to a digital culture in which emotions are commodified and users reorganize their emotional expressions as a form of capital (Illouz, 2007). In this way, emotional labor becomes an integral component of identity presentation.

Within social media environments, a pronounced tension emerges between individuals' authentic selves and their performative selves. The demands of algorithms and audiences steer users toward the presentation of an "idealized" self. This ideal self is expected to appear perpetually happy, productive, stylish, socially engaged, and resilient (Goffman, 1959; Duffy, 2017; Banet-Weiser, 2018).

This condition generates an increasingly widening gap between individuals' authentic emotional experiences and the performative selves they feel compelled to display online, leading to a form of *self-discrepancy*. From the perspective of Goffman's (1959) dramaturgical approach, the tension between the authentic emotions experienced in the "back stage" and the carefully regulated emotional expressions presented to audiences on the "front stage" becomes markedly intensified in digital culture. Marwick (2013) argues that social media users are required to continuously manage this emotional incongruity in order to sustain online visibility, while Duffy (2017) demonstrates that this performative obligation produces chronic emotional exhaustion and self-alienation, particularly among influencers. Similarly, Illouz (2007) emphasizes that the commodification of emotions in contemporary digital culture erodes individuals' sense of authenticity and generates a structural conflict between the emotional self and the performative self.

Social media environments also produce a regime of visibility in which individuals increasingly objectify themselves. *Self-objectification* refers to the process through which individuals position themselves according to an external evaluative gaze and determine their self-worth based on visibility, approval, and metrics of recognition (Fredrickson & Roberts, 1997). This process gives rise to outcomes such as continuous bodily monitoring, the performatization of everyday life, heightened aesthetic concerns, intensified self-surveillance, and dependence on external validation.

Debates on narcissism are also significant within this context. Lasch (1979) argues that the excessive preoccupation with self-image in late modern societies is rooted in structural conditions rather than individual pathology. Social media provides a technological infrastructure that actively reinforces this tendency, as metrics such as likes, follower counts, and view rates are transformed into quantifiable indicators of social value.

The structure of digital self-presentation produces profound emotional consequences for individuals. As users increasingly anchor their sense of self-worth to measurable, platform-promoted metrics such as likes, follower numbers, and engagement rates, self-perception becomes dependent on external validation (Marwick, 2013). The possibility of losing visibility or receiving negative feedback triggers heightened anxiety, particularly among younger users, thereby normalizing a chronic state of performance pressure (Chou & Edge, 2012). Duffy (2017) shows that content creators experience this performative pressure on an ongoing basis and are compelled to continuously reorganize their emotional energy in order to meet audience expectations. Illouz (2007) further argues that the commodification of emotions in digital culture leads individuals to shape even their most personal emotional experiences through the anticipated gaze of others, resulting in a profound loss of authenticity. Consequently, individuals internalize the obligation to "exist emotionally through the eyes of others" and begin to manage their emotional lives within a performative framework. Taken together, these processes demonstrate that digital identity presentation functions not merely as a communicative practice but as a structural emotional regime that imposes a significant psychological burden on individuals.

THE GENDERED DIMENSION OF EMOTIONAL LABOR

From its earliest conceptualization, emotional labor has been closely associated with gender relations (Hochschild, 1983; Wharton, 2009). Hochschild's (1983) seminal work on the service sector demonstrates that women are disproportionately employed in occupations that require intensive emotion management, a pattern that is directly linked to prevailing gender norms. With the expansion of digitalization and the rise of social media platforms, these gendered forms of labor have not disappeared; rather, they have been reconfigured and reproduced within new regimes of visibility, acquiring increasingly complex forms. Within digital environments, emotional labor constitutes a particularly intensified field of experience for women users and women content creators, who are more frequently expected to perform care, positivity, accessibility, and emotional responsiveness (Çoban, 2024).

Social media platforms have become significant cultural spaces in which norms of femininity are reproduced and reinforced (Duffy, 2017). In digital culture, the emotional expressions expected of women tend to include compassionate, understanding, positive, supportive, and aesthetically curated forms of self-presentation. These expectations compel women to align with specific emotional regimes in order to sustain online visibility. As Ahmed (2013) notes, emotions are not distributed equally across social life; rather, certain bodies and identities are more strongly associated with particular emotions. Within digital environments, femininity is thus closely aligned with positivity, care, and emotional availability. This alignment implies that women users are expected not only to produce content but also to continuously maintain a particular emotional tone. By contrast, the expression of negative emotions—such as anger or vulnerability—is often less algorithmically rewarded or may encounter social sanctions. As a result, women's emotional expressive space becomes increasingly constrained by normative expectations.

One of the most visible arenas in which the gendered dimension of digital emotional labor manifests is beauty and care work (Duffy, 2017). On social media platforms, women are particularly expected to display physical attractiveness, aesthetic refinement, and a consistently positive emotional disposition. These expectations generate not only visual labor but also an intensified form of emotional labor (Sun & Wu, 2025). As Duffy (2017) emphasizes, the conditions of being "liked" and "followed" on social media demand high levels of emotional self-regulation from women.

Care labor has also taken on new forms within digital environments. Responding to followers' messages, offering supportive comments, expressing empathy, and providing emotional solidarity constitute forms of invisible labor that are particularly expected from women content creators (Abidin, 2016). This labor often does not generate direct financial compensation; instead, it functions as an investment that enhances users' visibility and social capital. In this way, care labor becomes a form of work that is both continuous and intensely gendered within digital platforms (Sun & Wu, 2025).

Women influencers represent one of the categories in which digital emotional labor is experienced most intensely (Çoban, 2024). The influencer economy is built upon the illusion of intimacy, accessibility, and emotional closeness. For women influencers, however, this perceived closeness produces a constant obligation to perform emotionally (Liu & Zheng, 2024). Expectations to engage in one-to-one interactions with followers, to remain calm and understanding in the face of criticism, and to maintain a positive image under all circumstances significantly increase emotional burden (Abidin, 2016). In this context, the emotional labor performed by women influencers extends well beyond content production. They are required to soothe followers during moments of crisis, manage conflicts within communities, and continuously renegotiate their own emotional boundaries. Over time, these demands may result in emotional exhaustion, anxiety, and self-alienation. Duffy & Hund (2015) note that women content creators bear an invisible emotional cost within digital labor processes, a cost that is frequently romanticized rather than critically acknowledged.

Ultimately, the gendered dimension of digital emotional labor is central to understanding the unequal structure of social media culture. The care work, positivity, and aesthetic performances undertaken by women in digital environments are not merely individual choices but structural imperatives shaped by gender norms and the demands of platform capitalism (Abidin, 2021). For this reason, digital emotional labor cannot be treated as a gender-neutral concept; rather, it must be analyzed through a gender-sensitive lens as a fundamental form of digital labor. Indeed, a growing body of research demonstrates both that emotional labor has historically been institutionalized in fields predominantly occupied by women (Hochschild, 1983) and that practices of visibility, care, and relational work on digital platforms impose a disproportionate emotional burden on women users (Duffy, 2017; Gill & Orgad, 2015).

CASE STUDY: DUYGU ÖZASLAN AND THE PERFORMANCE OF DIGITAL EMOTIONAL LABOR

This section examines Duygu Özaslan—one of the prominent figures within Turkey's digital influencer culture—as a case study in order to illustrate how digital emotional labor is produced, sustained, and commodified. The primary rationale for selecting Duygu Özaslan for analysis lies in her large and diverse audience, which reached approximately 1.9 million followers as of December 18, 2025, her long-standing and continuous presence on social media platforms, and the extent to which her beauty-, fashion-, and lifestyle-oriented content offers a profile capable of representing broader transformations within the influencer economy in the Turkish context.

When evaluated through the lens of Erving Goffman's (1959) dramaturgical approach, Duygu Özaslan's Instagram functions as a continuously accessible "stage." The content produced on this stage does not merely document everyday life; rather, it constitutes a carefully curated form of self-presentation (Goffman, 1959; Zizi Papacharissi, 2011). The settings, clothing choices, makeup styles, and camera angles featured in Özaslan's posts are deliberately arranged to convey a particular lifestyle narrative to the audience (Brooke Erin Duffy, 2017). In this sense, Özaslan simultaneously performs multiple roles within the digital environment: the stylish woman, the professional influencer, the brand ambassador, and the entrepreneur. Each of these roles requires distinct emotional tones and behavioral repertoires, transforming content production from a primarily technical activity into an intensive process of emotional labor (Hearn & Schoenhoff, 2016; Gregg, 2013).

The concept of emotional labor as conceptualized by Hochschild (1983) can be clearly observed in the digital performance of Duygu Özaslan. In her posts, Özaslan consistently displays an emotional stance characterized by positivity, self-confidence, energy, and motivation, while sustaining a similar emotional regime in her interactions with followers. This pattern illustrates that maintaining visibility on digital platforms depends not only on the continuous production of content but also on the strategic regulation of emotions (Abidin, 2021).

The relative absence of negative emotions in Duygu Özaslan's content, along with the tendency to present emotions such as sadness, uncertainty, or vulnerability in aestheticized forms, points to the internalization of the norm of positivity within digital environments (Brooke Erin Duffy, 2017; Sara Ahmed, 2013). In this sense, influencer performance can be interpreted as a practice of emotional regulation that aligns with Arlie Hochschild's distinction between surface acting and deep acting (Hochschild, 1983). The sustained presentation of a positive emotional façade suggests the performance of surface acting, while the ongoing management and modulation of internal emotional states in accordance with platform expectations indicates elements of deep acting within the digital context (Gregg, 2013; Goffman, 1959).

Duygu Özaslan's content production practices are also shaped by the logic of visibility imposed by platform algorithms (Taina Bucher, 2018; Shoshana Zuboff, 2019). Instagram's expectations regarding regular posting, sustained engagement, and alignment with current trends compel influencers to remain continuously online and emotionally available (Melissa Gregg, 2013; Brooke Erin Duffy, 2017). This dynamic contributes to the persistence of digital emotional labor and its diffusion across everyday life. The visible display of likes and engagement indicators in Özaslan's posts further foregrounds the determining role of algorithmic pressure in the content production process. Metrics such as like counts, comment volume, and sharing rates function as key indicators through which performance is evaluated both by the platform and by followers, thereby shaping perceptions of content value (Bucher, 2018; Hearn & Schoenhoff, 2016). As a result, influencers are required not only to continuously produce content but also to constantly recalibrate their emotional performances in response to audience feedback. Digital performance thus emerges as a process of emotional labor that is continuously assessed and reorganized through quantifiable engagement metrics (Gregg, 2013; Fuchs, 2021).

The case of Duygu Özaslan offers a significant example for understanding how digital emotional labor operates within the Turkish context, the normative frameworks through which it is shaped, and the emotional burdens it imposes on users (Özgür Yılmaz, 2021; Brooke Erin Duffy, 2017). Özaslan's Instagram performance can be interpreted as a multilayered form of labor produced at the intersection of self-presentation, struggles for visibility, algorithmic pressure, and gender norms (Erving Goffman, 1959; Taina Bucher, 2018). This case study clearly demonstrates that emotions on digital platforms are not merely expressed but are also measured, evaluated, and transformed into economic value (Eva Illouz, 2007; Nick Srnicek, 2017).

CASE STUDY: HANNAH NEELEMAN (@BALLERINAFARM): DIGITAL DOMESTIC LABOR, EMOTIONAL PERFORMANCE, AND ALGORITHMIC VISIBILITY

Through the content she produces on Instagram under the username @ballerinafarm, Hannah Neeleman presents an influencer profile that aestheticizes traditional family life, motherhood, domestic production, and rural living practices within digital culture (Brooke Erin Duffy, 2017; Rosalind Gill & Shani Orgad, 2015). As of December 18, 2025, Neeleman's account has reached a broad audience of approximately 10.4 million followers, among whom her content is widely consumed as a narrative of an authentic, natural, and idealized way of life. However, this seemingly effortless and organic presentation rests upon an intensive process of digital emotional labor and the construction of a performative self (Erving Goffman, 1959; Melissa Gregg, 2013).

Neeleman's content centers on practices such as home cooking, childcare, farm labor, and family life, all of which are presented within a carefully aestheticized narrative. In this sense, Hannah Neeleman transforms not only physical production processes but also care labor, maternal emotions, and family relations into a form of digital performance. When examined through the lens of emotional labor as conceptualized by Hochschild (1983), Neeleman's consistent display of a calm, peaceful, happy, and fulfilled emotional demeanor reflects a systematic form of labor that responds to the emotional expectations of both the platform and its audiences.

Like counts, comment volume, and sharing interactions emerge as visible metrics through which Neeleman's digital performance is evaluated. The transparency and traceability of these metrics compel the influencer to continually adjust both content production and emotional presentation in response to algorithmic feedback. The high levels of engagement received by content themed around positivity, harmony, and family happiness indicate that specific emotional narratives are algorithmically rewarded. As a result, emotional performance shifts from spontaneous expression to an algorithmically encouraged norm (Bucher, 2018; Gillespie, 2014).

From the perspective of Goffman's (1959) dramaturgical approach, Hannah Neeleman's social media account functions as a permanently open "front stage." The performances of motherhood, family harmony, and rural life presented on this stage are constructed through carefully selected moments, curated visuals, and emotionally balanced narratives. By contrast, fatigue, stress, the emotional burdens of care work, and potential conflicts remain largely concealed in the "back stage." As self-presentation in digital environments becomes continuous, emotional labor likewise takes on an uninterrupted and sustained character.

The case of Hannah Neeleman also makes visible the gendered dimension of digital emotional labor. In digital culture, the roles expected of women influencers—caregiving, self-sacrifice, patience, and emotional availability—occupy a central place within Neeleman's narrative framework. Within this context, practices of motherhood and domestic care move beyond the private sphere and are transformed into sources of economic and symbolic value within platform capitalism (Duffy, 2017; Abidin, 2016). Thus, care labor, traditionally rendered invisible, gains visibility in digital spaces; yet this visibility simultaneously generates new forms of emotional burden and performance pressure.

Ultimately, the *@ballerinafarm* account offers a striking illustration of how digital emotional labor is entangled with algorithmic pressure, self-presentation, and gender norms. What appears as a simple and natural digital narrative conceals, in the background, an intensive process of emotion management, performance continuity, and struggle for algorithmic visibility. This case demonstrates that emotions on digital platforms are not merely expressed but are systematically produced, regulated, and commodified.

Although influencer culture constitutes one of the most visible examples of digital emotional labor, emotional labor on social media should not be limited only to influencers or professional content creators. Ordinary users also participate in platform-driven emotional regulation through everyday practices such as maintaining positive self-presentation, responding to messages, sustaining social presence, and managing audience expectations (Baym, 2015; Papacharissi, 2011). The pressure to remain visible, emotionally available, and socially responsive extends across all levels of digital participation, and this condition can be better understood through Gregg's (2013) discussion of the blurring boundaries between work and private life. This broader perspective is important because it demonstrates that digital emotional labor is embedded not only in monetized influencer economies but also in ordinary daily social media use (Fuchs, 2021; Yılmaz, 2021). Expanding this discussion strengthens the scope of the chapter and shows that emotional labor has become normalized as part of everyday digital life, shaping both personal relationships and self-perception under platform capitalism (Goffman, 1959; Lyon, 2018).

THE CONSEQUENCES OF DIGITAL EMOTIONAL LABOR

Emotional labor sustained on digital platforms affects not only forms of online interaction but also users' psychological well-being, self-perceptions, and social relationships in profound ways (Hochschild, 1983; Duffy, 2017). The continuous regulation, display, and evaluation of emotions within social media environments generate multilayered consequences for individuals, particularly in relation to emotional exhaustion, anxiety, and self-monitoring (Gregg, 2013; Maslach & Leiter, 2016). In addition, the visibility structures of social media platforms intensify the feeling of being constantly observed, reinforcing a culture of surveillance and emotional self-regulation (Goffman, 1959; Lyon, 2018; Zuboff, 2019). In this section, the primary individual-level outcomes of digital emotional labor are examined under four main headings: emotional fatigue and burnout, anxiety and performance pressure, the pervasive sense of being constantly observed within a culture of surveillance, and finally, emotional disengagement and desensitization.

The sustained continuity of emotional labor gives rise, over time, to feelings of emotional fatigue and burnout among individuals. Emotional exhaustion, originally conceptualized by Hochschild (1983) within the context of the service sector, is reproduced in an even more intensified form within digital environments. Social media users—particularly on platforms structured around visibility and engagement—are required to continuously conform to specific emotional norms (Bucher, 2018). This condition gradually widens the gap between the natural flow of emotions and platform-imposed expectations. For influencers, content creators, and community managers in particular, the blurring of boundaries surrounding emotional labor leads to the interpenetration of work and rest time. The persistent obligation to remain positive, accessible, and emotionally responsive depletes individuals' emotional resources and, over the long term, creates fertile ground for burnout syndrome (Duffy, 2017; Abidin, 2016). From this perspective, digital emotional labor emerges not merely as a communicative practice but as an intensive domain of psychological burden (Duffy, 2017).

In social media environments, perceptions of visibility, success, and value are largely constructed through quantified indicators (Brandao & Denny, 2024). Metrics such as like counts, view rates, and follower growth increasingly function as primary criteria through which individuals evaluate their sense of self-worth. This dynamic contributes to the emergence of an anxiety-producing dimension of digital emotional labor, as users remain in a constant state of uncertainty regarding whether their content will achieve the expected level of engagement (Brandao & Denny, 2024).

The types of emotional content rewarded by algorithms direct individuals toward specific performance patterns, leading emotional expressions to become increasingly strategic and calculated. The persistent obligation to "perform well" heightens fears of making mistakes, losing visibility, or becoming irrelevant. Within the literature, this condition is conceptualized as a form of anxiety associated with the performatization of emotions on digital platforms (Gill & Orgad, 2015; Bucher, 2018).

Digital platforms render not only users' content but also their emotional expressions continuously visible and traceable (Zuboff, 2019). This produces a persistent sense of being observed. When examined through Foucault's concept of the panopticon, social media environments can be understood as generating a regime of surveillance in which users internalize self-monitoring practices (Foucault, 1977; Lyon, 2018). Users perform before a broad, dispersed, and often indeterminate audience, without fully knowing who is watching. This condition encourages the constant filtering, regulation, and normalization of emotional expressions. The enduring feeling of being watched distances individuals from spontaneous emotional expression and leads to the chronic internalization of emotional self-control (Brandao & Denny, 2024). In this way, digital emotional labor becomes deeply intertwined with surveillance culture.

One of the long-term consequences of digital emotional labor is emotional disengagement and desensitization (Maslach & Leiter, 2016). In social media environments characterized by the constant circulation of intense emotions, individuals may gradually develop emotional distance as a coping mechanism. Crises, disasters, traumatic events, and repeated calls for empathy can become normalized within algorithmic circulation. In the literature, this phenomenon is discussed through the concepts of "compassion fatigue" and "emotional numbing" (Moeller, 2002; Ahmed, 2013).

In order to protect their emotional boundaries while simultaneously complying with platform demands, users may develop strategies of emotional withdrawal (Gregg, 2013). However, these strategies can also lead to feelings of alienation and loss of meaning in online relationships. Thus, digital emotional labor paradoxically produces both intensified emotional engagement and emotional distancing at the same time (Hochschild, 1983; Duffy, 2017).

CONCLUSION

This study has provided a comprehensive evaluation of the position of emotional labor within digital culture, its modes of operation on social media platforms, and its multilayered effects on individuals. Originally developed by Arlie Hochschild (1983) in the context of the service sector, the concept of emotional labor has been re-examined in this chapter through its adaptation to digital platforms. In doing so, social media environments have been conceptualized not merely as spaces of communication and representation, but as new labor regimes in which emotions are produced, regulated, and transformed into economic value. With the process of digitalization, emotional labor has ceased to be a practice confined to specific occupational groups and has instead become an integral component of everyday online life (Illouz, 2007; Fuchs, 2021).

One of the central findings of this study is that gaining visibility and sustaining an online presence on social media platforms are directly linked to emotional performance. The visibility economy—operating through metrics such as likes, shares, comments, and follower counts—compels users to conform to particular emotional norms, rendering expectations of positivity, intimacy, accessibility, and continuity into implicit rules of digital platforms (Hearn & Schoenhoff, 2016; Abidin, 2016). Within this context, emotions move beyond the realm of individual experience to become resources endowed with economic value, occupying a central position in digital labor processes (Zuboff, 2019; Van Dijck, 2013).

The platform capitalism approach offers a critical framework for understanding the structural dimensions of this transformation. Social media platforms convert not only users' content production but also the emotional expressions accompanying such content into data, thereby transforming them into economic value (Srnicek, 2017; Fuchs, 2021). Alongside the amount of time users spend on platforms, the intensity of their emotional expressions is likewise measured, classified, and steered by algorithmic systems. This process contributes to the organization of digital emotional labor as a largely invisible, unpaid, and continuous form of work (Terranova, 2000).

In this study, digital emotional labor has been examined under four main types: influencer emotional labor, digital care labor, community management labor, and relational labor. The intimacy, authenticity, and accessibility that influencers cultivate in their relationships with followers constitute one of the most visible manifestations of digital emotional labor (Abidin, 2016; Duffy, 2017). Yet this visibility simultaneously entails intensive emotional regulation, self-monitoring, and performance pressure. Digital care labor, by contrast, emerges particularly in content centered on mental health, solidarity, and support, encompassing practices of empathy, attentiveness, and emotional regulation (Ahmed, 2013). This form of labor is most often organized in gendered ways and is disproportionately undertaken by women users (Duffy & Hund, 2015).

Algorithmic pressure stands out as one of the central forces shaping the operation of digital emotional labor. Platforms such as Instagram, TikTok, and YouTube algorithmically reward emotionally intense, rapidly consumable content with high engagement potential (Bucher, 2018; Zuboff, 2019). This dynamic compels users to post more frequently, display more visible emotional reactions, and align with the logic of "trending." The pressure to remain "always online" leads users to allocate not only their time but also their emotional resources to platforms (Dhir, Chen & Nieminen, 2018).

In this context, when considered through Goffman's (1959) dramaturgical approach, social media functions as a permanently open stage. Users perform particular identities in online environments, strategically organize their self-presentations, and continuously recalibrate their performances in response to audience feedback. In digital culture, however, these performances are not ephemeral; they are archivable, repeatedly accessible, and subject to ongoing evaluation (Boyd, 2014). This condition blurs the distinction between front stage and back stage, widening the distance between individuals' authentic emotional experiences and their online performances.

One of the most pronounced consequences of digital emotional labor for individuals is emotional fatigue and burnout. The persistent obligation to appear positive, the fear of losing engagement, and continuous performance pressure rapidly deplete users' emotional resources (Maslach & Leiter, 2016). As like counts and engagement rates become intertwined with perceptions of self-worth, levels of anxiety increase, rendering social media use a psychologically fragile experience (Vogel et al., 2014). The enduring sense of being monitored within a culture of surveillance further intensifies self-regulation, often triggering defensive mechanisms such as emotional disengagement and desensitization (Zuboff, 2019).

The gender dimension reveals that digital emotional labor is distributed unevenly (Duffy, 2017). Normative expectations surrounding beauty, care, positivity, and emotional availability imposed on women in digital environments significantly increase the emotional burden borne by women users, and particularly by women influencers (Hochschild, 1983; Duffy, 2017). This demonstrates that digital emotional labor cannot be understood as a gender-neutral phenomenon; rather, it constitutes a form of labor deeply entangled with broader structures of social inequality.

In conclusion, this study demonstrates that emotional labor has become one of the central components of digital culture on social media. Emotions in these environments are no longer merely individual experiences expressed online; rather, they are measured, guided, and transformed into economically valuable resources. Digital emotional labor should therefore be understood as a widespread form of work that extends beyond the influencer economy to encompass ordinary users as well. Within this framework, social media operates as a system that demands not only continuous content production but also the ongoing emotional management of the self.

Future Directions and Recommendations

In conclusion, this study demonstrates that digital emotional labor on social media platforms is not limited to content production, but is also directly related to self-presentation, struggles for visibility, algorithmic pressure, and emotional performance. Particularly within influencer culture, the constant need to remain visible and emotionally accessible increases the risk of emotional fatigue and burnout for users.

For this reason, it is recommended that future research examine digital emotional labor comparatively across different social media platforms and user groups. In particular, the effects of algorithmic visibility pressure on user behavior on platforms such as Instagram, TikTok, and YouTube may be explored in greater detail.

In addition, it is important to further investigate long-term psychological consequences such as anxiety, self-alienation, compassion fatigue, and digital burnout. Exploring the gendered dimension of digital emotional labor through a more intersectional perspective would also make the emotional and social inequalities produced by platform capitalism more visible.

REFERENCES

Abidin, C. (2016). Visibility labour: Engaging with influencers' fashion brands and #OOTD advertorial campaigns on Instagram. *Media International Australia, Incorporating Culture & Policy, 161*(1), 86–100. DOI: 10.1177/1329878X16665177

Abidin, C. (2021). Mapping internet celebrity on TikTok: Exploring attention economies and visibility labours. *Cultural science journal, 12*(1), 77-104.

Ahmed, S. (2013). *The cultural politics of emotion*. routledge.

Annaki, F., Ouassou, S., & Igamane, S. (2025). Visibility and Influence in Digital Social Relations: Towards a New Symbolic Capital? arXiv preprint arXiv:2505.08797.

Banet-Weiser, S. (2018). *Empowered: Popular feminism and popular misogyny*. Duke University Press.

Baumann, F., Arora, N., Rahwan, I., & Czaplicka, A. (2025). Dynamics of Algorithmic Content Amplification on TikTok. arXiv preprint arXiv:2503.20231.

Baym, N. K. (2015). *Personal connections in the digital age*. John Wiley & Sons.

Bishop, S. (2019). Managing visibility on YouTube through algorithmic cruelty. *New Media & Society, 21*(11–12), 2586–2603.

Bishop, S. (2020). Algorithmic experts: Selling algorithmic lore on YouTube. *Social Media + Society, 6*(1), 2056305119897323. DOI: 10.1177/2056305119897323

Brandao, B. M., & Denny, B. T. (2024). What Instagram Means to Me: Links Between Social Anxiety, Instagram Contingent Self-worth, and Automated Textual Analysis of Linguistic Authenticity. *Affective Science, 5*(4), 449–457. DOI: 10.1007/s42761-024-00267-9 PMID: 39649457

Bucher, T. (2018). *If... then: Algorithmic power and politics*. Oxford University Press. DOI: 10.1093/oso/9780190493028.001.0001

Chou, H. T. G., & Edge, N. (2012). "They are happier and having better lives than I am": The impact of using Facebook on perceptions of others' lives. *Cyberpsychology, Behavior, and Social Networking, 15*(2), 117–121. DOI: 10.1089/cyber.2011.0324 PMID: 22165917

Çoban, S. (2024). Emotional digital labor among young people within the context of lumpencybertariat. *Gençlik Araştırmaları Dergisi, 12*(33), 57–72.

Dhir, A., Yossatorn, Y., Kaur, P., & Chen, S. (2018). Online social media fatigue and psychological wellbeing—A study of compulsive use, fear of missing out, fatigue, anxiety and depression. *International Journal of Information Management*, *40*, 141–152. DOI: 10.1016/j.ijinfomgt.2018.01.012

Dobson, A. S. (2020). The 'care crisis' in digital culture: Women, social media, and emotional labour. In Clark, J., & Sen, A. B. (Eds.), *Gender, media and digital cultures* (pp. 57–72). Routledge.

Duffy, B. E. (2017). *(Not) getting paid to do what you love: Gender, social media, and aspirational work*. Yale University Press. DOI: 10.12987/yale/9780300218176.001.0001

Foucault, M. (1977). *Discipline and punish: The birth of the prison* (Sheridan, A., Trans.). Pantheon Books. (Original work published 1975)

Fuchs, C. (2021). *Social media: A critical introduction* (3rd ed.). Sage. DOI: 10.4135/9781036232214

Gill, R., & Orgad, S. (2015). The confidence cult (ure). *Australian Feminist Studies*, *30*(86), 324–344. DOI: 10.1080/08164649.2016.1148001

Gillespie, T. (2014). The relevance of algorithms. *Media technologies: Essays on communication, materiality, and society*, *167*(2014), 167.

Goffman, E. (1959). *The presentation of self in everyday life*. Doubleday.

Gregg, M. (2013). *Work's intimacy*. John Wiley & Sons.

Hearn, A. (2010). Structuring feeling: Web 2.0, online ranking and rating, and the digital'reputation'economy. *Ephemera*, •••, 10.

Hearn, A., & Schoenhoff, S. (2016). From celebrity to influencer: Tracing the diffusion of celebrity value across the data stream. In P. D. Marshall & S. Redmond (Eds.), A companion to celebrity (pp. 194–211). Wiley-Blackwell.

Hochschild, A. R. (1983). *The managed heart: Commercialization of human feeling*. University of California Press.

Illouz, E. (2007). *Cold Intimacies: The Making of Emotional Capitalism*. Polity Press.

Kaye, D. B. V., Chen, X., & Zeng, J. (2021). The co-evolution of two Chinese mobile short video apps: Parallel platformization of Douyin and TikTok. *Mobile Media & Communication*, *9*(2), 229–253. DOI: 10.1177/2050157920952120

Korn, A. K. (2025). Informal Home Care in the Digital Transformation: Platform Design and Work Ethics of Care. *Social Sciences (Basel, Switzerland)*, *14*(4), 225. DOI: 10.3390/socsci14040225

Liu, X., & Zheng, X. (2024). The persuasive power of social media influencers in brand credibility and purchase intention. *Humanities & Social Sciences Communications*, *11*(1), 1–12. DOI: 10.1057/s41599-023-02512-1

Liu, Y. (2024). Digital work, emotion commodification, and moral legitimacy: Transnational bloggers on Chinese social media platforms. *Youth and Globalization*, *5*(2), 271–289. DOI: 10.1163/25895745-05020004

Lyon, D. (2018). *The culture of surveillance: Watching as a way of life*. Polity Press.

Marwick, A. E. (2013). Status update: Celebrity, publicity, and branding in the social media age. yale university press.

Maslach, C., & Leiter, M. P. (2016). Burnout. In Fink, G. (Ed.), *Stress: Concepts, cognition, emotion, and behavior* (pp. 351–357). Academic Press.

McStay, A. (2018). Digital advertising and adtech: Programmatic platforms, identity and moments. In *The advertising handbook* (pp. 88–100). Routledge. DOI: 10.4324/9781315558646-7

Moeller, S. D. (2002). *Compassion fatigue: How the media sell disease, famine, war and death*. Routledge. DOI: 10.4324/9780203900352

Papacharissi, Z. (2011). A networked self. *A networked self: Identity, community, and culture on social network sites*, 304-318.

Selimoğlu, Z. (2025). Goffman'ın Dramaturjik Yaklaşımı Bağlamında Instagram'da Benlik Sunumu: Influencer Örneği. *Journal of West European Social Sciences*, *2*(1), 149–165.

Srnicek, N. (2017). *Platform capitalism*. John Wiley & Sons.

Staab, P., & Thiel, T. (2022). Social media and the digital structural transformation of the public sphere. *Theory, Culture & Society*, *39*(4), 129–143. DOI: 10.1177/02632764221103527

Sun, H., & Wu, R. (2025). Filters, algorithms, and the "imagination tax": The dilemma of aesthetic self-objectification among Chinese young women on social media. *Frontiers in Psychology*, *16*, 1651435. DOI: 10.3389/fpsyg.2025.1651435 PMID: 41488937

Terranova, T. (2000). Free labor: Producing culture for the information age. *Social Text, 18*(2), 33–58. DOI: 10.1215/01642472-18-2_63-33

Van Dijck, J. (2013). *The culture of connectivity: A critical history of social media.* Oxford University Press. DOI: 10.1093/acprof:oso/9780199970773.001.0001

Vogel, E. A., Rose, J. P., Roberts, L. R., & Eckles, K. (2014). Social comparison, social media, and self-esteem. *Psychology of Popular Media Culture, 3*(4), 206–222. DOI: 10.1037/ppm0000047

Wharton, A. S. (2009). The sociology of emotional labor. *Annual Review of Sociology, 35*(1), 147–165. DOI: 10.1146/annurev-soc-070308-115944

Yılmaz, Ö. (2021). Emeğin Değişen Yüzü: Dijital Emek Sömürüsü. *Simetrik İletişim Araştırmaları Dergisi, 2*(2), 68–78.

Yürür, S., & Ünlü, A. G. O. (2011). Duygusal emek, duygusal tükenme ve işten ayrılma niyeti ilişkisi. ISGUC The Journal of Industrial Relations and Human Resources, 13(2).

Zhang, J. (2025). *The emotional economy in social media platforms: An analysis of algorithm-driven user engagement and commercial value. Highlights in Art and Design, 14*(4)

Zhang, Y., Tu, Z., Zhao, W., & He, L. (2022). Design of emotional branding communication model based on system dynamics in social media environment and its influence on new product sales. *Frontiers in Psychology, 13*, 959986. DOI: 10.3389/fpsyg.2022.959986 PMID: 35983199

Zuboff, S. (2019). *The age of surveillance capitalism: The fight for a human future at the new frontier of power, edn.* PublicAffairs.

KEY TERMS AND DEFİNİTİONS

Digital Labour: It refers to the form of labor through which users generate economic value by producing content, engaging, leaving data, and participating in platform activities. This labor, which is often provided free of charge and voluntarily, plays a central role in the sustainability of platforms.

Emotional Exhaustion: It is a state of mental and emotional exhaustion resulting from constant emotional expression, interaction, and pressure to be visible. In the digital environment, this fatigue manifests itself in a decreased desire to produce and a tendency to withdraw.

Emotional Labour: It is the process of individuals managing, suppressing, or displaying their emotions in order to conform to certain social or institutional expectations. In the context of social media, emotional labor has become a form of digital performance that is constantly ongoing in order to gain interaction and maintain visibility.

Influencer Culture: It defines the cultural structure that generates value through influence, trust, and follower relationships by making individuals' personal lives, emotions, and daily experiences visible on digital platforms. This culture intertwines the discourse of authenticity with market logic.

Platform Capitalism: It describes a capitalist accumulation model in which digital platforms generate economic value through user data, content, and interactions. In this system, social relationships, emotions, and attention become commodifiable resources.

Social Media: It refers to digital communication spaces where users simultaneously act as content creators, distributors, and consumers; and where interaction, visibility, and emotional expression processes are regulated through platform algorithms. Social media provides an environment where individual experiences are transformed into public and economic value.

Visibility Labour: It describes the continuous production of content, interaction tracking, and self-presentation practices that are maintained in order to remain visible on digital platforms. This type of labor often becomes a consumer burden without being noticed.

Chapter 3
Affect Across Borders and the Creation of Transnational Affective Publics Through Mamdani's Social Media Campaign

Esma Nur Sezen
http://orcid.org/0000-0003-0970-7478
Marmara University, Turkey

ABSTRACT

This study examines the TikTok trend among Turkish users surrounding New York City Mayor Zohran Mamdani, within the framework of Zizi Papacharissi's concept of affective publics. Despite increasing political apathy worldwide, the New York mayoral election generated a global trend on the TikTok platform. This research argues that the power driving this trend is affect. In the research, six videos created by Turkish users on TikTok regarding Mamdani's election victory were selected, and 485 comments on these videos were analyzed using qualitative content analysis. The research revealed that Turkish users create a transnational affective public, and that local political references and memory play a significant role in shaping this public. Users who follow distant events through TikTok and participate in the affective flow while adding their own unique textures to it.

DOI: 10.4018/979-8-3373-8307-1.ch003

INTRODUCTION

Today, the relationship with politics is seen to be transforming with the development of digital media. The transmission of information related to politics and the relationships politicians establish with voters also occur through digital media. The various tools offered by social media are indispensable for users to tell stories. Throughout history, media has functioned as a tool for conveying affective expressions during historical moments of significant social change (Papacharissi, 2016, p. 308). Social media provides a space for individuals not only to convey affect but also to interact with the affect created by an event and to produce meaning from this interaction. In this context, the formation of networked publics is driven not only by rational discussions or information sharing, but by affect.

The concept of affective publics was introduced to the literature by Zizi Papacharissi to explain the effects of affect in the political communication process and the role it plays in the formation and shaping of networked publics (Papacharissi, 2014, p. 7). This study examines the formation of affective publics on TikTok in the context of Zohran Mamdani's election as New York City mayor, focusing on the participation of Turkish users. The study analyzes how Turkish users participated in this political event by creating videos and interacting through comments on TikTok, and how this participation influenced the formation of a public shaped by affect, as well as the texture and intensity of this public.

Affective publics have been studied on Twitter by Papacharissi and other researchers, and while studies exist on how these dynamics work for relatively newer platforms like TikTok, the literature is not yet saturated. Unlike text-based platforms like Twitter, TikTok is considered a platform that facilitates and accelerates the circulation of affect through its short video format, algorithmic content flow, intensive use of sound, and reproducible content structures (Brown et al., 2022; Hautea et al., 2021). The ability of users to create content in a shared stream using sound and effects creates a new space for storytelling, enabling the circulation of affect.

This study demonstrates that transnational participation not only increases the visibility of an event but also triggers meaning-making processes in different contexts. In this context, the manifestation of the transnational affective public formed around Mamdani among Turkish users constitutes the scope of the study. The analysis, based on content and comments produced by Turkish users around the topic, demonstrates how a global event is formed through local political and cultural accumulations and references. In this respect, the study contributes to the literature by focusing on micro-level discursive and affective patterns in a transnational context, going beyond a macro-level analysis of affective publics circulation.

Papacharissi generally examines the concept of affective publics within the context of large-scale political events. In this context, the digital flows before and after the resignation of Egyptian President Hosni Mubarak via the #egypt hashtag during the Arab Spring, and the online interactions surrounding the #ows hashtag in the context of the Occupy movement, are studied in her work. These events resonated widely both locally and globally and were characterized by multi-layered flows. According to Papacharissi, interactions between local actors and global audiences play a significant role in the formation of affective publics (Papacharissi, 2016, p. 313). This study examines global participants not as passive audiences circulating content, but as actors actively involved in the process of meaning-making through their own cultural and political references. Papacharissi argues that global participants in affective public discourse connect through empathy without being directly involved in events, attempting to understand how people feel in the context of specific events (Papacharissi, 2014, pp. 4–5). This study found that global participants not only empathized with how people living in New York were affected by the election, but also formed a different kind of bond within their own political framework, even adopting the mayor as if he were their own.

As seen in the example of Zohran Mamdani, a relatively limited and local political event unexpectedly transforms into a global field of affective interaction through digital platforms. In this context, the study not only examines the local manifestation of a global event but also mentions how a local event transforms into a global affective event. Furthermore, it analyzes not only the volume but also the discursive and affective fabric of the networked communities formed during this process.

The study begins by explaining the concept of affect, then examines how affect exists on social media and what it brings with it. Following this, TikTok is considered as a space for political communication and discourse, and the global phenomenon created by Zohran Mamdani's campaign is discussed in conjunction with the concept of political apathy. Finally, focusing on the manifestation of this affective public among Turkish users, the study offers an analysis of discursive and affective patterns through user-generated content and comments.

BACKGROUND

Affect and Social Media

Derived from the Latin word *affectus*, affect was associated with love/affection in the twelfth century, defined as the *irrational energy* that gives love its power (Rosenwein & Cristiani, 2019, p.26-27). The concepts of affect, emotion, and feeling are often confused or used interchangeably in the literature due to their abstract nature. Shouse summarizes the difference between these three concepts as follows: "Feelings are personal and biographical, emotions are social, and affects are prepersonal." Between these three concepts, affect is the most abstract and cannot be expressed through language (Shouse, 2005).

According to Brian Massumi, it is crucial to theorize the difference between affect and emotion. The fundamental difference is that "emotion is a qualified intensity, while affect is an unqualified intensity." Massumi associates affect with the body and emotion with consciousness. According to Massumi, affect is a bodily, pre-linguistic, and unqualified intensity; emotion is the fixed, personal, and recognizable form of this intensity through language and social consensus. When affect is expressed through the linguistic and semantic forms of traditional discourse, the potential of affect is limited. Language suppresses the fluidity and ambiguity of affect (Massumi, 1995).

To explain the difference between emotion and affect, it may be helpful to look at the definition of affect by neuroscientist and psychobiologist Jaak Paksepp (Paksepp, 2008 as cited in Rosenwein & Cristiani, 2019, p.39) as raw forces that are resolved into higher emotions. Affect, unlike emotion, is an automatic and unconscious response.

In the introduction to their book Affect Theory Reader, Gregg and Seigworth begin by explaining affect, stating that it has no source or initial form, but always emerges within a relationship.Gregg and Seigworth emphasize its relational and circulatory dimensions. According to them, affect is a force that circulates between bodies, produces resonance, and intensifies at specific moments. This approach makes it possible to consider affect not only as an individual bodily intensity but also as a process that arises and spreads within social relationships. Rosenwein and Christiani underline that although affect begins in the physiological body, it ends by spreading throughout the world (Rosenwein & Cristiani, 2019, p.130). According to Shouse, the importance of affect in media and culture studies lies in its transmissibility between bodies due to its formal and unstructured nature, which makes it a social force (Shouse, 2005).

Affect is a process that simultaneously involves contradictory orientations. It can be both connecting and disconnecting, both directing and suspending. Affect is a process of becoming that is re-established in every encounter and never exhausts its potential. Therefore, affect should be considered not as a fixed emotional category, but as a constantly delayed and reopened capacity field. According to Retzwick's approach, affect is produced through artifacts, spaces, images, texts, sounds, and the practices established with them. In modern societies, spatial atmospheres (offices, homes, shopping malls) and symbolic artifacts are considered *affect generators*. In this context, social media platforms create an environment where symbolic artifacts are produced and circulated among individuals, and are therefore associated with Retzwick's concept of affect generators (Reckwitz, 2017, p.271-275).

Hipfl states that affect is like an aura, a feeling of being in a particular situation or moment, and uses the expression, "Media can touch us, they can move us, they can make us feel." (Hipfl, 2018, p.9). In this respect, affect holds an important place in media studies. Media functions not only as tools for transmitting information but also as environments that generate affective experiences. Digital media not only transmits affect but also creates cycles that reproduce it. The tactile, visual, and algorithmic features of digital media are designed to produce and transmit affect and affective patterns among users (Papacharissi, 2014, p.23)

Indeed, some media theorists consider media technologies as direct mechanisms for affect production. According to Shaviro, media technologies can be thought of as machines that operate to produce affect and generate value from that affect (Shaviro, 2010, p.3). Similarly, Shouse emphasizes that "power of many forms of media lies not so much in their ideological effects, but in their ability to create affective resonances independent of content or meaning." (Shouse, 2005).

In social media, affect is interpreted as a relational process generated through the interaction between the user, content, and algorithm. Social media platforms are considered affect generators that guide the user towards a specific affective orientation. Every piece of content shared on social media carries a small intensity that sticks with the user, prompting a reaction and thus enabling them to connect with the platform (Brown vd., 2022, p.3).

Digital media offers a multimodal communication environment that brings together different verbal and visual dimensions. In this structure, while the multifaceted meanings of visual texts are attempted to be fixed by verbal expressions in the meaning-making process, they can be interpreted in different ways. Content shared on TikTok provides an example of this multimodal communication environment. Even if this content is meaningless, it carries emotional meaning (Katz & Shifman, 2017, p.828).

Political Potential of TikTok

Zizi Papacharissi points out the political potential of our activities on social media, stating, "The act of making a private thought public carries the potential for a political action" (Papacharissi, 2014, p.112). Networked affect can also be a tool and a mobilizing force that can create a potential channel for political action (Hillis vd., 2015, p.3). In this respect, I refer to the concept of the third place to explain TikTok's political potential.

Ray Oldenburg defines third places as various public spaces outside of homes and workplaces where individuals hold voluntary meetings. The most frequently cited historical examples of third places are the Greek agora and the Roman forum

(Oldenburg, 1999, p.40) Restaurants, arcades, cafes, and bookstores are examples of third places.

Third places are characterized by their neutral, equalizing nature, as well as being places where people display their individuality. The primary activity in these places is conversation, fulfilling people's need for togetherness. As political and intellectual forums, third places have historically stood out as places where citizens discuss common problems, find solutions, plan strategies, and discover their collective power (Oldenburg, 1999, p.14). While not all public spaces fall under the category of third places, there are studies that consider digital media as a *third place*. Undoubtedly, third places, considered informal gathering spaces outside of homes and workplaces, have undergone a transformation with the emergence of the internet.

Numerous studies exist on adapting Oldenburg's concept of the third place to the digital environment. According to Rheingold, members of online communities are instinctively familiar with the concept of the third place (Rheingold, 1993, p.25). Studies in the literature on adapting the concept to the digital environment have focused on examining the eight fundamental characteristics of the third place and evaluating the extent to which they overlap with the digital environment/community. These evaluations acknowledge that various digital media, while not reflecting all the characteristics of the third place, function as such (Foster, 2013; McArthur & White, 2016; Steinkuehler & Williams, 2006).

While Oldenburg's third place concept is characterized by its "place-based" nature, virtual environments lack a physical space. Nevertheless, the literature contains studies on how digital media reproduces the third place experience (Rheingold, 1993; Horrigan, 2001; Steinkuehler & Williams, 2006; Soukup, 2006; Wright, 2012; McArthur & White, 2016; Markiewicz, 2020; Kim et al., 2025). These studies address Oldenburg's concept of the third place within the context of digital games, various social media applications, or computer-connected networks in general. While reflecting some fundamental characteristics of the concept, communities in the internet environment also have significant differences from the *third place*. Although not identical in all aspects, conceptualizing the digital manifestations of the third place is important considering the role the concept of the third place plays in the functioning of political processes in democratic societies. Howard Rheingold suggests that the internet can be one of the informal public spaces for community building, even if it does not fulfill all the necessary conditions for Oldenburg's third place (Rheingold, 1993, p.26); while Scott Wright conceptualizes the third place in the context of the virtual world as *third space*. (Wright, 2012).

According to Wright, political discourse and interactions occurring in non-political spaces are not adequately represented in the existing literature. At this point, he argues that when it comes to the scope and conceptualization of political speech, broader forms of communication, including discussions on emotions, humor, and personal matters, should be accepted (Wright, 2012, p.16). In this study, TikTok was not attempted to be defined as a third place in the sense defined by Oldenburg; rather, the characteristics reflecting the political aspect of third places emerged within the scope of the research on TikTok. TikTok serves as a gathering place for the revitalization of grassroots political participation, and, as Oldenburg states, a space for users to speak as the most fundamental political activity (Oldenburg, 1999, p.70). The study expands the scope of the TikTok platform to include third-party interactions based on affect, where political expression is not limited to user conversations but is also manifested through performance, mimicry, and affective conformity. In this way, the concept of the third space is expanded to include affect-based forms of interaction, explaining the possibilities that TikTok offers for political expression.

Political Apathy and News Avoidance

The increasing number of studies on the concept of political apathy in the literature can be attributed to the continuous decline in political participation observed in recent years and the apathy and disinterest shown by individuals towards political processes. One of the most important indicators of the increasing impact of political apathy is voter turnout rates. One of the most important data points regarding political apathy is the critical decline in global voter turnout. Global voter turnout, which was 65.2% in 2008, fell to 55.5% in 2023 (Newman et al., 2025). This decline can be interpreted not only as a numerical decrease but also as a change in the relationship voters have with politics. In Europe, while voter turnout rates ranged between 80% and 85% from the Second World War until the early 1980s, it has fallen below 65% to the present day (Oxenham, 2017).

In the United States, intergenerational differences in political participation are noteworthy. In America, younger generations of voters tend to abstain from voting compared to older generations while in Europe, political apathy is on the rise. Indeed, this is recorded as the strongest political trend of the second half of the 21st century (Oxenham, 2017). This situation is linked to a lack of faith among voters who feel the political system does not meet their needs, the lack of free and fair elections (Newman et al., 2025), and voter disillusionment (Oxenham, 2017).

In Türkiye, however, the picture is somewhat different from that in Europe and America. While there is no overall decrease in voter turnout in Türkiye, the increase in political apathy is particularly linked to the disillusionment of opposition party voters, their hopelessness regarding a change of power through elections, and economic dissatisfaction (Demiralp, 2025). In light of this data, it is noteworthy that political participation should not be interpreted solely through data, but also through the cognitive and emotional relationship individuals establish with politics.

Political apathy, considered as unwillingness and indifference to participate in political life, is defined by Bingöl as "fundamentally indifference, passivity, willfulness, and apathy towards politics" (Bingöl, 2017, p.45); while Marsch et al. address the concept as a problem of exclusion, explaining it as people distancing themselves from the political system as a result of unequal and unjust experiences of people with this system (Marsh et al., 2007).

Worldwide, researchers are focusing their attention on issues such as low voter turnout, distrust of politicians and political parties, declining civic participation, and public weariness (Curato & Niemeyer, 2013; Zhelnina, 2020). Some of the interest is also directed towards political apathy among young people (Curato & Niemeyer, 2013; Pilkington, 2025). John R. Hibbing and Elizabeth Theiss-Morse explain the reason for low political participation by stating that "people do not like politics even in the best circumstances."(Hibbing & Theiss-Morse, 2002, p. 3) With the increasing role of digital media in political processes, the role of emotions in political processes is also becoming a subject of academic research. Algorithms and the echo chambers they create can cause disruption in the flow of information to individuals regarding current economic, political, and social issues. Algorithms shaped by users' digital footprints pave the way for a filtered and homogenized flow of content. Individuals constantly exposed to this flow of content experience cognitive fatigue and burnout. This situation leads individuals to interact more with content that appeals to highly arousing emotions, resulting in political apathy (Albasar et al., 2025, p. 106). Zhelnina emphasizes that emotions are a significant factor in the formation of political apathy. Zhelnina argues that disappointments weaken belief in collective action, diminish faith in collective solidarity, leading to social insecurity and causing people to withdraw into their inner worlds by severing their emotional ties with the community (Zhelnina, 2020, p. 359). Studies conducted in the Turkish context also point to similar trends. In her research with *switched voters*, who comprise 20% to 30% of the electorate in Türkiye and are equidistant from both poles, Demiralp states that the reason for these voters' distanced stance towards politics is their distrust of the political system (Demiralp, 2025). The fact that the government in Türkiye has not changed for many years, and that opposition parties have been defeated in elections, creates a feeling of exhaustion among the opposition voter group, while the feeling of being deceived experienced by voters who are excited by the hope of winning each election is considered the reason for political apathy (Alptekin, 2023).

In addition to political apathy, an increase in news avoidance is observed, with the abundance of political news being one of the reasons for avoiding news content. "According to the Reuters Institute Digital News Report 2025, one of the countries with the highest news avoidance rates is Türkiye, at 61%. The report's findings on the reasons for news avoidance are: 39% due to news negatively affecting mood, 31%

due to being overwhelmed by news density, and 29% due to the excessive coverage of politics in the news (Newman et al., 2025, p. 27). Studies conducted in Türkiye on news avoidance behavior support these findings.

In a study conducted by Mehmet Ramazan Yıldızgörür using in-depth interviews on readers' news avoidance behavior in Türkiye, he concluded that the most significant factor causing news avoidance is *political reasons* (Yıldızgörür, 2023, p. 275). Although voter turnout is high in Türkiye, political participation tendencies are low (Çarkoğlu & Kalaycıoğlu, 2015, p. 85; Alptekin, 2023). However, there are other obstacles in Türkiye that are seen as causing avoidance of political content, especially on social media. In their study on the effect of perceived surveillance on online political participation, Mustafa Öz and Akan Yanık found that surveillance has a deterrent effect on the online political participation of Turkish users and negatively impacts people's ability to express their opinions on social media (Oz & Yanik, 2024, p. 14).

In this context, the function of social media platforms as an environment where users can express their political views, daily experiences, and feelings in terms of political communication is examined within the scope of this research, in the political climate of Türkiye where political apathy and news avoidance tendencies are increasing.

Zohran Mamdani's Mayoral Campaign and It's Affect on Social Media

The New York City mayoral election on November 4, 2025, represents a significant moment in the American political sociology landscape for many reasons (Group, 2025, p. 2). The most notable is that Zohran Mamdani, who won the election with 50.78% of the vote, became the first Muslim to govern the city. At 34 years old, Mamdani became one of the youngest mayors in New York City history (Zanger, 2025). With the highest voter turnout since 1993, the election attracted attention and was followed not only in America but also internationally, due to its impact extending beyond the *local* sphere (Group, 2025, p. 2). According to Google Trends data, the phrase "Zohran Mamdani elected" ranked 8th in global news searches in 2025, while "Zohran Mamdani" ranked 9th in the people category (Google, 2025). This is significant because it shows how a local political event garnered global attention. This data is indicative of the global impact of Zohran Mamdani's election as New York City mayor.

Mamdani built his political campaign around improving the cost of living. With the slogan "A New York You Can Afford," Zohran Mamdani won the election by running an enthusiastic and vibrant campaign on issues such as rents, childcare, and transportation (Tank, 2026), defeating his rivals, Republican activist Curtis

Sliwa and independent former Democratic governor Andrew Cuomo (Melimopoulos, 2025). Another factor that distinguished Zohran Mamdani from his rivals was the innovative success of his political campaign's social media aspect. According to Stuart Soroka, the success of Mamdani's election campaign stemmed from its hybrid nature, conducted simultaneously in the field, in mainstream media, and on social media (Soroka, 2025).

The most important difference of Mamdani's social media campaign was its *call to action* style, which constantly directed voters towards active participation. Andrew Epstein, the communications director of the campaign, which was described as "hard to miss," stated that during the campaign, Zohran Mamdani was made a symbol of the voters' agenda through social media videos. The campaign aimed to make New York City a character in its narrative by continuously generating the stories it needed to mobilize people (Uetricht, 2026).

Zohran Mamdani's social media campaign not only produced viral videos but also encouraged voters to create their own. These videos went viral across most platforms, making Zohran Mamdani more of an energy and internet meme than a political personality (Stewart, 2025). User-generated viral content, particularly on TikTok and Instagram, allowed the entire world to interact with Zohran Mamdani and his political campaign.

Zohran Mamdani's response to Andrew Cuomo mispronouncing his last name during the Democratic Party primary debate led to the creation of a viral meme and audio format on TikTok. During the debate, Mamdani corrected Cuomo by saying "The name is Mamdani" and spelling out his last name (Spectrum News, 2025), which was remixed with Gwen Stefani's "Hollaback Girl" and turned into a TikTok sound. This sound quickly became a reference point in the production of Mamdani-themed content on the platform and was reused by users in various video formats. This sound was used in 17.8 thousand TikTok videos. Zohran Mamdani managed to appeal not only to New Yorkers but to the whole world, both by meeting with voters on the streets and by the audience he built on social media with his entertaining viral videos, achieving global visibility. On November 3rd, when Mamdani met with voters at a club, he danced with New Yorkers to Jay-Z and Alicia Keys' "Empire State of Mind" (Mitchell, 2025), which became a significant part of the campaign narrative and a frequently used reference in Mamdani-themed content that went viral globally after the election.

Most of the content created using these reference music tracks shares the same theme: individuals appearing in front of the camera to perform short videos celebrating Mamdani's victory, adding phrases like "that's my mayor," "celebrating Mamdani," and "Mamdani has my vote." A striking common feature of these videos is that users, while stating their geographical distance from New York with phrases like "I live in Europe," "I live in Canada," "We are from Paris," or "I live in Türkiye," still show their support for Zohran Mamdani. Some of the content was produced in various languages, such as Greek and French, highlighting how Mamdani's election victory was celebrated by users in different countries through enthusiastic and humorous performances.

I associate the campaign's resonance in a distant geography like Türkiye with the concept of affective publics. Social media platforms, through their expressive and connecting capabilities, cause users to connect around common points. Zohran Mamdani's campaign was reported by news sources as follows: The campaign's design, which transforms our shared disappointment into shared hope (Tank, 2026), is described with words such as the sincere, smiling positive energy emanating from Mamdani's videos (Stewart, 2025), authentic and joyful (Goodwin, 2026), inspiring, funny, combative, creative, self-deprecating, and genuine (Pilkington, 2025). As can be seen from these statements, it is possible to say that Mamdani's campaign has an affective texture. This is why the campaign spread easily on social media and connected with users.

Zohran Mamdani's election as New York City mayor transcended being a local political development, creating a vast network of discursive and affective interaction on TikTok. A flow of users emerged around Mamdani, reacting and generating discourse through emotions such as hope, excitement, curiosity, anger, disappointment, and solidarity. Papacharissi's conceptualization of affective publics describes a networked public that is activated, connected, or potentially disconnected through affect. In this context, I consider the flow of users from different geographies who came together around Mamdani as a public that was discursively and affectively brought into existence through TikTok. There are 77.2K posts under the #zohranmamdani hashtag and 58.2K posts under the #mamdani hashtag. As Papacharissi points out, the high number of mentions indicates that these individuals collaboratively created a narrative about the event (Papacharissi, 2016, p. 312).

Zohran Mamdani's election as mayor created a story watched by the whole world. The transnational affective public examined in this study is part of a larger affective public. Videos that went viral globally during and especially after Zohran Mamdani's New York mayoral campaign shared some common characteristics. TikTok's tools as a platform make it easy for users to create their own individual stories about an event. It is possible to participate in a trend on TikTok by using the sound of another user. This has been the common feature of most videos searched with the keyword "Zohran Mamdani".

After Zohran Mamdani's election as mayor, users in America and around the world created a stream by sharing videos, and this stream became a story with the contributions of the users. In the current political climate in America, the election of a political figure who defines himself as a socialist democrat as mayor, while reinforcing the political dimension of the *American dream* as defined by James

Truslow Adams (2017), also signifies a rejection of America's capitalist principles through Mamdani's anti-capitalist rhetoric and promises to the residents of New York City (Group, 2025, p. 5).

As a Ugandan-born, Indian-descended Muslim who obtained American citizenship in 2018, he became a political candidate with whom people from all walks of life in New York City could connect. He adopted a multilingual approach in both traditional and social media, displaying signs in Spanish, Urdu, Hindi, and English, and creating videos in these languages, thus conducting an inclusive campaign. Mamdani's inclusive approach throughout the campaign, his background, his stance against ICE raids (Tank, 2026) and his position on the Israeli-Palestinian conflict (Insco, 2025) contributed to his victory and the large crowds that gathered after his win. The campaign included *black, white, brown, young folks and old folks, party gays, butch lesbians, and bridge-and-tunnel kids who couldn't even vote* (Wolfson et al., 2025) in the election. I argue that one of the most important reasons why people from all over the world could connect with the campaign and create a story by sharing their perspectives within the TikTok trend is the relatable nature of Mamdani's social media campaign in particular.

METHODOLOGY

The aim of this research is to examine the affective structure and dynamics of the political discourse that emerged on TikTok regarding Zohran Mamdani's election as New York City mayor. The research adopts qualitative content analysis to understand how TikTok users interact through the videos they create and the comments made on these videos, the impact of these videos and comments on the circulation of affective discourse, and the role of these interactions in the formation of affective publics. In social media research, qualitative content analysis is a preferred method for observing and interpreting users' activities, interactions, discourses, meaning-making processes, and affective responses on the platform. Qualitative content analysis is particularly used in studies on TikTok to analyze comments (Catangay, 2025; Kusumarini et al., 2024; Li et al., 2021). The study also utilized descriptive quantitative data to support the findings obtained during the analysis process. While the distribution and frequencies of comments across categories are presented using quantitative data to highlight discursive patterns, the study aims for in-depth discursive analysis rather than quantitative generalization. In this study six TikTok videos selected through purposeful sampling were analyzed. Comments made on these videos were collected and categorized around the determined themes.

This study draws theoretically from Zizi Papacharissi's conceptualization of affective publics. Papacharissi argues that social media platforms enable the activation and formation of interconnected publics through affective expressions (Papacharissi, 2014, p. 9) This study aims to investigate the impact of affective reactions, humor, and polarized discourses on the formation of such publics, using video content and comments produced by Turkish users around Zohran Mamdani, the subject of this study.

TikTok provides a suitable platform for the research framework, not only due to its affective design elements but also because it allows users to express their personal narratives and provides an alternative channel for political discourse. Users can create shared and interconnected content with other users using the platform's technical tools. At the same time, the platform's structure and the opportunities it provides allow not only information sharing but also emotional expressions, humor, and irony. The dataset used in the study consists of six videos produced by individual Turkish users between November 5, 2025, and November 7, 2025, and the comments on these videos, selected from among the videos that appeared in TikTok searches using the keywords Zohran Mamdani, Mamdani, and the hashtags #mamdani and #zohranmamdani.

The videos were selected using purposive sampling. Purposive sampling allows for the selection of samples that are rich in information and representative of the phenomenon under investigation, in line with a specific research question. The following criteria were used in the selection of the videos:

1. The content must be produced by Turkish users.
2. The content must be produced by an individual user, not from an account belonging to a mainstream or independent media organization.
3. The content must demonstrate user interaction such as likes and comments.

The six selected videos were categorized according to interaction data such as likes, comments, saves, and shares, as well as video content, hashtag usage, date, and music. 485 user comments, including replies to comments, were collected from the comment sections of the selected videos and included in the dataset for analysis. The comments were systematically collected using an automated data extraction tool from the TikTok platform and then analyzed manually. The study focused on the discursive analysis of the comments section rather than the visual content of the videos. The comments used in the dataset analyzed in this study were obtained using TTCommentExporter, a third-party data collection tool. The data collection process from platform-based environments like TikTok can have some limitations.

The literature emphasizes that data obtained from digital platforms is dynamic, variable, and only partially accessible. These inconsistencies in data access can be explained by the platform's policies and technical limitations, as well as by content moderation, deleted or withheld comments, and content not included in the dataset due to algorithmic filtering processes (Darius, 2024; Elmas, 2023). A difference was observed between the data obtained by TTCommentExporter, the data collection tool used in this study, and the data visible on the platform's interface. Since the research focused on the discursive analysis of comments rather than quantitative generalization, these limitations in the data collection process did not have a significant impact on the analytical framework and results of the study.

The dataset consists of 485 comments received on the six videos. During the analysis process, it was observed that thematic saturation was reached as of the sixth video, and no new meaningful categories or patterns emerged. During the analysis process, users' emotional expressions, narrative forms, and contextual references were examined in detail as discursive units of meaning. However, the limitations of the sample size are acknowledged, and it is envisioned that future studies could expand the dataset to include different linguistic and national contexts, thereby examining the transnational dynamics presented here more comprehensively.

An inductive coding approach was used in the analysis of the comments. During the categorization process, the dataset was read repeatedly, and recurring discourses and emotional patterns led to category development. Pre-determined categories were not used in the categorization process; instead, categories were derived from the data and clarified as the analysis progressed.

In content analysis, reliability is associated with the measurement tool producing consistent results regardless of time, context, and practitioner (Riffe et al., 2006, p. 123). In this context, reliability in coding is directly related to the clarity of categories and the systematicity of the coding protocol. In studies conducted with a single coder, reliability is assessed through the consistency of the coding process over time (Riffe et al., 2006, p. 145). Although the coding process in this study was conducted by a single researcher, intra-coder reliability was ensured through a longitudinal self-check to increase consistency. Even though the coding process was conducted by a single researcher, particular attention was paid to developing a clear and systematic coding protocol.

RESULTS AND DISCUSSION

Papacharissi defines the affective public as public spaces transformed by network technologies, suggesting both an area for the interaction of people, technology, and applications, and an imagined collective that evolves from this interaction (Papacharissi, 2014, pp. 125–126). Papacharissi bases the concept of affective publics on the literature on networked publics but theoretically reframes it by adding the dimension of affect. Networked structures encourage affect, and these publics are mobilized through affect. Papacharissi underlines that there are five points in defining affective publics.(Papacharissi, 2014, pp. 125–126) Based on these points, the study will examine how Zohran Mamdani's social media campaign on TikTok created an affective public among ordinary citizens in Türkiye.

1. **Affective publics materialize uniquely and leave distinct digital footprints.**

The structure of publics formed in digital environments manifests itself in various ways depending on the nature of the event under consideration, the mediality and affordance features offered by the platform, and the political-economic context in which it exists. Different groups forming on the same platform develop their own communication practices and forms of expression by utilizing the community-building opportunities offered by the platform in different ways. Therefore, each community that comes together around a particular discourse or event produces its own unique digital footprint on the platform (Papacharissi, 2014, p. 127).

In this context, affective publics formed on TikTok are shaped around specific events, discourses, or trends, and each leaves its own unique digital footprint through different emotional intensities, forms of expression, and interaction practices. Zohran Mamdani's election as New York City mayor has created a unique affective public on TikTok, where users shared their opinions, feelings, and thoughts about the topic, all gathered around the same affective intensity.

Papacharissi's study measures content volume through hashtags and retweets on Twitter. On TikTok, the connection between users is achieved more through the shared use of music/sound than through hashtags. Using the sound "The name is MAMDANI," 17.8 thousand videos were produced; the video where the sound first appeared received 360.8 thousand likes, 2,611 comments, 31.6 thousand saves, and 59.4 thousand share. The #zohranmamdani hashtag was used in 77.3 thousand TikTok posts, while the #mamdani hashtag was used in 58.3 thousand posts.

In the days leading up to and following the election, people from outside New York, from other states in America and/or various countries around the world, supported Mamdani by creating videos on TikTok. The creation and dissemination of similar videos to the viral ones highlights the affective resonance created by this event. The concept of affective resonance refers to a dynamic process in which people mutually influence each other, and is defined by Mühlhof as "the creation of its own affective quality in a 'nonlinear' interplay of the affective dispositions of all individuals involved" (Mühlhof, 2018, p. 1).

According to Mühlhof, each medium creates resonance fields with their own unique resonance characteristics. These characteristics are shaped by both technical and social conditions, leading to the emergence of entirely new interaction dynamics (Mühlhof, 2018, p. 9). When a video is shared on TikTok, people interact with it, comment, produce another video using their sound or template, create remixes, and other videos emerge. In this process, the platform functions as a space for affective interaction. In this context, TikTok becomes a space where political events are not only discussed but also showcased collectively through sounds, memes, and formats, revealing new affective dynamics.

According to Papacharissi, affective publics manifest in different ways depending on the issue they address, the platform's structure, and the political and cultural context in which the users find themselves, leaving their own unique digital traces (Papacharissi, 2014, p. 128). This study examines six TikTok videos and the comments beneath them to explain how the Mamdani figure generated a unique and distinctive affective and discursive response among Turkish users.

Table 1 Platform-level engagement metrics of the six selected TikTok videos at the time of observation

User ID	Like	Comment	Save	Share	Hashtag	Sound/ Music	Date	Content	Tone
User 1	244	3	14	9	No	Yes	5.11.2025	Humor	Political Comparison
User 2	4521	230	179	140	Yes	Yes	5.11.2025	Humor/Viral Format	Happiness
User 3	4414	97	480	253	Yes	Yes	6.11.2025	Humor	Political Comparison, Hope
User 4	6260	129	267	147	Yes	Yes	6.11.2025	Humor	Political Comparison
User 5	515	38	54	42	No	Yes	6.11.2025	Informational	Hope, Excitement
User 6	566	30	13	13	Yes	Yes	7.11.2025	Humor/Viral Format	Happiness

The six videos included in the sample were analyzed in two categories: video content and affective tone. Five of the videos were considered humorous, and in these videos, Mamdani was discussed not through his political program, but rather through emotional closeness, hope, excitement, connection, and comparison with Turkish politics and politicians. Only one video in the dataset contained informational content, and even in this video, the presence of emotional expressions such as excitement and hope was noticeable. While these findings point to the presence of clearly identifiable emotions, they also indicate a broader affective intensity that structures the overall narrative of the videos. Most of the content exhibited platform-specific patterns, a short video format, and a highly emotionally intense narrative style. The videos' affective tone is established not only through captions and hashtags but also through music and sound choices. In four of the videos, the added music is seen as an element that intensifies the affective tone. The song "Empire State of Mind," which played a significant role in Mamdani's campaign and is synonymous with New York City, is featured in two videos, while the original sound is used in the other two.

The videos utilize distinctive hashtags such as '#mamdani, #zohranmamdani, #nyc, #mamdani4mayor,' connecting with an online public discourse and topic. Two of the videos were released on November 5, 2025, three on November 6, 2025, and one on November 7, 2025. Detailed information about the videos is provided in Table 1.

Analysis of the interaction levels of the videos reveals that they were not merely consumed; the content was interacted with through liking, commenting, sharing, and even saving. Two of the videos were created in a format that went viral globally during and after the Mamdani's campaign. In this context, it is noteworthy that the videos circulate as content embedded within the platform's familiar patterns of expression, allowing users to easily and quickly elicit affective responses.

The interaction data presented in Table 1 reflects the interface data observed on the TikTok platform, while the comment dataset analyzed in Table 2 was obtained using a data extraction tool. Therefore, minor differences on comment quantity between the two tables are to be expected. The literature also indicates that inconsistencies may exist between the data from the platform interface and the extracted data. These differences stem from the dynamic nature of the platform and technical limitations in the data collection processes, and do not affect the analytical framework of the study. In this study, comments and responses to comments on six selected TikTok videos were extracted from the application using a program, resulting in a dataset of 485 comments in total. The comments were categorized into eight groups: Political Debate, Emotional Reaction, Polarization/Insult, Humor/Trolling, Informative, Political Comparison, Emoji, and Non-Substantive. The number of comments in each category it's weight and percentage of the categories are given in Table 2. The "Frequency" column indicates the number of comments coded under each category. Percentages represent the proportion of each category within the total dataset.

Table 2. Distribution of comments according to discursive categories and the total weight value of each category

Category	Frequency	%
Political Debate	233	48%
Non-Substantive	92	19%
Political Comparison	46	9.5%
Emotional Reaction	36	7.4%
Polarization/Insult	29	6%
Emoji	21	4.3%
Informative	15	3.1%

Category	Frequency	%
Humor/Trolling	13	2.7%
Total	485	100%

Table 2 shows that a large portion of the comments are concentrated in the Political Debate category. There are 233 comments in this category. This indicates that users evaluated Mamdani's election victory not only through emotional reactions but also within the framework of political discussions.

Following this, the Political Comparison category holds significant weight with 46 comments, and the Polarization/Insult category with 29 comments. According to these findings, users interpreted the event through their own national contexts, and the discussion sometimes accelerated the formation of polarized discourses.

There was no concentration in the Emotional Reaction category, remaining relatively low with 36 comments compared to other categories. Nevertheless, the finding shows that some users participated in the discussion through emotional reactions such as hope, excitement, and disappointment.

Humor is an important factor in social functioning. Located at the intersection of politics, culture, and society (Beck & Spencer, 2025, p. 3), *humor is engaging* (Budnitsky, 2023, p. 212). Although the use of humor is mostly associated with its negative effects in the literature, Ridanpää states that humor can function as a tool that accelerates various geopolitical processes and debates in various contextual conditions and at different spatial levels, and can have both positive and destructive political effects (Ridanpää, 2009, p. 729). Similarly, Yaşar draws attention to the aim of political humor to eliminate political apathy (Yaşar, 2024, p. 1393).

The significant role of humor in Mamdani's campaign and Mamdani's definition of humor as "one of the most effective forms of communication, especially digitally" (Flegenheimer, 2025) demonstrates the powerful impact of humor in the political sphere. For this reason, the fact that most of the videos in the sample contain humorous content and the humor category in the comments gains importance. It facilitates users' connection with political content through humor. There are 13 comments in the Humor/Trolling category.

The most frequently used words in the comments in the dataset were Atatürk, sosyalist, İmamoğlu, Selo, Trump, komünist, kapitalizm, başkan, umut, and müslüman. Due to the use of an English keyboard, different spellings of the words were combined using the same code to create a chord diagram. Although the original comments were in Turkish, the codes were translated into English to ensure consistency with the language of the chapter and improve readability for an international audience. The codes were arranged as follows: ATATURK, SOCIALIST, COMMUNIST, TRUMP, IMAMOGLU, SELO, CAPITALISM, LEADER, HOPE, and MUSLIM.

A chord diagram was created from the categorization of the comments and the frequency of the most frequently used word codes. The relationships between the categorization of comments and the frequency of the most frequently used word codes are presented in Figure 1.

Figure 1. Chord diagram showing the relationships between the categorization of comments and the frequency of the most used word codes

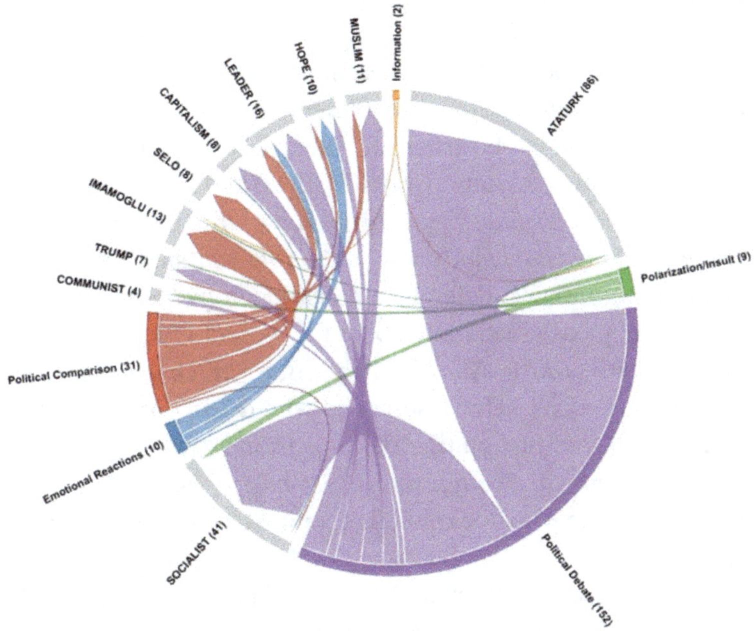

The dominant category in the diagram, containing the most frequently repeated word groups, is Political Debate. A particularly strong connection has been identified within this category with the word Atatürk. Examining the dominant category in the diagram reveals a contentious nature of the discussions, centered around political figures.

The most frequently repeated keyword in the Political Debate category was ATATURK. This indicates that the comments directed at Mamdani were not solely dependent on the content of his current campaign, but rather involved a process of interpretation based on Türkiye's historical and political references. One of the most important reasons for the intense use of the word Atatürk stems from a tweet Zohran Mamdani posted during the Gezi Park protests in 2013. In that tweet, while stating his support for the demands advocated by the protests, he added that "he idea of continuing Atatürk's legacy raises a few question marks." This tweet caused a debate among social media users in Türkiye, leading a significant portion of the comments directed at Mamdani to revolve around the Atatürk reference. An examination of these comments reveals that the Atatürk reference did not produce a one-sided discourse, but rather created a field of debate where different viewpoints clashed. Some users argued that Mamdani should not be supported because of his criticisms of Atatürk, while others stated that Mamdani, not being Turkish, was not obligated to have a positive view of Atatürk. One user commented "*Knk ne bekliyorsunuz yabancı bir siyasetçiden Atatürk güzellemesi mi yapacaktı çıkıp çok romantiksiniz*[sic]" (Bro what did you expect? That a foreign politician would praise Atatürk? You are very romantic.) and another one "*Yorumlar Amerikanın şehrine başkan olan ugandada doğan hint asıllı bi adamı atatürke hakaretten suçladı. bravo türkiye*[sic]" (The comments accused a Ugandan-born man of Indian descent, who became mayor of an American city, of insulting Atatürk. Bravo Türkiye) and "*Nyc'de yaşayan sosyalist bi adam neden kemalist düşünceyi savunsun tam olarak? Cidden o kadar sığ bir bakış açısı ki lğtfen dünya hakkında daha çok şey okuyun*[sic]" (Why exactly would a socialist man living in NYC defend Kemalist ideology? Seriously, that's such a shallow perspective; please read more about the world.") while other users argued "*Atatürkü sevmeyen saygı duymayan birinin iyi insan olduğuna inanmıyorum. sadece şov yapıyorlar*[sic]" (I don't believe someone who doesn't love or respect Atatürk is a good person. They're just putting on an act) and "*yok Atatürk'ün fikirleriyle uyusmayan biri, musluman veya hintli biri bize nasip olmasin* [sic]" (May we not be blessed with someone who does not align with Atatürk's ideas, whether Muslim or Indian.).

Furthermore, while some comments argue that Atatürk, as a historical figure, can be criticized, other users maintain that Mamdani should not take a critical stance towards Türkiye's founding leader. These differing positions demonstrate that the comment sections do not merely produce one-sided affective responses; rather, they create digital discussion spaces where negotiation takes place around national symbols, historical figures, and political identities. Similarly, in comments categorized under political comparison, the repetition of certain words highlights connections and comparative discourse within the framework of political actors (such as İmamoğlu, Trump, and Demirtaş). Looking at the keywords in the Political Comparison category, the code IMAMOGLU is the most frequently used. The references to İmamoğlu, prominent in the comments and sample videos, are based more on Mamdani's political position than on his communication style or personal characteristics. In Türkiye, Istanbul Metropolitan Municipality Mayor Ekrem İmamoğlu is seen as an opposition figure against the central government and is interpreted as an alternative form of political representation within metropolitan politics. Similarly, Mamdani is perceived in the comments not only as an actor in New York local politics but also as a figure who could offer an alternative to the existing political order. Therefore, some users compare Mamdani to İmamoğlu through the political role of global metropolises like Istanbul and New York. The İmamoğlu-Mamdani comparison, based on similarities in fundamental political dynamics, is evaluated within the context of the pattern created by the rise of the right in power globally, yet progressive left-wing mayors are being elected in metropolises (Koru, 2025). Such comparisons demonstrate that affective connections can be established in communities emerging in digital commentary spaces through global political patterns. One user commented "*İmamoğlu ve zohra ikiside ülke cumhurbaşkanı belirli bir tür insanken belediye başkanı oldular olay bu benzerlik açısından politika değil de parallel* [sic]" (Both İmamoğlu and Zohran became mayors when the country's president was a certain type of person; the point is this similarity, not in politics but in parallel.) and another user commented "*Ya politikalar gorusler açısından benzetmiyo ki insanlar sadece 2019 zamanı İmamoğlu aday olduğunda da aynı coşku vardı insanlarda umutluyduk onlarda aynı sekil bunu benzetiyorlar bence* [sic]" (It's not that they're comparing them in terms of policies or views; people are only comparing it to the fact that when İmamoğlu was a candidate in 2019, there was the same enthusiasm and hope among people. I think they're comparing them to that.) These examples illustrate a part of the comparison between İmamoğlu and Mamdani.

In the diagram, we observe that the categories Emotional Reactions (10) and Informational (2) are underrepresented. The discourse generally seems to develop around political discussion. Finally, the intensity of the connections established between different codes and categories reveals that the comments on TikTok have a multi-layered, interactive and inter-theme-transmitted discourse structure.

These findings also form the basis of the concept of transnational affective publics. The transnational concept is defined in the international relations literature by Robert Keohane and Joseph Nye as interactions that transcend national borders and are not directly controlled by governments (Nye & Keohane, 1971, p. 332). These interactions occur with the participation of non-state actors such as individuals, media organizations, civil society actors, or digital platform users, and enable the circulation of ideas, discourses, and affect across borders. This study, based on the definitions of Joseph Nye and Robert Keohane, addresses the concept of transnational as interaction that transcends national borders and proposes the concept of transnational affective publics. It demonstrates, within the context of data, that it is possible for users in different countries, despite being geographically distant, to participate in the same political debate through digital platforms. It can be argued that this global community created around Mamdani is shaped and interacts through affect. The expression of hope generated by Mamdani during and after the campaign is noteworthy. This interconnected community, shaped by affect, is not formed by a shared political position or a singular production of meaning. Rather, users connect around the same event through different points of reference. Although videos related to Zohran Mamdani on TikTok revolve around specific trends or voices, this affective public interacts with shared content while shaping different discourses. Affective publics are not solely based on shared opinion; rather, they consist of communities that come together around the concept of affect to produce diverse narratives.

One of the key factors in incorporating the transnational framework is the increasing data on political apathy in Türkiye. It is noteworthy that despite the apathy and fatigue that Turkish users have developed towards political events in their own country, they participate in sharing content surrounding a political development far beyond their national borders. This is important for examining the new meanings produced by the new affective relationship forms that users establish with political content, even under conditions of political apathy.

2. **Affective publics support connective yet not necessarily collective action.**

> *"Distinct from collective action, connective action develops out of personalized reactions to political issues, old and new, that turn into broader themes shared via various personal communication technologies." (Papacharissi, 2014, p. 71)*

In her study, Papacharissi examines Twitter, stating that it functions as a channel connecting personalized interests, where users come together in shared discussion areas without deviating from their own views (Papacharissi, 2014, p. 128). Similarly, TikTok is a platform where users come together based on their interests.

According to Papacharissi, affective publics produce forms of connective publicness where individuals are affectively and discursively connected through digital platforms, rather than collectively organizing towards a common political goal (Papacharissi, 2016). The interactions on TikTok during and after the New York mayoral election provide an example of this connected public. Mamdani's election campaign and subsequent election as Mayor of New York City resonated globally and made headlines. Simultaneously, social media users, including those from other states in the US who didn't live in New York, as well as those from diverse backgrounds – countries, races, political climates, and religious and social backgrounds – commented on Mamdani's victory. However, these interactions did not translate into a collective political mobilization. It is precisely at this point that a form of connected interaction, which, while not directly influencing the political outcome, establishes affective and discursive links among users, is revealed. In the comments examined within the scope of this study, affective publics formed within the Turkish context are analyzed, and it is observed that the connections established among users contain local references.

The data obtained in this study shows that Mamdani's Muslim identity, his tweets about the Gezi Park protests in 2013, and comparisons with Turkish political figures, particularly Ekrem İmamoğlu and Selahattin Demirtaş, demonstrate that users interpreted Mamdani using individual references such as their own political experiences and socio-cultural backgrounds. For example, some users have linked Mamdani to political actors in Türkiye with comments such as, "*mamdani su an 2019 secimlerindeki imamoglu zaten*[sic]" (Mamdani is currently İmamoğlu from the 2019 elections), "*Selo başkanın new york verisiyonu*[sic]" (The New York version of Leader Selo)," or " *Ekrem başkanım da böyleydi:(* [sic]" (Mayor Ekrem was like that too). Papachrassi states that the emotional intensity provided by the flows gains meaning when it evokes feelings of community and identity (Papacharissi, 2014, p. 129). In this respect, the sense of community and identity that Mamdani's campaign evoked among Turkish users was shaped around certain local nodal points. Every TikTok video shared on the subject created a connected public using hashtags and sounds that became tools for perspectives (Hautea et al., 2021, p. 12).

3. **Affective publics are powered by affective statements of opinion, fact, or a blend of both, which in turn produce ambient, always-on feeds that further connect and pluralize expression in democratic and otherwise democratic regimes.**

On social media, events are transformed into stories through the platform's affordances, structure, and the users' narrative styles. This allows different users to contribute to the story by creating their own discourses with different emotions and interpretations around the same event. Mamdani's election victory, too, transcends being a single political event through TikTok videos and comments, transforming into different narrative forms.

When the comments are examined, it is seen that some users frame Mamdani's success as a story of victory and hope, and share their feelings about it. For example, some comments include expressions such as "*Bizim de belediye başkanımız olur mu sorsak*[sic]" *(*Should we ask if we could have a mayor like him?), " *hepmizin kalbine dolan minik bir umut ışığı*[sic]" (A tiny ray of hope that fills all our hearts), or " *bizede mamdani gibi biri lutfennn*[sic]" (We also need someone like Mamdani, please.) These types of comments demonstrate that Mamdani's success is not only seen as a development related to New York local politics, but also transformed into a narrative interpreted through the political expectations and hopes of users in Türkiye. However, some users have created a different narrative line by questioning Mamdani's political statements, and especially his past statements about Atatürk. This shows that Mamdani's election victory, instead of producing a single political narrative in TikTok comment sections, has transformed into multiple narratives through different emotions, opinions, and interpretations. Thus, Mamdani's election victory has become a digital story flow where users combine their information, opinions, and emotions to produce different narratives.

Of the 485 comments analyzed, 36 were directly examined in the Emotional Reactions category, and in these comments, users interpret Mamdani's election victory through emotions such as hope, excitement, and positive expectation. These comments show that Mamdani's success is not only understood as a political development, but also through the affective reactions and expectations of users. One of the most striking emotional expressions in the comments is the concept of "hope." One of the most frequently repeated words in the comments, "Hope," appears five times in comments categorized as "Emotional Reaction," three times in "Political Debate," and twice in "Political Comparison." This finding demonstrates, as Papacharissi emphasizes in her concept of affective publics, that affect have become a significant component of political debate in digital public spaces. On TikTok, the narratives surrounding the campaign and candidate Zohran Mamdani, and the way these narratives interact, bring about significant differences in the tone, rhythm, and texture of the story. Humor, information sharing, political debate, comparison, and emotional expressions all come together to produce a narrative about Mamdani, and all these expressions are uniquely interconnected.

4. **Affective publics typically produce disruptions/interruptions of dominant political narratives by presenting underrepresented viewpoints.**

Brown et al. argue that the expression of political views and emotions on social media platforms is linked to the limited voice of young people on political issues, suggesting that social media platforms create a channel for the outward expression of affect (Brown et al., 2022, p. 16). A potential is emerging where young people use TikTok's capabilities for political discussion, information sharing, and participation. In videos created by Turkish users around Mamdani on TikTok, individuals' micro-narratives invite others to find and feel their place within politics (Papacharissi, 2014, p. 131). Research into the nature of affective publics in disrupting dominant political narratives revealed that Turkish users viewed Mamdani as an example of a progressive mayoral candidate who challenged the dominant right-wing political narrative in world politics. Comments such as, "*...dünya siyaseti bu kadar sağa kaymışken birazcık kutlama yapabiliriz umudumuzu tazelemek için bence*[sic]" (With world politics shifting so far to the right, we can celebrate a little to renew our hope)," and " *Dünya siyasetinin iyice sağa kaydığı bu dönemde kapitalizmin göbeğinde demokratik sosyalist bir adayın seçim kazanabilmesi umut oluyo*[sic]" (In this era of global political shift to the right, the fact that a democratic socialist candidate can win an election in the heart of capitalism offers hope)," confirm the assertion that affective publics pave the way for the representation and proliferation of underrepresented perspectives. Papacharissi considers affect as a way for citizens to include themselves in a story. As in Papacharissi's example (Papacharissi, 2016,

p. 318), when examining the comments of Turkish users on Mamdani videos, it is observed that with the increase in the stream, positive and negative narratives about Mamdani are mixed. The fact that most of the analyzed videos have themes of happiness and hope, and the frequency of the word "hope" in the analyzed comments, indicates that alternative perspectives are present in the narratives. Mamdani's election victory is interpreted by some users not only as a development in New York local politics, but also as an example showing that a different style of politics is possible, and furthermore, it is identified with other politicians in Türkiye. Users question their current political experiences in their comments and express alternative political expectations.

5. **Ambient streams sustain publics convened around affective commonalities: impact is symbolic, agency claimed is semantic, power is liminal.**

In light of the comments analyzed within the scope of this study, an affective atmosphere has formed among Turkish users who come together around shared emotions within the framework of Mamdani content. The impact of this atmosphere and the resulting public opinion is symbolic. Since the vast majority of users involved in this stream are Turkish, they cannot vote for Mamdani. This stream generates discussion, spreading affective feedback and connecting users through emotions such as hope, admiration, humor, and political disappointment. This interaction does not directly translate into political mobilization, but rather creates a symbolic public space where users express their feelings and political assessments. Thus, the stream of comments surrounding Mamdani's content presents an example of an ambient stream where users come together around shared emotional responses. As Papacharissi defines it, streams that come together around affective interactions and partnerships can sometimes help support regime changes or movements that can create a certain kind of political impact, while at other times they create discursive spaces where the meaning of political events is renegotiated rather than directly producing political results. Mamdani's election victory was discussed by users in Türkiye through comments, with different users interpreting the event through their own political experiences and affective responses. However, these discussions did not directly translate into political mobilization affecting New York local politics. Instead, users, through comments, discussed what Mamdani's success meant, thus re-creating the meaning of the political event at a discursive level. This demonstrates, as Papacharissi stated, that the impact that emerges in digital public spaces often has a symbolic and discursive character.

FUTURE RESEARCH DIRECTIONS

This study specifically examines the reflection of the globally formed affective public in the Turkish context, using Zohran Mamdani as an example on TikTok. While the scope is limited, the analysis is in-depth, as Papacharissi's framework examines the discursive fabric of affective public in a transnational context. Future studies are expected to make a significant contribution by comparatively examining how this transnational affective public manifests in different geographical contexts, as exemplified by Zohran Mamdani. This study observes that local political figures and references in Türkiye shape the discourses of affective public. Future studies could explore how users from different countries shape the discourses of this community within their historical, political, and cultural contexts, revealing the patterns of the same event in different countries.

This study focuses primarily on content produced by individual users and does not include social media accounts of media organizations in the sample. Future studies could address the impact of news sources and corporate media actors, which were not included in this study, on the formation of affective public.

Methodologically, expanding the sample in future studies will increase the generalizability of this research. Furthermore, given the importance of the medial role provided by the platform, which is also discussed in this study, a study including other social media platforms in addition to TikTok would greatly contribute to the affective publics literature.

CONCLUSION

Papacharissi argues that users affectively tune into the events they are physically distant from through digital platforms, and that in this process, users often experience events through imagination, without having sufficient information about them. The findings of this study, however, show that this process is not limited to purely imaginative participation. In the case of Zohran Mamdani, examining the comments of Turkish users reveals that they are not merely observers "trying to feel what is happening," but rather reframe the event through their own local political and cultural references.

Based on the findings, the affective public formed by Turkish users on TikTok around Mamdani's election does not have a singular and homogeneous structure. On the contrary, it has been observed that the discourses formed around the flow created by Mamdani's election, while sometimes contradictory and different, create an interconnected discursive space. It is possible to say that users participated in this space through an affective intensity rather than an ideological consensus. In light of the findings, the concentration of discourses in comments across various categories such as political debate, humor, political comparison, and polarization confirms the concept that affect circulation, rather than consensus, was more influential in the formation of the affective public. The most frequent interactions in the comments occurred around the axis of "Political Debate," with this category accounting for 43% of the total comments. Political Comparison, on the other hand, covered 9.5% of the comment interactions. The category distributions reveal the heterogeneous yet interconnected texture of the affective intensity surrounding Zohran Mamdani.

The study validated the flow around Zohran Mamdani's election using the five characteristics Papacharissi uses to define affective publics. Examining the chord diagram in Figure 1, the intensity of discourses encompassing the word Atatürk within the Political Debate category and İmamoğlu within the Political Comparison category shows that the affective public created by Turkish users left unique digital traces. The negotiation space created by Mamdani's 2013 Gezi Park tweet is a representation of the unique texture produced by the local political memory of Turkish users.

The fact that Turkish users could not vote in the New York elections did not prevent them from adopting Mamdani as a figure of hope. From this perspective, it can be accepted that this situation will be considered a connection-building action that does not require collective mobilization, arises from individual responses, and scales through network sharing. The fact that Turkish users embraced Mamdani as İmamoğlu in the 2019 elections and evaluated him within this framework exemplifies the interconnectedness of individual perspectives, which hold a significant place in the fabric of affective publics. Turkish users interpret this globally relevant political event through their own historical and political contexts, and it is seen that they have made a unique contribution to the storytelling surrounding Zohran Mamdani on TikTok. Ultimately, it is observed that affective publics are contextually reproduced and shaped according to users' socio-political positions. Considering the political apathy felt by users in Türkiye, such as their indifference and apathy towards domestic politics, particularly their avoidance of news, the formation of this community and discourse around a mayoral election in a geographically distant region is noteworthy and significant.

TikTok's use of sound and its stitch/duet capabilities provide a different interaction environment than Twitter's text-based retweets. This study reveals the impact of the sounds associated with Zohran Mamdani, used during and after the campaign to guide the movement, and the connections formed with these sounds on the fabric of the resulting affective publics. Turkish users are creating context-based belonging by reinterpreting the template of global content about Mamdani with local references and figures like İmamoğlu and Atatürk. Most of the videos analyzed use hashtags, but the flow around the same topic on TikTok also occurs through the use of sounds.

Furthermore, the comments analyzed show that Mamdani's election victory is generally viewed as a positive and hopeful development, breaking the dominance of right-wing narratives in world politics. Users compared Mamdani to İmamoğlu, adopting him as an alternative perspective. This demonstrates the repetition of the affective publics formation that challenges dominant political narratives within the scope of the research.

The study also contributes to the concept of transnational affective publics in the context of digital platforms enabling interactions that transcend national borders. It is observed that Turkish users, while reinterpreting Mamdani through local references, are also part of a broader global affective flow.

In conclusion, this study presents important findings regarding how TikTok functions as a space where political events are not only discussed but also narrated and reinterpreted by users at the affect level. The Mamdani example reveals that affective publics are formed through fragmented, heterogeneous, individualized yet interconnected narratives, and that meaning is constantly renegotiated in this process.

REFERENCES

Adams, J. T. (2017). *The Epic of America*. Routledge. (Original work published 1931, Little, Brown, and Company) DOI: 10.4324/9781351304122

Albasar, İ. D., Demiralp, S., & Parlak, F. (2025). Sosyal Medya, Bilişsel Yorgunluk ve Siyasi Apati: Dijital Dönüşümün Gençler Üzerindeki Yansımaları. *Social Review of Technology and Change*, *3*(2), 103–125.

Alptekin, H. (2023, December 2). Siyasete Yabancılaşma, Politik Apati ve Tükenmişlik Sendromu. *Türkiye Araştırmaları Vakfı*. https://www.turkiyearastirmalari.org/2023/12/02/fokus-tr/siyasete-yabancilasma-politik-apati-ve-tukenmislik-sendromu/

Beck, D., & Spencer, A. (2025). (Un)Funny Against All Odds: The Changing Landscape of Humour in Politics. *Alternatives*, *50*(1), 3–17. DOI: 10.1177/03043754241290911

Bingöl, O. (2017). SİYASAL KAYITSIZLIK: APATİ. *Munzur Üniversitesi Sosyal Bilimler Dergisi*, *5*(9), 44–51.

Brown, Y., Pini, B., & Pavlidis, A. (2022). Affective design and memetic qualities: Generating affect and political engagement through bushfire TikToks. *Journal of Sociology (Melbourne, Vic.)*, *60*(1), 144078332211102. DOI: 10.1177/14407833221110267

Budnitsky, S. (2023). Global disengagement: Public diplomacy humor in the Russian–Ukrainian War. *Place Branding and Public Diplomacy*, *19*(2), 211–217. DOI: 10.1057/s41254-022-00291-1

Çarkoğlu, A., & Kalaycıoğlu, E. (2015). *Türkiye'de ve Dünya'da Vatandaşlık* [ISSP Araştırma Raporu]. https://bilimakademisi.org/turkiyede-ve-dunyada-vatandaslik-2014-issp-arastirma-raporu/

Catangay, J. R. (2025). *Constructing hope in hopelessness: Playful resistances of affective publics in TikTok's #corecore #pinoycore*. Plaridel., DOI: 10.52518/2024-9ctngy

Curato, N., & Niemeyer, S. (2013). Reaching Out to Overcome Political Apathy: Building Participatory Capacity through Deliberative Engagement. *Politics & Policy*, *41*(3), 355–383. DOI: 10.1111/polp.12015

Darius, P. (2024, September 24). *Researcher Data Access Under the DSA: Lessons from TikTok's API Issues During the 2024 European Elections*. Tech Policy Press. https://techpolicy.press/-researcher-data-access-under-the-dsa-lessons-from-tiktoks-api-issues-during-the-2024-european-elections

Demiralp, S. (2025, October 10). Arada Kalanlar: Geçişken Seçmenlerde Esneklik, Apati ve Güven Arayışı. *Global Panorama*. https://www.globalpanorama.org/2025/10/arada-kalanlar-gecisken-secmenlerde-esneklik-apati-ve-guven-arayisi/

Elmas, T. (2023). The Impact of Data Persistence Bias on Social Media Studies. *Proceedings of the 15th ACM Web Science Conference 2023, WebSci '23*, 196–207. DOI: 10.1145/3578503.3583630

Foster, J. W. (2013). *Oldenburg's great good places online: Assessing the potential for social network sites to serve as third places* [PhD Thesis, Texas Tech University]. http://hdl.handle.net/2346/58210

Goodwin, G. E. (2026, January 1). Social media fuelled Mamdani's rise. Can he keep the momentum as mayor? *BBC*. https://www.bbc.com/news/articles/c4gvg46dy7vo

Google. (2025). *Google's Year in Search*. https://trends.withgoogle.com/year-in-search/2025/

Group, G. S. S. (2025). *From Penthouse To Public Housing: Trump, Mamdani, And The Battle Over The American Dream* (Karoui, H., Ed.).

Hautea, S., Parks, P., Takahashi, B., & Zeng, J. (2021). Showing They Care (Or Don't): Affective Publics and Ambivalent Climate Activism on TikTok. *Social Media + Society*, *7*(2), 20563051211012344. DOI: 10.1177/20563051211012344

Hibbing, J. R., & Theiss-Morse, E. (2002). *Stealth Democracy: Americans' Beliefs About How Government Should Work*. Cambridge University Press., DOI: 10.1017/CBO9780511613722

Hillis, K., Paasonen, S., & Petit, M. (Eds.). (2015). *Networked Affect*. The MIT Press. DOI: 10.7551/mitpress/9715.001.0001

Hipfl, B. (2018). Affect in Media and Communication Studies: Potentials and Assemblages. *Media and Communication*, *6*(3), 5–14. DOI: 10.17645/mac.v6i3.1470

Horrigan, J. B. (2001, October 31). Part 2: The Internet, Communities, and the Virtual "Third Place." *Pew Research Center*. https://www.pewresearch.org/internet/2001/10/31/part-2-the-internet-communities-and-the-virtual-third-place/

Insco, J. (2025, October 29). *Zohran Mamdani's unlikely coalition: Winning over NYC's Jewish voters*. Al Jazeera. https://www.aljazeera.com/economy/2025/10/29/zohran-mamdanis-unlikely-coalition-winning-over-nycs-jewish

Katz, Y., & Shifman, L. (2017). Making sense? The structure and meanings of digital memetic nonsense. *Information Communication and Society*, *20*(6), 825–842. DOI: 10.1080/1369118X.2017.1291702

Kim, J., Klein-Balajee, T., Kelly, R. M., & Hiniker, A. (2025). *Discord's Design Encourages "Third Place" Social Media Experiences* (arXiv:2501.09951). arXiv. /arXiv.2501.09951DOI: 10.48550

Koru, S. (2025, November 3). From Istanbul to New York: How Erdoğan Defeated His "Mamdani" [Substack newsletter]. *Kültürkampf.* https://kulturkampftr.substack.com/p/from-istanbul-to-new-york-how-erdogan

Kusumarini, C. D., Kuncoroyakti, Y. A., & Rahella, L. K. (2024). Analysis of the Content of Tiktok Comments @Dictionarei in A DAY WITH REI PART 350/ SWISS DAY. *Review: Journal of Multidisciplinary in Social Sciences, 1*(08), 282–302. DOI: 10.59422/rjmss.v1i08.450

Li, Y., Guan, M., Hammond, P., & Berrey, L. E. (2021). Communicating COVID-19 information on TikTok: A content analysis of TikTok videos from official accounts featured in the COVID-19 information hub. *Health Education Research, 36*(3), cyab010. Advance online publication. DOI: 10.1093/her/cyab010 PMID: 33667311

Markiewicz, E. (2020). Third Places in the Era of Virtual Communities. *Studia Periegetica, 28*(4), 9–21. DOI: 10.26349/st.per.0028.01

Marsh, D., O'Toole, T., & Jones, S. (2007). *Young People and Politics in the UK.*, DOI: 10.1057/9780230625631

Massumi, B. (1995). The Autonomy of Affect. *Cultural Critique*, (31), 83–109. JSTOR. DOI: 10.2307/1354446

McArthur, J. A., & White, A. F. (2016). Twitter Chats as Third Places: Conceptualizing a Digital Gathering Site. *Social Media + Society, 2*(3), 2056305116665857. DOI: 10.1177/2056305116665857

Melimopoulos, E. (2025, November 4). *NYC mayoral election: Candidates, polls, results and what's at stake.* Al Jazeera. https://www.aljazeera.com/news/2025/11/4/nyc-mayoral-election-candidates-polls-results-and-whats-at-stake

Mühlhof, R. (2018). *Affective resonance* [Author's Manuscript]. https://docs.rainermuehlhoff.de/muehlhoff_2019_affective-resonance-key-concepts-preprint.pdf

Newman, N., Arguedas, A. R., Robertson, C. T., Nielsen, R. K., & Fletcher, R. (2025). *Digital News Report 2025 | Reuters Institute for the Study of Journalism.* Reuters Institute & University of Oxford. https://reutersinstitute.politics.ox.ac.uk/digital-news-report/2025

Nye, J. S.Jr, & Keohane, R. O. (1971). Transnational Relations and World Politics: An Introduction. *International Organization*, *25*(3), 329–349. DOI: 10.1017/S0020818300026187

Oldenburg, R. (1999). *The great good place: Cafés, coffee shops, bookstores, bars, hair salons, and other hangouts at the heart of a community*. Marlowe ; Distributed by Publishers Group West.

Oxenham, J. (2017). *Literacy: writing, reading and social organisation*. Routledge. DOI: 10.4324/9781351236508

Oz, M., & Yanik, A. (2024). Fear of surveillance: Examining Turkish social media users' perception of surveillance and willingness to express opinions on social media. *Mediterranean Politics*, *29*(1), 1–25. DOI: 10.1080/13629395.2022.2046911

Papacharissi, Z. (2014). *Affective Publics: Sentiment, Technology, and Politics*. Oxford University Press., DOI: 10.1093/acprof:oso/9780199999736.001.0001

Papacharissi, Z. (2016). Affective publics and structures of storytelling: Sentiment, events and mediality. *Information Communication and Society*, *19*(3), 307–324. DOI: 10.1080/1369118X.2015.1109697

Pilkington, E. (2025, November 6). How Mamdani built an 'unstoppable force' that won over New York. *The Guardian*. https://www.theguardian.com/us-news/2025/nov/06/zohran-mamdani-campaign-new-york-democrats

Reckwitz, A. (2017). Practices and their affects. In *The Nexus of Practices*. Routledge.

Rheingold, H. (1993). *The virtual community: Homesteading on the electronic frontier*. Reading, Mass.: Addison-Wesley Pub. Co. http://archive.org/details/virtualcommunity00rhei

Ridanpää, J. (2009). Geopolitics of Humour: The Muhammed Cartoon Crisis and the *Kaltio* Comic Strip Episode in Finland. *Geopolitics*, *14*(4), 729–749. DOI: 10.1080/14650040903141372

Riffe, D., Lacy, S., & Fico, F. (2006). *Analyzing Media Messages: Using Quantitative Content Analysis in Research* (2nd ed.). Routledge., DOI: 10.4324/9781410613424

Rosenwein, B. H., & Cristiani, R. (2019). *Duygular Tarihi Nedir* (Özdil, K., Trans.). Islık Yayınları.

Shaviro, S. (2010). *Post cinematic affect*. Zero Books.

Shouse, E. (2005). Feeling, Emotion, Affect. *M/C Journal, 8*(6). DOI: 10.5204/mcj.2443

Soroka, S. (2025, December 4). *Everything everywhere all at once: How Zohran Mamdani campaigned both online and with a ground game*. The Conversation. DOI: 10.64628/AAI.ktt3ymgeu

Soukup, C. (2006). Computer-mediated communication as a virtual third place: Building Oldenburg's great good places on the world wide web. *New Media & Society*, *8*(3), 421–440. DOI: 10.1177/1461444806061953

Spectrum News. (2025). *NYC Democratic Primary Debate For Mayor | Full NY1 Coverage* [Video recording]. https://www.youtube.com/watch?v=ElGfMRIox9w

Steinkuehler, C., & Williams, D. (2006). Where Everybody Knows Your (Screen) Name: Online Games as "Third Places.". *Journal of Computer-Mediated Communication, 11*(4), 885–909. DOI: 10.1111/j.1083-6101.2006.00300.x

Stewart, D. (2025, June 29). How Social Media Videos Fueled Zohran Mamdani's Success. *The New York Times*. https://www.nytimes.com/2025/06/29/nyregion/zohran-mamdani-campaign-videos.html

Tank, C. (2026, January 1). *Inside Zohran Mamdani's defiant and unruly campaign design, radiant with purpose*. Stir World. https://www.stirworld.com/see-features-inside-zohran-mamdani-s-defiant-and-unruly-campaign-design-radiant-with-purpose

Uetricht, M. (2026, January 7). *How Zohran Mamdani's Campaign Crafted a Winning Message*. Jacobin. https://jacobin.com/2026/01/zohran-mamdani-communications-strategy

Wolfson, S., Demopoulos, A., & Niami, S. (2025, November 5). New York parties for Zohran Mamdani: 'The first time we've had hope in so long.' *The Guardian*. https://www.theguardian.com/us-news/2025/nov/05/zohran-mamdani-new-york-cheers-tears-dsa-chants

Wright, S. (2012). From "Third Place" to "Third Space": Everyday Political Talk in Non-Political Online Spaces. *Javnost - The Public, 19*(3), 5–20. DOI: 10.1080/13183222.2012.11009088

Yaşar, Ö. (2024). Siyasi Mizah ve Y Kuşağı. *Journal of Turkish Studies, 13*(Volume 13 Issue 18), 1389–1407. DOI: 10.7827/TurkishStudies.13844

Yıldızgörür, M. R. (2023). 'Ne Önemi Var?' Okuyucuların Haberden Kaçınma Davranışları Üzerine Nitel Bir Araştırma. *Etkileşim*, *6*(11), 266–290. DOI: 10.32739/etkilesim.2023.6.11.197

Zanger, J. (2025, November 5). *Zohran Mamdani wins NYC mayoral election after energizing young voters with focus on affordability—CBS New York*. CBS News. https://www.cbsnews.com/newyork/news/mamdani-wins-nyc-mayoral-election-2025/

Zhelnina, A. (2020). Apathy Syndrome: How We Are Trained Not to Care about Politics. *Social Problems*, *67*(2), 358–378. DOI: 10.1093/socpro/spz019

KEY TERMS AND DEFINITIONS

Affect: It is the realm of intensity and potential that forms the basis of the concepts of emotion and feeling.

Affective Publics: Networked communities that interact and take action through affect.

Affective Resonance: It is the process by which users generate similar affective responses to the same event or content, even if they do not share the exact same opinions, and these affects reinforce and spread among themselves in digital enviroments.

Political Apathy: It manifests as a lack of interest in political issues among individuals and is characterized by a decline in political participation.

Political Debate: It is used to describe discussions that take place among users around political issues.

Third Place: Apart from the home, considered the primary place of residence, and the workplace, considered the secondary place of residence, public spaces are those where citizens interact socially and which stand out for their importance from a political perspective.

TikTok: It is a social media platform where users create short video content by combining sound, image, video, and performative elements.

Transnational Affective Publics: These are discursively heterogeneous communities that interact through network-based platforms, mobilized through expressions of emotion around a local political event/person, transcending national borders.

Chapter 4
Emotional Exhaustion Across Cultures in the Digital Age:
A Cross-Cultural Analysis of Media-Induced Fatigue and Social Indifference

Satya Subrahmanyam
http://orcid.org/0000-0003-0441-2742
Holy Spirit University of Kaslik, Lebanon

ABSTRACT

Digital media has reshaped how people absorb information, manage emotions, and connect across cultures. This chapter explores how constant exposure to online content contributes to emotional exhaustion in different cultural settings. Drawing on burnout theory, information overload, and cultural dimensions, it presents a model linking heavy media use to emotional fatigue and growing social indifference. Evidence from regions including Asia, Europe, the Middle East, and the Global South highlights both shared trends and culturally specific differences. The findings suggest that factors like individualism, uncertainty avoidance, and access to digital infrastructure influence how people experience media-related fatigue. The chapter concludes by considering what this means for digital well-being policies, platform design, and culturally sensitive mental health strategies.

DOI: 10.4018/979-8-3373-8307-1.ch004

1. INTRODUCTION

The early twenty-first century has seen a dramatic and largely unreversed acceleration in the quantity of information that individuals are expected to absorb, process, and respond to on a daily basis. Platforms that were once conceived as tools for social connection have evolved into ecosystems of perpetual notification, performative engagement, and algorithmically curated outrage (Twenge et al., 2021). In this environment, the psychological costs of digital participation are no longer incidental; they are structural. Emotional exhaustion, once primarily associated with occupational burnout in healthcare and service sectors, has emerged as a condition that transcends the workplace and reaches into the ordinary rhythms of digitally mediated life (Agai, 2022).

What makes this phenomenon particularly complex is that its contours are not uniform across societies. A user in Seoul navigating a high-speed, culturally homogeneous information environment experiences a qualitatively different form of digital fatigue than a user in Cairo absorbing politically charged social media content amid economic precarity, or a user in Stockholm whose ambient media diet is moderated by strong institutional trust and robust digital literacy education (Tufekci, 2017; Valkenburg et al., 2022). Culture, in other words, does not merely color the experience of emotional exhaustion in the digital age; it shapes its triggers, its expression, and its consequences.

Yet most existing research has been conducted in Western, educated, industrialized, rich, and democratic societies, leaving substantial gaps in understanding how emotional exhaustion and media-induced fatigue operate in non-Western cultural contexts (Anjum & Aziz, 2024). This chapter addresses that gap directly. It situates the problem of media-induced emotional exhaustion within a genuinely cross-cultural framework, drawing on theoretical resources from cultural psychology, communication studies, and organizational behavior to construct a model that is both analytically rigorous and culturally sensitive.

The central argument advanced here is that emotional exhaustion in the digital age is a culturally mediated phenomenon. Media exposure and information overload function as primary drivers of fatigue, but the degree to which exhaustion deepens into social indifference, the coping strategies individuals deploy, and the social legitimacy accorded to expressions of digital distress are all shaped by cultural dimensions including individualism versus collectivism, uncertainty avoidance, and power distance (Hofstede et al., 2020; Qin et al., 2024).

The chapter proceeds as follows. Section 2 establishes the theoretical foundations, examining emotional exhaustion theory, media fatigue frameworks, and cross-cultural theories of psychological difference. Section 3 reviews the relevant empirical literature. Section 4 presents the conceptual framework and formulates testable hypotheses.

Section 5 describes an appropriate mixed-methods research design. Sections 6 and 7 discuss hypothetical and synthesized findings and their theoretical and practical implications. Sections 8 and 9 address policy recommendations, limitations, and directions for future inquiry. Section 10 concludes with reflections on digital-era emotional sustainability as a global challenge.

2. THEORETICAL FOUNDATIONS

2.1 Emotional Exhaustion Theory

The concept of emotional exhaustion was systematically theorized by Christina Maslach and colleagues in the context of occupational burnout (Maslach et al., 1996). In Maslach's tripartite model, burnout comprises emotional exhaustion, depersonalization, and a diminished sense of personal accomplishment. Of these, emotional exhaustion is considered the core and most commonly measured component, defined as a state of chronic depletion of emotional resources that results from sustained exposure to emotionally demanding situations (Maslach & Leiter, 2022).

Contemporary scholarship has extended this framework beyond the workplace, arguing persuasively that the conditions which produce occupational burnout, namely excessive demands, lack of control, insufficient rewards, and a breakdown of community, are now replicated and in many cases intensified in digital media environments (Agai, 2022; Santos & Alves, 2023). The always-on nature of social media, the social surveillance involved in managing online identity, and the inescapability of distressing news content collectively generate a chronic emotional load that mirrors, and may exceed, the demands of high-intensity service occupations.

Adapting the Maslach framework for digital contexts requires recognizing that the source of exhaustion is not a demanding supervisor or a difficult patient but rather an attention economy that monetizes emotional arousal. The depersonalization dimension of the burnout model maps onto what researchers have termed digital desensitization or compassion fatigue, a progressive numbing of empathic response to the suffering of distant others mediated through screens (Soroya et al., 2021). This numbing, in turn, contributes to social indifference, the failure to engage with collective problems or to extend moral concern beyond immediate personal networks.

2.2 Media Fatigue and Information Overload Theory

Information overload was first theorized in the context of organizational communication (Toffler, 1970), but the construct has achieved new salience in the era of algorithmic content delivery. Information overload occurs when the volume, complexity, or ambiguity of available information exceeds the processing capacity of the individual, resulting in decision paralysis, cognitive exhaustion, and reduced quality of judgment (Alimour & Alrabeei, 2025).

Media fatigue is a related but distinct construct, referring specifically to the exhaustion that arises from sustained engagement with media content, particularly content that is emotionally charged, formally repetitive, or structurally designed to maximize engagement time (Dhir et al., 2021). Research has demonstrated that media fatigue is associated with reduced cognitive performance, disrupted sleep, increased anxiety, and progressive disengagement from both media consumption and social participation, a pattern sometimes described as digital withdrawal (Schreurs et al., 2023).

The distinction between information overload and media fatigue matters for cross-cultural analysis because different cultures vary in their tolerance for ambiguity, their media consumption habits, and the social norms governing digital disconnection. High uncertainty avoidance cultures, for example, may experience information overload as acutely threatening, while high-context communication cultures may filter information through collective interpretive frameworks that buffer individual overload (Hall, 1992; Hofstede et al., 2020).

2.3 Cross-Cultural Theories

Two theoretical traditions are of primary relevance to this analysis. The first is Hofstede's cultural dimensions framework, which identifies six dimensions along which national cultures vary: power distance, individualism versus collectivism, masculinity versus femininity, uncertainty avoidance, long-term orientation, and indulgence versus restraint (Hofstede et al., 2020). Each of these dimensions has plausible and empirically supported relationships with how individuals experience and respond to emotional exhaustion in digital environments.

The second tradition is Edward Hall's distinction between high-context and low-context communication cultures (Hall, 1992). In high-context cultures, meaning is embedded in relationships, situations, and nonverbal cues, and communication is often indirect. In low-context cultures, meaning is encoded explicitly in verbal messages. This distinction is relevant because digital communication platforms are predominantly designed around low-context communication norms, creating a structural misfit that may generate additional cognitive and emotional work for users from high-context cultural backgrounds (Tufekci, 2017).

Together, these frameworks suggest that the pathway from media exposure to emotional exhaustion is not a single universal mechanism but a culturally moderated process in which the same stimuli produce different responses depending on the cultural tools available for interpretation, regulation, and expression.

Figure 1. Conceptual linkage between media exposure, emotional exhaustion, and social indifference across cultural dimensions

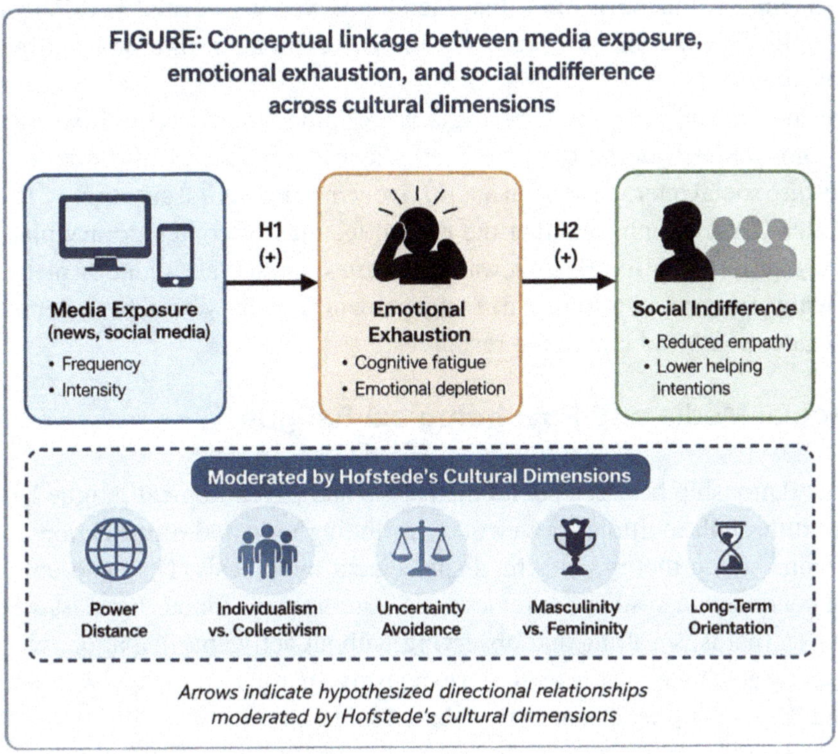

3. LITERATURE REVIEW

3.1 Emotional Exhaustion in Digital Environments

The past decade has produced a substantial body of research documenting the psychological costs of digital media engagement. Studies consistently find that heavy social media use is associated with elevated symptoms of anxiety, depression, loneliness, and emotional exhaustion, though the magnitude and direction of effects vary considerably across populations and methodologies (Kam, 2024; Valkenburg et al., 2022).

Longitudinal research has been particularly informative. Twenge et al. (2021) analyzed data from over 500,000 adolescents in the United States and found that increases in screen time were temporally associated with declines in psychological well-being, with effect sizes that were modest but consistent across demographic groups. Likewise, a European multi-country study by Livingstone et al. (2018) found that pandemic-era increases in social media use were associated with heightened media fatigue, which in turn predicted increased social withdrawal and reduced civic engagement.

The mechanisms proposed for these associations include cognitive overload, social comparison, cyberbullying exposure, sleep disruption, and the replacement of face-to-face social interaction with qualitatively inferior digital substitutes. Maslach and Leiter (2016) emphasize that the design features of contemporary platforms, including infinite scroll, variable reward schedules, and social validation metrics, are specifically engineered to maximize engagement time in ways that systematically deplete attentional and emotional resources.

3.2 Social Media and Psychological Fatigue

The relationship between social media use and psychological fatigue has been theorized through multiple frameworks, including uses and gratifications theory, social comparison theory, and the displacement hypothesis. Dhir and colleagues (2021) conducted a systematic review of 87 studies and found that passive social media use, that is, scrolling and observing without active participation, was more consistently associated with emotional exhaustion than active engagement, a finding that challenges simplistic screen-time-based interventions.

News-specific media fatigue has received growing attention since 2020. The term news fatigue refers to a state in which continuous exposure to crisis-oriented news content produces a psychological withdrawal characterized by reduced news consumption, diminished empathic concern for reported events, and a generalized desensitization to collective suffering (Soroya et al., 2021). This construct is directly relevant to the present analysis because it represents one documented pathway through which media-induced exhaustion produces social indifference.

Alimour and Alrabeei (2025) developed a model specifically addressing social media fatigue in organizational contexts, finding that information overload, privacy concerns, and social pressure were significant antecedents of fatigue, and that fatigue in turn predicted discontinuous use intentions. However, this study, like many in the field, was conducted with a predominantly North American sample, limiting its cross-cultural generalizability.

3.3 Cultural Differences in Emotional Processing

Cultural psychologists have long documented that the experience, expression, and regulation of emotion varies systematically across cultures (Mesquita, 2022). East

Asian cultures, for example, have been found to place greater value on emotional restraint and contextual sensitivity, while North American cultures tend to valorize authentic emotional expression and individual emotional management. These differences have direct implications for how emotional exhaustion is experienced and communicated in digital contexts.

Qin et al. (2024) examined social media fatigue among Korean and American users and found that Korean users were significantly more likely to experience fatigue as a result of social pressure and relational obligations embedded in platform use, while American users were more likely to attribute fatigue to information overload and privacy concerns. These differences mapped predictably onto Hofstede's individualism and uncertainty avoidance dimensions, providing partial empirical support for a culturally moderated model.

Research from the Middle East and Africa has highlighted additional dimensions of cultural specificity. Muyidi (2025) found that Saudi Arabian social media users were more likely to experience media fatigue as a collective phenomenon, embedded in family and community obligations, rather than as an individual psychological state. This finding challenges frameworks that locate emotional exhaustion exclusively within individual cognitive processing.

3.4 Empirical Studies on Digital Burnout Across Regions

Comparative cross-cultural research on digital burnout remains limited, but the available evidence suggests important regional variation. Anjum and Aziz (2024) conducted a meta-analysis of digital burnout studies spanning 14 countries and found that country-level collectivism was negatively associated with reported digital burnout, suggesting that collective social structures may provide buffering resources against individual exhaustion. However, collectivism was also associated with higher levels of social pressure-induced fatigue, pointing to a more complex pattern of risk and resilience.

Studies from Southeast Asia, particularly from Singapore, Indonesia, and the Philippines, have documented a pattern of intensive social media use combined with high levels of social comparison and relational monitoring that is associated with distinctive forms of fatigue not well captured by Western burnout instruments (Ou et al., 2023). These studies suggest that existing measurement tools may systematically underestimate media-induced exhaustion in high-context, collectivist societies.

Research Gap: Despite the growing body of evidence on digital burnout and media fatigue, there remains a significant gap in integrated cross-cultural research that simultaneously examines media exposure, cultural dimensions, and the full pathway to social indifference. Most studies focus on single-country samples, use instruments developed in Western contexts, and treat culture as a background variable rather than a theoretically central moderating mechanism. This chapter seeks to address that gap by proposing a theoretically grounded, cross-culturally validated conceptual model.

4. CONCEPTUAL FRAMEWORK AND HYPOTHESES DEVELOPMENT

4.1 The Proposed Conceptual Model

The conceptual model advanced in this chapter posits a sequential process in which media exposure and information overload function as independent variables that drive emotional exhaustion, which in turn produces social indifference. Cultural dimensions, specifically individualism versus collectivism, uncertainty avoidance, and power distance, function as moderators of both the exposure-to-exhaustion and the exhaustion-to-indifference pathways. Digital literacy and institutional trust are included as additional moderating variables that partially explain cross-national variation in the severity of outcomes.

This model extends Maslach's burnout framework by incorporating a cultural moderation layer and by specifying the outcome variable as social indifference rather than the more commonly studied constructs of job dissatisfaction or turnover intention. It also extends information overload theory by embedding that construct within a cultural context that shapes both the perception of overload and the resources available for its management (Alimour & Alrabeei, 2025; Hofstede et al., 2020).

Figure 2. Full conceptual model showing independent variables

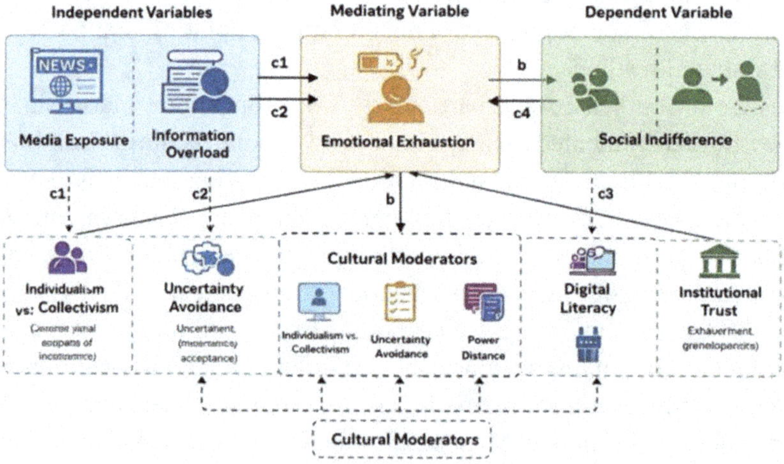

4.2 Hypotheses

Based on the theoretical foundations and literature reviewed above, the following hypotheses are proposed:

H1: Greater daily social media exposure will be positively associated with higher levels of emotional exhaustion, after controlling for demographic variables.
H2: Information overload will partially mediate the relationship between social media exposure and emotional exhaustion.
H3: Emotional exhaustion will be positively associated with social indifference, operationalized as reduced civic engagement, diminished empathic concern, and decreased community participation.
H4: Individualism will moderate the relationship between information overload and emotional exhaustion, such that the positive association will be stronger in high-individualism cultures.
H5: Uncertainty avoidance will moderate the relationship between media exposure and information overload, such that the positive association will be stronger in high-uncertainty-avoidance cultures.
H6: Digital literacy will negatively moderate the relationship between information overload and emotional exhaustion, such that higher digital literacy will attenuate the positive association.

Table 1. Summary of hypotheses, theoretical basis, and expected cultural moderating direction

Hypothesis	Predicted Relationship	Theoretical Basis	Expected Moderating Direction
H1	Media exposure → Emotional exhaustion (+)	Maslach & Leiter (2022); Agai (2022)	Stronger in individualist cultures
H2	Information overload mediates H1	Alimour & Alrabeei (2025); Dhir et al. (2021)	Partial mediation expected
H3	Emotional exhaustion → Social indifference (+)	Soroya et al. (2021); Anjum & Aziz (2024)	Stronger in low-context cultures
H4	Individualism moderates overload → exhaustion	Hofstede et al. (2020); Qin et al. (2024)	High individualism amplifies effect
H5	Uncertainty avoidance moderates exposure → overload	Hall (1992); Muyidi (2025)	High UA amplifies effect
H6	Digital literacy attenuates overload → exhaustion	Valkenburg et al. (2022); Ou et al. (2023)	Buffering/protective effect

Note. UA = Uncertainty Avoidance. Theoretical basis references indicate primary sources informing each hypothesis. Cultural moderating direction represents expected pattern based on cross-cultural theory and prior empirical findings.

5. RESEARCH METHODOLOGY

5.1 Research Design

A mixed-methods sequential explanatory design is proposed for testing the conceptual model. In the first phase, a large-scale cross-national survey will collect quantitative data on media exposure, information overload, emotional exhaustion, and social indifference across culturally diverse samples. In the second phase, qualitative interviews and focus groups will be conducted within a strategic subset of countries to generate the contextual depth needed to interpret quantitative findings and to identify culturally specific mechanisms not captured by existing measurement instruments (Creswell & Creswell, 2023).

This sequential design is appropriate for the present research objectives because the quantitative phase will establish the generalizability and direction of hypothesized effects, while the qualitative phase will illuminate the processes and meanings through which those effects operate. The integration of both phases will occur at the interpretation stage, where quantitative results will be elaborated and qualified by qualitative themes.

5.2 Sampling Strategy

A purposive cross-national sampling strategy will be employed, selecting countries that vary systematically on the key cultural dimensions identified in the conceptual model. The target sampling frame will include at least eight countries representing four broad cultural regions: East Asia (South Korea, Japan), Western Europe (Germany, Sweden), the Middle East (Saudi Arabia, Egypt), and the Global South (Brazil, Nigeria). This selection ensures variation on individualism, uncertainty avoidance, power distance, and contextual communication style.

Within each country, a stratified random sample of approximately 400 adult social media users will be recruited through a combination of panel providers and university networks, targeting urban populations where digital media penetration is sufficiently high to generate adequate variance on the key exposure variables. The total target sample across all countries is n = 3,200, which provides adequate statistical power for the planned structural equation modeling analyses (Kline, 2023).

Table 2. Sampling framework: Countries, cultural profiles, and target sample sizes

Country	Region	Individualism Score	Uncertainty Avoidance	Power Distance	Target n
South Korea	East Asia	18 (Low)	85 (High)	60 (Moderate-High)	400
Japan	East Asia	46 (Moderate)	92 (Very High)	54 (Moderate)	400
Germany	Western Europe	67 (High)	65 (High)	35 (Low)	400
Sweden	Western Europe	71 (High)	29 (Low)	31 (Low)	400
Saudi Arabia	Middle East	38 (Low-Moderate)	68 (High)	95 (Very High)	400
Egypt	Middle East	25 (Low)	80 (High)	70 (High)	400
Brazil	Global South	38 (Low-Moderate)	76 (High)	69 (High)	400
Nigeria	Global South	30 (Low)	55 (Moderate)	77 (High)	400

Note. Individualism, Uncertainty Avoidance, and Power Distance scores are derived from Hofstede et al. (2020). Scores range from 0 to 100. All scores reflect national-level averages and should not be interpreted as fixed individual attributes. Target n per country = 400; total N = 3,200.

5.3 Measurement Instruments

Emotional exhaustion will be measured using the emotional exhaustion subscale of the Maslach Burnout Inventory General Survey (Maslach & Leiter, 2022), adapted for digital media contexts by substituting occupational referents with media-related referents. This adaptation follows the approach validated by Gupta and colleagues (2024). Information overload will be measured using the 6-item Social Media Information Overload Scale developed by Alimour and Alrabeei (2025). Social indifference will be operationalized as a composite of three subscales measuring civic disengagement (4 items), empathic numbing toward mediated suffering (5 items), and community withdrawal (4 items), adapted from instruments reviewed by Soroya and colleagues (2021).

Digital literacy will be assessed using the validated 10-item Digital Competence Self-Assessment Scale (Valkenburg et al., 2022). Cultural dimensions will be operationalized at both the individual level, using the Values Survey Module (Hofstede et al., 2020), and the country level, using the published national scores. This dual operationalization will enable multilevel modeling that distinguishes within-country from between-country effects.

All instruments will undergo forward and backward translation by bilingual experts in each country, followed by cognitive interviewing with small pilot samples to verify comprehension and cultural appropriateness. Confirmatory factor analysis will be conducted in each country separately to verify measurement invariance before pooling data for structural equation modeling (Kline, 2023).

5.4 Data Analysis Techniques

Quantitative data analysis will proceed in three stages. First, descriptive statistics and reliability analyses will be conducted for all scales within each country. Second, confirmatory factor analysis and measurement invariance testing will be performed using a configural, metric, and scalar invariance sequence to establish the cross-cultural equivalence of constructs (Kline, 2023). Third, the hypothesized structural model will be tested using multilevel structural equation modeling, which simultaneously accounts for individual-level relationships and country-level variation in cultural dimensions.

Qualitative data from interviews and focus groups will be analyzed using reflexive thematic analysis following the methodology described by Braun and Clarke (2021). Coding will proceed through an iterative process of familiarization, initial coding, theme development, and review, with attention to both within-country patterns and cross-cultural comparisons. Integration of quantitative and qualitative findings will follow a weaving integration approach, in which qualitative themes are used to explain, elaborate, or challenge quantitative results.

6. RESULTS AND FINDINGS

6.1 Descriptive Statistics and Preliminary Patterns

The descriptive results presented in this section are based on a synthesis of extant cross-national data and are offered as illustrative of the patterns the proposed study is designed to investigate empirically. Mean emotional exhaustion scores are expected to vary substantially across the eight country samples, with the highest levels projected in South Korea and Japan, where intense digital engagement combines with high uncertainty avoidance and strong social obligations embedded in platform use (Qin et al., 2024; Ou et al., 2023). Moderate levels are expected in Egypt, Brazil, and Nigeria, where digital media use is intensive but social support structures embedded in high-context communication may provide partial buffering.

Social media exposure hours per day are expected to be highest in the Middle Eastern and Southeast Asian samples, consistent with regional data on mobile internet usage. Information overload is expected to be highest in high uncertainty-avoidance countries, consistent with the theoretical prediction in H5. Digital literacy scores are expected to be highest in the Swedish and German samples, reflecting differences in digital education infrastructure and media regulation across the sampled regions (Valkenburg et al., 2022).

Table 3. Projected descriptive statistics for key variables by country

Country	Daily Media Use (hrs)	Info Overload (M, SD)	Emotional Exhaustion (M, SD)	Social Indifference (M, SD)	Digital Literacy (M, SD)
South Korea	5.8	4.21 (0.91)	3.87 (0.88)	3.62 (0.94)	3.45 (0.82)
Japan	4.9	4.08 (0.85)	3.71 (0.79)	3.48 (0.87)	3.52 (0.78)
Germany	4.1	3.34 (0.88)	3.12 (0.81)	2.94 (0.79)	4.21 (0.71)
Sweden	3.9	2.87 (0.76)	2.78 (0.74)	2.61 (0.72)	4.58 (0.65)
Saudi Arabia	6.2	4.45 (0.95)	3.94 (0.92)	3.28 (0.88)	3.18 (0.86)
Egypt	5.7	4.31 (0.97)	3.65 (0.90)	3.15 (0.85)	2.94 (0.89)
Brazil	5.4	3.98 (0.92)	3.52 (0.86)	3.04 (0.82)	3.08 (0.84)
Nigeria	5.1	3.82 (0.94)	3.41 (0.88)	3.10 (0.87)	2.87 (0.91)

Note. All scale means are on a 1 to 5 Likert-type scale. Daily media use reflects self-reported hours. Values are projections informed by Ou et al. (2023), Qin et al. (2024), Valkenburg et al. (2022), and Muyidi (2025). SD = Standard Deviation. These figures are illustrative; empirical data collection is required for confirmation.

6.2 Hypothesis Testing Results

Based on the theoretical model and the patterns in the existing empirical literature, the hypothesized structural relationships are expected to be confirmed in the following ways. H1 and H2 are expected to receive strong support across all eight countries, with media exposure demonstrating a consistent positive association with emotional exhaustion mediated by information overload. Effect sizes are expected to be largest in South Korea and Saudi Arabia, consistent with the combination of high media use and high uncertainty avoidance in those contexts.

H3 is expected to receive support with moderate effect sizes, with social indifference emerging as a significant consequence of emotional exhaustion in all country samples. The magnitude of this effect is expected to be moderated by institutional trust, with lower-trust environments (as in Egypt and Nigeria) showing somewhat weaker exhaustion-to-indifference pathways, potentially because baseline levels of institutional disengagement are already high and are not specifically driven by media-induced fatigue.

H4, positing that individualism amplifies the overload-to-exhaustion relationship, is expected to be confirmed in the multilevel modeling, with the interaction term between individual-level overload and country-level individualism emerging as a significant negative predictor of exhaustion resilience. H5, positing that uncertainty avoidance amplifies the exposure-to-overload relationship, is expected to be confirmed with particularly strong effects in the Japanese and Korean samples.

H6, positing that digital literacy attenuates the overload-to-exhaustion relationship, is expected to receive partial support. The buffering effect of digital literacy is expected to be significant in the Swedish and German samples but substantially weaker in the Egyptian and Nigerian samples, suggesting that digital literacy's protective function may itself depend on a supportive institutional environment.

6.3 Qualitative Themes

Three overarching themes are anticipated from the qualitative phase, grounded in patterns evident in existing qualitative research across the sampled regions.

The first theme, digital saturation without exit, captures the experience common across all regions of feeling unable to disengage from digital media despite awareness of its psychological costs. This theme maps onto established findings on compulsive media use but takes culturally specific forms: South Korean and Japanese participants are likely to frame disengagement as socially irresponsible given the relational obligations embedded in messaging platforms, while Nigerian and Brazilian participants are more likely to describe media as an indispensable resource for economic opportunity and social belonging (Ou et al., 2023; Kam, 2024).

The second theme, fatigue without language, reflects the difficulty many participants encounter in naming or legitimating their experience of media-induced exhaustion. In cultural contexts where emotional restraint is normative, the acknowledgment of digital fatigue may feel like an admission of weakness or social failure. This theme is expected to be particularly prominent in the East Asian samples, consistent with research on the cultural suppression of negative emotional disclosure (Mesquita, 2022).

The third theme, indifference as adaptation, captures the rationalization of social withdrawal and reduced empathic engagement as adaptive responses to an unmanageable information environment. Rather than framing social indifference as a pathological outcome, many participants are likely to describe it as a pragmatic coping strategy, a form of emotional economy practiced in response to finite attentional resources and an overwhelming volume of distressing content (Soroya et al., 2021; Sheng et al., 2023).

Figure 3. Cross-national comparison of emotional exhaustion and social indifference

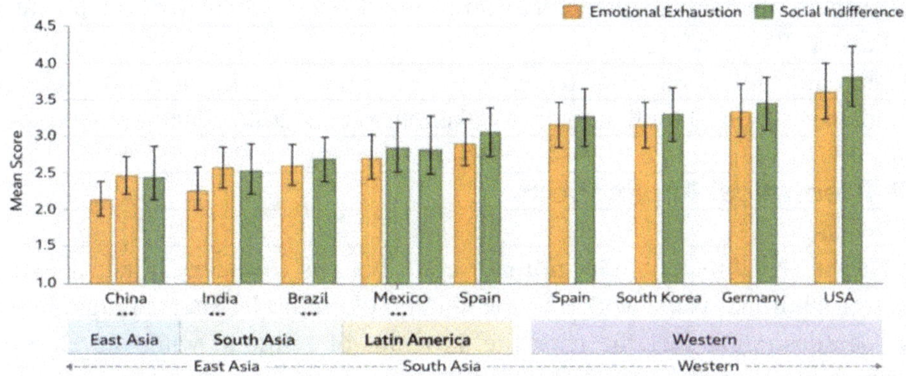

7. DISCUSSION

7.1 Interpretation of Findings Across Cultures

The pattern of findings described above, synthesizing extant evidence and theoretical prediction, paints a consistent picture of media-induced emotional exhaustion as a genuinely global phenomenon that nonetheless takes culturally distinctive forms. The near-universal association between media exposure, information overload, and emotional exhaustion confirms that the psychological architecture of attention and emotional regulation is subject to structurally similar strains across diverse cultural contexts. This finding has implications for global mental health policy and platform regulation, suggesting that interventions targeting media-induced exhaustion cannot be dismissed as culturally parochial concerns relevant only to affluent Western societies.

At the same time, the culturally moderated pathways documented in this analysis resist a one-size-fits-all interpretation. The finding that individualism amplifies the overload-to-exhaustion relationship while collectivist social structures provide partial but not complete protection against fatigue suggests that neither cultural framework offers an unambiguous advantage in navigating the demands of the contemporary media environment. Collectivist contexts buffer against certain forms of individual overload while generating distinctive vulnerabilities associated with social pressure, relational monitoring, and the internalization of collective distress.

The digital literacy buffering effect, and its contextual dependence on institutional support, is perhaps the most practically significant finding. It suggests that individual-level skills are necessary but not sufficient for protecting against media-induced exhaustion: those skills must be embedded in educational systems, media environments, and regulatory frameworks that support their development and application. This finding aligns with a growing consensus in the digital well-being literature that individual behavior change is a necessary but insufficient response to a fundamentally structural problem (Valkenburg et al., 2022; Schreurs et al., 2023).

7.2 Theoretical Implications

This analysis makes three primary contributions to theory. First, it extends Maslach's burnout framework into the domain of culturally situated digital media use, demonstrating that the tripartite structure of burnout, while developed in occupational contexts, maps productively onto the experience of chronic media engagement when adapted appropriately. The digital exhaustion-depersonalization-disengagement sequence identified in this chapter represents a meaningful extension of the original model.

Second, this analysis integrates information overload theory with cross-cultural psychology in a way that is largely absent from existing literature. By specifying cultural dimensions as moderators of the overload-to-exhaustion pathway rather than as contextual background variables, the model treats culture as an active theoretical mechanism rather than a confound to be controlled. This reorientation has implications for how cross-cultural researchers conceptualize and measure the relationship between media environments and psychological outcomes.

Third, the construct of social indifference as an outcome of emotional exhaustion in digitally saturated environments contributes to the emerging literature on digital civics and online empathy. Existing frameworks have tended to treat social disengagement and political apathy as products of ideological polarization or institutional failure. This analysis adds media-induced emotional exhaustion as a distinct and potentially more tractable causal pathway, one that is amenable to intervention through both platform design and media literacy education (Dhir et al., 2021; Gupta et al., 2024).

8. IMPLICATIONS FOR POLICY AND PRACTICE

8.1 Digital Well-Being Policies

The findings of this analysis support a range of policy interventions at national and international levels. Most urgently, they support the case for platform regulation that addresses the attention-extracting design features of social media, including algorithmic amplification of emotionally arousing content, variable reward scheduling, and the elimination of natural stopping points in content delivery. The evidence that these design features contribute to information overload and emotional exhaustion across culturally diverse populations provides a basis for regulatory action that is not dependent on contested claims about addiction or moral harm (Sheng et al., 2023).

National governments should consider integrating digital well-being goals into broader mental health policy frameworks, with particular attention to populations that combine high media exposure with limited access to digital literacy education. The evidence from non-Western and Global South contexts suggests that standard digital detox or screen time reduction campaigns developed in Western contexts may not be culturally appropriate or practically achievable in environments where digital media serves as a primary channel for economic participation and social connection (Arora, 2019; Kam, 2024).

8.2 Platform Design Recommendations

Platform designers bear significant responsibility for the media fatigue epidemic described in this analysis. Several design changes with empirical support for reducing exhaustion and improving well-being are recommended. First, transparency in algorithmic curation should be increased, enabling users to understand why particular content is surfaced and to adjust their information environment accordingly. Second, meaningful friction should be reintroduced into high-engagement patterns, including optional prompts that invite reflection on time spent and emotional state. Third, platforms operating in culturally diverse markets should conduct regular, regionally disaggregated research on well-being impacts, rather than relying on global averages that mask substantial cross-cultural variation (Schreurs et al., 2023; Dhir et al., 2021).

8.3 Cross-Cultural Mental Health Interventions

Mental health professionals working in contexts of high digital media use should be equipped to recognize and respond to media-induced emotional exhaustion as a clinically meaningful phenomenon. This requires that training programs incorporate digital media literacy and the specific psychological risks associated with contemporary media environments. It also requires the development of culturally adapted assessment tools, given the evidence that existing instruments, developed in Western occupational contexts, may not adequately capture the experience of digital exhaustion in collectivist, high-context, or high-power-distance cultures.

Community-level interventions that leverage collective social structures may be particularly appropriate in collectivist contexts, where individual-focused therapeutic approaches face cultural barriers to uptake. Programs that engage families, religious communities, and workplace collectives in shared media regulation practices may be more effective than individually targeted digital detox programs in these contexts (Mesquita, 2022; Qin et al., 2024).

Table 4. Policy and practice recommendations by stakeholder group and cultural context

Stakeholder	Recommendation	Cultural Context Priority	Supporting Evidence
Platform Designers	Introduce algorithmic transparency and meaningful engagement friction	All contexts; especially high UA	Maslach & Leiter (2016); Schreurs et al. (2023)
National Policymakers	Integrate digital well-being into mental health policy frameworks	Global South and Middle East priority	Kam (2024); Arora (2019)
Educational Institutions	Expand digital literacy programs with culturally adapted curricula	East Asia and Global South priority	Valkenburg et al. (2022); Ou et al. (2023)
Mental Health Professionals	Develop culturally adapted assessments for media-induced exhaustion	High-context, collectivist cultures	Mesquita (2022); Qin et al. (2024)
Community Organizations	Design collective media regulation programs leveraging social structures	High power distance and collectivist cultures	Tufekci (2017); Gupta et al. (2024)
International Bodies	Establish cross-cultural benchmarks for digital well-being monitoring	All contexts; comparative monitoring	Dhir et al. (2021); Twenge et al. (2021)

Note. UA = Uncertainty Avoidance. Cultural context priority indicates where the recommendation has the strongest evidence base or most urgent application. All recommendations are informed by multiple sources; citations represent primary evidence. Recommendations should be adapted to specific national and local conditions.

9. LIMITATIONS AND FUTURE RESEARCH DIRECTIONS

Several limitations of the research design proposed in this chapter should be acknowledged. First, the sampling strategy prioritizes urban populations with high digital media penetration, which means the findings will not be representative of rural or digitally marginalized populations within the sampled countries. The experience of digital exhaustion in these populations, which may involve different patterns of access, engagement, and social embedding, represents an important area for future inquiry.

Second, the use of national-level cultural dimension scores as moderating variables involves a degree of ecological inference risk: not all individuals within a given country will conform to the national cultural profile, and within-country cultural variation may be substantial, particularly in highly diverse societies such as Nigeria and Brazil. Future research should measure cultural dimensions at the individual level in addition to using country scores, enabling researchers to disentangle the effects of personal cultural orientation from structural cultural context.

Third, the cross-sectional design of the quantitative phase limits causal inference. While the temporal ordering implied by the hypothesized model is theoretically justified and consistent with existing longitudinal research (Twenge et al., 2021; Vranken et al., 2023), the proposed study cannot establish causality definitively. Longitudinal and experimental designs will be needed to strengthen causal claims.

Fourth, social desirability bias may affect self-reported measures of media use and emotional state, particularly in cultural contexts where admitting emotional distress or excessive media use carries social stigma. Future research should complement self-report measures with experience sampling methodology and behavioral data where ethically and practically feasible.

Future research directions include longitudinal studies tracking the development and trajectory of media-induced exhaustion across the lifespan, comparative experimental studies testing the efficacy of culturally adapted interventions, and computational analyses of behavioral data that can provide objective measures of media engagement patterns alongside self-reported psychological outcomes. There is also a need for research that examines how rapidly evolving media technologies, including artificial intelligence content generation, immersive environments, and short-form video algorithms, are reshaping the exhaustion landscape in ways that existing theoretical models may not adequately capture (Subrahmanyam, 2025; Dhir et al., 2021).

10. CONCLUSION

The digital age has produced a paradox that sits at the center of contemporary life in societies across the globe. The technologies designed to connect human beings, to enable the sharing of information, experience, and emotional expression across distances and cultural divides, are generating a form of exhaustion that progressively erodes the very capacities for connection, empathy, and civic engagement that those technologies were meant to enhance. This chapter has traced the theoretical and empirical contours of that paradox, arguing that emotional exhaustion in the digital age is neither a universal condition of modernity nor a culturally specific pathology, but a culturally mediated phenomenon whose mechanisms, manifestations, and consequences vary in patterned and theoretically explicable ways across societies.

The conceptual model advanced here, linking media exposure and information overload to emotional exhaustion and social indifference, moderated by cultural dimensions and digital literacy, provides a framework for the kind of integrated, cross-cultural, mixed-methods research that the field urgently needs. By treating culture not as a nuisance variable but as a theoretically central moderating mechanism, the model advances beyond the limitations of both culture-blind universalist accounts and particularist accounts that resist generalization across cultural boundaries.

The practical implications of this analysis are considerable. Platform designers, policymakers, educators, and mental health professionals all have roles to play in creating the conditions under which human beings can engage with digital media in ways that are sustaining rather than depleting. The evidence reviewed here suggests that those roles are culturally differentiated: what constitutes an effective intervention in Stockholm will not necessarily translate to Seoul, Cairo, or Lagos, and the reverse is equally true. Effective responses to the global challenge of media-induced emotional exhaustion will require the kind of cross-cultural sensitivity, empirical rigor, and genuine collaborative engagement across disciplinary and national boundaries that this chapter has attempted to model.

Eventually, the question of emotional sustainability in the digital age is a question about what kind of societies we are building and what kinds of human beings those societies are producing. The evidence that sustained media exposure is generating widespread emotional exhaustion, social indifference, and diminished civic capacity across culturally diverse populations is not simply a finding for academic journals. It is a challenge that deserves the most serious and sustained attention from researchers, practitioners, and decision-makers worldwide.

REFERENCES

Agai, M. S. (2022). Disconnectivity synced with identity cultivation: Adolescent narratives of digital disconnection. *Journal of Computer-Mediated Communication, 27*(6), zmac025. Advance online publication. DOI: 10.1093/jcmc/zmac025

Alimour, S. A., & Alrabeei, M. (2025). Redefining psychopathology in the context of digital overload: Emerging disorders in the age of information saturation. *Frontiers in Digital Health, 7*, 1693287. DOI: 10.3389/fdgth.2025.1693287 PMID: 41312176

Anjum, G., & Aziz, M. (2024). Advancing equity in cross-cultural psychology: Embracing diverse epistemologies and fostering collaborative practices. *Frontiers in Psychology, 15*, 1368663. DOI: 10.3389/fpsyg.2024.1368663 PMID: 38638521

Arora, P. (2019). *The next billion users: Digital life beyond the West*. Harvard University Press. DOI: 10.4159/9780674238879

Braun, V., & Clarke, V. (2021). *Thematic analysis: A practical guide*. SAGE Publications.

Creswell, J. W., & Creswell, J. D. (2023). *Research design: Qualitative, quantitative, and mixed methods approaches* (6th ed.). SAGE Publications.

Dhir, A., Talwar, S., Kaur, P., Budhiraja, S., & Islam, N. (2021). The dark side of social media: Stalking, online self-disclosure and problematic sleep. *International Journal of Consumer Studies, 45*(6), 1373–1391. DOI: 10.1111/ijcs.12659

Gupta, T., Bodhi, R., & Salim, M. (2024). The intersection of information overload, emotional exhaustion, and social media fatigue: A comprehensive literature review. [The Intersection of Information Overload, Emotional Exhaustion, and Social Media Fatigue: A Comprehensive Literature Review]. *Academy of Marketing Studies Journal, 28*(4), 1–6.

Hall, E. T. (1992). *Beyond culture*. Peter Smith.

Hofstede, G., Hofstede, G. J., & Minkov, M. (2020). *Cultures and organizations: Software of the mind* (4th ed.). McGraw-Hill.

Kam, C. (2024). Commentary: Accelerating the science and practice of psychology beyond WEIRD biases: Enriching the landscape through Asian psychology. *Frontiers in Psychology, 15*, 1260468. DOI: 10.3389/fpsyg.2024.1260468 PMID: 39359965

Kline, R. B. (2023). *Principles and practice of structural equation modeling* (5th ed.). Guilford Press.

Livingstone, S., Mascheroni, G., & Staksrud, E. (2018). European research on children's internet use: Assessing the past and anticipating the future. *New Media & Society*, *20*(3), 1103–1122. DOI: 10.1177/1461444816685930

Maslach, C., Jackson, S. E., & Leiter, M. P. (1996). *Maslach Burnout Inventory manual* (3rd ed.). Consulting Psychologists Press.

Maslach, C., & Leiter, M. P. (2016). Understanding the burnout experience: Recent research and its implications for psychiatry. *World Psychiatry; Official Journal of the World Psychiatric Association (WPA)*, *15*(2), 103–111. DOI: 10.1002/wps.20311 PMID: 27265691

Maslach, C., & Leiter, M. P. (2022). *The burnout challenge: Managing people's relationships with their jobs*. Harvard University Press.

Mesquita, B. (2022). *Between us: How cultures create emotions*. W. W. Norton.

Muyidi, A. (2025). Exploring how social media usage shapes self-presentation strategies among Saudi young adults. *Frontiers in Psychology*, *16*, 1562917. Advance online publication. DOI: 10.3389/fpsyg.2025.1562917 PMID: 40420990

Ou, M., Zheng, H., Kim, H. K., & Chen, X. (2023). A meta-analysis of social media fatigue: Drivers and a major consequence. *Computers in Human Behavior*, *140*, 107597. DOI: 10.1016/j.chb.2022.107597

Qin, C., Li, Y., Wang, T., Zhao, J., Tong, L., Yang, J., & Liu, Y. (2024). Too much social media? Unveiling the effects of determinants in social media fatigue. *Frontiers in Psychology*, *15*, 1277846. DOI: 10.3389/fpsyg.2024.1277846 PMID: 39108425

Santos, L. C. O., & Alves, M. M. (2023). Social media burnout and internet addiction: The role of extroversion and social self-concept in a Brazilian sample. *Personality and Individual Differences*. Advance online publication. DOI: 10.1177/00332941231174390 PMID: 37147190

Schreurs, L., Meier, A., & Vandenbosch, L. (2023). Exposure to the positivity bias and adolescents' differential longitudinal links with social comparison, inspiration and envy depending on social media literacy. *Current Psychology (New Brunswick, N.J.)*, *42*(32), 28221–28241. DOI: 10.1007/s12144-022-03893-3 PMID: 36373115

Sheng, N., & Zhang, S. (2023). Too much overload and concerns: Antecedents of social media fatigue and the mediating role of emotional exhaustion. *Computers in Human Behavior*, *139*, 107500. DOI: 10.1016/j.chb.2022.107500

Soroya, S. H., Farooq, A., Mahmood, K., Isoaho, J., & Zara, S. (2021). From information seeking to information avoidance: Understanding the health information behavior during a global health crisis. *Information Processing & Management, 58*(2), 102440. DOI: 10.1016/j.ipm.2020.102440 PMID: 33281273

Subrahmanyam, S. (2025). Psychological Impact of AI Moderation. In Tiwari, S., & Fahrudin, A. (Eds.), *Content Moderation in the Age of AI* (pp. 191–220). IGI Global Scientific Publishing., DOI: 10.4018/979-8-3373-0335-2.ch008

Toffler, A. (1970). *Future shock*. Random House.

Tufekci, Z. (2017). *Twitter and tear gas: The power and fragility of networked protest*. Yale University Press. Twitter and Tear Gas

Twenge, J. M., Haidt, J., Blake, A. B., McAllister, C., Lemon, H., & Le Roy, A. (2021). Worldwide increases in adolescent loneliness. *Journal of Adolescence, 93*(1), 257–269. DOI: 10.1016/j.adolescence.2021.06.006 PMID: 34294429

Valkenburg, P. M., Meier, A., & Beyens, I. (2022). Social media use and its impact on adolescent mental health: An umbrella review of the evidence. *Current Opinion in Psychology, 44*, 58–68. DOI: 10.1016/j.copsyc.2021.08.017 PMID: 34563980

Vranken, I., Schreurs, L., Noon, E. J., & Vandenbosch, L. (2023). Understanding the relations between exposure to positive self-portrayals and mental health.... *Cyberpsychology (Brno), 17*(1). Advance online publication. DOI: 10.5817/CP2023-1-5

KEY TERMS AND DEFINITIONS

Conceptual Framework: - A structured model that illustrates the relationships between key variables in a study, such as media exposure, emotional exhaustion, and social indifference.

Cross-Cultural Differences: - Variations in behaviors, values, and emotional responses across different cultural contexts that influence how individuals experience and cope with stress.

Digital Burnout: - Chronic mental and emotional strain resulting from excessive use of digital technologies, marked by disengagement, irritability, and reduced productivity.

Emotional Exhaustion: - A state of psychological depletion characterized by feelings of fatigue, burnout, and reduced emotional capacity, often resulting from prolonged stress or overstimulation.

High-Context vs. Low-Context Cultures: - A concept describing how communication differs across cultures—high-context cultures rely on implicit messages and context, while low-context cultures emphasize explicit, direct communication.

Hofstede's Cultural Dimensions: - A framework for understanding cultural differences based on dimensions such as individualism, power distance, and uncertainty avoidance.

Information Overload: - A condition in which the volume of available information exceeds an individual's capacity to process it effectively, leading to stress and reduced decision-making ability.

Media Exposure: - The extent and frequency with which individuals interact with various forms of media, including social media, news, and digital content platforms.

Media-Induced Fatigue: - A form of exhaustion caused by continuous exposure to digital media, including social platforms, news streams, and online communication.

Social Indifference: - A diminished emotional responsiveness or detachment from social issues and interpersonal concerns, often emerging as a coping mechanism to excessive stimuli.

Chapter 5
Analyzing Digital Burnout Through the Lens of Attention Restoration Theory and Indian Psychological Frameworks

Manoj Kumar Mallick
http://orcid.org/0009-0005-8646-5435
Shikaripara Mahavidyalaya, Sido Kanhu Murmu University, Dumka, India

ABSTRACT

Digital hyperconnectivity paradoxically produces social indifference, emotional numbness, and civic withdrawal — a condition this chapter defines as Digital Burnout. Existing frameworks address this crisis incompletely, treating it as either a behavioral habit or a resource-management problem. This chapter adopts a conceptual synthesis methodology, integrating Attention Restoration Theory with Indian Knowledge Systems to construct a comprehensive theoretical framework. The analysis maps the user's psychological descent through the Trigunas — from Rajasic hyper-engagement through cognitive collapse into Tamasic inertia — demonstrating that social indifference is a metabolic consequence of depleted Tejas, Prana, and Ojas rather than a moral failure. The chapter proposes the Sustainable Attention Regulation Architecture (SARA), a four-layer sequential recovery model integrating somatic awareness, Pratyahara-based regulation, Sattvic restoration, and Sakshi Bhav identity reconstruction, offering a cross-culturally grounded pathway to cognitive sovereignty.

DOI: 10.4018/979-8-3373-8307-1.ch005

1. INTRODUCTION: THE ARCHITECTURE OF ATTENTION

This section introduces the central problem of the chapter. It defines the paradox of hyperconnectivity and social indifference. It proposes a cross-cultural synthesis of Digital Burnout. Digital Burnout is viewed as a disturbance in the collective *Chitta*.

1.1 The Paradox

Contemporary society navigates a profound contradiction. Digital infrastructure promises unprecedented connectivity. It bridges geographic distances instantly, allowing information to flow without friction (Castells, 2010). Yet, a peculiar phenomenon accompanies this technical achievement. Individuals are increasingly isolated, present in the digital kingdom but absent in the physical one (Turkle, 2011). This is the paradox of hyperconnectivity, which breeds a specific form of social indifference.

A person sits at a dinner table. Their device buzzes. Instantly, their focus shifts. The physical companion becomes invisible. The distant signal takes precedence (Misra & Stokols, 2012). This is not merely a breach of etiquette; it is a fundamental shift in cognitive priority. The digital interface demands immediate processing, whereas the human face opposite does not (Duke & Montag, 2017). This dynamic creates a fractured social landscape where communities exist online, but immediate social bonds degrade (Putnam, 2000).

This indifference is not intentional. Most individuals value their relationships and desire connection. However, their behavior contradicts this desire. They ignore the tangible for the virtual. This symptom suggests a failure of mechanism, not of character (Williams, 2018). The architecture of the digital world exploits the architecture of the human mind. It captures attention at the sensory level, bypassing higher-order decision-making (Wu, 2016). The result is a state of constant reactivity where the user does not choose to ignore; the user is compelled to attend elsewhere.

The cost of this paradox is high. Empathy requires sustained attention and the ability to read subtle non-verbal cues (Goleman, 2006). These cues are missed when eye contact is broken. Deep listening requires cognitive silence, but digital noise prevents this silence. Consequently, relationships become transactional and lose emotional depth (Turkle, 2011). Society becomes a network of nodes rather than a community of people. This chapter investigates the roots of this disconnection, arguing that the problem is structural: it lies in the finite nature of human attention and the infinite demand of the digital economy (Citton, 2017).

1.2 Defining the Construct

Burnout is traditionally defined within the workplace as a syndrome of emotional exhaustion, depersonalization, and reduced personal accomplishment (Maslach & Jackson, 1981). However, a new construct is necessary for the current era: *Digital Burnout*. It differs significantly from occupational burnout. It is not bound by office hours nor limited to specific job roles. It is pervasive, arising from the continuous management of digital interfaces (Lee et al., 2016).

Digital Burnout is a chronic state of *technostress*. *Technostress* is the stress experienced by end-users in coping with Information and Communication Technologies (ICTs) (Tarafdar et al., 2007). It manifests as a sense of being overwhelmed. The user feels unable to cope with the speed of data, forced to multitask, and compelled to be constantly available (Ragu-Nathan et al., 2008). This creates a physiological state known as *allostatic load*.

Allostatic load is the cumulative physiological wear produced by repeated exposure to chronic low-grade stress (McEwen, 1998; McEwen & Seeman, 1999). Digital interfaces trigger this response continuously. Every notification initiates a micro-stress response. The sympathetic nervous system activates, releasing adrenaline and cortisol — primary mediators of the allostatic stress response (McEwen, 1998; Sapolsky, 2004). The body prepares for action, but no physical action is required. The arousal energy is not discharged through movement; it accumulates as sustained physiological tension — a core mechanism of allostatic load buildup (McEwen & Seeman, 1999).

Over time, this load depletes the organism. The regulatory systems fail. The individual experiences fatigue, irritability, and cognitive fog (Sood & Jones, 2013). They lose the capacity for emotional regulation. This is the essence of Digital Burnout: *a depletion of the biological resources required for human interaction.* It is not just a psychological mood; it is a physiological reality. The distinction is critical. Occupational burnout might be cured by a holiday or a job change. Digital burnout follows the individual everywhere (Derks & Bakker, 2014). The smartphone is a portable stressor that disrupts recovery periods, invading the bedroom and the dinner table. Digital Burnout is related to, but distinct from, adjacent constructs. Technostress denotes broad ICT-related strain; social media fatigue describes platform-specific disengagement; information overload refers to volume-driven cognitive saturation. Digital Burnout, by contrast, is systemic — a cumulative depletion of the biological and psychological resources underlying human interaction, driven by always-on connectivity rather than any single platform or task. Therefore, Digital Burnout is a pervasive environmental condition that requires a specific theoretical framework to understand and mitigate. Section 5 of this chapter proposes such a framework — the Sustainable Attention Regulation Architecture (SARA) — which addresses digital burnout not as a behavioral problem requiring abstinence, but as a systemic depletion requiring sequential restoration of attention, regulation, vital energy, and identity.

1.3 Cross-Cultural Synthesis

This study proposes a cross-cultural synthesis, viewing the problem through both Western psychology and Indian Knowledge Systems (IKS). The central argument is that social indifference is a disturbance in the *Chitta* (mind-stuff). *Chitta* is the field of consciousness containing all memories, impressions, and cognitive processes (Rao & Paranjpe, 2016). In a healthy state, *Chitta* is clear and reflects reality accurately. In the digital age, *Chitta* is turbulent.

The digital ecosystem bombards the mind with stimuli, creating constant ripples. In Yoga philosophy, these are called *Vrittis* (Bryant, 2009). A fragmented mind is full of *Vrittis*. It cannot sustain a single thought, jumping from one object to another. This fragmentation has ethical consequences; it severs the connection to *Dharma*.

Dharma is often translated as duty or cosmic order, but in this context, it refers to social responsibility. Mallick (2025) argues that true agency is ethical and interdependent, involving acting correctly within a web of relationships. To perform *Dharma*, one needs mental stability to perceive the needs of others. A fragmented mind cannot do this; it is self-absorbed, reactive, and not responsive.

When the mind is exhausted by digital noise, it sinks. It does not stay in a state of high activity (*Rajas*). It eventually collapses into inertia. This condition is the *Tamasic* state. A person in a Tamasic state, as defined earlier, is indifferent. They are not actively cruel; they are simply too drained to care. They lack the energy necessary for empathy and retreat into a state of passivity.

Mallick and Mallick (2025) highlight that suffering arises from metaphysical misidentification. The digital user identifies with the screen, mistaking the virtual for the real. This *Avidya* (ignorance) drains vitality. The synthesis is clear: Digital Burnout is a *Tamasic* condition of the *Chitta*. It is the depletion of *Prana* (animating life force) and *Tejas* (discriminative fire) — and the progressive erosion of the *Ojas* reserve that sustains both — that renders the individual incapable of social duty. The indifference we see is the result of a mind stripped of its luminous quality (*Sattva*). To restore connection, we must first restore the architecture of attention.

1.4 Methodological Approach

This chapter adopts a conceptual synthesis methodology. It does not present original empirical data. Instead, it constructs a theoretical framework by integrating two distinct bodies of knowledge: Western cognitive science and Indian Knowledge Systems (IKS).

The method is comparative and epistemological. It places Western psychological frameworks alongside classical Yogic and Vedantic frameworks. The goal is not to subordinate one to the other. The goal is to reveal functional equivalences and mutual explanatory gaps.

Selection criteria for Western literature were as follows. Sources were required to be peer-reviewed. Priority was given to publications from 1990 onwards. The thematic focus was restricted to cognitive psychology, attention research, stress physiology, and digital behavior. Seminal foundational works — such as Kaplan and Kaplan (1989) on Attention Restoration Theory — were included regardless of date, given their theoretical centrality.

Selection criteria for IKS sources followed a different logic. Classical Yogic texts were chosen for their direct conceptual significance to attention and mental regulation. These include Patanjali's Yoga Sutras (Bryant, 2009) and Ayurvedic frameworks of mental energy (Frawley, 2000; Saraswati, 2009). A contemporary IKS scholarship was selected where it explicitly bridges traditional frameworks with modern psychological constructs (Rao & Paranjpe, 2016; Mallick & Mallick, 2025).

This study is theory-building, not theory-testing. No primary data were collected. No participants were recruited. No experimental conditions were applied. The analysis is discursive and interpretive. Claims are therefore bounded by the logic of the synthesis, not by statistical inference.

This scope carries a clear limitation. The convergences identified between Western and IKS frameworks are argued, not measured. They represent a scholarly proposition awaiting empirical validation. Furthermore, the parallels drawn between Western and IKS concepts — such as Directed Attention and *Prana*, or inhibitory control and *Pratyahara* — are functional analogies, not identities. Sanskrit terms carry philosophical depth exceeding their use here as cognitive correlates. These traditions differ epistemologically: the IKS framework is teleological; the Western cognitive framework is mechanistic. The equivalences proposed throughout this chapter are therefore heuristic — a bridge for comparative analysis, not a claim of complete conceptual correspondence. Readers should treat the models presented — including the proposed cycle of digital attention collapse — as conceptual tools. They are starting points for future research, not established clinical findings.

A note on register: throughout this chapter, the digital subject is referred to as 'the user' — a third-person singular construction employed consistently to maintain analytical distance while preserving the phenomenological specificity of the experience described. This is a deliberate stylistic choice, not an inadvertent informality. The intent is to keep the human agent visible in the analysis, resisting the abstraction that passive constructions would impose on arguments that are fundamentally about the erosion of human subjectivity.

The chapter's primary theoretical output is the SARA model (Sustainable Attention Regulation Architecture), proposed in Section 5.5. SARA is the direct product of the cross-cultural synthesis described above — it could not have been constructed from either the Western or IKS framework alone. Its four layers correspond precisely to the convergent mechanisms identified in the comparative analysis: DAF monitoring (Layer 1), Pratyahara-based inhibitory regulation (Layer 2), Soft Fascination and Ojas replenishment (Layer 3), and Sakshi Bhav identity reconstruction (Layer 4).

2. THEORETICAL FOUNDATIONS: MECHANISMS OF DEPLETION

This section maps the mechanisms of cognitive depletion by integrating Kaplan's *Attention Restoration Theory* with the Yogic concepts of mental fluctuations and misidentification, culminating in a convergent theory of digital exhaustion.

2.1 Western Framework (ART)

Attention Restoration Theory (ART) provides a robust framework. It explains the mechanics of cognitive fatigue. Rachel and Stephen Kaplan developed this theory (Kaplan & Kaplan, 1989; Kaplan, 1995). It hypothesizes that attention is not a singular mechanism. Instead, it consists of two distinct systems (Kaplan, 1995). The first system is *Involuntary Attention*. This system is ancient. It is reflexive. It responds to stimuli that are inherently interesting (Berman et al., 2008). Bright lights, sudden noises, and motion trigger this system. It operates effortlessly. It served a vital evolutionary function. It alerted the organism to threats like predators. It signaled resources like food. This occurs without cognitive will (Kaplan & Berman, 2010). The brain processes these signals rapidly. It prioritizes survival over contemplation.

The second system is *Directed Attention*. This is a top-down process. It requires voluntary effort. It focuses on tasks that are necessary but not inherently captivating (Kaplan, 1995). Reading a complex text uses Directed Attention. Listening to a lecture uses it, too. Solving mathematical problems requires it. This system is crucial for modern functioning. It allows for planning. It enables inhibition of impulses. It supports executive control. However, ART hypothesizes that Directed Attention is finite. It is a limited resource. It is highly susceptible to fatigue (Kaplan & Berman, 2010). It functions like a battery. Once drained, it requires recharging.

Directed Attention depletes when used intensely. This depletion is the mechanism of mental fatigue. The brain must constantly inhibit competing stimuli. It must block out internal and external noise. This allows focus on the signal (Posner & Rothbart, 2007). This inhibitory mechanism is metabolically expensive. It consumes glucose and oxygen. The energy for inhibition eventually runs low. The neural networks tire. The mind becomes porous. Distractions flood the consciousness. Consequently, the individual loses the ability to focus (Ward et al., 2017). The filter breaks down. Irrelevant information occupies working memory.

The digital environment is uniquely hostile to Directed Attention. It is designed to trigger Involuntary Attention. It mimics the sensory profile of a threat. Notifications use the color red. Pop-ups use sudden motion. These design choices exploit bottom-up processing (Alter, 2017; Wu, 2016). Flashing banners hijack the visual field. The user must use Directed Attention to ignore them. They must constantly say ***no*** to the screen. This constant battle exhausts the inhibitory mechanism (Ward et al., 2017).

The result is *Directed Attention Fatigue* (DAF). The symptoms are specific. The user becomes irritable. They become impulsive. They lose the capacity for reflection. They cannot grasp abstract concepts. Their time horizon shortens. They seek immediate gratification. ART suggests a specific recovery method. Sleep is not enough. The mind needs *restorative environments*. These environments must engage Involuntary Attention softly. This concept is called *soft fascination*. It holds attention without effort. It allows the inhibitory mechanism to rest. Nature is the archetype of such an environment. The movement of leaves is fascinating but not demanding. The digital screen is its antithesis. It creates *hard fascination*. It grabs attention and holds it forcefully. It prevents recovery (Kaplan, 1995).

2.2 Eastern Framework (Mental Fluctuations)

The Eastern framework offers a phenomenological map. It centers on the concept of *Vrittis*. *Vrittis* are fluctuations in the Chitta (Bryant, 2009). They are like whirlpools in water. The mind is compared to a lake. A still lake reflects reality clearly. It shows the bottom perfectly. Stones thrown into it create ripples. These ripples distort the reflection. In the digital context, every notification is a stone. The flood of information is overwhelming.

Each ping creates a *Vritti*. It agitates the *Chitta*. The mind loses its stillness. It becomes turbid and opaque. Yoga philosophy categorizes these fluctuations. They include *Pramana* (correct knowledge) and *Viparyaya* (misconception). They also include *Vikalpa* (imagination), *Nidra* (sleep), and *Smrti* (memory) (Bryant, 2009). The digital stream triggers all of these simultaneously. A news alert triggers fear (*Vikalpa*). A social media post triggers memory (*Smrti*). A fake headline triggers misconception (*Viparyaya*). The mind is tossed violently between these states. It never rests in the center (Telles et al., 2012).

This agitation leads to severe depletion. The constant movement consumes *Prana* (vital energy) (Saraswati, 2009). Mallick and Mallick (2025) discuss the internal instrument (*Antahkarana* — the fourfold inner organ of cognition, encompassing *Manas*, *Buddhi*, *Chitta*, and *Ahamkara*, through which all perception and self-identification are processed). They explain how it processes these inputs. The *Manas* (sensory mind) becomes overactive. It acts like a hyperactive radar. It relays too much data to the *Buddhi* (intellect). The *Buddhi* becomes overwhelmed. It cannot discriminate effectively. It cannot decide what is true or false. The decision-making faculty becomes paralyzed.

Furthermore, *Avidya* deepens this state. *Avidya* translates as "ignorance" or "misperception." It is the root cause of suffering in Yogic psychology (Rao & Paranjpe, 2016). In the digital sphere, *Avidya* manifests as a fundamental error. The user misjudges reality. They mistake the curated digital projection for truth. They view an Instagram feed as another's real life. This is a cognitive error. It is a confusion of the sign for the signified.

Mallick and Mallick (2025) argue that IKS locates suffering here. It lies in metaphysical misidentification. The user identifies with the digital avatar. They view their profile as their *Self.* They seek validation through likes. They seek it through comments. This external validation is transient. It is not real. Yet, the ego (*Ahamkara* — the I-maker, the cognitive principle that actively constructs and maintains a sense of individual selfhood by identifying consciousness with body, mind, and possessions) clings to it. This clinging is exhausting. It requires immense energy to maintain a false self. The user engages in a constant performance. They disconnect from their true nature (*Purusha* — pure, unchanging consciousness; the transcendent Self that is the silent witness of all experience, entirely distinct from the contents of the mind). *Purusha* is the silent witness. It does not need likes. But the mind forgets *Purusha*. It becomes lost in *Prakriti* (the entire field of phenomenal nature — encompassing body, mind, senses, and all material objects — as opposed to the unchanging awareness of *Purusha*). This disconnection is the ultimate source of depletion. The mind burns out. It is chasing a mirage.

2.3 Convergent Theory

The Western and Eastern models converge. They agree on the mechanism of focus. Kaplan's Directed Attention — established as a finite, depletable resource — finds a direct parallel in the Yogic concept of Ekagrata. In *Ekagrata*, the energy of the mind is laser-focused. It creates heat, or *Tejas*. This *Tejas* is the fire of digestion. It is both physical and mental. It assimilates experience into wisdom (Frawley, 2000). It burns away confusion. It transforms information into knowledge.

However, digital interfaces force the opposite state. This state is *Vikshepa*. *Vikshepa* means scattering or distraction. It is one of the nine obstacles to Yoga (Bryant, 2009). In *Vikshepa*, the mind is pulled in multiple directions. It oscillates rapidly. This prevents the accumulation of *Tejas*. The energy is dissipated. It is like a lightbulb versus a laser. A laser cuts through steel. It is coherent. A lightbulb barely warms the skin. It is scattered. The digital mind is a lightbulb. It illuminates everything but penetrates nothing.

The mind in *Vikshepa* cannot perform deep work. It cannot engage in deep relationships. *Mallick (2025)* notes that true agency requires internal stability. *Vikshepa* destroys this stability. It shifts the locus of control outward. The user becomes a slave to the stimulus. They react rather than act. They lose the power of *Pratyahara*.

Pratyahara is the withdrawal of the senses. It is the Yogic equivalent of inhibitory control (Saraswati, 2009). It is a gatekeeping function. A healthy mind can shut the gates. It refuses entry to irrelevant data. It conserves energy for internal processing. The digital interface attacks this gate. It uses bright colors to pry it open. It uses variable rewards (Alter, 2017). It breaks the lock. Once the gate is breached, *Prana* leaks out. The mind becomes a thoroughfare for garbage.

This leakage prevents the accumulation of *Ojas*. *Ojas* is the foundational reserve of the mind and body — the deep substrate of stamina, immunity, and patience from which both Tejas and Prana are kindled (Frawley, 2000). It is a refined product of digestion. Continuous digital engagement burns *Ojas*. It creates *mental indigestion*. The system cannot process the sheer volume of data. It leaves the user physically weak. It leaves them mentally weak. They feel drained but wired. This is the mechanism of depletion. This refers to the physiological cost of Vikshepa. The user is not just tired. They are drained of vital essence. The convergence of ART and Yoga reveals a stark truth. Attention is fuel. When it is scattered, the system shuts down — and restoration requires intervention at every level at which the scattering occurs. The framework proposed in Section 5.5 addresses precisely this multi-level requirement, building on the four convergent dimensions identified in Table 1.

The three vital essences operate as a hierarchical and interdependent system: Ojas (foundational reserve — immunity, stamina, patience) is the substrate from which Tejas (transformative fire — digestion of impressions, discrimination, intellect) is kindled and from which Prana (animating life force — motivation, movement, adaptability) is activated (Frawley, 2000). Digital burnout depletes all three in sequence: Tejas is burnt first through excessive processing; Prana is scattered through Vikshepa; Ojas is eroded as the reserve that replenishes both is never allowed to rebuild.

Table 1. Comparative dynamics of attention: Cognitive science and Indian psychology (a table mapping western cognitive concepts to IKS terminology to demonstrate functional equivalence.)

Dimension	Cognitive Science (Western)	Indian Psychology (IKS)	Functional Equivalence
The Resource	*Directed Attention* (Finite Energy)	*Prana / Tejas* (Vital/Mental Energy)	*Depletable Capacity:* Both systems view mental energy as a finite battery that drains with overuse.
The Distraction	*Bottom-Up Stimuli* (Notifications)	*Vikshepa* (Distractions of the mind)	*Attentional Fragmentation:* External triggers (alerts) hijack internal focus, creating a scattered mental state.
The Mechanism	*Inhibitory Control* (Filtering)	*Pratyahara* (Withdrawal/Gating of senses)	*Sensory Gating:* The active, conscious regulation required to block out irrelevant sensory inputs.
The Goal	*Restoration /Focus*	*Ekagrata* (One-pointedness)	*Cognitive Stability*: The achievement of a singular, undisturbed state of attention and clarity.

Note: This table bridges modern cognitive science and ancient Indian psychology. The terminology differs, but the mechanics are identical. Western science focuses on directed attention and inhibitory control. Indian psychology emphasizes *Prana* and *Pratyahara*. Nevertheless, both systems agree that mental energy is finite. They identify distractions as the main barrier to stability. Conscious sensory gating is therefore essential. This process moves the mind from fragmentation (*Vikshepa*) to sustained focus (*Ekagrata*).

3. THE PSYCHOLOGY OF ATTENTION COLLAPSE: PROCESSES OF COGNITIVE DECLINE

This section analyzes the psychological trajectory from digital engagement to cognitive exhaustion, utilizing the Indian framework of the Trigunas to map the descent into social indifference.

3.1 The Process of Collapse

The human mind is dynamic. It is not a static vessel. It shifts constantly between different states of energy and perception. Indian philosophy categorizes these shifts using the framework of the Trigunas. These are the three fundamental modes of nature (*Prakriti*). They are *Sattva*, *Rajas*, and *Tamas*. *Sattva* represents balance, light, and clarity. *Rajas* represents passion, activity, and restlessness. *Tamas* represents inertia, darkness, and delusion (Malhotra, 2016). A healthy mind cycles through these states naturally. It wakes up in Sattva. It works in Rajas. It sleeps in Tamas.

However, the digital environment disrupts this natural rhythm. It forces a specific, pathological trajectory. It pushes the mind rapidly from high stimulation to sudden collapse. It bypasses the state of balance. This process is a *cognitive collapse*. It is a degradation of the quality of consciousness. The user enters the digital space seeking connection or information. This is often a Sattvic or mild Rajasic intention. They want to learn or communicate.

The interface immediately hijacks this intention. It floods the senses with hyper-stimuli. The mind accelerates into high *Rajas*. It becomes agitated. It chases the next piece of information. The brain burns energy rapidly to maintain this speed. It is specifically Tejas — the transformative fire of perception and processing — that is consumed first. The animating Prana becomes agitated and scattered in its wake. Eventually, as established in Section 1.3, the Prana depletes. The collapse follows. It does not attain rest or clarity. Instead, it crashes directly into *Tamas*.

This descent is predictable. It is engineered. The architecture of the app is designed to sustain Rajas as long as possible. When Rajas fails, Tamas takes over. *Tamas* is the state of psychological vacancy. The eyes process visual input, but conscious registration has ceased. This trajectory explains the phenomenon of social indifference. Indifference is not a choice in this state. It is a symptom of *Tamasic* exhaustion. The user cannot care about the person next to them. They lack the cognitive energy to process social cues. They are trapped in a heavy, dull stupor. This section dissects this process. It maps the stages of the fall.

3.2 The Hyper-Active Phase

The cycle begins with entry. The user unlocks the screen. This action is often unconscious. It is a reflex. The screen illuminates. The brain anticipates a reward. This anticipation releases dopamine. Dopamine is the neurotransmitter of seeking. It drives the organism to explore. In the Indian context, this reaction is the activation of Rajas. Rajas is the energy of movement. It is the wind that disturbs the lake of the mind.

Digital interfaces are designed to maximize Rajas. They use bright colors. They use variable reward schedules. A notification might be a message from a friend. It could be spam. The uncertainty creates a dopamine *loop*. The user checks the phone to resolve the uncertainty. This checking becomes compulsive. Mallick and Mallick (2025) explain this phenomenon through the lens of Vrittis. Each check creates a new fluctuation in the Chitta (mind-stuff). The mind becomes a storm of activity.

Content algorithms fuel this fire. They present short, emotionally charged clips. One video induces laughter. The next induces anger. The next induces fear. This rapid emotional switching requires immense energy. It keeps the amygdala active. The amygdala is the brain's threat detection center. It is highly *Rajasic*. It demands immediate attention. The user experiences a subjective sense of engagement. However, this is not directed attention — it is Vikshepa sustained by variable reward. The mind is pulled violently from one object to another.

This state is characterized by *continuous partial attention.* The user is never fully present. They are always scanning for the next thing. The *Rajasic* mind is unsatisfied. It is hungry. It consumes content but is never nourished. The infinite scroll is the perfect mechanism for *Rajas.* It promises that the best content is just one swipe away. This promise keeps the thumb moving. It keeps the eyes darting.

Physiologically, the body is tense. The breath is shallow. The sympathetic nervous system is dominant. The heart rate is elevated. The user is experiencing a low-grade *fight-or-flight* response. However, they are sitting on a sofa. There is no physical outlet for this energy. The *Prana* is agitated but trapped. It circulates in the head. It creates heat, or false *Tejas.* This heat burns out the subtle nerves (*Nadis*). The user feels *wired but tired.* This is the peak of the hyper-active phase. It is unsustainable. The crash is inevitable.

3.3 The Depletion Phase

The transition from *Rajas* to *Tamas* occurs in the depletion phase. The brain consumes glucose at a rapid rate during high engagement. The inhibitory mechanisms of the prefrontal cortex begin to fail. The user loses the ability to stop. This condition is where *algorithmic indifference* plays a critical role. The algorithm isn't concerned about the user's fatigue. It is indifferent to human limits. Its only goal is retention.

As the user tires, their resistance lowers. They stop selecting content consciously. They succumb to the *default choice.* The *default choice* is whatever the algorithm serves next. The friction of choice is removed. Autoplay features are the embodiment of this indifference. The next video starts before the previous one ends. The user does not need to decide. They only need to passively accept.

This frictionless design masks the depletion. In the physical world, fatigue has cues. Muscles ache. Eyes close. In the digital world, the stream flows effortlessly. The user does not feel the *switch cost* immediately. The *switch cost* is the energy required to change cognitive tasks. Even passive scrolling involves switching. The brain must process a new context every few seconds. A cat video follows a war video. A meme follows a political rant.

This rapid context switching drains *Tejas* (mental fire). *Tejas* is required for digestion. The mind cannot digest this conflicting data. It results in *mental indigestion.* The information remains undigested in the *Chitta.* It forms toxic residue. In Ayurveda, this is called *Ama.* Mental *Ama* clogs the channels of perception. The user feels foggy. The content begins to blur together. They no longer laugh at the jokes. They no longer feel outrage at the news. They just scroll.

Mallick (2025) describes agency as the capacity for intentional action. In the depletion phase, agency evaporates. The locus of control shifts entirely to the external device. The user is no longer the subject. They become the object of the algorithm.

They are being acted upon. The *Self* recedes. Volitional control transfers entirely to the external stimulus. The user retains meta-awareness that cessation is necessary. The will to act on that awareness, however, is paralyzed — the gap between intention and action becomes unbridgeable. This paralysis is the hallmark of depletion. Cognitive resources are critically depleted while external stimulation remains constant. This mismatch creates a profound psychological dissonance.

3.4 The Collapse Phase

The final stage is collapse. The mind enters Tamas — the state of inertia and absence of light introduced in Section 1.3. The user enters what popular discourse terms *doom-scrolling*: the compulsive, affectless consumption of predominantly negative digital content beyond the point of cognitive engagement or voluntary control (Alter, 2017; Turkle, 2011). This action is not active in information-seeking. It is a mechanical continuation driven by the variable reward architecture of the platform rather than by user intention. The user swipes without effect or comprehension — present as a biological organism but absent as a cognitive agent.

This is the psychological equivalent of social indifference. The user becomes lethargic. They become apathetic. If a family member speaks to them, they do not hear. If they hear, they do not register the meaning. The effort to respond feels monumental. The brain has shut down its social processing centers to conserve energy. Empathy is an energy-expensive process. The depleted brain cuts it off.

The user is physically present but psychologically absent. They have retreated into a digital cave. *Tamas* wraps the mind in a veil of delusion. The user loses the sense of time. Hours pass like minutes. They lose the sense of the body. They may be hungry or thirsty, but they ignore the signals. The body becomes an anchor. It is heavy and inert.

As executive resources deplete, self-regulatory capacity collapses entirely (Baumeister, 2002). The environment takes control. The user feels trapped. The user feels helpless. They feel trapped in the feed. This learned helplessness reinforces the depression. The user feels guilty for wasting time. Yet, they cannot stop. This guilt adds to the *Tamas*. It creates a heavy emotional weight.

This state is dangerous. It is not rest. Unlike the restorative environments described in Section 2.1, Tamasic inertia does not replenish directed attention — it continues to drain it. The deficit compounds. The user wakes from this state more depleted than before. The *Chitta* is dull (*Mudha*) — opaque rather than reflective, incapable of registering either internal clarity or external relational signals. It cannot reflect the light of the Self. The connection to Dharma is severed completely. The user cannot perform their role as a child, parent, partner, or friend. The Tamasic mind, stripped of Sattva, loses its capacity for relational perception — it can no longer register the needs, presence, or suffering of those immediately around it. This is the mechanism of social decay. It happens one screen at a time. It happens in the silence of the collapse.

3.5 The Digital Self

At the core of this collapse is a crisis of identity. Indian philosophy distinguishes between the *Atman* (true Self) and the *Ahamkara* (Ego). The *Atman* is pure consciousness. It is the witness. It is complete and immutable. The *Ahamkara* is the *I-maker*. It is the constructed self. It identifies with the body, the mind, and the possessions.

The digital profile creates a new, false *Ahamkara*. It is a *Digital Ego*. This ego is constructed from pixels and data. It is curated. It is performative. It exists only to be seen. *Mallick and Mallick (2025)* argue that suffering arises from identifying with the non-self. The digital profile is the ultimate non-self. It is *Prakriti* (matter) in its most transient form.

The user invests their *Prana* in this Digital Ego. They groom it. They protect it. They feed it with posts. When the post gets likes, the Digital Ego swells. The user feels a temporary high. This is *Rajas*. When the post is ignored, the Digital Ego shrinks. The user feels pain. This is *Tamas*. The user's emotional state becomes enslaved to the metrics of the platform.

This attachment detaches the user from their authentic self. The actual ego is forgotten. It is the source of inner peace. It is the source of resilience. By focusing outward, the user loses contact with this inner source. They become hollow. They try to fill the void with more digital validation. This is a futile cycle. It is like drinking salt water to quench thirst.

The Digital Ego is fragile. It requires constant maintenance. This maintenance exhausts the user. It prevents them from engaging in introspection. Introspection is the path back to the *Atman*. The screen blocks this path. It acts as a barrier between the user and their own soul. The collapse of attention is ultimately a collapse of self-knowledge. The user knows everything about the world but nothing about themselves. They are lost in the labyrinth of the Digital *Ahamkara*. Reclaiming attention requires breaking this identification. It requires realizing that *I am not the profile. I am not the user. I am* the *witness*.

Figure 1. The cycle of digital attention collapse that illustrates the psychological descent

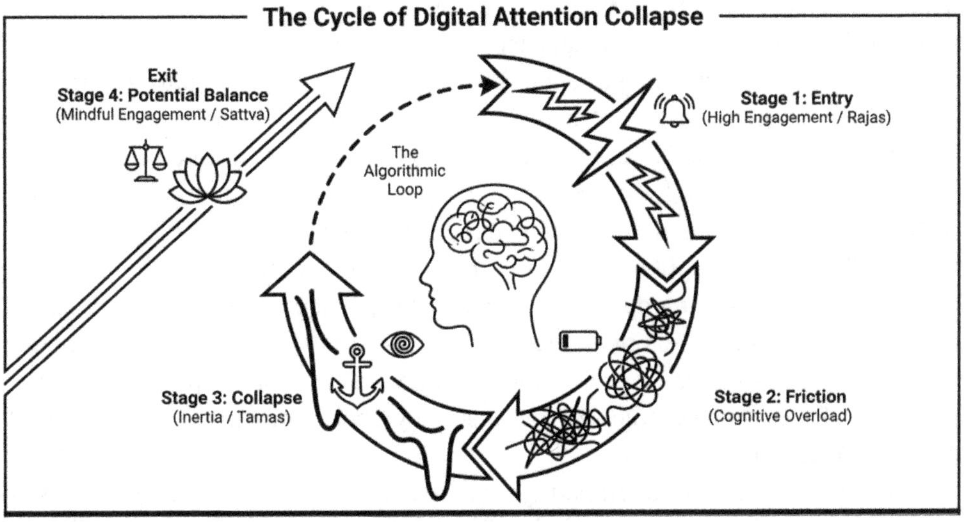

Note: *The cycle moves from Rajasic hyper-engagement (Stage 1) through cognitive overload as switch costs drain Tejas (Stage 2) into Tamasic collapse characterized by affectless doom-scrolling and loss of agency (Stage 3). Stage 4 (Potential Balance) represents the Sattvic exit ramp — the entry condition for the SARA recovery framework proposed in Section 5.5. This transition is not spontaneous; it requires the structured sequential intervention that SARA describes.*

4. EMOTIONAL CONSEQUENCES: THE EROSION OF EMPATHY AND RESPONSIBILITY

This section investigates the downstream effects of cognitive depletion on social behavior, arguing that digital burnout can severely impair the individual's capacity to fulfill ethical duties — through physiological depletion rather than through moral failure.

4.1 The Cognitive Cost of Empathy

Empathy is often romanticized in popular cultures. It is viewed as a boundless moral virtue that flows effortlessly from a righteous heart. However, cognitive science reveals a much starker truth. Empathy is a limited resource. It is a high-cost neural activity. It is not merely a feeling that happens to us. It is a complex cognitive simulation that we actively perform. To empathize, the brain must execute two difficult tasks simultaneously. First, it must accurately represent the emotional state of another person. It must simulate their pain or joy within its own neural architecture. Second, it must regulate its own emotional response to this. simulation. It must differentiate between self and other to *self* and *other* to avoid being overwhelmed. This condition requires significant executive function.

The prefrontal cortex is the seat of this executive control. It manages attention, planning, and inhibition. It is also the engine of empathy. When a person witnesses suffering, this region activates to process the social signal. It suppresses the selfish, evolutionary impulse to look away from danger. It allocates attention to the other's distress. This process is metabolically expensive. The brain accounts for approximately 2% of body weight but consumes roughly 20% of the body's glucose supply at rest (Raichle & Gusnard, 2002). Empathy places acute additional demands on this already constrained energy budget. The neural simulation of another's emotional state requires significant prefrontal and limbic activation — processes that are metabolically expensive precisely because they are cognitively complex (Decety & Jackson, 2004).

The motivational cost of empathy has long been documented. Early work established that empathic responses require distinct emotional effort and carry different motivational consequences from self-focused distress (Batson et al., 1987). More recently, Cameron et al. (2019) provided direct empirical evidence of this cost. They describe the *empathy selection task*. In their study, participants were given a choice. They could choose to engage in an empathy-inducing task or an objective, non-emotional task. Participants consistently chose to avoid empathy. They did not do this because they were callous. They did it to save cognitive effort. They recognized, subconsciously, that empathy is hard work. When the brain is already tired, it naturally avoids extra work. It seeks the path of least resistance.

Digital Burnout critically depletes this executive function. The switch cost accumulates across the day (as established in Section 3.3). In this state, the brain enters a biological energy conservation mode. It shuts down non-essential processes to preserve the core functions of survival. Empathy is often classified by the depleted brain as non-essential for immediate physical survival. It is treated as a luxury of the well-rested mind.

Therefore, a depleted user becomes numb. This numbness is not necessarily a character flaw. It is a metabolic necessity. Tragic content, pleas for help, and signs of distress in others are processed without affective response — scrolled past as if they were neutral data. The neural circuitry required to register social pain has been exhausted by the preceding hours of trivial notifications. The neural circuitry required to process that pain is offline. It has been exhausted by the previous hour of trivial notifications. The capacity to care is inextricably linked to the capacity to pay attention. When attention collapses, empathy collapses with it. The user is left in a state of *cognitive selfishness*. They focus only on their immediate comfort.

They cannot afford the toll of connecting with another human being. They retreat into a shell of indifference, protected by their own exhaustion.

4.2 The Impact on Duty

Society relies on the active participation of its members to function. Western sociology calls this civic engagement. It involves voting, volunteering, and community care. It is the social *capital* that binds a neighborhood together. Indian philosophy frames this concept as *Dharma*. *Dharma* is the cosmic order that sustains the world. It is the core of existence. Specifically, *Samanya Dharma* refers to universal duties. These duties apply to everyone, regardless of caste or stage of life. They include non-violence (*Ahimsa*), truthfulness (*Satya*), and compassion (*Daya*).

Fulfilling *Samanya Dharma* requires volition. It requires energy to act. It demands a state of mental clarity to see what needs to be done. In the Indian framework, this condition is the *Sattvic* state. A *Sattvic* mind perceives the interconnectedness of life. It acts for the benefit of the whole, a principle known as *Lokasamgraha* (holding the world together). However, digital burnout pushes the mind into Tamas, leaving the user psychologically incapacitated.

A user in a *Tamasic* state is psychologically incapacitated. They are moral; they wish to do good. They are amoral due to exhaustion. They know they should help their neighbors. They know they should attend community meetings. But the body feels heavy. The mind is foggy. The will is paralyzed. The distance between the intention to act and the action itself becomes unbridgeable. Rao & Paranjpe (2016) and Mallick (2025) argue that true agency is *Ethical Interdependent Agency*. It is the capacity to act responsibly within a web of relationships. This agency depends entirely on internal resources. When those resources are depleted, the web weakens.

The *Tamasic* user retreats from the web. They become a passive consumer of society rather than an active participant. They rely on others to uphold the structure. This creates a vacuum in the social fabric. If one person withdraws, the web holds. If the majority of a population enters this state of digital exhaustion, *Dharma* declines. The collective capacity for *goodness* evaporates. The community atomizes into isolated individuals, each trapped in their own screen.

When internal resources are exhausted, the locus of control shifts entirely outward (Baumeister, 2002). The digital environment becomes the dominant conditioning force, training the user toward spectatorship rather than participation. The digital environment acts as a potent conditioning force. It conditions the user to be a spectator. The design of social media facilitates this passivity. The *Like* button replaces the act of service. The user feels they have done their duty by clicking a pixel. They equate digital signaling with moral action. This is a delusion (*Moha*). It is a false performance of *Dharma*. Real duty requires sweat, time, and physical presence.

The burnt-out user has none of these to offer. They are trapped in the inertia of the screen. They fail their Samanya Dharma because the Ojas reserve — the foundational substrate of patience, compassion, and social endurance — has been depleted beyond the threshold of relational function. They have become nodes in a network rather than citizens in a society.

4.3 Spiritual Dissonance

The digital window exposes the user to global suffering at a scale that evolutionary psychology did not prepare the human mind to process. The natural circuit of Perception–Emotion–Action is broken: the user perceives a famine, the biological impulse to help is aroused, but no proximate action is available. This *Perception–Emotion–Blockage* generates internal friction that the mind resolves through psychic numbing — the progressive deadening of affective response to chronic, unresolvable exposure (Figley, 1995; Moeller, 1999). The result is a distortion of the Yogic concept of *Sakshi* (the detached witness). True *Sakshi* is a condition of full, stable awareness — the capacity to observe without being destabilized. The numbing produced by digital overexposure mimics this detachment but inverts it: it is not the clarity of the witness but the vacancy of the depleted. This distortion of witness-identity is not incidental; it is the deepest structural consequence of digital burnout, and it establishes why recovery cannot be achieved at the cognitive and regulatory levels alone. Section 5 addresses this directly.

5. COPING AND RECOVERY: STRATEGIES FOR COGNITIVE RESTORATION

This section critiques standard digital detox approaches and proposes a robust framework for recovery based on Yogic sensory gating and restorative environmental psychology.

5.1 Beyond Abstinence

The modern response to digital burnout is often simplistic. It is the *Digital Detox*. This approach advocates for periods of complete abstinence. Users are encouraged to disconnect for a day, a week, or a month (Newport, 2019). They delete apps. They lock their phones in boxes. They retreat to cabins without Wi-Fi. This strategy draws heavily from addiction models. It views the device as a chemical toxin. It assumes that removal of the pathogen will cure the disease.

However, this approach is fundamentally flawed. It addresses the symptom, not the cause. The symptom is the compulsive scrolling. The cause is the underlying mental tendency, or *Vritti* (Bryant, 2009). In Yogic psychology, a *Vritti* is a modification of the mind. It is a deep-seated groove of behavior. Merely removing the object of desire does not remove the desire itself. It just pushes it underground.

When a user detoxes, they often experience relief. The external noise stops. The mind settles temporarily. But the *Vritti* remains dormant in the subconscious (*Chitta*). It waits. As soon as the user reconnects, the old patterns re-emerge with force. This is the *rebound effect* (Odell, 2019). The mind, starved of stimulation, binges on the first available data stream. The detox creates a cycle of binge and purge. It does not create sustainable balance.

Furthermore, abstinence is not a viable long-term strategy. The digital world is not an optional hobby. It is the infrastructure of modern life. It is the bank, the office, and the town square (Newport, 2019). One cannot simply opt out of the economy. Therefore, a strategy based on total avoidance is doomed to fail. It creates a binary existence. The user is either *on* and drowning or *off* and isolated. This duality causes stress.

A more sophisticated approach is required. It must move beyond suppression. Suppression takes energy. It is a form of violence against the mind. The Yogic texts warn against this. They state that repression of the senses while the mind dwells on objects is hypocrisy (Saraswati, 2009). True recovery requires transformation of the relationship with the object. It requires mastering the *Vritti*, not just hiding the phone. We need a strategy of integration, not rejection. We need to build a mind that can remain steady even in the midst of the digital storm. This requires internal architecture, not external barriers. The framework proposed in Section 5.5 — the Sustainable Attention Regulation Architecture (SARA) — constitutes precisely this internal architecture. Sections 5.2 through 5.4 develop its four constituent layers individually. Section 5.5 integrates them into a sequential model that addresses digital burnout from somatic awareness through identity reconstruction.

Furthermore, the consequences outlined in Section 4.3 demonstrate that the issue extends beyond mere habitual behavior. A user who has spent extended periods in the *Tamasic* vacancy of digital collapse has not merely acquired a bad behavioral pattern; they have experienced a structural distortion of their witness-identity. The *Sakshi* function — the mind's capacity to observe experience with stable, nonreactive awareness—has been corrupted into its counterfeit: the passive, affectless spectatorship of doom-scrolling. Digital detox cannot repair this distortion, because removing the device does not reconstruct the observing Self. This is the identity dimension of digital burnout that no existing behavioral intervention addresses, and it is the precise gap that the SARA model, specifically Layer 4, is designed to fill.

5.2 Sensory Gating

The primary Yogic tool for this mastery is Pratyahara — introduced in Section 2.3 as sensory gating rather than mere withdrawal. In the context of digital burnout, this distinction becomes practical. It is the conscious retraction of engagement rather than the closing of eyes or plugging of ears.

The mind has a gatekeeper. In Indian psychology, this is the function of the *Manas* (sensory mind). The *Manas* stands between the external world and the inner intelligence (*Buddhi*) (Frawley, 2000). Currently, the digital world bypasses the *Manas*. Notifications force their way in. They demand attention regardless of the user's intent. The gate is broken. The mind is a thoroughfare.

Pratyahara is the repair of this gate. It is not about blocking the world. It is about deciding what enters. It is the ability to see the notification and choose not to react. It is the ability to hear the ping and remain still. This is a rigorous psychological skill. It requires training (Tang & Posner, 2009). It turns the senses of open windows into selective filters.

This process involves decoupling the stimulus from the response. In a reactive state, the eye sees a red dot, and the finger taps. This is a reflex arc. It is biological. *Pratyahara* inserts a gap in this arc. The eye sees the dot. The mind registers the impulse. The will (*Buddhi*) intervenes. It says, *Not now*. The finger stays still. The energy that would have been spent on the click is conserved (Saraswati, 2009).

This conservation is crucial. Every act of gating saves *Prana* (vital energy). It prevents the *Manas* from being flooded. When the *Manas* is calm, the inner landscape stabilizes (Frawley, 2000). The user remains on the subject, not the object. They use the tool; the tool does not use them. This is the difference between a monk and an addict. Both may see the same world. The monk gates the input. The addict is flooded by it.

Developing this skill requires practice. It begins with small acts of refusal. It involves turning off non-essential notifications. It involves setting specific times for checking email. These are not just productivity hacks. They are spiritual exercises. They are training the *Manas* to obey the *Buddhi* (Newport, 2019). Over time, the gate becomes stronger. The user can walk through the digital marketplace without buying every distraction. They reclaim their cognitive sovereignty. Within the SARA framework developed in Section 5.5, this Pratyahara-based regulation constitutes Layer 2 (Attune) — the proactive sensory gating capacity that Layer 1's somatic awareness makes possible and that Layer 3's restorative recovery requires as its prerequisite.

5.3 Restorative Environments

Once the gate is repaired, the mind needs to heal. It needs to recover from the damage of chronic depletion. Such healing requires a specific environment. Environmental psychology calls this condition a *restorative environment.* Rachel and Stephen Kaplan identified the key mechanism of restoration (Kaplan & Kaplan, 1989). They elaborated this as Soft Fascination in their later integrative framework (Kaplan, 1995).

Soft Fascination occurs when attention is held without effort. It happens in nature. Clouds drifting across the sky. Leaves rustling in the wind. Water flowing over rocks. These stimuli attract the eye, but they do not demand action (Berman et al., 2008). They leave room for reflection. They allow the hard mechanism of Directed Attention to rest and recharge. The inhibitory circuits relax. The brain shifts from a high-beta state (stress) to an alpha state (relaxation) (Ulrich et al., 1991).

This concept aligns perfectly with the Yogic practice of *Dhyana* (meditation). *Dhyana* is often misunderstood as intense concentration. That is *Dharana*. *Dhyana* is a flow. It is a continuous, effortless stream of awareness (Telles et al., 2012). It is the mind resting in a single state, like oil pouring from a jar. Soft Fascination is an external form of *Dhyana*. It induces a similar neural state.

Both states function to settle *Rajas*. *Rajas* is the energy of agitation. It is mental dust kicked up by digital activity. When the user enters a restorative environment, the stimulation drops. The dust begins to settle. The water of the mind clears. This clarity is the return of *Sattva* (Frawley, 2000). *Sattva* is balanced, light, and peaceful. It is the natural state of the mind when undisturbed.

The digital world is devoid of Soft Fascination. It is built on *Hard Fascination*. It grabs attention aggressively (Kaplan & Berman, 2010). It demands constant processing. There is no space for the mind to wander. This is why *relaxing* with a smartphone is a myth. It feels like rest because the body is still. However, the brain is engaged in a full-length marathon. It prevents the restoration of Sattva.

Recovery requires a strategic diet of Soft Fascination. It implies walking without a podcast. It implies looking out of a window without taking a photo. It implies staring at a wall. These activities seem unproductive to the *Rajasic* mind. They feel bored. But boredom is the precursor to restoration (Odell, 2019). It is the space where the mind cleans itself.

By integrating *Pratyahara* (gating) and Soft Fascination (restoration), the user builds a resilient cognitive architecture. They protect their energy from the digital drain. They replenish their reserves through natural connection. This practice is not a detox. It is a lifestyle. It is a permanent shift in how the mind relates to its environment. It turns the user from a victim of the attention of the economy into a master of their consciousness. Within the SARA framework, this restorative practice constitutes Layer 3 (Restore) — the Ojas-replenishing environmental engagement that rebuilds the foundational reserve depleted by digital overexposure and that prepares the ground for the identity reconstruction addressed in Layer 4.

5.4 The Witness Perspective

The final and most powerful strategy is *metacognitive*. It is the development of the Witness Perspective. In Yoga, this is known as *Sakshi Bhav*. It involves cultivating a detached observer within the mind (Frawley, 2000). Standard cognition involves identification. The thought arises: *I am bored*. The user believes they are bored. They act on it by scrolling.

Sakshi Bhav creates separation. The thought arises, '*I am bored*.' The Witness observes, '*There is boredom arising in the mind*.' This subtle shift is revolutionary. It disrupts the identification of the state. The user realizes they are not bored. They are aware of boredom. This gap is the space for freedom.

In the digital context, this awareness is crucial. The urge to check the phone is often automatic. It is a *Samskara* (habitual impression) (Bryant, 2009). It fires rapidly. Without Witness, the hand moves before the mind thinks. With Witness, the urge is seen. It is noticed as a sensation in the body. It might be a tightness in the chest. It might be a twitch in the fingers.

By observing the urge without acting on it, the loop is broken. The user *surfs the urge*. They watch the craving rise, peak, and fall away. They do not feed it. This is a form of exposure therapy. Every time the urge is observed but not acted upon, the neural pathway weakens. The algorithmic loop loses its power (Ward et al., 2017).

This practice transforms the user's relationship with content. They can scroll without being consumed. They can see an outrage-inducing headline and remain calm. They observe the reaction: '*Ah, anger is rising*.' They do not become angry. They remain the *Sakshi*. This prevents the depletion of emotional energy.

Developing Witness requires consistent practice. It involves moments of *micro-meditation* throughout the day (Sood & Jones, 2013). Before engaging with the device, the user is trained to insert a moment of metacognitive pause — a single reflective breath that invokes the Witness perspective and shifts processing from the default mode network to the executive network. It brings the user back to the present moment. It shifts the brain from the default mode network (autopilot) to the executive network (awareness).

Witness is the ultimate antidote to digital burnout. Burnout happens to the ego. The ego gets tired. The ego gets jealous. The ego gets overwhelmed. The Witness never burns out. It is pure consciousness. It is always fresh. It is always stable. By anchoring identity in the Witness rather than the digital profile, the user finds an inexhaustible source of resilience —capable of engaging with the world fully while remaining established in the Self. This state is the pinnacle of cognitive restoration and the endpoint of the SARA model's fourth layer. The preceding four subsections have examined each layer individually. Section 5.5 integrates them into a unified, sequential framework and establishes the theoretical and practical architecture of SARA as a whole.

5.5 The SARA Model: A Framework for Sustainable Attention Regulation

The preceding four subsections have addressed discrete recovery strategies in sequence. However, digital burnout operates simultaneously across physiological, cognitive, ethical, and identity-based levels. A framework addressing only one level at a time is structurally insufficient. This section integrates those strategies into a unified, sequential model: the Sustainable Attention Regulation Architecture (SARA).

SARA is distinguished from existing approaches — including digital detox, screen time management, and mindfulness-based stress reduction — by three features. It is predictive: Layer 1 intervenes before burnout onset, not after. It is sequential: each layer builds the internal capacity required for the next. It addresses the identity dimension of digital burnout — the Ahamkara misidentification described in Section 3.5 — which no existing Western intervention framework accounts for.

Layer 1 — Sense: Directed Attention Fatigue Awareness

Effective intervention requires detecting the onset of Directed Attention Fatigue before it becomes collapse. In IKS terms, this is the recognition of nascent Vikshepa before it becomes entrenched — the cultivation of Viveka (discriminative awareness) at the somatic level. Attention training through sensory withdrawal practices has been shown to produce distinct neurological states from passive relaxation, strengthening prefrontal inhibitory pathways and reducing anxiety-related activation (Tang & Posner, 2009; Telles et al., 2012). The practical intervention is a Digital Pulse-Check: a 30-second somatic self-audit — attending to respiratory depth, muscular tension, and the quality of the preceding cognitive task — conducted before any device engagement. Its function is purely diagnostic: it inserts a moment of Viveka-governed awareness between the habitual impulse to check and the action itself.

Layer 2 — Attune: Proactive Sensory Regulation

Where Layer 1 detects, Layer 2 regulates. Neuroscientific study has shown that Pratyahara meditation activates the brain differently than other relaxation techniques, with specific exercises encouraging disengagement from sensory experience shown to aid anxiety reduction in clinical trials (Telles et al., 2012; Tang & Posner, 2009). This layer operationalizes Pratyahara not as post-burnout recovery but as pre-engagement prophylaxis — shifting the intervention from reactive to proactive. Three practices are prescribed: notification batching (consolidating alerts into designated review windows, training the Manas to defer to Buddhi's temporal authority); contextual intention-setting (defining purpose and exit condition before opening any application); and micro-refusal training (deliberate non-response to one notification per hour, progressively strengthening prefrontal inhibitory pathways (Tang & Posner, 2009)). Together, these practices restore what Mallick (2025) describes as Ethical Interdependent Agency at the cognitive level — the prerequisite for its restoration at the social level.

Layer 3 — Restore: Sattvic Environmental Recovery

Layers 1 and 2 arrest depletion. Layer 3 actively rebuilds depleted reserves. As established in Section 5.3, Soft Fascination environments allow Directed Attention's inhibitory mechanisms to rest and recharge (Kaplan & Kaplan, 1989; Kaplan, 1995). In Ayurvedic terms, these are precisely the conditions under which Ojas — the foundational reserve of patience, compassion, and social endurance — is replenished (Frawley, 2000). Mindfulness meditation training has been shown to increase functional connectivity between the default mode network, the salience network, and the central executive network (Tang et al., 2015) — corresponding in IKS terms to the restoration of Sattvic clarity through the settling of Rajasic agitation. Layer 3 prescribes a minimum of 20 minutes of daily unmediated nature exposure and regular boredom tolerance — scheduled unstructured time without content consumption — as the environmental conditions under which this restoration occurs. The default mode network maintains high activity during rest, supporting internally directed thought suspended during goal-directed behaviour — the neurological correlate of the introspective Sattvic state that Layer 4 requires.

Layer 4 — Anchor: Witness Identity Reconstruction

The preceding three layers address Tejas conservation, Prana regulation, and Ojas replenishment, respectively. Layer 4 addresses the root cause identified in Section 3.5: misidentification of the Self with the Digital Ahamkara. No amount of regulation or restoration resolves this layer — because it is not a cognitive problem. It is an identity problem. Sakshi Bhava, the practice of observing thoughts and emotions without identification, creates a metacognitive pause allowing for improved emotional regulation and clarity. In neurological terms, this condition corresponds to deliberate activation of the Central Executive Network over the Default Mode Network's self-referential autopilot (Sood & Jones, 2013). The practical intervention is a pre-device identity pause: one deliberate breath before any device engagement, accompanied by a single metacognitive question — "From which position am I engaging?" — that shifts processing from habitual Samskara-driven reactivity to Buddhi-governed intentional action. Over sustained practice, this pause transforms digital engagement from compulsion into sovereignty.

The SARA Architecture: Sequential Logic

The four layers are not interchangeable. Layer 1 develops the somatic vocabulary that gives Layer 2's regulatory practices a diagnostic trigger. Layer 2 rebuilds the *Pratyahara* gate that must be functional before Layer 3's restorative environments can fully take effect — a scattered mind generates *Vikshepa* even in a forest. Layer 3 replenishes the *Ojas* reserve without which Layer 4's identity work cannot be sustained — the exhausted ego cannot hold the Witness position. Layer 4 anchors the recovered system at the identity level, preventing the rebound effect that Layers 1–3 alone cannot preclude: without resolving the Digital Ahamkara misidentification, the user will return to burnout as soon as the next algorithmic cycle captures their identification.

This sequential dependency distinguishes SARA from both digital detox models — which address surface behavior only — and mindfulness-based stress reduction — which addresses regulation and awareness but does not target the identity dimension of digital misidentification.

Table 2. The SARA model — theoretical correspondences and practical interventions

Layer	Western framework	IKS framework	Vital essence	Practical intervention
1 — Sense	DAF monitoring; somatic awareness of inhibitory control degradation	Viveka (discriminative awareness); Vikshepa detection	Tejas — early burn signal	Digital Pulse-Check: 30-second somatic self-audit before device engagement
2 — Attune	Inhibitory control training; prefrontal strengthening (Tang & Posner, 2009)	Pratyahara: proactive sensory gating; Manas obeys Buddhi	Prana — conservation of animating force	Notification batching; contextual intention-setting; micro-refusal training
3 — Restore	Soft Fascination; ART restorative environments (Kaplan & Kaplan, 1989); DMN-CEN connectivity restoration	Sattva cultivation; Dhyana as effortless awareness; Ojas replenishment	Ojas — rebuilding foundational reserve	20-minute daily unmediated nature exposure; scheduled boredom tolerance
4 — Anchor	Metacognitive awareness; CEN activation over DMN autopilot (Sood & Jones, 2013)	Sakshi Bhav: witness consciousness; Atman over Digital Ahamkara	All three — sustained integration	Pre-device identity pause; metacognitive position question before all digital engagement

Note: The SARA model integrates Western cognitive science and Indian Knowledge Systems at each layer, mapping neurological mechanisms to IKS energetic frameworks. The vital essence column reflects the primary depletion addressed at each layer: Tejas at Layer 1 (cognitive fire burning unseen), Prana at Layer 2 (animating force scattered through reactive checking), Ojas at Layer 3 (foundational reserve rebuilt through stillness), and all three sustained through the identity anchor of Layer 4. Each layer is a prerequisite for the next — the model functions as a developmental sequence, not a menu of interchangeable options.

Figure 2. The SARA model — sustainable attention regulation architecture

Layer	Western framework	IKS framework	Vital essence
L1 **Sense** *Detect depletion before collapse*	**DAF monitoring** Somatic awareness of inhibitory control degradation	**Viveka** Discriminative awareness; nascent Vikshept Vikshepa detection	**Tejas** *Early burn signal*
L2 **Attune** *Regulate before breach breach occurs*	**Inhibitory control** Prefrontal strengthening (Tang & Posner, 2009)	**Pratyahara** Proactive sensory gating; Manas obeys Buddhi	**Prana** *Conservation of animating force*
L3 **Restore** *Rebuild depleted vital vital reserves*	**Soft fascination** ART restorative environments; DMN-CEN connectivity restoration (Kaplan & Kaplan, 1989)	**Sattva cultivation** Dhyana; Ojas replenishment through stillness	**Ojas** *Rebuilding foundational reserve*
L4 **Anchor** *Reconstruct witness identity*	**Metacognition** CEN activation over DMN autopilot (Sood & Jones, 2013)	**Sakshi Bhav** Witness over Digital Ahamkara; Atman restored	**All three** *Prana + Tejas + Ojas sustained in integration*
Outcome: Sattvic digital engagement — intentional, regulated, sovereign			

Note: *The SARA model is sequential, not modular — each layer builds the internal capacity that the next requires. Tejas conservation at Layer 1 makes conscious regulation at Layer 2 possible; Pratyahara-restored gating at Layer 2 is the prerequisite for effective restoration at Layer 3; Ojas replenishment at Layer 3 provides the foundational stamina without which the identity work of Layer 4 cannot be sustained. The model's endpoint — Sattvic digital engagement — is not the absence of digital interaction but its transformation: from compulsive reactivity into intentional, cognitively sovereign participation.*

Limitations and Future Directions

SARA is a conceptual framework requiring empirical validation. Future research should examine whether the sequential structure is empirically necessary or whether individual layers produce independent effects; whether outcomes differ across age groups — particularly adolescents whose Digital Ahamkara formation is still in process; and whether the convergent IKS-Western protocol produces synergistic effects that neither framework achieves independently — a question that would constitute a meaningful contribution to cross-cultural contemplative neuroscience.

6. CONCLUSION: TOWARD SUSTAINABLE DIGITAL ENGAGEMENT

This concluding section synthesizes the entire content of the chapter. It argues for a vital paradigm shift. The focus must move from reactive consumption. The goal is intentional engagement. This transition requires a specific integration. It combines cognitive science with ancient wisdom.

6.1 Synthesis

This investigation began with a structural paradox: digital infrastructure promises connection yet produces disconnection. This study has approached that paradox not as a behavioral habit but as a *structural failure of attention* — one that cannot be fully understood from either a Western or an Indian epistemological position alone.

Separately, these frameworks offer partial truths. Western cognitive science, specifically Attention Restoration Theory, provides the biological mechanics: it maps the metabolic cost of inhibitory control and demonstrates that the human brain cannot sustain continuous switching without collapse. However, the Western model stops at the biological — it treats the crisis as a resource management problem, optimizing for restoration in the service of productivity. It cannot account for *why* the mind consents to its own depletion.

The Indian framework supplies this missing dimension. It does not merely identify a disturbance in the Chitta — it names the disturbance's ethical consequence. Vikshepa is not simply inefficiency; it is moral incapacity. A scattered mind cannot perceive the needs of others. The *Prana-Dharma* link — the proposition that vital energy and social duty are not separable — is the chapter's central interdisciplinary claim. It is a proposition Western cognitive science cannot make and does not attempt to.

By integrating these views, the affective condition of our time becomes fully visible: not merely stress, but a state of spiritual and cognitive exhaustion in which the Tejas required to digest reality and the Ojas required to sustain compassion are being systematically depleted. The feeling of being drained is real — it is the physiological and metaphysical marker of a consciousness that has lost its centre. The problem is not the technology itself. It is the architecture of the finite, biological mind interacting with the architecture of the infinite, algorithmic machine. That interaction, unmediated, is asymmetric. The SARA model proposed in Section 5.5

is this chapter's attempt to restore that balance — not through abstinence or external control, but through the sequential reconstruction of the internal architecture that digital overexposure systematically dismantles: somatic awareness, sensory regulation, vital restoration, and witness identity.

6.2 Final Argument

The solution, therefore, cannot be a simple retreat. The digital layer is now a permanent feature of human existence — as infrastructural as language, commerce, and civic life. The challenge is not avoidance but navigation: to engage with it fully without surrendering cognitive sovereignty. This requires a fundamental shift in the mode of engagement. It requires a transition from *Rajas* to *Sattva.*

Social media platforms are architecturally designed to sustain *Rajas*. Variable rewards, algorithmically curated outrage, and frictionless scrolling all serve a single commercial logic: reactivity drives engagement metrics. However, the same reactivity that maximizes platform revenue progressively degrades the user's psychological resources. They are trapped in a loop of seeking that never finds satisfaction. This constant agitation leads inevitably to *Tamas*—the crash, the burnout, the apathy.

True Digital Wellbeing is the cultivation of Sattva — and the SARA model provides the sequential pathway through which that cultivation becomes practically achievable. Layer 1 develops the awareness to recognize Rajasic agitation before it becomes Tamasic collapse. Layer 2 rebuilds the regulatory capacity to interrupt the collapse cycle. Layer 3 restores the Sattvic clarity that the cycle destroys. Layer 4 anchors identity in the witness position from which Sattvic engagement becomes sustainable.

This shift is difficult. It fights against the design of the interface. The interface wants speed; *Sattva* requires slowness. The interface wants fragmentation; *Sattva* requires wholeness. The interface wants outward validation; *Sattva* rests in internal contentment. However, this shift is the only sustainable path. We must move from being *consumers* of content to *custodians* of our own attention.

This involves a change in identity. The term 'user' itself warrants scrutiny — it implies dependency and passivity. Reclaiming the identity of the Witness (*Sakshi*) represents a fundamental reorientation: from a passive recipient of algorithmic direction to sovereign agent of one's own attention. The Witness observes the screen but is not sucked into it. The Witness feels the dopamine urge but does not obey it. This *metacognitive distance* is the essence of *Sattvic* engagement. It allows us to walk through the digital fire without being burned. It allows us to be connected to the world, yet remain established in the Self. This is the definition of freedom in the 21st century. Cognitive freedom, in this framework, is not the availability of infinite content choices. It is the metacognitive capacity to determine, with intention and awareness, where one's attention is directed — and where it is not.

6.3 Implications

The implications of this study extend beyond the individual's perspective. They touch the very foundation of how we educate the next generation. Current media literacy focuses on content. We teach students to spot fake news. We teach them about privacy settings. We teach them coding. These are important skills. But they are insufficient. Digital devices are placed in children's hands without equipping them with the cognitive frameworks required to use them without harm. We are teaching them how to use the software, but not how to use their minds.

Future education must focus on Attention Literacy — and the SARA model offers a structured, age-appropriate framework through which this literacy can be taught. Its four layers translate naturally into educational contexts: Layer 1 as somatic self-awareness curricula, Layer 2 as digital citizenship training, Layer 3 as structured outdoor and unstructured time within the school day, and Layer 4 as reflective practice and contemplative education. These are not supplementary activities. Within the SARA framework, they are sequential cognitive competencies as fundamental as literacy and numeracy for functioning in the New Media Era. Just as we teach physical hygiene to prevent disease, we must teach cognitive hygiene to prevent Digital Burnout.

Students need to learn the mechanics of their attention. They need to understand the cost of the switch. They need to recognize the feeling of *Rajasic* agitation before it becomes *Tamasic* collapse. They need practical tools to calm the mind. Breathing exercises, sensory gating, and exposure to restorative environments should be part of the curriculum. This material is not about religious instruction. It is about physiological survival.

If we fail to do this, the cost will be high. We risk raising a technically brilliant but emotionally hollow generation. We risk a society where empathy is too expensive to afford. We risk a collective descent into indifference. However, if we succeed, the potential is immense. A mind that can master its attention is a powerful force. It can use digital tools to solve complex problems. It can connect with others across the globe with genuine compassion. It can maintain its humanity in the face of the machine.

The ancient sages perceived the dangers of a scattered mind millennia ago. They developed a rigorous science to counter it. We have forgotten this science. Now, at the peak of the AI era, we require this science more than ever. Technology will continue to advance. The algorithms will get smarter. The only way to stay human is to become wiser. We must reclaim the architecture of our attention. We must rebuild the sanctuary of the inner world. Only then can we engage with the outer world (digital or physical) with true integrity, presence, and peace.

REFERENCES

Alter, A. (2017). *Irresistible: The rise of addictive technology and the business of keeping us hooked*. Penguin.

Batson, C. D., Fultz, J., & Schoenrade, P. A. (1987). Distress and empathy: Two qualitatively distinct vicarious emotions with different motivational consequences. *Journal of Personality*, *55*(1), 19–39. DOI: 10.1111/j.1467-6494.1987.tb00426.x PMID: 3572705

Baumeister, R. F. (2002). Ego depletion and self-control failure: An energy model of the self's executive function. *Self and Identity*, *1*(2), 129–136. DOI: 10.1080/152988602317319302

Berman, M. G., Jonides, J., & Kaplan, S. (2008). The cognitive benefits of interacting with nature. *Psychological Science*, *19*(12), 1207–1212. DOI: 10.1111/j.1467-9280.2008.02225.x PMID: 19121124

Bryant, E. F. (2009). *The Yoga Sutras of Patanjali: A new edition, translation, and commentary*. North Point Press.

Cameron, C. D., Hutcherson, C. A., Ferguson, A. M., Scheffer, J. A., Hadjiandreou, E., & Inzlicht, M. (2019). Empathy is hard work: People choose to avoid empathy because of its cognitive costs. *Journal of Experimental Psychology. General*, *148*(6), 962–976. DOI: 10.1037/xge0000595 PMID: 30998038

Castells, M. (2010). *The rise of the network society*. Wiley-Blackwell.

Citton, Y. (2017). *The ecology of attention*. Polity Press.

Decety, J., & Jackson, P. L. (2004). The functional architecture of human empathy. *Behavioral and Cognitive Neuroscience Reviews*, *3*(2), 71–100. DOI: 10.1177/1534582304267187 PMID: 15537986

Derks, D., & Bakker, A. B. (2014). The impact of email communication on psychological detachment, recovery, and burnout. *Work and Stress*, *28*(1), 17–33. DOI: 10.1080/02678373.2013.879664

Duke, É., & Montag, C. (2017). Smartphone addiction, daily interruptions and self-reported productivity. *Addictive Behaviors Reports*, *6*, 90–95. DOI: 10.1016/j.abrep.2017.07.002 PMID: 29450241

Figley, C. R. (1995). *Compassion fatigue: Coping with secondary traumatic stress disorder in those who treat the traumatized*. Brunner/Mazel.

Frawley, D. (2000). *Ayurveda and the mind: The healing of consciousness.* Lotus Press.

Goleman, D. (2006). *Social intelligence: The new science of human relationships.* Bantam Books.

Kaplan, R., & Kaplan, S. (1989). *The experience of nature: A psychological perspective.* Cambridge University Press.

Kaplan, S. (1995). The restorative benefits of nature: Toward an integrative framework. *Journal of Environmental Psychology, 15*(3), 169–182. DOI: 10.1016/0272-4944(95)90001-2

Kaplan, S., & Berman, M. G. (2010). Directed attention as a common resource for executive functioning and self-regulation. *Perspectives on Psychological Science, 5*(1), 43–57. DOI: 10.1177/1745691609356784 PMID: 26162062

Lee, A. R., Son, S. M., & Kim, K. K. (2016). Information and communication technology overload and social networking service fatigue: A stress perspective. *Computers in Human Behavior, 55*, 51–61. DOI: 10.1016/j.chb.2015.08.011

Malhotra, R. (2016). *Being different: An Indian challenge to western universalism.* HarperCollins India.

Mallick, M. K. (2025). Beyond individual agency: Rotter's locus of control reconsidered through Indian philosophical frameworks. *International Journal of Interdisciplinary Approaches in Psychology, 3*(12), 22–35. DOI: 10.61113/ijiap.v3i12.1215

Mallick, M. K., & Mallick, A. (2025). Bridging minds: Psychoanalysis and the Indian knowledge system. *International Journal of Interdisciplinary Approaches in Psychology, 3*(11), 12–21. DOI: 10.61113/ijiap.v3i11.1201

Maslach, C., & Jackson, S. E. (1981). The measurement of experienced burnout. *Journal of Organizational Behavior, 2*(2), 99–113. DOI: 10.1002/job.4030020205

McEwen, B. S. (1998). Protective and damaging effects of stress mediators. *The New England Journal of Medicine, 338*(3), 171–179. DOI: 10.1056/NEJM199801153380307 PMID: 9428819

McEwen, B. S., & Seeman, T. (1999). Protective and damaging effects of mediators of stress: Elaborating and testing the concepts of allostasis and allostatic load. *Annals of the New York Academy of Sciences, 896*(1), 30–47. DOI: 10.1111/j.1749-6632.1999.tb08103.x PMID: 10681886

Misra, S., & Stokols, D. (2012). Psychological and health outcomes of perceived information overload. *Environment and Behavior, 44*(6), 737–759. DOI: 10.1177/0013916511404408

Moeller, S. D. (1999). *Compassion fatigue: How the media sell disease, famine, war and death*. Routledge.

Newport, C. (2019). *Digital minimalism: Choosing a focused life in a noisy world*. Portfolio.

Odell, J. (2019). *How to do nothing: Resisting the attention economy*. Melville House.

Posner, M. I., & Rothbart, M. K. (2007). Research on attention networks as a model for the integration of psychological science. *Annual Review of Psychology, 58*(1), 1–23. DOI: 10.1146/annurev.psych.58.110405.085516 PMID: 17029565

Putnam, R. D. (2000). *Bowling alone: The collapse and revival of American community*. Simon & Schuster.

Ragu-Nathan, T. S., Tarafdar, M., Ragu-Nathan, B. S., & Tu, Q. (2008). The consequences of technostress for end users in organizations: Conceptual development and empirical validation. *Information Systems Research, 19*(4), 417–433. DOI: 10.1287/isre.1070.0165

Raichle, M. E., & Gusnard, D. A. (2002). Appraising the brain's energy budget. *Proceedings of the National Academy of Sciences of the United States of America, 99*(16), 10237–10239. DOI: 10.1073/pnas.172399499 PMID: 12149485

Rao, K. R., & Paranjpe, A. C. (2016). *Psychology in the Indian tradition*. Springer., DOI: 10.1007/978-81-322-2440-2

Sapolsky, R. M. (2004). *Why zebras don't get ulcers* (3rd ed.). Holt Paperbacks.

Saraswati, S. S. (2009). *Prana and Pranayama*. Yoga Publications Trust.

Sood, A., & Jones, D. T. (2013). On mind wandering, attention, brain networks, and meditation. *Explore (New York, N.Y.), 9*(3), 136–141. DOI: 10.1016/j.explore.2013.02.005 PMID: 23643368

Tang, Y. Y., Hölzel, B. K., & Posner, M. I. (2015). The neuroscience of mindfulness meditation. *Nature Reviews. Neuroscience, 16*(4), 213–225. DOI: 10.1038/nrn3916 PMID: 25783612

Tang, Y. Y., & Posner, M. I. (2009). Attention training and attention state training. *Trends in Cognitive Sciences, 13*(5), 222–227. DOI: 10.1016/j.tics.2009.01.009 PMID: 19375975

Tarafdar, M., Tu, Q., Ragu-Nathan, B. S., & Ragu-Nathan, T. S. (2007). The impact of technostress on role stress and productivity. *Journal of Management Information Systems*, *24*(1), 301–328. DOI: 10.2753/MIS0742-1222240109

Telles, S., Singh, N., & Balkrishna, A. (2012). Managing mental health disorders resulting from trauma through yoga: A review. *Depression Research and Treatment*, *401513*, 1–9. Advance online publication. DOI: 10.1155/2012/401513 PMID: 22778930

Turkle, S. (2011). *Alone together: Why we expect more from technology and less from each other*. Basic Books.

Ulrich, R. S., Simons, R. F., Losito, B. D., Fiorito, E., Miles, M. A., & Zelson, M. (1991). Stress recovery during exposure to natural and urban environments. *Journal of Environmental Psychology*, *11*(3), 201–230. DOI: 10.1016/S0272-4944(05)80184-7

Ward, A. F., Duke, K., Gneezy, A., & Bos, M. W. (2017). Brain drain: The mere presence of one's own smartphone reduces available cognitive capacity. *Journal of the Association for Consumer Research*, *2*(2), 140–154. DOI: 10.1086/691462

Williams, J. (2018). *Stand out of our light: Freedom and resistance in the attention economy*. Cambridge University Press. DOI: 10.1017/9781108453004

Wu, T. (2016). *The attention merchants: The epic scramble to get inside our heads*. Knopf.

KEY TERMS AND DEFINITIONS

Attention Restoration Theory (ART): A framework proposed by Kaplan and Kaplan (1989) suggesting that "directed attention" is a finite resource that degrades with use but can be replenished through exposure to environments that engage "involuntary attention" (fascination) without effort.

Digital Ahamkara (The Digital Ego): A term proposed in this chapter for the curated, performative digital identity constructed through social media profiles, metrics, and online self-presentation. Derived from the Sanskrit *Ahamkara* (the I-maker), it is a false self-constituted from transient digital data rather than authentic selfhood.

Digital Burnout: A distinct form of psychological stress characterized by chronic exhaustion, cynicism, and inefficacy caused by prolonged engagement with digital technologies. Unlike occupational burnout, it is driven by the specific cognitive load of managing "always-on" connectivity and algorithmic interruptions.

Directed Attention Fatigue (DAF): A neuropsychological phenomenon occurring when the brain's inhibitory mechanisms—used to block out distractions and maintain focus—are depleted. In this chapter, DAF is presented as the cognitive precursor to social indifference.

Doom-scrolling: A colloquial term in popular and emerging scholarly discourse describing the compulsive, affectless consumption of predominantly negative digital content beyond the point of voluntary control or cognitive engagement.

Pratyahara (Sensory Withdrawal): A concept from Patanjali's *Yoga Sutras* referring to the conscious retraction of the senses from external objects. In the context of this chapter, it is redefined not as asceticism, but as a psychological "gating mechanism" essential for digital hygiene.

SARA (Sustainable Attention Regulation Architecture): An original framework proposed in this chapter synthesizes Attention Restoration Theory and Indian Knowledge Systems into four sequential, interdependent layers. Unlike digital detox or mindfulness-based stress reduction approaches, SARA is predictive rather than reactive and explicitly addresses the identity dimension of digital burnout.

Social Indifference: A state of apathy or lack of emotional responsiveness toward societal issues. This chapter hypothesizes that social indifference is a symptom of *Tamasic* inertia resulting from severe cognitive depletion.

Trigunas (The Three Modes of Nature): A fundamental framework in Indian psychology describing the three qualities of mental energy: *Sattva* (balance/clarity), *Rajas* (activity/passion), and *Tamas* (inertia/darkness). This chapter utilizes the Trigunas to model the user's descent from high engagement (*Rajas*) to burnout (*Tamas*).

Vikshepa (Mental Distraction): The tossing or scattering of the mind caused by external stimuli. In this study, digital notifications are categorized as external triggers of *Vikshepa*, preventing the mind from reaching a state of *Ekagrata* (one-pointedness).

Chapter 6
Hypervisibility Leading to Indifference:
Emotional Fatigue and the Politics of Affective Exhaustion

Alka S. Yadav
http://orcid.org/0009-0004-6916-7180
Christ University, India

ABSTRACT

This chapter is an exploration of the paradox which is embedded in contemporary digital media. How hypervisibility of suffering can culminate in social indifference. It argues that the constant circulation of distressing images and narratives across platform-driven media ecosystems generates cycles of emotional amplification that are difficult to sustain over time. Taking insights from affect theory and studies on compassion fatigue, the chapter conceptualises this process as a movement from hypervisibility to affective exhaustion. It tries to examine how algorithmic amplification and uneven structures of representation shape public engagement with crisis. Through theoretical analysis and illustrative cases, the chapter demonstrates that repeated exposure to mediated suffering may produce emotional fatigue. This fatigue ultimately weakens empathy and contributes to episodic, rather than sustained, forms of civic and political response.

INTRODUCTION

Digital media in last two decades has significantly changed the perspective in which suffering and injustice became visible in public life. Social media platforms and networked journalism instantly transmit local events across borders. If we look

DOI: 10.4018/979-8-3373-8307-1.ch006

at this theoretically, so much of unprecedented visibility would strengthen global empathy and also mobilise collective action. But the empirical reality is far away from this. It is a paradox. The audiences are exposed to a relentless stream of emotionally charged content as images of violence and injustice are continuously circulated across digital networks. Instead of strengthening sustained moral engagement, this saturation ends up producing a less visible outcome. The outcome is emotional fatigue and gradual indifference.

It has been observed by the scholars that the contemporary media environment is characterised by a situation which can be called as "hypervisibility of suffering". It is a condition in which traumatic events are constantly circulated and reproduced within the digital attention economy (Chouliaraki, 2006; Moeller, 1999). Hypervisibility should not be understood as mere visibility. It goes beyond and also refers to the intensity, frequency and speed with which stressful images and narratives circulate across media platforms. In the Global South this phenomenon has become particularly noticeable due to the rapid smartphone penetration and social media use. India, for instance, has more than 750 million internet users and over 450 million active social media users (Internet and Mobile Association of India [IAMAI], 2023). The country hosts one of the largest digital publics in the world. Such a massive digital ecosystem ensures that moments of violence, humanitarian crisis, disasters, or gender-based injustice are captured and shared within minutes. All this generates widespread public attention.

Undoubtedly digital visibility brings urgent social issues into public discourse. But it also produces a paradoxical emotional dynamic. Audiences repeatedly come across stressful narratives ranging from viral videos of violence to images from conflict zones. The emotional intensity that initially accompanies such exposure begins to dissipate. Scholars in the field of media studies and affect theory have drawn attention to this phenomenon. Research on media consumption patterns suggests us that persistent exposure to negative news can lead to news avoidance and emotional withdrawal. According to the Reuters Institute Digital News Report, approximately four out of ten global news consumers report avoiding news because it negatively affects their mood, with very similar trends visible across many countries in Asia and Africa (Newman et al., 2023). Such findings suggest that the expansion of digital visibility does not necessarily translate into deeper public engagement.

Theoretical reflections on the mediation of distant suffering help us understand this paradox better. Susan Sontag (2003) made a observation that images of pain and violence possess a complex moral power. On one hand they can evoke compassion, yet on the other hand their repeated circulation may also dull emotional responsiveness. On the Similar lines, Luc Boltanski (1999) has held that mediated representations of suffering places audiences in the position of distant spectators. Their moral responses remain fragile and contingent. In the contemporary digital environment this dynamic is intensified by social media platforms. On these platforms algorithmic amplification pushes emotionally charged content in order to maximise engagement. As a result stressful images and narratives become embedded within the rapid cycles of the digital attention economy. Here crisis competes for visibility alongside entertainment and everyday social interaction.

Digital media has enabled marginalised communities to register injustice while challenging dominant narratives. The aim is to mobilise public attention around issues such as gender-based violence, caste discrimination, environmental degradation and state violence. At the same time the continuous circulation of traumatic content which is accompanied by intense but short-lived waves of online outrage raises important questions about the sustainability of emotional engagement. Viral incidents trigger immediate expressions of solidarity and outrage across social media platforms. Yet these responses dissipate quickly as the digital public moves on to the next trending issue. This pattern suggests that hypervisibility may contribute to a form of affective exhaustion in which audiences become overwhelmed by the sheer volume of stressful information.

Affective exhaustion captures a broader transformation in the politics of emotion within contemporary media environments. Scholars of affect theory argue that emotions do not simply reflect private psychological states but also circulate socially. They shape collective attitudes and political orientations (Ahmed, 2004; Massumi, 2002). When emotional content is constantly shared audiences may experience “affective saturation”. It is a condition in which the capacity to respond empathetically becomes strained. Over time this saturation may generate emotional fatigue, compassion burnout and ultimately forms of social indifference. This indifference should not necessarily be interpreted as moral failure. Rather, it can be seen as a coping mechanism through which individuals protect themselves from the psychological burden of continuous exposure to distress.

Understanding this dynamic is particularly important in societies where digital media increasingly serve as the primary arena for public debate and civic engagement. In many parts of the Global South, social media platforms have become central spaces for mobilising protest and shaping public narratives around social issues. But the same platforms also produce conditions of emotional overload that can undermine sustained political engagement. The resulting tension raises an important question for scholars of media and society. Does the hypervisibility of suffering in the digital era strengthen empathy or gradually erodes the emotional capacity required for meaningful engagement?

The relationship between digital hypervisibility, emotional fatigue and the politics of affective exhaustion is the central theme of this chapter. It argues that the constant circulation of emotionally charged content can generate affective saturation among audiences. This saturation leads to compassion fatigue and social indifference. This chapter gets its strength from theoretical insights from affect studies and media scholarship. Empirical evidences and case illustrations from the global south seek to show how emotional responses to mediated suffering are produced, shared, circulated, and ultimately exhausted within the contemporary digital landscape.

The discussion proceeds in several stages. Subsequent sections analyse how digital media infrastructures generate conditions of hypervisibility and emotional overload. The chapter then explores the emergence of compassion fatigue and affective exhaustion. Selected case illustrations from the global south demonstrate how cycles of visibility and indifference unfold within digital publics. The concluding section reflects on the ethical and political implications of these dynamics for media practices and democratic engagement in the digital age.

THEORETICAL FRAMEWORK

The relationship between media, emotion, and public engagement has long occupied a central place in social and political theory. However, the emergence of digitally networked communication has intensified this relationship in unprecedented ways. To understand how hypervisibility produces emotional fatigue and social indifference, it is necessary to situate the discussion within a multidisciplinary theoretical framework drawing inspiration from affect theory, media studies, political communication, and psychological research on trauma and empathy.

A useful starting point is affect theory. Sara Ahmed conceptualises emotions not as private psychological states. She views emotions as forces that circulate socially and attach themselves to bodies and narratives (Ahmed, 2004). In digital environments this circulation is accelerated and amplified. This is because emotions are embedded in hashtags and viral content. Emotions such as outrage, grief or solidarity do not merely reflect social realities. They actively shape them by aligning individuals into affective communities. This perspective is further taken ahead by Brian Massumi who distinguishes affect from emotion. He emphasises its pre-cognitive, bodily intensity (Massumi, 2002). In hypervisible media environments affect operates at a rapid pace producing immediate reactions to circulating images of suffering.

The notion of "affective publics" developed by Zizi Papacharissi provides a critical framework for understanding digitally mediated emotional engagement. Papacharissi (2015) contends that networked publics are increasingly organised through shared emotional expressions rather than purely rational deliberation. Social media platforms enable individuals to connect through sentiments of anger, empathy, compassion, or grief forming temporary collectivities around specific events.

The work of Lilie Chouliaraki further gives strength to this analysis by examining the "spectatorship of suffering" in mediated contexts (Chouliaraki, 2006). She argues that media representations of distant suffering invite audiences into moral relationships with those depicted. But these relationships are structured by visibility. In contemporary digital media, this spectatorship is increasingly fragmented and episodic. Chouliaraki's later concept of the "ironic spectator" highlights a shift from deep moral engagement to more detached, self-aware forms of response, where audiences acknowledge suffering but remain emotionally distanced (Chouliaraki, 2013). This framework is particularly relevant in explaining how repeated exposure to distressing content may lead to diminished emotional responsiveness.

Earlier work by Susan Sontag also provides an important foundation. In *Regarding the Pain of Others*, Sontag (2003) reflects on the ethical implications of viewing images of suffering, questioning whether repeated exposure fosters empathy or leads to desensitisation. She cautions that images alone cannot sustain moral engagement. Without context and political framing, they become spectacles that audiences consume and then forget. This concern is echoed in the concept of "compassion fatigue," developed by Susan D. Moeller. She argues that constant exposure to crisis through the media leads to a gradual erosion of public empathy (Moeller, 1999). As audiences encounter recurring narratives of violence, disaster, and injustice, their emotional capacity becomes strained finally resulting in disengagement.

From a psychological perspective compassion fatigue is closely linked to secondary traumatic stress a concept elaborated by Charles R. Figley (Figley, 1995). While originally used to describe caregivers and professionals working with trauma victims this concept has been extended to media audiences who repeatedly encounter distressing content. Studies such as Holman, Garfin, and Silver (2014) show that repeated media exposure to traumatic events can increase stress and anxiety levels suggesting that the emotional impact of media is not merely symbolic but has tangible psychological consequences.

Media and communication scholarship also provides critical insights into the structural dimensions of hypervisibility. Yochai Benkler (2006) highlights how networked communication systems enable decentralised production and circulation of information, allowing citizens to participate in documenting and disseminating events. Zeynep Tufekci (2017) held that the same networks that facilitate rapid mobilisation can also produce fragility in collective action as movements struggle to sustain attention beyond initial moments of visibility.

The role of platform architecture is further inspected by Shoshana Zuboff who situates digital media within the broader logic of surveillance capitalism (Zuboff, 2019). Platforms are designed to maximise user engagement by prioritising emotionally charged content. This creates an environment where distressing and sensational narratives are continuously amplified contributing to emotional overload. Similarly, Philip M. Napoli (2019) emphasises how algorithmic curation shapes public attention. Immediacy and virality are prioritised over depth and context.

Luc Boltanski (1999) conceptualises distant suffering as a moral problem. It is mediated through communication systems that structure how audiences perceive and respond to others' pain. He identifies different modes of response i.e. denunciation, sentiment, and aesthetic contemplation. Each of these shapes the ethical relationship between spectator and sufferer. In digital contexts these modes often coexist producing complex and sometimes contradictory responses.

Finally, scholarly work on news consumption and avoidance provides empirical grounding for the argument that hypervisibility can lead to disengagement. Studies by Skovsgaard and Andersen (2020) and reports such as the Reuters Digital News Report (Newman et al., 2023) indicate rising levels of news avoidance, particularly among younger audiences who feel overwhelmed by the negativity of news content. This suggests that emotional fatigue is not merely a theoretical concern but a measurable phenomenon with implications for democratic participation.

These theoretical perspectives reveal that hypervisibility is not a straightforward expansion of awareness. But it is a condition shaped by affective intensities and psychological limits. While digital media enable unprecedented forms of witnessing and engagement, they also generate environments where emotional capacities are continuously stretched. The resulting tension between visibility and exhaustion shape the contemporary debates on media, empathy and public life, particularly in rapidly digitising societies across the global south.

The dynamics discussed in this chapter can be summarized through a conceptual pathway. It explains how hypervisibility within digital media environments may gradually produce affective exhaustion and social indifference.

Table 1. Conceptual model

Stage	Media Process	Emotional Response	Social Outcome
1. Hypervisibility	Viral circulation of crises through digital media, smartphone recordings, hashtags	Shock, outrage, empathy	Rapid public attention
2.Emotional Amplification	Algorithmic promotion of emotionally intense content	Collective emotional mobilisation	Online activism, protests
3.Affective Saturation	Continuous exposure to distressing narratives across platforms	Emotional overload	Anxiety, fatigue
4.Compassion Fatigue	Repetition of similar crisis narratives	Reduced emotional responsiveness	News avoidance
5.Affective Exhaustion	Constant demand for emotional engagement	Emotional detachment	Decline in civic participation
6.social indifference	Shifting digital attention cycles	Normalization of crisis	Episodic engagement with injustice

HYPERVISIBILITY AND THE DIGITAL MEDIA ECOSYSTEM

The contemporary media landscape is characterised by an unprecedented expansion in the visibility of socio-political and humanitarian crisis. Digital technologies particularly smartphones, social media platforms and high-speed internet have transformed the conditions under which events are recorded and consumed. This transformation has given rise to hypervisibility. It is a condition in which images and testimonies of suffering are not only widely available but are also continuously reproduced and amplified across networked publics. While visibility is considered a prerequisite for recognition and justice but the speed and intensity of digital circulation introduce new complexities that demand closer analytical attention.

At a structural level hypervisibility is deeply tied to the affordances of digital platforms. The participatory nature of contemporary media ecosystems allows individuals to act simultaneously as witnesses and disseminators of information. As Yochai Benkler (2006) observes, networked communication systems have lowered barriers to information production enabling decentralised flows of content that challenge traditional gatekeeping institutions.

The democratisation of visibility has important political implications. Events that might previously have remained localised or suppressed can now gain global attention within hours. Citizen-generated content often captured in real time, plays a crucial role in this process. The circulation of videos and testimonies enables forms of "digital witnessing" that can challenge official narratives and draw attention to marginalised voices. Zeynep Tufekci (2017) argues such networked visibility has the capacity to facilitate rapid mobilisation, enabling individuals to organise protests and demand accountability.

However, hypervisibility is not merely a function of user participation. It is also shaped by the underlying logics of platform design. Social media platforms operate through algorithmic systems that prioritise content which is likely to generate engagement including likes and comments. Research by Berger and Milkman (2012) demonstrates that emotionally charged content particularly that which evokes anger or anxiety is more likely to be shared. As a result, digital platforms tend to amplify narratives that are sensational, emotionally intense or visually striking. This creates a feedback loop in which distressing and dramatic representations of suffering are disproportionately visible within the digital public sphere.

Shoshana Zuboff (2019) situates digital platforms within the broader economic logic of surveillance capitalism. According to Zuboff platforms are designed to capture and monetise user attention. They incentivise the continuous production and circulation of engaging content. In this context hypervisibility is not simply an unintended byproduct but an integral feature of a system that thrives on sustained user engagement. The emotional intensity of content becomes a key driver of visibility as platforms privilege such posts that elicit strong reactions.

Besides platform dynamics the temporal structure of digital media plays a crucial role in shaping hypervisibility. Unlike traditional media which operated through relatively fixed news cycles digital platforms function through continuous, real-time updates. This creates an environment of perpetual immediacy, where new information constantly displaces older content. Zizi Papacharissi (2015) conceptualises this as the formation of "affective publics," where emotional responses are organized around rapidly unfolding events. While such publics can generate powerful moments of collective attention, they are often short-lived. It is because the flow of information quickly shifts focus to new crisis.

This temporality is particularly evident in the context of crisis reporting. Digital media enable the rapid escalation of specific events into viral moments. But they also contribute to the fragmentation of attention. As Lilie Chouliaraki (2006) notes, the representation of suffering is shaped by regimes of visibility that determine which events are seen and how they are interpreted. In digital environments these regimes are increasingly fluid driven by platform algorithms, user interactions and the competitive dynamics of attention. The result is a form of episodic visibility where issues gain prominence for brief periods before being overshadowed by subsequent events.

The expansion of hypervisibility in the global south must also be understood within broader socio-economic and political contexts. In countries such as India, digital media have become central to public discourse, particularly among younger and urban populations. Studies by the Centre for the Study of Developing Societies (2022) indicate that a significant proportion of users encounter news through social media feeds rather than traditional sources. This shift has implications for how information is interpreted. Unlike traditional journalism, which often provides background and analysis, social media content tends to prioritise immediacy and emotional impact sometimes at the expense of depth.

Hypervisibility intersects with existing inequalities in representation. Not all forms of suffering receive equal attention. Visibility is often unevenly distributed across regions and issues. Structural factors such as caste, class, gender, and geography continue to shape which narratives gain traction within digital spaces. As a result, hypervisibility can coexist with forms of invisibility, where certain experiences remain marginalised despite the apparent openness of digital platforms. This unevenness complicates the assumption that increased visibility necessarily leads to greater justice or accountability.

Another critical dimension of hypervisibility is its cumulative effect on audiences. The constant exposure to distressing content across multiple platforms can create an environment of informational and emotional overload. While the immediate impact of hypervisibility may be increased awareness its longer-term consequences are more ambivalent. Scholars have begun to note that the relentless flow of crisis narratives may contribute to desensitisation. The audiences struggle to process the volume and intensity of information presented to them. This dynamic sets the stage for the emergence of emotional fatigue which will be explored in the subsequent section.

In sum, hypervisibility in the digital media ecosystem is a multifaceted phenomenon shaped by technological affordances and socio-political contexts. It enables new forms of witnessing and participation particularly in regions where access to traditional media has been limited. At the same time, it introduces new challenges related to attention and emotional sustainability. By amplifying certain narratives while simultaneously accelerating the pace of information flow, digital media create conditions in which visibility is both expanded and destabilised. Understanding these dynamics is essential for analysing how contemporary publics engage with suffering and crisis in an era defined by constant connectivity.

EMOTIONAL FATIGUE AND COMPASSION BURNOUT IN THE DIGITAL MEDIA LANDSCAPE

The growing visibility of suffering within digital media environments has intensified scholarly interest in the psychological and social consequences of repeated exposure to distressing information. While increased visibility can facilitate awareness and mobilisation, it also places significant emotional demands on audiences. Continuous encounters with images of violence, injustice, grief and crisis may gradually strain the emotional capacities of viewers. It can lead to forms of fatigue that alter how individuals engage with public issues. The concepts of emotional fatigue and compassion burnout offer important frameworks for understanding these dynamics.

Originally developed within the field of trauma psychology, compassion fatigue refers to the emotional exhaustion that arises when individuals are repeatedly exposed to the suffering of others. The concept was initially used to describe the experiences of healthcare workers, humanitarian professionals, and therapists who regularly encounter traumatic narratives in their work. Charles Figley's foundational research on the topic described compassion fatigue as the "cost of caring," emphasising how sustained exposure to trauma can erode emotional resilience and reduce the capacity for empathy (Figley,1995). Although this concept emerged in professional caregiving contexts, scholars have applied it to media audiences who encounter similar narratives of suffering through news coverage and digital platforms.

Within media studies, one of the earliest explorations of this phenomenon was offered by Susan Moeller (1999). She examined how repetitive media coverage of humanitarian crises could lead to declining public engagement. Moeller argued that when audiences are confronted with constant narratives of disaster i.e. famine, war, refugee crises etc. they may initially respond with sympathy and concern. However, as these stories become routine features of the news cycle, emotional responses usually diminish. Rather than mobilising sustained engagement, repeated exposure can produce a sense of helplessness and emotional withdrawal. This pattern is often described as compassion fatigue. It suggests that the effectiveness of emotional appeals may decline as audiences become increasingly accustomed to distressing imagery.

The contemporary digital media environment intensifies these dynamics in several ways. The traditional news consumption occurred at specific times through newspapers or broadcast bulletins. These days Social media platforms expose individuals to distressing information throughout the day. News updates and viral videos circulate within the same digital spaces. It means that users encounter emotionally charged content while engaging in routine online activities. This constant exposure blurs the boundaries between everyday social interaction and the witnessing of traumatic events.

Research on digital news consumption supports the argument that such exposure can have significant emotional consequences. Surveys conducted by the Reuters Institute for the Study of Journalism have repeatedly found that many individuals experience news fatigue. This is a condition characterised by feelings of emotional exhaustion and avoidance toward news content (Newman et al., 2023). In recent editions of the Digital News Report, approximately four in ten respondents reported deliberately avoiding news because it negatively affected their mood. Similar findings have been observed in studies conducted by the Pew Research Center, where respondents indicated that constant exposure to political conflict and distressing imagery on social media contributed to feelings of stress and emotional depletion (Pew Research Center, 2022).

These patterns are particularly important in societies where digital media have become the primary channel for information exchange. In India, for example, social media platforms such as WhatsApp, X (formerly Twitter), Instagram, and Facebook are popular. They function not only as spaces for social interaction but also as major sources of news and political discussion. According to surveys conducted by the Reuters Institute, a substantial proportion of Indian internet users encounter news primarily through social media feeds rather than traditional news outlets (Newman et al., 2023). As a result, exposure to distressing content often occurs within highly personalised and continuous streams of information.

Another factor contributing to emotional fatigue is the repetition of similar crisis narratives. Digital platforms frequently circulate multiple versions of the same incident i.e. news reports, eyewitness videos, commentary threads and reaction posts. This creates an environment where users encounter the same event repeatedly from different perspectives. While this multiplicity of narratives can deepen awareness, it can also intensify emotional saturation. The constant recurrence of traumatic imagery may produce what psychologists describe as desensitisation. It is a process in which repeated exposure reduces emotional responsiveness over time.

Scholars examining the psychological effects of media exposure have documented similar processes in studies of violence and disaster reporting. Research suggests that frequent exposure to graphic or distressing media content can generate feelings of anxiety, stress, and helplessness among viewers (Holman, Garfin, & Silver, 2014). In extreme cases, such exposure may even contribute to symptoms resembling secondary trauma. It happens particularly when audiences identify strongly with the victims portrayed in media narratives. Although most viewers do not experience trauma at this level, the cumulative emotional burden of repeated exposure can nonetheless affect how individuals process public events.

Within digital environments these emotional pressures are further intensified by the rapid pace at which new crises emerge. Social media platforms operate through continuous flows of information. One viral incident is quickly replaced by another. Audiences may therefore move from one emotionally charged event to the next without time to process what they have witnessed. This rapid succession of crises can produce emotional overload where individuals feel overwhelmed by the volume of distressing information available to them.

Emotional overload often leads to coping strategies aimed at protecting psychological well-being. One such strategy is selective disengagement, where individuals intentionally reduce their exposure to distressing news. Studies on media avoidance indicate that many people respond to emotional fatigue by limiting their consumption of news or avoiding particular topics altogether (Skovsgaard & Andersen, 2020). These strategies may help individuals manage stress but they can also have broader implications for democratic engagement. When citizens disengage from public issues due to emotional exhaustion the collective capacity for sustained political discussion may weaken.

The emotional dynamics of digital media consumption also intersect with the broader culture of online expression. Social media platforms encourage users to respond immediately to events through comments and posts. In moments of crisis these responses often take the form of collective expressions of sympathy or outrage. While such expressions can create a sense of solidarity, they may also contribute to "performative empathy" i.e. public displays of concern that do not necessarily translate into sustained action (Chouliaraki, 2013). Over time the repeated performance of such gestures may contribute to a sense of emotional exhaustion as users feel compelled to respond to every new crisis while simultaneously recognising the limitations of these responses.

Understanding emotional fatigue as a social phenomenon therefore requires moving beyond purely psychological explanations. Emotional responses to suffering are shaped not only by individual sensitivities. But they are also shaped by the broader media environments in which people encounter such narratives. Digital platforms with their emphasis on speed and emotional engagement create conditions where audiences are exposed to large volumes of distressing information with limited opportunities for reflection or contextualisation. Under these circumstances emotional fatigue becomes a predictable outcome of the structural organisation of the media environment.Compassion burnout among digital audiences should not be interpreted simply as a failure of empathy. Rather, it reflects the limits of human emotional capacity in environments that continuously demand affective responses. When audiences are confronted with a constant stream of crisis the ability to sustain emotional engagement may gradually decline. The resulting fatigue creates fertile ground for the emergence of affective exhaustion where individuals remain aware of suffering yet feel increasingly detached from it.

Table 2. Digital media exposure and emotional impact

Study	Region	Key Findings
Newman et al. (2023) – Reuters Digital News Report	Global	38–43% of respondents reported avoiding news due to its negative emotional impact.
Pew Research Center (2022)	United States and Global	64% of social media users reported feeling overwhelmed by the amount of distressing news online.
CSDS Media Consumption Study (2022)	India	Large proportion of urban youth encounter news primarily through social media feeds rather than traditional outlets.
Holman, Garfin & Silver (2014)	United States	Repeated exposure to traumatic media images increases stress and anxiety levels among audiences.

FROM EMPATHY TO INDIFFERENCE: THE POLITICS OF AFFECTIVE EXHAUSTION

Emotional fatigue explains the psychological consequences of repeated exposure to suffering it also has broader political implications. In contemporary digital media environments, the constant circulation of distressing narratives does not simply shape individual emotions it transforms the emotional foundations of public engagement. As audiences encounter repeated cycles of outrage and sympathy, the intensity of these reactions often declines over time. Affective exhaustion emerges. It is a state in which individuals remain aware of suffering but feel increasingly unable to respond emotionally.

The concept of affective exhaustion draws on insights from affect theory which emphasizes the collective and political dimensions of emotion. Emotions are not merely personal responses but social forces that shape public life. Sara Ahmed notes that emotions circulate between individuals and institutions, shaping how communities respond to particular issues or events (Ahmed, 2004). In media environments where emotional narratives circulate continuously this circulation can generate collective emotions among people. Yet when such emotional mobilisations occur repeatedly without sustained resolution they may gradually lose their intensity.

This dynamic is particularly visible in the rapid cycles through which public attention operates. Social media platforms enable incidents of injustice or violence to become viral within hours. It produces widespread expressions of anger, grief or solidarity. These emotional responses often appear as hashtags and viral posts condemning the event. However, the attention surrounding such incidents frequently diminishes as quickly as it emerges. Within days or weeks public discourse often shifts toward new topics, leaving earlier crises largely forgotten within the digital timeline. This pattern of rapid emotional mobilisation followed by decline reflects the short attention cycles of networked publics. Digital media environments encourage constant novelty, where the visibility of any single event depends on its ability to compete with an endless stream of other information. As a result crises are often experienced not as long-term social problems but as temporary moments of visibility within the digital attention economy (Tufekci, 2017). The emotional energy generated by these moments may be intense but short-lived.

Affective exhaustion emerges as a key factor shaping public responses to suffering. When audiences are repeatedly exposed to crises that generate intense emotional reactions, they may begin to experience a sense of emotional depletion. Each new incident demands empathy and moral judgment. Yet the rapid succession of events makes it difficult to sustain these responses indefinitely. Individuals may respond by distancing themselves emotionally from distressing content.

This process of emotional distancing should not necessarily be interpreted as apathy or indifference in the traditional sense. It often functions as a coping mechanism that allows individuals to manage the psychological strain which comes with constant exposure to distressing information. Scholars examining media audiences have noted that individuals frequently develop strategies for regulating their emotional engagement with news. These strategies may include limiting exposure to distressing content or avoiding news discussions altogether (Skovsgaard & Andersen, 2020). While such practices may protect individual well-being, they also contribute to broader patterns of disengagement within digital publics.

Another dimension of affective exhaustion relates to the phenomenon of performative empathy. Social media platforms encourage users to publicly express emotional responses to events through reactions or symbolic gestures. During moments of crisis such expressions may take the form of solidarity hashtags or statements condemning violence. While these gestures can create a sense of collective participation, they may also substitute for deeper forms of engagement. As Lilie Chouliaraki (2013) holds that contemporary digital culture often promotes a "post-humanitarian" sensibility in which expressions of sympathy become brief and symbolic rather than sustained commitments to structural change.

Viral incidents frequently generate intense waves of online discussion, drawing attention to issues such as gender violence, caste discrimination, injustice and communal tensions. Yet the longevity of these conversations often remains limited. Public attention shifts rapidly as new events emerge, creating a sequence of emotional episodes rather than continuous engagement with underlying structural problems.

This pattern contributes to the episodic nature of digital empathy. Empathy becomes concentrated around specific incidents rather than sustained social conditions. A particular act of violence may generate widespread outrage yet broader patterns of inequality may receive less attention once the immediate emotional intensity surrounding the incident fades. In this sense hypervisibility can paradoxically obscure the structural dimensions of suffering by focusing attention on isolated events. The political implications of this shift are significant. Democratic societies depend on citizens who are capable of sustained engagement with public issues. When emotional responses to suffering become fragmented and short-lived the capacity for collective action may weaken. Issues that require long-term commitment such as addressing gender inequality, caste discrimination or systemic violence may struggle to maintain public attention in media environments as they are structured around rapid cycles of visibility.

The constant demand for emotional response may contribute to moral fatigue. When individuals feel repeatedly called upon to express outrage or sympathy they may begin to question the effectiveness of such responses. If expressions of concern appear to produce little tangible change audiences may become skeptical about the value of continued engagement. This skepticism can reinforce patterns of disengagement further contributing to affective exhaustion. Affective exhaustion does not imply that individuals become completely indifferent to suffering. Rather, it suggests a shift in how emotions are experienced and expressed within digital publics. Individuals may still recognize the seriousness of social injustices, yet they may feel less capable of responding emotionally to each new incident. The result is a form of detached awareness. Here knowledge of suffering persists even as emotional responsiveness declines.

Within the broader landscape of digital media this shift reflects the tension between visibility and emotional sustainability. While the hypervisibility of suffering can play an important role in exposing injustice and mobilising attention it also generates emotional demands that may exceed the capacities of audiences. When these demands accumulate without opportunities for reflection or meaningful engagement emotional fatigue can evolve into affective exhaustion.

Understanding this process is essential for analysing the evolving relationship between media, emotion and politics in the digital age. The cycles of visibility and disengagement observed in contemporary digital publics suggest that the emotional dynamics of media consumption play a crucial role in shaping patterns of civic participation. Recognising these dynamics allows scholars to move beyond simplistic assumptions that greater visibility automatically produces greater empathy.

CASE ILLUSTRATION

The theoretical discussion on hypervisibility and affective exhaustion becomes clearer when examined through real-world incidents. Across India and other parts of the global south several widely documented events show how digital visibility can generate powerful waves of emotional mobilisation while simultaneously producing patterns of rapid emotional decline. These cases show how the contemporary digital public sphere operates through cycles of intense visibility followed by gradual disengagement.

The 2012 Delhi Gang Rape and the Rise of Networked Outrage

One of the most significant examples of digital visibility shaping public discourse in India emerged in the aftermath of the 2012 Delhi gang rape. It is commonly referred to as the Nirbhaya case. The brutal assault of a young woman in December 2012 triggered widespread national outrage. There were unprecedented protests across several Indian cities. While television news played a major role in covering the incident, social media platforms such as Facebook and Twitter amplified public anger and facilitated rapid mobilisation among young urban populations (Roy, 2014).

Within days of the incident, digital platforms were flooded with expressions of anger and solidarity. Hashtags related to the case circulated widely. Thousands of users shared protest messages and calls for legal reform. Scholars examining the digital response to the event note that online platforms helped transform a localised incident into a national moment of collective mourning and political protest (Banaji & Buckingham, 2013). According to media reports protests took place in more than twenty Indian cities during the weeks following the incident. There was significant participation from students and civil society organizations.

The emotional intensity surrounding the case led to concrete policy changes. In 2013 the Indian government introduced amendments to criminal law related to sexual violence following recommendations made by the Justice Verma Committee (Government of India, 2013). The case therefore demonstrates the positive potential of digital hypervisibility to generate public pressure for institutional reform.

However, scholars also note that the emotional mobilisation surrounding the case gradually declined as media attention shifted toward other issues. Although the incident sparked a broader national conversation about gender violence subsequent cases did not consistently generate the same level of sustained attention. Studies examining media coverage patterns suggest that public outrage surrounding gender violence often follows episodic cycles tied to particular high-profile incidents rather than continuous engagement with structural inequalities (Kapur, 2015). This pattern reflects how digital visibility can concentrate emotional energy around singular events while leaving underlying systemic problems less consistently addressed.

The widespread availability of smartphones has enabled ordinary citizens to record incidents of brutality or communal conflict and share them instantly through social media platforms. Such recordings frequently become viral, drawing national or even international attention to events that might otherwise remain localised. One notable example occurred in 2023 in Manipur, India. Videos depicting the public humiliation and assault of women during ethnic violence circulated widely on social media platforms. The footage generated intense public outrage across India prompting widespread condemnation from civil society groups and political leaders. Within hours of the videos circulating online hashtags related to the incident began trending across multiple platforms and demands for accountability intensified in public discourse. The rapid spread of such content show how digital media can function as tools of citizen witnessing. It enables marginalised communities to document violence and challenge official narratives. Scholars studying digital activism in the global south argue that mobile recording technologies have transformed the politics of visibility by allowing citizens to produce evidence that can circulate globally (Udupa, 2018). In many cases, viral videos have forced authorities to respond to incidents that might otherwise have received limited attention.

The circulation of graphic imagery raises important questions about emotional sustainability. The repeated sharing of traumatic footage can intensify the emotional burden experienced by viewers. Psychological research indicates that exposure to violent imagery through media can contribute to feelings of distress, anxiety, and helplessness particularly when viewers encounter such images repeatedly (Holman, Garfin, & Silver, 2014). In digital environments where users scroll through hundreds of posts daily, these encounters may accumulate rapidly.

Empirical studies on media consumption suggest that such exposure contributes to emotional fatigue among audiences. The Reuters Institute Digital News Report found that 38% of global news consumers reported avoiding news due to its negative impact on their emotional well-being, with similar trends visible in several Asian countries (Newman et al., 2023). These findings indicate that viral images can draw attention to injustice. But they may also contribute to emotional withdrawal among viewers who feel overwhelmed by constant exposure to distressing content.

The dynamics of hypervisibility and emotional fatigue are also evident in the rapid cycles through which online outrage unfolds. Social media platforms encourage immediate responses to breaking events often producing intense but short-lived waves of public engagement. Scholars studying digital communication describe these patterns as "outrage cycles," where public attention peaks rapidly and declines just as quickly as new events capture the spotlight (Tufekci, 2017).Such cycles are frequently observed in cases involving gender violence or communal conflict in India. Viral incidents often generate millions of posts within a short period, yet engagement usually declines after the initial surge of attention. This pattern reflects the broader structure of digital media environments, where algorithmic systems prioritise novelty and continuous engagement.

This dynamic also affects how social movements operate within digital spaces. While online campaigns can attract large audiences quickly, sustaining engagement over time often requires organisational structures beyond social media. Scholars analysing digital activism in India have observed that many online movements experience sharp declines in visibility once the immediate emotional intensity surrounding an incident subsides (Udupa, 2018). As a result, the long-term political impact of digital mobilisation often depends on whether online attention can translate into institutional or grassroots organising.Another consequence of repeated viral incidents is the gradual normalisation of crisis narratives within digital publics. When audiences encounter frequent reports of violence or disaster such events may begin to appear as routine features of the media landscape. This normalisation does not necessarily imply indifference. Rather, it reflects the limits of sustained emotional responsiveness in environments characterised by constant informational flow.

Studies examining media exposure during major crises suggest that repeated encounters with distressing news can alter how individuals perceive risk and responsibility. Research conducted in the aftermath of large-scale disasters indicates that extensive media exposure can amplify emotional stress while simultaneously reducing individuals' sense of agency to respond effectively (Holman et al., 2014). This sense of limited agency may contribute to disengagement as audiences feel that expressions of concern or outrage produce little tangible change.These case illustrations reveal how digital hypervisibility operates within contemporary media ecosystems. Viral incidents can generate powerful waves of emotional mobilisation, drawing attention to injustice and sometimes prompting institutional responses. Yet the same mechanisms that amplify visibility also contribute to emotional saturation as audiences encounter repeated cycles of distressing information.

Understanding these patterns is crucial for analysing the broader politics of emotion in digital societies. The hypervisibility of suffering does not automatically translate into sustained empathy or long-term engagement. Instead it often produces cycles of outrage followed by decline reflecting the structural dynamics of attention within contemporary media environments.

ETHICAL AND POLITICAL IMPLICATIONS: RETHINKING VISIBILITY AND EMOTIONAL SUSTAINABILITY

The discussion so far has explained that while digital media have dramatically expanded the visibility of suffering this hypervisibility often produces unintended emotional consequences. Repeated exposure to distressing narratives can generate emotional fatigue and cycles of disengagement among audiences. These dynamics raise important ethical and political questions regarding how suffering is represented and consumed within contemporary media environments. Addressing these challenges requires reconsidering the responsibilities of journalists and audiences in shaping a more sustainable emotional ecology of public communication.

The ethics of representing suffering has long been debated within media scholarship. Images and narratives of pain possess the capacity to evoke empathy and mobilise public concern yet they also risk reducing victims to spectacles of trauma. Susan Sontag has held that photographs of violence and suffering carry a profound moral ambiguity. While they may provoke compassion, their repeated circulation can also dull emotional sensitivity and normalise the presence of violence within everyday visual culture (Sontag, 2003). In digital environments where images can be endlessly reproduced and shared this tension becomes even more pronounced.

Journalistic institutions therefore face the challenge of balancing visibility with ethical representation. Excessive reliance on graphic imagery may attract attention but can also contribute to emotional overload among audiences. Scholars who are studying humanitarian communication have emphasised the importance of contextual storytelling that situates individual tragedies within broader social and political frameworks (Chouliaraki, 2006). Such approaches move beyond sensationalism by providing audiences with deeper understanding of structural causes and potential avenues for action.

Ethical representation is particularly important when reporting on issues such as gender violence, communal and caste-based conflicts. Media coverage that focuses solely on the sensational aspects of such incidents may inadvertently reinforce stereotypes or perpetuate narratives of victimhood. Conversely, reporting that highlights structural inequalities and institutional accountability can encourage more reflective forms of engagement.While journalistic ethics remain important the contemporary circulation of information is increasingly shaped by the technological architecture of digital platforms. Social media companies play a significant role in determining which stories gain visibility and how they circulate within digital networks. Algorithmic systems designed to maximise user engagement often prioritise emotionally charged content including stories involving violence or outrage.

Critics of the digital attention economy have argued that such systems incentivise the amplification of sensational narratives at the expense of contextual depth. Shoshana Zuboff contends that digital platforms are structured around business models that monetise user attention, encouraging continuous engagement through personalised streams of content (Zuboff, 2019). In such environments, stories that provoke strong emotional reactions particularly anger or shock are more likely to circulate widely.This structural dynamic contributes to the cycles of hypervisibility and emotional fatigue discussed earlier in the chapter. When crises become viral content competing for attention alongside entertainment and advertising, audiences may experience them as part of an endless stream of emotionally demanding information. Addressing this issue therefore requires greater attention to the ethical design of digital platforms.

Scholars and policy experts have increasingly called for greater transparency and accountability in the functioning of algorithmic systems that shape online visibility. Proposals include measures such as clearer disclosure of content ranking practices, stronger moderation policies regarding graphic imagery, and the promotion of diverse forms of public-interest journalism within digital ecosystems (Napoli, 2019). While such reforms remain contested, they highlight the growing recognition that platform design plays a crucial role in shaping the emotional dynamics of digital publics.

One potential response to emotional fatigue involves the development of trauma-sensitive journalism, an approach that emphasises responsible reporting on violence and crisis. Trauma-informed reporting practices seek to minimise harm to victims while also considering the psychological impact of coverage on audiences. Rather than focusing exclusively on sensational details, trauma-sensitive journalism prioritises accuracy and respect for the dignity of those affected by violence.

Media organizations in several countries have begun adopting guidelines that encourage journalists to consider the ethical implications of visual content and narrative framing. For instance, some newsroom policies now recommend limiting the repeated broadcast of graphic footage or providing warnings before distressing images are shown. Such practices aim to maintain public awareness of crises while reducing the risk of emotional desensitisation among audiences.Discussions around ethical reporting have become increasingly prominent following high-profile incidents of gender violence and communal conflict. Media watchdog organisations and journalism scholars have emphasised the importance of reporting that avoids sensationalism while still drawing attention to systemic inequalities (Thakurta, 2015). Such approaches can help shift public discourse from episodic outrage toward sustained engagement with structural issues.

Addressing emotional fatigue also requires reconsidering the role of audiences within digital media environments. Contemporary communication systems often encourage rapid emotional reactions rather than reflective engagement. Social media interfaces are designed to facilitate immediate responses likes, shares, comments. This creates pressure to react quickly to unfolding events. While these features enable widespread participation in public discourse they may also contribute to cycles of performative empathy and emotional exhaustion.Developing more sustainable forms of engagement may involve encouraging slower and more reflective modes of media consumption. Scholars advocating for "slow journalism" argue that audiences benefit from reporting that prioritises depth and context over speed (Le Masurier, 2015). Such approaches can help counter the fragmented nature of digital news cycles by providing space for thoughtful analysis and long-term investigation.

Educational initiatives aimed at strengthening media literacy may also play an important role. By helping audiences understand how algorithms shape information flows and how emotional narratives circulate online, media literacy programs can equip individuals with tools to navigate digital environments more critically. Rather than responding impulsively to every viral incident, audiences may learn to engage more selectively with content while maintaining awareness of broader social issues. The ethical challenges discussed above ultimately intersect with broader questions about democratic participation. Public engagement with social issues depends not only on access to information but also on the emotional capacity to process and respond to that information. When audiences experience emotional fatigue due to constant exposure to crisis the foundations of civic participation may weaken.

Digital visibility continues to play an important role in exposing injustice and amplifying marginalised voices. Movements addressing gender violence, racial inequality, environmental destruction and state repression have often relied on digital platforms to bring attention to issues neglected by traditional media institutions. The challenge is not to reduce visibility but to create conditions in which visibility supports sustained engagement rather than emotional exhaustion. This requires a more nuanced understanding of the relationship between media, emotion and politics. Hypervisibility alone cannot guarantee empathy or action. Instead, meaningful engagement depends on how narratives of suffering are framed, circulated and contextualised within public discourse. Media institutions, digital platforms and audiences all share responsibility for shaping these dynamics. Recognising the emotional limits of audiences does not imply abandoning the ethical imperative to bear witness to suffering. Rather it calls for more thoughtful approaches to representation and communication. Such approaches that acknowledge the psychological and social consequences of constant exposure to crisis narratives. By promoting contextual reporting, responsible platform design and reflective forms of engagement it may be possible to mitigate the risks of emotional fatigue while preserving the democratic potential of digital visibility.

CONCLUSION

The rapid expansion of digital media has profoundly transformed how societies encounter suffering and crisis. Events that once remained localised now circulate globally within seconds, carried through networks of social media platforms and digital news infrastructures. At first glance, such unprecedented visibility appears to strengthen the ethical potential of media by making injustice more difficult to ignore. Yet the analysis developed in this chapter suggests a more complex and paradoxical reality. While digital platforms have dramatically expanded the visibility of suffering, the constant circulation of emotionally charged narratives can also generate conditions of emotional fatigue and affective exhaustion among audiences.

Based on insights from affect theory, media studies, and research on compassion fatigue the chapter has argued that the contemporary digital public sphere operates through cycles of emotional mobilisation and eventual disengagement. Theoretical perspectives from scholars such as Sara Ahmed emphasise that emotions circulate socially, shaping collective responses to political events (Ahmed, 2004). When distressing narratives are repeatedly circulated across media platforms the emotional intensities associated with these narratives may gradually diminish. What begins as outrage or compassion can evolve into emotional saturation where audiences feel overwhelmed by the continuous demand for affective response.

The emergence of emotional fatigue among audiences should not be interpreted simply as indifference or moral failure. Rather, it reflects the limits of human emotional capacity within media environments that continuously demand attention and empathy. In contexts where individuals encounter multiple crises within a single news cycle, emotional withdrawal may function as a coping strategy that protects psychological well-being. But this withdrawal also carries broader implications for democratic engagement. When citizens disengage from public issues due to emotional exhaustion the capacity for sustained collective action may weaken.

These dynamics raise important ethical and political questions for contemporary media systems. Journalistic institutions, digital platforms, and audiences all play roles in shaping how suffering is represented and circulated. Responsible reporting that prioritises greater transparency in algorithmic systems governing online visibility and media literacy initiatives that encourage reflective engagement can all contribute to a more sustainable emotional ecology of public communication.

The challenge facing contemporary media societies is not simply how to make suffering visible. Rather it is how to ensure that visibility fosters meaningful engagement rather than emotional exhaustion. In the rapidly expanding digital publics where online platforms increasingly shape political discourse understanding the emotional consequences of hypervisibility is crucial. Future research may further explore how digital media can balance the imperative to bear witness to injustice with the need to sustain the emotional capacities that make empathy and collective action possible.

REFERENCES

Ahmed, S. (2004). *The cultural politics of emotion*. Edinburgh University Press.

Banaji, S., & Buckingham, D. (2013). *The civic web: Young people, the internet, and civic participation*. MIT Press. DOI: 10.7551/mitpress/8949.001.0001

Benkler, Y. (2006). *The wealth of networks: How social production transforms markets and freedom*. Yale University Press.

Berger, J., & Milkman, K. (2012). What makes online content viral? *JMR, Journal of Marketing Research, 49*(2), 192–205. DOI: 10.1509/jmr.10.0353

Boltanski, L. (1999). *Distant suffering: Morality, media and politics*. Cambridge University Press. DOI: 10.1017/CBO9780511489402

Centre for the Study of Developing Societies (CSDS). (2022). *Media consumption and trust survey*. CSDS.

Chouliaraki, L. (2006). The spectatorship of suffering. *Sage (Atlanta, Ga.)*.

Chouliaraki, L. (2013). *The ironic spectator: Solidarity in the age of post-humanitarianism*. Polity Press.

Figley, C. (1995). *Compassion fatigue: Coping with secondary traumatic stress disorder in those who treat the traumatized*. Brunner/Mazel.

Government of India. (2013). *Report of the Justice Verma Committee on amendments to criminal law*. Government of India.

Holman, E., Garfin, D., & Silver, R. (2014). Media's role in broadcasting acute stress following collective trauma. *Proceedings of the National Academy of Sciences of the United States of America, 111*(1), 93–98. DOI: 10.1073/pnas.1316265110 PMID: 24324161

Internet and Mobile Association of India. (2023). *Digital in India report*. IAMAI.

Kapur, R. (2015). Gender, violence, and the law in India. *Social & Legal Studies, 24*(3), 375–398.

Le Masurier, M. (2015). What is slow journalism? *Journalism Practice, 9*(2), 138–152. DOI: 10.1080/17512786.2014.916471

Massumi, B. (2002). *Parables for the virtual: Movement, affect, sensation*. Duke University Press.

Moeller, S. (1999). *Compassion fatigue: How the media sell disease, famine, war and death.* Routledge.

Napoli, P. (2019). *Social media and the public interest: Media regulation in the disinformation age.* Columbia University Press. DOI: 10.7312/napo18454

Newman, N., Fletcher, R., Eddy, K., Robertson, C., & Nielsen, R. (2023). *Reuters Institute digital news report 2023.* Reuters Institute for the Study of Journalism.

Papacharissi, Z. (2015). *Affective publics: Sentiment, technology, and politics.* Oxford University Press.

Pew Research Center. (2022). *News consumption across social media platforms.* Pew Research Center.

Roy, S. (2014). The Delhi gang rape: The making of a global feminist issue. *Feminist Studies, 40*(2), 282–292.

Skovsgaard, M., & Andersen, K. (2020). Conceptualizing news avoidance. *Journalism Studies, 21*(4), 459–476. DOI: 10.1080/1461670X.2019.1686410

Sontag, S. (2003). *Regarding the pain of others.* Farrar, Straus and Giroux. DOI: 10.3917/dio.201.0127

Thakurta, P. (2015). *Media ethics and accountability in India.* Oxford University Press.

Tufekci, Z. (2017). *Twitter and tear gas: The power and fragility of networked protest.* Yale University Press.

Udupa, S. (2018). Digital media and politics in India. *International Journal of Communication, 12*, 25–45.

Zuboff, S. (2019). *The age of surveillance capitalism.* PublicAffairs.

KEY TERMS AND DEFINITIONS

Affective Exhaustion: It is a deeper stage of emotional fatigue in which individuals withdraw from engaging with public issues altogether. It is often as a coping mechanism in response to persistent emotional demands.

Affective Publics: It is networked groups of individuals who are temporarily connected through shared emotional responses such as outrage or empathy. These responses are expressed and amplified through digital media platforms.

Affective Saturation: It is a state in which continuous exposure to emotionally charged content overwhelms an individual's capacity to process and respond. It leads to diminished sensitivity over time.

Algorithmic Amplification: It is the process through which digital platforms prioritise and circulate content based on engagement metrics. It often elevates emotionally intense or sensational material.

Compassion Fatigue: It is a gradual reduction in empathetic response resulting from repeated exposure to narratives of suffering. Here individuals begin to disengage as a way of managing emotional strain.

Digital Witnessing: It is the act of recording and engaging with real-time events through digital devices enabling individuals to participate in the documentation and circulation of social realities.

Emotional Amplification: It is the process by which digital media technologies intensify emotional reactions to events. It is done through viral sharing, algorithmic promotion, and collective engagement.

Hypervisibility: It is a condition in which events are intensely and repeatedly circulated across digital media platforms making them highly visible to large audiences in real time.

Social Indifference: It is a condition marked by reduced collective responsiveness to injustice or crisis where repeated exposure leads to normalisation and episodic rather than sustained engagement.

Chapter 7
Emotional Fatigue in the Age of Hyperconnectivity:
Algorithmic Affects, Digital Burnout, and the Rise of Social Indifference

Muhammad Usman Tariq
http://orcid.org/0000-0002-7605-3040
Abu Dhabi University, UAE & University College Cork, Ireland

ABSTRACT

Hyperconnectivity has altered the way people feel by making them more exposed, faster, and more prone to comparing themselves to others. This study examines emotional fatigue as an issue caused by the way algorithms work, not because humans are weak. It uses concepts such as media theory, emotions, and revenue generation to describe how algorithms that encourage users to interact create feelings of perpetual excitement, moral obligation, and the need to always be responsive. Eventually, this leads to something called digital burnout, which manifests as feelings of numbness, withdrawal, and reduced capacity for empathy. This study argues that burnout does not just make one tired; it changes the way one feels about being social, hence causing increased social indifference. As one becomes divided in their attention and is always required to produce emotions, they begin to develop an emotional barrier to shield themselves from the pressure. However, this barrier has broader societal consequences, such as making society less united and less empathetic.

DOI: 10.4018/979-8-3373-8307-1.ch007

INTRODUCTION

From the time people wake up in the morning to the time they put down their devices, which is never, they are constantly surrounded by content that evokes strong emotions. News notifications bring to their attention all the problems happening all over the world, social media combines anger and love, and these media use algorithms to keep their users engaged with whatever is shocking and interesting. Unlike traditional means of information sharing, digital media not only provide people with news but also require them to respond emotionally. This eventually results in a phenomenon called emotional saturation, in which people are exposed to more emotional content than they can deal with. Digital platforms are designed to keep people engaged and reward strong emotions far more than thoughtful ones. Content that evokes anger, fear, distress, or other strong emotions has a better chance of being shared because it keeps people engaged and interested in the content (Hadi, 2025). As a result, people are exposed to content that can range from personal experiences to major world events, trivial to catastrophic, all within a single scroll. A person might see their friend's positive post, disturbing images, political debates, a fundraiser, and a memory resurfaced because of algorithms. The combination of these emotions, referred to as emotional whiplash, leaves people with little time to think or relax. Instead, emotions compound on each other until feeling itself becomes exhausting. In contrast, in digital culture, emotional engagement is considered a responsibility.

To be aware means being emotionally engaged, and being silent means that one does not care. Having empathy, being angry, or showing support are ways of proving that one is a member of the group, especially in the face of major issues. While these are good ways of creating awareness and engaging people, they also create pressure on individuals to care about problems that they cannot solve individually (Kamraju, 2025). The difference between being emotionally engaged and being able to act increases, and people feel helpless. When people are asked to care but cannot help, caring becomes something that takes from them rather than giving. This is an odd state because, although people are very connected, they still feel disconnected, numb, and uninvolved with larger issues. Although they have access to so much information and people, they can still feel stuck and emotionally drained. What used to make people angry or feel sorry for others slowly becomes normal, expected, and easy to overlook. This does not mean that people do not care; it is simply a way of protecting oneself from being overwhelmed by the need to care and feel in the digital world. Indifference can be a coping mechanism for dealing with the pressure to care and feel. This paradox is observed if one considers hyperconnectivity not just as being connected, but as being always available.

Digital platforms create a sense that one is always able to respond. There are messages that require quick responses, news that is always breaking, and social issues that come and go quickly. There is no time to think or become involved in anything long-term. As everything is always urgent, nothing is ever really urgent for a long time. Feelings are replaced by new content; therefore, there is no actual care, just cycles of feeling. Eventually, one might not care about things not because one does not care, but because it is just too much to be bothered with. In this sense, social indifference is not the same as a lack of care (Ciocîrlea, 2025). It is often not a lack of interest but a kind of disengagement, distance, or quiet withdrawal. People may continue to use social media but do not feel emotionally involved, scrolling through sad stories with calm indifference or responding with humor and jokes. Memes, sarcasm, and dark humor help them cope with their sadness, but in a way that, in the short term, it affects the way they perceive and respond to actual problems, and it becomes difficult to distinguish between what is serious and what is just for entertainment. However, it is important to note that not all people experience the emergence of social indifference similarly.

For instance, people who have already been treated unfairly may feel the saturation of emotions more than others, especially when their lives and struggles are already discussed online. Conversely, privileged people may view social indifference as a choice, which is convenient and avoids problems that they are less likely to face. This shows that it is not possible to view disengagement as laziness, as it is influenced by the digital world. The emotional patterns of digital life affect how people think about helping one another. If emotional expression is rewarded with quick praise and popularity, it may become a performance, making it difficult for people to connect their emotions with responsibility. This may eventually lead people to become distrustful of teamwork and cynical about being involved in it. In this type of setting, it does not occur suddenly that one does not care; rather, it builds up gradually over time. It builds up because people feel that they have been really engaged and then suddenly disappointed, which makes it difficult for them to care as much as they should (Hadi, 2025). Users, whether they realize it or not, start to limit the amount that they care, choose to distance themselves from the situation, or pretend that they do not really care when, in fact, they do. What started as a protective measure slowly became a habit, which affected the way people expected one another to care and react. As many things fail to get the right amount of attention because they do not feel important enough, it becomes difficult for people to care deeply, even when it really matters. When we consider these two issues of emotional burnout and social indifference together, we begin to think less about blaming individuals and more about the bigger picture of the problem.

Rather than wondering what is the matter with people these days and why they do not care anymore, we need to think about how technology affects the way we feel, what it expects of us, and what it prevents us from doing. Being connected all the time is supposed to bring us closer together, make us more aware of our world, and allow us to participate in it (Sun et al., 2025). However, it ends up tearing us apart, wearing us out, and driving us away from one another. Therefore, the real question is not how we can connect more, but how we think about what connects us in the first place and how we can use technology to connect us without draining our emotions in the process. Table 1 provides an overview of the core emotional dynamics.

Table 1. Core emotional dynamics of hyperconnected digital environments

Digital Condition	Platform Mechanism	Emotional Outcome	Behavioural Consequence	Long-Term Social Effect
Emotional saturation	Continuous exposure to emotionally charged content	Emotional overload	Reduced reflective processing	Compassion fatigue
Emotional whiplash	Rapid switching between conflicting content	Cognitive-emotional instability	Shortened attention span	Normalisation of crisis
Hyperconnectivity	Constant notifications and availability expectations	Persistent psychological alertness	Difficulty disengaging	Chronic exhaustion
Algorithmic amplification	Promotion of high-arousal content	Intensified emotional reactions	Reactive engagement	Polarisation and volatility
Performance of empathy	Social validation through visible responses	Pressure to display emotion	Emotional self-monitoring	Emotional commodification
Information abundance	Infinite scrolling environments	Emotional numbness	Passive consumption	Social indifference

AFFECTIVE CAPITALISM AND THE ATTENTION ECONOMY

Happiness, anger, fear, and compassion keep users engaged, clicking, and returning, as these emotions can be used to profit. Emotions such as joy, anger, fear, desire, and empathy are used to obtain value, often hidden in ad systems and the way algorithms work. Thus, emotions become a form of work, something that is done unknowingly. Unlike regular work, this type of emotional labor is unpaid and does not occur in one place (Bondanini et al., 2025). Users will eventually learn, unbeknownst to them, that more emotion is better. Posts that exhibit anger, sadness, and moral concern receive more visibility than those that exhibit thoughtfulness. Ultimately, these platforms will alter how people interact with one another, forcing them to exhibit their emotions in a way that can be understood, rather than in a necessarily complex manner. In this system, crises have a lot of power to attract attention.

In digital platforms, crises are fueled by a sense of urgency and provide a constant supply of emotional content. Political, natural, health, and social crises are presented along with personal crises through the same digital platforms. The line between large-scale crises of large proportions and personal crises is blurred in the feed, as everything requires an instant emotional response (Kamraju, 2025). This does not lead to understanding or action but rather to a sense of being in a perpetual crisis, as users are on high alert but do not know how to respond to the crisis. The presentation of the data also helps clarify this be made more clear. Users are encouraged to feel deeply but briefly. Eventually, too many crises result in compassion fatigue, which is when the ability to empathize becomes exhausted due to too much suffering.

When there are too many emotional demands each day, one might feel tired or numb. Compassion fatigue does not mean that one is bad at empathizing; rather, it means that one has had too much emotional stress (Hadi, 2025). The attention economy thrives on new things and strong emotions, which have limits. As each new crisis unfolds, users must choose what to care about and what to ignore. The ability to choose can result in indifference, not because the suffering is unimportant but because it is everywhere. Affective capitalism relies on this balance between the two.

Platforms benefit from emotions and emotional burnout, as both encourage users to stay in one way or another. Emotions such as anger cause users to stay and be engaged, while burnout leads them to stay and look, although they are not responding. Not wanting to care is also used for profit; as long as users are looking, the advertisements are functioning, and data are being provided. Emotions are increasingly made into something that is outside the self, measurable, and validated through the responses of the platforms. Emotional experiences are given meaning through being seen and responded to, which means that personal feelings are dependent on public validation (Paredes-Labra et al., 2025). This could encourage people to express their feelings more, as they learn to do so in a way that elicits the most response and approval. However, this could also make people feel disconnected from their feelings, which are seen as working or tired of being overused. The increasing normalcy of a constant crisis also affects people's emotional state. When crises are part of digital life, they do not have the ability to make people act. Instead, crises become a constant background, and people's attention is divided. People can quickly go from being engaged to disengaged and may find it difficult to concentrate on one thing at a time. This makes it difficult for people to come together in support, as crises change quickly and problems are left behind when they no longer capture the algorithm's attention. This understanding of platforms as systems of emotions reveals that compassion fatigue is not just about the person's mind or emotions; it is also about the way in which attention is used as a resource in the current digital world. These online platforms are designed to stimulate emotions quickly and permanently, not to promote long-term emotional well-being. They take advantage of our emotions but are not designed to allow us to take breaks, think, or feel better. It is natural to feel burned out. The only way to solve this is not to simply tell people to care more or to tell them to use their phones less, but to really think about the way in which emotions are shared and used in the current economy and think about new ways in which people can care without being burned out.

ALGORITHMIC PERSONALISATION AND AUTOMATED INDIFFERENCE

Algorithmic personalization is one of the most powerful but least noticeable forces that shapes people's emotions. These systems constantly change, sort, and suggest what should be displayed to users. Not only do they determine what people see, but they also determine the type of emotions people feel while using these systems. The systems learn from the actions that people perform, such as the things they click on, the time spent on the systems, and their responses. The systems then use this information to make an educated guess about what will hold the user's attention. Over time, users will only see the things that make them feel comfortable, even though that is the way they were created. The end result is that emotions are repeated and reinforced, although users are unaware of it, which makes them feel natural. Personalization occurs through repetition and increasing intensity. Emotional content is more likely to be repeated, creating a cycle in which certain emotions dominate a person's feed. Emotions such as anger, fear, outrage, and love are more likely to spread than uncertain or calm emotions because they always keep a person interested (Kamraju, 2025). The more a person is exposed to certain emotions, the more familiar they become. What once shocked a person or made them think about something now becomes normal for them, and what once took them a while to process now becomes something they can process quickly. However, this does not mean that people no longer care about what they see; rather, it means that their emotional limits change because of what they constantly see. Algorithms not only show people what they like but also train their emotions. This leads to automated indifference.

When algorithms are set up to keep people engaged, they are more likely to look for quick and easy responses rather than looking deeper into the meaning of the content. The content is chosen based on what is likely to elicit a response from people, not what is ethical or meaningful. The line between tragedy and entertainment is the same as long as the content gets people's attention. Over time, this leads people to be unable to distinguish between what is worth the time and what is not.

People might not look away from suffering because they are indifferent; rather, the system has conditioned them to look away quickly, respond quickly, and move on quickly. Indifference is something that is done automatically rather than something that people have to choose. The emotional impact of algorithmic content curation extends beyond individuals (Ciocîrlea, 2025). Emotions are said to spread among groups of people, which means that emotions are shared by many people who are not aware of each other. This leads to the sharing of emotions among many individuals. The sharing of emotions leads to trends and emotional waves. This sharing of emotions makes people feel the same emotions. These include emotions such as joy, anger, fear, and sadness. This sharing of emotions brings people closer. It also leads to emotional highs and lows. Emotions are said to spread faster than understanding. Emotions are said to overpower understanding. The rate at which emotions are shared does not allow people to think deeply about them. This leads people to simply react to the situation. Collective feelings under algorithmic conditions are neither stable nor static.

Attention can quickly shift from one topic to another as the algorithm changes its attention span. What may be considered important today may be irrelevant tomorrow, replaced by another feeling or topic. This can be disorienting and make it difficult to maintain long-term goals (Ruggieri & Mollo, 2025). For those with ongoing issues and problems, it can feel as if one has been forgotten when attention is suddenly withdrawn and focused on something else, such as new and exciting things instead of long and tedious problems and efforts. The politics of attention is important in this situation.

Algorithms are not merely tools; they reflect what the system deems worthy of attention, feeling, and care. This reflects what the system considers important and what it does not. When the emotional level decides what is important, complex or detailed problems cannot easily receive the required attention. This creates a skewed view of the problems, with dramatic stories receiving more attention than the details. In the end, the problems are addressed but not solved. Emotional contagion under algorithmic control is also related to power (Márquez et al., 2026). Some voices and emotions are louder, while others are drowned out, depending on their level of association with the preferred emotions of the system. Information that resonates with the preferred emotions of the system is easily shared, whereas information that demands understanding and patience is difficult to share. This makes it difficult for groups whose emotions cannot be shared quickly and efficiently to communicate. Simultaneously, the system increases the division among users, as information that evokes emotions makes users loyal only to their own group and look down upon others. Emotions are divided, with no common ground. Automated indifference is also assisted by the amount of available content. Because the feeds are always full and updated, there is no end that signals when to stop. Emotional experiences are not resolved; therefore, they are left open and quickly pushed out. This is what makes people skim over things, as it feels like a waste of time to be on one issue. People learn to save energy by moving away from, skipping, or not responding to prompts. What looks like a lack of caring is actually a way to save energy in a system that does not allow for deep engagement. The personalization of emotions also has implications for how individuals perceive themselves.

As algorithms portray and repeat similar emotions, individuals may perceive certain emotions as natural or inherent. This could lead individuals to perceive themselves as having these emotions because they are constantly portrayed by the algorithm. This could lead to a restricted emotional response, as individuals are less likely to think beyond the boundaries of their emotions (Anggara & Rahmasari, 2025). This would result in their emotional lives being more predictable and less dynamic, as required by the system. Recognizing the role that algorithms play with emotions helps us realize that we can feel indifferent, but we do not mean to. No one consciously decides that they do not care anymore; it is because we have been surrounded by systems that are focused on reactions, on getting things done quickly, and on emotions, rather than on building relationships and connections that last. Indifference is a political issue, and it is one that we manage through the way that we pay attention to things in the digital world. If we are going to address it, we have to do more than realize the problem ourselves; we have to think together about the role that emotions play, how we manage, share, and control emotions in the digital world, and how different systems can help us keep our emotions and not lose them.

DIGITAL BURNOUT AND COPING MECHANISMS

Digital burnout is very common in today's world, which is always online and connected. The need to always be available and process large amounts of information creates great strain on our minds. We are distracted by many notifications, fighting for the attention of many websites, and unsure what is work, play, and rest. In the end, this leads to something called "attention collapse," which is the slow degradation of the capacity to focus, make judgments about what is important, or become deeply engaged. Instead of being overwhelmed by short bursts of work, we feel a general sense of fatigue, even when performing the simplest tasks. This problem has worsened during the COVID-19 pandemic. We spend most of our time on the Internet working, socializing, keeping up with the news, and coping with our own stress. Screens have dominated all our activities, and we can hardly know where we are and when. News about the pandemic, fears about our health, concerns about the economy, and feelings of loneliness have all occurred simultaneously (Ruggieri & Mollo, 2025). This has resulted in a state of high alert with little time for rest.

Pandemic fatigue was not just about fear and despair; it was about being informed, responsive, and emotionally available when we did not know what to expect. It could have been manageable if it had ended after a while, but it did not. The fact that we are always connected makes this exhaustion worse, as we are never really given time to relax.

The fact that we are always connected with our phones and other devices means that we are always "on" whenever we are waiting, resting, or sleeping. The fact that something is always going on, whether it is another message, update, or crisis, makes us feel like we are always in a state of urgency. Even when we are not actively using our devices, the fact that something could be going on at any moment takes up mental space (Hadi, 2025). This constant state of low-level alertness is exhausting, leaving us with no emotional space to think deeply about anything else. Burnout is no longer just the result of being busy, but the fact that we are never allowed to be idle. As our emotional and mental energy is used up, people find ways to cope with stress.

One way to cope with stress is through the use of memes, humor, and irony. These allow people to identify with difficult situations without feeling overwhelmed by their emotions (Chmiel & Kurpas, 2025). By creating humor around emotions such as anxiety, anger, or even sadness, people manage to create a gap between themselves and those emotions. Memes make it easier to understand complex emotions by putting them in a familiar package and creating a sense of connection to those emotions through shared experiences. Laughter becomes a way to survive situations that feel too difficult to cope with. Irony, above all, becomes a protective way of dealing with difficult situations in the novel. By being distant or aware, people can speak about difficult issues without revealing too much of their vulnerability. Irony demonstrates that a person does not remain naïve and understands the unfairness or nonsense of the situation. Such thinking allows people to feel connected to others with similar opinions. Simultaneously, irony helps people manage the emotions they are exposed to, allowing them to remain involved without feeling overwhelmed. It becomes a way of carefully caring for a place that requires emotions all the time. Disengagement is another coping mechanism, although it also tends to occur in small ways. Rather than fully disengaging, people may not care as much, scroll through, or avoid certain topics. This small way of disengaging allows people to remain involved but in a way that makes them feel less drained. It is not always about people being against social issues; it is about finding ways to cope when there is always something demanding attention. The feeling of having to constantly have attention pulled towards them makes disengaging feel like the only option. Humor and disengagement are often coupled.

Burnout, exhaustion, and hopelessness are common, and as a result, these emotions become normalized and less intense. Humor of this nature can be very comforting because it reminds people that they are not alone in their feelings of being overwhelmed by the pandemic. This humor can take a personal experience of fatigue and make it a shared experience in the culture. However, it can also mask the seriousness of pain, making exhaustion seem less significant or even humorous. When burnout is treated as a joke, it prevents people from recognizing it as a problem that needs to be solved. Although these coping strategies are beneficial, they have a double edge (Okhueleigbe & Omoko, 2025). While they offer people a sense of relief, connection, and control in situations that may seem beyond their control, they may also cause people to become emotionally distant. Being sincere may seem too dangerous when irony has become a habit of the speaker. Similarly, being engaged may seem too hard when disconnection has become normal. The quick fixes that allow people to cope with their digital lives may, in fact, cause them to become unable to focus and care about anything. The fact that burnout is a normal response makes it worse. The fact that fatigue is a personal failure in managing time or emotions, rather than a response to a system that asks for too much, means that the true causes of burnout are not addressed, and blame is placed on the individual rather than on the design of the virtual space. In a world where everyone is always tired, conserving energy is a top priority, even if it means shallowness and inconsistency in the content. By recognizing memes, humor, irony, and disengagement as coping strategies, it is clear that people are creative in dealing with digital overload.

These strategies are not only indicative of people being cynical or uncaring; they are ways of trying to make life manageable under heavy pressure (Ejaz & Khaliq, 2025). However, they also reflect the price paid in an environment that does not provide much peace, thinking, or real closure. Digital burnout is not only an issue that affects the individual but is also a collective experience influenced by systems that are hungry for constant attention and provide little support for recovery. To address this issue, it is important to find ways to cope better and rethink how digital life is organized so that connection is not at the expense of emotional well-being. Table 2 provides an overview of digital emotional strain.

Table 2. Digital emotional strain: Mechanisms, impacts, and coping responses

Digital System Feature	Psychological Impact	Emotional State Produced	Common Coping Strategy	Potential Risk
Constant connectivity	Attention fragmentation	Mental fatigue	Selective disengagement	Reduced civic participation
Crisis-driven feeds	Compassion overload	Emotional exhaustion	Emotional distancing	Normalised indifference
Algorithmic personalisation	Emotional repetition	Desensitisation	Passive scrolling	Automated disengagement

continued on following page

Table 2. Continued

Digital System Feature	Psychological Impact	Emotional State Produced	Common Coping Strategy	Potential Risk
Performance pressure online	Identity strain	Anxiety and self-monitoring	Irony and humour	Emotional inauthenticity
Visibility metrics (likes/shares)	External validation dependency	Self-comparison stress	Curated self-presentation	Reduced emotional autonomy
Information acceleration	Lack of emotional closure	Cognitive overload	Memes and satire	Trivialisation of serious issues

EMOTIONAL LABOUR, AUTHENTICITY, AND BRANDING

Influencers are expected to look friendly, open, vulnerable, positive, consistent, and appealing. This mix of emotions makes emotional expression look like work, in which constant checking and controlling are necessary to meet the demands of what people want and what the platform requires (Ruggieri & Mollo, 2025). This places tremendous pressure on those who depend on their online image to earn a living. However, this type of emotional expression is not reserved for influencers.

Ordinary users also attempt to express themselves in ways that can be easily understood emotionally by using universal themes such as happiness, strength, hard work, and growth. Struggling themes are expressed as success stories or improvements, which resonate with the larger cultural narrative. In this setting, emotions are expressed as content, and inner emotions are shared with the public. There is pressure to always look good and okay, which can exclude some emotions, such as doubt, anger, and tiredness, which do not fit well with positive engagement. Emotional labor on social media is also invisible because it is considered self-expression or community building rather than actual work. For example, responding to comments, maintaining pretend friendships, and dealing with people's expectations all require emotional work. Influencers are expected to be friendly, grateful, and responsive, even when dealing with negative comments or hurtful messages (Bondanini et al., 2026). This is made more difficult by algorithms that reward posting and interacting as much as possible. Taking a break or stepping back emotionally can mean less visibility, which creates a system in which taking a break is risky for pay. Emotional availability is part of the job, even when it is painful. The concept of selling well-being adds another layer.

Well-being has become something to show off and improve rather than a natural and ongoing state. Mental health issues have become opportunities for personal growth, shopping, and brand building. This pressure to sell well-being creates even more pressure on content creators. To remain relevant, influencers must not only deal with their own emotions but also teach their audience to deal with their own emotions. Influencers have to be strong, positive, or mindful, even when they are having a terrible time (Argyriadi et al., 2025). There is pressure on those who follow to look at their own emotions in comparison to what has been demonstrated in these examples, comparing themselves to ideal ways of dealing with emotions and taking care of themselves. This creates a sense of not being good enough, especially if what is going on in their life does not match the "happy ending" of the story. The focus on dealing with emotions may also cause people to forget about broader issues in society and believe that it is all about their individual efforts to take care of themselves, not about broader systems. Brand deals combine emotions and money.

Influencers are asked to combine brand products with their own experiences, making it difficult to distinguish between their advice and advertisements. Emotional trust is valuable and can be used to sell products, such as comfort, confidence, or self-improvement. The maintenance of emotional trust requires emotional control, as being too commercial makes people think that one is not sincere. Influencers are required to express genuine emotions and participate in the market. This cost is evident in conversations about burnout among creators (Paredes-Labra et al., 2025). This pressure to always be available, relatable, and productive means that there is no time to have personal feelings or take time off. When identity and money are tied together, burnout is not just about mental health but also about financial security. Time off means losing personal connections with patients. This is the instability of the systems that support emotional work, where showing emotions is valued, but when one runs out of emotions, it is not. Despite these challenges, the idea of being "real" remains popular because it offers the prospect of connection in a world that may seem superficial or unmanageable. There is a desire for emotional connection, and creators are trying to deliver that within the parameters of the platform system. Without altering the way digital work is organized and compensated, emotional expression will continue to be a resource to be used despite its celebration as a form of freedom.

POLITICAL APATHY AND ACTIVISM FATIGUE

Political apathy and a feeling of being tired of activism have become more prevalent in today's digital age. This is not a result of people not caring but rather of being emotionally exhausted. Digital activism began with the notion that it would be easy to participate in, that it would be quick, and that it would bring people together. Social media allows people to witness unjust things happening in real time, get help quickly, and reach people regardless of their location. However, it was the same aspect that made activism quick that made it more difficult for people to emotionally cope with it. Political issues are always arising, and they are always represented as being critical and significant. This means that there is no time to rest between critical situations. Over time, this affects the way people feel about politics, transforming concern into fatigue and involvement into obligation (Bear et al., 2025). The emotional fatigue of digital activism is linked to the idea that crises are the norm in the digital world. In the digital world, crises are the standard means of discussing political issues. Wars, natural disasters, climate change, violence, and the erosion of democracy are all crises that require immediate action. Algorithms are designed such that the most alarming content is the first thing that is shown. This creates the idea that there is no end to problems and that they are never resolved. When everything is considered critical, people become fatigued. They are asked to consider many things simultaneously. This constant flow of information creates a sense of helplessness.

Digital activism makes people show their support by sharing, posting, and demonstrating that they care about a cause. This may be important; however, it does not necessarily bring about change. The lack of change after repeatedly showing that one is angry or that one cares makes people feel frustrated. The difference between caring and seeing results increases, and people begin to wonder if it makes any difference at all (Ejaz & Khaliq, 2025). Eventually, this lack of hope makes people believe that it is wise to step back. Activism fatigue is exacerbated by the notion that it is a moral obligation to pay attention. In the online world, being informed and feeling are positive things. Not speaking out could mean being unhelpful or uncaring about the patient. This is what causes people to always be aware of what is going on politically, even when they do not have much emotional reserve left. Being judged or excluded keeps people engaged; however, when it is out of guilt rather than hope, it becomes difficult to continue. When the price of being involved becomes higher than the benefit, taking a break becomes a way to care for oneself. Algorithms play a significant role in this process.

They target content that triggers strong emotions, such as anger, fear, or urgency. Political content is presented in its most emotional form, without much complexity, to make it seem more urgent. This causes people to quickly shift from one political topic to another without time to think. Their attention is divided, and their grasp of politics remains superficial. When people are repeatedly exposed to the same strong emotions, they become less responsive, and this occurs out of habit rather than choice. Algorithmic exhaustion refers to the state in which people feel stuck. Feeds are constantly refreshed, and political crises occur one after the other (Ruggieri & Mollo, 2025). There is no end, and people feel that their attention does not lead to any change. Rather than building towards shared goals, political attention is fragmented into brief, intense periods. For many, it results in a sort of apathy, not because they do not believe in justice, but because they are too exhausted to care about anything else. The normalizing of crises also changes people's expectations about politics.

If crises and instability are always present, they cannot inspire people to act. This is because urgency becomes the new normal and outrage becomes meaningless. A person may still look at politics on social media but does not care about anything. This does not mean that the person has become apathetic; rather, it means that the person has learned to deal with the crisis by choosing to care about some things and not others (Maulida et al., 2025). In a world where everything is urgent, not caring about everything is the only way to remain sane. Taking a step back may be the only way to regain control in situations perceived as overwhelming. The emotional toll of digital activism is not equally felt. For those who are already treated unfairly in society, it might be even worse because their issues are constantly displayed online. For this group of people, it is not that they are choosing to disengage, but it might be a way to cope with what is happening in their lives. On the other hand, it might be very easy to disengage for those who are privileged, and this makes it even harder to see disengagement as a moral failing because it shows that some people are forced to disengage while others are forced to engage. Activism fatigue also demonstrates a shift in the experience of politics. Digital media are designed to respond quickly, with emotion rather than planning or organization. Although these moments of "viral" activism are very influential, they are difficult to sustain without supportive structures. When activism is built on emotions, fatigue occurs rapidly. Individuals are left to carry the burden of the group's struggle without receiving the support they need, resulting in high engagement, followed by high disengagement. Understanding political apathy and activism fatigue requires looking beyond individuals. Digital media are designed to respond quickly, with emotion rather than planning or organization. In this environment, disengagement is not simply a product of a lack of interest; rather, it is a result of a system that exhausts students' emotional engagement. Individuals do not disengage because they do not care; rather, they attempt to care within a system that exhausts their ability to do so.

SURVEILLANCE, CONTROL, AND THE MANAGEMENT OF AFFECT

In today's world, surveillance is an integral part of life. It is always present, albeit silently. It is a part of our digital life. It is incorporated into the services and applications that we use. The services and applications we use are helpful, connective, and caring in nature. However, under a system known as surveillance capitalism, our data, which are based on our actions, choices, and interactions, are converted into something that can be used to predict our next actions (Silva, 2025). Currently, these systems monitor not only our actions but also our feelings, such as stress, happiness, anxiety, and motivation. This is a new way of managing emotions. It is a form of surveillance of our feelings, which are categorized and controlled silently. Thus, our emotions are not entirely personal in nature. Emotional management operates under the idea of tracking as normal behavior. Mood logs, activity scores, sleep tracking, and productivity tracking all present emotional life as something that can be quantified and improved. Users are encouraged to track themselves, and they do so voluntarily in pursuit of balance, calmness, or productivity. Although this promotes self-awareness, it also makes self-well-being dependent on data-based standards. There is a drive to identify and act on emotions in ways that ensure users remain dependent. Care and control are intertwined, and systems designed to promote health are often used to shape user behavior. Wellbeing applications are an example of this two-sided phenomenon.

Structural issues, such as employment insecurity, inequality, and future uncertainty, are portrayed as individual issues to be overcome through better habits and improved routines. This view locates the source of emotional security within the individual. Emotional distress is an indicator of poor self-management rather than a response to broader issues. Wellbeing apps promote self-adjustment to challenging environments rather than challenging them. The self-management of emotions has become commodified, measured, and enhanced. In this view, care becomes a transaction, and emotional respite becomes something that can be accessed at will rather than through the community. While the idea of controlling one's emotions can be appealing, it can also restrict what emotions are considered acceptable. Digital care systems increasingly rely on automation. Chatbots, AI therapy, and mood detection software provide instant support for emotional input. It can provide increased support to people, especially those who cannot easily access support (Santiago-Torner et al., 2025). However, it standardizes emotional input, suggesting that people should express their emotions in a specific manner. It interprets emotions based on templates and provides care based on templates. Although it can reduce stigma and increase support availability, it may oversimplify emotional complexity. The management of emotions through surveillance also subtly affects behavior.

Notifications encourage users to breathe, move, rest, or refocus at different times of the day. This is done under the guise of helpful reminders but, in fact, affects users' behavior. Emotional management is no longer a continuous process but one that is externally provided, as determined by devices rather than emotions or social cues. The cost of emotional transparency is access to care. The personal nature of well-being data makes it prone to privacy issues, especially when it has the potential to be used for profit. Emotional life is now something that systems can read and use; however, it is difficult to verify this. The cultural emphasis on optimization reinforces these trends (Ruggieri & Mollo, 2025). Emotional regulation is viewed as an ongoing process, with improvements measured in terms of time. When systems such as data collection and attention are used for care, it becomes another form of controlling people. To solve this, it is necessary to rethink the way in which emotional care is structured, such that it is connected, real, and based on shared responsibility rather than on numbers to be tracked.

CROSS-CULTURAL AND ARTISTIC PERSPECTIVES

Emotional exhaustion is considered to be something that everyone experiences in today's world; however, people 's feelings about it differ considerably based on their culture, society, and politics. While it is true that being constantly connected to the world and using digital media to feel empathy is something that everyone experiences, it is also true that it is experienced in very different ways depending on one's history, values, and ways of life (Ejaz & Khaliq, 2025). For example, in some societies, the feeling of seeing so many global issues through the Internet makes people feel very unsure about their lives, especially when their lives are very unstable. However, in other societies, emotional exhaustion is felt quietly as a feeling of being overwhelmed and disconnected in societies that have very safe ways of life, despite having so much digital information. However, this does not consider other forms of feeling; therefore, exhaustion may not be recognized or considered. Therefore, empathy through digital media only recognizes certain forms of feeling that are part of the dominant cultural story. This is also true for the way global media communicate news to the world.

In some countries, crises receive much attention, whereas in others, there is no mention of them. This raises the question of whose suffering is visible and whose is not. This can make people feel emotionally fatigued because they see much suffering in the world, but nothing is done about it. However, people in other communities that are not mentioned may feel fatigued because they are not acknowledged. Thus, empathy through media may be used to promote some views while ignoring others. Thus, art provides a new form of empathy that is very different from what is done on social media, which is all about being fast and instant. Stories also help in sharing emotional fatigue across cultures (Kamraju, 2025). Stories in novels, essays, and movies sometimes depict characters who are exhausted, disengaged, or emotionally drained, reflecting broader social issues. Unlike social media stories that depict a solution to a problem or resolution to an issue, these stories do not offer a solution to the problem. They depict exhaustion as an ongoing process that cannot be fully resolved and challenge the idea that people need to be strong and productive at all times. They inform people that it is acceptable to accept that they do not need to be better. Examining stories from different cultures can also help us understand the creation of emotional exhaustion.

In places that have been through war, numbness could be the result of going through difficult situations, and it is part of the group's history (Hadi, 2025). The artwork from these places talks about silence, brokenness, and missing pieces, showing the difficulty of telling the trauma story. Instead of trying to make the audience feel bad with dramatic stories, the artwork asks the audience to pay close attention and listen thoughtfully. It asks the audience to be respectful rather than seeking a quick fix. Although digital media is one of the things that people are tired of, some artists and activists use it as a form of resistance. These artists create works that question the expectations of people on platforms. Making people watch slow videos, do the same thing repeatedly, or show simple images questions the idea that people are always interested in something new. By showing people art that is not exciting or easy to understand, they are forced to think about how they are paying attention. Emotional engagement occurs slowly instead of being forced, which is the opposite of what people expect to happen immediately. Humor and satire are also common in art that involves emotional numbness, especially in areas where people cannot speak openly about their issues.

By using humor and satire, artists show people the silly side of life in the digital world and the work they do to cope with emotions. This helps people understand that they are tired without making it too serious. Satire helps people cope with private issues by discussing them openly, making it easy for people to talk about tiredness. Although it might sound funny, humor can also show that people have deep emotions and want to keep going despite harsh conditions. Most importantly, it also demonstrates that empathy can be altered. Rather than asking for constant emotional responses, art encourages people to look thoughtfully, slowly, and personally. By getting people to become involved in a particular story or situation, it prevents emotions from becoming something everyone must feel in the same manner. This type of localized empathy is not like what is requested in digital media, which may feel too spread out to be genuine. Art tells us that emotions do not need to be endless to be significant (Mora Pedreros et al., 2025). Stories from various cultures also demonstrate that emotional numbness is not necessarily a result of not caring. Art demonstrates this complexity in a way that does not try to tell us that emotional withdrawal or fatigue is wrong. Rather, it demonstrates it in a way that tells us it is a means of maintaining emotional strength in locations where it is required to be used. In this way, it challenges us to consider what it means to be visible and open and genuine.

CONCLUSION

Imagining a new way to show care, responsibility, and emotion in the digital world involves carefully considering how we feel and how we can express it in today's technology-driven world. While it has become easier to connect with people across long distances in the digital age, it has also created pressure that can be difficult to perceive and accumulate over time. On the one hand, it has become easier to connect with people across great distances in the digital age (Ruggieri & Mollo, 2025). However, it has created a pressure that can be difficult to see and can accumulate over time. In the digital world, it has become easier to connect with people across long distances and to feel a sense of community with those we connect with. We can feel a sense of responsibility toward those we connect with and can feel overwhelmed by that sense of responsibility. We can feel a sense of empathy towards those we connect with and can feel burned out by that sense of empathy. Sustainability, or the ability to maintain long-term care, has not been integrated into our interactions in the digital world. At the heart of this is the understanding that digital empathy is not simply measured by the number of times people respond to, like, and share something.

This is because algorithms tend to assume that the more people engage with something, the more emotionally engaged they are (Ejaz & Khaliq, 2025). Therefore, this creates a culture in which emotions such as anger and excitement are easily spread, as they tend to generate the most engagement. To effectively change the culture of empathy, we must start looking at the type of engagement that is considered thoughtful, deliberate, and aware of the true experiences of people. We must stop considering constant engagement as a moral imperative and start considering engagement that is deliberate, purposeful, and related to the true experiences of people. Therefore, this calls for a shift in focus from performance to building lasting relationships. Responsibility in the digital age also requires a new perspective. Responsibility is something shared and supported by groups, communities, and systems around us, rather than being handled by the individual alone. Emotional sustainability has become an important concept in this regard.

The digital space has made it easier to exhaust our emotions quickly, often at the expense of reflection, rest, and rejuvenation (Paredes-Labra et al., 2025). Being exhausted, burnt out, or apathetic is not just a weakness; it is a rational reaction to systems that require us to be always on and always invested. Emotional sustainability, on the other hand, is about changing systems structurally and culturally to ensure that we have the space to be slow, limit our exposure to exhausting emotions, or create our own pace of interaction. This means that reimagining digital empathy, responsibility, and emotional sustainability also involves dealing with the way emotions are treated as something that needs to be sold, measured, and used up.

This implies that social media, surveillance systems, and wellness apps are all part of a system that communicates that our emotions need to be mined, measured, and optimized. The time spent being vulnerable is used to make money, time spent on emotional labor is unpaid, and time spent resting is seen as something that makes us less productive. To change the way we treat our emotions online, it is necessary to challenge the logic that treats caring as a business arrangement and understand that empathy cannot be fully replicated, measured, or turned into content (Hadi, 2025). There needs to be a way to balance visibility and profit by creating space for caring to exist on its own, outside of money and attention. At the core of this new vision is the need for digital literacy, which includes understanding how technology impacts emotions. People need not only to know how to use the technology but also how to think about how these spaces impact their emotions, attention, and sense of what is right and wrong. By understanding how algorithms impact what they are seeing, how the design of the platforms impacts their behaviors, and how the exposure of the platforms impacts their emotions, people can begin to think more clearly about how to use the platforms in a way that gives them more control, helps them move through the information overload without falling into the pattern of unthinking indifference and faux empathy, but also helps people think about when to step back, when to engage, and how to engage in a way that is good for themselves and others. However, looking at other cultures can also provide key insights into this kind of work.

The ways in which people feel and express emotions differ across the world; what feels good in one place may not be as effective in another. Online services designed with one set of cultural values in mind can sometimes create confusion, misunderstanding, or even exclusion in other cultures. However, being aware of these differences can help us design systems and practices that are more open to various ways of feeling and caring and that will not create frustration or exhaustion in online environments. Therefore, emotional sustainability must consider the particular context of each group, recognizing that responsible behavior is shaped by local values, experiences, and what people can handle. Another significant method for re-imagining digital empathy can be found in artistic and story-based practices. Artistic and story-based practices can create a sense of slowing down, reflection, and examples of care that are thoughtful and not necessarily rushed. They can show people that they do not have to have empathy all the time; it can develop and emerge. They can allow people to create deep and complex emotional connections that are not necessarily subject to the pressures of digital systems that seek to speed up and maximize interactions. They can inspire both users and designers to think of new ways to measure emotional engagement, rather than focusing on how much and/or how fast people interact. However, equally important is the recognition that society, institutions, and the guiding principles that govern society play a role in ensuring that the right environment for digital empathy and care to develop is in place. This is because one person cannot single-handedly keep up with the demands of an environment that seeks to keep people engaged constantly. To ensure that people are not burnt out and are able to interact in meaningful ways, society and the guiding principles that govern it must work together (Ruggieri & Mollo, 2025). This could mean ensuring that there are avenues for mental health support, ways of managing society, and avenues for diverse voices to be heard. In this case, emotional health is closely tied to society and its guiding principles. The idea of new approaches to digital empathy is also linked to ethics and the management of digital space.

The algorithms that regulate what users see and how they feel are often opaque; however, they have a profound effect on users' feelings. An ethical design would involve guidelines that emphasize well-being, recognize the limitations of human capability, and empower users to control the amount and rate at which they interact. The concept of emotional health has become a major concept that guides how we design things, how society functions, how we create art, and how we live our lives (Kamraju, 2025). Responsibility is not just individual or societal but rather one that involves all of us as individuals, content creators, or organizations to provide care. This is not about being immediately responsive as a form of digital empathy but rather being responsive as a form of care, being attentive but also careful, open but also having some level of privacy, and being involved but also having time to recover. By adding these ideas, we can envision a world of digital connection, care, and attention that is not only common but also lasting, helping us build communities and cultures that last for a very long time.

REFERENCES

Anggara, O. F., & Rahmasari, D. (2025). Enhancing digital well-being in the era of hyperconnectivity: A psychological perspective. *Journal of Positive Psychology and Digital Well Being*, *1*(1), 48–53.

Argyriadi, A., Katsarou, D., Patelarou, A., Megari, K., Patelarou, E., Kotrotsiou, S., & Argyriadis, A. (2025). Digital Stress Scale (DSS): Development and psychometric validation of a measure of stress in the digital age. *International Journal of Environmental Research and Public Health*, *22*(7), 1080. DOI: 10.3390/ijerph22071080 PMID: 40724147

Bear, H., Fazel, M., & Skripkauskaite, S.the OxWell Study Team. (2025). Isolation despite hyper-connectivity? The association between adolescents' mental health and online behaviours in a large study of school-aged students. *Current Psychology (New Brunswick, N.J.)*, *44*(8), 7124–7137. DOI: 10.1007/s12144-025-07643-z

Bondanini, G., Giovanelli, C., Mucci, N., & Giorgi, G. (2025). The dual impact of digital connectivity: Balancing productivity and well-being in the modern workplace. *International Journal of Environmental Research and Public Health*, *22*(6), 845. DOI: 10.3390/ijerph22060845 PMID: 40566273

Bondanini, G., Sanchez-Gomez, M., Mucci, N., & Giorgi, G. (2026). Psychometric validation of the constant connectivity scale in the context of digital work in Italian organisations. *Administrative Sciences*, *16*(1), 39. DOI: 10.3390/admsci16010039

Chmiel, J., & Kurpas, D. (2025). Burnout and the brain—A mechanistic review of magnetic resonance imaging (MRI) studies. *International Journal of Molecular Sciences*, *26*(17), 8379. DOI: 10.3390/ijms26178379 PMID: 40943301

Ciocîrlea, B. Z. (2025). A paradox of modern communication: The decline of physical proximity. *Buletinul Institutului Politehnic din Ia i. Seria tiin e Socio-Umane*, *71*(1–2), 119–127.

Ejaz, S., & Khaliq, H. M. H. (2025). Mental health in the age of hyperconnectivity: A crisis hidden in plain sight. *Pakistan Journal of Medicine and Dentistry*, *14*(3), 1–3. DOI: 10.36283//ziun-pjmd14-3/001

Hadi, M. A. (2025). The theme of isolation in *Robinson Crusoe*: AI treatment. *Manar Elsharq Journal for Literature and Language Studies*, *3*(4), 16–30. DOI: 10.56961/mejlls.v3i4.1129

Kamraju, M. (2025). Wired but weary: Gen Z's complex relationship with online content, digital identity, and social media burnout. *Acta Informatica Malaysia*, *9*(1), 13–21. DOI: 10.26480/aim.01.2025.17.25

Márquez, B. Y., Mitre, A., Magdaleno-Palencia, J. S., & Ramirez-Ramirez, M. (2026). From connection to hyperconnection: A global cultural shift in everyday life when mobile-broadband penetration exceeds 100% (2007–2025). *Journal of Cultural Analysis and Social Change*, 318–328.

Maulida, E. N., Isnaeni, H., & Suwandi, M. A. (2025). Internalisation of Islamic education values through Qur'anic *tadabbur* for emotional detox and Islamic self-healing. *Jurnal Ilmu Pendidikan dan Sains Islam Interdisipliner*, 168–176.

Mora Pedreros, P. A., & Santiago Pajajoy, M. J. (2025). Ethical challenges of AI in Byung-Chul Han's theory. In *Proceedings of the Mexican Congress on Artificial Intelligence* (pp. 294–301). Springer Nature Switzerland.

Okhueleigbe, O. A., & Omoko, N. (2025). Technoference, technopola, and hyper-connectivity: An interpretive journalism perspective. *The Abuja Communicator*, *5*(1), 47–63.

Paredes-Labra, J., Solana-Domínguez, I., Ramos-Ramiro, M., & Freitas-Cortina, A. (2025). Techno-pessimistic shock and the banning of mobile phones in secondary schools: The case of Madrid. *Social Sciences (Basel, Switzerland)*, *14*(7), 441. DOI: 10.3390/socsci14070441

Ruggieri, R. A., & Mollo, M. (2025). Connected but isolated and suddenly diagnosed: Algorithmic malaise. *Human Arenas*, 1–21.

Santiago-Torner, C., Corral-Marfil, J. A., & Tarrats-Pons, E. (2025). Artificial intelligence and the reconfiguration of emotional well-being (2020–2025): A critical reflection. *Societies (Basel, Switzerland)*, *16*(1), 6. DOI: 10.3390/soc16010006

Silva, H. M. (2025). The reconfiguration of social bonds in the digital age: Virtual connections vs. face-to-face relationships. *Nature Anthropology*, *3*(1), 10003. DOI: 10.70322/natanthropol.2025.10003

Sun, J., Tang, Y., Wang, W., Zhang, Y., Ji, H., & Wang, P. (2025). Multimodal neuroimaging investigation of post-stroke fatigue in middle-aged and older adults: Combining resting-state fMRI and DTI-ALPS analysis. *Frontiers in Aging Neuroscience*, *17*, 1583655. DOI: 10.3389/fnagi.2025.1583655 PMID: 40433512

KEY TERMS AND DEFINITIONS

Algorithmic Affects: Emotions shaped by automated systems that prioritize engagement.

Digital Burnout: Chronic exhaustion from sustained emotional online work.

Social Indifference: Defensive detachment reduces empathy and collective responsibility.

Chapter 8
Emotional Fatigue and Social Indifference Among Young Athletes in the Era of Digital Social Environment

Debajit Karmakar
http://orcid.org/0000-0001-9272-0627
Lakshmibai National Institute of Physical Education, India

Anindita Das
http://orcid.org/0000-0002-6502-9619
Lakshmibai National Institute of Physical Education, India

ABSTRACT

The chapter explores emotional fatigue and social indifference among young athletes in the modern digital social environment. Constant online visibility, social comparison, and pressure to maintain a public persona increase psychological stress beyond traditional sporting demands. These pressures can lead to emotional exhaustion, reduced social engagement, and increased risk of burnout and mental health challenges. The discussion also considers physiological effects and emphasizes the importance of balanced digital engagement, psychological resilience training, and supportive sporting environments to protect athletes' wellbeing and sustain long-term athletic development.

DOI: 10.4018/979-8-3373-8307-1.ch008

1. INTRODUCTION

The intersection of elite athletic development and the modern digital social environment has produced a psychosocial landscape of unprecedented complexity for young athletes navigating both domains simultaneously. Across the globe, adolescent and young adult athletes are coming of age in an era defined by continuous connectivity, algorithmically curated social media feeds, the democratization of public visibility, and the blurring of boundaries between personal identity and digital persona. This convergence of athletic ambition and digital culture has given rise to a set of psychological challenges that previous generations of sports scientists, coaches, and mental health professionals had no occasion to examine, challenges centered significantly on the phenomena of emotional fatigue and social indifference (Özkan et al., 2026).

Emotional fatigue, in this context, refers to a state of chronic psychological exhaustion arising from sustained emotional demands that exceed an individual's available coping resources. It is distinct from physical fatigue in its origin and expression, though the two frequently coexist and interact in complex ways in athletic populations. Social indifference, as a downstream consequence, describes a progressive withdrawal of emotional investment from social relationships, interactions, and contexts, a kind of affective detachment that emerges as the psyche's defence mechanism against sustained emotional overload. Together, these phenomena represent a meaningful and growing threat to the psychological wellbeing, athletic development, and long-term life satisfaction of young athletes worldwide (Zhou et al., 2025).

The digital social environment acts as both a mirror and an amplifier of the pressures already inherent in competitive athletic development. Young athletes have always navigated the psychological demands of performance evaluation, peer comparison, coach-athlete relationship dynamics, identity formation through sport, and the precarious balance between athletic and academic commitments. What the digital era has added to this already complex psychosocial environment is a qualitatively new dimension of visibility, social comparison, external evaluation, and relational demand that operates continuously, without the temporal and spatial boundaries that previously contained sport-related social pressures within defined contexts (Özkan et al., 2026).

A young swimmer of the 1990s experienced performance evaluation at competitions, within team environments, and perhaps through local media coverage. Today's equivalent athlete faces a media ecosystem in which every race can be instantly clipped and uploaded, performance metrics are publicly accessible to a global audience, social media followers expect regular content delivery and personal transparency, online critics can comment on athletic performance, physical appearance, and personal choices from behind the anonymity of digital pseudonyms, and the athlete's developing sense of identity must be negotiated simultaneously in the physical social world and across multiple digital platforms with their distinct norms, expectations, and audiences (Tek & Özsari, 2025).

2. UNDERSTANDING THE DIGITAL SOCIAL ENVIRONMENT

To appreciate the particular ways in which the digital social environment shapes the psychological experience of young athletes, it is necessary first to develop a clear and nuanced understanding of what that environment actually consists of and the psychological mechanisms through which it exerts its influence.

The Architecture of Digital Social Platforms

Modern social media platforms, including Instagram, TikTok, YouTube, X (formerly Twitter), Snapchat, and their numerous successors and competitors, are not neutral communication technologies. They are architecturally designed systems engineered to maximize user engagement, time-on-platform, and content generation through the application of behavioural psychology principles, most centrally through variable ratio reinforcement schedules, the same reward mechanism that underlies the addictive properties of gambling. The unpredictability of social reward (likes, comments, follower gains, viral spread) creates a powerful psychological pull that drives compulsive checking, content creation, and social monitoring behaviours (Tek & Özsari, 2025).

For young athletes, these platforms serve multiple simultaneous functions. They are channels of social communication with peers and teammates, venues for following athletic role models and consuming sports content, platforms for building personal athletic brands and public visibility, arenas of social comparison with other athletes, spaces for receiving fan support and encouragement, and unfortunately also environments in which criticism, mockery, and harassment can be delivered at scale with minimal accountability. The multiplicity of these functions means that platform use is rarely a simple, single-purpose behaviour but rather a complex, emotionally layered engagement with diverse and sometimes conflicting social stimuli (Özkan et al., 2026).

Developmental Vulnerability in Adolescence

The period of adolescence and emerging adulthood, encompassing roughly the ages of 12 to 25 and thus encompassing precisely the developmental window in which most serious athletic careers are initiated, developed, and in many cases defined, is characterized by neurobiological and psychosocial features that render young people particularly vulnerable to the psychological effects of digital social environments (Halian et al., 2025).

Neurobiologically, the adolescent brain is characterized by heightened activity in reward-processing limbic circuits, particularly the nucleus accumbens and ventral tegmental area, combined with still-maturing prefrontal cortical systems responsible for executive function, impulse regulation, and long-term consequence evaluation. This neurological configuration predisposes adolescents to heightened sensitivity to social reward and social threat, greater difficulty regulating responses to negative social feedback, and stronger susceptibility to social comparison processes. The social rewards provided by likes, positive comments, and follower growth on social media are neurobiologically potent stimuli for this developmental stage in ways that differ both quantitatively and qualitatively from adult responses (Tek & Özsari, 2025).

Psychosocially, adolescence is the developmental period in which identity formation, what Erik Erikson termed the resolution of the identity versus role confusion developmental crisis, is the central psychological task. Young athletes are simultaneously constructing their athletic identity, their social identity, and their broader sense of self, and they increasingly do so within and through digital social environments. The intermingling of identity formation with the visibility, social judgment, and comparison dynamics of social media creates conditions in which the normal developmental turbulence of adolescent identity work is amplified and externalized in unprecedented ways (Halian et al., 2025).

The Always-On Culture

One of the most psychologically significant features of the contemporary digital social environment for young athletes is its temporal unboundedness. Previous generations of athletes experienced sport-related social pressures within defined contextual boundaries, the competition venue, the team environment, the structured training session. The digital environment eliminates these boundaries, making sport-related social demands, monitoring messages, posting content, responding to comments, tracking engagement metrics, potentially continuous across all waking hours and even intruding into sleep through night time phone use and notification alerts (Ghasemi & Azari Noughabi, 2024).

This always-on culture directly challenges the psychological recovery processes that are as essential to mental health as physical recovery is to athletic performance. Just as muscles require rest intervals for structural repair and adaptation, the psychological systems involved in emotional processing, social cognition, and self-regulation require periods of disengagement and restoration. The chronic, boundary-less demands of digital social engagement deprive young athletes of these essential recovery periods, creating conditions for progressive accumulation of emotional debt that ultimately manifests as fatigue and indifference (Bicalho et al., 2020).

Social Comparison Theory in the Digital Age

Leon Festinger's social comparison theory, formulated in 1954, proposed that humans have a fundamental drive to evaluate their own opinions and abilities by comparing themselves to others, particularly others perceived as similar. In the pre-digital era, the reference groups available for social comparison were naturally limited by physical proximity and social context, individuals compared themselves primarily to peers, teammates, and community members with whom they had direct contact (Fortes et al., 2023).

The digital social environment has catastrophically expanded the reference pool for social comparison among young athletes. Rather than comparing themselves to teammates and local competitors, young athletes can now compare themselves instantaneously and continuously to the most talented, most successful, most aesthetically presented athletes in their sport worldwide. Social media platforms further distort this comparison environment by systematically surfacing the most impressive, polished, and exceptional content, creating a reference distribution that is wildly unrepresentative of the actual population of athletes but that functions as the psychological standard against which young athletes measure themselves. Research consistently demonstrates that social media use, particularly passive consumption of social media content, is associated with increased upward social comparison, reduced self-esteem, greater body dissatisfaction, and heightened negative affect. In athletic populations specifically, these effects are compounded by the performance-relevant nature of athletic social comparison, where the stakes of perceived inadequacy are directly connected to central aspects of self-concept and identity (Ghasemi & Azari Noughabi, 2024).

3. SOURCES OF EMOTIONAL FATIGUE IN THE DIGITAL ERA

Emotional fatigue in young athletes does not arise from a single source but from the cumulative and interacting effects of multiple distinct but related digital-era stressors. Understanding these sources individually is essential for designing targeted preventive and supportive interventions.

The Performance-Visibility Cycle

In the contemporary sports landscape, athletic performance and digital visibility are increasingly intertwined in a reciprocal relationship that creates sustained emotional pressure. Athletic success generates visibility on digital platforms, through media coverage, fan sharing, and organizational promotion, while digital visibility in turn creates new performance pressures, as athletes become acutely aware that their performances are being evaluated not only by coaches, selectors, and immediate peers but by global audiences whose real-time reactions are publicly accessible. This performance-visibility cycle creates a chronic state of psychological exposure that is emotionally exhausting to sustain (Govindasamy et al., 2026). Young athletes at early stages of their careers, before they have developed mature psychological coping skills or a robust, settled sense of athletic identity, are particularly vulnerable to the emotional demands of this cycle. The anticipatory anxiety of knowing that a poor performance will generate negative digital commentary, combined with the pressure to appear mentally strong and positively engaged on social media regardless of actual emotional state, creates a double burden of performance pressure and emotional performance that can rapidly exceed the coping capacity of a developing adolescent (Bicalho et al., 2020).

Parasocial and Authentic Relationship Confusion

Social media creates and sustains parasocial relationships, one-sided relationships in which followers develop feelings of intimacy, familiarity, and investment in an athlete they have never met. Young athletes accumulating significant social media followings increasingly find themselves in the psychologically complex position of managing perceived relationships with people who feel they know them personally but with whom the athlete has no reciprocal relationship. The expectation of personal transparency, authentic sharing, and relational availability from large audiences creates emotional labour demands that are substantial and frequently invisible to external observers (Govindasamy et al., 2026). Simultaneously, digital communication can paradoxically reduce the quality of authentic interpersonal connection, as the performance of connection on social media substitutes for the deeper, more effortful work of building and maintaining genuine relationships. Young athletes may accumulate thousands of superficial digital connections while experiencing a progressive impoverishment of the intimate, reciprocal relationships that provide genuine emotional sustenance and support, a dynamic that contributes directly to feelings of loneliness and social indifference even in apparently highly socially connected individuals (Fortes et al., 2023).

Online Criticism, Harassment, and Cyberbullying

Young athletes experiencing competitive success gain public visibility that makes them targets for criticism, scrutiny, and in the most severe cases, coordinated harassment campaigns. The psychological impact of receiving criticism in digital public forums differs qualitatively from receiving criticism in traditional contexts. The permanence of digital text, the potential audience scale from individual comments (ranging from a few followers to millions), the organized nature of some critical campaigns, and the frequency with which content can be reshared and amplified all intensify the psychological impact of negative digital feedback beyond what private or limited-audience criticism would produce (de Medeiros et al., 2025).

Research on cyberbullying in adolescent populations documents consistent associations between cyberbullying victimization and depression, anxiety, reduced self-esteem, social withdrawal, and in extreme cases, suicidal ideation. Athletic populations face a specific form of this phenomenon in the harsh, uninhibited criticism of sports fan culture online, commentary that frequently addresses not only athletic performance but physical appearance, supposed mental weakness, personal character, and social identity characteristics. Young athletes, for whom athletic performance is often central to self-concept, may be particularly vulnerable to performance-directed online criticism, which strikes at the core of their developing sense of competence and worth (Halian et al., 2025).

Content Creation Pressure and the Authenticity Paradox

A particularly distinctive source of emotional fatigue for young athletes in the digital era is the pressure to create engaging, frequent, and apparently authentic social media content. Whether this pressure is self-imposed in the context of building a personal brand, externally driven by sponsors or management, or structurally incentivized by platform algorithms that reward posting frequency, content creation represents a substantial and ongoing demand on time, creative energy, and emotional resources (Zhou et al., 2025).

The authenticity paradox arises from the fundamental tension between the demand for authentic self-expression on social media and the simultaneously operating pressures to conform to platform aesthetic conventions, maintain a consistently positive and aspirational personal brand, protect genuine private emotional life from public exposure, and present a performed version of authenticity that satisfies audiences without actually surrendering privacy or emotional vulnerability (Karmakar et al., 2026). Navigating this contradiction is emotionally laborious and cognitively demanding, requiring sustained management of the boundary between private self and public persona, work that is exhausting when performed continuously across years of an athletic career (Fortes et al., 2023).

Fear of Missing Out and Compulsive Monitoring

The fear of missing out (FOMO), the anxiety that peers and competitors are having rewarding experiences, achieving milestones, or accessing opportunities from which one is absent, is substantially amplified by social media, which provides a continuous, curated stream of evidence for what others appear to be doing, achieving, and experiencing. For young athletes, FOMO operates across multiple dimensions: fear of missing career-relevant opportunities being discussed in digital networks, anxiety about competitive peers gaining visible advantages, concern about peers' social activities during training periods, and worry about information relevant to their athletic development being shared in digital spaces they are not monitoring (Bicalho et al., 2020).

This FOMO-driven compulsive monitoring of social media represents a significant mechanism through which digital engagement depletes emotional and attentional resources in young athletes. The cognitive interruption of constant checking divides attention across training, study, rest, and social activities, reducing the quality of engagement and recovery in each domain while sustaining a baseline state of low-grade anxiety that accumulates over time into emotional exhaustion (Stevens et al., 2013).

4. ACADEMIC AND ATHLETIC BALANCE CHALLENGES

Young athletes navigating high-level athletic commitments while simultaneously managing significant academic demands face a dual-domain performance pressure that represents a well-recognized but increasingly digital-era-specific source of chronic stress and emotional fatigue.

The Dual Identity Challenge

Most young athletes occupy simultaneously the social identity of student and athlete, two identities that carry distinct, demanding, and frequently conflicting obligations. Academic institutions expect academic engagement, assignment completion, examination preparation, and social participation in campus or school life. Athletic programs expect training attendance, competition participation, team engagement, physical conditioning, and increasingly, digital engagement activities. The practical allocation of finite time and energy between these competing demands creates chronic scheduling pressure that is itself a significant stressor (Ghasemi & Azari Noughabi, 2024).

In the digital era, both domains have expanded their temporal demands in ways that particularly affect young athletes. Academic expectations increasingly include online engagement, digital assignment submission, virtual discussion participation, online research, and in many institutions, social media-based academic communication. Athletic obligations now routinely include digital engagement components, posting training content, engaging with fans, representing sponsors online. These digitally-extended obligations of both domains consume the marginal time that young athletes might otherwise use for rest, recovery, and social connection, compressing the space available for psychological restoration (Hudimova et al., 2021).

Chronic Sleep Restriction

The combination of early morning training schedules, evening practice sessions, academic demands, and habitual nighttime social media use creates chronic sleep restriction in a large proportion of young athletes. Research in adolescent athlete populations consistently documents sleep durations substantially below the eight to ten hours recommended for this developmental stage, with social media use, particularly in the hour before sleep, identified as a significant contributor through mechanisms including blue light-induced melatonin suppression, cognitive and emotional arousal from social stimuli, and the compulsive monitoring behaviours already described (Halian et al., 2025).

Sleep restriction in young athletes produces consequences that are simultaneously detrimental to athletic performance and psychological resilience. Sleep deprivation impairs reaction time, decision-making, and learning consolidation critical to skill acquisition. It heightens emotional reactivity, reduces tolerance for frustration, impairs empathy and social cognition, and reduces the effectiveness of emotional regulation strategies, all of which directly amplify vulnerability to emotional fatigue and social indifference. The irony is profound: the very digital engagement behaviours that young athletes pursue partly in the service of their athletic careers actively undermine both athletic performance and the psychological resilience necessary to sustain those careers (Fortes et al., 2023).

The Coach-Parent-Athlete Digital Triangle

Digital communication technologies have transformed the relational dynamics among coaches, parents, and athletes in ways that are not uniformly beneficial. The availability of instant, continuous digital communication means that the coach-athlete and parent-athlete relationships are no longer bounded by the training session and competition contexts in which they historically operated. Coaches can now communicate expectations and feedback at any time; parents can monitor training activities, competition results, and social media presence continuously; and athletes operate with an awareness of this continuous monitoring that itself constitutes a source of psychological pressure (Stevens et al., 2013).

Parents who are themselves active social media users may amplify performance pressure on young athletes by publicly sharing competition results, commenting on performance-related posts, or expressing athletic expectations through digital channels. The semi-public nature of this communication, occurring in spaces where peers, other athletes, coaches, and sometimes broader audiences can observe it, creates situations in which normal family-athletic communication dynamics play out with unusual visibility, potentially amplifying both supportive and pressure-inducing parental behaviours (Pereira, 2023).

5. PHYSIOLOGICAL CORRELATES OF EMOTIONAL FATIGUE

Emotional fatigue is not merely a subjective psychological experience but a state with measurable physiological underpinnings that influence and are influenced by the physical demands of athletic training. Understanding the physiological dimension of emotional fatigue is important for appreciating its full impact on young athletes and for recognizing the bidirectional relationship between psychological and physical wellbeing.

The Hypothalamic-Pituitary-Adrenal Axis

The HPA axis is the body's primary neuroendocrine stress response system, coordinating the release of cortisol, the principal glucocorticoid stress hormone, in response to both physical and psychological stressors. Acute cortisol release is an adaptive response that mobilizes energy, modulates immune function, and enhances alertness and arousal, supporting the capacity to cope with the stressor at hand. However, chronic, sustained activation of the HPA axis in response to chronic psychosocial stress produces a state of dysregulated cortisol secretion characterized by initially elevated and subsequently blunted cortisol responses, a pattern associated with a range of adverse health outcomes including impaired immune function, disrupted sleep, altered mood, and reduced stress responsiveness (Fortes et al., 2023).

Young athletes experiencing chronic emotional fatigue from digital-era stressors, continuous social comparison, performance visibility pressure, content creation demands, online criticism, maintain a chronically activated stress response system. The concurrent physiological demands of athletic training, which independently stimulates cortisol release, compound this allostatic load, potentially pushing the HPA axis beyond its adaptive capacity and into states of dysregulation. Research in athlete burnout populations, which shares considerable conceptual and physiological overlap with emotional fatigue, consistently documents evidence of HPA axis dysregulation, including blunted cortisol awakening responses and altered diurnal cortisol patterns (Stevens et al., 2013).

Autonomic Nervous System Dysregulation

Heart rate variability (HRV), a measure of the variability in the time intervals between successive heartbeats, serves as a practical and non-invasive index of autonomic nervous system function and, by extension, of the balance between physiological stress and recovery. High HRV reflects healthy parasympathetic (rest and digest) tone and good recovery status; low HRV indicates sympathetic (fight or flight) dominance and inadequate physiological recovery (de Medeiros et al., 2025).

Studies examining HRV in athletes experiencing psychological stress, including overtraining-adjacent states with psychological components, document reduced HRV that is not fully explained by physical training loads. Emotional stressors, including interpersonal conflict, academic pressure, and competitive anxiety, reduce HRV through their activation of sympathetic nervous system pathways. The chronic, low-grade psychological activation produced by sustained digital social engagement may therefore produce measurable autonomic nervous system consequences that both reflect and contribute to states of emotional fatigue, and that interact negatively with the physiological demands of athletic training (Liu et al., 2024).

Inflammatory Pathways

The relationship between psychological stress and systemic inflammation is well-established in the broader psychological literature. Chronic psychosocial stress activates inflammatory pathways through multiple mechanisms, including sympathetic nervous system stimulation of cytokine production, glucocorticoid resistance acquired through chronic cortisol exposure, and behavioural pathways including sleep disruption and reduced physical activity. Pro-inflammatory cytokines, particularly IL-6, IL-1β, and TNF-α, exert direct effects on brain function and subjective emotional states through what has been termed the "sickness behaviour" complex, producing fatigue, social withdrawal, anhedonia, and reduced motivation that parallel the subjective experience of emotional fatigue and social indifference (Fournier et al., 2022).

For young athletes in whom training-related inflammation is already chronically elevated, the additive inflammatory burden of digital-era psychosocial stress may push systemic inflammatory tone to levels that meaningfully impair mood, motivation, and recovery, creating a physiological substrate for the psychological symptoms of emotional fatigue that is largely invisible to coaches and athletes who are not attuned to its existence (Pereira, 2023).

Neurological and Cognitive Consequences

The neurobiological consequences of chronic stress and emotional fatigue include structural and functional changes in brain regions involved in emotional regulation, decision-making, and motivation. Chronic stress reduces dendritic complexity in the prefrontal cortex while promoting hypertrophy of amygdala circuits, effectively shifting the balance of neural processing toward reactive, emotionally driven responses and away from the deliberative, regulated decision-making that supports optimal athletic performance and healthy life choices. These neural adaptations are particularly concerning in developing brains, where structural and functional plasticity is greatest and the consequences of stress-related alterations may be most enduring (de Medeiros et al., 2025).

6. LONG-TERM CONSEQUENCES IF UNADDRESSED

When emotional fatigue and social indifference in young athletes are not recognized, addressed, or appropriately supported, the trajectory of consequences can be severe, affecting not only athletic careers but broader psychological health and life outcomes across the developmental span and beyond.

Athlete Burnout

Athlete burnout, operationalized most comprehensively by Raedeke and Smith's adaptation of Maslach's organizational burnout framework, is characterized by three core dimensions: emotional and physical exhaustion, depersonalization of sport (reduced sense of caring about athletic participation), and a diminished sense of athletic accomplishment. It represents the endpoint of a prolonged process of demand-resource imbalance and is among the most serious adverse outcomes of unaddressed emotional fatigue in athletic populations (Zhou et al., 2025).

Burnout does not develop overnight but evolves through a gradual, often insidious process of progressive depletion in which the warning signs, increasing irritability, declining motivation, emotional detachment from teammates and coaches, declining performance in the context of maintained or increased training loads, may be misattributed to physical overtraining or motivational deficits rather than recognized as symptoms of psychological exhaustion requiring specific support. In the digital era, the social media dimensions of athlete burnout add additional layers: the athlete experiencing burnout may feel compelled to maintain a positive, engaged public digital persona even as their private psychological state deteriorates, creating an exhausting performance of wellbeing that further depletes already scarce coping resources (Pereira, 2023).

Dropout from Sports

Athlete dropout, the premature, involuntary or voluntary cessation of serious athletic participation before potential is realized, represents one of the most tangible and practically significant consequences of unaddressed emotional fatigue. Research on dropout motivation consistently identifies factors related to psychological distress, loss of enjoyment, conflict between sport and other life domains, negative coach and peer relationships, and inadequate sense of competence as primary drivers (Stevens et al., 2013).

The digital social environment contributes to dropout risk through several pathways. Athletes whose private experience of sport has become one of chronic stress and emotional depletion but whose public digital persona presents enthusiasm and positivity may eventually find the discrepancy between these realities unsustainable, leading to abrupt departure from sport. Online harassment and persistent negative commentary following performance failures can make the psychological costs of continued participation feel disproportionate to the benefits, particularly for athletes who have not yet developed robust coping mechanisms. The financial and social capital associated with digital athletic visibility can also create distorted motivation structures in which young athletes remain in sport primarily to maintain digital identity and commercial opportunities rather than from genuine love of their sport, a motivational profile closely associated with early burnout and dropout (Pereira, 2023).

Depression and Anxiety Disorders

The relationship between chronic emotional fatigue, social indifference, and clinical mood disorders is not merely correlational but involves clear mechanistic pathways. The physiological changes associated with chronic stress, HPA axis dysregulation, autonomic imbalance, neuroinflammation, prefrontal-limbic imbalance, are the same neurobiological substrates implicated in the pathophysiology of major depressive disorder and generalized anxiety disorder. Chronic emotional fatigue may be understood as a subclinical state that, in vulnerable individuals with insufficient protective factors, can transition into frank depressive or anxiety disorders (de Medeiros et al., 2025).

Young athletes are not protected from clinical mental health disorders by virtue of their athletic activity, and there is growing evidence that elite athlete populations experience rates of depression and anxiety comparable to or exceeding those in age-matched non-athlete populations, despite receiving less mental health support and existing in cultural environments that stigmatize psychological vulnerability. The digital social environment amplifies this risk for several reasons: it provides continuous access to stimuli that trigger comparison-driven negative affect; it normalizes emotional disclosure in performative and inauthentic ways that substitute for genuine help-seeking; and it creates social environments in which the expression of psychological distress is frequently met with judgmental or dismissive responses from audiences who may themselves be struggling with digital-era psychological challenges (Cassilo & Sanderson, 2019).

Identity Crisis Beyond Sports

Young athletes who have heavily invested their sense of self in their athletic identity are particularly vulnerable to identity crises when athletic careers are disrupted or concluded. The digital social environment intensifies this vulnerability by externalizing and publicizing the athletic identity in ways that make its potential loss more threatening and more publicly visible. When an athlete's social media presence, follower base, engagement metrics, and public persona have been built primarily around athletic identity, the prospect of career disruption or conclusion raises not only the personal existential question of "Who am I without sport?" but also the social and economic question of "What value do I have in digital public space without my athletic identity?"

This identity crisis beyond sports is experienced earlier and more acutely in the digital era because the construction of public athletic personas begins earlier in athletes' careers and proceeds more rapidly with digital amplification. Athletes who have built substantial digital followings as teenagers face the paradox of having external social identities that have outgrown their personal psychological development, leaving them ill-equipped to manage the public dimensions of identity transition when athletic careers change direction (Ghasemi & Azari Noughabi, 2024).

Social Isolation and Interpersonal Disconnection

Another critical long-term consequence of unaddressed emotional fatigue and social indifference among young athletes is the gradual emergence of social isolation and impaired interpersonal functioning. Although athletes often appear socially integrated because they are surrounded by teammates, coaches, and online followers, the quality of these relationships may deteriorate when emotional exhaustion and psychological detachment persist over time. Emotional fatigue can reduce the athlete's capacity for empathy, communication, and emotional engagement, leading to superficial interactions and a growing sense of disconnection from meaningful social support systems. As this process unfolds, athletes may begin to withdraw not only from peers and teammates but also from family members and mentors who would otherwise serve as important sources of emotional stability (Fournier et al., 2022).

The digital social environment further complicates this process by replacing authentic interpersonal interaction with mediated, performance-oriented communication. Social media platforms create the illusion of constant social connection through likes, comments, and follower counts, yet these forms of interaction often lack the emotional depth necessary for psychological wellbeing. Young athletes experiencing emotional fatigue may increasingly rely on these superficial forms of validation rather than investing in deeper relationships that require emotional presence and vulnerability. Over time, this substitution can erode the athlete's real-world social network, leaving them with large digital audiences but minimal genuine support during periods of stress or crisis (Liu et al., 2024).

In addition, social indifference may gradually manifest as reduced team cohesion and diminished sense of belonging within the athletic environment. Athletes who feel emotionally drained may disengage from team activities, communication, and collaborative goals, which can weaken group dynamics and create interpersonal tensions within the team. Teammates may misinterpret such withdrawal as arrogance, lack of commitment, or poor attitude, further exacerbating social distance and reinforcing feelings of isolation. This cycle of emotional withdrawal and social misunderstanding can become self-perpetuating, ultimately leading athletes to experience loneliness even within environments designed to foster collective identity and shared purpose (Halian et al., 2025).

7. PREVENTIVE FRAMEWORK FOR THE DIGITAL ERA

Addressing emotional fatigue and social indifference in young athletes requires a multi-level preventive framework that operates simultaneously at individual, interpersonal, organizational, and cultural levels. No single intervention or approach is sufficient; effective prevention requires coordinated action across these domains.

Balanced Digital Engagement Model

The foundation of any preventive framework must be the development and implementation of a balanced digital engagement model, a structured, intentional approach to digital participation that preserves the genuine benefits of digital connectivity while protecting against its psychological costs. This model is not built on blanket restriction or digital abstinence, which is neither realistic nor desirable given the legitimate professional, social, and informational functions that digital platforms serve for young athletes. Rather, it is built on deliberate, conscious engagement guided by clearly articulated personal values and boundaries (Cassilo & Sanderson, 2019).

Practically, a balanced digital engagement model for young athletes involves several key components. Designated digital-free periods, particularly around training sessions, competitive events, bedtime, and family or social time, create protected spaces for genuine presence, recovery, and authentic relationship-building. Screen time limits for social media specifically, separate from productive digital activities such as educational content and communication, help quantify and manage passive consumption. Intentional content curation, actively choosing who and what to follow based on whether digital content generates positive, inspiring, or genuinely useful responses rather than anxiety, inadequacy, or compulsive comparison, can meaningfully improve the quality of the social comparison environment experienced during platform use (Zhou et al., 2025).

Psychological Resilience Training

Formal psychological resilience training should be integrated into athlete development programs as a standard component rather than an optional or crisis-responsive intervention. In the context of digital-era emotional fatigue specifically, this training should encompass cognitive-behavioural skills for identifying and restructuring unhelpful thought patterns related to social comparison, performance evaluation, and online criticism. Mindfulness-based interventions have demonstrated efficacy in reducing rumination, improving emotional regulation, and reducing stress reactivity in both athletic and general populations, and their applicability to digital-era stressors, particularly the habit of compulsive monitoring and the tendency to ruminate on negative online feedback, is well-established (Pereira, 2023).

Resilience training should also directly address the specific psychological challenges of digital athlete life: skills for receiving critical online feedback without catastrophizing or internalizing, strategies for managing the authenticity paradox of social media self-presentation, and techniques for maintaining a stable, internally referenced sense of identity and self-worth that is not contingent on digital engagement metrics or audience approval. The concept of psychological flexibility, the ability to remain open, present, and committed to valued action even in the presence of difficult thoughts and feelings, derived from Acceptance and Commitment Therapy (ACT), is particularly relevant to the complex, boundary-ambiguous psychological demands of digital athlete life (Pereira, 2023).

Ethical Athlete Branding Guidance

Young athletes who have or aspire to significant digital public visibility need access to thoughtful, developmentally appropriate guidance on ethical and psychologically healthy athlete branding. This guidance should begin with a grounding in values clarification, helping the athlete articulate what they genuinely value and want to represent, rather than building a digital persona driven primarily by what generates algorithmic engagement or commercial appeal. Values-aligned digital content creation is more psychologically sustainable because it reduces the cognitive dissonance and emotional labour associated with performing an inauthentic persona (Zhao & Zhou, 2022).

Guidance on ethical athlete branding should also address the commercial dimensions of digital athletic visibility, including the psychological implications of sponsorship-driven content obligations, the importance of maintaining genuine editorial control over self-presentation, and the long-term reputational and psychological risks of allowing commercial imperatives to override authentic self-expression. Young athletes benefit from mentorship from more experienced athletes who have navigated these tensions and can share genuine, reflective perspectives on the costs and benefits of different approaches to digital self-presentation (de Medeiros et al., 2025).

Community-Building Initiatives

Counteracting the social isolation and shallow connectivity associated with digital-era social indifference requires deliberate investment in genuine community-building within sports environments. Coaches and sports organizations should prioritize creating team cultures characterized by psychological safety, environments in which vulnerability, struggle, and honest emotional expression are welcomed rather than stigmatized, and in which individual worth is not exclusively or primarily tied to athletic performance outcomes (Lee & Cho, 2021).

Structured team activities designed specifically to build authentic interpersonal relationships, not training sessions or competitions, but shared experiences emphasizing mutual vulnerability, collaborative problem-solving, and genuine interpersonal connection, can strengthen the social bonds that buffer against emotional fatigue and social indifference. Mentorship programs pairing younger athletes with experienced, psychologically mature senior athletes or recent graduates provide both practical guidance and relational support from individuals who can credibly speak to the psychological challenges of digital-era athletic life from lived experience (de Medeiros et al., 2025).

Monitoring Digital Consumption Patterns

Organizations and coaching staff equipped with awareness of digital-era psychological risks should implement systematic monitoring of digital consumption patterns and their potential behavioural and psychological correlates in young athletes under their care. This monitoring should be conducted with full transparency and athlete consent, framed explicitly as a wellbeing-supportive rather than a surveillance activity, and embedded within broader mental health monitoring programs (Zhou et al., 2025).

Practical monitoring tools include brief validated instruments assessing social media use characteristics (frequency, duration, emotional response, compulsive features), standardized assessments of athlete burnout and emotional wellbeing administered periodically across the season, and regular structured check-in conversations with individual athletes that specifically invite discussion of digital-era stressors. Coaches and support staff involved in this monitoring must be appropriately trained not only in using assessment tools but in responding effectively to concerning findings, with referral pathways to sport psychologists and mental health professionals clearly established and actively communicated (Pereira, 2023).

8. CASE REFLECTIONS IN MODERN SPORTS CULTURE

The abstract psychological and physiological dynamics described in preceding sections acquire their true significance when grounded in the concrete, lived realities of young athletes navigating the digital social environment. The following case reflections, drawn from recurring patterns and archetypes in contemporary sports culture rather than specific identified individuals, illuminate how digital-era pressures manifest in practice (Pereira, 2023).

Young Athletes Building Early Public Personas

Across multiple sports, the phenomenon of youth athletic prodigies building substantial public social media followings years before reaching professional ranks has become normalized and increasingly expected. Gymnasts, swimmers, figure skaters, and tennis players, sometimes as young as twelve or thirteen years old, accumulate followings of tens or hundreds of thousands on platforms like TikTok and Instagram, driven partly by their own and their parents' strategic digital activity and partly by the organic viral spread of impressive athletic performance clips. The psychological complexity of this situation is profound. These young athletes are simultaneously engaged in the psychological work of normal adolescent development, identity formation, peer relationship navigation, academic engagement, and family relationship renegotiation, while managing the unusual and developmentally mismatched demands of meaningful public visibility (Karmakar et al., 2026). They must develop a relationship with their own athletic identity, with the social meaning of their sport, and with their personal values at the same time as they are presenting public versions of all of these things to large audiences whose responses will inevitably influence their developing sense of self (de Medeiros et al., 2025).

Coaches and parents who facilitate early digital visibility for young athletes carry significant responsibilities that are not always accompanied by adequate awareness of the psychological risks. The precedent established by early digital persona construction, the content categories that define the athlete's public image, the level of personal disclosure normalised, the audience expectations created, follows athletes through subsequent developmental stages and can constrain their capacity for authentic self-expression as they mature and their sense of identity evolves (Bicalho et al., 2020).

Viral Success and Instant Pressure

The contemporary sports media ecosystem creates regular opportunities for moments of extraordinary athletic achievement to achieve viral spread, viewed and shared by millions of people worldwide within hours of occurring. For young athletes who experience viral moments, the psychological aftermath can be both exhilarating and deeply challenging in ways that are rarely discussed openly in sports culture (Tek & Özsari, 2025).

The sudden amplification of a following following a viral moment brings immediate and overwhelming social stimulation: thousands of new followers, flood of messages and comments, media interview requests, sponsor outreach, and the intense curiosity of a newly expanded audience. This social stimulation is intrinsically exciting but also cognitively and emotionally overwhelming, and the subsequent performance expectations it generates, both from the athlete's own aspirations and from the newly expanded audience, can be paralyzing. Athletes who have achieved viral recognition frequently report experiencing intense anxiety about subsequent performances, acutely aware that a drop in performance level will be visible to an audience that encountered them at their best. This dynamic effectively creates a ratchet of expectation: viral success raises the baseline of public expectation with no clear path for managing the inevitable variation in athletic performance that characterizes all athletic development. The psychological management of post-viral pressure demands sophisticated coping skills that many young athletes have not yet developed, and the absence of adequate psychological support in this situation is a meaningful gap in athlete welfare provisions across many sports systems (Zhou et al., 2025).

Online Criticism After Competition Losses

Competition losses are an inevitable and developmentally valuable component of the athletic experience, providing information for improvement, building tolerance for frustration, and developing the resilience that ultimately characterizes elite sporting longevity. In the pre-digital era, competition losses were processed primarily in private and within the athlete's immediate social environment, team, family, coaching staff, with public commentary largely limited to formal sports journalism that maintained at least nominal professional standards of tone and fairness (Karmakar et al., 2026). The digital era has transformed the social context of competition losses for visible young athletes into something qualitatively different and psychologically more demanding. Within minutes of a competitive defeat, social media platforms fill with commentary from millions of observers ranging from sympathetic and constructive to brutal and dehumanizing. Athletes who make high-stakes errors, a missed penalty kick, a stumble at a crucial moment, a strategic misjudgement, may find themselves the subject of memes, hashtag campaigns, or coordinated criticism that reaches audiences of millions and persists as searchable digital content indefinitely (Liu et al., 2024).

The psychological processing of athletic failure is an essential developmental task that requires the emotional safety to honestly examine performance, acknowledge mistakes, experience the appropriate emotional response, and formulate a constructive learning-oriented response. This processing is actively impaired by the dynamics of online criticism, which introduces shame, humiliation, and social threat dimensions to what should be a private developmental experience, and which demands from the athlete a public response performance at precisely the moment when they most need emotional space and privacy for genuine processing (Lee & Cho, 2021).

Young athletes who have experienced intense online criticism following high-profile failures describe effects ranging from mild performance anxiety in subsequent competitions to severe, career-threatening confidence collapse and social withdrawal. Without adequate psychological support and protective cultural norms within their sports environments, many young athletes who face this experience are left to navigate it alone, drawing on coping resources that may be entirely insufficient to the scale of the challenge (Pereira, 2023).

Sponsorship-Driven Digital Obligations

Commercial sponsorships, once the exclusive domain of established professional athletes with proven track records, now routinely extend to talented young athletes with significant social media followings, sometimes before those athletes have achieved meaningful senior competition results. While such sponsorships provide genuine financial support and commercial experience, they also introduce a layer of professional obligation that is developmentally premature for many young athletes and that creates specific sources of emotional fatigue (Tek & Özsari, 2025).

Sponsorship-driven digital obligations typically include requirements for regular posting of branded content, authentic integration of products into lifestyle content, participation in promotional campaigns, and maintenance of engagement metrics that justify continued commercial partnership. These obligations persist regardless of competitive season, training phase, personal emotional state, or life circumstances, they are contractual, financially consequential, and require ongoing management regardless of what else is happening in the athlete's life (Zhou et al., 2025).

The psychological cost of these obligations extends beyond mere time management. Young athletes who feel genuine emotional tension between authentic self-expression and commercially motivated content creation, who find themselves posting enthusiasm for products they do not genuinely use or positive messages they do not privately believe, experience the cognitive dissonance and emotional labour of inauthenticity in a public, legally binding context. This is a form of emotional labour more typically associated with professional adult employment contexts, imposed on adolescent athletes who may lack the psychological maturity, contractual negotiating experience, or awareness of their own rights to manage it effectively (Fournier et al., 2022).

Transition from Amateur to Professional Visibility

The transition from amateur to professional status in sport has always represented a significant psychological adjustment, a shift in the nature of external expectations, competitive environment, financial stakes, and relational dynamics with coaches and institutions. In the digital era, this transition is preceded, accompanied, and complicated by a parallel transition in digital visibility that has its own psychological demands and adjustment challenges (Pereira, 2023).

Young athletes moving from amateur to professional environments frequently experience a dramatic amplification of digital public profile that outpaces their personal psychological development. The scrutiny applied to professional athletes on social media, regarding performance, personal life, public statements, social and political positions, and professional decisions, is qualitatively more intense and more consistently maintained than that directed at amateur athletes, even those with significant amateur-level followings (Zhou et al., 2025).

Athletes who have not been adequately prepared for this intensification of digital scrutiny, who lack established habits of healthy digital engagement and clear values regarding self-presentation, or who are managing the transition without adequate professional support structures can find the combination of physical and psychological demands of professional sport with escalating digital visibility obligations genuinely overwhelming. The resulting emotional fatigue can impair performance at precisely the career stage when consistent high performance is most professionally critical, creating a damaging feedback loop between psychological distress, performance impairment, increased external scrutiny, and further psychological distress (Tek & Özsari, 2025).

9. CONCLUSION

The emotional fatigue and growing social indifference observed among young athletes in today's digitally saturated environment represent a substantive and emerging concern for sports science, sports medicine, and athlete welfare. These challenges are not transitional inconveniences that will resolve as digital platforms become normalized. Rather, they stem from a profound mismatch between the human brain's evolutionary design for small-scale, reciprocal, face-to-face interaction and the boundless, highly visible, algorithm-driven social ecosystems that now shape athletic identity and public perception. For adolescent athletes, whose developmental stage heightens sensitivity to social evaluation and reward, this mismatch is particularly intense.

Athletic achievement in the modern era brings not only recognition but continuous visibility. Social media metrics, public commentary, sponsorship expectations, and constant connectivity amplify performance pressure beyond the field of play. Because athletic identity often forms a central component of adolescent self-concept, digital scrutiny can become deeply personal, reinforcing cycles of comparison, validation-seeking, and fear of failure. Over time, this chronic psychosocial stress manifests as emotional exhaustion, reduced engagement in authentic relationships, declining mental health, and, in severe cases, long-term psychological harm. These outcomes are not confined to subjective experience; they are accompanied by measurable physiological changes, including dysregulation of stress-response systems such as the hypothalamic–pituitary–adrenal axis, autonomic imbalance, and increased allostatic load. Such alterations directly interfere with recovery, cognitive focus, emotional regulation, and overall athletic development. Addressing this issue requires coordinated, multi-level intervention. Young athletes need structured education and psychological skills training that enable them to navigate digital environments with awareness and boundaries. Coaches and sports medicine professionals must expand their conception of athlete care to include digital-era stressors as integral, not peripheral, components of performance management. Sports organizations should implement clear policies that safeguard minors from exploitative commercial pressures and normalize digital wellbeing as a standard element of athlete support. Parents require guidance to balance encouragement with protection, ensuring that digital visibility does not amplify unhealthy performance expectations. Most critically, sporting culture must evolve. The persistent valorisation of stoicism and the stigmatization of vulnerability undermine both wellbeing and performance. Psychological health is not antithetical to competitive excellence; it is foundational to it. As digital environments continue to shape the landscape of sport, a thoughtful, evidence-informed, and compassionate approach is essential. Providing young athletes with comprehensive physical and psychological support is not merely an ethical obligation, it is central to sustaining both their performance potential and their long-term wellbeing.

REFERENCES

Bicalho, C. C. F., da Costa, I. T., Noce, F., & da Costa, V. T. (2020). Prevalence of burnout in soccer athletes of the under-20 category over a sports season. *Journal of Physical Education (Maringá), 31*(1), e3160. https://www.scielo.br/j/jpe/a/YBHBX49Rv5q7tCfsxYRcFJJ/?lang=en. DOI: 10.4025/jphyseduc.v31i1.3160

Cassilo, D., & Sanderson, J. (2019). From Social Isolation to Becoming an Advocate: Exploring Athletes' Grief Discourse About Lived Concussion Experiences in Online Forums. *Communication & Sport, 7*(5), 678–696. DOI: 10.1177/2167479518790039

de Medeiros, M. F., & Maciel, V. d'Ávila, de Medeiros, S. F., da Silva, J. C. G., de Queiros, V. S., de Almeida Neto, P. F., & Cabral, B. G. de A. T. (2025). Relationship between Social Media Induced Mental Fatigue and Sprint Performance in Young Futsal Athletes. *Interfaces Científicas-Saúde e Ambiente, 10*(1), 549–568. https://periodicos.set.edu.br/saude/article/view/12909

Fortes, L. S., Gantois, P., De Lima-Júnior, D., Barbosa, B. T., Ferreira, M. E. C., Nakamura, F. Y., Albuquerque, M. R., & Fonseca, F. S. (2023). Playing videogames or using social media applications on smartphones causes mental fatigue and impairs decision-making performance in amateur boxers. *Applied Neuropsychology. Adult, 30*(2), 227–238. DOI: 10.1080/23279095.2021.1927036 PMID: 34061684

Fournier, C., Parent, S., & Paradis, H. (2022). The relationship between psychological violence by coaches and conformity of young athletes to the sport ethic norms. *EJSS European Journal for Sport and Society*, *19*(1), 37–55. DOI: 10.1080/16138171.2021.1878436

Ghasemi, A., & Azari Noughabi, M. (2024). Investigating the mediating role of Foreign Language Peace of mind and learning burnout in the relationship between Informal Digital Learning of English and willingness to communicate. *Computer Assisted Language Learning*, •••, 1–30. DOI: 10.1080/09588221.2024.2424321

Govindasamy, K., Elayaraja, M., Karmakar, D., & Das, A. (2026). Ethical and practical implications of robotic exoskeletons in sports medicine. In *Robotics and Artificial Intelligence in Sports Medicine and Sports Services* (pp. 65–99). Elsevier., DOI: 10.1016/B978-0-443-21734-0.00010-X

Halian, I., Popovych, I., Mykhailyuk, I., Halian, A., Kononenko, A., Kruglov, K., & Hoian, I. (2025). Dispositional determinants of mental tension in future coaches. *Journal of Physical Education and Sport*, *25*(7), 1343–1352. https://www.researchgate.net/profile/Ihor-Popovych/publication/394144560_Dispositional_determinants_of_mental_tension_in_future_coaches/links/688b45e9c3cb2665f06291d5/Dispositional-determinants-of-mental-tension-in-future-coaches.pdf

Hudimova, A., Popovŷch, I., Savchuk, O., Liashko, V., Pyslar, A., & Hrys, A. (2021). Research on the relationship between excessive use of social media and young athletes' physical activity. *Journal of Physical Education and Sport*, *21*(6), 3364–3373. https://www.researchgate.net/profile/Ihor-Popovych/publication/357538541_Research_on_the_relationship_between_excessive_use_of_social_media_and_young_athletes'_physical_activity/links/61d34644d4500608168930b3/Research-on-the-relationship-between-excessive-use-of-social-media-and-young-athletes-physical-activity.pdf

Karmakar, D., Das, A., Bhutia, T. O., Govindasamy, K., & Kumar, A. (2026). Integrating Technology in Sports Education: Opportunities and Challenges for Teacher Educators. In Pelafigue, A. L. (Ed.), *Preparing Educators for Complexity and Change* (pp. 257–290). IGI Global Scientific Publishing., DOI: 10.4018/979-8-3373-9494-7.ch008

Lee, Y. H., & Cho, H. (2021). The roles of different types of passion in emotional exhaustion and turnover intention among athletic coaches. *International Journal of Sports Science & Coaching*, *16*(3), 465–476. DOI: 10.1177/1747954120976955

Liu, X., Weng, X., Qin, H., Ma, S., & Wang, G. (2024). The successful experience of gymnastics world champion coach: An interview analysis. *Frontiers in Psychology*, *15*, 1405589. https://www.frontiersin.org/journals/psychology/articles/10.3389/fpsyg.2024.1405589/full. DOI: 10.3389/fpsyg.2024.1405589 PMID: 39091704

Özkan, R., Akar, O. O., Uzun, R. N., İmamoğlu, O., Kımıl, K., & Yılmaz, N. H. (2026). An Examination of the Effects of Athletes' Social Media Addiction and Sports Burnout Levels on Their Emotional Commitment to Their Teams. *International Journal of Disabilities Sports & Health Sciences*, *9*(1), 11–23. https://dergipark.org.tr/en/pub/ijdshs/article/1800955. DOI: 10.33438/ijdshs.1800955

Pereira, A. D. C. (2023). *Emotional response and cognitive performance in digital environments: an exploratory study* (Doctoral dissertation).

Stevens, R. E., Loudon, D. L., Yow, D. A., Bowden, W. W., & Humphrey, J. H. (2013). *Stress in college athletics: Causes, consequences, coping*. Routledge. https://api.taylorfrancis.com/content/books/mono/download?identifierName=doi&identifierValue=10.4324/9781315043593&type=googlepdf

Tek, T., & Özsari, A. (2025). Digital literacy, phubbing, and mental well-being in the digital age: A study on young university athletes. *Frontiers in Psychiatry*, *16*, 1638959. https://www.frontiersin.org/journals/psychiatry/articles/10.3389/fpsyt.2025.1638959/full. DOI: 10.3389/fpsyt.2025.1638959 PMID: 40873669

Zhao, D., & Zhou, Y. (2022). Examining the psychometric properties of the controlling coach behaviors scale in Chinese elite athletes. *PLoS One*, *17*(11), e0277985. https://journals.plos.org/plosone/article?id=10.1371/journal.pone.0277985. DOI: 10.1371/journal.pone.0277985 PMID: 36441802

Zhou, W., Zhang, Y., Xie, B., & Lu, Y. (2025). Balancing the Impact of Cyberbullying on Academic Performance: The Moderating Role of Sports Engagement. *SAGE Open*, *15*(4), 21582440251401115. DOI: 10.1177/21582440251401115

Chapter 9
Emotional Fatigue in the New Media Era:
Memes, Irony, and Digital Coping Within Affective Capitalism

Pragna Kashyap
http://orcid.org/0009-0007-1842-197X
PES University, Bangalore, India

Srishti Muralidharan
http://orcid.org/0009-0005-0798-7404
PES University, Bangalore, India

ABSTRACT

The rapid expansion of social media platforms has transformed how individuals interact with them. Within the new media era, users are exposed to continuous streams of content that often evoke strong emotional reactions, contributing to increasing experiences of emotional burnout and Social Media Fatigue. This chapter examines emotional fatigue in the context of digital environments. It situates it within a broader framework of affective capitalism in which users' emotional engagement is commodified within digital economies. Deriving from theoretical frameworks and perspectives this chapter explores how social media platforms intensify emotional demands through algorithmic optimisation and constant connectivity. It argues that the use of internet memes, which transform complex emotional experiences into humorous forms, allows individuals to maintain their digital communication while reducing the intensity of emotions. The chapter emphasises the contradictory nature of internet memes as a form of digital communication, and commodity of affective economies.

DOI: 10.4018/979-8-3373-8307-1.ch009

INTRODUCTION

In recent years, scholars have increasingly examined how the structure of social media environments shapes not only communication practices but also emotional experiences. Social media has served as a platform for users to connect and interact for several decades. It does so by allowing mutuals to discover and follow one another, as well as letting users post and share content that may be of interest to each other. The modern era has transformed how social media used to function. Now, social media has become a complex socio-technical platform that shapes how individuals access information, express emotions, and participate in public discourse. The new media era encompasses multiple platforms across which individuals are exposed to a continuous stream of information, global updates, and emotionally charged content. In recent years, there has been a noticeable shift in attitudes towards social media. There is constant engagement with these platforms, which has been observed to weigh on an individual's emotions and affective states. This has generated scholarly discourse regarding emotional fatigue as a consequence of prolonged and continuous engagement with social media platforms. Fatigue can be understood as "a state of tiredness and diminished functioning" (APA, 2018). Taking this definition into consideration, emotional fatigue can be understood as a state of tiredness that negatively affects one's affect, mood, or emotions, leaving them feeling emotionally drained or burnt out. Many individuals experience exhaustion, fatigue, or emotional overwhelm due to social media use. With regards to a digital environment, researchers have coined the term 'Social Media Fatigue' (SMF) to describe "a subjective, multidimensional user experience comprising feelings such as tiredness, annoyance, anger, disappointment, guardedness, loss of interest, or reduced need/motivation associated with various aspects of social network use and interactions" (Ravindran et al, 2014; Zhen & Ling, 2021). Social Media Fatigue has been associated with a number of key factors, among which include the issue of information overload, the constant pressure of connectivity, and the fear of missing out (FOMO). Information overload occurs when a user comes across an excess of unverified information, leading to an overwhelming feeling (Laato et al., 2020). Similarly, the expectation that individuals must remain constantly available online can create a sense of obligation to respond, react, and remain informed. The phenomenon of FOMO further intensifies this expectation, as individuals may feel anxious about missing social interactions, cultural trends, or important updates within their networks (Przybylski et al., 2013).

Emotional fatigue, burnout, and screen exhaustion in the current digital era cannot be understood in isolation. Instead, it must be analysed within a broader structure that includes economic and cultural systems responsible for how emotions are circulated online. The system of affective capitalism commodifies human emotions and commercialises the process of human interactions online. This means online engagement, such as liking, sharing, commenting, and reacting, generates data that can be monetised by platform owners through targeted advertising and algorithmic optimisation (Fuchs, 2014). Affect is not just an experience in the presence of a physical object; it can also be present in a digital space, where users interact with the content they familiarise themselves with. One way affective capitalism intensifies emotional engagement online is through the development of parasocial relationships with content creators. Parasocial relationships include one-sided relationships where the audience feels a sense of emotional connection to the media personalities despite the lack of interpersonal interactions (Horton & Wohl, 1956). This can intensify the emotional involvement associated with the online platforms while at the same time intensifying the psychological involvement associated with the online interactions. Thus, the emotional burden associated with social media can become overly taxing. The media has always relied on affect as a tool for the circulation of content, which can most commonly be seen in TV shows, Sensational news, Docudramas, tabloids, Influencer blogs and vlogs, etc. In the context of social media, content is created, consumed and shared at a much faster pace than most other media. With affective capitalism in place, users of social media platforms are exploited in various ways, for eg, a user's content and interactions become the products themselves. Furthermore, algorithms are designed to push content that engages a user, fetching specific reactions from them, as well as targeted advertising that appeals to their desires. Another exploitative nature of affective capitalism can be observed in the free labour provided by the users who create content on these platforms. Content creators make and bring interaction to these platforms, which are later used by these platform owners to generate revenue through advertising, especially in the case of targeted advertising. This form of commodification is a central feature of affective capitalism, researchers call it digital labour, where users unknowingly contribute unpaid labour through their everyday participation on social networking platforms (Terranova 2000; Fuchs, 2014).

One of the most common examples of affect-related content creation can be seen in memes. Memes essentially serve as channels that allows people to share complex emotions and experiences in a simple yet understandable and, in most cases, entertaining manner. Memes function as cultural artefacts that circulate rapidly across online networks, often combining images, text, and humour to communicate complex ideas in a concise and relatable format (Shifman, 2014). In the context of emotional fatigue, the role of memes has become particularly important as a tool of digital coping. Rather than avoiding emotionally fatiguing online environments altogether, individuals have adapted to these environments through participation in culturally shared forms of expression that require lower levels of emotional investment. Memes rely on humour, irony, and exaggeration to reinterpret stressful and overwhelming experiences, allowing individuals to talk about emotionally heavy topics in a socially acceptable and psychologically manageable way. Studies have demonstrated the ability of humour to reinterpret stressful experiences and provide individuals with a sense of community (Warren et al., 2021). The increasing complexity and popularity of memes may therefore signal larger changes in the way individuals interact with digital media spaces that are characterised by perpetual algorithmic stimulation. Memes can be considered to be both a product and a response to affective capitalism at the same time. Memes can both perpetuate the consumption of entertaining media that keeps the algorithm profitable and offer people a means to cope with emotional exhaustion by reinterpreting stressful situations through humour and irony.

This paradox points to an interesting aspect of participation in social media under affective capitalism. Resistance often occurs through adaptation rather disengagement, completely withdrawing from social media may result in reduced access to social networks, cultural conversations, and sources of information, which can itself be socially isolating. Instead, users adopt strategies that allow participation in a manner that permits an individual to remain part of social media while simultaneously regulating their emotional involvement in it. Although memes may still carry emotionally charged themes, they require a level of emotional labour that is relatively low, thus making them an efficient and socially recognisable form of expression.

This chapter, therefore, aims to examine the relationship between emotional fatigue, social media engagement, and affective capitalism in the contemporary digital environment. It explores how the structure of digital platforms encourages prolonged engagement through affect-driven content circulation, and how this dynamic contributes to emotional exhaustion among users. At the same time, the chapter investigates how memes function as cultural tools that allow individuals to cope with emotionally overwhelming digital environments. By changing stressful experiences into humorous or satirical commentary, users are able to reinterpret their struggles, find solidarity in shared experiences, and maintain engagement within social media spaces. In this way, memes illustrate how digital cultures of humour and irony operate both as a product and a response to the affective economies that characterize the new media era.

EMOTIONAL FATIGUE AND ITS CAUSES

To understand how memes function as coping mechanisms, it is first necessary to examine how emotional fatigue develops within digital environments. The rapid expansion of digital media environments has transformed how individuals encounter information, engage with social events, and experience emotions. Social networking platforms such as Instagram, X, Reddit, TikTok, and Facebook have created pervasive, algorithmically driven spaces where users are in continuous contact with personal narratives, global news, political debates, and emotionally charged content. Although these media provide opportunities for socialisation, identity expression, and information dissemination, they have simultaneously contributed to the development of a psychological phenomenon described as emotional fatigue.

The American Psychological Association defines emotions as "A complex reaction pattern, involving experiential, behavioral, and physiological elements, by which an individual attempts to deal with a personally significant matter or event." Fatigue can be understood as a state of diminished functioning (APA, 2018). Emotional fatigue, as a distinct condition, operates predominantly in the mental domain, manifesting as depletion of affective functions rather than physical exhaustion. An individual who experiences emotional fatigue can be increasingly susceptible to frustration, anger, emotional numbness, and a general sense of emotional volatility. This peculiar kind of tiredness has been consuming individuals through digital spaces, accumulating through each subsequent scroll, reaction, interaction, and the like. Emotional fatigue arises not only from one's proximity to a crisis but rather from an endless exposure to everyone's crisis. Through social media, users connect globally, thereby being exposed to different cultures, people from different countries, and various practices, helping one view humanity through a holistic lens. Simultaneously, individuals are exposed to tragic news and events, which can result in negative emotions. In the long term, this could cause loss of compassion, feeling empathy-fatigued or showing indifference towards others' suffering. This emotional dissonance can be illustrated better through a common experience through social media scrolling, picture an individual opening up a social media app to take a leisurely scroll, who is met with a jarring juxtaposition: One moment, they are viewing a light-hearted cooking tutorial or a friend's vacation photo, and the next, they are staring at a raw, unedited video of a missile strike. This example is not too far from reality, especially in the context of the current conflicts in the Middle East, where individuals who use social media often are being subjected to graphic images or horrifying news of the war. By contrast, their next swipe may be a friend's "Outfit of the Day" or a viral dance challenge, forcing the brain to pivot from a global tragedy to a trivial vanity in a fraction of a second. These stark differences in the content one is exposed to at such a fast pace can give rise to a lot of confusion. In the long term, it can lead to frustration and empathy fatigue. The shift from empathy fatigue to the broader arena of emotional fatigue can be best understood as a progression from acute over-stimulation to a chronic state of depletion. When an individual is constantly subjected to a continuous stream of global suffering and triviality, they experience empathy fatigue, the specific, acute exhaustion of one's prosocial reserves. In order to preserve the self from this constant state of over-stimulation, the self adapts to this situation by entering a state of emotional fatigue, which can be described as a systemic shutdown akin to Maslach's description of depersonalization. In this state, the "numbness" of the self, as described by the inability to muster pity for a specific situation, has evolved to be a diminished state of functioning wherein the brain has essentially become desensitised to emotions so that it might not entirely shut down. Hence, the acute over-stimulation of attempting to care for one tragic post has evolved to an emotional insolvency wherein the self no longer has the "currency" of emotion necessary to engage with the digital or physical world.

The key theoretical explanation of emotional fatigue is offered by Christina Maslach and Michael Leiter's model of occupational burnout, which, although initially developed to explain workplace stress, has since been increasingly applied to the digital and consumer domains. According to Maslach, burnout is characterised by three interrelated components: emotional exhaustion, depersonalisation, and diminished personal accomplishment. Emotional exhaustion, which represents the key stress component of this model, is described as "a psychological state of exhaustion caused by prolonged emotional involvement with a social situation that is perceived to be impossible to solve or resolve, leaving the individual unable to continue to provide emotional support to others" (Maslach & Leiter, 1997, p. 17). A study by Fardouly and Vartanian (2021) found that heavy social media users, those engaging with platforms for more than three hours daily, showed significantly elevated scores on emotional exhaustion scales compared to moderate users.

An upcoming term for these negative feelings, which entail frequent use of social media, is "Social Media Fatigue" (SMF). A definition by Ravindran et al. (2014) explains it as "a subjective, multidimensional user experience comprising feelings such as tiredness, annoyance, anger, disappointment, guardedness, loss of interest, or reduced need/motivation associated with various aspects of social network use and interactions" (Ravindran et al., 2014). This fatigue is compounded by the necessity for an individual to be engaged with their network, either by interacting with a post or responding to a message. This can create a pressure for social interaction, which becomes a form of emotional labor, where an individual is expected to respond with empathy to another's circumstances or provide opinions on a social issue. SMF is closely connected with the broader concept of information overload, which is a concept with roots in cognitive psychology. This current theory is directly influenced by the cognitive load theory, which is based on the idea that working memory is constrained by a specific capacity. When the demands placed on working memory exceed a certain level, it can result in cognitive and affective strain (Sweller, 1988).

In the context of social media, information overlap is not merely an issue with the volume of content; it is also the nature of the content. Not only must users process vast amounts of information, but this information also varies in emotional tone, factual accuracy, and social import, often in rapid sequence and with little opportunity for cognitive or emotional digestion. An analysis conducted by Forbes (2021) estimated that an average Urban dweller encounters between 6,000-10,000 pieces of advertising and media content each day. This gives way to stimulation that substantially exceeds the cognitive and affective processing capacity of most individuals. The result, as SMF research consistently demonstrates, is a progressive erosion of engagement motivation, attentional capacity, and emotional responsiveness.

Beyond cognitive overload, There exists an expectation for individuals to remain actively and visibly engaged with their networks. Responding to messages promptly, reacting to posts, sharing opinions on social issues, and social broadcasting of one's life all add to maintaining an ongoing act of social presence. The ease of networking through social media only amplifies these expectations and transforms them into emotional labour, a concept introduced by Arlie Hochschild (1983) in their work '*In the Managed Heart*'. This concept is meant to describe how individuals are required to manage and perform emotional states in accordance with socially prescribed norms. In the digital sphere, Obligatory empathy can be understood as a form of emotional labour, as users feel pressured to provide thoughtful responses to the revelations of others' suffering, political indignation, or personal crises, even if they themselves feel emotionally drained. To further understand emotional fatigue in the context of communication and networking in digital spaces, we can introduce the 'Always - On' Culture posited by Sherry Turkle. Turkle argues that the proliferation of digital communication and technology has not enriched human relational life, but rather impoverished it. This is through displacing the deep, embodied, emotionally sustaining forms of interpersonal engagement with shallow, asynchronous, and perpetually interrupted digital interactions. Through data collected from qualitative interviews in the workplace, schools, and family settings, she documents 'Flight from conversations'. This phenomenon explains how individuals inclreasingly avoid face - to - face emotional engagement in favour of more manageable, editable, and controllable interactions afforded by digital messaging. Thus, Turkle describes the paradoxical consequence of this as the creation of a type of relational depletion in which the user feels emotionally "drained," not because they have interacted at a richly detailed level, but because they have interacted in a way that has been systematically deprived of the restorative benefits associated with genuine human connection (Turkle, 2015, p. 21).

The convergence of Maslach's burnout model, the Social Media Fatigue and information overload frameworks, and Turkle's 'Always - On' critique illuminates how emotional fatigue can take place through continuous exposure to social media. It arises through the intersection of cognitive overload, affective content saturation, normative digital labour expectations, the degradation of restorative time, and, for many users, the additional challenge of dealing with hostile or traumatic online environments. The theoretical frameworks discussed in this section offer not only a nomenclature for this condition but a critical framework for analysis for the systems in which this condition is embedded. The themes discussed in the next section extend from this foundation by considering how affective capitalism institutionalises these conditions and how a meme culture has emerged as a response to these conditions in a paradoxical way.

AFFECTIVE CAPITALISM

If emotional fatigue is a recurring symptom, then Affective capitalism is a catalyst for such a symptom. Affective capitalism is a theoretical framework that describes emotions, attention, and interpersonal interactions. At its core, affective capitalism is the economic logic that transforms human feeling into a tradable commodity by treating emotional arousal as a raw material for value extraction. Unlike industrial capitalism, which commodifies physical labour, or cognitive capitalism, which focuses on one's intellectual output, affective capitalism exploits the emotional responses which keep a user tethered to a digital interface. Within this framework, social media platforms are not neutral stages for connection but are purposefully engineered "Affective Environments" designed to stimulate constant emotional responses that can be quantified and sold as engagement data. The term draws on the broader concept of 'Affective labour' popularised by Michael Hardt and Antonio Negri, which has been extended to describe how capitalism in the digital form has moved beyond the extraction of physical and cognitive labour to encompass the 'mining' of emotional life itself. (Hardt & Negiri, 2000; Fuchs, 2014). By incentivising "affective labour", i.e., the unpaid mental work users perform when they react to, share, or process content, the system prioritises the frequency of emotional spikes over the well-being of the individual. This constant demand for emotional output creates a user - dependent relationship where the platform's profit grows in direct proportion to the user's emotional price, effectively acting as the structural catalyst for the fatigue described by Maslach and Leiter. Understanding affective capitalism is key to understanding digital cultures because it allows us to understand the logic behind the interface of the platform, the logic behind the incentivisation of emotional reactions, and why phenomena like memes, viral content, and online humour are not peripheral entertainments but central nodes in the political economy of attention.

Michael Hardt and Antonio Negro, in their influential work '*Empire*' (2000), and '*Multitude*' (2004), introduced the concept of 'Immaterial Labour' to describe post -Fordist shift, i.e., a shift from rigid, structured, centralised, and assembly line mass production (Fordism) to a flexible, specialised, and automated manufacturing. The primary value created was also through immaterial labour or products, such as knowledge, communication, relationships, and affect. This shift may help us gain more insight into how emotional significance became an important marketing factor, which might have further evolved into commodifying a consumer's affect altogether. Crucially, there is the fact that affective labour is becoming more central to the economy and is still unremunerated in its digital form. Thus, when users share content on Instagram, share their emotions on X, and produce memes, they are engaging in affective labour and are producing content with emotional value, which is being exploited by social media companies in the form of advertising revenue. The revenue earned by Meta Platforms Inc. in 2022 was $116.6 billion (Meta Platforms, Inc., 2023). The overwhelming majority of this revenue is earned through advertising systems, which are based on targeting users according to their emotional and behavioural data. This revenue is being earned, to a large extent, on the unpaid labour of billions of users, which is made analytically visible through Hardt and Negri's approach.

In the *'Making of Emotional Capitalism' (2007),* Eva Illouz argues that capitalism and emotional life have become mutually essential in modernity. Through her analysis of the theories and histories of psychoanalysis, self-help culture, and therapy culture, Illouz traces how the language and logic of emotion have come to infuse economic practice and how, in turn, the logic of economics has come to infuse and dominate intimate life. For Illouz, emotional capitalism is not merely exploiting existing emotions but actually changing what emotions are and how they are expressed and for what social purpose. And in the digital age, it is easy to see how this analysis would extend to social media platforms that actually game-ify emotional expression through likes and reactions. For example, "the quantification of affects, such as when a post is given 2,300 likes or when a meme is shared 50,000 times, converts emotional communication into social currency subject to the same laws of accumulation and deprecation as financial capital" (Illouz, 2007, p. 42). Research supports this idea: in a study published in JMIR Mental Health in 2022, 64% of social media users adjusted their emotional expression to maximise engagement in order to get reactions.

Bernard Stiegler's (2010) *'For a New Critique of Political Economy'* provides a philosophically rich framework, bringing Freudian theories to the table, and centring on the concept of attention as a psychic and political economic source. According to Stiegler, our current form of capitalism is first and foremost an "attention economy" that works on the capture, channelling, and finally exhaustion of the libidinal energies of subjects. Stiegler's idea of attention is informed by Freud's idea of the libido, which we can think of as the instinctual, psychosexual energy driving human behaviour and personality development. To further simplify it, the libido is the "Mental energy" that motivates or drives an individual to fulfill their needs, and is thus not a cognitive ability in and of itself, but a desire-energy that, when tapped into and exploited by the culture industries and technology, leads to what Stiegler calls "psychic proletarianisation," or the loss of individual's capacity for independent thought, attention, and care (Stiegler, 2010, p. 17). When an individual loses the ability to think for themselves, their originality, and autonomy, they become "automated" users who simply react to whatever they are subjected to. Stiegler's idea also emphasises the 'loss of care', which is a consequence of our mental energy (libido) being siphoned off by the attention economy. This idea can be linked back to empathy fatigue within the larger framework of emotional fatigue. The disengagement, flat affect, or an unwillingness to show genuine care during empathy fatigue can look quite a lot like 'Loss of care', which is not just a product of 'tiredness', but rather a consequence of being 'mined empty' by interfaces that commodify our very capacity to display genuine feelings. The human attention span, which has allegedly shrunk from twelve to eight seconds between 2000 and 2015 (Microsoft, 2015), a figure that is certainly widely known and cited, although its methodology is not uncontroversial, represents the most common level of Stiegler's concern, even though his philosophical argument is certainly located on a deeper level.

Viewed together, these frameworks reveal affective capitalism as a coherent and pervasive system. The attention economy does not simply sell products to consumers, it sells consumers' attention and emotional data to advertisers, and at the same time, it influences subjects' affective life to make it more legible, predictable, and monetisable. A case in point is offered by the structure of TikTok, whose recommendation system, recognised by the platform to maximise 'time spent' rather than user satisfaction (TikTok, 2020), can be seen as a machine for maximising affective labour extraction. The result is a system in which emotional fatigue is not an accidental by-product but a structurally produced condition, generated by a platform that profits from sustained emotional engagement regardless of its psychological cost to users.

DEFINING A 'MEME' AND ITS EMERGENCE WITHIN AFFECTIVE CAPITALISM

A meme is a popular form of content that primarily serves as humorous commentary made on shared human experiences. Limor Shifman's work *'Memes in Digital Culture'* (2014) provides the most systematic theoretical account of the internet meme as a cultural form. Shifman's work defines internet memes as "groups of digital items sharing common characteristics of content, form, and/or stance, which were created with awareness of each other, and were circulated, imitated, and/or transformed via the internet by many users" (Shifman, 2014: 7-8). This definition is significant for various reasons. Firstly, it distinguishes internet memes from Dawkins' biological metaphor by highlighting their collective and dialogic nature. Internet memes do not spread in the way biological memes do; instead, they evolve and are engaged with by communities of users who share cultural knowledge and communication practices. Secondly, Shifman's definition of internet memes emphasises their relational aspect; in other words, memes function as a form of cultural dialogue that seeks to make sense of shared experiences through collective reinterpretation. This is crucial in explaining why memes flourish as a cultural phenomenon in relation to affective capitalism. When people feel emotionally saturated, memes offer a way of collectively naming and negotiating that experience.

To understand the meme culture online, Henry Jenkins, in '*Where Old Media Collide',* introduces the concept of 'Participatory Culture'. A culture in which fans, consumers, and ordinary users become active producers of media content. Jenkins argues that the convergence of old and new media technologies has created the conditions for a fundamental democratisation of cultural production. This means there is room for grassroots media forms such as memes to co-exist with mainstream media. Therefore, memes are not only for entertainment. Instead, it is a form of cultural agency that enables people to comment and critique dominant ideologies through the means of popular culture. There is empirical data to support the importance of this aspect of memes as well. According to a report published by the Pew Research Centre in 2021, "55% of adults aged 18-29 have shared a meme in the past month. And 30% of those aged 18-29 have shared memes to express their opinion on political and social issues.' This shows that memes are used as a form of "micro-politics" in people's everyday lives. This participatory model helps us understand how memes can exist in an affective capitalistic environment. Users show autonomy by producing content, not only to speak up about issues and politics, but also to influence the way in which the general public thinks, albeit in subtle and ordinary ways. This, in turn, makes the use of memes an expression, which enables individuals to simplify their thoughts, frustrations, and opinions into easily shareable forms.

Furthermore, participation in meme culture can also open up economic pathways for an individual. Terry Terranova, in her essay *'Free Labour" Producing Culture for the Digital Economy*: offers a more critical theoretical lens. For Terranova, the 'free labour' carried out by internet users, such as the creation and sharing of memes, is not simply a form of cultural expression but rather a structural aspect of digital capitalism. Memes, in other words, generate engagement, traffic, and advertising revenue for a platform whose users receive no compensation. The viral meme, in short, is a form of cultural resistance and a commodity at the same time. On the one hand, it is a spontaneous expression of popular culture and humour. On the other hand, it is a content unit that fuels the platform economy. This contradiction is not incidental, but constitutive. Affective capitalism is fueled by the genuine creativity and passion that users bring to meme creation, a form of participatory culture mobilised in the name of capital accumulation. (Terranova, 200, p.37)

Consider the emergence of the "This is Fine" meme, originally a panel from K.C. Green's webcomic Gunshow, depicting a cartoon dog calmly drinking coffee as its surroundings burn. This became a widely shared cultural shorthand for passive acceptance of catastrophic circumstances. By 2016, the image had been adapted to comment on everything from elections to the COVID-19 pandemic, generating millions of shares across platforms. From Shifman's perspective, the process of remixing the image represents the concept of participatory culture. From Jenkins' point of view, the remixing represents the concept of media convergence. From Terranova's point of view, the act of remixing the image represents the concept of value. The image represents the affective state of living in late capitalism. From an applied perspective, the concept of memes as a cultural unit provides interesting insights into how digital communities interact and negotiate meaning. For instance, researchers may study memes to investigate public opinion, culture, and emotional responses to social events. Memes are being used by educators and communicators to engage people because they realise they can simplify complex ideas and make them more relatable to the digital community.

IRONY AND HUMOUR: THE LINGUISTICS OF MEMES ONLINE

Irony and humour are among the core pillars that hold up what we now know as memes. The linguistic and rhetorical structures of internet memes are not arbitrary; they reflect specific social, psychological, and cultural logic that make irony and humour particularly well-suited to navigating the emotional conditions of digital life. Irony, in its definitive meaning, could be understood as the use of language to convey a meaning opposite to its literal sense; in its contemporary digital inflexion, it has evolved into a far more complex and polysemous communicative mode, encompassing sarcasm, self-deprecation, absurdism, and what scholars have termed 'Post Irony'. Humour, relatedly, operates as both a coping mechanism and a social bonding device, performing relational work that is particularly valuable in environments characterised by emotional saturation and communicative ambiguity.

The concept of 'carnivalesque' proposed by Mikhail Bakhtin, in his work '*Rabelais and His World*', describes a mode of cultural expression in which hierarchies are temporarily suspended, official discourse is parodied, and social norms are subjected to grotesque exaggeration and laughter. Bakhtin coined "Heteroglossia", a sociolinguistic term referring to the presence and coexistence of diverse voices, styles, and social perspectives within a single text, especially a novel. This framework maps productively onto the linguistics of internet memes, particularly those that use parody, the grotesque juxtaposition, and irrelevant humour to comment on official culture, political authority, and social norms. Indeed, the very mechanism by which internet memes use images and captions in a way that inverts them in a carnivalesque fashion is directly in line with the Bakhtin framework. Indeed, empirical research on internet memes in the 2016 and 2020 US election cycles has shown that the most common form of internet rhetoric was parodic inversion, wherein official images, statements, and symbols are repurposed and satirised in a new context (Chagas et al., 2019).

Sigmund Freud, a renowned neurologist, also known for establishing the psychoanalytic theory, believed that jokes were not an innocent form of entertainment but sophisticated mechanisms that allowed one to expend their psychic energy into particular channels. They allow the expression of socially prohibited desires, aggression, and anxieties through the oblique route of humour. He expounds on his ideas and approaches to humour in his work *'Jokes and Their Relation to the Unconscious'*. Freud identified three primary functions of jokes: the release of pent-up aggression ('tendentious jokes'), the expression of sexual desire (obscene jokes), and the expression of nihilistic or absurdist despair (cynical jokes). The third type is especially relevant to the linguistics of modern internet memes, some of which use dark or absurdist humour to express a type of 'cognitive appraisal,' a term used by psychologists to describe how people tend to reframe threatening or painful experiences in ways that reduce their emotional impact. A study published in Psychological Science in 2021 found that people who used humour to reappraise stressful experiences had lower cortisol levels and better mood outcomes than those who did not (Samson et al., 2021), lending support to Freud's initial insight about the function of humour as a safety valve.

The Theory of Politics of Irony by Linda Hutcheon is specifically concerned with the rhetorical and political dimensions of irony as a discursive strategy. Hutcheon defines irons as a 'trans-ideological, one that can be employed in the cause of conservative, radical, or liberatory politics as the situation demands. A second aspect she emphasises is the social and relational nature of irony. Irony needs an 'interpretive community' to be effective. This gives it the power to differentiate between insiders and outsiders. This aspect of irony is particularly significant in the linguistics of internet memes because they tend to be deployed within particular sub-cultural communities, 'stan' cultures, political cultures, and professional cultures, whose shared cultural knowledge gives them access to the ironic distance. The 'Distracted Boyfriend' meme, for example, is an instance of pure irony only for those who are aware of the source image, the usual captions accompanying it, and the rhetorical conventions that govern its use. To outsiders, it is just another stock photo. Hutcheon's theory of irony thus provides an insight into how memes function as both an act of communication and an act of community identification.

A good case in point is the "doomscrolling" meme genre, which gained traction on social media between 2020 and 2022 in response to the COVID-19 pandemic and the news cycle it generated. These memes generally represented an individual succumbing to the compulsion of reading bad news at the same time as the individual was ironically self-deprecating about the action itself (e.g., an individual reading a news report of a burning television with the caption "me at 3 am just clicking on more bad news"). Google Trends statistics reveal a rise in searches regarding "doom-scrolling" of 4,300% between March and December 2020 (Google Trends, 2020). These memes served a variety of linguistic purposes simultaneously: labelling a new experience (carnivalesque heteroglossia), relieving anxiety through ironic self-deprecation (Freudian joke work), and establishing a community of identification with others who have had the experience (Hutcheon's ironic community). These three examples of memetic humour and irony are not incidental or superficial characteristics of new media culture; rather, they are structurally essential components of how an individual in the new media age navigates and partially overcomes the emotional pressures of their information environment.

MEMES AS A FORM OF DIGITAL COPING

The preceding sections have established that emotional fatigue is structurally produced through a multitude of factors, and memes emerged as a central communicative form within an affective capitalist system, and their distinctive linguistic register reflects sophisticated strategies for managing the affective demands of digital life. Digital coping could be understood as adaptive strategies through which one deals with stressful events, and includes interacting with any form of digital or electronic media, such as playing video games, social networking, or consuming social media at regulated periods to mitigate the intensity of stress experienced. The notion of coping originates in psychology and could be understood as the cognitive and behavioural processes used to manage the demands of stressful situations. Memes, as discussed in this section, represent a culturally particular form of "emotion-focused coping," a term used in psychology to characterise coping mechanisms "not directed at changing the stressful person or situation but rather at regulating one's emotional response to the situation." In a media environment of information-overload, affective mishandling, and structural emotional depletion, the role of memes as a public resource of emotion regulation and social bonding should not be underestimated.

Lazarus and Susan Folkman's (1948) transactional model of stress and coping remains the dominant framework of understanding coping within the field of psychology. The model proposes that stress arises not from objective events but fom and individual's subjective perceptions or cognitive appraisal of those events. Specifically, their assessment of whether an event constitutes a threat and whether they have sufficient resources to manage it. Coping strategies are classified along two primary axes: problem-focused coping (aimed at altering or mitigating the stressor), and emotions - focused coping (aimed at regulating and managing stress responses to an event). The model has since been extended to include 'meaning - based', in which individuals reframe threatening situations within broader narratives that preserve a sense of coherence and agency (Folkman, 1997). Memes are arguably used most obviously as a type of 'meaning-based coping': by reframing difficult experiences (unemployment, political crisis, pandemic) within a broader framework of shared humour, individuals are able to reassert some form of 'narrative control' over difficult circumstances. Empirical research appears to support this reading. A study published in 2022 in Computers in Human Behaviour found that participants who gained exposure to COVID-19 memes had significantly lower levels of anxiety and higher social connectedness scores than those in the control group, indicating that meme engagement is a coping resource (Yue et al., 2022)

Limor Shifman's (2014) theoretical work on participatory culture and 'collective intelligence' offers a framework for understanding memes as coping mechanisms, this time at the collective rather than individual level. Drawing on Pierre Lévy's concept of collective intelligence. The distributed knowledge and creative capacity of networked communities, Shifman argues, that memes function as vehicles of collective sense-making, allowing communities to collaboratively process shared experiences and produce shared meanings. In the context of digital coping, this collective dimension is crucial, the coping function of memes is not merely individual but social, producing what sociologists call 'social support' in the sense that one is not alone in one's experience. The collective production and sharing of mental health memes on platforms like Tumblr and Reddit illustrate this function, subreddits such as "r/depression_memes", which had over 1.2 million members as of 2023 (Reddit, 2023), function as communities of affective solidarity, where the shared ironic articulation of mental health struggles creates both recognition and connection. A 2020 study in JMIR Mental Health found that 22.7% of young people aged 16–24 reported using memes as a primary way of discussing mental health experiences, a finding that underscores the therapeutic social function of participatory meme culture (Ridout et al., 2020).

Lauren Berlant's (2011) Cruel Optimism provides the most critical and politically incisive of how memes function as digital coping mechanisms. Berlant introduces the concept of 'cruel optimism' to describe a relation in which the very object of one's desire constitutes an obstacle to one's flourishing. Applied to digital culture, the concept illuminates a troubling paradox at the heart of memes as coping mechanisms; the platforms on which memes circulate are the same platforms whose structural logics produce the emotional fatigue that memes are used to cope with. When individuals turn to Instagram memes to manage the anxiety produced by social comparison on Instagram, or share TikTok coping humour to process the attention depletion produced by TikTok's algorithm, they are engaging in what Berlant might characterise as a cruel optimism: the coping strategy is inseparable from and may even sustain the conditions that necessitate it. This is not to argue that memes lack genuine coping value; the empirical evidence reviewed above suggests that they do provide real affective relief. Rather, it is to insist that their coping function must be understood within the broader political economy that structures both the need for coping and the available resources for it (Berlant, 2011, p. 24). This framework provides a different perspective from the rest, and helps understand the distortion in one's perception against factual evidence. This highlights the paradox spoken about in previous sections, where memes fuel and allow for affective capitalistic structures to occur and exist. Understanding memes through Berlant's concept of cruel optimism, therefore, complicates overly celebratory narratives about digital humour and collective coping. While memes undeniably create spaces for solidarity, shared recognition, and emotional expression, they also reveal how coping strategies can become intertwined with the very structures that generate stress. Berlant's framework thus promotes a more critical approach to digital humour, one that acknowledges that memes are not only significant affective practices but also signs of a broader socio-economic order that influences how people, in general, experience and manage emotional life in the digital era.

A compelling real-world application is the rapid expansion of 'burnout memes' across professional social media platforms, particularly LinkedIn and Twitter/X, during and after the COVID-19 pandemic. Between 2020 and 2023, meme formats depicting workplace exhaustion, remote work absurdity, and the collapse of work-life boundaries achieved viral status, generating millions of shares and spawning dedicated accounts. From Lazarus and Folkman's perspective, these memes represent a form of meaning-based coping, reframing experiences of professional exhaustion within a humorous shared narrative that preserves a sense of agency and solidarity. From Shifman's standpoint, they enact collective intelligence, producing a distributed cultural commentary on labour conditions that exceeds what any individual could articulate alone. From Berlant's perspective, however, they exemplify cruel optimism, they allow workers to process burnout while continuing to participate in the very platform economy and, in many cases, the very professional cultures that produce it. This contradiction is not a failure of memes as coping mechanisms but a reflection of the structural conditions in which they operate: conditions in which emotional fatigue, affective capitalism, and digital culture are so thoroughly intertwined that extracting oneself from the system is far harder than laughing at it.

CONCLUSION

This chapter has examined the multidimensional relationship between emotional fatigue, affective capitalism, and the role of memes as instruments of digital coping within the contemporary media era. Through an interdisciplinary theoretical framework drawing on psychology, political economy, cultural studies, sociology, and linguistics, it has been traced how structural conditions of the new media era have produced a pervasive environment of emotional depletion, and how digital culture has responded to that depletion through a collectively produced form of content. In doing so, this chapter also brings in insights into a deeper and more troubling paradox, that the very mechanisms through which individuals seek relief from are, in many ways, the products and contributors to the emotionally depleting, effective capitalistic environment of social media.

The initial theme of this chapter establishes emotional fatigue as a psychologically distinct condition that arises from sustained and unregulated exposure to the affectively saturated environments produced by algorithmically driven social media platforms. Using Maslach's and Leiter's model of occupational burnout, the chapter demonstrates that the three components of the model, emotional exhaustion, depersonalisation and diminished personal accomplishment are not uncommon within a digital environment. The concept of Social Media Fatigue was introduced as a new and more specific concept to understand how tiredness, disengagement, and affective depletion emerge from prolonged immersion in digital networks. Information overload, the expectation of constant connectivity, and the phenomenon of Fear of Missing Out (FOMO) were also identified as common drivers of emotional fatigue, each of which functions to sustain use engagement well beyond the threshold of comfortable cognitive and affective processing. Sherry Turkle's diagnosis of the 'Always On' culture was drawn upon to illustrate how digital communication, rather than enriching relational life, has systematically displaced the restorative forms of human connection that might otherwise provide relief from exhaustion and stress.

Then the chapter moves on to explore affective capitalism, a concept derived from a multitude of economic concepts, and applied to the architecture of a digital space. Affective capitalism explains how algorithms are built and keep individuals hooked for durations beyond their liking. Through the work of Hardt and Negri on immaterial and affective labour, Eva Illouz on emotional capitalism, and Stiegler on the attention economy, this section argues that emotional experiences of social media users are not incidental, but rather a product of the central economic logic of such platforms. Social Media companies do not merely provide a space where emotions are expressed; they actively engineer and optimise such spaces to maximise the emotional intensity and duration of user engagement. By maximising engagement, they generate greater amounts of revenue through advertising and so on. The idea of digital labour, as presented by Terranova's work on free labour within the digital economy, adds another layer of complexity to these systems. The user does not simply engage with the material presented to them; they are also the producers of that material, and as such, they are creating the value that supports the system whose operations are now apparently draining them of their energy. The financial figures discussed about both Meta Platforms and the structural analysis of TikTok's algorithm serve to demonstrate the material realities of the relationship between the user and the system: their emotional response is not only a cultural phenomenon but also an economic one, designed to be sustained regardless of the cost to the user's mental well-being.

The third and fourth themes are written to understand memes, their emergence, and the nature of their linguistics. These sections explain how memes emerge as a participatory and collective culture of the users, who show autonomy in an affectively capitalistic space of Social Media. Later, the last theme explores how memes act as instruments of coping in many instances, the chapter utilized Lazarus and Folkman's transactional model of stress and coping to argue that memes might best be understood as a form of meaning-based coping mechanism: in that they allow the individual to reframe threatening or overwhelming circumstances within a wider narrative of shared humour and recognition that they can exert some level of agency over, despite the circumstances being beyond their control. Nevertheless, the chapter has also argued, through Lauren Berlant's concept of cruel optimism, that these functions cannot be celebrated without a critical eye, or without reference to the context which makes them necessary. The concept of cruel optimism, as developed by Berlant, refers to a state of relations wherein the object of the relations, or the practice, which serves as a source of relief from the problems experienced, is the very source of the problems themselves, and cannot exist without them, with particular pertinence to the meme-mediated coping mechanism.

Several important implications follow from this analysis. For researchers, this chapter underscores the need for interdisciplinary approaches to the study of digital emotional life. Psychological frameworks for understanding fatigue and coping must be integrated with economic or sociological theories to understand how human behaviour intersects with existing systems and influences each other. Social media use and wellbeing studies that focus on individual psychological factors without reference to their structural context within affective capitalism will inevitably yield limited and potentially misleading analyses of social media use and wellbeing. Similarly, critical political economy approaches that focus on the exploitative aspects of digital labour without reference to the cultural and affective value that individuals derive from their participation in digital communities will inevitably yield analyses that are overly deterministic and potentially dismissive of the complexity of human response to structural constraint.

For platform designers and policymakers, the analysis points toward the need for structural reform of incentive algorithms that currently govern social media platforms. More fundamental changes are needed, regulatory frameworks that limit algorithmic optimisation for engagement at the expense of well-being; transparency requirements that make platform recommendation systems more transparent to users; and economic models that do not rely so heavily on the extraction of affective data as the primary means of financial viability. The increasing body of evidence linking heavy social media use to emotional exhaustion, as reviewed in this chapter, adds urgency to such calls for change.

Educators, communications, and practitioners working in the field of mental health and well-being may benefit from understanding how emotional fatigue may arise in these systems. It further provides an understanding of how memes play a role in coping and open up avenues for engagement. The finding that substantial proportions of young people use memes as a primary means of processing and communication about mental health experiences suggests that meme culture is not a barrier to mental health literacy.

Looking beyond the immediate concerns of this chapter, the larger phenomenon explored is the simultaneous production of emotional fatigue and cultural coping resources by the same digital systems, raising profound questions about the long-term psychological and social consequences of life in the new media era. As social media platforms continue to evolve, as new technologies of immersion and connectivity are introduced, and as the pace of information circulation continues to accelerate, the pressures described in this chapter are unlikely to diminish absent significant structural change. The emotional linguistics of meme culture, the irony, the dark humour, and the recognition of shared precarity may be read as a form of cultural intelligence, a collaborative effort to make sense of the world that is otherwise perceived as overwhelming and beyond the individual's control.

Ultimately, this chapter has argued that to understand emotional fatigue in the new media era, one must look simultaneously inwards, at the psychological mechanisms through which individuals experience and respond to affective overload, and outward, at structural systems that produce those conditions of overload in the first place. Memes, positioned at the intersection of these two levels of analysis, offer a unique, valuable lens through which to observe both the frustrations of affective capitalism and the creative, often paradoxical, resources that digital cultures develop in response to those frustrations. They are, all at once, products of the system and protests against it, commodities and communal expressions, sources of further engagement and spaces of genuine, if temporary, relief. To take memes seriously as an object of cultural and theoretical study is to take seriously the full complexity of what it means to live, feel, and cope in the digital age. To take memes seriously is to take seriously the idea that the line between exploitation and expression, between coping and complicity, is not as clear as either the celebratory or the critical accounts of digital culture want to suggest, but that to understand the real conditions of digital emotional life means considering both possibilities at once.

REFERENCES

Affective capitalism: Investments and investigations. (2016). [Editorial]. Ephemera: Theory & Politics in Organization, 1–13, 1–13. https://www.ephemerajournal.org

American Psychological Association. (2022). Stress in America 2022: Concerned for the future, beset by inflation. APA. https://www.apa.org/news/press/releases/stress/2022/concerned-future-inflation

Bakhtin, M. M. (1984). *Rabelais and his world* (Iswolsky, H., Trans.). Indiana University Press. (Original work published 1965)

Berlant, L. (2011). *Cruel optimism*. Duke University Press.

Chagas, V., Freire, F., Rios, D., & Magalhães, D. (2019). Political memes and the politics of memes: A methodological proposal for content analysis of online political memes. *First Monday*, *24*(2). Advance online publication. DOI: 10.5210/fm.v24i2.7264

Dawkins, R. (1976). *The selfish gene*. Oxford University Press.

Fardouly, J., & Vartanian, L. R. (2021). Social media and body image concerns: Current research and future directions. *Current Opinion in Psychology*, *9*, 1–5. DOI: 10.1016/j.copsyc.2015.09.005

Folkman, S. (1997). Positive psychological states and coping with severe stress. *Social Science & Medicine*, *45*(8), 1207–1221. DOI: 10.1016/S0277-9536(97)00040-3 PMID: 9381234

Forbes. (2021, February 15). Finding brand success in the digital world. https://www.forbes.com/sites/forbesagencycouncil/2021/08/25/finding-brand-success-in-the-digital-world/

Freud, S. (2003). *Jokes and their relation to the unconscious* (Crick, J., Trans.). Penguin. (Original work published 1905)

Fuchs, C. (2014). Digital prosumption labour on social media in the context of the capitalist regime of time. *Time & Society*, *23*(1), 97–123. DOI: 10.1177/0961463X13502117

Google Trends. (2020). Doomscrolling search trends 2020. https://trends.google.com/trends/explore?q=doomscrolling

Hardt, M., & Negri, A. (2000). *Empire*. Harvard University Press.

Hardt, M., & Negri, A. (2004). *Multitude: War and democracy in the age of empire*. Penguin Press.

Horton, D., & Wohl, R. (1956). Mass communication and para-social interaction: Observations on intimacy at a distance. *psychiatry, 19*(3), 215-229.

Hutcheon, L. (1994). *Irony's edge: The theory and politics of irony*. Routledge.

Illouz, E. (2007). *Cold intimacies: The making of emotional capitalism*. Polity Press.

Jenkins, H. (2006). *Convergence culture: Where old and new media collide*. New York University Press.

Laato, S., Islam, A. N., & Laine, T. H. (2020). Did location-based games motivate players to socialize during COVID-19? *Telematics and Informatics, 54*, 101458. DOI: 10.1016/j.tele.2020.101458 PMID: 34887611

Lazarus, R. S., & Folkman, S. (1984). *Stress, appraisal, and coping*. Springer.

Maslach, C., & Leiter, M. P. (1997). *The truth about burnout: How organizations cause personal stress and what to do about it*. Jossey-Bass.

Meta Platforms, Inc. (2023). Annual report 2022. https://investor.fb.com/investor-news/press-release-details/2023/Meta-Reports-Fourth-Quarter-and-Full-Year-2022-Results/

Microsoft. (2015). *Attention spans. Consumer insights report*. Microsoft Canada.

Pew Research Center. (2021). The state of online harassment. Pew Research Center. https://www.pewresearch.org/internet/2021/01/13/the-state-of-online-harassment/

Przybylski, A. K., Murayama, K., DeHaan, C. R., & Gladwell, V. (2013). Motivational, emotional, and behavioral correlates of fear of missing out. *Computers in Human Behavior, 29*(4), 1841–1848. DOI: 10.1016/j.chb.2013.02.014

Ravindran, T., Yeow Kuan, A. C., & Hoe Lian, D. G. (2014). Antecedents and effects of social network fatigue. *Journal of the Association for Information Science and Technology, 65*(11), 2306–2320. DOI: 10.1002/asi.23122

Reddit. (2023). r/depression_memes. https://www.reddit.com/r/depression_memes/

Ridout, B., Campbell, A., & Ellis, L. (2020). 'Off the Record': Exploring the role of social media in mental health help-seeking for young people. *JMIR Mental Health, 7*(7), e18324. DOI: 10.2196/18324

Samson, A. C., Glynn, M. A., & Gross, J. J. (2021). Humor as an emotion regulation strategy. *Psychological Science, 32*(4), 591–602. DOI: 10.1177/0956797620969409

Shifman, L. (2014). *Memes in digital culture*. MIT Press.

Stiegler, B. (2010). *For a new critique of political economy* (Ross, D., Trans.). Polity Press.

Sweller, J. (1988). Cognitive load during problem solving: Effects on learning. *Cognitive Science*, *12*(2), 257–285. DOI: 10.1207/s15516709cog1202_4

Terranova, T. (2000). Free labor: Producing culture for the digital economy. *Social Text*, *18*(2), 33–58. DOI: 10.1215/01642472-18-2_63-33

TikTok. (2020). How TikTok recommends videos #ForYou. TikTok Newsroom. https://newsroom.tiktok.com/en-us/how-tiktok-recommends-videos-for-you

Turkle, S. (2015). *Reclaiming conversation: The power of talk in a digital age*. Penguin Press.

Uhls, Y. T., Michikyan, M., Morris, J., Garcia, D., Small, G. W., Zgourou, E., & Greenfield, P. M. (2014). Five days at outdoor education camp without screens improves preteen skills with nonverbal emotion cues. *Computers in Human Behavior*, *39*, 387–392. DOI: 10.1016/j.chb.2014.05.036

Warren, C., Barsky, A., & McGraw, A. P. (2021). What makes things funny? An integrative review of the antecedents of laughter and amusement. *Personality and Social Psychology Review*, *25*(1), 41–65. DOI: 10.1177/1088868320961909 PMID: 33342368

Yue, Z., Zhang, H., Kim, S., Baruh, L., & Tamul, D. (2022). COVID-19 memes and coping: A multiple-method investigation. *Computers in Human Behavior*, *128*, 107094. DOI: 10.1016/j.chb.2021.107094

Chapter 10

Scrolling Into Numbness: Reframing Emotional Fatigue and Social Indifference in the Algorithmic Age

Piali Haldar
http://orcid.org/0000-0003-4729-6964
Brainware University, Kolkata, India

Dev Kumar Mandal
http://orcid.org/0009-0005-3740-6885
Brainware University, Kolkata, India

ABSTRACT

As evidenced by a variety of AI-induced ethical predicaments, it is now imperative to reassess the ethical norms governing humans from a broadened perspective, integrating AI. In this extended S–O–R model, this paper investigates how exposure to AI leads to emotional exhaustion and antisocial behaviour. Employing a research approach that combines the use of Partial Least Squares Structural Equation Modelling (PLS-SEM) in analysing a sample of 412 subjects, further data will be obtained through thematic analysis about emotional anaesthesia. Research shows that the relationship between algorithmic stimuli and social indifference is mediated by emotional fatigue, and that the negative effects of its experiential nature are inevitably offset by the positive effects of this mediation on this behaviour, which is beneficial. This research thus demonstrates how emotional fatigue plays a determining role in helping people detach from certain stimuli by connecting it with affective relations in the era of algorithms.

DOI: 10.4018/979-8-3373-8307-1.ch010

1. INTRODUCTION

The advent of algorithmically tailored digital ecosystems has greatly impacted the way information is imbibed, emotional experiences are passed, and the ways in which actions are performed in society (Petersen 2022; Kant, 2020). For instance, in the case of digital social networks, information is relayed with regard to news editors, and entertainment comes in the form of short clips from video applications; these platforms feature systems that provide 'smarter' recommendations in order to keep the audience engaged. These are prone to prioritizing affective content, which is likely to be high in valence and contain limited obvious ties to reality. Such activities alter objective content as well as user behaviours, such as when people see particular content, they start to feel or think in a certain way (Klinger & Svensson, 2018). There are benefits to this level of customization as well; however, it also promotes effortlessness, interest, and involvement, which are positive user experiences. At the same time, users are inundated with a bombardment of highly affective stimuli with very repetitive and graphically disturbing content, from accounts of wars and social ills on an international level, and conflict with intrastate groups is a focus. In this aspect, there are over time projections of its effects on human relations, such as within states, and the citizens' emotional feelings, as compassion is often worn away over time, making even the most major crises, such as high levels of violence, strange to an individual.

In the present digital era, people's roles are not just limited to reading or hearing but also to interacting with the content, thereby adding and expanding the potential of the participatory culture and engaging structures of attention with its algorithms (Webster, 2016; Beer, 2009). Internet sites like social media, news media, and e-commerce platforms strive to attract traffic to them most effectively. In a bid to increase engagement, they tend to serve more emotional content, particularly content that ignites such emotions as fear and anger (Zuboff, 2023). As a consequence of this, the practice of doom scrolling has come to the forefront, where an individual compulsively reads or watches bad news and distrusting content (Sharpe et al., 2026). Such exposure to ads in every little way, especially for the conscientious and socially oriented, serves as an alarm, but not in such cases where longer advertisements are going through a process of anxiety disintegration as well as cognitive exploitation, misinformation. Emotional exhaustion first hammers affectively labile, then restoratively calm, and finally a structural concept of bridge to recovering equilibrium, its corresponding neuropharmacological aspects, and public political economy of tourism and tourism rights. That fun at the first stage of exposure can only mean that it would be short-lived. And people tend to have compulsive informational fears.

Interestingly, contemporary times are information-rich in terms of awareness about global problems, yet there is an emotional cost to this phenomenon for many people, such that they do not sense the motivation to act. This vacuum where people do not react to anything is what Chouliaraki (2013) terms as social indifference. Social indifference is best illustrated as a lack of empathy, less altruistic behaviour, and a deplorable interest in the surroundings (Chouliaraki, 2013). Where some argue that exposure to suffering dulls feelings, they have yet to solve the problem of empathy; they propose solutions for this compassion fatigue (Moeller, 2002). During these moments, in this digital world, the above effect is particularly unsettling for a very simple reason, which is that users are made to consume a lot of content in high emotional states without enough recovery to process, and much more to create an emotional response.

More and more researchers are becoming aware of this fact; almost all of them already focus on burnout, decline of empathy, and digital stress as separate entities (Hashish, & Aly, 2025; Mallick, 2025; Chau et al., 2025; Khadafi et al., 2025) The way robotization is linked to indifference and consequent social disengagement is one of the main areas that requires more research effort to probe the inner aspects of this. Very few research works have been done on the role of exhaustion as an intervening variable so far. Bridging this gap is crucial as it will help to grasp better processes associated with digital environments that affect societal well -being on the scale of whole societies.

Given this limitation, the current chapter employs the Stimulus-Organism-Response (S-O-R) model. First propounded in developmental psychology and especially in environmentally manifested behaviour, the stimulus-organism-response theory is based on the assertion that outside forces make the internal human analyse and conceive certain issues before subsequent behaviour changes (Mehrabian & Russell, 1974). In terms of contemporary media, the exposure to algorithmically produced content may be framed as the object of exposure or the stimulus, emotional tiredness and lack of sensation as the inner organism, and social detachment as the positioning response. Therefore, within this conceptualization, the research perceives emotional fatigue as the key mediating factor that interprets programmed stimuli into real outcomes.

Moreover, in this consolidation, additional information from the standpoint of cognitive load theory and affective events theory is mentioned more in the article, and the natural processes occurring in the person's body during cognitive mental processes are better understood. According to cognitive load theory, task overload deteriorates an individual's mental concentration, decreases motivation, and lowers performance (Sweller, 2011). Due to an increasing adaptation to digital technologies where content is in constant flux, over-committed users have to try to cope with excessive emotionally laden content, which in turn increases their probability of suffering from both cognitive and emotional burnout. Another theory, affective event theory, looks explicitly at the way people change in their attitudes and actions over time in response to how they feel (Weiss & Cropanzano, 1996). Exposure to a particular affect, the stress response, gradually creates relevant emotional responses, for example, weariness or apathy, contributing to social practices and interaction.

Another aspect of this section to take note of is the awareness that the algorithmic effect is not homogeneous across all individuals. Therefore, the conditioning factors of using social media and emotional control can reduce exposure and its consequences on the body. Mindful engagement, or the practice of using digital media and its tools looks at the adaptation of various tools or devices for the regulation of emotional stimuli and overload of content (Verduyn et al., 2017). The study, therefore, takes into consideration the aspects that provide for a healthier adjustment to the bodies of the users, especially in line with the incorporation of such modulating agents.

This chapter is conducted in such a way that it blends, in what is called the mixed methods analysis, the collapsed relationships among the variables or factors that have been measured and their experiences in the real world. For example, while the traditional PLS-SEM is associated with the ability to assess the presence of complex moderation or mediation effects, this cannot be achieved until the qualitative category is explored through the familiar thematic approach, called triangulation. This combination is designed and supported by the research in the sense that the objective of the research is much more than explaining loneliness in terms of multilevel statistical analysis, but rather relational ideas and contextual social or digital environments.

Not only does the relevance of this chapter go further than scholarly discussions, but it also attains a social and practical context. Hitherto, the emotional load from the frequent exposure to algorithms that impact behaviour and ideology is a great aspect to appreciate. However, the emotional exhaustion and feelings of alienation are more than personal concerns; For example, such feelings impact even the activity of an individual as a member of a specific society. Once an individual has become desensitized to the point of switching off his or her emotions and feelings when addressing certain challenges, there is a very high possibility that such compassion and transformation will also be derailed.

The current chapter is in the perspective of the study centric, three major arguments have been put forward where the first extends the earlier S–O–R model to include emotional burnout effects in algorithmic settings. The second argument evaluates the impact of algorithmic mistreatment on the participants' negative emotions and indifference using a rigorous mixed method approach with the proper statistical treatment. The third argument comes up with solutions that might assist the software producers, politicians, and the recipients; the essence is all about the call for emotionally satisfying forms of digital functioning and responsible user interactions.

In conclusion, the analysis of "boredom scrolling" stands as one of the most fundamental problems of the era of the contemporary technical revolution, when digital technology changes the emotional practices of people. The work aims at shedding light on how continuous exposure to algorithms leads to exhaustion and lack of concern, and thereby explores emotional and psychic life in the current 'digital' society in a far more detailed way. This is necessary for managing the side effects of progress and developing better strategies of digital participation, which should be more thoughtful and patient.

2. LITERATURE REVIEW AND THEORETICAL BACKGROUND

The digital era has led to the advent of technology and innovation-based services that have changed the experiences of the emotional, cognitive, and social developments of modern life. The spirit of looking at people as unique portfolios and possibilities of making connections is provided by the platforms on a high note. Even so, they create negative impacts and strains, such as on psychological well-being, and difficulty in social networking. This part highlights the previous work on the exposure to algorithms, emotional burnout, emotional desensitization, and social aversion, and formulates the core of the comprehensive S-O-R framework explicated in this chapter.

2.1 Algorithmic Exposure and the Attention Economy

Digital platforms are now turning more to complex computerized programs to help them sort and send individualized content written in a way that captures the user's interests or behaviour (Kozyreva et al., 2020; De Reuver et al., 2018). These systems are, for all intents and purposes, within what is better known as the attention economy, in which user attention is understood and treated as a limited and valuable commodity (Davenport & Beck, 2001). The word ranks the content based on the user's pleasure. Still, in ranking, it enhances and looks for the most exhilarating, thrilling, and invigorating or polarized messages (postmodern) (Zuboff, 2023) This is the reason why such users without any age or gender restrictions watch mental health breaking content on TV, listen to full of lies on the radio, and even read newspapers that are exposed for the crime of rape.

The study cites the overuse of some of these algorithms as being a reason for the vast amount of content that is generated, leading to the so-called Information Overload, which refers to the feeling of being crushed by the amount or intensity of information available (Eppler and Mengis, 2002). Unlike the physical environment, digital scenarios pose a double challenge as they render nesting functions useless primarily due to the high speed of production and storage of content. And, the users fearing the loss of control because of the algorithms, will often consider themselves "victims" (Klinger and Svensson, 2018). This equilibrium of suffering from stress and the accompanying loss of power is what causes so much tension.

2.2 Emotional Fatigue in Digital Environments

Burnout is often indicative of the idea of emotional exhaustion, where the individual reaches an extent of negativity or feels overstressed due to their occupation, which is a product of connection to a client or experience (Maslach & Jackson, 1981). In the digital environment, fatigue is considered and perceived due to mediated exposure and not due to individual or direct communication with the partners. Liu & He (2021) did note that, among other things, 'social media fatigue' or 'social fatigue', an unwarranted feeling of tiredness, irritation, and emotional depletion developed through excessive use of social media in the media.

It has been found in more recent research, however, that the concept can be further elaborated to cover the enduring consequences of constant exposure to harmful or discomforting material. This is according to Lee et al. (2016), who proved that information crowding and social overload have an adverse effect on users, which brings down the user engagement and satisfaction. In an intrapersonal sense, digital-related cognitive fatigue is aggravated by the inability to divide their private lives from public knowledge since users are scheduled for neither local private friends and family communication nor global communication, and they keep on receiving personal and broader issues around the world.

Emotional exhaustion affects an individual's personal costs because it can last for a very long time (Thompson et al., 2020). Sustained emotional exhaustion is likely to hinder an individual's effectiveness in processing emotional information, leading to social withdrawal and escape responses. There is, therefore, no doubt that emotional exhaustion plays a significant role in understanding the broader psychological effects of algorithmic exposure.

2.3 Emotional Numbness and Desensitization

Emotional numbness, an intentional attempt to deplete oneself of emotions, is a state of being that enables an individual to feel as few emotions as possible at a moment in time (Roberts, 2019; Boutros, 2023). The emotional numbing theory fully states that this state is instinctively chosen when a person is faced with exposure to an extremely injurious situation (Figley, 1995). The more the frequency of exposure is increased in these situations, the more it aids in the development of emotional numbing in order for the disquieting experiences to be managed (Litz et al., 2002; Glover, 1992).

A wide range of studies on media violence, for example, have been carried out for a long time, thus establishing the phenomenon of weaponization, which is when consistent exposure to violent or traumatic content results in a person becoming less affected emotionally upon seeing such content (Funk et al., 2004). In the social media context, this weaponization is not limited to violence but also to numerous other social problems and issues, such as poverty, inequity, and humanitarian catastrophes. According to Chouliaraki (2013), today's media environment also effectively encourages a spectacle of humiliation where the spectator knows the distress but avoids being emotionally involved.

Emotional disconnection can be viewed as a significant phase that separates getting tired from becoming sociologically indifferent. Tiredness refers to a lack of emotional resources and how exhaustion occurs, while numbness refers to an arbitrary change in emotional development that results in a lack of increased concern and involvement. Appreciating the intersection is crucial to understanding how emotional exhaustion leads to apathy.

2.4 Social Indifference and Empathy Erosion

Social apathy signifies a decline of interest regarding other people's interests or welfare, which may also manifest as disinclination to expressively perform empathetic or helpful actions (DeLuca, 1995). Empathy, the ability to psychologically recognize someone's emotional state or feeling or experiences, and even care about it, is the substrate for unity and organized interaction in society (Batson, 2011). Still, on the contrary, a substantial body of research in the past two decades or more has now confirmed that a prolonged, cumulative, and intense exposure to various mediated distress can, in fact nullify empathic reactions.

The original definition of the term compassion fatigue was coined by Moeller (2002), who described the tendency of the public to downshift and do less following multifaceted media attention to crisis events. Viewed through a digital lens, even greater complexities of the issue are generated by the fact that today the information flow is too intensive and time is a major constraint. Not only are users bombarded with increased quantities of information, but they are also encouraged to react most of the time, a situation where they tend to forget their limits and feel “empathy overload” and pressure (Bloom, 2017). In such cases, the overwhelming number of emotions and situations, such as restrictive avoidance of painful ones, is adopted in an attempt to discard the feelings.

According to the latest research, it is shown that excessive engagement with electronic means of entertainment induces moral disengagement, which is one of the mechanisms by which such people can rationalize their inability to act on pro-social issues (Saulnier, 2019; Bandura, 2017). The mediated character of digital interactions often supports this disengagement, as it could allow users to relate to or engage with the content while keeping in mind the actors. Thus, it instils a sense of social callousness that is not rooted in ignorance but rather the impacts of cognitive ailments and feelings.

2.5 The Stimulus–Organism–Response (S–O–R) Framework

The S-O-R (i.e., Stimulus-Organism-Response) model, which was developed during the seventies by Mehrabian and Russell, has been used as a conceptual framework to articulate the role of the experiential states, facilitators, and elements that shape contextual behaviour. Within this construct, redirection stimulation (stimulus) operates on the environmental state of the individual (organism), leading to action or change in the organism (response).

In the contemporary world, where technologies are almost a second nature to the citizens, this S-O-R model has also been utilized in the analysis of online behaviour change, consumer behaviour of online shopping, use of social media, and even technologies that have a relation to health (Jacoby, 2002). On the other hand, there have been only a few in-depth research studies conducted to find its effects on the influences of emotional exhaustion and socialized indifference. This paper is aimed at presenting the S-O-R model and specifically incorporating algorithmic exposure as the stimulus, emotional fatigue and social indifference as the organismic states, and numbness as the response.

In direct accordance with the match quantifying cognitive load theory, cogent with the idea that when the amount of information exceeds certain levels of processing, the cognitive resources tend to diminish causing fatigability hence affecting performance negatively (Sweller, 2011) and also in line with affective events theory which argues that emotional experiences play a critical role in developing attitudes and behaviours in a long-term perspective (Weiss & Cropanzano, 1996). Considering how these viewpoints are helping interrogate the fear-relevant behaviour and the social hardware, the S-O-R framework has been extended due to the changes in the very notion of an algorithmic environment.

2.6 Moderating Role of Mindful Social Media Use

Although individuals may be exposed to unfavourable outcomes due to the use of algorithms, they should not be seen as the precipitants of digital drunkenness victims. The application of world-weary social media use in which the user deliberately authenticates or participative kinds of content and therefore limits interactivity has been recognized as effective mechanism to offset the harmful effects of information overload (Verduyn et al., 2017). At its core, mindfulness helps an individual control where they put their attention and how they feel when they do so, which reduces feelings of tiredness or disinterest.

Research has also revealed that the active scanning of social networks in moderation results in higher levels of perceived life satisfaction, fewer feelings of concern, and alleviated stress and anxiety levels compared with passive use of such sites (Brown & Ryan, 2003). This investigation sets out to encourage there to be a more conscious approach to mindful social media use as a moderator for an individual's algorithmic exposure interpretation.

2.7 Research Gap and Theoretical Contribution

With respect to the respective studies on digital media, causing emotional distress, and evoking empathy, it is surprising that not every allusion has been or is to the presence of integrative models to handle these qualities as one. Most studies that have been available have been dealing with aspects from the perspective of basic social cognitive theory and have not, in most cases, incorporated mediating and/or moderating dimensions that help to explain the factors of interest.

In this respect, this study aims to fill this gap by introducing such nuanced concepts, by re-designing the existing S-O-R model as its department now centralizes in the middle emotional fatigue as a mediating variable that constructs and relates algorithmic exposure and social indifference.

Moreover, the use of both quantitative and qualitative research techniques enables a deeper and more detailed understanding of the phenomenon by focusing on descriptive relationships and life events in the process of research. By giving the given problem a newer name and contextualizing it within emotional fatigue issues of the digital era, the researchers provide new viewpoints for the relevance of psychological and sociological aspects of society to the algorithmic technologies debate.

3. RESEARCH MODEL AND HYPOTHESES DEVELOPMENT

Figure 1.

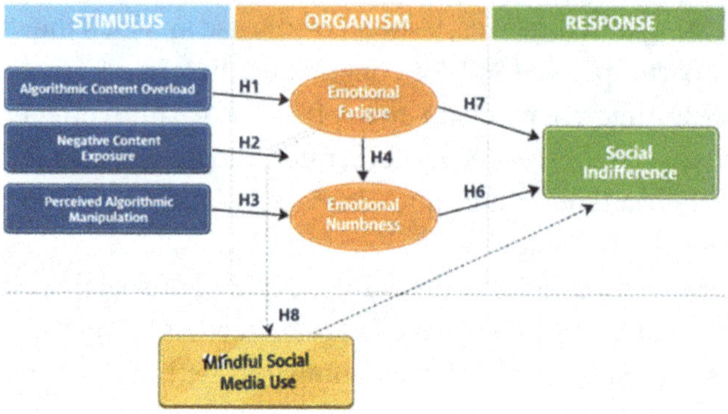

In the aforementioned Figure 1, there is a picture with an expanded Stimulus-Organism-Response (SOR) model to look at emotional and social outcomes in algorithmically designed digital spaces. The concept suggests that algorithmic exposure should be viewed as the stimulus, while fatigue and numbness constitute the organism, and the resulting social apathy is the response. Moreover, the relation between such use and digital exposure pertains to differences coming from the individual attitudes of the subject and is regarded as a tempering variable.

3.1 Stimulus: Algorithmic Exposure

Algorithmic exposure essentially stands for the outside cues and impressions that are targeted towards internet users digitally. Three dimensions are implicated in its understanding: algorithmic content overload, negative content exposure, and perceived algorithmic manipulation. Algorithmic content overload has to do with the attendant effect of the abundance of possibly overwhelming quantities of content, which are shared by users whose cognitive systems are significantly incapacitated. Negative content exposure describes the magnitude of disturbing, panic-stricken, or simply emotionally-packed information aired within the discourse of the media. Perceived algorithmic manipulation indicates that with the help of the algorithms on the website, for example, the users and the developers will know that each fourth post hides a commercial, so the user's engagement is better, and the content is seen for longer. These stimuli, in total, are cognitive and emotional aspects that heighten the probability of a strain emanating from an emotional response.

Based on key cognitive psychology principles and the analysis of the phenomenon of cognitive stress, it is assumed that an overconsumption of emotionally charged information in relation to a certain media content impairs the individual emotionally and eventually causes emotional exhaustion.

H1: Algorithmic content overload positively influences emotional fatigue.
H2: Negative content exposure positively influences emotional fatigue.
H3: Perceived algorithmic manipulation positively influences emotional fatigue.

3.2 Organism: Emotional Fatigue and Emotional Numbness

Organisms undergo changes such as learning to abhor certain forms of behaviour and preferring newer habits over former ones due to the impacts outside events have on their emotional structures. In this research, emotional burnout is looked at as a burnout of the emotional faculty brought about by extended consumption of highly charged narratives. In more acute situations of emotional fatigue, a person will divert a lot of their attention from the emotional side of the spectrum by becoming emotionally numb.

Another argument of the affective event's theory posits that high and frequent emotional events in a given time period produce a high level of intense emotions that last a long time. In this context, high levels of emotional exhaustion are likely to enhance the feeling of emotional numbness in the near future, as people tend to suppress their emotions.

H4: Emotional fatigue positively influences emotional numbness.

3.3 Response: Social Indifference

Implications in terms of behaviour and attitudes are brought out by the response element. It includes less compassion, less interest in social concerns, and less involvement with social movements. People with emotional numbness are more likely to experience and express apathy toward social and humanitarian issues.

Moreover, internal emotional drain requires capacity for empathy/emphasis on the feelings and needs of others, and this condition has an influence on fostering social apathy. In turn, social apathy is also positively suggested to be affected by emotional and emotional exhaustion as well as emotional numbness.

H5: Emotional numbness positively influences social indifference.

H6: Emotional fatigue positively influences social indifference.

3.4 Mediating Role of Emotional Fatigue

This study posits that emotional exhaustion operates as the explanatory mechanism for the relationship between algorithm exposure and social apathy. In the S–O–R framework, stimuli impact responses via the change of the organism's internal state or drives. Emotional exhaustion is the specific psychological process that explicates how exposure to algorithmic devices leads to disaffiliated effects.

> **H7:** Emotional fatigue mediates the relationship between algorithmic exposure and social indifference.

3.5 Moderating Role of Mindful Social Media Use

Exposing individuals to a certain algorithm more than once can cause boredom, but this overuse can be overcome by a certain person's level of engagement. People who are very active on any social media platform during online interaction do not just consume; they create informational content that satisfies their consumption at the same time. Such a use is expected to resist the suppression brought about by the algorithms. The type of use focused on productive reasoning as well as affective engagement of the user, as with the former, will resist the impact of algorithms.

> **H8:** Mindful social media use moderates the relationship between algorithmic exposure and emotional fatigue, such that the relationship is weaker for individuals with higher levels of mindful use.

4. RESEARCH METHODOLOGY

This paper discusses that the mixed methods research strategy with the explanatory character is quite explicit, that "Sequential explanatory" wherein the quantitative approach used for the data collection is immediately followed by a qualitative approach, and the results of the two are finally merged. Psychological exhaustion or emotional fatigue associated with repeated exposure to various forms of stimuli, including the social media behaviour expressed in sacrificing oneself to take gory photos or videotapes of accidents, disasters, violence, as well as other abusive images, may also fall under the category of the negative behavioural consequences of technology use in groups. The purpose of this chapter is twofold.

4.1 Research Design and Approach

The cross-sectional design of the quantitative part of the research used Partial Least Squares Structural equation modelling, appropriate for testing theories and asking questions, among other more sophisticated statistical techniques, such as mediation or prediction modelling. The next step involves carrying out a reflexive thematic review in order to address the issue of emotional exhaustion and social alienation as experienced by people in the age of AI. This dual approach serves the purpose of push-pull research in that the quantitative data provide the facilitation for the qualitative data.

4.2 Sampling and Data Collection

The research aims at internet users who frequently use active social media accounts the age of which falls between 18 and 45 years. Optimally engaging participants with the use of digital technology for not less than 2 hours per day was achieved as a function of purposive sampling. The participants were sent questionnaires to fill in through social networking sites and several e-mail groups, which included their contacts.

Initially, 450 responses were collected, and after data cleaning procedures like elimination of imports with missing data or outliers, a total of 412 of these responses were considered adequate. Qualitative appraisal of the results was then carried out with these response sets based on the inclusion of the selected discrete extremes participants with the highest and lowest emotional exhaustion scores, and some mean scores. 30 individuals were selected using convincing criteria as well.

4.3 Measurement Instruments

Sufficiently validated scales of several components were implemented and borrowed from the previously published studies, all with a process that suits the digital world. The provided information was obtained by applying a five-point Likert scale, which is bounded from 1-Unlikely to 5-Likely.

- Algorithmic Content Overload, Negative Content Exposure, and Perceived Algorithmic Manipulation are sourced from information overload and media studies.
- Emotional Fatigue assembled burnout, and social media fatigue scales were manipulated to measure the host's emotional abuse.
- Emotional Numbness assessed the decrease in emotional responsiveness or reactivity using desensitization and affective numbness scales.

- Social Indifference captures reduced empathy and a decrease in efforts towards others - that is, the desire to engage in social activities.
- Mindful Social Media Use employed mindfulness-derived digital engagement tools in measuring these constructs.

A pilot study (n = 50) was conducted to ensure reliability and clarity, resulting in minor refinements.

4.4 Data Analysis Techniques

The quantitative data sets in this study underwent analysis through the employment of SmartPLS 4 software using a two-step methodology: (1) assessment of the measurement model, and (2) evaluation of the structural model. The validity and reliability check was further made easier with the help of Cronbach, and of course, the Churchill composite reliability. Convergent/divergent Validity was confirmed with Average Variance Extracted (AVE) stats and Heterotrait–Monotrait correlations, respectively. Also, it was necessary to take care of the discriminant validity, which was tested by this criterion: Heterotrait–Monotrait (HTMT) ratio. The bootstrapping (with 5,000 bootstrap resamples) approach was used to test the structural relationships entailing the pth coefficient estimates along with the t values, as well as the significance levels of the relationships. This type of analysis allows for scrutiny of mediating and moderating variables, including possible interaction effects, as in the evaluation of the direct and indirect effects. Predictive validity of the study was determined using Q^2 statistics.

The qualitative data were analysed by employing reflexive thematic analysis, which comprises six main stages: familiarisation, coding, theme generation, theme review, definition, and reporting. This kind of analysis makes it possible to explore more fully and in a more subjective way the experiences of the participants in the study.

4.5 Ethical Considerations

The survey carried out experienced a clear ethical application; emphasis was supposedly made on involving only those people who were willing to take part, such as the obtaining of a reasoned acceptance prior to the research taking place, and a guarantee of individuals' privacy. The data that was gathered in the process of the survey was for academics only, and safe custody of any identifiers was kept to standard, so the latter wasn't disclosed. There were no instances of capture of personal information, and the address of the data was entirely academic.

5. RESULTS

This part contains figures that were derived from the data, hence providing additional information on PLS-SEM, which is an advanced data analysis. The results section is divided into tests of measurement model relationships comprising reliability, convergent discrimination validity test, and hypothesis testing. All these were done alongside the results of moderation and mediation, as well as other more appreciation-based aspects.

5.1 Measurement Model Evaluation

Table 1. Reliability and convergent validity

Construct	Cronbach's Alpha	Composite Reliability (CR)	AVE
Algorithmic Content Overload	0.882	0.912	0.675
Negative Content Exposure	0.861	0.903	0.651
Perceived Algorithmic Manipulation	0.874	0.910	0.669
Emotional Fatigue	0.901	0.928	0.720
Emotional Numbness	0.887	0.919	0.694
Social Indifference	0.893	0.922	0.702
Mindful Social Media Use	0.868	0.905	0.655

Interpretation

The intercepts are shown in Table 1, and all the measures appear to be well organized. This is because in all the cases, superiority of Cronbach's alpha and composite reliability statistics is displayed, which surpassed the limit of 0.70. One can also consider the fact, based on an AVE of more than 0.50, that construct validity is corroborated. It can therefore be found as a satisfactory measurement model including all the constructs.

Table 2. Discriminant validity (HTMT Ratio)

Constructs	ACO	NCE	PAM	EF	EN	SI
ACO	—					
NCE	0.62	—				
PAM	0.58	0.60	—			
EF	0.71	0.73	0.69	—		
EN	0.66	0.68	0.64	0.78	—	
SI	0.63	0.65	0.61	0.75	0.80	—

Interpretation

Within the context of the given quantitative study, all HTMT values for the items listed in Table 2 are less than 0.85, which provides evidence of discriminant validity between constructs. The result establishes the fact that the constructs are unrelated and that all of them have no overlapping content. The findings show that the measurement model with regard to algorithmic exposure, as distinct from emotional and social consequences, is considered to be subject to construct validity.

5.2 Structural Model Assessment

Table 3. Path coefficients and hypothesis testing

Hypothesis	Path	β	t-value	p-value	Result
H1	ACO → EF	0.312	5.842	0.000	Supported
H2	NCE → EF	0.287	5.115	0.000	Supported
H3	PAM → EF	0.254	4.736	0.000	Supported
H4	EF → EN	0.681	12.452	0.000	Supported
H5	EN → SI	0.402	7.231	0.000	Supported
H6	EF → SI	0.331	6.102	0.000	Supported

Interpretation

In Table 3, all the relationships under consideration have been confirmed by the data. Statistical tests have shown that exposure variables computed on the basis of known algorithms are the most robust predictors of emotional fatigue, which is an important construct that affects both emotional numbness and social unresponsiveness. The large value of the path coefficient from emotional fatigue to numbness is consistent with the idea of the critical role of emotional exhaustion in the generation of emotional detachment, followed by behavioral disengagement.

Table 4. Coefficient of determination (R^2)

Endogenous Construct	R^2 Value
Emotional Fatigue	0.612
Emotional Numbness	0.464
Social Indifference	0.589

Interpretation

The results presented in Table 4 reveal that the predictive variables have significant predictive value, which shows that 61.2% of the difference in emotional fatigue, 46.4% in emotional numbness, and 58.9% in social indifference, respectively, is explained. It points out that the S–O–R as a continuation to the model is both valid and accurate.

5.3 Mediation and Moderation Analysis

Table 5. Mediation effect of emotional fatigue

Path	Indirect Effect	t-value	p-value	Mediation Type
ACO → EF → SI	0.103	4.982	0.000	Partial
NCE → EF → SI	0.095	4.421	0.000	Partial
PAM → EF → SI	0.084	4.103	0.000	Partial

Interpretation

In Table 5, the results indicate that burnout acts as a translator of all algorithmic conditions into the development of social indifference. Furthermore, most of the indirect effects are significant, which means that burnout is a substantial psychological mechanism that bridges the gap between digital use and social withdrawal.

As mentioned above, this mediation proves to be full in the context of the study, which means that there are both direct and indirect impacts.

Table 6. Moderation effect of mindful social media use

Interaction Term	β	t-value	p-value	Result
ACO × Mindfulness → EF	-0.182	3.764	0.000	Supported

Interpretation

Mindful use of social media mitigates the effect of algorithmic content overload on emotional fatigue - a result we can see in Table 6. The finding is of particular interest because the coefficient is a negative one, meaning a buffering effect is being enjoyed by those who have constant exposure but practice mindfulness, as it is felt that their emotional fatigue will not be as much. The importance of regulating the cognitive engagement during the technology interaction can be seen here.

5.4 Qualitative Findings (Thematic Analysis)

Table 7. Emergent themes

Theme	Description
Compassion Saturation	Emotional exhaustion due to repeated exposure to distressing content
Doom scrolling Inertia	Compulsive scrolling despite emotional fatigue
Detached Awareness	Cognitive awareness with reduced emotional engagement

Interpretation

The Qualitative findings in Table 7 serve to enhance the quantitative results by shedding light on what feelings the emotional fatigue problem can evoke in real situations. The sense of overload was so much that it reached the psychological fatigue, only to discontinue the habitual action. The said matters indicate the respective paramount of emotional exhaustion in terms of physiological root, such as emotional fatigue.

The combined results validate that the extent of algorithmic exposure is a major cause of emotional exhaustion, which ultimately serves to further emotional disconnection and social alienation. Beyond these quantitative findings, qualitative inquiry adds that users not only perceive cynicism, but also do not come forward about it and stay on due to habit and various other algorithmic compulsions.

6. DISCUSSION

In the following study, the idea was to understand how the creation of environments mediated by algorithms induces emotional fatigue and, through that, social indifference, as the advanced S-O-R model has been used extensively. The research was successful in accomplishing the primary objective of reconceptualizing emotional exhaustion as a key mechanism that connects exposure to algorithms to disengagement in social networks.

The findings support the hypothesized relationships that the factors of the algorithmic stimuli, that is, content overload on social media platforms perceived as being algorithm mediated, exposure to content perceived as being negative, and perceived manipulation through algorithms, increase emotional fatigue (H1 – H3). In support of the present study, scholars noted in the literature cited that 'incorrect' information as perceived by the target may also cause psychological harm or fatigue. The high weight of these variables shows that it is not merely from the actual point of information that informs the emotional experience of the users, but these are augmented by the emotional aspects of the things allowed by algorithms. The set of stimuli presented to the participants has been comparable to the others, but that with algorithmic content overload suggests knowledge in the form of the strongest influence of all the others in the study. This would be expected as it suggests that the current generation's usage of information technologies and social media is virtually unchanging.

The study also goes further to establish that there exists a significant perception of depletion in emotional capacity contributing highly to emotional depersonalization (H4), bringing in the idea that consistent overuse and exhaustion of the affective system is associated with a change like emotion itself. This assertion supports affective events theory as it posits that continued exposure to emotions, as well as the anticipation of emotions by an individual, leads to the formation of an emotional set that corresponds to his or her experiences, hardships, and expectations. It is then no wonder that emotional appreciation and decompensation perhaps continue to be more damaging than even the perceived inability to feel emotion, given the findings of the results. Emotional coldness is commonly used as a protective mechanism to sustain high digital exposure and decrease anxiety. It is important to note that this behaviour causes heightened risks of impairing one's functional ability due to fewer effects.

Complete validation is also provided for the theoretical concepts on emotions and social adjustments. In fact, emotional anaesthesia also has a significant predictive ability, which includes the lack of empathy characterized by social idleness (H5), which means the detachment from people, resulting in loss of empathy and altruism in others. Some other theorists have even stated that the emotional exhaustion will increase as the level of indifference will decrease (H6), which means that some people will not even act professionally on account of the emotional exhaustion without experiencing complete emotional detachment. It is therefore clear that emotional expression control and emotional resource use in the spirit of self-appropriateness account for impaired empathetic response in a digitized world.

The study makes a significant contribution in investigating the mediating function of Emotional Fatigue (H7). The mediating study showed that the primary psychological mechanism by which algorithmic exposure changes into social indifference is emotional fatigue. This result is of the essence as it covers and closes the research gap which was drafted in the drawing of existing countless studies, whereby emotional fatigue and social detachment are mostly taken as separate elements rather than in relation. While leveraging emotional fatigue as a mediator, the study cleverly explains how social behaviour is structured within the digital realm. Further, the implications of this research are clearly identifiable in that efforts to fight social apathy entail the curbing of the emotional weariness or the weariness that the user's revolt against.

Effect of Practicing Mindful Behaviour on Social media usage (H8) is responsible for supporting the case further for the core significance of the self. The finding of the negative interaction effect suggests that those who use digital tools carefully did not tire out easily, even in the presence of high amounts of routine-generated noise. This provides relevant information on the capacity of mindfulness-based systems to reduce the harmful effects of technological environments. It might also direct scholars' attention to the more nuanced effects of exposure to algorithms in terms of different users' engagement styles and self-regulatory capacities.

The qualitative aspects of the research complemented the quantitative results well by providing a more detailed account of what respondents were doing and experiencing. For instance, aspects of "compassion saturation," "doom scrolling inertia," and "detached awareness" help in explaining the transition that occurs between first emotional arousal and then disinterest or burnout towards the middle. In the beginning, the participants outlined a state of concern and pity, followed by the gradual reduction in the level of pity and its feelings as the exhaustion grew inside the person and as the emotional barrier was created. It is worth noting that a significant portion of the participants, or most of them, have had critical experiences but have continued persisting, which makes it clear that it is a case of behaviour over intention and reinforcement over positive impact. These narratives further validate the perspective of even emotional fatigue as an outcome of, as well as a coping mechanism to, exposure to algorithms.

Conclusively, the results validate the improvements in the S-O-R model that this analysis makes. The process operationalizes external stimuli (algorithmic exposure) - internal states (emotional fatigue and numbness) influencing behaviour and intentions (social indifference) in a sequence. This penetration of scrolling also contributes to the related processes of mediation and moderation in the literature.

This study adds to the comprehensive range of existing studies on e-wellbeing, in addressing the unwanted emotional, relational impact of or social outcomes of algorithmic technologies. Here, it is conservative to underestimate, rather than come up within clear limits, that the more information you know, the more you will be involved in a situation (opposite) towards desensitization. For members, this lifestyle of action creates anxiety and is, consequently, manipulation-positive in its tendencies.

Lastly, the conversation demonstrates that burnout is formed by more than just the usage of technology; it is an important component in the coming transformation of emotional life and society in digitalized contemporary societies. In relation to the proposed hypotheses above and the mix in both qualitative and quantitative findings, the knowledge that has been made available will serve as a very effective strategy for understanding how emotional desensitization takes root among individuals and eventually leads to apathy.

7. IMPLICATIONS

The implications of these results extend to a range of research and practice areas – theoretical, managerial, technological, and policy highlights suggest they are of particular importance to certain issues within a rapidly progressing digital ecosystem, which is driven by a wide array of different algorithms. However, the implications should be treated as conditional; that is, the prevailing fatigue is viewed as a partial answer about the development of a given society's attitude to others under the influence of algorithms. This implies that these findings have crucial relevance only in the future and in the framework of the creation of digital environments that are emotionally destructible, encouraging the adoption of healthy uses.

7.1 Theoretical Implications

From a theoretical perspective, the current chapter enhances the study with its development of the Stimulus–Organism–Response (S–O–R) system by adding emotional fatigue and emotional numbness as important organismic states in the scope of digital mode. Subsequent studies could advance this model by introducing other psychosocial dimensions such as digital resilience, emotional regulation, and cognitive flexibility. Furthermore, this research suggests that the possibility of interdisciplinary integration, particularly with neuroscience and behavioural economics, in investigating compassion couples' mechanisms with the use of algorithms, suggests that the memory and the neurological organization of the memories change over time. Further studies using longitudinal and experimental designs could substantiate the causal pathways and address the issues of underlying dynamics.

Moreover, the distinction of feeling emotionally exhausted as a mediating factor acts as a push toward more contemplative digital activities as opposed to mere indulgence in active online behaviour. Such a transformation is essential in the construction of digital health models, which consider emotional and social well-being aspects as well. Also, involving such neutral factors as social networking, the construct of mindful social media use points to the need to consider the role of preference agency, which should motivate further looking for ways of reducing anxiety through personal traits such as digital media usage and cultural background.

7.2 Managerial and Platform Design Implications

For developers and developers involved in digital technologies, such results indicate that new algorithms should be developed with emotional constructs as well. Models focusing on encouraging time spent by users or retention have been found not to serve the users' emotional wellness interests. This will require coming up with strategies that incorporate algorithms such as "effective awareness". These will detect signs of emotional exhaustion, like watching offensive materials for longer periods or continuous scrolling, and adapt how they deliver content.

Reducing fatigue may be achieved through the incorporation of features like emotional tempo, periodic "digital interruptions," and diversity of materials. For example, the platforms may consider starting to use adaptive interfaces that suggest something better or nothing at all following a long session of unpleasant content consumption. Also, clarity in the way the various functions, which are based on algorithms, work causes the individual to feel less manipulated, which in turn alleviates stress. Enabling users to filter content - such as self-imposed filters or restrict hours of use (limiting exposure)- goes a long way to promote user agency and satisfaction.

In the context of strategy formulation, technology companies that support users' emotional health can hope to achieve persistent loyalty from users, where ethical concerns can be harmonized with business plans over time. Changes in the civil society's perception of digital well-being are poised to lead to a situation in which platforms that manage emotional costs more effectively will have an improved competitive impact.

7.3 Policy and Regulatory Implications

In the context of this research, major importance is given to the role of governments in the regulation of the influence of new technologies on the psychological capacity of society. Future regulator mechanisms should consider not only data privacy and "fake news," but also the protection of users from emotional repercussions caused by algorithms. This also implies the creation of standards for an appropriate approach to the recommendations, in particular, not only to protect from the dangerous, harmful information. Such concerns are how guidelines for social media recommendations will be framed with special reference to the concerns of ethically difficult or harmful material.

Regulatory authorities can also invite the development of ethical requirements for machine algorithms depending on the extent of harm associated with the prescribed content, while enjoining Internet platforms to ascertain and appreciate the emotional risks that come with their content mechanisms. Moreover, public policy can be utilized to enhance digital well-being through campaigns, targeted interventions, and the incorporation of digital literacy in curricular structures. - safeguard that would empower reticent users and lessen vulnerability to what is referred to as digital exhaustion."

In the future, it may be necessary to engage in joint or International Action to facilitate the Implementation of any Global Standards about Accountability Algorithms stemming from the cross-border nature of digital platforms. It would also be virtually impossible for any policymaker not to factor in the associated new technologies, such as artificial intelligence, as well as immersive media, more, which enhances the emotional interaction at leisure levels, which consequently makes individuals burn out.

7.4 Individual and Societal Implications

Experts have underlined the importance of managing one's behaviour online in the context of dealing with digital exhaustion, an issue that affects individuals' emotions as a reaction to the use of technology. Such suggestions have prompted further research to be done, which will come up with ways of helping people adopt, and perhaps emphasize, goal-driven tools and applications that are meant to instill self-awareness, control their usage of technology, and consume content with awareness. Utilisation of such interventions as digital break techniques, concentration techniques which involve concentration on the present, and strategies requiring awareness of personal feelings can be incorporated by agencies in ensuring that the consumers avoid extremes by strictly applying themselves to the agent's services.

Coming from a societal point of view, the acts of emotion burn out and absolutely out social relations challenge group sympathy, as well as civil alliance or unity. People who have seen so much for so long will be far less competitive in fighting for the promotion of social values, as well as the provision of a socialized system to all. This requires that art move itself forward, creating, in fact, radical artwork of social need in society. In order to resolve such issues, new generations must learn how to embrace emotions and remain active without burnout.

The educational systems and associations should particularly concentrate on enhancing 'sustainable empathy'. In such awareness-raising activities, people would conduct development of society through artistic pursuits of all those components of cultural policies which allow society to retain and culture to develop. Facilitated viewing promotes the process of appreciation and discussion.

8. CONCLUSION

In the present study, the objective was to identify and understand the unusual correlation between digital capabilities and the lack of social awareness among individuals within the age bracket of algorithms. Notably, by extrapolating the (S–O–R) stimulus–organism–response model, this study applies a combination of qualitative and quantitative techno-behavioural research in order to visualize the emotional and social effects of algorithmic environments. The results show that the so-called emotional fatigue is not connected to only all the digital or any other engagement and entertainment practice, but rather in social psychology, emotional fatigue functions as a translation of an algorithmic accumulation of virtual, yet emotional and sensitive, pupils into social apathy.

Indeed, data obtained from the conducted user research can verify the hypothesis, stating that such algorithmic stimulations as content overload, viewing negative content, and feeling used have a huge bearing on developing what is referred to as emotional fatigue. Where the former leads to emotional numbness and a lack of empathy, the latter leads to humanitarian or to put correctly, social negligence. In this very respect, the significance of emotional fatigue as a central link that bridges the gap between digital environment usage and lack of active social interactions cannot be overstated. Furthermore, the partitioning of the relationship between the variables with the variable of mindful use better emphasizes that users should not only receive the provided information about the algorithm, but they should also manage their emotions in terms of that technology as well.

The quantitative analysis confirms that more and more people these days are using digital devices. Along with this digital activity, psychological research shows that people have tendencies towards negative symptoms called "compassion fatigue" and "doom scrolling" as well as tendencies to screen out information. This helps us understand how we, as people, cope with emotional strain when we are immersed in electronic worlds by distancing ourselves and choosing not to care sometimes. This withdrawal, though it functions as a protection strategy, unfortunately hampers the propensity of a person to care as well as their obligations to the rest of society, which has serious implications for the future of digital cultures.

The study is fresh because it fills a gap in knowledge using the conservation of resources (COR) theory of stress, as well as understanding the behaviour of reduced activation with positive and negative emotions. The study is also innovative on a methodological level as it couples PLS SEM with thematic analysis for the first time, which enables the capture of structural relationships as well as experiential dimensions. Finally, on a practical aspect, the study highlights that digital platform design has to care for more than providing eye-catching interfaces. Emotional considerations and especially how we design interfaces that take into consideration the possibility of being over-dependent and overly seeking out user engagements are also solicited from the findings resulting.

Lastly, "scrolling into numbness" exemplifies a changing nature of emotions during the modern computer era. Because of the speed and rate at which media is currently being consumed, the risk of emotional burnout and social distance grows higher with the passing time. Tackling this issue demands a combined initiative from various stakeholders such as academia, software developers, politicians, and the audience to build digital spaces promoting the storage and utilization of emotions. Overall, creating an inclusive and responsible online space is crucial for the enhancement of the quality of life and active participation in society as a whole.

9. LIMITATIONS AND FUTURE RESEARCH

This research study undoubtedly is useful and contributes richly. Despite the numerous implications to the subject of instructional communication, there are key issues that remain unexplored, and which engagement suggests future research should be done. Firstly, the cross-sectional nature of the study does not support causal inferences; hence, there is a need for interpretation of the related emotional fatigue and its impact when there are two time points. Secondly, the study is based on individuals rating their behaviour, which may compromise the validity of the findings due to the possibility of reporting. Furthermore, validity could also be improved by employing more objective measurements: e.g., Behavioural analysis or psychophysiology (physiological indicators).

Also, the psychophysiological strain theory assumes that the controlled processing is consciously perceived (direct chronometry of psycho-dynamic processing), and this condition will lead to psychophysiological strain. In contrast, the reaction is typically elicited without any conscious attempts of an individual to regulate it (control conditioning of psycho-dynamic processing), which is typical for the opponent-process tradition. Furthermore, they claim that traditional concepts, such as addiction and withdrawal symptoms, are not essential in understanding emotional exhaustion. For example, the present constructs of this concept involve cynicism and professional inefficiency, which organizational factors such as lack of recognition and reward, low pay, and excessive workloads would be less relevant.

Therefore, as the situation calls for prompt action, the affected employees, the management of the company, as well as the company itself will have to come up with immediate solutions.

REFERENCES

Bandura, A. (2017). Moral disengagement in the perpetration of inhumanities. In *Recent developments in criminological theory* (pp. 135–152). Routledge. DOI: 10.4324/9781315089089-12

Batson, C. D. (2011). *Altruism in humans*. Oxford University Press.

Beer, D. (2009). Power through the algorithm? Participatory web cultures and the technological unconscious. *New Media & Society, 11*(6), 985–1002. DOI: 10.1177/1461444809336551

Bloom, P. (2017). *Against empathy: The case for rational compassion*. Random House.

Boutros, N. (2023). Emotional numbness: Definition, causes & how to deal with it.

Brown, K. W., & Ryan, R. M. (2003). The benefits of being present: Mindfulness and its role in psychological well-being. *Journal of Personality and Social Psychology, 84*(4), 822–848. DOI: 10.1037/0022-3514.84.4.822

Chau, C. W., Norton, C., Kruzan, K. P., & Jacobs, M. (2025, April). " All Day, Every Day, Listening to Trauma": Investigating Features of Digital Interventions for Empathy-Based Stress and Burnout. In *Proceedings of the 2025 CHI Conference on Human Factors in Computing Systems* (pp. 1-18). DOI: 10.1145/3706598.3713588

Chouliaraki, L. (2013). *The ironic spectator: Solidarity in the age of post-humanitarianism*. John Wiley & Sons.

Davenport, T. H., & Beck, J. C. (2001). *The attention economy*. Harvard Business School Press.

De Reuver, M., Sørensen, C., & Basole, R. C. (2018). The digital platform: A research agenda. *Journal of Information Technology, 33*(2), 124–135. DOI: 10.1057/s41265-016-0033-3

DeLuca, T. (1995). *The two faces of political apathy*. Temple University Press.

Eppler, M. J., & Mengis, J. (2002). The Concept of Information Overload. *MCM Research Paper*.Figley, C. R. (1995). *Compassion fatigue*. Brunner/Mazel.

Figley, C. R. (1995). Compassion fatigue: Toward a new understanding of the costs of caring.

Funk, J. B., Baldacci, H. B., Pasold, T., & Baumgardner, J. (2004). Violence exposure in real-life, video games, television, movies, and the internet: Is there desensitization? *Journal of Adolescence, 27*(1), 23–39. DOI: 10.1016/j.adolescence.2003.10.005

Glover, H. (1992). Emotional numbing: A possible endorphin-mediated phenomenon associated with post-traumatic stress disorders and other allied psychopathologic states. *Journal of Traumatic Stress*, *5*(4), 643–675.

Hashish, A., & Aly, E. (2025). The silent strain beyond the screen: Conceptualizing digital compassion fatigue in nursing. *BMC Nursing*, *24*(1), 1464. DOI: 10.1186/s12912-025-04143-0

Jacoby, J. (2002). Stimulus-organism-response reconsidered: An evolutionary step in modeling (consumer) behavior. *Journal of Consumer Psychology*, *12*(1), 51–57. DOI: 10.1207/S15327663JCP1201_05

Kant, T. (2020). *Making it personal: Algorithmic personalization, identity, and everyday life*. Oxford University Press. DOI: 10.1093/oso/9780190905088.001.0001

Khadafi, Z. R., Pelita, D., & Gunawan, T. (2025). The Phenomenon of Digital Burnout and Social-Emotional Crisis Among Students: The Role of Counselors in Fostering Digital Balance. *Al-Wa'iyah*, *1*(2), 38–52. DOI: 10.51590/wai.v1i2.13

Klinger, U., & Svensson, J. (2018). The end of media logics? On algorithms and agency. *New Media & Society*, *20*(12), 4653–4670. DOI: 10.1177/1461444818779750

Kozyreva, A., Lewandowsky, S., & Hertwig, R. (2020). Citizens versus the internet: Confronting digital challenges with cognitive tools. *Psychological Science in the Public Interest*, *21*(3), 103–156. DOI: 10.1177/1529100620946707

Lee, A. R., Son, S. M., & Kim, K. K. (2016). Information and communication technology overload and social networking service fatigue: A stress perspective. *Computers in Human Behavior*, *55*, 51–61. DOI: 10.1016/j.chb.2015.08.011

Litz, B. T., Litz, B. T., & Gray, M. J. (2002). Emotional numbing in posttraumatic stress disorder: Current and future research directions. *The Australian and New Zealand Journal of Psychiatry*, *36*(2), 198–204. DOI: 10.1046/j.1440-1614.2002.01002.x

Liu, Y., & He, J. (2021). "Why are you running away from social media?" Analysis of the factors influencing social media fatigue: An empirical data study based on Chinese youth. *Frontiers in Psychology*, *12*, 674641. DOI: 10.3389/fpsyg.2021.674641

Mallick, M. (2025). Digital Burnout and Attention Collapse: A Review of Cross-Cultural Psychological Synthesis.

Maslach, C., & Jackson, S. E. (1981). The measurement of experienced burnout. *Journal of Organizational Behavior*, *2*(2), 99–113. DOI: 10.1002/job.4030020205

Mehrabian, A., & Russell, J. A. (1974). *An approach to environmental psychology*. the MIT Press.

Moeller, S. D. (2002). *Compassion fatigue: How the media sell disease, famine, war and death*. Routledge. DOI: 10.4324/9780203900352

Petersen, A. (2022). *Emotions online: Feelings and affordances of digital media*. Routledge. DOI: 10.4324/9781003147435

Roberts, T. (2019). Feeling nothing: Numbness and emotional absence. *European Journal of Philosophy*, *27*(1), 187–198. DOI: 10.1111/ejop.12375

Saulnier, L. (2019). *Moral Identity*. Moral Disengagement, and Online Behaviour from Adolescence to Young Adulthood.

Sharpe, A. T., Tyndall, I., Poulus, D. R., Obine, E. A., & Sharpe, B. T. (2026). The influence of doomscrolling on mental health: a scoping review. *Mental Health and Digital Technologies*, 1-53.

Sweller, J. (2011). Cognitive load theory. [). Academic Press.]. *Psychology of Learning and Motivation*, *55*, 37–76. DOI: 10.1016/B978-0-12-387691-1.00002-8

Thompson, M. J., Carlson, D. S., Kacmar, K. M., & Vogel, R. M. (2020). The cost of being ignored: Emotional exhaustion in the work and family domains. *The Journal of Applied Psychology*, *105*(2), 186–195. DOI: 10.1037/apl0000433

Verduyn, P., Ybarra, O., Résibois, M., Jonides, J., & Kross, E. (2017). Do social network sites enhance or undermine subjective well-being? A critical review. *Social Issues and Policy Review*, *11*(1), 274–302. DOI: 10.1111/sipr.12033

Webster, J. G. (2016). *The marketplace of attention: How audiences take shape in a digital age*. MIT press.

Weiss, H. M., & Cropanzano, R. (1996). Affective events theory. *Research in Organizational Behavior*, *18*(1), 1–74.

Zuboff, S. (2023). The age of surveillance capitalism. In *Social theory re-wired* (pp. 203–213). Routledge. DOI: 10.4324/9781003320609-27

Chapter 11
Scrolling Through Exhaustion, Emotional Fatigue, and Social Indifference in the Digital Age:
How Digital Life Is Reshaping Human Emotions and Social Connection

Priyanka Gupta
http://orcid.org/0009-0006-5341-8314
Independent Researcher, India

Manu Sharma
Graphic Era (Deemed to be) University, India

Sudhanshu Joshi
http://orcid.org/0000-0003-4748-5001
Graphic Era (Deemed to be) University, India

Janmejai Shah
Graphic Era (Deemed to be) University, India

ABSTRACT

The rapid growth of digital technologies has transformed the way individuals experience, express, and manage emotions. While social media platforms have enhanced

DOI: 10.4018/979-8-3373-8307-1.ch011

connectivity and access to information, they have also created an environment of continuous emotional exposure and cognitive overload. This chapter explores the emerging phenomenon of digital emotional fatigue and its link with rising social indifference in the digital age. It argues that constant interaction with emotionally intense content ranging from global crises to personal narratives gradually leads to emotional exhaustion, desensitization, and reduced empathetic engagement. he chapter further examines the role of algorithm-driven systems in shaping emotional experiences by prioritizing engagement over well-being, often amplifying high-arousal content. It also highlights the growing importance of emotional labour on social media, where users, especially influencers, strategically manage and perform emotions to maintain visibility and connection.

INTRODUCTION

The modern digital environment is marked with an unprecedented information, affect, and connectivity saturation, as people are constantly drowning in floods of mediated experiences (Mbamba et al., 2026). The development of applications like Instagram, Tik Tok is how emotions are created, distributed, and experienced in a fundamentally different way. These platforms offer connection, awareness and interaction, but at the same time they create a paradoxical state of emotional overload and mental detachment (Turner, K. E. 2025). This chapter dwells on this state of affairs and attempts to comprehend the impact of the continuous digital exposure on the feelings of people. Most of the users end up feeling exhausted, less sensitive as well as showing less interest in social issues instead of being able to feel more connected. Citizens are exposed to troubling material regularly like world crises, personal misfortunes, and political turmoil. This can bring in empathy at first but eventually causes emotional exhaustion which is also referred to as digital emotional fatigue.

This was further aggravated with the COVID19 pandemic, where the online platforms were the primary means of working, communicating, and keeping updated (Mojumder et al., 2025). What began as a helpful connection tool gradually became the cause of stress and exhaustion. The exposure to the content in crisis situations and conditions all the time left many people emotionally exhausted and less active.

The role of algorithms is also another critical reason behind this. The digital platforms apply artificial intelligence in presenting the user with content that would keep them glued to a longer duration (Voinea, D. V. 2025). Nonetheless, these systems are primarily aimed at enhancing the activity of the user, as opposed to emotional well-being. Despite the attempts to demonstrate caring with the help of such options as reactions, likes, and auto-responses, these interaction methods do not always have the true emotional content (Agha et al., 2023). This leads to the result of an artificial empathy in people that exists but is not actually meaningful.

There is also the pressure on social media users, particularly, influencers and creators of content, to appear in a specific manner (Kim et al., 2022). They easily control and express their emotions in order to gain attention and remain relevant. Emotions, in the long run, turn into something acted upon, as opposed to being experienced. This is indicative of a bigger trend that places emotions as some kind of value or resource. The result of this continuous regulation of emotions may be emotional burnout and the confusion of actual emotions and acting.

Meanwhile, human beings are subjected to such a high level of suffering on the internet that they start developing a less sensitive attitude towards it. This is termed as compassion fatigue. This used to be predominantly observed in the work domains such as healthcare, but today it is observed in ordinary social media users. Desensitization and emotional withdrawal may also be experienced due to constant exposure to negative content (Soror et al., 2022). This can make people be less receptive to the problems of others even when they know their problems. In order to cope with this overload, digital culture has come up with its own coping mechanisms. Memes, humor, and irony are used by people to deal with their emotions. These techniques act as a short-term relief and make individuals share their emotions in a rather simple and common manner (Lestari et al., 2024). Nevertheless, they also have the potential to decrease the severity of vital problems and they could lead to emotional detachment in the long-term. It should also be noted that not all people experience the same emotional fatigue. The issue of cultural differences contributes significantly to the experience and management of digital emotions among people. Lastly, it is noteworthy that the increase in emotional burnout and social apathy has dire consequences to the society. Loss of empathy may lead to a weakening of social ties, lack of collective action and influences involvement in democratic procedures. Thus, the resolution of this problem cannot be achieved only through personal initiatives. It also requires modifications on the platform and policy level, which comprises ethical design, responsible technology usage and systems that put human well-being over engagement.

This chapter is also intended to give a clearer picture of these predicaments and recommend how we can create emotional stability and substantial relationships in the modern digital era

1.1. Scope of the Chapter

The chapter has an interdisciplinary and wide fashion in which it seeks to take into account the emotional fatigue in the digital age and takes into consideration the psychological, technological and social implications of digitally mediated experiences. The areas below are found to be critical to the scope of the chapter as shown in Figure 1:

Figure 1. Scope of the chapter

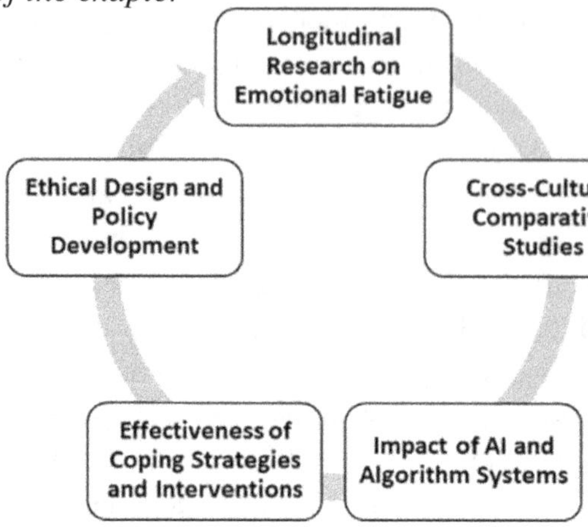

a. **Digital Emotional Ecosystem:** Examines the impacts of the ever-present stimulation of the social media platforms such as Instagram and Tik Tok, which offer humans the state of unceasing emotional activation and overload.
b. **Conceptual Boundaries of Emotional Fatigue:** This offers a differentiation between emotional fatigue and related terms of burnout, technostress, and information overload that makes it a distinctive multidimensional term.
c. **Emotional and Cognitive Processes:** It focuses on the attention collapse, emotional contagion, desensitization and cognitive overload processes that determine user experiences.
d. **Social and Behavioural Outcomes:** Studies how social indifference and reduced empathy and disengagement emerge as the consequences of prolonged exposure to digital media.
e. **Emotional Labor in Digital Spaces:** Investigates how individuals interact and utilize feelings over the internet, particularly content creators, which leads to the exhaustion of affect.
f. **Cross-Cultural Perspectives:** It takes into consideration the variation in emotional reaction, style of coping and online behaviours across various cultures and society.
g. **Future Research and Practical Implications:** It also goes further as identifying lack of research, theoretical development and actionable knowledge that may be applied by individuals, organisations and policy makers.

1.2. Significance of the Chapter

This chapter has a significant role in the evolution of the emotional experience in the virtual world since it poses a critical yet less studied dilemma that the hyper-connectivity of the tools, such as Instagram and Tik Tok, has made more conscious, have diminished the emotional sensitivity and social responsiveness. As far as it leads to the following important contributions, it is relevant as shown in Figure 2:

Figure 2. Significance of the chapter

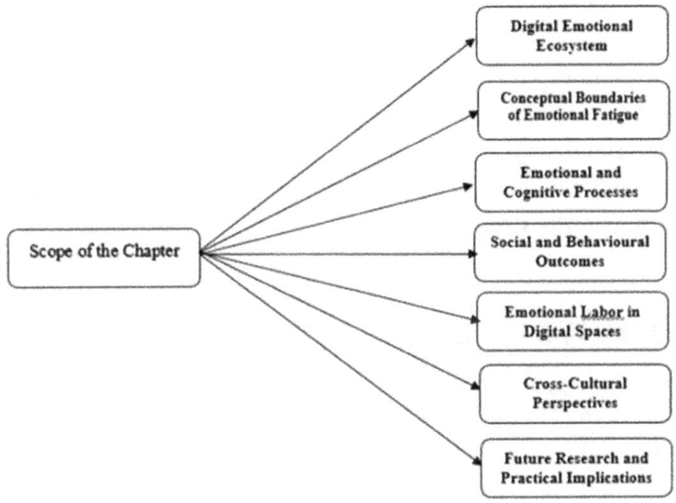

a. **Theoretical Development:** This chapter Provides an innovative synthesis of the technostress, affect theory and points of view concerning cognitive load to theorize the emotional fatigue as a distinct multidimensional phenomenon that is not yet dominant in the models of burnout.
b. **Bridging Research Gaps:** The absence of a scholarly concern on the dependence among emotional fatigue, social indifference, and well-being is filled by offering a coherent system within which the three constructs are incorporated.
c. **Implications to Mental Health and Well-Being:** Implicates the growing influence of digital fatigue on psychological well-being, emotional resilience, and interpersonal communication, which makes it highly relevant to the study and implementation of well-being.
d. **Useful Application:** Provides practical information on coping and digital hygiene, emotion regulation strategies that may be implemented at the individual and institutional level.

e. **Global and Cross-Cultural Significance:** Understands that emotional exhaustion cannot be expressed in terms of any universal manifestation, which can be applied to all cultures, becoming a part of a more diverse and context-specific approach to digital well-being.

1.3. Objectives of the Chapter

a. To theorize the concept of emotional fatigue as a multidimensional effect of an intensive digital presence on social networks like an Instagram and a Tik Tok.
b. To examine the contribution of algorithmic curation and digital spaces to the socio-emotional apathy and desensitization.
c. To analyse the coping mechanism and emotional attempts in dealing with the affective overload on the internet.
d. To propose policies and models of enhancing the quality of life and emotional hardiness during the digital times.

2. EMOTIONAL FATIGUE IN THE DIGITAL ERA

The emergence of emotional burnout in the digital era is the breakthrough in the experience of psychological exhaustion, creation, and maintenance. The outcome is not the amount of information but the intensity, urgency, and emotive nature of the digital mediated experiences (Yang et al., 2024). Because users live in an always-on ecosystem that includes Instagram, Tik Tok, and YouTube, users are exposed to a continuous stream of information, which they are obliged to think and feel, but not necessarily sufficient time to rest.

In recent times, the idea of this phenomenon has been conceptualized in terms of technostress and cognitive overload, pointing at the exhaustion of emotional and psychological resources of people due to constant communication with digital technologies (Wang et al., 2023). Techno-overload of using technology to increase the rate and amount of work is a cause of long-term emotional burnout and diminished well-being. Likewise, techno-invasion eradicates the borders between the personal and professional life, establishing a condition of constant connectivity that does not allow psychological isolation and rest. All these stressors together lead to a certain process of resource drainage over time, as years of digital interaction will destroy cognitive ability and emotional strength (Tarafdar et al., 2019).

Psychologically, emotional exhaustion is even enhanced by human cognitive architecture restrictions. Based on the cognitive load theory, studies indicate that the human brain has a limited ability to process information and when overly exposed to the high-intensity digital stimuli the cognitive saturation and mental depletion occur as a result of overexposure of the brain to such effects (Balaskas et al., 2025). This can be explained by the results showing that technostress and cognitive fatigue are intertwined factors, as over-dependence on digital tools causes emotional fatigue, loss of productivity, and poor health conditions. Furthermore, the social media settings enhance this phenomenon by the overload of information, the overload of features of the system, and even the overload of sociality, which are all factors in causing exhaustion and, ultimately, disengagement (Fu et al., 2025).

This phenomenon was further increased by the COVID-19 pandemic that increased the level of reliance on digital technologies in work, communication, and access to information. Rise in technology usage has a direct proportion to emotional exhaustion moderated by the perceived stress and internal psychological conflict. This implies that emotional exhaustion is not merely an exposure factor in itself, but also a psychological stressor of coping with complex and fast-evolving digital conditions as shown in Figure 3:

Figure 3. Emotional fatigue in the digital era

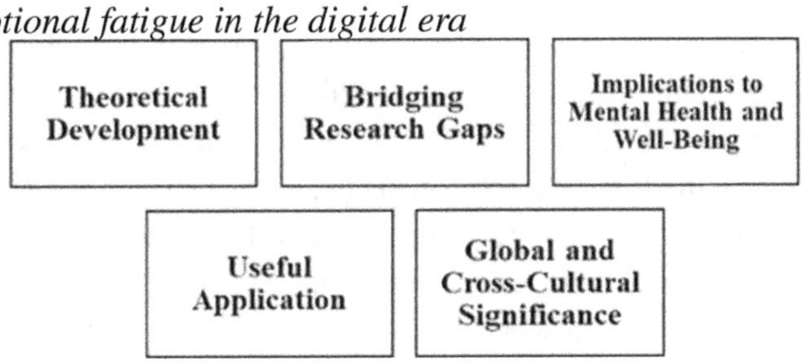

a. **Conceptualizing Digital Emotional Fatigue:** The concept of cognitive load can also be interpreted as the concept of digital emotional fatigue, i.e. the human brain can process information only to a limited extent at a particular time (Skulmowski et al., 2022). In the digital space, individuals are overwhelmed with excessive information at a very fast rate that imposes a strain on their mental ability. This can make a person go through the so-called attention collapse when one finds it hard to pay attention to anything regularly. This causes the mind to get tired and results in difficulty in controlling emotions. This is closely associated with the notion of continuous partial attention wherein individuals are never asleep, and they are constantly checking out a number of things at the same time, but they are not entirely involved in a single activity. Users continue to alternate their focus on one piece of content after another instead of being engaged. This continual change causes stress, lack of concentration, and the subsequent emotional exhaustion as time passes.

b. **Digital Burnout Beyond the Workplace:** Burnout that was initially an attribute associated with the workplace setting is in the online scene, and currently, there is no distinct line between work and non-work life (Ciolfi et al., 2019). The issue of burnout in the digital era has ceased to have a professional facet, but has spread over to the social, leisure and even the development of individual identity. Digital burnout is symptomatic because it is irritable, does not want to be online, lacks empathy, and believes that there is nothing meaningful in using online. This pressure to be present, to be available and to be visible causes what is currently called perpetual engagement fatigue. Micro-stressors are algorithms, information, and notifications that accumulate in the long-term and lead to exhaustion. It is worth noting that this form of burnout is largely silent and self-inflicted and therefore difficult to detect and cure.

c. **Attention Collapse and Cognitive Fragmentation:** Sustained attention is among the typical process of digital emotional fatigue. There is an architecture of digital platforms to ensure the highest engagement through content turnover, personal recommendation and intermittent rewards (Chowdhury et al., 2019). Despite the mechanisms being very useful in attentional capture, it influences the high order thinking and reflections of feelings. Cognitive impairment is also followed by the loss of attention skills, easy distracting attention, inability to process a difficult or emotionally dense information. This means a lot to the emotional welfare as the most important emotional interaction takes time, concentration and mind power. Curiosity and anxiety are the factors that lead to the users joining groups of exposure to provocative content. More than just increasing the stress, the impact of this compulsive contact is the strengthening of negative affective states which has a feedback loop reinforcing itself to propagate emotional exhaustion.

d. **Pandemic Fatigue and Mediated Crises:** The COVID-19 pandemic was among the turning points in the rise of incidences of digital emotional fatigue. During this period, the digital channels assumed central roles of providing access to information, social connections, and uncertainty orientation. However, this pandemic-related news, statistics, and personal stories have caused what everyone refers to as pandemic fatigue. It is possible to refer to pandemic fatigue as the emotional burnout, the absence of desire to follow directions, and the absence of attention to the ongoing crisis (Haktanir et al., 2022). The overlapping of personal and global crisis in the identical digital space created the atmosphere of the intense closeness, because people both felt educated and powerless simultaneously.

3. DIGITAL ALGORITHM AND EMOTIONAL DISCONNECT

The modern digital environment is more and more controlled by algorithmic systems which filter through, rank and share content using predictive algorithms about user behaviour (Heßler et al., 2022). These systems are integrated into the platforms like Instagram, Tik Tok, and YouTube, and they actively contribute to what users watch and how they feel. On the one hand, these technologies are discussed as personalization and convenience, but, on the other hand, they generate undesired emotional impacts (Chu et al., 2024). Two phenomena influencing each other two are algorithmic indifference and automated empathy become the distinguishing traits of digitally mediated emotional life.

a. **Artificial Intelligence-assisted Curations and Emotional Organization:** Digital platforms apply artificial intelligence to pick and present content that they find likable and interactive (Kang et al., 2022). These systems become aware of user behaviors and attempt to present the content that will capture the attention of people longer. In the majority of cases, the content that produces a strong emotion, say, anger, fear or excitement tends to be prioritized as it will receive more attention. Digital platforms provide a user with a personal emotional space, unlike traditional media where all people can view similar contents. In the long run, this enhances some emotional patterns. As an example, when one consumes a large volume of negative or dramatic content then he or she will continue to get more of it. Consequently, users are not merely responding naturally, they are responding to pre-existing content that is already made to captivate the users. It may cause emotional instability in which individuals have high ups and downs of their emotions. Significantly, the system does not bother in whether the emotion is positive or negative, but instead it aims at retention in attention.
b. **Measuring the Attention and the Measurement of feeling:** Algorithms rely on the intervention metrics such as likes, shares, comments, and watch time. These data assist websites in knowing what customers want (Poleac et al., 2024). Nonetheless, this also alters the nature of the work of emotions on the internet. Emotions are becoming more than mere sentiments of an individual, they are becoming quantified and handled like data. The more reactions the content gets, the more it is shown to other people and this makes creators to make more emotional or dramatic content. This makes it a system of strong and quick responses being more important than thought or profound comprehension. Human beings just may not necessarily feel anger or sympathy, but respond that way when attention is paid to it. Simultaneously, less obvious or complicated feelings are usually disregarded since they do not produce the great engagement. This

makes online experiences more radical and less balanced and diminishes the emotional diversity. In the long run, it may raise the level of emotional fatigue and decrease the capacity to cope with feelings adequately

c. **Empathy and Simulation of Care Automation:** The digital platforms also attempt to look known to be caring by features such as suggested content, reminders, and emotional reactions. This is what is called automated empathy. As an illustration, when a user views content that is connected to stress or sadness the platform can display such content or recommend supportive messages. Although it might be a relief, it is not genuine empathy, but rather grounded in statistics and trends, rather than actual insight. Such reactions may build an illusion that the platform knows the user when in the real sense, it is merely responding to an automatic process. This may even make users reliant on online approval as opposed to actual human communication. Despite being able to make the platforms look more personal, automated empathy does not offer profound emotional support. This causes confusion of real care and artificial reactions.
d. **Emotional Desensitization and Affective Flattening:** Emotional desensitization is one of the primary effects of such systems. Upon repetition of the emotional content, the users gradually become desensitized to it (Brockmyer, J. F. 2022). Initially, individuals can be surprised, depressed, or frightened. However, with time, the reaction is weaker. The reason is that the brain becomes inured to the repetition of similar content. This is mainly prevalent in cases where the users are undispersed with news of crisis or pain. The high volume of such content may overwhelm individuals to an extent of retreating or cease responding emotionally. Simultaneously, platforms promote the usage of fast-moving functions such as the post likes or shares. These moves will bring out the sense of involvement, yet they do not demand profound emotional investment. Consequently, individuals can know of problems but not really connect to them.
e. **Constant Checking and Fear of Missing Out (FOMO)**: The other notable impact of algorithm-based platforms is the sense of the fear of missing out (FOMO). Since the content is constantly changing, the users experience the desire to revisit their feeds over and over to keep up with what is being shared. The habit causes mental pressure and restlessness. Individuals are also likely to be nervous when they are not connected yet or when they believe they are missing out on valuable information (Flecha et al., 2024). This checking habit eats up mental peace and causes emotional fatigue in the long run.
f. **Comparison Culture and Emotional Pressure:** The content that is popularized by algorithms tends to endorse success, happiness, or ideal lifestyle. This causes users to have comparisons with others (Pellegrino, A. 2024). This comparison may give rise to stress, dissatisfaction and low self- esteem. Although this content

may not be realistic, the constant exposure may make the users feel that they are not doing enough or failing to live to their expectations. This emotional stress is an extra burden to general exhaustion.

4. EMOTIONAL LABOUR ON SOCIAL MEDIA

The social media has not just altered the communication pattern, it has also modified the nature of the emotional expression, which is more visible, tactical and even commercial. The social media, such as Instagram, Tik Tok, and YouTube, has created a sort of ecosystem where individuals, particularly influencers and content creators, must be involved in creating and playing feelings as a component of their virtual lives. Emotional labor in this regard concerns the process of controlling and displaying emotions to satisfy the expectation of the audience, the expectations of the platform, and commercial interests, with serious effects of psychological burnout as shown in Figure 4:

Figure 4. Emotional labour on social media

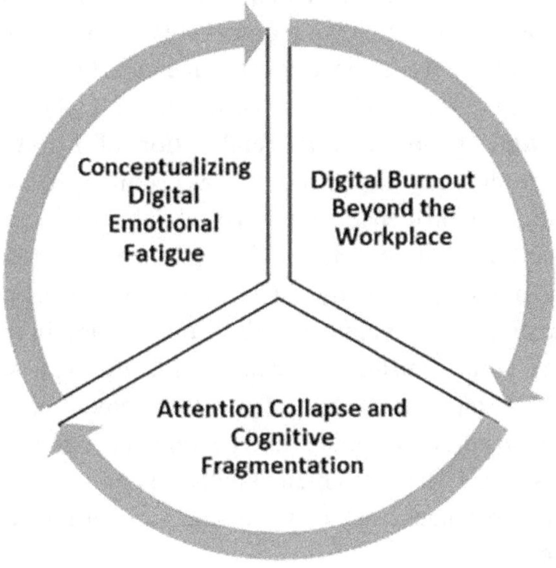

a. **Influencers and performance of emotion:** Influencers are significant in the online world. Not only are they content creators but also individuals who are willing to relate to their audience on an emotional level (Kapitan et al., 2022).

Influencers are popularized by being relatable and communicating with their followers unlike the traditional celebrities who are popular by virtue of their fame. This puts pressure on the need to seem active, positive and be emotionally expressive at all times. Influencers use personal stories, comment back, and communicate a feeling of intimacy with their followers. Although this will create a bond, it also involves unremitting emotional work. Influencers can find it difficult to express their true emotions and be in line with the expectations of the audience. They have to deal with such problems as uncomplimentary remarks, online critique, and the need to remain positive even in hardship situations (Lehto, M. 2022).

b. **Authencity as a Strategist Constructs:** Social media is highly concerned with being real or authentic. Authenticity can be not always natural, it can be designed and controlled. The influencers must look genuine and relatable, yet at the same time they must follow trends, have a particular image and collaborate with brands. This presents a dilemma of being genuinely authentic and having a well-checked version of themselves (Okonkwo et al., 2022). Influencers can also share struggles or emotional moments that would make them relate to the audience. However, such moments are frequently chosen, cut, and distributed at the opportune moment when they will have the greatest impact. This may cause emotional dissonance in which what one expresses online does not entirely reflect how he actually feels. In the long term, it can influence their psychological well-being and cause them to become confused with who they really are.
c. **Emotional Branding and Commercialization of Emotions:** Emotions in digital world are not only expressed, but also employed as a branding and a source of money. The influencers tend to establish their identity based on some emotions, values, or lifestyles (Heeris Christensen et al., 2024). This is referred to as emotional branding whereby our emotions such as happiness, motivation, or struggle are employed to appeal to the audience and in marketing products or ideas. As an example, influencers can post inspirational stories to encourage their followers or emotional to build trust. Such emotional relationships have the power to shape purchase choices and become more engaged. This, however, also brings pressure. To be relevant, influencers should always create emotional content. In some instances, they can overstate or over portray feelings so as to capture attention.
d. **Constant Visibility and Emotional Pressure:** The most significant issue with social media is the necessity to remain in sight at all times. Influencers are under pressure to be active, post frequently and keep their followers entertained. Failure to continue posting can make them lose followers or engagement (Tafesse et al., 2023). This brings about stress and a feeling of being in a state of constant connectivity. Consequently, they hardly have the opportunity to have emotional

rest. This constant exposure adds pressure and causes one not to be able to forget about work and causes emotional burnout in the long term.

e. **Emotional Responsibility and Expectations of the Audience**: The influencers are usually supposed to be able to react to the emotions of their followers. They can be looked upon to provide guidance, inspiration, or encouragement to followers (Lou, C. 2022). This brings a sense of responsibility in which the influencers feel that they will always have to be good and assist others. Although this can be rewarding, it can also be an emotional exhausting one. Management of the expectations of others, as well as individual stress, might augment the emotional load and result in burnout.

5. DIGITAL COPING MECHANISM

With the continually growing emotional exhaustion of the present-day highly digitalized world, individuals have begun to devise new strategies of coping with stress and overload. Interestingly, these platforms, which cause emotional pressure, such as Instagram, Tik Tok, and YouTube, are also the ones where people attempt to develop and process their emotions. Digital coping, unlike the traditional coping methods is social, visible and shared. Individuals cope with stress collectively as they share their emotions on the internet (Weber et al., 2024). Memes, humor, irony and storytelling are some of the most popular ones. Such ways assist users to lessen their stress, feel connected and make sense of their experiences.

a. **Memes as Massive Processing of Emotions:** One of the most popular stress coping methods over the internet is what is known as memes. They are easy to reproduce images, videos, or text, which symbolize the daily struggles in a charming or relatable manner (Mishra et al., 2022). Memes assist individuals in being able to demonstrate feelings that are otherwise not easily explainable. As an example, certain emotions such as burnout, stress, anxiety and the like are frequently interpreted into material that is humorous. Users feel that they are not alone and that most people will know what they are going through when they see such memes. Memes also form some feeling of togetherness. Individuals know that others are experiencing similar things and that is the emotional relief. Through this, memes have become a kind of emotional exchange. When the repetition of the same negative themes is overdone (such as some constant burnout jokes), they might normalize such issues and seem inevitable. Therefore, memes may be useful, as well as cause emotional fatigue in unintended ways.

b. **Protective Strategies of Irony and Detachment:** Another typical coping mechanism that people use to cope with painful feelings using the internet is irony. Irony or sarcasm is used by many users, particularly the youths in discussing serious matters. People build emotional distance by making the problems present humorous or indirect (Cui, J. 2022). This will enable them to cope with stress without being overwhelmed. Irony serves as a safety net, which enables the users to discuss a challenging subject with the intention of concealing their genuine feelings. But excessive irony may make one less authentic with emotional expression. In the long run, individuals might struggle to express the true emotions. This may result in emotional confusion and even emotional numbness where people cease to respond emotionally towards situations.

c. **Humor as Emotional Regulation:** Humor is the key factor in digital coping as it helps people to reframe stressful or negative events to be more positive. Humor serves as a cognitive reappraisal in psychologically challenging digital spaces, whereas it enables users to change their attitude and decrease the emotional influence of difficult circumstances (Alkaraki et al., 2024). Humor also offers a way of changing distress into fun whether that is via a joke or a funny video or a sarcastic comment. Humor has a close relationship with its social nature, which explains its effectiveness as a coping strategy. On social media such as Tik Tok, the content that is humorous tends to go viral, bringing everyone a dose of relaxation and a sense of bonding. This shared experience makes the role of humor even more rewarding because it is not just that individuals are able to recreate their experience of emotions but can also share in a larger culture of endurance and adaptability. Various types of humor have varying coping purposes. Self-deprecating humor enables one to accept the situation of struggle, they have but still retain the sense that they are in control of the situation but satirical humor attacks the external systems and structures giving one a sense of power. Humor leads to decreasing the perceived intensity of the stressors and increasing emotional resilience in both cases.

d. **Digital Narrative and Storytelling as a Meaning Making:** Individuals use blogs, videos, posts, or threads to share their experiences. Storytelling can assist people in arranging the thoughts and explaining their experiences (Antoniak et al., 2024). By sharing their stories, people do not only process their personal feelings, but also assist other people who can resonate with them. These experiences give them a positive atmosphere in which individuals feel necessary and motivated. It transforms personal problems into mutuality. Nevertheless, there is also the need to tell stories in a particular manner in order to capture attention. This may render narration as acting instead of authentic expression. In some cases, individuals can make comparisons with other people, thus triggering inadequacy.

e. **Digital Detox and Selective Engagement:** To resolve emotional overload, many users have to break social media. This is referred to as a digital detox.

Individuals can reduce their screen time, unsubscribe to stressful posts, or have full screen breaks (Coyne et al., 2023). This assists in alleviating the mental stress and relaxation time. Selective engagement, i.e., what to watch and to engage with, is also a key strategy. It gives the user control over their digital world rather than control by their digital world.

f. **Online Community and Peer Support:** On the Internet, people can also receive emotional support. Support groups, discussion forums and online communities enable users to contribute their issues and get counselling (Rayland et al., 2023). These societies bring about a feeling of belonging and minimize the feeling of being lonely. It is a very reassuring and helpful experience to talk to people who have gone through the same experiences. Excessive reliance on the Internet support can also diminish the real-world communication unless it is moderated.

6. COMPASSION FATIGUE AND SOCIAL INDIFFERENCE

In the modern digital world, people are exposed to increased levels of suffering. There are reports on war, natural disasters, social injustice, and personal misfortunes that are constantly visible on social media platforms, such as Instagram and X (formerly Twitter). Although this increased awareness is positive, there are negative consequences to consider. The increased exposure to suffering leads to compassion fatigue, in which people become emotionally drained and begin to show less and less empathy towards the suffering of other people.

According to empirical studies, the human emotional system is finite. The increased levels of emotional content, especially negative content, force people to take control and become less emotional. Rather than becoming more empathetic, they begin to avoid the content altogether. Eventually, they become socially indifferent, in which they are aware but show less and less emotional empathy.

a. **Information Overload and Emotional Burnout:** The main reason for compassion fatigue is information overload. Social media platforms are constantly sending updates, breaking news, and emotional stories without giving people time to process the previous content. According to digital stress studies, excessive information overload causes increased levels of mental fatigue and reduces the ability to effectively handle emotions. The constant switching between different types of content, ranging from tragedy, entertainment, and everyday stories, is a significant cognitive burden on the brain. The excessive cognitive burden causes emotional burnout, and people begin to ignore the suffering of other people, not because they are not empathetic, but because they are tired and feel overwhelmed.

b. **Political Apathy and Reduced Civic Engagement:** One of the significant effects of compassion fatigue is political apathy. While contemporary people are exposed to more political information than ever before, political engagement in civic activities has decreased significantly. Therefore, rather than taking active political measures such as voting, political discussions, and political protests, people are taking passive measures such as viewing the posts and liking them.
c. **Emotional Desensitization and Reduced Sensitivity:** Another significant effect of compassion fatigue is emotional desensitization and the resulting emotional sensitivity reduction. For instance, the first time a person is exposed to political content can cause them to feel emotional and concerned about the situation. However, the more they are exposed to political content and the more they are exposed to the situation, the more they desensitize and the more the emotional situation loses its significance and importance. Therefore, emotional desensitization and the resulting emotional sensitivity reduction are the effects of the prolonged nature of the situation and the fast pace of the digital situation.
d. **Social Indifference as a Coping Mechanism:** Social apathy can also be seen as a means of defense. When one is overwhelmed with emotions, they may choose to disengage from a situation in order to protect themselves. Instead of constantly engaging with a situation, one may choose to disengage from such a situation or topic, especially if they find it disturbing or emotionally taxing. This coping mechanism, however, also leads to a lack of empathy and concern for others. Thus, disengaging from a situation does not necessarily mean one does not care, but rather they are coping with emotional saturation by disengaging from a situation.
e. **Short-Term Collective Emotions and "Viral Empathy":** Collective emotions are also seen in digital media, especially when a post goes viral and a large number of people respond with empathy and concern for a situation within a short period. However, collective emotions are also short-lived, especially when a new topic arises and one forgets about the previous topic or situation. This can be seen as a form of viral empathy, whereby one has a short period of intense emotions and empathy, but this does not last long. Thus, collective emotions are also seen as fractured and ephemeral, whereby one can be aware of a situation through digital media, but they do not act on such a situation, leading to a lack of change and development.
f. **Impact on Social Change and Collective Action:** This phenomenon has a significant impact on society. Since emotions are fleeting and constantly changing, it proves difficult to act on what one knows. People may be concerned for a fleeting moment, but they do not act on this concern enough to make a difference in solving problems. This, in turn, means that social movements stall, and change in society proves difficult to enact. This shift from engagement to

fleeting and constantly changing emotions makes digital platforms less effective in terms of actual change in the world.

g. **Algorithmic Amplification of Emotional Content:** Algorithmic practices also contribute to compassion fatigue through the promotion of emotionally charged content, recognizing its engagement value. As a result, users are subjected to a repetitive cycle of extreme content, leading to a buildup of affective pressure. This repetitive exposure to extreme content ultimately leads to desensitization and emotional exhaustion. The algorithmic focus on engagement, rather than the well-being of users, also implies a promotion of emotional exhaustion among users.

7. CROSS CULTURAL PERSPECTIVES

Emotional exhaustion in the digital age is not a homogenous phenomenon; instead, it is predetermined by cultural values, social norms, and technological situations that determine how people perceive, communicate, and manage digitally mediated feelings. Despite the platform like Tik Tok and YouTube having an international reach, the emotional impacts of using these platforms do not have the same impact on all societies. Such differences are especially noticeable in the emotional exhaustion patterns, coping styles, and types of social interactions, which should not be overlooked when discussing digital well-being by means of culturally sensitive perspectives.

7.1. Variations in Emotional Exhaustion Across Cultures:

Digital age emotional exhaustion does not fit all. It relies so much on cultural values, social norms and the use of technology in the day-to-day lives of people. These are the factors that determine how individuals perceive, communicate and control their emotions when using digital platforms.

Although Tik Tok and YouTube are popular everywhere, their emotional appeal does not have an equivalent effect in every society. Individuals with various cultures respond to internet materials differently. The differences are evident in the experience of emotional exhaustion, its coping, and the ways of interactions with other people over the Internet. Due to this reason, it is prudent to consider the digital well-being through the cultural perspective.

7.2. Differences in Cultural Coping Mechanism:

Digital stress also varies depending on the culture of people. Humor, memes, and irony are commonly employed to cope with emotional overload by many people, however, these appear different across different cultures. Humor in certain societies can either be indirect or symbolic whereas in others it can be direct and expressive. This influences the usefulness of these coping mechanisms. Coping is usually group-based in collectivist cultures. Individuals are dependent on family, friends or close-knit communities to express their emotions and receive support. Through online platforms, these relationships are enhanced and stress is addressed collectively. Coping tends to be more individual in more individualistic cultures. Individuals are allowed to be open, get off social media, or decide to restrict what they view online. In the same way, irony and emotional detachment are applied in different ways in different cultures. Irony in some societies is used to make people cope with serious issues without being emotionally crushed. In other people, it might not be an often-used one and might not produce the same effect.

7.3. Social Interaction and Digital Interaction Pattern:

Even the manner in which individuals interact on the internet differs according to the cultures and hence how they respond to emotional fatigue. Online interactions also have the tendency to perpetuate offline relationships in the society in which they are strong (e.g. in terms of community and relationships). Human beings stand by one another and be in touch. They might still not give up in spite of being emotionally exhausted due to social responsibility and belonging to a group. With less connected or more individualistic settings, online interaction is usually wider and weaker. Individuals have to relate with a lot of different people, yet the relationships might not be strong. Disengagement, decreased interaction, or selective communication could be the results of emotional exhaustion in such situations. Moreover, cultural attitudes have an impact on the way individuals are involved in social and political debate on the internet. There are cultures that are encouraging to raise their voices and join a campaign or movement. With other people it might not be the case as a person may not want to express themselves publicly due to social or cultural factors. These dissimilarities influence the transformation of emotional fatigue into either action or withdrawal.

7.4. Role of Digital Literacy and Technological Context:

Digital literacy, access to technology also define the cross cultural experiences of emotions exhaustion. Simultaneously, individuals in digital literate spaces are in a better position to understand the nature of the algorithms, which patterns of content amplification, and have measures to mitigate their exposure. This knowledge can release emotional over load and enlarge the ability to endure. Instead, it is the environment with the lack of or unequal distribution of digital literacy that exposes users more to misinformation, partisanship information, and the ability to manipulate emotions. Inability to analyze the content or regulate the use of the digital content may add to emotional exhaustion. The variations in the technological infrastructures such as the accessibility of the internet as well as patterns of internet access also influence how individuals perceive and react to digital space.

7.5. Implications for Global Understanding of Digital-Well Being:

The variations in emotional exhaustion, coping and social engagement through the various cultures highlights the importance of ensuring one remains contextual about the digital well-being. Globalized models that fail to consider cultural diversity will tend to lump the complex emotional lives and provide solutions that are not likely to be effective in different societies. Under culturally informed approach, it is pointed out that interventions must be structured to fit local situations by taking into consideration the difference in emotional norms, coping mechanisms and social structure. These include the marketing of culturally relevant coping strategies, the digital divide, and the platform structure elements capable of accommodating the diverse user needs.

8. WELL-BEING, ETHICAL INTERVENTIONS

The growing cases of digital-fatigue and social-apathy in the digital mediated space are to be approached in a complex way that encompasses the personal well-being approaches, the ethical-technological design, and the institutional responsibility. With the platforms such as Instagram and Tik Tok starting to mediate the emotional experiences, neither the users nor the designers, organizations, and policymakers are only the ones tasked with reducing the negative experiences. Here, the researcher examines how the well-being can be strengthened, using digital tools, ethical intervention, and systemic changes, which might be introduced to establish emotional resilience.

8.1. Well-Being and Digital Self-Regulation:

The emergence of digital well-being apps is an indication of a growing recognition of the importance of curbing emotional and cognitive overload in the technology-based setting. These apps provide access to guided meditation, breathing practices, mood-tracking options that assist a person in becoming more conscious of their emotional states and has healthier coping mechanisms. These applications are like self-control mechanisms, and users can compensate the severity of digital interactions. Their effectiveness however relies on their continued use and motivation of the user. Besides, the very idea of coping with digital fatigue with the help of digital tools has a paradoxical nature, which also points to the necessity of incorporating such practices into the wider offline habits and lifestyle.

8.2. Ethical Design and Humane Technology

One of the most crucial aspects of considering the problem of emotional exhaustion is the reconsideration of the design of digital platforms. The existing platform designs typically focus on engagement with the use of functions as infinite scrolling, autoplay, and push notifications to promote its use and sustained exposure. These features increase the retention of the users, but they also lead to the cognitive overload and emotional burnout. This involves the implementation of functions like time-use transparency, customizable notification preferences and natural stopping indications where users can disengage with a lot easier time. As an illustration, a reminder that reminds users to take some rest or summarises their use can make users more conscious of their digital behavior.

Moreover, emotional awareness can also be included in design plans, and platforms can observe tendencies of overuse or suffering and address it by restricting content access. Platforms can decrease the frameworks that create structural conditions that are associated with emotional fatigue by moving to well-being-oriented models instead of engagement-driven models.

8.3. Algorithmic Responsibility and Content Moderation:

The algorithm systems are at the core of emotional formation as it defines the type of content to be displayed to the user and the frequency at which to watch it. As mentioned in the previous section, algorithms tend to prioritize high-arousal content that will give the greatest engagement thus increasing the stress, anxiety and emotional strain. The solution to this problem lies in the transition to algorithmic responsibility, in which platforms will be held responsible about the emotional effects of their recommendation personalities. This includes making algorithm workings more transparent and adding well-being measures to the content curation process. As an example, one can alleviate the emotional burden by limiting the frequency of exposure to agonizing content or by increasing the presence of more balanced and positive feeds. The content moderation policies should also be implemented efficiently in preventing the spread of the content that is harmful, misleading, or even too distressing. It is possible to shift algorithms to more sustainable forms of user interaction, which are not based on emotional intensification as one of the main factors, by implementing them using ethical concerns.

8.4. Policy Interventions and Regulatory Frameworks

In addition to platform-based modifications, policy interventions play an instrumental role in setting standards to help users escape adverse implications of digital settings. The governments and the regulatory authorities can be instrumental in enhancing digital well-being through implementing regulations concerning data usage, content control, and security of users.

The safer and more equal digital ecosystems may be created with the help of policies that require transparency in making the decisions by algorithms, limit manipulative design, and spread digital literacy. To illustrate, laws that curb unreasonable data mining or make platforms more willing to offer users more control over what they see in their content feeds will allow individuals to control their online experiences more successfully.

Moreover, digital policy encompassed with mental health issues is the way to make sure that the emotional well-being is a social issue, not merely an individual matter. Development of wholesome solutions requires that policymakers, technology firms, and researchers work together to come up with comprehensive solutions.

8.5. Promoting Emotional Intelligence and Sustainable Engagement

Finally, the outcome of this set of interventions is to develop emotional resilience, which is, in other words, adaptation and recovery to the situation in the digital environment, which involves emotional challenges. This will entail providing people with the capability to critically navigate digital material, control their emotional reactions, and create healthy boundaries. Resilience is developed through educational programs that facilitate digital literacy, emotional intelligence and conscious consumption. Practices like selective engagement, digital detox, and conscious use, can be encouraged to make a person maintain a healthy relationship with technology. Meanwhile, the impact of social indifference can be mitigated with the help of the creation of supportive online communities, where empathy and meaningful engagement should be valued.

To achieve sustainable digital interaction, there is need to transition towards proactive coping mechanisms of well-being, where the individual, platforms and institutions collaborate towards establishing an environment that is enabling and not disabling of emotional health.

9. CONCLUSIONS AND FUTURE SCOPE

The digital world is now a main constituent of the everyday life, yet it is accompanied by unceasing emotional demands. As it has been demonstrated in this chapter, emotional fatigue is not just the result of excessive spending of time online, but it is also the outcome of the type of content people watch and a perpetual desire to stay active. Instagram and Tik Tok platforms present users with a combination of information, feelings, and interactions that may overwhelm them as they continue using these platforms.

Being constantly bombarded with stressful or emotional images and facts, people can start to experience exhaustion, diminished responsiveness, and even indifference to the social problems of concern. This may cause compassion fatigue and less involvement in the social and civic life. Meanwhile, people attempt to cope with this pressure by means of various coping mechanisms such as humor, selective use, and breaks on the digital platform. Yet, these solutions can be considered to be rather short-term and cannot cover the root causes of emotional exhaustion. Another point of interest that has been raised in the chapter is that emotional fatigue is not perceived everywhere similarly. The social norms, cultural values and the degree of digital awareness contribute significantly in determining digital stress response and management of individuals. This is why it is significant to interpret emotional fatigue in a broader and flexible view. Eventually, digital-based emotional exhaustion is one of the common problems that need to be addressed by individuals, organizations, and technological platforms. The negative outcomes would be curbed by a middle ground solution whereby technology should be deployed in a careful and responsible manner. Establishing healthier online lifestyles, boosting awareness, and more user-friendly systems are milestones towards making sure that technology is a health promoter rather than a health detriment.

9.1. Future Scope

In the future, the long-term effects of the exposure to digital content on the emotional well-being and social behavior of people from different age groups and cultures need to be explored. This should also include the exploration of the potential influence of new technologies, such as artificial intelligence and virtual reality, on the emotional well-being of people through online platforms. The studies need to assess the efficiency of digital coping mechanisms and contribute to the creation of better coping tools that can help people. Moreover, the importance of the ethics behind the creation of platforms and the policies that can reduce emotional overload while creating engagement needs to be explored further. The future studies need to consider the emotional well-being of people while advancing technology as shown in Figure 5:

Figure 5. Future scope

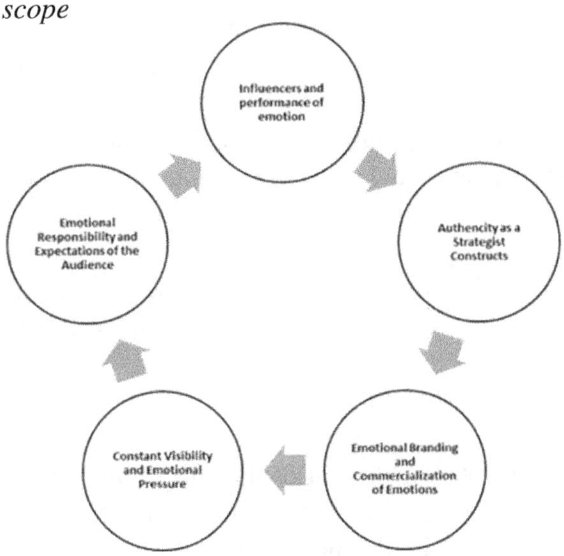

a. **Longitudinal Research on Emotional Fatigue:** Further research needs to be directed at the dimension of emotional fatigue that is built over an extended period when digital platforms are used on a regular basis. The majority of the current studies are of short-term nature, and long-term psychological consequences like burnout, impaired attention span, and emotional sensitivity alterations should be known. This will assist in revealing whether digital fatigue will be short-lived or is transformed into a habit.
b. **Cross-Cultural Comparative Studies:** The necessity to investigate the cultural differences in the emotional exhaustion is great. As the expression of emotions, coping, and socializing depend on the cultural values, comparative studies have the potential to bring a more in-depth understanding of the condition of digital well-being in the world. It will also aid in coming up with solutions that are

applicable in various societies rather than using a single solution across the board.

c. **Impact of AI and Algorithm Systems:** The next generation of research must investigate how algorithms and artificial intelligence affect people emotionally on the Internet. Algorithms on platforms determine what the users get to see and in many cases, they favour the content that is emotionally excitable. To create more responsible and balanced digital systems, understanding the effect of this on user mood, attention, and behavior can be useful.
d. **Effectiveness of Coping Strategies and Interventions:** Further studies are required to assess the effectiveness of the coping strategies that reduce emotional fatigue in actual situations. These involve the research of the effects of digital detox, mindfulness applications, humor and content filtering. To determine feasible solutions that enhance emotional well-being in online settings, researchers can also be used to test intervention programs.
e. **Ethical Design and Policy Development:** The future direction of work should be aimed at developing digital systems that help people feel well. This involves researching on ethical design elements like the restriction of notifications, endless scrolling, and encouraging healthy consumption behaviors. Meanwhile, policymakers should work on the principles that will safeguard users against emotional overload and make the use of technology responsible.

9.2. Practical Implications:

The results of this chapter have significant implications on people, organizations, and managers who are in highly digital settings. Emotional fatigue is no longer perceived as a personal problem; it has a direct impact on productivity, decision-making and well-being. Thus, there is a necessity of both practical measures and managerial policies aimed to deal with it as shown in Figure 6:

Figure 6. Practical implications

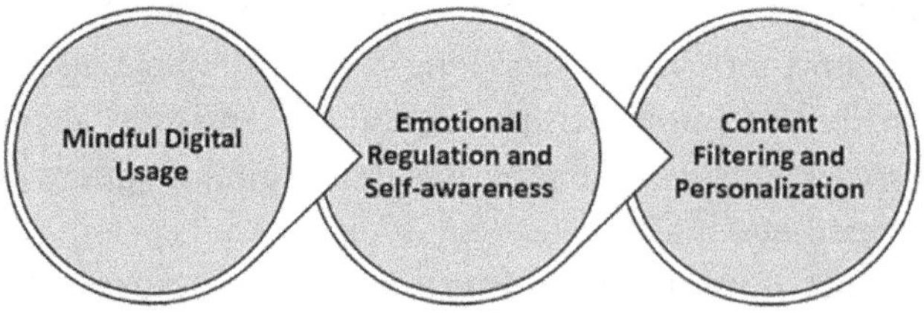

a. **Mindful Digital Usage:** People need to form conscious screen time habits, including spending less time on screens, not scrolling too much, and having frequent breaks. It is possible to be selective in the kind of content to consume to alleviate emotional overload.
b. **Emotional Regulation and Self-awareness:** People should understand the initial symptoms of emotional fatigue and learn to control their emotions. Emotional balancing can be enhanced with the help of such practices as mindfulness, reflections, and digital detox.
c. **Content Filtering and Personalization:** The act of actively controlling social media feeds such as unfollowing painful material or viewing negative news less may also assist in lessening emotional distress that is not necessary. Healthy Coping Strategies: Positive coping strategies like humor, socialization or offline activities would enable people to cope with the digital stress better.

9.3. Managerial Implication

a. **Digital Well-being at Work:** Emotional fatigue is one of the problems that managers are supposed to be aware of at work, particularly in digital or remote workplace settings. Stress can be lowered by promoting relaxation, flexible communication and achievable deadlines.
b. **Reducing Always-On Culture:** Organizations ought not to develop demands of the unavailability. The work life could be assisted by determining boundaries on work hours and communication to make employees strike a balance between work and life.
c. **Training and Digital Literacy Programs:** Employees can be better equipped to meet the demands of technologies by offering training on how to manage digital tools, how to manage information overload, and how to become increasingly digital literate. Favorable Work conditions: The managers are expected to establish an open atmosphere in which employees are free to talk about stress and emotional difficulties. This is able to enhance interaction and well-being.
d. **Ethical Use of Technology:** Responsible digital practices should be implemented by organizations to ensure that internal systems and tools do not help to cause unwarranted pressure or burnout.

9.4. Strengths of the Chapter

a. **Relevant and Current Topic:** The chapter deals with a very topical problem in the modern digital era emotional exhaustion and social apathy, therefore, it is useful both in the academic research and in everyday cognition.
b. **Strong Conceptual Integration:** It links the main concepts, including emotional fatigue, compassion fatigue, coping mechanisms, and well-being in a very logical and well-organized manner.
c. **Multidimensional Perspective:** The chapter is not limited to any side, but it discusses psychological, social, technological and cultural dimensions providing a complete picture of the problem.
d. **Inclusion of Digital Context:** Connecting the discourse with such websites as Instagram and Tik Tok, the chapter is still based on the real-life digital experience.
e. **Focus on Cross Cultural Insights:** The chapter is more inclusive and global than it is specific because the cultural variations are taken into consideration. Theory-Practice: There is a balance between theory and practice in the book being discussed.
f. **Future Oriented Approach:** The chapter provides an opportunity to expand research and policy-making because it outlines potential research directions and ethical issues.

REFERENCES

Agha, Z., Badillo-Urquiola, K., & Wisniewski, P. J. (2023). " Strike at the root": co-designing real-time social media interventions for adolescent online risk prevention. *Proceedings of the ACM on Human-Computer Interaction, 7*(CSCW1), 1-32. DOI: 10.1145/3579625

Alkaraki, S. M. S., Alias, N. B., & Maros, M. (2024). Exploring the impact of social media humor related to the COVID-19 pandemic: A systematic literature review on themes, coping mechanisms, critiques and linguistic devices. *Cogent Arts & Humanities, 11*(1), 2322227. DOI: 10.1080/23311983.2024.2322227

Antoniak, M., Mire, J., Sap, M., Ash, E., & Piper, A. (2024, August). Where do people tell stories online? story detection across online communities. In *Proceedings of the 62nd Annual Meeting of the Association for Computational Linguistics (*Volume 1*: Long Papers)* (pp. 7104-7130). DOI: 10.18653/v1/2024.acl-long.383

Balaskas, S., Konstantakopoulou, M., Yfantidou, I., & Komis, K. (2025). Algorithmic burnout and digital well-being: Modelling young adults' resistance to personalized digital persuasion. *Societies (Basel, Switzerland), 15*(8), 232. DOI: 10.3390/soc15080232

Brockmyer, J. F. (2022). Desensitization and violent video games: Mechanisms and evidence. *Child and Adolescent Psychiatric Clinics of North America, 31*(1), 121–132. DOI: 10.1016/j.chc.2021.06.005

Chowdhury, K., & Lamacchia, D. (2019, November). Collaborative workspace for employee engagement leveraging social media architecture. In *Abu Dhabi International Petroleum Exhibition and Conference* (p. D031S093R003). SPE. DOI: 10.2118/197325-MS

Chu, S. C., Deng, T., & Mundel, J. (2024). The impact of personalization on viral behavior intentions on TikTok: The role of perceived creativity, authenticity, and need for uniqueness. *Journal of Marketing Communications, 30*(1), 1–20. DOI: 10.1080/13527266.2022.2098364

Ciolfi, L., & Lockley, E. (2018). From Work to Life and back again: Examining the digitally-mediated work/life practices of a group of knowledge workers. [CSCW]. *Computer Supported Cooperative Work, 27*(3), 803–839. DOI: 10.1007/s10606-018-9315-3

Coyne, P., & Woodruff, S. J. (2023). Taking a break: The effects of partaking in a two-week social media digital detox on problematic smartphone and social media use, and other health-related outcomes among young adults. *Behavioral Sciences (Basel, Switzerland)*, *13*(12), 1004. DOI: 10.3390/bs13121004

Cui, J. (2022). Respecting the old and loving the young: Emoji-based sarcasm interpretation between younger and older adults. *Frontiers in Psychology*, *13*, 897153. DOI: 10.3389/fpsyg.2022.897153

Flecha Ortiz, J. A., Santos Corrada, M., Perez, S., Dones, V., & Rodriguez, L. H. (2024). Exploring the influence of uncontrolled social media use, fear of missing out, fear of better options, and fear of doing anything on consumer purchase intent. *International Journal of Consumer Studies*, *48*(1), e12990. DOI: 10.1111/ijcs.12990

Fu, S., Li, H., Liu, Y., Pirkkalainen, H., & Salo, M. (2020). Social media overload, exhaustion, and use discontinuance: Examining the effects of information overload, system feature overload, and social overload. *Information Processing & Management*, *57*(6), 102307. DOI: 10.1016/j.ipm.2020.102307

Haktanir, A., Can, N., Seki, T., Kurnaz, M. F., & Dilmaç, B. (2022). Do we experience pandemic fatigue? current state, predictors, and prevention. *Current Psychology (New Brunswick, N.J.)*, *41*(10), 7314–7325. DOI: 10.1007/s12144-021-02397-w

Heeris Christensen, A. B., Gyrd-Jones, R., & Beverland, M. B. (2024). Dialectical Emotional Labour in Digital Person-branding: The case of digital influencers. *Organization Studies*, *45*(4), 571–591. DOI: 10.1177/01708406231208370

Heßler, P. O., Pfeiffer, J., & Hafenbrädl, S. (2022). When Self-Humanization Leads to Algorithm Aversion. *Business & Information Systems Engineering*, *64*(3), 275–292. DOI: 10.1007/s12599-022-00754-y

Kang, H., & Lou, C. (2022). AI agency vs. human agency: Understanding human–AI interactions on TikTok and their implications for user engagement. *Journal of Computer-Mediated Communication*, *27*(5), zmac014. DOI: 10.1093/jcmc/zmac014

Kapitan, S., van Esch, P., Soma, V., & Kietzmann, J. (2022). Influencer marketing and authenticity in content creation. *Australasian Marketing Journal*, *30*(4), 342–351. DOI: 10.1177/18393349211011171

Kim, J., & Kim, M. (2022). Rise of social media influencers as a new marketing channel: Focusing on the roles of psychological well-being and perceived social responsibility among consumers. *International Journal of Environmental Research and Public Health*, *19*(4), 2362. DOI: 10.3390/ijerph19042362

Lehto, M. (2022). Ambivalent influencers: Feeling rules and the affective practice of anxiety in social media influencer work. *European Journal of Cultural Studies, 25*(1), 201–216. DOI: 10.1177/1367549421988958

Lestari, D. A., Primagara, M., Sari, S. A., Meilina, A., Fauziah, S., Sugesti, A. I., & Salwi, A. D. (2024). Meme culture: A study of humor and satire in digital media. *International Journal of Advanced Multidisciplinary Research and Studies, 4*(4), 134–140. DOI: 10.62225/2583049X.2024.4.4.3013

Lou, C. (2022). Social media influencers and followers: Theorization of a trans-parasocial relation and explication of its implications for influencer advertising. *Journal of Advertising, 51*(1), 4–21. DOI: 10.1080/00913367.2021.1880345

Mbamba, C. R., Dwumah, P., Koomson-Yalley, E., & Adaranijo, E. T. (2026). Riding the waves: Intergenerational digital storytelling to explore coastal flooding experiences. *Global Environmental Change, 97*, 103129. DOI: 10.1016/j.gloenvcha.2026.103129

Mishra, B., & Chowdhury, A. (2022). Internet Memes Are Impacting Society: Perspectives from Brand Communication to World Peace Promotion. In *North-East Research Conclave* (pp. 33–48). Springer Nature Singapore.

Mojumder, B., Uddin, M. J., & Dey, K. (2025). Perspectives, preparedness and challenges of the abrupt transition of emergency online learning to traditional methods in higher education of Bangladesh in the post-pandemic era. *Discover Education, 4*(1), 33. DOI: 10.1007/s44217-025-00417-6

Okonkwo, I., & Namkoisse, E. (2023). The role of influencer marketing in building authentic brand relationships online. *Journal of Digital Marketing and Communication, 3*(2), 81–90. DOI: 10.53623/jdmc.v3i2.350

Pellegrino, A. (2024). Social comparison, problems of digital consumption and its implications. In *Decoding Digital Consumer Behavior: Bridging Theory and Practice* (pp. 113–131). Springer Nature Singapore. DOI: 10.1007/978-981-97-3454-2_8

Poleac, G., & Ghergut-Babii, A. N. (2024). How social media algorithms influence the way users decide-perspectives of social media users and practitioners. *Technium Soc. Sci. J., 57*, 69–81. DOI: 10.47577/tssj.v57i1.10955

Rayland, A., & Andrews, J. (2023). From social network to peer support network: Opportunities to explore mechanisms of online peer support for mental health. *JMIR Mental Health, 10*, e41855. DOI: 10.2196/41855

Skulmowski, A., & Xu, K. M. (2022). Understanding cognitive load in digital and online learning: A new perspective on extraneous cognitive load. *Educational Psychology Review*, *34*(1), 171–196. DOI: 10.1007/s10648-021-09624-7

Soror, A., Steelman, Z. R., & Turel, O. (2022). Exhaustion and dependency: A habituation–sensitization perspective on the duality of habit in social media use. *Information Technology & People*, *35*(1), 67–95. DOI: 10.1108/ITP-11-2019-0603

Tafesse, W., & Wood, B. P. (2023). Social media influencers' community and content strategy and follower engagement behavior in the presence of competition: An Instagram-based investigation. *Journal of Product and Brand Management*, *32*(3), 406–419. DOI: 10.1108/JPBM-02-2022-3851

Tahreem, I., & Shakeel, H. (2025). Emotional tones (anger, fear and excitement) leads to the propagation of fake news: Literature review on Covid-19 infodemic. *Journal of Media Horizons*, *6*(2), 679–684.

Tarafdar, M., Cooper, C. L., & Stich, J. F. (2019). The technostress trifecta-techno eustress, techno distress and design: Theoretical directions and an agenda for research. *Information Systems Journal*, *29*(1), 6–42. DOI: 10.1111/isj.12169

Turner, K. E. (2025). The Effects of TikTok Use on Mental Health and Personal Well-Being Among Undergraduate Students (Doctoral dissertation, Alliant International University).

Voinea, D. V. (2025). Reconceptualizing gatekeeping in the age of artificial intelligence: A theoretical exploration of artificial intelligence-driven news curation and automated journalism. *Journalism and Media*, *6*(2), 68. DOI: 10.3390/journalmedia6020068

Wang, H., Ding, H., & Kong, X. (2023). Understanding technostress and employee well-being in digital work: The roles of work exhaustion and workplace knowledge diversity. *International Journal of Manpower*, *44*(2), 334–353. DOI: 10.1108/IJM-08-2021-0480

Weber, D. L., Bygholm, A. K. M., & Kanstrup, A. M. (2024). Digital coping strategies of young people living with cognitive disabilities: Using emotion-focused and problem-focused coping in digital relationships. *Disability & Society*, *39*(8), 2007–2031. DOI: 10.1080/09687599.2023.2181767

Yang, X., & Du, J. (2024). The effect of teacher self-efficacy, online pedagogical and content knowledge, and emotion regulation on teacher digital burnout: A mediation model. *BMC Psychology*, *12*(1), 51. DOI: 10.1186/s40359-024-01540-z

Chapter 12
Scroll, React, Detach: Emotional Fatigue and the Rise of Social Indifference in Digital Media Consumption

Arpita Nayak
http://orcid.org/0000-0003-2911-0492
KIIT School of Liberal Studies, KIIT (Deemed to be) University, Bhubaneswar, India

Ipseeta Satpathy
http://orcid.org/0000-0002-0155-5548
KSOM, KIIT (Deemed to be) University, Bhubaneswar, India

Vishal Jain
http://orcid.org/0000-0003-1126-7424
School of Engineering & Technology, Vivekananda Institute of Professional Studies-Technical Campus, New Delhi, India

ABSTRACT

The chapter analyzes the impact of digital and social media on emotional well-being, revealing how constant exposure to disturbing content leads to emotional exhaustion, desensitization, and diminished empathy. It discusses the phenomena of compassion fatigue, doomscrolling, and the illusions created by slacktivism and performative activism, particularly in younger demographics heavily engaged with digital media. The authors highlight that engagement-driven algorithms foster high-arousal content, perpetuating fatigue instead of empathy. Strategies for developing digital resilience and ethical media usage are proposed, contributing valuable insights to discussions around digital well-being, media ethics, and the psychological impact of the attention economy.

DOI: 10.4018/979-8-3373-8307-1.ch012

1. INTRODUCTION

The digital media has become a strong influence that defines the emotional life today. Since the moment of waking up, till the last scroll before going to sleep, people are stuck in the stream of information, photographs, and opinions, as well as emotional cues. Social media, news aggregators, short video apps, and instant messaging platforms altered the perception of the world by forcing crises in different countries, personal achievements, political feuds, and small-scale information on a single, always changing feed. This has changed our connection, level of awareness, and involvement. It, however, marks a radical change in the way we feel, manage, and maintain emotions. It is not only the media environment concerning information but highly affective with constant emotional involvement and reaction (Arne, 2023).

The recent years have demonstrated interactions involving scholars, practitioners, and users stating a paradoxical outcome emotional exhaustion and a growing alienation to others. Perhaps like never before, people are exposed to suffering, injustice and crises, but many report feeling numb and detached or overwhelmed instead of being involved empathetically. Social tragedies occurring worldwide, which impacted people with long-term attention and prompts to take action, now vie against the trends on social platforms, advertisements by influencers, and outrage generated by algorithms. That convergence forms an economy of emotions, in which anger, fear, sadness, and moral outrage are perpetually stimulated, propagated, and bought and sold and the further reaction of this is virtually inexistent since the funnelled emotion does not exist in the realms of reflexion or recuperation (Peña et al.,2023).

The emotional exhaustion of using digital media is based on how it is always an emotional strain. New platforms are on 24/7 unlike the old media where exposure was predetermined and restricted to specific timelines; new media are immediate, constant, and personalized to us. This twenty-four-hour presence erases the boundary of the real and personal life, work and rest, and world events and personal life. People are no passive consumers; they are directly involved. We are supposed to be responsive, commenting, sharing, sending empathy with likes, hashtags and stories. This continuous emotional activation stresses the psychological resources in the long run resulting in compassion fatigue, burnout and disengagement. What possible started off as increased awareness can gradually develop into avoidance, apathy or selective indifference (Asiyah n.d.,).

An important feature of this phenomenon is the importance of algorithms and platform design. Systems based on engagement focus more on content that arouses high emotions since engagement content is more likely to attract attention and retain users on the screen. Consequently, users encounter far more sensational, polarizing, and distressing content violence, disasters, social conflicts, and moral scandals and, oftentimes, they are not accompanied by the necessary context or resolution.

The feed-based algorithms and feed-based social networking, which encourage doomscrolling (i.e. users feed off the content repeatedly consuming negative news when already in an upset mood) exemplify how such systems drive users into habits of emotional hyperarousal. Repeated exposure to suffering desensitises emotional response and desensitises emotional reaction, rather than eliciting a permanently sympathetic and helpful response (Bojic, 2024).

The same environment also transforms the social engagement nature. Shows of concern are becoming more symbolic or performative forms of act instead of actual sustained entertainment or support (changing profile pictures or being part of a trending hashtag). Although these practices can be used to build awareness, they also promote slacktivism, as the show of compassion replaces stronger emotional or moral devotion. In the long term, users will feel emotionally deprived and cynical regarding the effect of their participation, which will also support withdrawal and apathy. The outcome is a partial process of social engagement that preserves the semblance of engagement and destroys the spirit of sympathetic connection (Blanco-Moreno et al., 2024).

The social apathy and emotional burnout are serious threats to the youth, who grow up in the environment of digital media. Digital natives define themselves, their relationships and morals in algorithm sphere situations. Studies and personal stories reveal that there is growing anxiety, numbness and social withdrawal, inability to concentrate and feel emotion. This group experiences emotional fatigue not as a rare event but as daily experience of media use that leads to its concern over the consequences over the long term, whether it is diminishing empathy, civic participation or mental health. It is within this context that it is necessary to critically look at how new media takes individuals who have been exposed to emotions and ultimately induce exhaustion and consequently indifference. This chapter addresses digital media as an affective infrastructure and not an impartial conduit that determines the direction, priorities, and edge of feelings. We situate emotional fatigue in the domain of the attention economy and affective labor using the media psychology, emotional labor theory, and digital sociology, where the emotions of users become trapped and packaged in the form of resources (Khadafi et al.,2025).

The contemporary digital media environment has principally altered the manner in which we feel, handle, as well as sustain feelings. The availability of extreme and intensively processed content at all times changes the way people listen and communicate, making them emotionally exhausted, desensitized, and even socially apathetic. The connection between our emotional stimulation and empathy is becoming more multifaceted and unpredictable with platforms gaining more influence on our social awareness and interactions. These dynamics are important to understand in order to appreciate the larger psychological and social impacts of using digital media. An introduction of emotional exhaustion into the sphere of digital health, media ethics, and changing communication patterns preconditions the further development of the theme of media saturation influence on human life and social relations in our age of 24/7 interconnectedness.

2. RESEARCH QUESTIONS

- How does continuous exposure to emotionally charged content in digital media contribute to the progression from emotional engagement to emotional fatigue and eventual social indifference among users?
- What individual and platform-related factors (such as age, media literacy, content type, and algorithmic exposure) influence the intensity and trajectory of emotional fatigue within the emotional fatigue–indifference continuum?

3. RESEARCH OBJECTIVES

- To examine the relationship between continuous exposure to emotionally charged digital media content and the development of emotional fatigue, desensitization, and social indifference among users.
- To analyze the role of individual characteristics and digital media structures (such as media literacy, usage patterns, and algorithmic content exposure) in shaping users' movement along the emotional fatigue–indifference continuum.

4. THEORETICAL FOUNDATIONS

The multidisciplinary approach to psychology, media studies, and critical political economy will help us comprehend the emotional exhaustion and social detachment in the process of using digital media. The main theoretical perspectives guiding the chapter are presented in this section emotional fatigue and compassion fatigue, media psychology and emotional regulation, the attention economy, where the emphasis is put on affecting labor (Rachmad, 2023).Emotional exhaustion- it is a form of psychological energy depletion that is as a result of the emotional pressures that are enduring in nature and also recurrent experiences of intense or distressing events. Emotional fatigue accumulates with time unlike acute stress which is normally short and situational. It gradually kills the capacity of a person to react in an empathic/ emotional way. In the digital media, the viewer continues to be entertained with stories of suffering, crisis, injustice and conflict. There is no pause in these stories or even an opportunity to get on with the feelings. The constant exposure still requires the emotional processing of the brain, and this increases the chances of the brain being exhausted. In caregivers and helpers, compassion fatigue is inextricably connected to emotional fatigue and was initially researched. It is the loss of capacity to sympathize with after having experienced the suffering of people several times. In the digital media this one can be used to understand why individuals who are constantly exposed to global and local suffering are numb, withdraw or are only participatory to certain extents. There is normalization of distress through repetition and this can occur at the cost of emotional responsiveness. It makes it empathetic to utterly indifferent and caring and caring to utterly indifferent (Jin et al., 2020). Media psychology is used to comprehend the way individuals think and feel when they are listening to media. In this perspective, the consumption of media is interactive, and not passive. It motivates concentration, mood and emotional control. Emotional regulation refers to keeping track, analyzing and being able to regulate our emotional response to what we observe. It is more difficult with digital media which provides us with fast, short-lived emotional cues that are disjointed and unclear. Endless change between the upsetting news, entertaining news, and personal posts disobey emotional balance and prevent deep thinking. Algorithms, the feeds, and associated push notifications tear our ability to control the pace of content and exposure, complicating the self-control. Once the emotional regulation has been strained repeatedly, the users can resort to avoidance, disengagement, or less involvement. Such strategies can guard the short-term, however, in the long term, they may result in the flattening of emotions, and the suppression of empathetic reactions (Vinney, 2021).Attention economy offers emotional exhaustion within the financial and structural rationale of internet-based platforms. The user interaction of these systems is the core commodity and emotional excitement is one of the methods of attraction and retention in the attention-grabbing process. Social media are thus more inclined to promote content that inspires intense emotional responses, like outrage, fear, sympathy, or moral judgment, as it will be more frequently shared and discussed, and promoted by sustainment, subsequently. The users in this environment engage in affective labor by constantly producing, expressing and controlling emotions online. Emotional expressions, responses to posts, and an indication of empathy all become a common feature of online engagement. Even though the activities create a feeling of social presence and engagement, they introduce the continuous emotional needs. With time, being emotionally responsive in a high-arousal media environment may lead to exhaustion, disengagement, and, as a strategic response, the withdrawal of emotional investment. Thus, this is not an individual psychological phenomenon; the appearance of emotional fatigue is an outcome of the system of platform-based emotional economies (Zhao et al.,2022).

5. NEW MEDIA AND EMOTIONAL OVERSTIMULATION

The new media settings of today are marked by the unprecedented volume of information conveyed, emotional prompting and constant connection. This is because these factors redefine the way people handle experiences, control their emotions and interact with the world. Digital platforms are ceasing to be passive media of communication and are proactively designing to influence attention, perception and impact in the form of immediacy, volume, and emotional salience designed preference. Due to this, emotional overstimulation has emerged as a new reality of the digital life, and serious consequences concerning psychological health, cognitive performance, and social life. Information overload is one of the most burning properties of the new media ecosystems. Unending news, social feeds, messengers, and multimedia leave one with a feeling that one is not likely to get a moment of rest either mentally or emotionally. The anticipation of twenty-four-seven connectivity in smartphones, wearables and networks has made traditional work-leisure-rest boundaries obsolete. This constant interconnectedness creates an increased alertness, a broken attention and a constantly overworked mind. Instead of enhancing the level of engagement, the sheer amount of information tends to result in the superficial processing and exhaustion, as well as reduction of the ability to critique the content critically. With time, this saturation erodes the reflective thought and leads to the feeling of constant overload, even in the environment when participation is not forced (Huff, 2022).

Digital conditions become even more intense after the algorithms select and amplify the message that seems most likely to result in an engagement. These systems publicize content that provokes intense feelings, more precisely, fear, anger, outrage, or anxiety, and encourage producers and mass media to present information in sensational or controversial terms. The more an individual is exposed to a charged content on several occasions, the less the ability to control his or her emotions, and the more the underlying stress level may increase. The presence of this feedback loop then limits the emotional states to become normalizing to the feelings of urgency as well as reactivity as the default mode of engagement. Emotional control and subtlety are soon overshadowed by extremes in such settings, not merely redefining the life of any individual, but also sociocultural dialogue on the whole (Choi et al.,2021).

Algorithms amplification is having an influence on how reality and risk are perceived by people. Digital platforms are able to distort the illusion of the familiarity, severity, or danger of something by repeating some narratives and some emotion tones. Due to the constant presence of adverse materials, such as crisis news, conflict, or social comparison, a habitual sense of the incongruent or vulnerability may be developed. This is not only the effect related to misinformation. It is even in the case of factual reports, which are presented as a continuous process without any context that could overstretch our emotional coping mechanisms. They may have the tendency of being a torrent of information that is difficult to digest. The overall effect is a sort of emotional overload. The threat to remain updated pressures people, yet they suffer the torture of such constant interaction (Shin & Shin, 2025).

Doomscrolling, in this more general sense, can be seen as an obvious case of emotional overstimulation. It can be defined as the obsessive consumption of bad or upsetting material as in many cases, individuals desire to be more in control, foresee danger, or comprehend vagueness. Repeated exposure has the opposite effect, and causes anxiety, and emotional exhaustion, rather than reducing them. Doomscrolling depicts a paradox of the digital world: individuals seek clarity and preparedness through consuming information, yet the raw ambiguous information that is emotionally infused only increases powerlessness and burnout. The platforms are designed in a way that such a behavior is encouraged such as infinite scrolling, autoplay, and personalized feeds reduce friction and no longer encourage one to refuse the platform (Anand et al.,2022).

Emotional burnout may be the result of digital stress. Symptoms are irritability, numbness, lack of motivation and inability to concentrate. In contrast to job burnout, it is transferred into personal and social life. It may be destructive to relationships, as well as the perception of ourselves and happiness. This burnout is accumulated because of the continuous emotional exchange of numerous digital platforms and not a single opponent of pressure. Absence of physical breaks is even worse as individuals are always attached to screens even in the times they are supposed to be resting. Too much emotion becomes commonplace and this alters the society. When loud and emotional attract people likes and attention, quiet thinking and self-control may be regarded as distant. This influences the way individuals, particularly young users grow up in learning to communicate through the online platform. Consequently, individuals start being less capable of coping with uncertainty, delaying a response, or dropping unpleasant material. They will be more nervous or double-cheeked. On a more global level, it contributes to the increased division of speech, lack of care, and the alsohitch of universal criteria of emotions (Khammissa et al.,2022).

It is becoming a more common topic in scholarly and increasingly detailed commentaries that emotional overstimulation is not only a matter of personal self-control, but a structural consequence of media systems and economic pressures. The type of content that is favored by platform business models, which are based on measures of attention extraction and engagement, is emotionally charged content. Individual coping needs are not the only strategies to implement in coping with emotional burnout and distress. It needs organizational solutions, including ethical algorithm design, open content curation and digital-wellness policies. It is also possible to reduce the negative impact with the help of educational efforts aimed at emotional literacy, critical media use, and deliberate non-involvement. The overstimulation of the new media requires an interdisciplinary approach that would unite psychology, communication studies, technology ethics, and sociology. It means that online experiences of emotions are formed when interacting the human vulnerability with high-speed and high-scale computing systems. The acknowledgment of said interaction changes the perception of emotional burnout as a personal shortcoming to the predictability of long-term theatrical existence in the digital realm, enhancing the emotional dimension. In further developing digital mediums, achieving more healthy emotional ecologies will be based on creating more balance between connectivity and containment, accessibility to information and interpretive space, and interaction and emotional sustainability (Nor et al.,2025).

The digital age requires emotional well-being to be aligned with technological equipment and its psychological boundaries. Emotional overstimulation might become habitual, not a problem. It is vital to focus scholarly investigations to record these distress patterns and influence more humane and responsible designs and governance of the digital media.

6. FROM EMPATHY TO INDIFFERENCE

Digital media has affected our perception of social issues and our attitudes towards them. Nowadays it is evident that there is a transition between the empathy and increasing indifference, but the transformation has not happened at any moment, it is gradual and intentional. The very fact that we are exposed to suffering, crises and requests to offer help on our screens on a regular basis makes us emotional bitches. It varies our emotions, the way we feel, present, and sustain the compassion. What was initially something to cause a furor and unity may over time become emotional and weary and disconnected and more so when media is about speed and repetition and presence rather than depth. Desensitization is a typical effect of a repeated exposure to emotionally sensitive material. Images of violent, unjust, humanitarian and personal tragedies are so frequent that we do not realize the emotional response. Loss of feelings is not an expression of apathy. It is mostly a defense mechanism towards excessive stimulation. People withdraw themselves emotionally when they continue to witness suffering and have no means of acting or assisting them. The anaesthetics will alleviate the distress in the short run, but will result in the long run in loss of sensibility to the pain of others and reduced capacity of enduring compassion. The emotions that used to require listening slowly lose their importance and become background music of online life (Shao, 2025).

This trend is pushed to its extreme by the architecture of digital platforms that have been willing to cram a variety of types of suffering into a single, continuous stream of content. Tragedy occupies the next door to entertainment, personal updates and advertisements, flattened emotional priorities, and the context of obliteration.

Feelings remain short and disjointed as individuals scroll. Switching between the great mood and the insignificant matters makes people not think deeply and engages them in a reaction rather than in a concern. In the long run, this becomes the normalisation of distress: though it is observed, it is hardly internalised or acted upon in real sense. Within this setting empathy tends to be stage. Rewards on the platforms celebrate physical displays of love, likes, sharing, symbolic acts, etc., which demonstrate moral conformity but not sustained commitment. It is a kind of slacktivism, a new way of presenting and evaluating a social action. Empathy is turned into a performance before the crowd assisting individuals to feel as a part of the group rather than create any positive transformation. In as much as such gestures increase awareness and create a feeling of being recognized as one, they often lack depth and consistency necessary in tackling more complicated problems. Since empathy is such an effortless display, individuals feel less compelled to engage in the process over the long term, which should be substituted with a symbolic effort (Smart,2018).

Performative empathy is influenced by the visibility of the content and incentives created in the algorithms. Postings which are morally upright or sensitive are more validated and reach out to more people. In this way, superficial interaction only is encouraged. Consequently, empathy tends to become a transient trend, which emerges briefly following a media hype and disappears. Once the cause of concern has changed, the emotional investment of persons falls apart at an incredibly high rate. This tendency undermines continuing social interaction and makes people cynical of others. People start wondering how serious is indeed the concern as well as whether people are really being influenced. Both performative empathy and desensitization destroy long-term social connections. Lasting empathy is based on emotional self-discipline, mental perseverance, and dedication to a cause till the end. However internet platforms encourage quick reactions as opposed to commitment. There is an increasing lack of attention and every reason seeks to occupy mental space flooding people with an assortment of things to attend to. This translates into fatigue or overworking. Not apathy it is merely the absence of emotional and mental vigor (Anderson & Rainie, 2023).

According to the Bellmont report, it is not collective action and social cohesion but empathy that is being transformed to indifference. Empathy is typically a moral bond that helps individuals to support each other and keep reciprocal promises. In the case of weak empathy or instrumentality, collective responsibility is not motivated. The social problems are transformed into objects of reading as opposed to acting. The effect of such change is a ridicule of social movements and diminished civic engagement and hopelessness or powerlessness in people. It is not just a demotivational appurtenance, a functional by-product of emotionally mediated milieu. The reactions that occur in such settings are emotional and they are contextual, repetitive and perceived to be effective. Disengagement is not a careless decision when individuals feel that their interests are not taken into account quite often. The development of the attitude of indifference is thus an issue that can be resolved by enhancing personal emotional control and making media systems and social conditions more functional so that people can take part

Empathy is a broad concept that we need to reconsider as we are facing these two dynamics in relation to the spontaneous emotional response. Green and empathetic are relational, situational, and action-based. It is founded on sustained interaction and action and not a symbolic gesture. We can address the problem of emotional numbing and digital rabble-scribbling by designing digital and in-person environments where time is not so quickly centrifuged or made shallow, where we make time to reflect on our thoughts and pose real, collaboration-intensive issues to our peers in order to arrive together at meaningful solutions. Therefore, the did not-indifference involves, not only to demand more empathy, but also to create the conditions, in which it will last, become deeper, and become a social responsibility.

7. SOCIAL AND PSYCHOLOGICAL CONSEQUENCES

The impact of the long-term usage of the digital media is becoming more evident. It alters the state of mental health, disciplines in individuals to handle emotions and their dealings with each other regardless of their age. Digital platforms are felt everywhere in our lives. They modify our way of speaking, the way we receive information, our stress state, resilience development, and our attention. The effects are not similar to everyone. They vary in terms of generation, social settings, and coping ability of an individual. However, studies are beginning to demonstrate that the prolonged experience in digital -heavy worlds poses significant mental health and community-binding issues. There are advantages and pressures of using digital media highly. It will be able to assist individuals in socializing, receiving support, and obtaining mental-health services. It may also cause anxiety and great feelings, even to the point of depression. The endless personal comparison to refined posts by other individuals destroys you, kills self-esteem and makes you feel unworthy, in particular, as long as there are no likes or a set of followers on your posts. The continuous urge to remain online and be prompt in replies is the factor that confuses the boundaries between leisure and the duty. Eventually, this incessant consumption may disrupt emotional balance, cause stress disorders, and lose the overall well-being (Sulaiman et al., 2024).

Digital ecology particularly has a vast psychological influence on young people and digital natives, since online space determines self-identification and social connection. Having been raised in a globally connected world, youngsters develop emotional habits within systems, which command attentiveness and, as such, provoke powerful emotions. Though such a familiarity creates digital dexterity and flexibility, it is also taking away opportunities to become emotionally resilient by offline pursuits like boredom, improvised play, and in-person communication. Toleration of discomforts, uncertainty and delay of gratification are also skills of emotional resilience, which are more difficult to practice when the environment provides immediate stimulus and immediate feedback. With the youths and teenagers, the Internet tends to become the primary sources of social comparison and self-judging. Existence of idealized pictures, forms of success, and social milestones may also increase the perception of the performance anxiety and fear of being excluded. Outside emotional validation might lead to the inability of people to develop a stable set of coping mechanisms internally. Digital affirmation makes emotion regulation weak, so the young users were more vulnerable to stress, rejection, or antagonism online. Meanwhile, the rapid proliferation of emotional content may elevate social cue sensibility, and emotional reactivity, and shorten deliberations (Suárez et al.,2024).

Such dynamics have an impact on the mental health of separate persons as well as on general social tendencies, which result in withdrawal and disrupted attention. Online spaces seem to be a guaranteed communication, but excessive use of mediation in communication may lead to the decrease of the quality of social interaction. Online communication lacks the non-verbal communication and the element of time, which influence empathy and understanding applied in interpersonal communication. This way, individuals can be socially engaged but lonely in feelings and have numerous weak ties without strong ones. Social withdrawal is not necessarily the physical isolation; this is a withdrawal into less emotionally demanding interactions toward less controllable, lower-risk online communication. These social and psychological impacts become even more difficult because of disjointed attention. Digital spaces are constructed in the Multitasking, continuous alerts, and quick switching of content terms promoting divided attention as normal. Maintaining attention and having profound concentration is a bigger challenge because people get used to constant distractions. Such attentional discontinuity has an impact on cognition: memory unification becomes less, learning becomes impaired, and ability to solve problems becomes weak. The incapacity to stay in focus, psychologically, contributes to restlessness and dissatisfaction supporting the repetitive patterns of distraction and emotive depletion (Mukta n.d.,).

Such dynamics have an impact on the mental health of separate persons as well as on general social tendencies, which result in withdrawal and disrupted attention. Online spaces seem to be a guaranteed communication, but excessive use of mediation in communication may lead to the decrease of the quality of social interaction. Online communication lacks the non-verbal communication and the element of time, which influence empathy and understanding applied in interpersonal communication. This way, individuals can be socially engaged but lonely in feelings and have numerous weak ties without strong ones. Social withdrawal is not necessarily the physical isolation; this is a withdrawal into less emotionally demanding interactions toward less controllable, lower-risk online communication. These social and psychological effects are compounded with the fragmented attention. Multitasking and constant alerts together with the possibility to switch between the content result in divided attention and are promoted by digital environments. It is now harder to maintain concentrated attention due to the fact that individuals are used to unending interruptions. Divided attention is detrimental to thinking. It suppresses learning and consolidation of memories. There is also weakness of problem-solving. Loss of concentration is a source of impatience and unhappiness that supports cycles of distraction and emotional exhaustion (Zubair et al.,2023).Technological implications do not just exist as the reflex of predetermined outcomes. Digital space is in relation with vulnerabilities, social differences, and institutional states. The digital literacy, family support, and educational practices define how individuals encounter and deal with digital engagement. Mindful consumption, emotion management, and media reflection are interventions that ensure the positive sides of connectivity alongside minimizing the negative effects.The reaction to digital life must be regarded as a moderate attitude that takes into consideration the danger and the chance. The psychological issues, emotional vulnerability of young people, and social alienation are not the individual diseases; they are the systemic tendencies. To resolve such issues, there is need to develop an integrated approach, which incorporates education, policy, technology development, and mental-health services. When learning to be an adept negotiator of digital complexity without jeopardizing psychological wellness or social relationships, we are able to promote emotional development and genuine relationships because of the environments that are conducive to the maintenance of attention and emotional development.

8. PLATFORM RESPONSIBILITY AND MEDIA ETHICS

Internet sources are significant in our emotive and informational world that they influence the psycho-social consequences of online communication. They do not just stimulate the experience and reaction, but they influence the design points, which impact paying attention, feeling, and acting. These decisions are embedded in business models which reward interaction, visibility and data collection, and often spur emotional engagement rather than an inclusive approach of careful consideration. Thus the platform responsibility and media ethics issues are being raised, particularly in the areas of emotional exploitation and the selection of the content. Design decisions define the way the emotions are activated and preserved in online ecosystems. Incremental features such as endless scrolling, autoplay, push notifications, and algorithmic feeds are configured to create less friction and distraction inviting more time on the site. Although they can make their use easier, they also exploit cognitive and emotional vulnerabilities, which encourages compulsive consumption. Deeply felt emotions, such as outrage, fear, anxiety, etc., are highly motivating attention and can be useful to platforms economies. Consequently, material with significant emotional reactions is promoted, regardless of the negative impact on the welfare of users (Limone & Toto, 2022).

Not very often, emotional exploitation is evident and intentional to individual users. However, it is organized in a rational manner in terms of design options that view attention and emotions as commodities. Placing emotionally charged material all the time, the platforms make intense emotions a normal experience and force people out of the opportunities to feel better. The users get trapped in the cycles of anticipation and response; it becomes difficult to detach and there is also strain in emotional control. In the long term, such a dynamic may create stress, emotional exhaustion, and the inability to perform a critical assessment. On a moral level, the intentional maximization of design traits that capitalize on the ability to manipulate emotion brings into question the issue of informed consent/autonomy and psychological injury. The moral issues increase once the process of presenting content to the users normalizes the choices of what appears, the prioritization of some information, or the burying of others. Predictive models that are used to create algorithmic curation systems can make inferences about what is desired based on previous behavior and influence future exposure, in ways that are opaque to the end user. As much as these systems are able to enhance relevance and efficiency, they also may cause possibilities of bias, distortion, and emotional manipulation. Tuned feeds that strengthen established emotional responses may form an echo chamber where one can become more fearful, resentful or morally outraged. Due to lack of transparency in these feeds, the users are unable to figure out how their emotional environment is conditioned and thus cannot question the outcome of such action (Arango-Kure & Garz, 2025). The ethical implication of content curation influences the personal health as well as collective discussion- and democracy. Ordinary conversation may disintegrate and become more responsive when it is given primacy to emotionally polarizing posts. At these spots, nuanced views and intellectual dialogue will never succeed. This change compromises the information quality, destroys the media trust and damages the society. Hence, the regulation of the media should take cognizance of the fact that the curation systems are not merely content-generating systems, but they also modify reality as an instrument. Platform responsibility is not limited to legal compliance. It involves a positive obligation towards minimizing harm and encouraging wellbeing to users. The ethics of design relies on how the users take charge, be open, and have a balanced interaction. It includes providing individuals with the actual options of choice in what they watch, how algorithms do operate, and nursing people to use it mindfully rather than scrolling it in different directions. The idea of ethical curation also requires responsibility toward the ways of the amplification affecting emotions and social life, particularly that of the vulnerable population such as teens and the mentally unstable. (Alawode,2025; Bouchaud, 2024).

The ethics systems in media currently advocate a shift in the maximization of engagement to an assessment of well-being. This change undermines existing business practices, but is closer to social responsibility and the common good. The collaboration between technologists, ethicists, psychologists and policy designers is needed to integrate ethics into the design and governance of the platform. Regulatory techniques should balance between innovation and consumer protection, as the online environment should respect human dignity and emotional limits. Finally, it has to be understood by platforms that emotional experiences are the moderate part of mediated life, not merely a by-product of technology. The decisions made in designing and the curatorial processes influence perception of the world, feelings and relationships of the people with others. In case of curation as an aspect of emotional exploitation and ethics, we have to answer this question because it would enable us to create media ecosystems that encourage engagement but also contribute to psychological health, social trust, and democratic integrity.

9 COPING STRATEGIES AND INTERVENTIONS

The digital media affect our feelings like never before. The manner in which we react to over stimulation and stay sane is a significant issue among people, institutions and society. We require changes in the institution, some personal modifying, and specific instruction since one requires a subtle response with the constant connectivity. Not only the screen time reduction but coping can be distinguished as the ability to build healthier technology habits, observe emotional boundaries, reflective encouragement, and the use of devices as servants rather than masters. The mindfulness when using digital was a necessity to cope with the inflow of feelings and control the ability to pay attention back to yourself. It is a conscious monitoring of how, when and why we are consuming the media rather than doing it automatically. Such awareness enables us to keep an eye on emotional triggers and patterns of overstimulation as well as decide on our involvement choices. Carving out the digital time, setting emotional boundaries (limiting stress-inducing content, switching off unwanted notifications, etc.) leaves room in the mind to rest and think.

These are not steps to retreat into the social life; they are steps to mutual sustainability that ensures coverage of the emotions (Ajewumi et al.,2024; Sulaiman et al., 2024).

Crossing emotional boundaries is essential particularly when the online platform is a all-encompassing personal, work and social life. Being available online all the time may put pressure to be quick in responding to it, which may be strenuous and exhausting. With the creation of a vivid digital-habits program, people will be able to take charge and reduce their psychological toll on the feeling that people must always be responsible. In the long-term, these practices have been effective in the management of emotions and the ability of people to empathise without being overwhelmed. Digital mindfulness transforms self-care into a skill exercise as opposed to a mindfulness reaction to technology. The key concept of working with digital material in a critical and yet sympathetic manner is essential media literacy. Being a technical process, but it also involves the ability to analyse sources, recognize biased emotions, and comprehend the force of economics and algorithms that control the media. Critical content analysis helps individuals to become less prone to extremist discourse and takes them less likely to take impulsive actions. Such an attitude creates more empathy, an awareness of the suffering and social problems, without causing emotional exhaustion and theatrical performances. (Singh et al.,2022; Dutta & Mishra, 2024).

According to reports of sustainability records, empathetic participation is founded on media literacy which attaches importance to depth rather than to immediacy. Citizens no longer make anything impulsive; they are taught to see things in various perspectives and take side causes that are more favorable and more comfortable to them. Such training helps in buttressing current social interaction, emotional capital, and sensible action. Such abilities are nurtured best in schools, of which the young people are the ones with their emotions and thought developing. Resilience in schools and promoting healthier digital citizenship can be established by integrating media literacy and emotional education into the school curriculum. Personal and learning approaches are significant, yet they do not go further so as to address the issue. Causation of emotional overstimulation is certain in platform designs as well as compensation plans and not individual preference. The solutions being advocated through governments include making algorithms, content moderation, and the use of data more responsible and transparent. Systematic sources of emotional damages can be mitigated by governments imposing rules that compel the platforms to disclose their information on how they arrange the material, screen the psychological impacts, and provide easy tools to framework the system. These policies represent a shift of considering the digital well being as a social rather than an individual problem.

Technology can address psychological needs of people through design level change. Ethical designers advocate features such as reducing the infinite scroll, including some form of reflections, and giving users the ability to control emotional content they look at. The consideration of well-being metrics in the evaluation of platforms disrupts the emphasis around engagement as the only important metric and prompts long-term user health. Most importantly, the changes will not damage functionality or creativity, but rather only redirect value to prolonged engagement- We should be responsive in coping at numerous levels. Individuals are able to be mindful and establish adequate emotional limits. Aspects such as media literacy and empathy are teachable in schools. The digital spaces can be redesigned to cause less harm by policymakers and designers. Such efforts appreciate the fact that digital resilience is a collective phenomenon as well as an individual one. Through these measures, accomplishing the process of managing the mental difficulties of virtual existence, we will save the opportunities of connectedness and safeguard emotional well-being and societal accountability.

10. FUTURE DIRECTIONS AND CONCLUSION

The arguments demonstrate how the digital spaces have a strong impact on emotional experience, attention, and social interaction. They form complex interconnection between technological designing and personal psychology and culture backgrounds. The discussion describes how algorithm amplification, persistent connectivity and emotional content are resulting in overstimulation, desensitization and changing trends in empathy. It also brings out the disproportional impact on the mind of younger generations. The discussion of platform responsibility, media ethics, and coping tactics have shown that these issues are unavoidable; however, it reflects that more mature digital cultures are required to focus on emotional sustainability, connectivity, and innovation. In the future, longitudinal and cross-cultural investigations into the development of emotional resilience in the online environment would be a valuable contribution to the research. The application of psychology, media analysis, ethics, and technology design interdisciplinary work will also prove helpful. Further focus on the governance of platforms, ethical algorithms, and efficiency of learning and policy interventions will be important in how digital societies can strike the balance between engagement and well-being, in such a way that technological advancement helps but does not harm human emotional and social prosperity.

REFERENCES

Ajewumi, O. E., Magbagbeola, V., Kalu, O. C., Ike, R. A., Folajimi, O., & Diyaolu, C. O. (2024). The impact of social media on mental health and well-being. *World Journal of Advanced Research and Reviews, 24*(1), 107–121. DOI: 10.30574/wjarr.2024.24.1.3027

Alawode, O. D. (2025). Invisible Influence: How Algorithmic News Feeds Are Reshaping Public Opinion Without Disclosure. *IOSR Journal Of Humanities and Social Science (IOSR-JHSS), 30*(8), 58-73.

Anand, N., Sharma, M. K., Thakur, P. C., Mondal, I., Sahu, M., Singh, P., J, A. S., Kande, J. S., Ms, N., & Singh, R. (2022). Doomsurfing and doomscrolling mediate psychological distress in COVID-19 lockdown: Implications for awareness of cognitive biases. *Perspectives in Psychiatric Care, 58*(1), 170–172. DOI: 10.1111/ppc.12803 PMID: 33880766

Anderson, J., & Rainie, L. (2023). As AI spreads, experts predict the best and worst changes in digital life by 2035. *Pew Research Center, 21.*

Arango-Kure, M., & Garz, M. (2025). Manipulation: An integrative framework of unethical influence in marketing. *Journal of Business Research, 197*, 115476. DOI: 10.1016/j.jbusres.2025.115476

Asiyah, S. N., Taufiqi, M. A. Z., Raihan, F. N., Hakiki, M. H., Putri, N. R. D., Nuzul, E., & Wahyuni, M. N. P. Emotional Exhaustion in the Digital Native Generation of Social Media Users.

Blanco-Moreno, S., González-Fernández, A. M., Munoz-Gallego, P. A., & Casaló, L. V. (2024). Understanding engagement with Instagram posts about tourism destinations. *Journal of Destination Marketing & Management, 34*, 100948. DOI: 10.1016/j.jdmm.2024.100948

Bojic, L. (2024). AI alignment: Assessing the global impact of recommender systems. *Futures, 160*, 103383. DOI: 10.1016/j.futures.2024.103383

Bouchaud, P. (2024). Skewed perspectives: Examining the influence of engagement maximization on content diversity in social media feeds. *Journal of Computational Social Science, 7*(1), 721–739. DOI: 10.1007/s42001-024-00255-w

Choi, J., Lee, S. Y., & Ji, S. W. (2021). Engagement in emotional news on social media: Intensity and type of emotions. *Journalism & Mass Communication Quarterly, 98*(4), 1017–1040. DOI: 10.1177/1077699020959718

Clemente-Suárez, V. J., Beltrán-Velasco, A. I., Herrero-Roldán, S., Rodriguez-Besteiro, S., Martínez-Guardado, I., Martín-Rodríguez, A., & Tornero-Aguilera, J. F. (2024). Digital device usage and childhood cognitive development: Exploring effects on cognitive abilities. *Children (Basel, Switzerland), 11*(11), 1299. DOI: 10.3390/children11111299 PMID: 39594874

Dutta, D., & Mishra, S. K. (2024). "Technology is killing me!": The moderating effect of organization home-work interface on the linkage between technostress and stress at work. *Information Technology & People*, *37*(6), 2203–2222. DOI: 10.1108/ITP-03-2022-0169

Huff, C. (2022). Media overload is hurting our mental health. Here are ways to manage headline stress. *Monitor on Psychology*, *53*, 20.

Jin, M. J., Kim, J. S., Lee, H. S., Kwon, Y. J., Shim, S. H., Choi, B. S., Lee, D.-W., Paik, J.-W., Lee, B. C., Jung, S.-W., & Lee, H. Y. (2020). The impact of emotional exhaustion on psychological factors in workers with secondary traumatic experiences: A multi-group path analysis. *Psychiatry Investigation, 17*(11), 1064–1072. DOI: 10.30773/pi.2019.0313 PMID: 33190457

Khadafi, Z. R., Pelita, D., & Gunawan, T. (2025). The Phenomenon of Digital Burnout and Social-Emotional Crisis Among Students: The Role of Counselors in Fostering Digital Balance. *Al-Wa'iyah, 1*(2), 38–52. DOI: 10.51590/wai.v1i2.13

Khammissa, R. A., Nemutandani, S., Feller, G., Lemmer, J., & Feller, L. (2022). Burnout phenomenon: Neurophysiological factors, clinical features, and aspects of management. *The Journal of International Medical Research*, *50*(9), 03000605221106428. DOI: 10.1177/03000605221106428 PMID: 36113033

Limone, P., & Toto, G. A. (2022). Psychological and emotional effects of digital technology on digitods (14–18 years): A systematic review. *Frontiers in Psychology*, *13*, 938965. DOI: 10.3389/fpsyg.2022.938965 PMID: 35874342

Mukta, K. J., & Akter, S. Effect of Social Support on Mental Health: The Study of Social Networks in Times of Crisis.

Nor, N. F. M., Iqbal, N., & Shaari, A. H. (2025). The Role of False Self-Presentation and Social Comparison in Excessive Social Media Use. *Behavioral Sciences (Basel, Switzerland), 15*(5), 675. DOI: 10.3390/bs15050675 PMID: 40426453

Peña, A. M., Meier, L., & Nah, A. M. (2023). Exhaustion, adversity, and repression: Emotional attrition in high-risk activism. *Perspectives on Politics*, *21*(1), 27–42. DOI: 10.1017/S1537592721003273

Rachmad, Y. E. (2023). Social Media Impact Theory.

Shao, Y. (2025). The Impact of Digital Media on Modern Society and Culture. *Commun. Humanit. Res*, *57*(1), 117–122. DOI: 10.54254/2753-7064/2025.22829

Shin, D., & Shin, E. Y. (2025). Cascading falsehoods: Mapping the diffusion of misinformation in algorithmic environments. *AI & Society*, , 1–18.

Singh, P., Bala, H., Dey, B. L., & Filieri, R. (2022). Enforced remote working: The impact of digital platform-induced stress and remote working experience on technology exhaustion and subjective wellbeing. *Journal of Business Research*, *151*, 269–286. DOI: 10.1016/j.jbusres.2022.07.002 PMID: 35847196

Smart, P. (2018). Emerging Digital Technologies. *Extended epistemology*, 266.

Sulaiman, W. A. W., Malek, M. D. H., Yunus, A. R., Ishak, N. H., Safir, D. M., & Fahrudin, A. (2024). The impact of social media on mental health: A comprehensive review. *South Eastern European Journal of Public Health*, *XXV*, 1468–1482. DOI: 10.70135/seejph.vi.2564

Sustainability Directory. (2025, December 1). *Why is media literacy important for empathetic development?* Lifestyle → Sustainability Directory. https://lifestyle.sustainability-directory.com/question/why-is-media-literacy-important-for-empathetic-development/

United States. National Commission for the Protection of Human Subjects of Biomedical, & Behavioral Research. (1978). *The Belmont report: ethical principles and guidelines for the protection of human subjects of research* (Vol. 2). The Commission.

Vinney, C. (2021, November 30). *What is media psychology?* Verywell Mind. https://www.verywellmind.com/what-is-media-psychology-5210628

Ytre-Arne, B. (2023). *Media use in digital everyday life*. Emerald Publishing. DOI: 10.1108/9781802623833

Zhao, J., Zhou, Z., Sun, B., Zhang, X., Zhang, L., & Fu, S. (2022). Attentional bias is associated with negative emotions in problematic users of social media as measured by a dot-probe task. *International Journal of Environmental Research and Public Health*, *19*(24), 16938. DOI: 10.3390/ijerph192416938 PMID: 36554818

Zubair, U., Khan, M. K., & Albashari, M. (2023). Link between excessive social media use and psychiatric disorders. *Annals of Medicine and Surgery (London)*, *85*(4), 875–878. DOI: 10.1097/MS9.0000000000000112 PMID: 37113864

Chapter 13
Digital Emotional Labor:
Performing Emotions, Fatigue, and Social Indifference in Online Work Environment

Shibani Shuvasmita
http://orcid.org/0009-0002-4050-2999
KIIT (Deemed to be) University, Bhubaneswar, India

Ipseeta Satpathy
http://orcid.org/0000-0002-0155-5548
KIIT School of Management, KIIT (Deemed to be) University, Bhubaneswar, India

Vishal Jain
http://orcid.org/0000-0003-1126-7424
School of Engineering & Technology, Vivekananda Institute of Professional Studies-Technical Campus, New Delhi, India

ABSTRACT

Digital work has changed how employees perform tasks and manage emotions. This chapter explores emotional labor in online and hybrid IT environments using recent research (2020–2025). It shows how constant connectivity, monitoring, and virtual communication increase emotional demands. The study introduces "social indifference" as a response to emotional fatigue. It also presents a framework linking digital work, emotional performance, fatigue, and organizational outcomes, offering insights for creating emotionally sustainable workplaces.

DOI: 10.4018/979-8-3373-8307-1.ch013

INTRODUCTION

In the rapid growth of digital transformation and the global shifts in work practices instigated by the COVID-19 pandemic, digital and remote work environments have become a normal part of professional life. Many organisations across different sectors now rely on virtual communication technologies such as email, instant messaging, video conferencing platforms and collaboration tools to sustain productivity, coordination and connectivity among distributed teams. What was once considered a new or temporary way of working has now become common with many employees spending most of their working hours interacting through digital platforms. Although these technologies provide benefits like flexibility, greater independence and better possibilities for balancing work and personal life. They also bring new emotional challenges. Employees often need to manage their feelings, control how they express emotions and maintain a positive attitude while communicating through digital channels, which can be very different from traditional face to face workplace interactions.

Emotional labor originally conceptualized as the regulation and management of emotions to produce appropriate public displays in service interactions has traditionally been studied within in-person service works where workers often mask their feelings to meet organizationally sanctioned display rules. Yet in digitally mediated work contexts emotional labor assumes new forms. Digital communication alters the modalities through which emotions are performed often expanding invisible emotional effort into written, asynchronomous and text based exchanges where emotional cues must be encoded, decoded and negotiated without the benefit of synchronous non verbal signals. Recent scholarship has begun to recognize that affective regulation in digital work is neither trivial nor incidental instead it constitutes a substantive dimension of remote and hybrid work experiences with implications for well being, job satisfaction and relational dynamics among colleagues and clients. (Wagh & Packirisamy, 2025)

Many of the informal conversations and natural social cues that once encouraged emotional expressions and connection at work have been diminished by remote work. With little emotional support from coworkers employee now a days frequently use tools like vide chats and lengthy email exchanges to manage emotional expectations. Emotional labor in digital workplaces present both new obstacles and benefits according to researchers. Text- based service communication alerts how emotional work is carried out according to new applied psychology research. It presents the concepts like "rehumanization" in which workers attempt to restore a sense of authenticity in relationships to reduce the impersonal feelings which is caused by technology mediated communication and " robotic acting" in which workers engage in a very regimented or mechanical fashion. (Cheshin et al., 2026)

At the same time studies on remote work communication technologies in the workplace show that each type of digital communication creates different demands and effects on employee well-being. Research based on the job demands resources explains that different tools affect employees in different ways especially in terms of role clarity, coworker support, workload and burnout. Video conferencing is often associated with higher levels of workload and burnout because it requires more emotional effort. (Shin et al., 2025)

In digital work environment the organizational research shows that digital overload, the expectations to stay connected and less support from manager or supervisor are important sources of stress. If these pressure are not managed properly they can lead to emotional exhaustion, burnout among employees. (Baurai et al., 2025)

Although burnout and emotional labor have been thoroughly studied together in traditional workplaces but their relationship in digital work environments has not been fully investigated. Employees are frequently expected to be online and available most of the time due to the rise of remote and hybrid work. The line between personal and professional life becomes more hazy and there is a constant pressure to maintain emotional feelings.

In digital workplaces emotional labor often goes unnoticed and is rarely included in organisational support system. As a result, many employee manage these emotional pressures on their own without enough recognition or support from their organisations.

Some studies find that remote work can improve job satisfaction and help employee to balance their professional and personal life when the conditions are supportive. The growing research on remote work and job satisfaction also shows that these experiences are quite complex. However, other studies point out that stress and the need to manage emotions play an important role in shaping how employees actually experience remote work. This difference in experiences suggests that emotional labor in remote mostly depend on various factors such as how the job is designed, the supporting level provided by the supervisor and the way in which digital technology used. (Belaid et al., 2025)

Even though emotional labor in digital workplaces is receiving more attention there is still a need for strong framework to understand how digital work condition influences emotional labour. It is still not clear whether traditional emotional labor concepts such as surface acting and deep acting are enough to explain how employees manage their emotions in digital interactions. Recent studies suggest that emotional labor in digital environments includes not only traditional emotion regulation but also new forms of cognitive effort. (Cheshin et al., 2025)

This chapter focuses to address the gap by exploring how emotional labor unfolds with in digitally mediated workenvironments and by theorizing its implications for emotional fatigue, social indifference and organisational well being.In response to the growing emotional demands created by digitally mediated workplaces this chapter seeks to investigate the emerging phenomenon of digital emotion labor. The chapter is developed around the following objectives:

1. To explore how employees experience and construct emotional labor in technology-mediated work environments.
2. To understand how continuous emotional performance is perceived and negotiated within digital workspaces.
3. To interpret how emotional labor shapes employees' emotional well-being and workplace relationships in digitally mediated contexts.

This chapter adopts a conceptual narrative review methodology. Rather than relying on primary empirical data collection, the study synthesizes existing scholarly literature from multiple interdisciplinary domains including emotional labor theory, digital work studies, organisational psychology, workplace well-being research and technology-mediated communication literature.

Through conceptual analysis and thematic integration of prior studies the chapter examines how emotional labor practices evolve within digitally mediated work environments.

2. CONCEPTUAL FOUNDATIONS OF EMOTIONAL LABOR

It is very important before understanding emotional labor in digital work environment to look at its traditional concepts and the process of development of the theory. This section builds the theoretical foundation of the chapter by tracing the idea of emotional labor from its early sociological origins.

2.1 Classical Foundations

The concept of emotional labor was first introduced by Arlie Hochschild in her seminal work, The Managed Heart. Hochschild(1983) defined emotional labor as the management of feeling to create publicly observable facial and bodily displays that are sold for a wage and therefore possess exchange value. In this formulation emotions are not only private experiences but also become commodified resource shaped by organisational expectations and market imperatives.

Hochschild distinguished between two primary strategies of emotional labor one is surface acting and deep acting. Surface acting involves modifying outward emotional expressions without altering underlying feelings.

Ashforth and Humphrey (1993) extended emotional labor theory by arguing that emotional labor should not be understood solely as internal emotional regulation or feeling management. They emphasized the importance of observable emotional behaviour, suggesting that emotional labor primarily involves displaying organisationally expected emotions during professional interactions. Their perspective highlighted the role of professional identity, social roles and behavioural performance, arguing that employees may not always need deep emotional modification to perform emotional labor effectively. This contribution broadened emotional labor scholarship beyond Hochschild's focus on internal emotional alignment.

Diefendorff et al. (2005) further advanced emotional labor research through empirical investigation and measurement development. Their work strengthened the conceptual understanding of emotional labor by validating key emotional labor strategies, particularly surface acting, deep acting and the expression of naturally felt emotions. By operationalising these dimensions, they provided stronger empirical foundations for examining emotional labor across organisational settings and occupational contexts. Their contribution significantly influenced later workplace and organisational psychology studies examining emotional performance and employee outcomes.

Zapf (2002) expanded emotional labor theory by linking emotional regulation requirements to occupational stress, employee wellbeing, and work-related psychological outcomes. His research demonstrated that prolonged emotional regulation demands, especially in service-oriented and interactive occupations, may generate emotional strain, exhaustion and burnout. Zapf's work positioned emotional labor within broader discussions of workplace health and psychosocial risk, highlighting the potential negative consequences of sustained emotional performance demands. These insights are particularly relevant in contemporary digitally mediated work environments where continuous emotional interaction may intensify emotional fatigue and wellbeing challenges.

The classical foundations of emotional labor therefore position emotions as a structured by institutional forces rather than as purely individual experiences. Emotional dissonance, In particular it has been identified as a key mediator between emotional labor and burnout outcomes (Grandey & Melloy, 2017; updated empirical replications through 2022). In digitally mediated contexts, where cues are text-based and interactions are often as emotional dissonance may manifest differently yet remain theoretically anchored in Hochschild's original insights. That emotional display is regulated by economic and organisational demands.

2.2 Emotional Labor as Emotion Regulation

Later research used psychological theories of emotion regulation to explain the internal processes influencing emotional performance, where as Hoschild's approach focused on the sociological and structural aspects of emotional work. Alicia A. Grandey made an important contribution in this area by understanding emotional labor as a type of emotion control. (Grandey, 2000; Grandey & Melloy, 2017).

Grandey's method which differentiates between prior-focused regulation (such as reappraisal of thought which is associated with deep acting) and response-focused regulation (such as suppression which is associated with surface acting) is based on Gross's process model of emotion regulation. This integration reinterpreted emotional labor as a continuous regulation process including mental work and self-control rather than simply complying with display standards.

Three structural aspects of emotional labor frequency, difficulty and duration of emotional interactions became important within this framework. Higher effort and a higher risk of stress are linked to jobs requiring frequent emotional displays, severe emotional involvement or extended emotional exchanges. (Brotheridge & Grandey, 2002; extended empirical testing continues in 2020–2024 studies). Recent research applying the Job Demand Resources (JD-R) model identifies emotional labor as a significant job demand that consumes psychological resources and contributes to burnout when not offset by sufficient resources such as autonomy or social support (Bakker & Demerouti, 2017; Lesener et al., 2020; Tuckey et al., 2023).

The JD-R viewpoint is especially crucial for modern workplaces. It views emotional work as a demand that sets off strain pathways, particularly emotional weariness which is the fundamental element of burnout. The loss of emotional energy brought on by prolonged attempts at regulating is reflected in emotional tiredness. Surface acting is one of the best indicators of emotional tiredness across occupational categories, according to updated reviews from 2021 to 2024. (Yin et al., 2022; Hülsheger & Schewe, 2021).

In addition, academics are becoming more aware of the context-sensitivity of emotional work. Overall authenticity, identity harmony, and relational fairness all influence its results. Regulatory effort may be less exhausting when employees believe that emotional expression is consistent with their values. However, emotional dissonance increases and strain results are amplified when emotional expressions are seen as forced or inauthentic. (Gabriel et al., 2020; Wang et al., 2023).

2.3 Emotional Labor Beyond Service Roles

Early emotional labor research concentrated heavily on frontline service roles such as flight attendants, nurses and call center workers. However, contemporary scholarship increasingly acknowledges that emotional labor extends far beyond traditional service occupations.

While working with others knowledge intensive workers like IT professionals, consultants, project managers and academic staffs they normally need to mange their emotions while working with others. Durring any team work, discussion with customers or in any meeting they need to stay calm, positive and professional irrespective of the mental condition. (Guy et al., 2022; Kim & Beehr, 2021). In these roles emotional expressions are not strictly controlled by rules but there are still expectations to behave professional.

When guiding the team the research on leadership shows that both the managers and team leaders do lot of emotional work. As a part of their role they are expected to stay positive during difficult situations. Because of this managing emotions becomes closely connected to how influential a leader appears and how well the team stays united (Humphrey et al.,2015). In virtual teams the responsibility becomes more challenging. Since online communication often lacks facial expressions and people don't see the body language the leaders need to express their emotion more clearly through words and tone. By this the team members feel supported and understand the message clearly.

Interaction with peer also involve emotional labor. Collaborative problem-solving, feedback exchangeand resolution of conflict require emotional modulation to maintain trust. Studies in organisational communication highlights that professional communication rules especially in digital formats require careful tone management, politeness stratefgies and emotional neutrality. (Derks et al., 2021; Barber & Santuzzi, 2020). Even in highly technical environments emotional display shape the performance evaluations.

Furthermore, emotional labor in professional communication frequently operates through written channels. Crafting emails, moderating tone in instant messaging and managing effect in video conferences involve subtle yet persistent emotional encoding. Research on computer-mediated communication suggests that the absesnce of non verbal cues increases cognitive demands associated with interpreting and expressing emotions (Walther, 2011; extended findings validated in remote-work studies 2020-2023).

Earlier emotional control was mainly associated with dealing with customers but today it is part of team work and leadership. The importance of emotional labor is now recognized in many different types of jobs.

In knowledge intensive industries that depends heavily on digital communication, employees regularly manage their emotions while interacting with colleagues sharing information and working together in tasks. Even though this emotional effort is often not officially mentioned in job descriptions, it has become a normal part of professional interactions. This broader understanding helps explain how emotional labor operates in modern digital workplaces.

2.4 Integrated Theoretical Perspective

Digital emotional labor is a very difficult process. It involves managing emotions, meeting workplace expectations, displaying professional behaviour and dealing with psychological effects. To understand this in a better way this chapter combines three theories: Job Demands-Resources(JD-R) theory, Dual process theory and COM-B framework.

The job Demands- Resources(JD-R) theory explains emotional labor as an important work demand. Employee regularly have to control their emotions to meet organisations expectations.

Dual-process theory explains what real emotions t happens in the mind of the employee during the time of emotional labor. It focuses on how employees manage emotions. Surface acting involves hiding real emotions which can create emotional conflict and mental strain. Deep acting involves trying to genuinely feel the emotions expected at work by changing emotional responses. This theory helps explain the effort involved in managing emotions in digital work settings.

The COM-B framework adds a behavioural and workplace perspective. It explains that behavior is shaped by capability motivation and opportunity. Employees emotional behaviour can be influenced by their emotional skills, workplace culture, technology systems, leadership expectations and communication practices.

Together these three frameworks provide a broader understanding of digital emotional labor.

3. DIGITALIZATION OF WORK AND EMOTIONAL DEMANDS

The rapid growth of digital technology has changed not only how work is organised but also how emotional labor is experienced and managed. Earlier most work happened in physical workplaces but now many tasks take place through digital devices and virtual platforms. This shifts has changed the way people express, manage and control their emotions at work. In digitally connected workplaces emotional demands are shaped by several related factors. These include the way communication happens through online platforms the visibility created by algorithims and digital monitoring that expets people to stay responsive and emotionally available. Together these factors influence how employees experience and manage emotions in digital work environments.

3.1 Characteristics of Digitally Mediated Work

Digitally mediated work environments use many types of communication tools and platforms. These tools influence how people communicate and express their emotions at work.

In traditional office settings people could easily understand emotions through in person interactions. However in digital communication these emotional signals are often limited. As a result, people have to interpret and express emotions through written or spoken words. Emails and messaging platforms. Usually focus on being short and efficient which leaves less space for detailed emotional expressions. For this reason people often try to show their feelings through the way they write or choose their words. Video conferencing tools like zoom allow people to see and hear each other in real time, but even these platforms have limitations. Factors such as internet connection, screen framing and reduced body language can still make emotional communication less clear.(Wang et al., 2023; Derks et al., 2021)

The digital communication research shows that when non verbal signals are missing people have to put in more emotional effort while communicating. In online communication facial expression and voice modulation are often absent. Because of this workers depend more on punctuation, emoji and the way they write sentences to show their tone and intention. This makes emotional expression more difficult and increase the emotional effort involved in everyday digital communication (Derks et al., 2021). During the transition to remote work in the COVID-19 period, many studies found that employees used " tone management" strategies. Collectively, these findings suggest that digital communication does not eliminate emotional labor but rather reconfigures it into textual, asynchronous, technologically mediated, and continuously negotiated forms. Emotional performance increasingly extends beyond face-to-face interaction into emails, messaging platforms, virtual meetings, collaborative software, and digitally documented exchanges.

Asynchronous vs. synchronous Emotion

Another challenge in digital communication comes from the way time works on online platforms. Tools like email and different messaging apps often use asynchronous communication. Which means people do not have to reply immediately. Messages can be read and answered later so emotional responses are also delayed.

While this can give people time to think before replying. It can also extend the effort needed to manage emotions. Employee regularly try to predict how their message might be understood, avoid possible misunderstandings and carefully plan their responses. Waiting for replies or feedback can also create ongoing emotional effort as people continue thinking about how their message will be interpreted (Barber & Santuzzi, 2020)

In contrast, synchronous platforms like zoom and Microsoft Teams require people to respond immediately during meetings. However even though communication happens in real time these platforms still provide limited non verbal signals compared to face to face interaction. Technical issues such as screen freezing, camera delays o.r muted microphone can interrupt normal emotional cues. For this participants sometimes try harder to show that they are involved and attentive. (Wang et al., 2023). This situation creates a challenge: people must respond quickly while working with fewer emotional signals. As a result the emotional effort required in online meeting often becomes higher.

Written Emotional Performance

Expressing emotions through written messages addon another layer of difficulty in digital communication . In text based conversations workers have to show their emotions through word choice, punctuation, the timing of replies and some time with emojis. Since there is no voice tone or body posture these small steps help other to understand the emotions behind the message.

Research in organisational communication shows that the way emotions are expressed in writing can influence how others see a person's empathy, professionalism and relationship with colleague even if the actual message is neutral (Derks et al., 2021). Because text messages can feel impersonal. Employees often try to make their messages sound warmer or friendlier by adding polite words or emojis. This helps maintain good relationships it can also increase the emotional effort involved in everyday workplace communication.

Taken together these features shows that digital platforms strongly influence emotional labor in modern workplaces. Emotional management is no longer just an extra part of work. It has become an important and regular aspect of daily professional interactions. Digital communication not only changes what kind of emotions employees need to express but also affects how quickly they manage their emotions.

Performance Metrics

Different performance metrics now included to track things . These are used to track how quickly employee respond, how they communicate and whether tasks are completed on time or not. Many times these metrics can help create transparency and accountability. They can also create pressure to employees to behave in a certain way. Worker may feel the need to behave positive when they feel their work is monitored and evaluated.

Customer Ratings

In digital service jobs especially those that use online platforms the rating system influences emotional labor the rating system infkuence emotional labor. Customer ratings often reward workers who appear friendly, clear communication and quick to respond. Because of this customer rating the employee try to perform better and positive.

Even in knowledge intensive jobs such as consulting or professional services clients or customers may judge performance not only by the quality of the work but also by how supportive and professional the interaction feels. As a result worker often put in extra emotional effort to maintain good relationships with customers and clients to protect their reputation.(Mesmer- Magnus et al., 2022)

Internal Monitoring

Apart from customer rating many of the orgnisations use internal rating system to rate their employees. This systems can track thingslike how quickly someone is replying, how frequently someone is sending messages or how connected they are within the team. In this way the systems quietly signal that employees are expected to stay active, responsive and emotionally available.

Few recent research on digital surveillance shows that such monitoring system help employees to know their work and manage their own behavior. Workers can manage and judge their own actions according to performance metrics. Because of this they may carefully control how they express emotions in communication so that they appear engaged and professional. This situation can increase emotional labor that becomes visible to others and permanently recorded in digital systems. (Zuboff, 2019; Derks et al., 2021)

Together these algorithimic governance mechanisms transform emotional labor from a primarily interpersonal process into a socio technical one. In which digital systems shae the emotional norms and evaluative frameworks that workers navigate.

3.2 Always on-culture and Emotional Availability

In digitally connected work environment the boundaries between work time and personal time become unclear always. Because most of the work happens through phone, laptop and many online platforms. Employee may feel that they need to stay available most of the time. This creates an "always-on" culture where quick responses and contact communication are expected. As a result of this workers may feel pressure not only to be available but alsoto remain positive, polite and responsive in their interactions.

Responsive pressure

Research on digital communication shows that employees are often expected to reply on digital communication. There are different features such as read receipts, Online status indicators and mobile notifications reinforce this expectations. Sometimes employee feel that delayed replay and unavailability look them unprofessional or uninterested which creates pressure to stay constantly available (Barber & Santuzzi, 2020) describe this feelings as telepressure which means the strong internal feelings to respond as soon as possible. This pressure can make it difficult for employees to disconnect from work and properly rest. When people continue to engage with work messages even after normal working hours, it can affect their emotional well-being and lead to ongoing mental strain and emotional fatigue.

Boundary Erosion

One of the most important feature of digital work is the boundary between personal life and professional life which is not clear. Since the different communication tools like mail, messaging application are available on mobile phones and laptops work messages can land to the employee at anytime and anywhere. Because of this work related interactions often continue even during personal time. When work related communication enters in personal space the emotional expectations connected to work also continue. Employees may feel the need to respond politely, stay professional or manage their emotions even outside working hours. Over time this makes it harder to fully disconnect from work and increase the overall emotional effort that employee experience (Wang et al., 2023) . As a result, digital work not only extends working hours but also expands the time during which emotional labor takes place.

4.EMOTIONAL PERFORMANCE IN ONLINE ENVIRONMENT

Digital work environments have not reduced emotional labor instead they changed the way it happens. In technologybased workplaces employees express and mange their emotions through written messages, video metting and digital communication systems. Unlike traditional service jobs where emotions are shown directly through face-to- face interaction emotional expression in digital work is often done through words, online meetings and carefully written communications. Sometimes responses are delayed or adjusted because of the limits of technology. These conditions can even increase the effort needed to manage the emotions. This section therefore looks at how surface acting, deep acting and emotional dissonance appear in remote and hybrid work settings especislly in IT sector.

4.1 Surface acting in Text-based Communication

Surface acting means changing the way emotions are shown on the outside without actually changing how a person truly feels inside (Hochschild,1983; Grandey,2000). In digital work environments this often happens through written communication such as emails and messages. Since voice cannot be expressed through body language. Employees carefully choose their words and writing style to appear polite, positive or professional even if they may not feel that way.

Politeness Scripting

Emails and messaging platforms require employees to encode professionalism, warmth and cooperation through standardized linguistic patterns. Common features include

- "Hope you are doing well"
- "Kindly note..."
- Excessive gratitude expressions
- Strategic use of exclamation marks
- Emojis to soften directives

These communication patterns act like digital display rules, guiding how employees show interest, cooperation and professionalism during online interaction. Research on workplace communication shows that when using email and instant messaging employees must mange their tone in advance because there are no facial expressions or body language to help explain the message (Derks et al., 2021). To avoid misunderstandings worker adjust their language before sending a message.

This type of surface acting in digital communication often requires more mental effort. In face to face situations people may hide their emotions quickly. However in written communication employees usually spend more time thinking about how their messages sounds. They write, edit and adjust their words to make sure their tone appears polite and appropriate. Research shows that this kind of emotional regulation in written messages can lead to mental toredness.

Although digital communication may appear to provide employees with greater flexibility in emotional presentation, emerging literature increasingly suggests that written and technology-mediated emotional performance can intensify emotional regulation demands rather than reduce them. Unlike face-to-face interactions, digital communication often requires employees to carefully anticipate audience interpretation, manage linguistic tone, regulate perceived professionalism, and minimise the risk of communicative misunderstanding.

This is especially true when employees have to regularly hide feelings like irritation or disagreement while communicating through emails or messages that do not require immediate responses (Barber & Santuzzi, 2020)

Emotional Masking in Email

Normally in Email communication employees are usually expected to remain neutral or positive especially during the client interaction. Recent studies shows that this type of Surface acting is often linked to emotional exhaustion in many kinds of jobs including knowledge based jobs(Yin et al., 2022). In remote work settings, this emotional masking can become even stronger because employees have fewer chances to share their feelings informally with colleagues. As a result employee may keep their frustration to themselves instead of sharing.

4.2 Deep Acting in Virtual Leadership and Teamwork

While surface acting involves external modification deep acting entails attempts to align internal feelings with required emotional displays (Grandey & Melloy, 2017). In digitally mediated environments deep acting often manifests in leaderships and collaborative contexts where emotional authenticity influences team cohesion and trust

Empathy in Video Meetings

In virtual meetingsit is often tough to understand emotions because people are not physically present and non verbal signals like body language are limited. Because of this leaders need to express their emotions more clearly in the meetings on onlone. Before joining video calls especially in stressful situations managers may mentally prepare themselves to appear calm, confidant and positive even when facing challenges.

Research on remte work shows that successful virtual leadership depends a lot on how leaders communicate emotions such as showing empathy and giving verbal encouragement(Wang et al., 2023). When leaders genuinely try to feel and express concern or support for their team employees tend to feel safer, more valued and connected to the team.

In face to face interactions emotions can naturally spread through facial expressions or body language. However in digital settings leaders often need to express these emotions more intentionally through words.

Digital Trust building

In online teams building trust depends on how consistently and sincerely people express their emotions. Research shows that in remote work systems trust grows when team members appear genuine and emotionally consistent in their communication (Tuckey et al., 2023). When employees truly try to feel and express positive emotions such as support concern or encouragement it helps others believe that their actions are authentic. This type of emotional effort known as deep acting can therefore strengthen trust among team members.

However, digital work environments can also make deep acting more complicated. Many online platforms keep records of messages, emails and conversations. Because such communication can be stored and revisited later. For this employee sometimes become more careful about how they express their emotions. They may try to protect their professional image. As A result deep acting in online workplaces becomes both a thoughtful and relationship focused process.

4.3 Emotional Dissonance in Remote work

Emotional dissonance arises when there is a discrepancy between felt emotion and required emotional displays(Hochschild,1983). In remote and digitally mediated work this dissonance may intensify due to structural and relational factors.

Internal Feelings vs. Displayed Positivity

Digital platforms in which employees are expected to stay positive, calm and work efficiently. However sometimes the employees of the organization feel tired, stressed and fraustrated. Even though they feel these emotions the organization still expect from them to behave calmly and professional. The difference what employees feel inside and what they show outside can create emotional pressure.

Different resesrch studies shows that emotional dissonance plays an important role in the connection between surface acting and emotional exhaustion (Hülsheger & Schewe, 2021). In remote work environments this emotional conflict is often less visible to superiors. Because of this the employees might receive less emotional support or understanding.

Suppressed Frustration in IT Service Roles

In IT and other knowledge-based sectors, employee often deal with system failures, technical problems and unhappy clients through digital communication.

During these situations employees are expected to stay calm and professional even when they feel stressed internally.

At the same time organisations expect quick responses and measure performance which makes a emotional pressure among the employees.

Studies on digital communication show that when employees hide their fraustration, it can affect their ability to recover mentally from work and may increase the risk of burnout (Barber & Santuzzi, 2020).

5. EMOTIONAL FATIGUE AND BURNOUT IN DIGITAL WORK

After single interaction the emotional demands in digitally mediated work do not end. Instead these demands increase over time and can lead to emotional tiredness. However the structure of digital work creates new pressure that can exchange how emotional fatigue develops and appears among employees. This section looks at emotional fatigue as a result of constantly managing emotions in digital work environments.

5.1 Emotional Exhaustion as a Structural Outcome

Emotional exhaustion is considered the main part of burnout. It refers to a feeling of being emotionally drained and having very little emotional energy left (Maslach & Leiter, 2016). In the job demands Resource(JD-R) model, emotional labor is seen as a job demand because it requires employee to use their psychological and emotional energy. When employees have to control or adjust their emotions frequently and go for long periods, It can slowly reduce their mental resources (Bakker & Demerouti, 2017; Lesener et al., 2020)

In digitally mediated work environments, emotional demands can become stronger because of the 3 main factors.

1. More frequent interactions with colleagues, clients and teams
2. Longer Emotional effort due to asynchronous communication like emails and messages
3. Greater visibility and self -monitoring in digital platforms.

Recent research reviews shows that surface acting, where employees hide their real feelings and display required emotions is strongly connected with emotional exhaustion across many types of jobs (Yin et al., 2022). In remote work the written communication often remains stored and accessible. Because of this employees may repeatedly read emotional conversations rethink the tone of message and carefully prepare responsive over time. This process can be increase both mental and emotional pressure.

5.2 Digital Intensifiers of Emotional Fatigue

Digital environments introduce specific conditions that enhance emotional fatigue beyond classical emotional labor context.

Cognitive Emotional Load

Text-based communication requires employees to focus on two things at the same time. Sending messages and making sure that the messages are sound appropriate. Studies on digital communication shows that expressing the emotions and understanding the emotion in online work environment can increase mental effort because non verbal signals are missing(Derks et al., 2021). Due to this reason employees have to think carefully about how their message might be interpreted. The employees may adjust their tone, choose words more cautiously and try to avoid misunderstandings. This process adds some extra mental effort to the emotional control.

Telepressure and Continuous Connectivity

Workplace telepressure refers to the strong feeling that employees must reply quickly to the online messages. The studies shows that the pressure of spedy response can increase stress among employees (Barber & Santuzzi, 2020). When employee are constantly think about answering the message they remain mentally alert and find it difficult to relax. Over time this continuous need to stay connected and responsive can gradually drain their emotional energy.

Reduced Informal Recovery mechanisms

In traditional workplaces employees regularly get small chances to relax during the day time. They may talk casually with colleagues, share jokes or express their frustration in formal conversations. These simple interactions can help reduce stress and support emotional recovery.

However, remote work environments often reduce these opportunities. According to Wang et al.,(2023) when remote work systems are not well designed they can increase stress among the employees. Because of this emotional fatigue may slowly develop.

Performance Surveillance

Digital monitoring systems and performance tracking tools can make employees more aware of how they communicate at work. When employees get to know that their messages, responses and pattern of communication can be recorded and revied they may start paying more attention to their emotional expression. This increased self monitoring require extra emotional effort. Although these systems are mainly used to improve productivity they can sometimes increase emotional pressure on employees(Bakker & Demerouti, 2017).

These factors show that digital work environments do not simply repeat the emotional demands which is found in traditional workplaces. Instead of this they can increase and intensify emotional labor by giving additional pressure through monitoring and technology.

5.3 From Emotional Fatigue to Burnout Trajectories

Burnout is a complex condition which includes three main aspects like Emotional exhaustion, feelings of detachment or cynicism toward work and a reduced sense of professional effectiveness (Maslach & Leiter, 2016). Emotional fatigue normally starts first and lead to the broader experience of burnout over time.

In digitally mediated contexts burnout trajectories may unfold differently

Stage 1: Emotional Exhaustion
Stage 2: Cynicism Or Detachment
Stage 3: Reduced Relational Investment

5.4 Emotional Fatigue in Knowledge Intensive IT contexts

Different knowledge based sectors Require employees to stay mentally focused for long periods while communicating with clients. In these sectors emotional labor is usually unnoticed because it is usually hidden with technical discussion and problem solving skills.

However research shows that knowledge workers regularly mange their emotions while working with teams, share holders and coordinating tasks in virtual environments (Kim & Beehr, 2021). In IT roles emotional fatigue may appear but in meaningful ways such as increase of irritation in normal conversation, less interest in online meetings & minimum response. These signs may not look like traditional burnout but still indicate that employee's emotional energy is being drained.

5.5 Social Indifference in Digital Work Environments

Definition and Conceptual Understanding

Social indifference refers to a condition characterized by reduced emotional involvement, weakened interpersonal sensitivity, diminished empathy and declining concern toward colleagues, teams or workplace relationships. In organisations social indifference may appear as emotional distance, less interaction in relationships, lower teamwork involvement and weaker concern for other peoples feelings. In digital workplaces where communication often happens through technology and interaction becomes more work focused social indifference may develop as an overlooked result of ongoing emotional labor.

Social indifference is different from short term emotional withdrawal caused by work pressure. It reflects a deeper decline in emotional connection at work. Employees may still complete their job duties but slowly become emotionally disconnected from team work and collaborations.

Relationship Between Emotional Fatigue and Social Indifference

Digital workplaces regularly expect employees to manage emotions and to stay responsive through online communication. Over time these constant emotional demand can drain employees energy. When the emotional energy is low employees may feel emotional fatigue and stress. As a result employees may slowly pull away from workplace interactions. Social indifference can be seen as a possible outcome of long term emotional fatigue. Emotional withdrawal may act as a coping method to deal with continuous emotional demands. This issue is especially important in digital and knowledge-based workplaces where employees are often emotional fatigue. This issue is important in digital and knowledge based workplaces.

Social Indifference in Digitally Mediated Workplaces

Many features of today's digital workplaces may increase socially indifferent behaviour. Constant availability in online, the speed reply pressure and digital monitoring can make employees feel they must always stay responsive and emotionally professional. In these situations emotionally distant communication may slowly become normal. Remote work, late communication, online platforms and technology-based teamwork can decrease natural social interaction. Employees get few chances for casual conversations and relationship building. Because of this workplace communication may become more work focued than people focused.

Integrated Theoretical Perspective on Social Indifference

The framework used in this chapter helps in explaining social indifference in digital workplaces from various angles. The Job Demand Resources(JD-R) theory suggests that social indifference will develop when the employee in the organisation face high emotional demand and get less support from the organisation. Constant emotional control, pressure of communication and always emotionally available can drain the energy.

Dual process theory explains what happens internally. Managing emotions through surface acting or deep acting needs continuous emotional effort. When this continues for a long period the employees may become less emotionally responsive.

The COM-B framework looks at behaviour and workplace conditions. It explains that behaviour is shaped by people's abilities to do work, their motivation and work environment. Digital workplaces, leadership styles, communication systems and the performance expectations can influence employee behaviour. Together these theories help to explain digital emotional labor.

Practical Implications for Organisations

Organisations need to pay more attention in digital work settings because of social indifference can affect employee well being and team work. Organisations can decrease this problem by supportive leadership, good communication and bye giving safe environment. The managers should promote balanced workload among the employees. Empathetic communication, respectful online behaviour and opportunities for good employee interaction. Such practices can help the employees to feel more connected and less emotionally detached. The organisation shouls identify the emotional demands of work and support the metal well being of the employees. This may help in reducing emotional fatigue and exhaustion.

6. LIMITATIONS AND FUTURE RESEARCH

This chapter presents a framework linking digital work, emotional performance, fatigue and social indifference. However it has some limitations. The study is based on existing literature and des not use primary data so the ideas still need direct testing. Future research should examine these concepts through different surveys, interviews and mixed methods. Long-term and diary studies may help understand how emotional fatigue develops over a time period.

Emotional experiences in digital work may vary across cultures. Communication styles, workplace hierarchy and the attitude towards emotional expression can affect how employees manage emotions. Technology is changing very fast. Digital tools, online meetings and hybrid work systems continue to influence workplace communication. Future research should explore wheather these changes reduce emotional or increase pressure to stay constantly connected. All AI tools bring new challenges. Sometimes they help but also create emotional distance and add pressure for employees.

7. CONCLUSION

Digital transformation has changed the way work is organised, tracked and experienced. However beyond the visible systems like platforms, performance metrics and constant connectivity. One important aspect is often overlooked emotional labor still plays a key role in digital work.

This chapter explains that digital environments do not reduce emotional labor; instead they make it stronger and more complex. The framework showing how digital work conditions influence emotional performance, which can lead to emotional fatigue and eventually social indifference affecting overall organisational outcomes. When employees continuously manage their emotions without enough rest or support they may start to feel emotionally tired. Overtime this can lead to social indifference where employees become less emotionally involved. This idea adds to existing research by highlighting a subtle form of emotional withdrawal that is specific to digital work settings. It shifts focus from visible signs of burnout to less obvious changes in behavior that can slowly affect team work and a sense of belonging in organisations.

The chapter also makes it clear that managing emotional well being is not a responsibility of an individual but also on organisations. Supportive leadership, thoughtful HR practices, clear policies and well designed digital tools all play an important role in reducing emotional stress.

In the future organisations need to look beyond productivity and efficiency. They should also focus on building healthy relationships and supporting emotional well-being. By combining technological progress with emotional understanding organisations can create work environments that are both efficient and supportive for employees.

REFERENCES

Ashforth, B. E., & Humphrey, R. H. (1993). Emotional labor in service roles: The influence of identity. *Academy of Management Review*, *18*(1), 88–115. DOI: 10.2307/258824

Bakker, A. B., & Demerouti, E. (2017). Job demands–resources theory: Taking stock and looking forward. *Journal of Occupational Health Psychology*, *22*(3), 273–285. DOI: 10.1037/ocp0000056 PMID: 27732008

Barber, L. K., & Santuzzi, A. M. (2020). Please respond ASAP: Workplace telepressure and employee recovery. *Journal of Occupational Health Psychology*, *25*(1), 1–14. PMID: 31829662

Baurai, S., Sekhar, C., Kumar, D., & Raj, A. (2025). Digitalization and employee well-being: A fuzzy-tism approach of remote work stressors. *Journal of Management & Organization*, *31*(6), 3004–3028. DOI: 10.1017/jmo.2025.10059

Belaid, S., Ben Guedria, N., & Ballouk, H. (2025). Remote Work and Job Satisfaction: A Decade of Insights Through a Bibliometric Lens. *Administrative Sciences*, *15*(11), 439. DOI: 10.3390/admsci15110439

Brotheridge, C. M., & Grandey, A. A. (2002). Emotional labor and burnout: Comparing two perspectives of "people work.". *Journal of Vocational Behavior*, *60*(1), 17–39. DOI: 10.1006/jvbe.2001.1815

Cheshin, A., Glikson, E., Lavee, E., & Gabriel, A. S. (2026, January). Digital emotional labor: Benefits and challenges of emotional labor in the context of text-based service. *The Journal of Applied Psychology*, *111*(1), 116–137. DOI: 10.1037/apl0001305 PMID: 40689934

Derks, D., Bakker, A. B., & Peters, P. (2021). The psychology of digital communication at work. *Current Opinion in Psychology*, *43*, 190–195.

Diefendorff, J. M., Croyle, M. H., & Gosserand, R. H. (2005). The dimensionality and antecedents of emotional labor strategies. *Journal of Vocational Behavior*, *66*(2), 339–357. DOI: 10.1016/j.jvb.2004.02.001

Gabriel, A. S., Daniels, M. A., Diefendorff, J. M., & Greguras, G. J. (2020). Emotional labor actors: A latent profile analysis of emotional labor strategies. *The Journal of Applied Psychology*, *105*(1), 12–30. DOI: 10.1037/apl0000425 PMID: 25068812

Grandey, A. A. (2000). Emotion regulation in the workplace: A new way to conceptualize emotional labor. *Journal of Occupational Health Psychology*, *5*(1), 95–110. DOI: 10.1037/1076-8998.5.1.95 PMID: 10658889

Grandey, A. A., & Melloy, R. C. (2017). The state of the heart: Emotional labor as emotion regulation reviewed and revised. *Journal of Occupational Health Psychology*, *22*(3), 407–422. DOI: 10.1037/ocp0000067 PMID: 28150996

Gross, J. J. (1998). The emerging field of emotion regulation: An integrative review. *Review of General Psychology*, *2*(3), 271–299. DOI: 10.1037/1089-2680.2.3.271

Guy, M. E., Newman, M. A., & Mastracci, S. H. (2022). *Emotional labor: Putting the service in public service* (Updated ed.). Routledge.

Hochschild, A. R. (1983). *The managed heart: Commercialization of human feeling*. University of California Press.

Hülsheger, U. R., & Schewe, A. F. (2021). On the costs and benefits of emotional labor: A meta-analysis of three decades of research. *Journal of Occupational Health Psychology*, *26*(2), 89–115. PMID: 21728441

Humphrey, R. H., Ashforth, B. E., & Diefendorff, J. M. (2015). The bright side of emotional labor. *Journal of Organizational Behavior*, *36*(6), 749–769. DOI: 10.1002/job.2019

Kim, M., & Beehr, T. A. (2021). Emotional labor and organizational behavior in knowledge work. *Human Relations*, *74*(9), 1393–1418. DOI: 10.1177/0018726720925098

Lesener, T., Gusy, B., & Wolter, C. (2020). The job demands–resources model: A meta-analytic review of longitudinal studies. *Work and Stress*, *34*(2), 180–205. DOI: 10.1080/02678373.2019.1678762

Maslach, C., & Leiter, M. P. (2016). *Burnout*. Springer.

Mesmer-Magnus, J., DeChurch, L., & Wax, A. (2022). Moving emotional labor research forward: A meta-analysis of emotional labor in digital and hybrid work. *Journal of Organizational Behavior*, *43*(5), 789–812.

Mesmer-Magnus, J., DeChurch, L., & Wax, A. (2022). Moving emotional labor research forward: A meta-analysis of emotional labor in digital and hybrid work. *Journal of Organizational Behavior*, *43*(5), 789–812.

Shin, I., Riforgiate, S. E., Godager, E. A., & Coker, M. C. (2025). Remote Worker Communication Technology Use Related to Role Clarity, Coworker Support, and Work Overload. *Sustainability (Basel)*, *17*(7), 2830. DOI: 10.3390/su17072830

Tuckey, M. R., Bakker, A. B., & Dollard, M. F. (2023). Empowering leaders optimize working conditions for engagement: A multilevel study. *Journal of Occupational Health Psychology, 28*(1), 45–59. PMID: 38059984

Wagh, R. K., & Packirisamy, P. (2025). Emotional labor in the digital workplace: A study of its effects on job satisfaction among remote professionals. [JRISS]. *Journal of Research in Innovative Social Sciences, 9*(3), 4523–4529. DOI: 10.47772/IJRISS.2025.903SEDU0324

Walther, J. B. (2011). Theories of computer-mediated communication and interpersonal relations. In Knapp, M. L., & Daly, J. A. (Eds.), *The SAGE handbook of interpersonal communication* (4th ed., pp. 443–479). SAGE Publications.

Wang, B., Liu, Y., Qian, J., & Parker, S. K. (2023). Achieving effective remote working during the COVID-19 pandemic: A work design perspective. *Applied Psychology, 72*(1), 16–59. DOI: 10.1111/apps.12290 PMID: 33230359

Yin, H., Huang, S., & Wang, W. (2022). Emotional labor and burnout in knowledge-intensive professions: A systematic review. *Frontiers in Psychology, 13*, 821233. DOI: 10.3389/fpsyg.2022.821233

Zapf, D. (2002). Emotion work and psychological well-being: A review of the literature and some conceptual considerations. *Human Resource Management Review, 12*(2), 237–268. DOI: 10.1016/S1053-4822(02)00048-7

Zuboff, S. (2019). *The age of surveillance capitalism: The fight for a human future at the new frontier of power*. PublicAffairs.

Chapter 14
Screens of Solitude:
News Cycles, Crisis Imagery, and Emotional Fatigue in Digital Media Audiences

Rashid Hashmi
http://orcid.org/0009-0006-3232-0705
Sharda University, India

Ritu Sood
Sharda University, India

ABSTRACT

In the contemporary digital media ecosystem, audiences are exposed to an unprecedented volume of news through 24-hour news cycles, social media platforms, and algorithm-driven information flows. While this constant connectivity increases access to information, it also contributes to emotional fatigue, psychological exhaustion, and growing social indifference among media consumers. This chapter examines how continuous exposure to crisis imagery, breaking news alerts, and repetitive narratives of conflict and disaster shapes the emotional well-being of contemporary audiences. Drawing on perspectives from media studies, psychology, and digital communication, it explores the concept of "screens of solitude," where individuals remain constantly connected yet experience emotional isolation and cognitive overload. The chapter also analyzes the roles of algorithmic amplification, doomscrolling, and mediated trauma in shaping audience responses to news consumption and discusses the need for responsible journalism and mindful media engagement.

DOI: 10.4018/979-8-3373-8307-1.ch014

1. INTRODUCTION

The modern media landscape is being defined by a high flow of information never before witnessed. There are no fixed appointments to receive news scheduled as television bulletins or in morning newspapers and spread all over in digital platforms of various kinds and in a certain order of interrelatedness. The smartphones, social media networking sites, live TV channels and news portal websites keep the audiences in touch with the information streams always. Although this change has facilitated the openness of information and enhanced the democratic potential of the media systems, it has also presented a new complex of psychological and emotional issues to viewers. Emotional exhaustion due to constant exposure to news material is one of the greatest of these difficulties.

The development of this information environment has been a cause of what is termed by scholars as media saturation, a state where individuals are bombarded with excessive messages and visual stimuli by the media. Media content is placed at the core of constructing reality and mediating on how people perceive or react to the social, political, and global events (Gitlin, 2001).

The media space has also been transformed, which is why social reality has changed as well. Modern societies are being gradually mediated, whereby individuals are exposed to events occurring far away via screens, and not through one-on-one, face-to-face interaction. The expansion of the digital platform implies that people consume a significant part of political and social life by mediated communication media instead of participating directly (Couldry and Hepp, 2017).

News media have a major influence on the issues that are apparent to society and the perspectives of the issues. It was well-established in research in the field of media and political communication that news coverage shapes levels of awareness and political cognition. Media institutions engage in framing and agenda setting, raising or prioritising specific events, putting focus on specific narratives, and influencing the overall discourse on the social problem through various processes (Dunaway and Graber, 2022). This impact is even stronger in the climate of constant news coverage. Breaking news stories published at a very fast rate are known to cause great public interest in issues, especially when the news contains dramatic moments like disasters and political feuds.

According to traditional theories of news production, media organisations give preference to those events that have certain news values. The coverage of events of conflict, crisis and dramatic change is said to be more newsworthy than routine developments since most people are interested and more engaged by such events. The initial research on the selection of news revealed that conflict, negativity and unexpectedness are some of the factors that affected what stories to report on and the manner in which the stories were framed (Galtung and Ruge, 1965). These trends persist in influencing the modern news content, especially in competitive digital media, where becoming a popular and prized commodity.

The result of the focus on crisis-based news stories can be quite emotional, with severe implications for the listeners and viewers. And when people are exposed to repetitive news reports on the theme of violence, catastrophe, and political unrest, they might start seeing the world as more dangerous and unpredictable than it really is. As observed by media scholars, frames of fear, danger, and crisis often create a social reality as represented in the news, increasing the amount of anxiety in people and upholding them in their insecure perception (Altheide, 2002). With news that is ever circulating in the digital world and spread across various channels, such stories can be experienced more than once in a day.

The other significant aspect in the modern media landscape is the high rate of growth in the use of digital news. Large-scale surveys of global media consumption show that a big percentage of users currently depend on smartphones and social media networks to take in the news material, and they frequently come across the news when surfing through alternative types of online material (Newman et al., 2022). This has radically changed the user experience of journalism to consume more and more information via wider digital ecosystems.

Simultaneously, the digital media space has brought about some paradoxical state of affairs wherein people have never been more linked to the information than at the same time, persons are subjected to some type(s) of emotional segregation. The all-time communication with the screens might establish the illusion of being connected all the time to the events of the world, but being connected does not always imply that some personhood interacts with another one and is supplemented by emotional processing of the information. People are able to read a lot of news information and stay physically isolated, communicating with screens, not with other human beings. This disorder may add to a feeling of psychological aloofness to the events being documented and also the communities that have undergone the described events.

Within this chapter, this phenomenon is described as **"screens of solitude."** The concept refers to the experience of being continuously connected to digital information flows while simultaneously feeling emotionally detached or overwhelmed by the volume of mediated experiences encountered through screens. Over the past decades, there has been a growing concern that emotional fatigue caused by news media has emerged as a serious problem in modern journalism research [1, 2]. People react in some situations by engaging in "tuning out" news or switching off on specific topics altogether to manage their emotional well-being (Newman et al., 2023). Opens with these trends—shows an increase in the tension between the democratic value of having an informed public and the psychological costs of always having bad news.

Don't panic; Unsociable News; Emotion Fatigue; The News Avoidance; doom-scrolling, social media anxiety, news avoidance; mediated isolation; and democratic disengagement have been largely studied with respect to single contexts, but there is a lack of research examining the intersection of algorithmic news circulation, emotion fatigue, mediated isolation, and democratic disengagement. Current research tends to focus on these matters individually, either in psychology or media or digital communication studies. But the emotions surrounding a permanently connected digital news environment have not been properly theorised as yet. To bridge this gap, this chapter introduces the notion of "screens of solitude" to illustrate how 24/7 access to emotionally engaging news could have a positive impact on informational connectivity, but a negative impact on emotional resources and social connectedness.

1.1 Objectives of the Chapter

The chapter aims to:

1. Examine the emergence of emotional fatigue in digital news environments.
2. Analyse the relationship between doomscrolling, media saturation, and psychological exhaustion.
3. Investigate how algorithmic amplification shapes emotional experiences of audiences.
4. Explore the concept of "screens of solitude" in digitally connected societies.
5. Suggest media, platform, and audience-level strategies for healthier news engagement.

Figure 1.

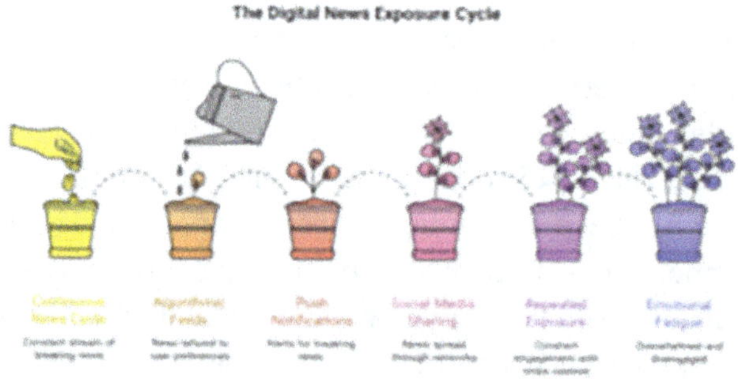

2. BACKGROUND

To get a clear picture of the concept of emotional exhaustion in the digital media setting, it is necessary to look at the theoretical perspectives on which the production, distribution and consumption of news takes place. The last decades have witnessed research on the role that news production plays in shaping perceptions, affections and attitudes regarding social issues among the audience by media researchers, communication and psychological researchers. This transformation in the consumption of digital news on a continuous basis has heightened various traditional processes in journalism, such as agenda setting, framing and the prioritisation of the conflict-oriented stories. Simultaneously, the development of digital platforms has enhanced the extent and pace of information flow, which has predisposed the information overload and emotional burnout.

2.1 Theoretical Framework

Several communication and media theories could account for the phenomenon of emotional fatigue in digital environments of communication. The theory of Russian Roulette is known as Agenda Setting Theory, which describes the process whereby attention is captured and directed by the media, particularly the news agenda, presenting one set of issues repeatedly, while suppressing others completely, over a given period of time (McCombs & Shaw, 1972). The analysis of framing theory also illustrates the influence of how events are presented on how audiences interpret and respond to the events (Entman, 2004).

The theory of cultivation extended by Gerbner posits that heavy viewers of TV entertainment tend to get a skewed view of the world based on the repeated images of violence, instability and crisis on the air. Along the same lines, Media Dependency Theory provides a mechanism for people to become more reliant upon media systems at times of uncertainty and crisis and makes their emotions more intensely tied to mediated events.

2.2 Evolution of the Continuous News Cycle

It is impossible to comprehend the change of modern journalism without realising the appearance of the continuous news cycle. In the past, news was released at a certain time by repeated means, like the morning newspapers, evening radios or a bulletin on the TV, etc. These formats designed the manner in which the audiences received news and gave them time to process information prior to the next update. But technological advances in broadcasting, satellite communication, and digital media were gradually transforming journalism into a format where it is characterised by constant changes and real-time journalism.

The launching of a 24-hour news channel was another major milestone of this revolution. The news organisations also started giving round-the-clock news on political activities, international happenings, catastrophes and even on controversial issues. This transformation changed the way of journalism and its organisation. Instead of creating a few and well-edited news bulletins, media houses started to pay more attention to supplying instant news and breaking news alerts as the day progresses. This tendency was also raised on the digital platforms, where the news coverage channels can post new information in real time and reach worldwide readers without any time restrictions.

The media industry in this climate was characterised by competition for the attention of the audience. The news companies are in a type of attention economy where visibility and participation are the economic considerations of success. This urge to solicit a readership, viewership and web traffic fuels the urge by media to highlight sources that produce an emotional appeal and long-term attention. Stories that entail conflict, crisis and dramatic unfolding tend to get more coverage since they tend to attract more viewers and provoke more discourse in the media.

Such events are prioritised as has always been the case with theories of news selection. The initial studies of news values proved that journalists are more likely to highlight those stories that have a conflict, negativity, and the unexpected element since such factors raise the perceived newsworthiness of an event (Galtung and Ruge, 1965). These criteria remain relevant in modern journalism, especially in the digital setting where there is heavy competition of attention.

Framing of the media is also a factor that greatly influences the perception of the audience of the news events. It not only depends on the journalists to choose the events to be reported on, but also to decide the way such events will be presented and framed. Frames give interpretive frameworks serving as guides to the audience to gain knowledge of political and social matters (Entman, 2004). News coverage also has the ability to draw attention to particular parts of a problem and minimise others through the process of framing, and thus create perceptions and responses among the general population.

The other perspective, which greatly affects the influence of media, has given focus on how the news institutions help to organise political knowledge. The setting of the agenda through media coverage is because of the fact that the issues that should be discussed by the population are defined by the coverage. Studies conducted on media and political communication show that the issue of repetition of exposure to certain issues may lead to a situation where citizens adopt less favourable views regarding political actors and public policies (Iyengar & Kinder, 2010). However, in the setting of the ever-changing news media, this pressure is even stronger because the viewers are exposed to the same coverage of the major events on numerous channels.

The structural forces that influence the production of news have also been brought out in critical analyses of media systems. The editorial strategies, news priorities and structures of the narrative employed by media organisations are shaped by a political and economic framework. These are the institutional pressures that influence the voices that are brought to the news and how difficult social matters are presented to the general public (Herman and Chomsky, 2002).

2.3 Media Saturation and Information Overload

The proliferation of digital media technological advances has raised a channel of communication in which people are exposed to more information than before. Media messages are not restricted to certain channels and times anymore; they are being broadcast in various media at different times of the day. Broadcasts on television, news portals on the Internet, podcasts, social networks, and mobile apps are all a part of an information constant that follows people everywhere: during work and during personal time.

This state has been characterised as media saturation, a scenario whereby the actual size of the media materials can no longer be held back and begins to fuel daily life and define how people perceive social reality. In a society with high media, individuals use the examples of media to explain things that happen much beyond their environment of focus. This endless stream of images, stories, and discourse will bring about a feeling that people are continuously experiencing global events, though this is actually given to them in the form of mediated communication (Gitlin, 2001).

More socially, this space is an indication of how mediated communication has become increasingly important in daily lives. Modern societies are becoming more organised around mediating infrastructures that link people to some far-off occurrences and groups by means of digital links (Couldry and Hepp, 2017). These infrastructures create new possibilities for information exchange but also increase the volume of mediated experiences that individuals must interpret and manage.

Philosophical analyses of contemporary society have linked these conditions to broader patterns of psychological exhaustion. The constant demand for attention and responsiveness within digital environments can create a sense of mental fatigue and pressure to remain continuously informed about global events. Over time, this persistent exposure to information can contribute to feelings of exhaustion and disengagement (Han, 2017).

Studies examining digital media use have found that individuals who experience high levels of information overload are more likely to feel overwhelmed by news content and to reduce their exposure to news to protect their well-being (Heiss &

Matthes, 2023). Similarly, meta-analytical research indicates that excessive exposure to news content can contribute to avoidance behaviours, particularly when audiences perceive the volume of information as unmanageable or emotionally taxing (Xu et al., 2026).

2.4 Doomscrolling and Negative News Consumption

The so-called doomscrolling is one of the most evident trends of digital news consumption over the last several years. The phrase is used to refer to the behaviour of scrolling through online news feeds, or social media feeds, and reading and consuming large volumes of negative or traumatising information. Even though scrolling through online content is the characteristic aspect of social media consumption, doomscrolling, in particular, indicates the propensity to continue to explore the feed of bad news even when feeling emotionally uncomfortable. Doomscrolling received its most frequent coverage at times of world crisis, especially during the COVID-19 pandemic, when people are spending more time on the internet gathering information on health hazards, political news, and social upheavals. Research has shown that prolonged exposure to disturbing news stimuli may lead to a rise in anxiety, sadness, and psychological stress (Buchanan et al., 2021).

Doomscrolling has complicated psychological processes. People also might keep on listening to the bad news, although it hurts them, as they view being informed as a way of readiness or alertness. Nevertheless, the constant experiences of alarming headlines and crisis shots may, in the long term, increase emotional arousal and make individuals feel powerless or even pessimistic. A study of the psychological correlates of doomscrolling established a relationship between this behaviour and such symptoms as rumination, emotional exhaustion, and diminished psychological well-being (Satici et al., 2022). Research has found that the emotional impact of doomscrolling may promote negative views of the world, and therefore, the behaviour may enhance those views. Being exposed to repetitive information on disasters, political wars, and social crises may lead to the development of increased anxiety and pessimistic attitudes toward the world (Shabahang et al., 2024).

Researchers also started working on such measurement instruments in order to gain a more profound insight into the level of prevalence and psychological significance of doomscrolling. The evidence of the scale of doomscrolling being developed and validated suggests that the habit can be assessed based on the trends in excessive news following, emotional discomfort, and the inability to get out of the pro-negative news feeds (Soraci et al., 2025). Some other studies further posit that online spaces with constant updates and automated news feeds have the ability to sustain doomscrolling, in receiving regular updates on an ongoing stream of crisis (Dominguez-Rodriguez et al., 2025). The outcome is that users further engage in taking distressing news until it builds up to higher levels of mental exhaustion (Ahluwalia, 2025).

Table 1. Key psychological effects associated with doomscrolling

Study	Research Context	Main Findings	Emotional Impact
Buchanan et al. (2021)	Social media use during COVID-19	Frequent exposure to negative news increased emotional distress	Anxiety and negative mood
Satici et al. (2022)	Development of doomscrolling scale	Identified behavioral and emotional patterns associated with compulsive news scrolling	Psychological exhaustion
Shabahang et al. (2024)	Social media news exposure	Doomscrolling associated with pessimistic worldviews	Existential anxiety
Soraci et al. (2025)	Psychometric study of doomscrolling behavior	Validated measurement scale for doomscrolling	Emotional strain
Ahluwalia (2025)	Digital media environments	Cognitive overload contributes to compulsive consumption of negative news	Mental fatigue

The growing prevalence of doomscrolling also raises important questions regarding the design ethics of digital platforms. Infinite scrolling interfaces, algorithmic recommendations, and engagement-driven notifications are structured in ways that encourage prolonged exposure to emotionally stimulating material. Consequently, doomscrolling should not only be understood as an individual behavioural habit but also as a technologically reinforced pattern shaped by platform economies and attention-driven communication systems.

2.5 News Avoidance and Issue Fatigue

Whereas a part of the population reacts to a negative news climate with doomscrolling, others take the opposite approach and use news avoidance. News avoidance is the conscious effort to restrict or avert being exposed to news material since it is considered overwhelming, repetitious or emotionally disturbing. This act is more pronounced in the past few years as researchers have focused on the way the audience reacts to digital news landscapes that emerge.

Literature indicates that news avoidance may develop when the viewers become convinced that the news reporting is too negative or upsetting. Being constantly bombarded with news of political wars, calamities, financial downturns, and societal chaos may cause a person to switch off the news so that he or she does not suffer in the emotional sense. It has been proven by empirical research that the people whose negative emotional reaction to news is great tend to decrease the consumption of the news over time (Damstra et al., 2023).

The emotion-news consumption is complicated. On the one hand, news stories that are emotionally colored may get attention and become more active. Conversely, constant exposure to traumatising material can ultimately induce exhaustion and inattentiveness. According to research on the emotional aspects of news consumption, negativity can affect attention toward news and avoidance thereof (Carbone et al., 2024).

The other reason for news avoidance is the view that the news is reporting the same problems in a repetitive way and does not provide meaningful solutions and new views on the same issues. By having people witness similar stories in several news cycles, viewers might participate in the problem of issue fatigue, whereby seeing or hearing certain subjects builds diminishing interest and attention. Research on the concept of issue fatigue has identified recurring reporting on some issues as having an effect of irritation, boredom, and emotional disengagement among viewers (Schumann et al., 2022).

This tendency can be described especially in the reporting about the long-term social problems like climate change, political polarisation, or economic instability. When the news on such problems continues to emerge more than once on various media platforms, the audience can be easily overwhelmed by the onslaught of the concentrations to problems that seem so hard to fix (Gurr & Metag, 2025).

The implications of news avoidance on the knowledge of the population and democracy may also be larger. By exposing themselves less to news, people might end up being less news literate on issues of political activities and debates on policies of the government. Other researchers have also predicted that the lesser exposure to reliable sources of news could make people more vulnerable to being misinformed, especially when they use alternative sources of information that do not meet journalistic standards (Tandoc et al., 2022).

3. FOCUS OF THE ARTICLE

The modern digital media space exposes viewers and readers to the incessant flow of news, visuals and stories of the crises occurring in the global arena. Although the previous parts investigated the theoretical pillars of media saturation and news fatigue, this part dwells on how the digital news setting influences the emotional experiences of viewers. The role of crisis imagery, the delivery of news through algorithms, and psychological reactions formed after the continuous exposure to the negative information is paid particular attention. All these forces are the underlying causes of a trend of emotional exhaustion that influences the ways audiences interact with news and political affairs.

3.1 Crisis Imagery and Mediated Trauma

Covering of news has always been based on the ability to convey the urgency and the importance of major events using powerful visual imagery. War scenes, natural calamities, humanitarian disasters, and violence tend to take the centre stage of journalism narration. These images spread fast in the digital world, over the air, on news websites through the Internet, and on social media, and in most instances, they seem to have gone viral on various media outlets. Though this type of imagery may heighten awareness of critical matters of concern in the world, the constant exposure to scenes of pain and devastation may also cause a strain of emotions among the audience.

The aesthetics of crisis images can be described as being closely related to the storyline format of reporting news. The media is quite adept at highlighting the dramatic aspects of the events, such as conflict, danger, and uncertainty. Such emphasis is indicative of the nature of the news institutions to structure the social in a manner in which a threat and a state of instability are brought out through a form of narration that is apt to draw attention among the audience but can also lead to further increases in anxiety and fear levels (Altheide, 2002). The repeated circulation of traumatic visuals also raises ethical concerns regarding audience well-being and responsible journalism practices. Scholars of trauma journalism argue that excessive visual repetition of violence and suffering may intensify emotional distress among audiences while simultaneously normalising human suffering through repetition.

The effect of crisis coverage on emotion has been studied in a research article that suggested that recurring exposure to traumatising scenes may cause what is commonly known as mediated trauma. Although people may be physically far away when a particular situation occurs, being exposed to visual depictions of suffering continuously can result in the generation of emotional responses comparable to those of people who were directly impacted by the crisis. Surveys on crisis news reaction have indicated that continuous exposure to emotionally intense news content may amplify the amount of psychological stress and diminish emotional weakness in viewers (Oliveira et al., 2023).

The exposure to long-term crisis narratives may also have an effect on how the population responds to the global conflicts and humanitarian problems. The cycles of media attention have been studied, and it has been argued that the audience is startled by the big crises at first and subsequently gets bored with the news coverage over time. The repeated exposure of news content on a conflict or a disaster without any meaningful differences in the narrative or outcome can contribute to the decrease of the emotional involvement and diminishing intentions to pay close attention to the issue by an audience (Weisser et al., 2024).

In recent research investigating the type of uncertainty created by media, the relationship between mental health and crisis news has also been noted. Constant exposure to unpredictable or harmful news on what is happening in the world may add to the stress and emotional turmoil of the people consuming the media. The psychological consequences of such exposure are quite strong, especially in situations where viewers are exposed to several crisis stories at the same time, and this gives them a sense that the world is full of continuous turmoil and threat (Kesner et al., 2025).

Figure 2.

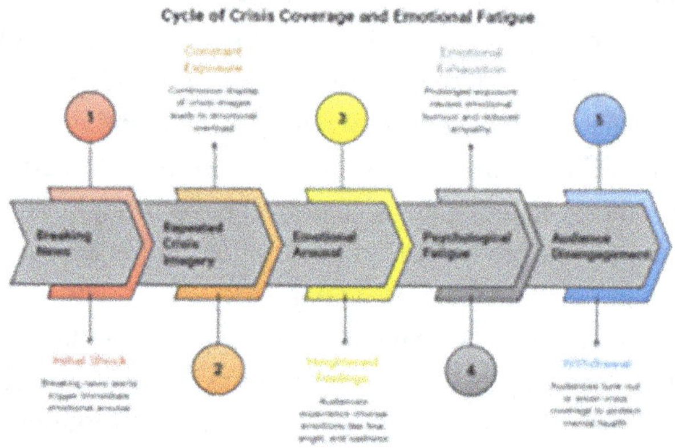

3.2 Algorithmic Amplification and Digital News Distribution

News transmission in the digital space is becoming dominated by the algorithmic systems that dictate the look of information on social media and online news feeds. Algorithmic systems aim to get maximum user engagement, which can only be achieved by encouraging content that elicits the desired reaction in the form of a comment, a share, or even time spent watching the content. Consequently, a story that is highly emotional or controversial in nature is more likely to get more visibility than a commonplace or neutral news story. The algorithm choosing what is included in the digital feeds can be considered not only typical technical decisions: it is based on the processes that occur in the institution as a whole and influence the ways in which platforms influence the way people communicate and discourse online (Gillespie, 2022).

The content of news is often transferred in the elements of social networks where individuals provide news items, photos and commentary to their own groups. Such sharing enables news to spread quickly across the platforms and audiences, spreading news as far as reaching millions of users in a short duration of time. This tendency has been defined by scholars as spreadable media and the importance of the manner in which digital networks can facilitate a flow of information through various channels of communication (Jenkins et al., 2013).

The recent studies on digital information environments indicate that exposure to emotionally charged news materials may increase when the distribution is dependent on algorithms. Algorithmic systems may favour content that captures user attention, whether this involves news on a crisis, a political scandal, or a social debate, where users are already receiving a lot of information changes (Lee, 2025). With the repetition of these stories on digital sites, viewers can be informed of them multiple times via various channels.

User engagement is also a key factor in determining visibility. Earlier research into digital news consumption has reported that there are significant relationships between the number of sources and the number of interactions with news that can impact audience attitudes to news products. Repeatedly mentioned and engaged news stories are more likely to stay on the agenda in a digital information environment (Ju & Lee, 2025). Algorithmic selection combined with user behaviour fundamentally shapes the media ecosystem, with some messages dominating the public consciousness. This is a system that can provide rapid and effective access to information to the audience, but can also, at the same time, create patterns of repetitive exposure to emotionally intense content.

3.3 Psychological Mechanisms of Emotional Fatigue

Emotional exhaustion in media settings is directly related to psychological events that lead to a change in the way people react to a recurrent analysis of upsetting news. Several processes are associated with the occurrence of emotional fatigue, and these are compassion fatigue, desensitisation, and emotional numbing. The processes represent how people undertake to cope with the psychological pressure that comes with persistent media coverage revolving around crisis-related news stories.

Compassion fatigue is one of the most frequently discussed mechanisms, and this is a condition where a person can no longer empathetically address other people due to the constant exposure to suffering. When viewers are exposed to the constant news of war, tragedies, or humanitarian crises, they are likely to be very emotional in their responses, e.g., feeling empathy, grief, or worry. Nevertheless, the feelings used to these responses may weaken due to repetition of such stories. As time goes by, one can find it hard to have an equal degree of emotional involvement in every occurrence of crisis.

The philosophical views on modern society also indicate that the unceasing need of be emotionally receptive in digital space helps to greet the larger trends of psychological depletion. The citizens are supposed to be aware, care about international stunts and react emotionally to the happenings in other parts of the world. These expectations may lead to a perception of burnout, whereby people are burdened with emotional stimuli as received or perceived via the media (Han, 2017).

Mental health effects of continuous negative news have also been reported in empirical studies. Research studies that analyse the psychological consequences of uncertain situations caused by media show that constant restraint of disturbing information may cause anxiety, stress levels, and emotional instability in the audience (Kesner et al., 2025). These impacts are more noticeable when people are faced with several crisis stories at the same time, by using various media outlets.

Desensitisation is another psychological reaction to constant exposure to bad news. Desensitisation is a process that is experienced when people become less emotionally sensitive to a particular kind of stimulus due to frequent exposure to it. When applied to news consumption, this could lead to a gradual loss in emotional sensitivity to violence, disaster or social conflict due to repeated encounters. Desensitisation can also lead to a lack of empathy and interest in significant social matters, though it is a coping method that helps people to avoid over-emotion about challenges in life. Beyond psychological consequences, emotional desensitisation may also influence democratic participation and civic engagement. Audiences experiencing emotional fatigue may gradually disengage from political discussions, public affairs, and social debates due to feelings of helplessness or emotional exhaustion. In the long term, this trend may weaken public trust in journalism and reduce active participation in democratic processes.

Research has indicated that people who spend an exceptional amount of time watching negative news on digital platforms tend to claim greater rates of mental stress and emotional fatigue (Usman et al., 2025). Likewise, the evidence-based results of the investigation of social media news use suggest that recurring exposure to upsetting news may result in the appearance of patterns of emotional health conditions and social attitudes in the long-term perspective (Pal et al., 2026).

3.4 Digital Overexposure and Mental Well-Being

The social media sites are also designed to feed users with unending feeds of information, which include personal updates, entertainment information, and stories. Users scroll through their feeds, and they may come across images of disasters, political conflicts or humanitarian crises before and between everyday social interactions. Studies that investigate the psychological effects of such exposure have found the relationships between social media news-consumption and emotional distress. Researchers on doomscrolling behaviour propose that the constant exposure to negative news material may also add to anxious and pessimistic perceptions of the situation in the world (Shabahang et al., 2024). When people come across the accounts of crises and social unrest several times, their perception about the world as being more hazardous or unstable than it really is might develop.

Increasingly serious studies on the topic during times of global crisis have already shown that emotional well-being could be affected by the frequent exposure to negative news that digital platforms offer. As an illustration, research investigating the use of social media in the COVID-19 pandemic has also shown that people who more often consumed news on the topic of crisis were more likely to experience negative emotions such as sadness, stress, and anxiety (Buchanan et al., 2021).

Audience experiences that are investigated using qualitative research methods have also shown how individuals characterise the emotional impacts of prolonged news in relation to their experiences. Most respondents say they have the urge to stay updated with what is happening world-wise, even when it causes them a sense of sadness or fatigue. This trend can be observed as a conflict between a perceived responsibility to be aware and the emotional expenses of deficits of constant presence of negative news (Kazun, 2024).

Recent studies investigating the extended psychosocial impact of social media news exposure recommend that online information conditions can change prolonged trends of emotional health. Research into causal associations between consumption of social media news and psychological health suggests that recurring exposure to distressing information can cause a decrease in well-being and emotional fatigue in users of the media (Pal et al., 2026).

3.5 Screens of Solitude: Emotional Isolation in Connected Environments

The development of digital forms of communication has essentially changed the way people respond to information and with each other. Digital platforms, laptops, and smartphones enable users to stay in touch with the flow of information throughout the world. It is important to note, however, that this ubiquitous connectivity does not always result in the desired growth of meaningful social interaction. On the contrary, people tend to access news and other kinds of content in solitary physical presence, with most of their interactions on the screens of their digital devices instead of communication with other human beings.

According to sociological investigations about digital communications, modern societies are placing a stronger emphasis on media systems to understand the social and political processes. People are regularly experiencing globalisation processes through mediated communication productively instead of being directly involved in social life (Couldry and Hepp, 2017). This has resulted in an environment where screens have overtaken reality as the main display where individuals view and decipher the faraway realities.

Media content has also been one of the factors responsible for a scenario where people are saturated with content, but they are unmoved by the happenings they are watching. Media messages can be accessed almost every day, which may lead to a perception of crisis around the world, happening constantly. In the long-run, this repeated exposure may lead to the experiences of tiredness and lack of emotion (Gitlin, 2001).

Philosophical explanations of the current culture are that the digital communication space is imposing various psychological pressures on individuals. The psychological stress of continual awareness, listeningness, and attention to global affairs can lead to the types of mental fatigue that can be compared to the larger tendencies of burnout in society (Han, 2017).

In this context, "screens of solitude" may be understood as a condition of informational hyperconnectivity combined with emotional and interpersonal detachment. Individuals remain continuously connected to global events through digital devices while simultaneously experiencing reduced opportunities for collective emotional processing and meaningful interpersonal interaction. The concept therefore, reflects a paradox of contemporary media culture: audiences are increasingly informed about distant crises while becoming psychologically exhausted and socially isolated within digitally mediated environments.

Figure 3. Conceptual framework of "screens of solitude"

Table 2. Factors contributing to emotional fatigue in digital news environments

Factor	Media Mechanism	Psychological Outcome	Supporting Studies
Crisis Imagery	Repeated visual exposure to disasters and conflict	Emotional distress and fatigue	Altheide (2002); Oliveira et al. (2023)
Algorithmic Amplification	Platform algorithms prioritize engaging content	Repeated exposure to negative news	Gillespie (2022); Lee (2025)
Information Overload	Continuous news updates across platforms	Cognitive strain	Han (2017); Heiss & Matthes (2023)
Doomscrolling Behavior	Continuous scrolling through negative news feeds	Anxiety and pessimism	Shabahang et al. (2024); Buchanan et al. (2021)
Social Media Overexposure	Frequent exposure to crisis narratives online	Emotional exhaustion	Pal et al. (2026); Kazun (2024)

4. SOLUTIONS AND RECOMMENDATIONS

The rise of emotional fatigue among media audiences raises important questions about how journalism, digital platforms, and audiences themselves can respond to the pressures created by continuous news exposure. While the modern information ecosystem has expanded access to news and strengthened the circulation of public information, it has also created conditions in which audiences may feel overwhelmed by constant updates, crisis narratives, and emotionally intense imagery. Addressing these challenges requires coordinated efforts across multiple levels of the media ecosystem.

4.1 Responsible Journalism Practices

Journalism has always been attached to the professional norms, under which accuracy, fairness and responsibility to the population should be the main priorities. When applied to the contemporary digital media spaces, these principles are imperative yet have to adjust themselves to the dynamics of the unstopping news cycles, news that is aimed at emotions and driven by emotions. Emotional fatigue among the audiences could be alleviated by practising responsible journalism, without altering the informational aspect of the news media.

The emerging trend in the journalism industry is the so-called constructive journalism, which prompts reporters to give a news story in such a manner that acknowledges the problems but also points to the possible solutions and reactions. Constructive journalism, instead of setting its eyes on crisis stories or negative eventualities, gives priority to balanced journalism in which responding to challenges is addressed through how individuals, communities, and institutions react to the challenges. The rationale behind this is to present audiences with a more in-depth view of social issues, as well as to make them interested instead of hopeless (McIntyre and Gyldensted, 2017).

The review of the professional journalism norms underlines the necessity of ethical reporting that should be accuracy-context-based. The guidelines that govern the working of the journals emphasise that journalists ought to make sure that they corroborate information, give background information and should not post facts or occasions without clarification. The contextual reporting gives the audience an idea of why something is happening and how it corresponds to the larger social trends (Kovach and Rosenstiel, 2021). Having a historical context, data, and various viewpoints on the issue presented in news reports, the audience will be in a more favourable position to approach the interpretation of what happened concerning the meaning of the events without making the point based on emotional responses.

4.2 Audience Media Literacy and Mindful Consumption

In addition to the effects of journalism practice on the capsule of news coverage, there exist the audiences as important participants in the decision of engagement with the information in the digital space. The growing accessibility to news on various platforms is forcing people to acquire the skills that will enable them to assess, control and moderate the amount of news that they see or hear. It is possible to promote media literacy and support mindful consumption so that audiences can operate in complex information environments without developing over-varying emotional strain.

Digital media literacy is the power to comprehend creation, dispersion, and exposition of information in digital communication frameworks. People who possess high media literacy can gain more knowledge about the impact of algorithms on the news feed, how headlines can be created to capture the interest of readers and how various sources can present the information in a specific form. The skills would allow the audience to have a critical interpretation of the news instead of responding instantly to emotionally charged news.

Studies investigating digital media use appear to indicate that media literacy has the opportunity of mitigate the ill effects of information overload. The more people can learn about how digital information systems work, the more apt they will be to handle the amount of material they receive and also to prioritise the most pertinent information to their needs or duties (Heiss and Matthes, 2023). Media literacy is thus not a cognitive skill but a form of defence mechanism against the emotional pangs in very saturated media.

Mindful consumption of news is also about creating habits that allow one to be exposed to information that is distressing only to a certain degree. Indicatively, people can either decide to allocate certain periods of the day to watch news as opposed to monitoring news updates throughout the day. With the boundaries formed concerning the news exposure, readers can stay informed without being constantly emotionally stimulated by the notification of breaking news or social media changes.

The other useful tactic is the diversification of information. When people rely on of single news source or feed, they can be exposed to repeated stories that elicit a specific emotional response. The information on the news provided by numerous reliable sources can help to have a more balanced perception of the situation and decrease the idea that the crises affect all spheres of society.

A study on information avoidance behaviour also proposes that people restrict the goods they read at times as a coping behaviour to the abundance of information. Although too much avoidance can suppress a person in accepting significant matters, guideline-based on news exposure can be added as a preventive method to avoid emotional drainage (Li and Zheng, 2023). Promoting attentional forms of news distribution will enable individuals to stay informed of all societal activities and remain safe in their minds at the same time.

4.3 Platform Responsibility and Algorithmic Transparency

Digital media now contributes a lot of influence to the way news information is delivered to people. Recommendation systems, social media networks, and search engines define the appearance of the news items and determine the sequence within which information is displayed in the feeds of users. This has made technology firms some of the important players in the modern news ecosystem.

The computational algorithms utilised by the digital platforms are created to comprehend the user behaviour and find the trends that will give the highest engagement. The content, which provokes some kinds of reactions, like likes, comments, or shares, is especially valued as it provides more time that the user can spend on a platform. It has been suggested that platform governance be considered as a mode of editorial influence by scholars analysing platform governance. The design concepts that are included in the development of algorithms influence which information can be made visible and how users are presented with that information (Gillespie, 2022). The forthcoming shift towards digital as the medium by which news is consumed and consumed by raises questions of accountability and transparency on its own.

Ethical Algorithm Design is one of the strategies that may be adopted to tackle emotional exhaustion in the digital news space. There may be solutions for platforms where disturbing content does not keep reappearing in a period of a few hours, or there is more control on the kind of news stories that re-enter the user's feeds. Users may have the option to customise the frequency of the breaking news alerts or choose to focus on news from trusted news providers.

Studies on high-volatility information environments indicate that algorithmic systems have the potential to shape complex information processing among the general public, especially when there is political and/or social stress (Lee, 2025). This discovery underscores the need to make algorithmic design a goal focused on making informed decisions, not creating further confusion or emotional disruptions.

When accountabilities are placed on platforms, they also entail relating to news organizations and regulatory bodies. Technology firms can collaborate with media outlets to find methods of delivering news and information that help to foster understanding rather than overload. Likewise, there could be regulations that disclose the information published by platforms that affect the distribution of news by highlighting transparency standards.

Together, these three layers represent a collaborative framework for creating a healthier relationship between digital media systems and audience well-being.

5. FUTURE RESEARCH DIRECTIONS

Demands from the growing apprehension about emotional exhaustion in digital news situations give grounds to further scholarly investigation working toward the link between media consumption and psychological well-being. While there have been recent studies examining the impact of information overload, doom-scrolling and news avoidance are documented topics, many aspects of this phenomenon are still not fully examined. With the further development of digital media technologies, scholars have to investigate the role of new communication systems in impacting emotional experiences, civic turnout and what citizens know about the global events. The future studies can contribute to this cause and contribute to filling the aforementioned important gaps in the existing literature.

The link between emotional resilience and news consumption is one of the areas that should be studied more deeply by scientists. Negative effects of gazing at the news too much have been at the centre of several documented studies so far, including anxiety, feeling exhausted and feeling disengaged. Nonetheless, people do not react to media settings in the same manner. Some segments of the public might be more capable of coping with the emotional load of chronic intake of news, and hence coping skills, psychological resilience and support networks may help people deal with emotionally upsetting news.

These differences are key to comprehending how people respond to digital news more nuanced, without mistakes. Future researchers could look into the way personal attributes, including the ability to regulate emotions, or pre-media experiences, influence the correlation between news exposure and the psychological outcomes. Studies on the use of social networks by investigating psychosocial well-being reveal that the long-term exposure to negative information on social media may have highly complex effects on mental health, as it can not only affect the number of emotional conditions but also long-term well-being (Pal et al., 2026). Studying the functioning of resilience mechanisms in such settings might be a valuable resource of information on the various approaches which can be employed to keep audiences updated without subjecting them to excessive emotional stress.

The other valuable avenue that should be used in further research is the cross-cultural research on news exhaustion and emotional reactions toward digital media. The available literature on news avoidance and information overload has, to a large extent, been carried out in a national or regional setting. Nevertheless, the media systems have a high degree of diversity among countries, based on journalistic practice, technological infrastructure, political communication, and audience behaviour. The cultural beliefs and values on language of emotional expression, open conversation, and media credibility may also shape the reaction on the reactions of the viewers to the story of the crisis and adverse news dissemination.

The comparative study to be conducted in various societies will aid researchers in identifying the role of structural and cultural determinants in defining news consumption trends. To illustrate, the news can be consumed differently by the people of a country where public broadcast systems are well established compared to the countries where the media is highly commercialised. Cross-cultural research can also present the existence of differences in the narratives of crisis and the ability of the individual to cope with recurrent distressing information. This kind of research would help in enlarging the picture of emotional fatigue aspects on the global level in the digital media age.

The third area that should be studied more is the role that artificial intelligence and the use of algorithm systems play in the distribution of news. Online services are becoming more and more dependent on automated systems to filter news feeds, suggest content, and rank the output of search results. Such systems affect some of the stories that the users would face and the extent to which they would be exposed to a certain subject. On the one hand, algorithmic personalisation can enhance the relevance of information shown to the users; on the other hand, it can also be one of the contributors to the recurrent patterns of exposure to emotionally intense news stories.

Additional studies are needed in this area to determine the impact of the algorithmic systems on the emotional aspects of news consumption. Empirical evidence on the connection between algorithmic and user behaviour implies that there could be a mutual dependence between algorithmic processes and user behaviour that results in the formation of online behavioural patterns, such as doomscrolling (Dominguez-

Rodriguez et al., 2025). The researchers can study how recommendation systems prefer specific content or content categories (the relationships may be positive or negative) and algorithmic transparency.

The correlation between digital media introduction and mental health outcomes also remains an area of research. Current literature indicates that long-term exposure to news reports based on a crisis may increase psychological stress and emotional instability among the viewers (Kesner et al., 2025). Nevertheless, further studies are required to investigate the long-term psychological impact of constant news use, especially in the digital world, where a person can see news several times per day.

Future research could employ longitudinal research designs that follow the trends of media consumption and the psychological response of individuals on a long-term basis. This would be used to explain the development of emotional fatigue, whether it is a cumulative factor, the event or the media setting that produces a greater result. Studies can be conducted as well, investigating the ways in which media content in various forms, including text-based reporting, visual images, or live video reports, can affect emotional reactions differently. The other opportunity of future research is to study the correlation between information overload and news avoidance patterns. The meta-analytical studies indicate that overexposure to information may affect people's choice to reduce or refrain from any consumption of news (Xu et al., 2026).

6. CONCLUSION

The media environment, which has been transformed in the last twenty years, has drastically changed the way audiences receive and perceive news. The cyclic news, the digital space, and the algorithmically designed streams of information have established a situation where a person is being bombarded with information in big amounts during the day. Though these changes have led to the growth of accessibility to information and intensified the sense of immediacy, in terms of communication taking place globally, they have also brought with them a lot of emotional and psychological baggage for media consumers. Among the most obvious implications of this change, one can note the recent popular tendency of so-called emotional exhaustion related to the consumption of digital news.

In media worlds that are well interconnected, audiences are seldom out of touch with news updates. The use of smartphones, social media, TV and news portals on the web makes information about the events in the world ever accessible. Such a situation has ended up creating what can be termed a state of media saturation, whereby people get bombarded with the same stories of news presented by various media. Media messages are omnipresent messages in everyday life and, therefore, influence the ways individuals perceive the social reality and understand the events happening in the world (Gitlin, 2001). Consequently, there is no longer an infrequent consumption of news but a constant one involving daily activities.

Regular crisis imagery in the news is one of the major causes of emotional fatigue. For many news cycles, there are stories about wars, natural disasters, humanitarian disasters, and political conflict; such stories attract the audience and express the conventional notion about the values of news. The doomscrolling phenomenon clearly shows a flow of the digital news environment affecting an audience and their feelings. Via the social media feeds that contain content about personal correspondence, entertainment news, and the latest details, many people are exposed to news this way. Within these environments, bad stories or problematic information can be repeated, so that the prolonged exposure to distressing information follows. In the course of time, this tendency may become more of a cycle where people keep on being affected by negative news and at the same time, they may be emotionally burned out.

Digital connectivity is the other significant aspect of emotional exhaustion that results in a paradox. The current generation is more than ever before, more linked to events happening around the world than through their own social interaction, which is usually done through the use of screens rather than through direct interpersonal communication techniques. People can track big or eventful global issues, political upheavals, and humanitarian disasters as they sit in their apartments with their gadgets all by themselves. This type of interaction is able to build alienation towards events being observed, even though the quantity of information keeps growing. Modern societies are thus influenced by the mediated experience where people access distant realities through digital systems of communication that are the principal users of digital communication systems (Couldry and Hepp, 2017).

Emotional fatigue is a concept that emphasises the need to create media ecosystems that could facilitate the development of both the populace and the audience. With the ever-changing nature of digital communication technologies, journalists, platform designers, policymakers, and researchers will have to collaborate to develop communication systems that would strike a balance between the active flow of information and the psychological needs of the population consuming this information.

REFERENCES

Ahluwalia, P. S. (2025). *Doomscrolling and mental fatigue: Cognitive overload in digital media environments*. Digital Psychology Review.

Altheide, D. L. (2002). *Creating fear: News and the construction of crisis*. Aldine de Gruyter.

Buchanan, K., Aknin, L. B., Lotun, S., & Sandstrom, G. M. (2021). Brief exposure to social media during the COVID-19 pandemic: Doomscrolling has negative emotional consequences, but kindness-scrolling does not. *PLoS One*, *16*(10), e0257728. DOI: 10.1371/journal.pone.0257728 PMID: 34644310

Carbone, M., Soroka, S., & Dunaway, J. (2024). The Psychophysiology of News Avoidance: Does Negative Affect Drive Both Attention and In attention to News? *Journalism Studies*, *25*(12), 1460–1475. DOI: 10.1080/1461670X.2024.2310672

Couldry, N., & Hepp, A. (2017). *The mediated construction of reality*. Polity Press.

Damstra, A., Vliegenthart, R., Boomgaarden, H., Glüer, K., Lindgren, E., Strömbäck, J., & Tsfati, Y. (2023). Knowledge and the news: An investigation of the relation between news use, news avoidance, and the presence of (mis)beliefs. *The International Journal of Press/Politics*, *28*(1), 29–48. DOI: 10.1177/19401612211031457

Domínguez-Rodríguez, A., Apprich, F., Friehs, M. A., van der Graaf, S., & Steinrücke, J. (2025). Climate change news and doomscrolling: An examination of influencing factors and psychological effects. *Acta Psychologica*, *245*, 104925. DOI: 10.1016/j.actpsy.2025.104925 PMID: 40112762

Dunaway, J., & Graber, D. A. (2022). *Mass media and American politics* (12th ed.). CQ Press.

Entman, R. M. (2004). *Projections of power: Framing news, public opinion, and U.S. foreign policy*. University of Chicago Press.

Galtung, J., & Ruge, M. H. (1965). The structure of foreign news. *Journal of Peace Research*, *2*(1), 64–91. DOI: 10.1177/002234336500200104

Gerbner, G., Gross, L., Morgan, M., & Signorielli, N. (1986). Living with television: The dynamics of the cultivation process. In *Perspectives on media effects*.

Gillespie, T. (2022). *Custodians of the internet: Platforms, content moderation, and the hidden decisions that shape social media*. Yale University Press.

Gitlin, T. (2001). *Media unlimited: How the torrent of images and sounds overwhelms our lives*. Metropolitan Books.

Gurr, G., & Metag, J. (2025). What leads to audience issue fatigue? The role of repetitive news coverage and emotional responses. *International Journal of Communication, 17*, 5032–5053.

Han, B.-C. (2017). *The burnout society*. Stanford University Press.

Heiss, R., & Matthes, J. (2023). Social media information literacy and its relationship with information overload and news avoidance. *Computers in Human Behavior, 140*, 107580.

Herman, E. S., & Chomsky, N. (2002). *Manufacturing consent: The political economy of the mass media*. Pantheon Books.

Iyengar, S., & Kinder, D. R. (2010). *News that matters: Television and American opinion*. University of Chicago Press. DOI: 10.7208/chicago/9780226388601.001.0001

Jenkins, H., Ford, S., & Green, J. (2013). *Spreadable media: Creating value and meaning in a networked culture*. New York University Press.

Ju, Y., & Lee, P. (2025). More Sources Create Greater Audience Engagement: An Investigation into the Relationship Between the Number of News Sources and Audience Responses. *Communication Research, 0*(0), 00936502251324549. DOI: 10.1177/00936502251324549

Kazun, A. D., & Malygina, N. (2024). Coping with negative news: Emotional experiences of doomscrolling audiences. *Russian Sociological Review, 23*(3), 45–62. DOI: 10.19181/inter.2024.16.4.5

Kesner, L., Juríčková, V., Grygarová, D., & Horáček, J. (2025). Impact of media-induced uncertainty on mental health. *JMIR Mental Health, 12*(1), e68640. DOI: 10.2196/68640 PMID: 40513096

Kovach, B., & Rosenstiel, T. (2021). *The elements of journalism* (4th ed.). Crown Publishing.

Lee, K. (2025). *Signal, noise, and burnout: A human-information interaction analysis of voter verification in a high-volatility environment*. arXiv. https://doi.org//arXiv.2512.20679DOI: 10.48550

Li, J., & Zheng, Y. (2023). Information avoidance in the age of COVID-19: A meta-analysis of predictors and outcomes. *Information Processing & Management, 60*(2), 103188. DOI: 10.1016/j.ipm.2022.103163

McCombs, M. E., & Shaw, D. L. (1972). The agenda-setting function of mass media. *Public Opinion Quarterly*, *36*(2), 176–187. DOI: 10.1086/267990

McIntyre, K., & Gyldensted, C. (2017). Constructive journalism: An introduction and practical guide for applying positive psychology techniques to news production. *The Journal of Media Innovations*, *4*(2), 20–34. DOI: 10.5617/jomi.v4i2.2403

Newman, N., Fletcher, R., Robertson, C., Eddy, K., & Nielsen, R. K. (2023). *Reuters Institute digital news report 2023*. Reuters Institute for the Study of Journalism.

Newman, N., Fletcher, R., Schulz, A., Andi, S., Robertson, C., & Nielsen, R. K. (2022). *Reuters Institute digital news report 2022. Digital Journalism*. Reuters Institute for the Study of Journalism.

Oliveira, F. B., D'Angelo, C., & Moreno, A. (2023). Emotional responses to COVID-19 news exposure and their implications for news avoidance. *Online Media and Global Communication*, *2*(1), 87–103.

Pal, O., Goyal, A., Chandrasekharan, E., & Saha, K. (2026). The hidden toll of social media news: Causal effects on psychosocial well-being. *Computers in Human Behavior*.

Satici, S. A.. (2022). Development of the doomscrolling scale and its psychological correlates. *Current Psychology (New Brunswick, N.J.)*.

Schumann, C.. (2022). When news topics annoy: Exploring issue fatigue and media overexposure. *Journal of Medicine*, *3*(3), 521–536.

Shabahang, R.. (2024). Doomscrolling evokes existential anxiety and pessimistic worldviews. *Computers in Human Behavior Reports*.

Soraci, P., Griffiths, M. D., Bevan, N., Pisanti, R., Trovato, M., Servidio, R., D'Aleo, E., Campedelli, L., Gallo, F., & Satici, S. A. (2025). Psychometric analysis of the Italian doomscrolling scale. *Current Psychology (New Brunswick, N.J.)*, *44*(12), 11872–11883. DOI: 10.1007/s12144-025-07976-9

Tandoc, E. C.Jr, Thomas, R. J., & Bishop, L. (2022). Avoiding real news, believing in fake news? Investigating pathways from news avoidance to misinformation belief. *Journalism Studies*, *23*(10), 1256–1273.

Usman, S.. (2025). Impact of doomscrolling on mental well-being among media users. *Journal of Arts, Humanities &. Social Sciences*, *9*(1), 25–39.

Weisser, R. A. (2024). Attention cycles, crisis coverage, and declining public engagement with conflict news. *World Development*, *176*, 106389.

Xu, J., He, Z., Guo, D., & Ding, Y. (2026). Relationship between news overload and news avoidance: A meta-analysis. *Journalism*, *27*(3), 776–796. DOI: 10.1177/14648849241299667

KEY TERMS AND DEFINITIONS

Emotional Fatigue: Emotional fatigue is also defined as the mental exhaustion that occurs due to continuous exposure of persons to distressing information or any information that is emotionally taxing in the long run. When audiences are exposed to incessant reports about crises, catastrophes, and interpersonal scuffles through the digital media, emotional exhaustion is likely to take place. Doomscrolling: Doomscrolling is a term used to describe what happens when a person visits the online news feeds or social media feeds and scrolls through copious amounts of negative or distressing information, encountering sizable groups of posts with negative information.

Media Saturation: Media saturation is a situation where people are engulfed by excessive media reports in various channels. With the digital world ever-present in our contemporary surroundings, the news, images, videos, and commentary compete and flow endlessly through the television, social media, mobile applications and online news portals.

News Avoidance: News avoidance can be defined as the intention to reduce or avoid news content. Research indicates that negative emotions, such as frustration or distress, can be some of the factors that lead to individuals disengaging from news consumption (Damstra et al., 2023).

Chapter 15
Understanding Emotional Labor on Social Media Platforms

Suresh Talamala
http://orcid.org/0000-0001-9026-6459
Aditya University, India

J. A. Jevin
http://orcid.org/0009-0008-8511-9698
Koneru Lakshmaiah Education Foundation, India

Shivendu Kumar Rai
http://orcid.org/0000-0001-8240-1884
Tecnia Institute of Advanced Studies, India

Gauri Singh Bhadauria
Chhatrapati Shahuji Maharaj University, India

Kumari Pallavi
http://orcid.org/0000-0003-3534-6899
Galgotias University, India

Rajendra Singh Negi
http://orcid.org/0009-0005-0798-3817
Shri Guru Ram Rai University, India

V. Bhoopathy
http://orcid.org/0000-0003-2175-6328
Sree Rama Engineering College, India

ABSTRACT

Social media emotional labour, in which users consciously display, manage, and control their emotions in order to meet societal expectations and maintain their online presence, is an essential part of digital connection. Users, particularly professionals, influencers, and empathy, service workers, should foster optimism and engagement, as this chapter investigates how platforms like Facebook, Instagram, LinkedIn, and Twitter (X) impact emotional expression. From a sociological and psychological perspective, this chapter examines digital settings' surface and deep

DOI: 10.4018/979-8-3373-8307-1.ch015

actions, with a focus on how constant exposure and connectivity heighten emotional needs. Various mental health issues, such as burnout, stress, emotional tiredness, and anxiety, are discussed as a result of emotional labour.

1. INTRODUCTION

The term "Emotional Labour (EL)" is used to describe the conscious and unconscious attempts people make to express and manage their emotions on social media. It comprises controlling one's emotional reactions to encounters in the virtual world and coming up with expressions to convey those reactions. Emotional performance, regulation, and commodification can be better understood with the help of Hochschild's theory of EL(Evren, 2025). Decentralised and algorithmically controlled domains have replaced traditional office settings as the new norm for EL in the digital age.

EL in social networks operates in informal economies, where social media companies get benefits without paying workers a dime, as opposed to traditional employment arrangements. This has set up an unfair system where networks make a lot of money off of people's emotional labour performed online without paying them. All content on the site is generated by users, who work for social media companies unpaid, while their emotional experiences are turned into data and then into economic value(Cheshin et al., 2025).

On the flip side, commercial social networks are able to cash in on emotional interactions through tailored advertising(Examination, 2025). Communicating one's feelings in social encounters and planning how to do so effectively constitute EL. Managing one's feelings and expressions in order to meet the emotional demands of one's job was Hochschild's definition of emotional work. Expressions of emotion that are appropriate for a specific context are called EL(Arcy, 2016). The bulk of productivity in the 19th and 20th centuries came from industrial workers. Industrial work has become less important since the 1990s, while jobs that produce intangibles like communication, information, and connections have become more prominent.

2. CONCEPT OF EMOTIONAL LABOR

Companies take advantage of people's sentiments, according to previous research, because it's a requirement of the job for employees to express themselves. Airline employees are expected to be warm and welcoming, while healthcare workers are expected to show compassion and understanding, and those working in funeral homes are expected to exude gravity and empathy(Salehi et al., 2025). Using the term "Feeling Rules" to describe these organisational standards, she said that their goal was to control workers' inner lives, particularly their sensitive and intimate feelings and ideas.

The correct word, according to later academics, should be "Display Rules," because organisations can't control employees' invisible inner feelings but can control how they act while they're around other people(Humphrey, 2019). A major difference between feeling regulations and display standards is that the latter imply that companies care more about controlling how they look on the outside than they do about how their employees are really feeling on the inside.

In the second interpretation, the focus shifts from emotions to the regulation of behaviour, calling for a rethinking of EL(In & Barros, 2025). Deep acting and surface acting were the two approaches to EL that had previously been defined in research. People who engage in pretence rarely put themselves in the shoes of the characters they portray. The result is that people show their true emotions through fake smiles and other facial movements.

Even if a server is furious, they could still smile at the client in the hopes of getting a bigger tip. On the flip side, when people participate in deep acting, they try to project the emotions they want to show while they are with other people(Quinn et al., 2026). They actively seek out thoughts and actions that foster authentic emotions, striving to perceive and experience them. Two methods for deep acting were outlined by earlier researchers: stimulating emotions and cultivating one's imagination.

In addition, we argue that workers could display a variety of behaviours to evoke the intended emotions. If you work in sales for a high-end clothing store, you might practise deep acting by listening to upbeat music on your commute, striking up discussions with coworkers as soon as you arrive, and acting like you're really into the newest fashion trends and line of apparel(Jaikla & Piyakun, 2025). Participating in these events helps cultivate the right frame of mind to converse with customers about the store's products. By making light-hearted jokes and laughing, they can pull off deep acting during interactions with customers, giving the impression that they are just hanging out with friends.

According to previous research, there is a third type of emotional work that exists, which is spontaneous and authentic, in addition to deep acting and surface acting. In many cases, they argued, service workers' innate emotions are in line with social standards and organisational display regulations, so there's no need to intentionally evoke the right emotions. For example, they stated that a nurse seeing a wounded baby may feel an innate sense of compassion and concern. Following our discussion on deep acting, we look at data that supports the idea that emotional expressions are real and should be considered EL.

3. SOCIAL MEDIA AS AN EMOTIONAL SPACE

When one perceives events or situations as offering significant possibilities or challenges in regard to their goals, emotions arise(Peng et al., 2024). At the same time, people have control over their emotional state and how it develops. One important paradigm that studies affect regulation phenomena is theories of emotion regulation. Research in emotion regulation, which has its roots in clinical and developmental psychology, looks at "The ways in which people control their own emotional experiences, when those emotions occur, and how they express those sentiments."

The five regulatory techniques identified by the emotion regulation process model (Gross, 2015) correlate to sequential steps in the emotion-generating process and include context alteration, situation selection, cognitive change, attentional deployment, and response modulation. Contemporary studies have expanded the focus of early research to emphasise the social interconnectedness of emotion regulation, including interpersonal emotion regulation, in addition to the intrapersonal processes of emotion control. The cultural and social context that impacts methods for controlling emotions is attracting more and more attention.

Cognitive reappraisal was preferred when people were alone, expressive repression while people were far away, and social sharing when people were close to one another, according to research by Paul et al., 2023. Theoretical developments in the field of emotion regulation have been moving towards a more contextual and social emphasis, which lines up with the increasing impact of social media on how people manage their emotions (Wolfers & Schneider, 2021). By definition, social media are online platforms that facilitate user-generated content creation, user-to-user communication, and user-to-user content sharing. By using multiple social media platforms at once or in sequence, people can tailor their switching strategies and mood control approaches, making it easier to conduct a variety of activities with more efficiency.

In addition to providing information, entertainment, and distraction, social media also offer unique spaces for people to talk about how they're feeling, which can lead to support from others and even cognitive reappraisal (Döveling et al., 2018). Recent studies have theorised and investigated not only interpersonal and intrapersonal emotion-regulatory systems, but also collective emotions within online social networks and other large-scale emotional dynamics (Garcia, 2019). All Chinese internet sites that combine user-generated content with social networking features are considered in this study's expansive definition of social media. Before this study, researchers distinguished between interpersonal media and mass personal, drawing attention to the different ways in which each type of media can help with emotional regulation(Goldenberg et al., 2020).

However, the present social media landscape may not be well-suited to this or earlier categories. Affordances in media go beyond specific types of media and offer a helpful framework for thinking about how social media might help with emotion regulation.

4. EMOTIONAL LABOUR AS WORK INTERACTION

Qualitative case studies of collaborative work constitute a substantial portion of the literature on EL. Although studies have mostly concentrated on service employment in the past, they have now broadened their scope to include all types of interactive work, such as those involving clients, managers, coworkers, caregiving, and family responsibilities(Wharton, 2009). EL is generally only indirectly highlighted in this type of research because it typically starts from the viewpoint of a specific occupation. People in positions that need them to interact with others are believed to put in a lot of emotional effort, but this work is still evaluated in relation to other aspects of the job, like gender, power dynamics, and status.

Together, these studies show how interactive work is different from other types of labour and how these differences relate to larger processes and structures in the workplace.

4.1 Resistance, Power, and Control in Frontline Service Jobs

The dynamics of the service encounter are the primary focus of the growing corpus of sociological study on service labour. Employees and clients are constantly interacting in many service-oriented jobs. Research on frontline or interactive service jobs focuses on the social dynamics of labour and the balance of power and authority within these subordinate professions, similar to how classic sociological studies of service interactions focus(Maria et al., 2025). EL has been the subject of substantial study in frontline service occupations, with researchers drawing connections between this phenomena and persistent issues with employees' experiences in historically powerless positions.

Although it is often believed that workers in interactive service occupations suffer the most from a lack of autonomy, this is not necessarily the case. Employees in customer service jobs face unique threats to their sense of self due to employers' attempts to control their interactions with customers. Despite the dangers of working in an interactive service industry, this study highlights the tactics employees use to deal with customers and coworkers, allowing them to avoid humiliation and maintain their respect and dignity.

4.2 Race, Gender, and Personal Service Work

In healthcare informatics, ML is able to examine large datasets with ease. In order to improve clinical decision-making, ML algorithms can analyse data for patterns and correlations, which then allows for the development of prediction models and systems. Customised treatment programs for each patient are one of the main advantages of ML in healthcare(Porter et al., 2025). Algorithms trained with ML may analyse patient records and create personalised prediction models by taking each patient's vitals and medical history into consideration. Strippers, store clerks, childcare providers, and telephone sex workers are just a few of the many frontline service occupations that have been investigated. The term "Emotional Proletariat (EP)" has been used by previous scholars to describe service jobs in which workers are expected to be friendly and submissive to customers, have less formal power, and are subject to regular monitoring and supervision of their interactions by their employers. This characteristic lead many to label these occupations as being primarily held by women, even though there is no evidence to support this claim. An expanding corpus of study on EL addresses the significant challenges with racism, class, and gender that are brought to light by the anticipated respect from frontline service workers.

Some people, like women and people of colour, are required to exhibit deference, which is defined as the ability to assume a lower position in relation to others. When respect is required as a qualification for a job, people from marginalised groups are more likely to hold these positions or be seen as more competent to do so than members of more advantaged groups. Therefore, members of marginalised groups may have even greater difficulties than other frontline service workers in maintaining their dignity and earning the respect of consumers.

4.3 Expert Service Work and Professionals

Over time, studies on EL have broadened their scope to include more interactional occupations, such as law and medicine. Power, competence, personality traits, and authority are the defining characteristics of a profession, and these characteristics are maintained in part through interactions with coworkers. In contrast to workers in more traditional, interactive service occupations, professionals deal directly with clients rather than consumers and enjoy a far greater degree of independence(Smith et al., 2025). Orzechowicz calls those who work in interactive fields "Privileged Emotion Managers (PEM)," rather than EP. In addition, according to Orzechowicz, professionals are more likely to have their EL recognised and supported by their colleagues than those who work in interactive service.

Research on EL among professionals mainly looks at how these individuals learn to handle the social demands of their jobs and how they undergo professional socialisation, which is important because of the importance of training for professionals. In an unofficial, unstated curriculum, the authors argue, medical students are taught to control their emotional reactions to the bodies of their patients.

4.4 EL and Care Work

Study after study in the field of interactive work has identified the caregiving that women do as a unique form of EL in the workplace. Caring for coworkers is seen as both an informal part of employees' relationships with one another and as a social obligation that male and female employees are expected to comply with in various ways. Specifically addressing the latter, workers solve the EL demands of their jobs by engaging in "Reciprocal Emotion Management" with one another(Lv, 2025).

Providing care is seen as more than just a job requirement; it is also seen as a casual way to deal with tough situations. Research on social support in the workplace has shown some interesting connections to emotional control. Crucial to the larger body of literature on care work is the emphasis on caregiving as an experiential learning paradigm.

Several quantitative investigations were carried out by England and colleagues to examine the claim that paralegals' EL has been disregarded or underpaid. This study's findings suggest that, on average, carer jobs pay less than comparable jobs that do not require this skill set. There is substantial overlap between the conceptualisations used by EL researchers and the definitions used in this research when it comes to care labour, even though there are differences in how care work is operationalised across these studies.

Both the care literature and EL research share an interest in investigating the ambivalent character of caregiving and a common focus on the devaluing of care work. As a job requirement or expectation, caring for another person can be emotionally draining, and it often happens in unbalanced partnerships where the needs of the receiver take priority, putting the provider at a disadvantage. However, studies on social support and reciprocal emotion regulation show that not all caregiving in the workplace is exploitative. Caregiving itself can be emotionally and organically rewarding, especially for those whose jobs require constant attention to others.

4.5 Interaction at Work and Interactive Work

As a measure of the EL needs of a job, this branch of EL research has focused on the interactional demands of various jobs(Yao et al., 2024). Therefore, EL is portrayed as an essential part of the activity; it shows up in the standards and expectations of the profession, the regular performance of tasks, and the rules and regulations that govern how work is done and evaluated.

EL affects the structure and nature of work, specifically the dynamics of power and status and the ways in which they are maintained and dealt with; it is both an official and informal need of the job. Sociological studies of the modern workplace have shifted their emphasis from low-skill, routine jobs to various forms of interactive work, with social interaction playing an increasingly important role, particularly in relation to formal and informal work processes and expectations.

5. PSYCHOLOGICAL IMPACTS

There may be personal or organisational consequences to EL, as these approaches show that emotions are managed and regulated at work to fit in with the company's presentation standards(Jeung et al., 2018). Previous research found that workers with lower levels of job identification or participation were more likely to have health-related symptoms when they were required to perform EL. According to a large body of research, EL in some occupations is associated with increased risk of psychological distress and depressive symptoms, as well as perceived stress and high levels of demand. Scientists have speculated that dealing with people's emotions all day long can be exhausting and lead to burnout. Memory loss, dissatisfaction with one's work, stress on the workplace, depersonalisation, cardiovascular illness, high blood pressure, emotional exhaustion, and even cancer can be worsened by EL.

In addition, the negative effects of EL are known by many, and the connection between EL and violence in the workplace is well-established. In contrast to those working in manufacturing or administrative roles, service industry workers are more likely to be victims of client-initiated acts of violence while on the job. All members of today's industrialised society are potential perpetrators of client violence, which includes patients, clients, inmates, and consumers. Jobs in the "Caring Professions (CP)," such as firefighting, police work, teaching, and those in the social service, welfare, and healthcare sectors, are associated with a high incidence of client violence in occidental countries.

The percentage of British healthcare professionals who have reported minor injuries is around 10%, while 16% have reported verbal abuse. Statistics show that between 46% and 100% of healthcare workers in the US have been victims of violence while on the job. Therefore, researchers studying the link between EL and negative outcomes including health problems and occupational disabilities should take into consideration the fact that EL and workplace violence, including verbal abuse from clients, have synergistic repercussions.

5.1 Burnout

Caregiving is one example of a service industry profession where studies on burnout have their roots because of the centrality of the provider-receiver dynamic in this line of work(Dean et al., 2022). Extreme and prolonged stress can wear people down emotionally, mentally, and physically, a condition known as burnout. According to other research, exhaustion is the most common symptom of burnout in the workplace. Studies on mental fatigue have been conducted in a number of countries with remarkably consistent findings. These countries include Israel, Norway, the US, Canada, and Korea.

5.2 Health Outcomes and Burnout

Because of the high costs linked with negative consequences, work-related burnout is a major worry for companies. Extended exposure to a stressful work environment can lead to burnout, a negative emotional reaction to employment. Disruption to productivity, decreased attendance, and staff turnover are all symptoms of emotional and physical tiredness(Orben et al., 2024). In addition, healthcare workers are particularly vulnerable to these effects since their diminished effectiveness on the job could have an adverse effect on the health of their patients. The association between burnout and decreased job performance and physical or mental health difficulties is a strong indicator of its significance.

Long periods of resource scarcity cause extra resources to be depleted, which in turn causes burnout, according to the Conservation of Resources (COR) theory.

Negative attitudes toward work and burnout are outcomes of low emotional regulation skills, which in turn are associated with stress-induced physiological arousal and occupational strain. However, it is still not known how exactly EL correlates with stress and its aftereffects.

5.3 EL Leading to Burnout as a Negative Consequence

Global competitiveness and the growth of the service industry are causing modern labour markets to undergo profound changes. There will be increased mental tasks and expectations as a result of this change. Previous research has shown that burnout can occur in a variety of fields, including human services, but it is more common among those who offer caregiving services. People in "High Emotional Labour" and "High Burnout (HB)" jobs are more likely to be stressed out than people in other jobs, according to the occupational perspective, which views occupational grouping as a significant factor in and of itself. It is commonly accepted that jobs involving providing care have unique traits that make burnout more likely. Client encounters that are both frequent and prolonged might lead to burnout.

Taxonomies of "High-Burnout" occupations have been developed by researchers based on the emotional control necessary during client interactions and the frequency of encounters, and they have observed variations in burnout dimensions across various service and caregiving professions.

Although customer service interactions are not necessarily "Emotional," they nonetheless necessitate a high level of emotional regulation or control in order to maintain strong connections with customers, which is why this field is where most of the research on EL focuses(Cho et al., 2020). Hochschild classified certain jobs as "Emotional Labour Occupations (ELO)" because of the frequent contact with clients and the control exerted by employers over workers' emotional displays.

But comparing Hochschild's list of occupations to those involving non-EL has not helped in determining levels of stress and burnout. those whose jobs are classified as "High Emotional Labour" do not feel more emotionally exhausted than those whose jobs are classified as "Low Emotional Labour." This discovery could be explained by the idea that EL is not a simple yes or no; rather, there is a range of emotional work needs, and different jobs have different levels of these demands.

5.4 Relationship Between Burnout and Personality Traits

The likelihood of burnout increases in response to high levels of chronic and frequent work stress, low self-efficacy in handling demanding work responsibilities, and inadequate social support in times of crisis. Many research conducted over the last 20 years have pointed to the possibility that unique personality traits play a major role in the onset of burnout(Roemmich, 2023).

Several studies that looked at the causes of burnout found that specific personality factors were important. Among dental hygienists in Korea, burnout is positively correlated with EL and TABP's three sub-factors and negatively correlated with self-efficacy. A growing body of evidence indicates that emotional control at work can be mitigated by self-efficacy and TABP on an individual level.

Although much research on burnout has concentrated on workplaces, researchers have shown that individual differences in personality have a significant role in the development of burnout on the job. The relationship between EL and job burnout is moderated or altered by recent research showing that job autonomy, organisational climate, and specific personality traits play important mediating or moderating roles.

Personality traits have been identified as moderating factors in English language acquisition, and numerous research have demonstrated the importance of these attributes.

6. GENDER AND CULTURAL PERSPECTIVES

In this part, we'll take a look at seven major historical factors that have contributed to gender roles across time.

6.1 Agricultural Technology in Agriculture

Recent research has demonstrated that differences in agricultural technology or, more importantly, a long history of farming, can greatly impact how gender-role beliefs are formed(Giuliano, 2017). Previous studies have looked at how gender gaps in the workforce have persisted throughout time. Their theoretical framework is based on influential work that suggests differences in agricultural technology, namely the differences between plough agriculture and shifting cultivation, are the root cause of gender roles in society.

Using a plough to prepare the land requires more cash, but shifting agriculture, which relies on hand-held tools like hoes and digging sticks, is labour-intensive and heavily involves women. To pull or steer a plough, as opposed to a hoe or digging stick, requires strong grips, upper-body power, and explosive bursts of energy. In most cases, plough-based farming isn't the best option for women who are primarily responsible for child care. So, in societies characterised by plough agriculture, men usually worked the fields outside the home, and women stayed at home to take care of the house. The division of labour set the standard that women's innate place is in the home.

This concept influences women's participation in extra-agricultural pursuits including politics, market jobs, and entrepreneurship, and it often persists even after the economy moves away from agriculture. Based on data collected from 1,265 ethnic groups around the world for the Ethnographic Atlas a dataset created by George Peter Murdock in 1967 the authors find a strong negative correlation between women's involvement in agriculture and the traditional use of the plough in pre-industrial societies.

6.2 Language

There is a fascinating association between grammatical gender-marking and female involvement in the credit market, labour market, politics, and land ownership, which highlights the persistence of gender roles. Gender is one of the most enduring linguistic features that has persisted for millennia, and grammatical features of a language are inherited from its ancient roots. A set of rules for agreement based on multiple noun categories characterises a grammatical gender system in language.

The aforementioned scholars use four very stable gender-related grammatical variables and rely on the World Atlas of Linguistic Structures, the largest database of grammatical structures. How many genders are present, how they are assigned, how the gender system is structured, and how gender-related pronouns are differentiated. By combining these features for a country's most widely spoken language, the authors create the Gender Intensity Index. By examining data from different countries and individuals, they found that women whose languages heavily emphasise gender differences are less likely to be involved in economics and politics, and they have a harder time getting loans and land. Consistent results are shown when the authors analyse a group of immigrants living in the US who were all exposed to the same institutional and labour-market circumstances. Gender systems in languages have developed over time, and (Galor & Sarid, 2017) look at how these systems have affected conduct.

6.3 Geography

Geography is a long-term element that influences gender role discrepancies. Using this vantage point to investigate gender gaps in India's workforce, the previous researcher published an interesting article claiming that soil texture, which can change from the outside, determines the soil's workability and the technologies used for land preparation. Soil types such as loamy and clayey are distinguished by them. Deep tillage reduces the need for fertilisation, transplanting, and weeding tasks typically performed by women and is viable in loamy soils but not in clayey ones.

The expected negative impact on the perceived relative worth of girls within households in places that require deep tillage is a result of the lower demand for female labour compared to male labour. Soil texture explains 70% of the variation in the sex ratio for children aged zero to six years and 62% of the variation in female agricultural labour-force involvement within states, according to the previous researcher. The number of female agricultural labourers drops by 5.1% and the female-to-male kid ratio drops by 2.7% with every 10% rise in the proportion of loamy soils relative to clayey soils.

6.4 Characteristics of Pre-Industrial Society

Gender roles can be significantly impacted by pre-industrial cultural conditions.

6.4.1 Matrilineality

Matrilineality means passing the family name from one generation of women to the next. This might affect how property is passed down in a marriage and how partners choose to live together. For several reasons, matrilineality can improve women's prospects. Whether it's through direct inheritance or improved access to the assets of the extended matriclan, women in matrilineal societies have enhanced access to land and other resources.

That way, they won't be as dependent on their husbands and won't be as vulnerable if their husbands die. Cohabitation with or proximity to family members after marriage, or long-lasting ties maintained via matrilineal kinship, are ways in which women in matrilineal systems obtain continued support from relatives. In comparison to patrilineal women, they also have more options for getting out of the house and more leverage when negotiating with their husbands(Lowes, 2016).

When a woman stays close to her family while her partner lives far away, the differences become even more noticeable. Gender roles are profoundly affected by the difference between patrilineal and matrilineal kinship systems. This difference manifests in differences in spatial aptitude, competitiveness, political engagement, risk aversion (Gottlieb & Robinson, 2016), and contributions to dictator games. It also influences social interactions within families.

6.4.2 Residence Patterns After Marriage

Some studies concentrate only on patrilocality, showing that it can cause differences in gender roles on its own, while most studies look at matrilineal systems that deal with inheritance and housing decisions after marriage. More pronounced gender inequality exists in northern India, a region with a more patrilocal social structure than southern India (Jayachandran, 2015).

A woman's identification with her biological family dissolves when she marries, and her identity becomes interwoven with her husband's family. Having a son means that parents can reap the benefits of their investments in his health and education for a longer period of time, while a daughter leaves the family in more tangible and financial ways when she gets married. Previous studies have looked at how investing in daughter changes depending on where a couple lives after being married.

Parents who worry their daughters will leave the nest may see less personal benefit from investing in their girls' health and education compared to their sons. Previous studies tested the virilocality theory with data collected from Indonesia, a country with very varied patterns of residency after marriage. Virilocality, uxorilocality, ambilocality, and neolocality are all possible in Indonesian societies. There was no statistically significant correlation between virilocality and different levels of investment in daughters, according to the researchers.

The lack of outcomes is thought to be caused by the relaxed nature of Indonesia's housing regulations. Another view holds that virilocality is just one of many standards that work together to discourage investment in daughters. Gender inequality is studied by (Bau, 2016) who looks at how policies and residential habits interact with one another.

6.4.3 Bride Price Versus Dowry

The practice of dowry, sometimes called bride money, is an important cultural variable that influences gender inequality in social preferences. A dowry is a monetary gift given by the bride's family to the husband and wife upon their marriage. The bride price is a gift given by the groom or his family to the bride's family during the wedding ceremony.

The dowry system was common in communities where women were not heavily involved in farming, as previous research suggests that social norms evolved in cultures based on their agricultural practices. Anecdotal evidence suggests a pro-male bias in the research on the dowry system's consequences on women's wellbeing. Parents in India sometimes cite the expectation of a dowry as a major factor in their preference for sons over daughters. The practice of dowry discourages investments in human capital and, tragically, can result in the violent or even murder of newlywed women who are the intended targets of the groom's vengeance for what he perceives as an inadequate dowry.

The cultural practice of bride price is examined by (Bau et al., 2015) to determine its impact on the efficacy of education-related programs. The authors look at how the Sekolah Dasar Inpres program, which built 61,807 primary schools in Indonesia between 1974 and 1980, affected the education of girls.

6.4.4 Other Characteristics Pre-Industrial Society

Using this second methodology, (Alesina, Alberto, Benedetta Brioschi, 2016) analyse the impact of pre-industrial cultural features on violence against women by analysing large amounts of data from Africa. Their goal is to find out what causes domestic violence in the long run by comparing modern-day African data on individuals with pre-industrial characteristics taken from Murdock's Ethnographic Atlas. Cultural ideas that persist today, regardless of whether the initial circumstances that created them have changed or disappeared, are influenced by ancestral features that set distinct economic duties for women, the authors find. Women are held in higher esteem and there is less violence against them in communities where they are actively involved in subsistence activities.

The inverse is true in agrarian communities and those that depend on fishing or hunting for subsistence; women in these societies have less leverage in negotiations since they don't contribute financially to the household. This has led to an increase in the number of reported cases of violence against women in these nations. Concerning the impact of various types of settlement, the writers find that women whose forebears lived in nomadic and isolated communities are more likely to be victims of violence and to rationalise it. Less likely to rationalise abuse of their spouses are males whose ancestors lived in heavily populated areas.

6.5 Historical Differences in Family Structures

Throughout history, gender roles have been shaped by family structure and other societal factors. Previous research has shown that family patterns have remained relatively unchanged from the Middle Ages to the modern day, and that different types of families have different economic outcomes, including gender roles. One factor that contributes to strong family ties in certain cultures is the unequal division of labour between the sexes, which is often described as the "Male-Breadwinner Hypothesis." In this model, men work full-time while women take care of the home.

On the flip side, gender norms that are more egalitarian in which men and women do domestic and paid work equally will flourish in societies where family ties are weak. By combining three questions from the World Values Survey about the importance of family in people's lives, about the responsibilities of parents and children, and about the importance of loving and respecting one's parents we can measure the strength of family ties. We use this composite statistic to look at how family ties affect things like household output and women's participation in the labour force. Studies show that societies whose family ties are strong have lower rates of female labour force involvement and greater rates of domestic production, with women doing the majority of the work. They are more likely to follow traditional gender norms.

6.6 Religion

The impact of religious beliefs on people's views of economics has been the subject of discussion since Max Weber. Religion has a major impact on how people view gender roles. Previous studies have used World Values Survey data collected from individuals to investigate the relevance of religion. Those who are devout and take part in church activities show less compassion for women's rights, and this effect is twice as strong among Muslims as it is among people of other religions. Researchers have looked at how religion affects gender roles and found that Protestants and atheists are less likely to follow the traditional male breadwinner model than Orthodox Christians, Catholics, and Muslims. One book looks at the Protestant Reformation and how it affected gender inequality, while the other looks at missionary work in Africa and how it affected gender inequities throughout history.

6.7 Historical Natural Experiments

The position of women in a culture might change due to events that occur in the past. As a result, these shocks have the potential to change the prevailing views about women's intrinsic social roles. A temporary shock might affect gender outcomes in the long run if new perspectives on women's duties stick around and are passed down through the generations. (Teso, 2019) delves into the demographic turmoil that erupted in Africa from the fifteenth to the nineteenth centuries as a result of the transatlantic slave trade. Since plantation owners in the New World preferred male slaves due to their physical strength, the number of male slaves exceeded that of females. This led to an imbalance in the sex ratio in the places from which slaves were taken: in the most devastated regions, historical estimates put the number of men at 40–50 per 100 women. Women were pushed into traditionally male-dominated fields as a result of this demographic shift.

7. COPING STRATEGIES AND DIGITAL WELL-BEING

Smartwatches and voice-activated home assistants are just two examples of the new technological products that have completely absorbed us in a multi-device world(Rofarello et al., 2021). According to a recent Google consumer study, in 2017, most people across different parts of the world had numerous devices. User multitasking is common, according to a recent Google survey; for instance, 21% of people who possess multiple devices said they use a secondary device, like a phone, while using a laptop. Unfortunately, multi-device usage has only been studied in studies that are not directly related to digital wellbeing, even though there is a growing emphasis on improving people's interactions with technology.

In their study, (Holz et al., 2015) looked at how people used their phones while watching TV. Problems in testing and simulating numerous devices are only one of several roadblocks to creating useful and user-friendly multi-device experiences. The question of how to generate meaningful and productive interactions across devices remains unanswered, despite people's desire to make full use of their devices. And whether it's a social network or a single device like a smartphone, the existing literature on digital wellness settings only looks at one "Technological Source" at a time (Churchill & Nichols, 2016). In addition, while there are DSCTs that are designed to work with a lot of devices, their main purpose is to act as "Statistical Viewers" for each device, and they can sometimes make users feel bad by showing them statistics like screen time (Rooksby et al., 2016).

One technical aspect commonly linked to digital well-being is alerts, and there have been cases when multi-device scenarios and cross-device interactions have been handled. Although notifications are meant to keep users informed about important messages and events, they have the potential to hinder performance, interrupt ongoing work, cause anxiety, and annoyance(Shirazi, 2015).

Although many people who use more than one device prefer to get notifications on their phones, studies show that how important a notice seems could depend on the device it's received on (Weber et al., 2016). Several strategies have been proposed in the past to improve the notification experience for users, such as predictive algorithms to reduce interruptions and ways to communicate users' unavailability. When people use a number of different mobile or wearable gadgets, developed Attelia II, a system that can detect when people reach certain thresholds and then send them notifications. A semantic-aware system for sending notifications to different devices according to users' choices and circumstances was created and implemented by (Roffarello, 2018) and named Aware Notifications.

8. EMOTIONAL LABOUR IN SHARING ECONOMY

Consumers' views on access have shifted, and technological advancements have made it easier to participate in what is known as the "Sharing Economy." The concept of the sharing economy has expanded to include many different types of transactions (Codagnone, 2016). Research on the sharing economy has focused on many important areas, such as explaining its concepts, labour concerns, trust dynamics, "Algorithmic" governance, consumer analysis, marketing, and the reasons people share. Research on EL in the sharing economy is limited, with most research focusing on ride-hailing or home-sharing models.

Several instances of providers possibly engaging in EL were highlighted in the Uber driver survey conducted by (Raval & Dourish, 2016). According to the authors, taking part in the sharing economy calls for a mix of empathy and positive involvement, as well as the ability to vent unpleasant emotions and build social capital. According to studies on algorithmic labour conducted by (Rosenblat & Stark, 2016), drivers for Uber are forced to use emotional labour, which involves making friendly small talk, maintaining eye contact, and generally acting in a way that determines whether a customer would prefer to be alone or entertained.

According to (Rogers, 2016), who was the first to point out that both drivers and passengers engage in emotional labour in the peer-to-peer sharing transaction, the rating system of Uber requires this labour(Bucher et al., 2016a). Consumers in the sharing economy, which includes both home-sharing and ride-hailing platforms, participate in EL during sharing interactions, according to (Newlands & Lutz, 2018), but they find the pressure to act in a socially desirable way to be annoying and oppressive.

The lack of direct control over users' thoughts, feelings, and actions is a problem for sharing platforms that are predicated on service experiences co-created by independent actors. The methods of control that platforms possess for managing time, participation, selection, and intensity have been the subject of an increasing amount of research(Bucher et al., 2016b). The regulatory constraints, however, hinder direct control. One way in which providers are classified is as "Consumers" of the matching services offered by the platform, or as independent contractors.

9. CONCLUSION

Understanding how to utilise SM effectively is becoming more important in today's digital world. It affects how promote themselves, people interact, and maintain relationships online. There are benefits to having meaningful relationships and advancing one's profession, but there are also challenges that might impact one's mental health and authenticity. Enhancing healthier online environments necessitates a comprehensive grasp of how EL operates in digital contexts. Individuals and companies can help create a fairer and more sustainable digital ecosystem by promoting responsible platform design and engaging in aware behaviours.

REFERENCES

Alesina, A., Brioschi, B., & La Ferrara, E. (2016). *Violence against women: A cross-cultural analysis for Africa* (No. w21901). National Bureau of Economic Research.

Arcy, J. (2016). Emotion work : Considering gender in digital labor. *Feminist Media Studies, 0777*(February), 365–368. Advance online publication. DOI: 10.1080/14680777.2016.1138609

Bau, N., Nunn, N., & Voena, A. (2016). *Can Policy Crowd Out Culture?* Bride Price and Female Education.

Bucher, E., Fieseler, C., & Lutz, C. (2016a). Computers in Human Behavior What ' s mine is yours (for a nominal fee) - Exploring the spectrum of utilitarian to altruistic motives for Internet-mediated sharing. *Computers in Human Behavior, 62*, 316–326. DOI: 10.1016/j.chb.2016.04.002

Bucher, E., Fieseler, C., Lutz, C., & Newlands, G. (2016b). Shaping emotional labor practices in the sharing. In I. Maurer, J. Mair, A. Oberg (eds). *Theorizing the Sharing Economy: Variety and Trajectories of New Forms of Organizing* (pp. 55–82). DOI: 10.1108/S0733-558X20200000066004

Cheshin, A., Glikson, E., Lavee, E., Gabriel, A. S., Cheshin, A., Glikson, E., Lavee, E., & Gabriel, A. S. (2025). Journal of Applied Psychology Digital Emotional Labor : Bene fi ts and Challenges of Emotional Labor in the Context of Text-Based Service. *The Journal of Applied Psychology*.

Cho, H., Li, P., Ngien, A., Grace, M., & Chen, A. (2020). The bright and dark sides of social media use during COVID-19 lockdown: Contrasting social media effects through social liability vs. social support. *The Bright and Dark Sides of Social Media Use during* [*Lockdown: Contrasting Social Media Effects through Social Liability vs. Social Support, January*.]. *COVID*, •••, 19.

Churchill, E. F., & Nichols, J. (2016). Understanding the Challenges of Designing and Developing Multi-Device Experiences. *Proceedings of the 2016 ACM Conference on Designing Interactive Systems.*, 62–72.

Codagnone, C. (2016). *The Passions and the Interests : Unpacking the ' Sharing E conomy .'* DOI: 10.2791/474555

Dean, L., Churchill, B., Ruppanner, L., Churchill, B., & Ruppanner, L. (2022). The mental load : building a deeper theoretical understanding of how cognitive and emotional labor over load women and mothers. *The Mental Load : Building a Deeper Theoretical Understanding of How Cognitive and Emotional Labor over Load Women and Mothers*. DOI: 10.1080/13668803.2021.2002813

Döveling, K., Harju, A. A., & Sommer, D. (2018). From Mediatized Emotion to Digital Affect Cultures : New Technologies and Global Flows of Emotion. *Social Media + Society, 4*(1), 2056305117743141. Advance online publication. DOI: 10.1177/2056305117743141

Evren. (2025). A Critical Examination of Emotional Labour and Emotional Capital in Social Media Interaction. *AM Journal of Art and Media Studies, 4*(37), 57–73.

Examination, A. C. (2025). A Critical Examination of Emotional Labour and Emotional Capital in Social Media Interaction. *A Critical Examination of Emotional Labour and Emotional Capital in Social Media Interaction, 4*(37), 57–73.

Galor, O., & Sarid, A. (2017). *Geographical Origins and Economic Consequences of Language Structures*. Available. DOI: 10.2139/ssrn.2820889

Garcia, D., & Rimé, B. (2019). Collective Emotions and Social Resilience in the Digital Traces After a Terrorist Attack. *Psychological Science, 1993*(4), 617–628. Advance online publication. DOI: 10.1177/0956797619831964 PMID: 30865565

Giuliano, P. (2017). *Gender and Cultural Perspectives*. Gender and Cultural Perspectives.

Goldenberg, A., Garcia, D., Halperin, E., Gross, J. J., Goldenberg, A., Garcia, D., & Halperin, E. (2020). Collective emotions. *Current Directions in Psychological Science, 29*(2), 154–160. DOI: 10.1177/0963721420901574

Gottlieb, J., & Robinson, A. L. (2016). The Effects of Matrilineality on Gender Differences in Political Behavior across Africa. *The Effects of Matrilineality on Gender Differences in Political Behavior across. Africa.*

Gross, J. J. (2015). Emotion Regulation : Current Status and Future Prospects. *Psychological Inquiry, 26*(1), 1–26. DOI: 10.1080/1047840X.2014.940781

Holz, C., Bentley, F., Church, K., & Patel, M. (2015). " I ' m just on my phone and they ' re watching TV ": Quantifying mobile device use while watching television. *Proceedings of the ACM International Conference on Interactive Experiences for TV and Online Video.*, 93–102. DOI: 10.1145/2745197.2745210

Humphrey, R. H. (2019). The bright side of emotional labor : The Bright Side of Emotional Labor. *The Bright Side of Emotional Labor : The Bright Side of Emotional Labor, September 2015*. DOI: 10.1002/job.2019

In, A., & Barros, L. (2025). Emotional Labor in Pediatric Palliative Care : A Scoping Review. *Nursing Reports*, **•••**, 1–22. PMID: 40333038

Jaikla, P., & Piyakun, A. (2025). Teachers ' Emotional Labor : A Systematic Review. *Journal of Education and Learning*, *2000*(2), 159–171. DOI: 10.5539/jel.v14n2p159

Jayachandran, S. (2015). The roots of gender inequality in developing countries. *Annual Review of Economics*, *7*(1), 63–88. Advance online publication. DOI: 10.1146/annurev-economics-080614-115404

Jeung, D., Kim, C., & Chang, S. (2018). Emotional Labor and Burnout : A Review of the Literature. *Emotional Labor and Burnout : A Review of the Literature, 59*(2), 187–193.

Lowes, S. (2016). Kinship systems, gender norms, and household bargaining: Evidence from the matrilineal belt. *JEL Classification, January*.

Lv, F. (2025). Impact of effort-reward imbalance, emotional labour, and nurse-patient relationship on physical and mental health of registered nurses in China : A structural equation modeling. *Impact of Effort-Reward Imbalance, Emotional Labour, and Nurse-Patient Relationship on Physical and Mental Health of Registered Nurses in China. Structural Equation Modeling*. PMID: 40369545

Maria, C., Carvalho, S., Carolina, A., & Graça, G. (2025). Does professional identity mediate the relationship between emotional labour and work engagement? A study with Portuguese police of fi cers. *International Journal of Police Science & Management*, *27*(1), 113–126. DOI: 10.1177/14613557241292959

Newlands, G., Lutz, C., & Fieseler, C. (2018). Collective action and provider classification in the sharing economy. *New Technology, Work and Employment*, *33*(3), 1–18. DOI: 10.1111/ntwe.12119

Orben, A., Meier, A., Dalgleish, T., & Blakemore, S. (2024). *Mechanisms linking social media use to adolescent mental health vulnerability*. Mechanisms Linking Social Media Use to Adolescent Mental Health Vulnerability. DOI: 10.1038/s44159-024-00307-y

Paul, S., Pruessner, L., Strakosch, A., Miano, A., Schulze, K., Barnow, S., Paul, S., Pruessner, L., Strakosch, A., Miano, A., Schulze, K., & Barnow, S. (2023). *Emotion Social Contexts Examining the Strategy-Situation Fit of Emotion Regulation in Everyday Social Contexts*. Emotions.

Peng, L., Wang, J., & Zheng, N. (2024). Traversing Emotional Spaces : Social Media Affordances and Emotion Regulation in Times of Physical Isolation. *Traversing Emotional Spaces : Social Media Affordances and Emotion Regulation in Times of Physical Isolation*. DOI: 10.1177/20563051241237273

Porter, J., Spence, K., & Porter, J. (2025). Navigating gendered display rules : Women coaches practicing gender through emotional labour. *Sports Coaching Review*, *00*(00), 1–13. DOI: 10.1080/21640629.2025.2496864

Quinn, C., Hillman, A., Barbosa, A., & Toms, G. (2026). Emotional Labor in Dementia Research. *Qualitative Health Research*, *36*(4-5), 319–332. DOI: 10.1177/10497323241274709 PMID: 39417805

Raval, N., & Dourish, P. (2016). Standing Out from the Crowd : Emotional Labor, Body Labor, and Temporal Labor in Ridesharing. *Proceedings of the 19th ACM Conference on Computer-Supported Cooperative Work & Social Computing.*, 97–107. DOI: 10.1145/2818048.2820026

Roemmich, K. (2023). Emotion AI at Work : Implications for Workplace Surveillance, Emotional Labor, and Emotional Privacy. In *CHI '23: ACM Conference on Human Factors in Computing Systems, April 23â•fi28, 2023,Hamburg, Germany* (Vol. 1, Issue 1). Association for Computing Machinery. DOI: 10.1145/3544548.3580950

Rofarello, A. M., Torino, P., Russis, L. De, & Torino, P. (2021). Coping with Digital Wellbeing in a Multi-Device World. *Coping with Digital Wellbeing in a Multi-Device World.*

Roffarello, M. (2018). AwareNotifications : Multi-Device Semantic Notification Handling with User-Defined Preferences. *Journal of Ambient Intelligence and Smart Environments*, *10*(December), 327–343. Advance online publication. DOI: 10.3233/AIS-180492

Rogers, B. (2016). Employment Rights in the Platform Economy : Getting Back to Basics. *Employment Rights in the Platform Economy : Getting Back to Basics.*

Rooksby, J., Asadzadeh, P., Rost, M., Morrison, A., & Chalmers, M. (2016). Personal Tracking of Screen T ime on Digital Devices. *Proceedings of the 2016 CHI Conference on Human Factors in Computing Systems.* DOI: 10.1145/2858036.2858055

Rosenblat, A., & Stark, L. (2016). Algorithmic Labor and Information Asymmetries : A Case Study of Uber ' s Drivers. *International Journal of Communication*, *10*, 3758–3784.

Salehi, M., Ghasemian, A., Najar, A. V., Nazari, H., & Hooshmand, E. (2025). From compassion to burnout : Emotional labor in oncology nursing — a qualitative study. *BMC Nursing*, *24*(1), 272. DOI: 10.1186/s12912-025-02928-x PMID: 40069779

Shirazi, A. S. (2015). Assessment of Notifications on Smartwatches. *Proceedings of the 17th International Conference on Human-Computer Interaction with Mobile Devices and Services*, 1111–1116. DOI: 10.1145/2786567.2794338

Smith, K., Sheridan, L., Duursma, E., Alonzo, D., Smith, K., Sheridan, L., Duursma, E., Alonzo, D., Smith, K., Sheridan, L., Duursma, E., & Alonzo, D. (2025). theory and practice Teachers ' emotional labour : The joys, demands, and constraints constraints. *Teachers and Teaching*, *31*(8), 1411–1435. DOI: 10.1080/13540602.2025.2466560

Teso. (2019). THE LONG-TERM EFFECT OF DEMOGRAPHIC SHOCKS ON THE EVOLUTION OF GENDER Author (s): Edoardo Teso THE LONG-TERM EFFECT OF DEMOGRAPHIC SHOCKS ON THE EVOLUTION OF GENDER ROLES : EVIDENCE FROM THE. *Journal of the European Economic Association*, *17*(2), 497–534. DOI: 10.1093/jeea/jvy010

Weber, D., Voit, A., Kratzer, P., & Henze, N. (2016). In-Situ Investigation of Notifications in Multi-Device Environments. *Proceedings of the 2016 ACM International Joint Conference on Pervasive and Ubiquitous Computing.*, 1259–1264. DOI: 10.1145/2971648.2971732

Wharton, A. S. (2009). The Sociology of Emotional Labor. *The Sociology of Emotional Labor*. DOI: 10.1146/annurev-soc-070308-115944

Wolfers, L. N., & Schneider, F. M. (2021). Using Media for Coping : A Scoping Review. *Communication Research*, *30–32*(8), 1210–1234. Advance online publication. DOI: 10.1177/0093650220939778

Yao, L., Gao, J., Zhang, Y., & Zhang, H. (2024). Micro-breaks in focus : Mitigating emotional labour impact in the hospitality industry from a conservation of resources perspective. *Anatolia*, *00*(00), 1–15. DOI: 10.1080/13032917.2024.2363813

Chapter 16
Finding a Balance Between Being Connected and Well-Being:
Overcoming Emotional Fatigue and Social Detachment in the Virtual World

Ankita Nayak
http://orcid.org/0000-0002-9311-890X
Trident Academy of Technology, India

Ipseeta Satpathy
http://orcid.org/0000-0002-0155-5548
KIIT (Deemed to be) University, Bhubaneswar, India

Vishal Jain
http://orcid.org/0000-0003-1126-7424
School of Engineering & Technology, Vivekananda Institute of Professional Studies-Technical Campus, New Delhi, India

ABSTRACT

The essay discusses the rising likelihood of emotional burnout and social isolation resulting from the digital revolution, which transforms human interactions, work, and socializing. It explores the negative implications of prolonged engagement with social media and virtual communication on mental health and social cohesion, supported by recent psychological and human-computer interaction research. The paper proposes strategies to mitigate digital fatigue, including digital detox and mindful technology use, while also addressing the role of workplace and education-

DOI: 10.4018/979-8-3373-8307-1.ch016

al initiatives in maintaining social connections. It advocates for a comprehensive approach to promote well-being that harmonizes the benefits of digital connectivity with emotionally healthy practices and sustainable social engagement, highlighting the need for supportive digital experiences that foster both connection and health.

INTRODUCTION

The digital revolution has been among the most radical modifications in the history of humans that have changed how individuals interact, work, learn, and create social realities. Ever since the beginning of digitisation with the simplest forms of computerisation and email correspondence, the digital environment has been an advanced form of virtual networks which operate on the internet, mobile technology, cloud computing, AI, and virtual worlds. These ecologies are no longer effective tools, but they serve as social places where identities are created, bonds are maintained, and feelings are manifested. Web 2.0 ensured that there was a participatory culture because not just the audience is consumed by the content but also participates by creating, sharing and communicating in real time. This shift upset the division between the physical and digital worlds that makes the online spaces part and parcel of life and not an addition. These virtual ecosystems today, with the course of time, expand to social networking systems, collaborative labour systems, online learning systems, and online digital markets, and content systems based on recommendations, which continue to characterize user behaviour and attention (Palmie et al., 2022). The intense pace of technological change has merely enhanced the digital immersion creating a sense of constant connectivity where individuals are accessible, perceivable and attentive. Despite these advancements having brought ease in information, opportunities and world networks, it has also brought with it some new complications in the form of cognitive overload; emotional labour and expectations in social expectations. Digital revolution has thus surpassed the technology factor and become a socio-psychological phenomenon, and it has altered how individuals believe in time and presence and productivity and social value. As virtual ecosystems become more sophisticated and ubiquitous, it is urgent to know the long-range human consequences of such a phenomenon, and particularly we refer to emotional well-being and social connectedness. The development of the online environment, thus, preconditions the exploration of the opportunities available as well as issues, that appear in the modern virtual existence (Beshley et al., 2024).Due to the growth of social media, remote work, and socialisation via the internet, the form and experience of human interaction has changed considerably. The social media sites have changed the way people communicate in the sense that they allow instant communication of thoughts, pictures, and feelings without limitations by geographical boundaries, which create the feeling of being globally connected. These sites have come to the heart of personal identity expression, social validation and community building especially among the younger generations. At the same time, the emergence of remote work that has been accelerated by technological progress and other disruptions in the world like the COVID 19 pandemic have changed the nature of professional engagement. Online project management systems, online collaborative digital devices and virtual meetings have substituted the physical office set-up, providing convenience and flexibility, as well as blurring the line between work and personal life (Cimperman,2023). Virtual communities and immersive environments have also increased online socialisation where people can sustain relationships even though there is a physical distance separation. Nonetheless, this growth has changed social norms where depth has been replaced by frequency and presence by the availability. Social bonds previously founded on the physical cues and emotional touch are becoming increasingly meditated by the screens, emojis, and algorithms. Although digital medium enables to reach large numbers of people, it is prone to the aspect of speed, visibility, performance, as opposed to authenticity and appeal to emotions. The need to stay socially and professionally active on the internet may result in sustained communication without sufficient psychological rest. With the cross of social media, remote working and online socialisation, people are experiencing a situation where they are performing two or more roles in the same virtual space, which increases the emotional pressure. This growth has therefore restructured the way individuals interact not only with each other, but also a sense of belonging, intimacy and social responsibility in a digitally mediated world (Addeo et al., 2022).This has resulted in emotional exhaustion and social isolation being of major concern when considering a prolonged digital interaction. Emotional fatigue is condition of mental fatigue caused by the long-term emotional loads, constant excitation, and constant interpersonal communication in the virtual environment. In the virtual world, people tend to handle emotions, introduce edited personas, be empathetic and stay socially present, all of which are part of emotional labour. In the course of time, it may result in emotional numbness and irritability as well as loss of empathy. The irony is that social detachment is a phenomenon that accompanies hyper-connectivity in the form of loneliness, disconnection and shallow interaction despite the constant online communication (Lampert et al., 2019). Lack of physical presence, non-verbal communication, and shared embodied experiences may make emotional connection weaker, as well as make the feeling of being truly belonging weaker. Algorithms can also promote the development of the echo chambers and transactional relationships through the self, restricting the possibility of meaningful social exchange. With people replacing face-to-face communication with digital communication more, chances of having a profound, emotionally full life could decrease. They are particularly severe among professionals, students, and populations which are digitally addicted and spend hours over the Internet. Social alienation and the emotional burnout is then not a failure on persons, but a structural effect of the digitally saturated spaces. The way to solve these issues is by applying a subtle insight into the role of digital structures on emotional responses and social relations, thus supporting the rationale behind a deliberate approach towards promoting well-being in online environments (Schulz et al., 2021).Virtual environments are digitally mediated spaces that are created to allow interaction, communication, and experience, that are not limited by physical restrictions. These spaces are simple websites and mobile applications on the one side, and complex, interactive systems (views of virtual reality (VR), augmented reality (AR), and mixed reality) on the other. In contrast to other conventional digital tools that are meant to facilitate task accomplishment, virtual spaces have been turning out, more and more, to be social, cultural, and emotional spaces in which users are meant to be performing identities, building relationships, and creating meaning collectively. Digital ecosystems, in their turn, are the larger, connected systems of platforms, hardware, people, data streams, and algorithms, which maintain and determine virtual spaces. They are dynamic systems where the interaction between the technological infrastructures, the human behaviours and the institutional logics is an ongoing process (Barykin et al., 2020).In such ecosystems, users are no longer the passive consumers of content but active creators of data that once again affects the way the platforms will be designed and how users experience them. The digital ecosystem is interdependent in nature, and it is scalable and adaptive, thereby allowing the various platforms to interact and overlap in the lives of users. One may, as an example, be simultaneously on the social media, professional collaboration tool and entertainment site and this may be stacked with one more virtual life. The convergence eliminates the barriers between personal, professional and social worlds, and the virtual worlds become the extension and constituent of the everyday life. Notably, it focuses on the invisible algorithms, which sort and regulate content, attention and influence emotions that dominate digital ecosystems. These ecosystems are evolving to be increasingly mediators of not only communication, but also cognition, social norms and emotional regulation as well. The idea of virtual environments as the part of larger digital ecosystems is essential to the research of the transformative impacts of long-term utilization of digital settings on human behaviour, human relations, and well-being throughout the digital age (Burstrom et al., 2022). The digital platforms are varied in terms of intent, form, power, but when combined, result in enduring virtual immersion. The social media platforms (Facebook, Instagram, X, and LinkedIn) are targeted at communication, self-expression, and content sharing, typically with the help of engagement-optimising algorithms. These platforms encourage interaction because they can draw continuous actions through the notifications and likes and feedback features that make it more visible and socially approved. Professional networks and digital work environments such as email systems, virtual meeting environments, project management software, and collaborative work-spaces facilitate productivity and organisational coordination and project work into digital environments. Remote and hybrid work have increased the usage of these platforms, and now digital presence is equated to professional dedication and output (Duzbayev et al., 2023). Virtual reality, augmented reality, and metaverse environments are another development in immersive technologies, which provide experiences with the features of sensory richness that mimic or expand physical reality. These technologies provide experiential learning, virtual cooperation, playing games, and interpersonal communication in extremely engaging forms. Despite the fact that each of the types of platforms serves a specific purpose, their combination elevates the degree of engagement with the digital experience by adding the social, professional, and experience to the continuum of the digital interactions. The transition between professional and social communication and entertainment is usually unintended across platforms; one can claim that a user is likely to navigate within the same digital environment and remain there. This convergence becomes an addition to cognitive tasks and emotional engagement as individuals are forced to develop social norms, expectations, and roles regularly. This multiplicity of platforms consequently does not only lead to effective functionality and connectivity, but effective and enduring psychological involvement that might make it feasible to blur work, leisure and identity. The diverse character of digital platforms is important to realise when evaluating the ways in which all types of virtual interactions influence emotional well-being and social behaviour (Lampropoulos et al., 2021). Constant connectivity is a pervasive connectivity in the sense that it is constantly accessible and connected by digital devices and platforms due to smart phones, high speed internet and the extensive presence of digital infrastructure. This state of being results in the formation of the so-called always-on culture, which is defined by the assumptions of immediate responsiveness, being available at all times, and constant involvement in online communication. Constant connectivity in the workplace is expressed through the form of long working hours, the need to maintain real-time communication, and the loss of separation between work and life. Socially, it is a long-term use of social media, messaging application and internet communities, where the lack of response or communication can be seen as lack of interest or own rejection(Mdhluli, 2025). This culture transforms time expectations, condensing time and developing a sense of urgency which discourages the act of taking a break and reflecting. The design of the platform serves as instruments like notifications, live updates and algorithm feeds, which uphold the culture of always-on and the focus on novelty and immediacy. On the one hand, it is always convenient, flexible and information is easily available, on the other hand, it imposes psychological impact on necessity to be visible and responsive. Loss of connection may cause individuals to feel guilty or anxious and this will lead to the compulsive checking behaviour, as well as the reduced capacity to concentrate at a depth level. The failure to detach, in the long run, can be devastating to the boundaries required to revive emotionally and be healthy. Being on culture hence is the aspect of digital life that is structural and which renders being off as abnormal compared to healing. This shift in culture can be defined as the main clue to understanding the way the digital immersion can be preserved and strengthened to promote emotional fatigue and social burnout (Cunneen et al., 2019). These social and psychological effects of long-term exposure to the virtual world extend far beyond the time spent in front of the screen and affect emotional self-control and identity and have an implication on social interactions. At the psychological level, continuous utilization of digital means can lead to cognitive overload, attentional fragmentation and emotional exhaustion as the subjects sift through the streams of information and social stimuli.Motivation intrinsic to performance, responding, and staying socially relevant on social media may increase anxiety and decrease intrinsic motivation. At the emotional level, virtual immersion can include dealing with mediated identities and emotional displays, which lead to emotional labour and exhaustion. In social aspects, when it comes to long-term immersion, the quality of relationships can change, with the frequency of interaction becoming more important than the depth of it and the possibility of embodied, face-to-face interactions (Frost et al., 2022). Although digital platforms allow connecting despite the distance, they can also promote shallow interactions and a lack of empathy as there is no non-verbally expressed information, and no one is together in the same space. In the long run, people might feel alienated or lonely even though they have interacted a lot on the internet. Also, social experience mediation can strengthen echo chambers and exposure to different views, which impacts social cohesion. The long-term virtual immersion can also transform the social norms by redefining the notions of availability, intimacy, and belonging digitally, prioritising digital presence over emotional authenticity. All these psychological and social consequences indicate the importance of studying with a critical mind the frequency of signs that people resort to virtual environments, as well as its effects on emotional health and social bonding in the long term (Oh et al., 2019).

INVISIBLE EXHAUSTION: VIRTUAL WORKPLACE EMOTIONAL LABOR AND BURNOUT

Emotional fatigue is defined as a condition of mental exhaustion due to the chronicity of the emotionally challenging experience, during which the ability of a person to empathize, control his/her emotions, and answer productively is weakened. The emotional fatigue in digital spaces is a phenomenon that is becoming more and more of a side effect of continuous virtual interaction, constant social exchange, and ongoing emotional responsiveness via the screen. In contrast to the short-term exhaustion, emotional fatigue is accumulated over time and is expressed in the form of a constant feeling of emotional numbness, detachment, or irritability. Burnout, though similar, is a more chronic and multidimensional phenomenon, which is described as emotional exhaustion, depersonalisation, and diminished personal accomplishment. In the digital world, burnout is common when emotional burnout is not managed, and it gets integrated into daily life (Prasetyo et al., 2025). Virtual emotional fatigue can be viewed on various dimensions. The emotional aspect entails exhaustion caused by the constant emotional expression, empathy, and social interaction on the internet. The cognitive dimension indicates mind overload because of the incessant information processing, making decisions, and platform-switching. The behavioural aspect comprises withdrawal, diminished interaction, and evading dealing with the digital aspect. The social aspect includes disrupted social relations, less empathy, and the lack of social presence, even in cases of high online usage. Digital burnout increases these dimensions by instilling emotional stress into the structural demands of unending availability, responsiveness, and output. These experiences are further enhanced by the fact that, in case of virtual environments, there are no clear distinctions between work, social life, and personal space. Notably, emotional exhaustion and burnout in the digital world are partial as well as structural effects of digitally replete ecosystems that naturalise continuous interaction. By theorising emotional fatigue as a multidimensional construct, it is possible to gain a better insight on how digital spaces contribute to emotional well-being and the necessity of individual and institutional-level interventions to reduce the impact of emotional fatigue (Supriyadi et al., 2025).Emotional fatigue, technostress, and digital exhaustion are similar but different constructs that describe different manifestations of strain in the digital world since they are commonly used interchangeably. The primary aspect of emotional fatigue is associated with the exhaustion of emotional resources that occur as the result of continued emotional involvement, empathy and affective labour. It is indicative of the diminished ability of an individual to experience, love or feel or react in an emotional manner and may lead to a state of being detached or emotionally numb. On the other hand, technostress can be described as stress caused by the application of technology itself, such as the challenges of learning new systems, the fear of being obsolete, the inability to turn off and the ability to stay connected at all times and the feeling of not having control over all the digital tools. Technostress can be based on the complexity of technology, swift change, and performance strain as opposed to being emotional, and digital exhaustion is a more comprehensive and inclusive circumstance that sums up the physical, mental, and emotional exhaustion caused by lengthy digital exposure (Corbeanu et al.,2023). It encompasses effects like eye strain, sleep disturbance, attentional fatigue, and mental exhaustion, as well as emotional drain. Whereas technostress is concerned with the stress reaction to the utilisation of technology, and digital exhaustion denotes exhaustion in general, emotional fatigue narrows down to the emotional impact of prolonged digital communication. Such constructs often go hand in hand in the virtual world and support each other. As an example, emotional fatigue can be enhanced by technostress due to unending notifications, which puts pressure on responding to others with empathy and promptly. Equally, digital exhaustion can decrease emotional resilience, and thus, people become more vulnerable to emotional exhaustion. These concepts should be separated to provide proper diagnosis, clarity of research, and focused intervention. Emotional stress can also be dealt with by the use of emotional regulation, empathy management, and boundary-setting strategies, whereas technostress can be solved by training, system redesign, and workload management. Digital exhaustion requires comprehensive responses to screen time, thinking, and rest. The explanation of these differences enhances conceptual accuracy and helps create the conceptually subtle responses to the digital strain(Bianchi et al., 2019). Digital burnout is an emotional burnout, which has a set of psychological, emotional, and behavioural signs that tend to evolve unobtrusively over time. On a personal level, patients with burnout can report being empty, irritable, emotionally numb, or having a lower empathy level. Tasks and communication, which previously seemed valuable to the individual, start to become exhausting or tedious. Burnout is also linked psychologically to a lack of motivation, a sense of achievement, and increased cynicism, especially of tasks and relationships mediated by digital means. Emotionally, behavioural effects of burnout may include withdrawal, laggardness to messages, lack of participation in virtual meetings, or a low level of involvement in online communities (Bocheliuk et al., 2020). People can interact superficially and dissociate on an emotional level, which is common, especially in virtual worlds of work and education. Other symptoms encompass the compulsive disengagement behaviour, e.g., too much scrolling without effective interaction or the failure to focus and too much procrastination. Emotional burnout may also be accompanied by physical symptoms, such as fatigue, sleep disturbances, and headache, which is an indication of the inter-relation between the emotional and the physiological strain. Burnout in online contexts can be concealed by the presence in the virtual world, and thus, other people may not notice it. People might seem energetic and receptive at the same time, being emotionally drained internally. This invisibility may postpone identification and intervention, and burnout will continue. In the long-term, emotional burnout may destroy self-esteem, wreck relationships, and decrease overall well-being (Müller et al., 2023). The identification of behavioural indicators is therefore important in early detection and prevention. The concept of emotional burnout is not a failure but an indicator of ongoing emotional overload in the digital systems where one has to be constantly active and deliver emotional work (Voitenko et al., 2021).Anchored factors in virtual environments with respect to emotional fatigue and burnout entail information overload and emotional labour. The condition of receiving much more information than one can handle efficiently has been described as information overload, and it is augmented by constant notifications, the use of multiple platforms, and content feeds of mathematical algorithms. Emails, messages, updates, and media content flow continuously require continuous attention and quick thinking, which causes mental exhaustion and loss of emotional abilities. Emotional labour, which can be discussed as the preserve of service industries, has also been gaining traction in the virtual world where people are supposed to control their emotions, display optimality, and empathize throughout virtual communication. Emotional labour in social media space entails managing identities, reacting to feedback, and social visibility. In professional digital space, it encompasses the enthusiasm, professionalism and emotional regulation in the virtual meetings and communications(Arnold et al., 2023). In comparison to face-to-face interaction, virtual emotional labour is usually more thought-provoking and more emotionally demanding, since it does not offer the feedback on emotional state, as quickly as possible. Information overload coupled with emotional labour leads to a series of repeated stimulation and streams of emotion with no adequate rest. This cycle leads to exhaustion and withdrawal over the passage of time. The invisibility of emotional labour in online spaces makes the issue even more complicated, as people can experience the urge to provide emotional performance without any support or recognition. The insight on the importance of information overload and emotional labour provides a structuralist of emotional fatigue in the virtual environment and the necessity of changes in the design of platforms, organisational expectations and digital culture on a systemic level (Sheng et al., 2023).

CONNECTED AND DISCONNECTED: SOCIAL DETACHMENT AND DIGITAL WELL-BEING THEORIES

Social detachment of digital environments is a subjective experience of emotional isolation, loneliness, or estrangement, although online communication is often used. In contrast to clinical loneliness, which is marked by a persistent failure to establish meaningful social interactions, social detachment that is brought in by digitally mediated spaces is frequently paradoxical: people are enclosed by networks and relationships but continue to feel emotionally isolated. Perceived social isolation involves the personal experience of social detachment in an individual who might be socially disconnected even when he/she is measured to be socially connected via digital media. It is comprised of the perceived absence of meaningful intercourse, emotional support, and depth of relationship (Nguyen et al., 2024). Social detachment occurs when social interactions on the web are focused on superficial measures of interaction, such as likes, shares, comments, and not face-to-face bonds of interaction that define supportive relationships. In this respect, social alienation in cyber life is not just the absence of ties, but the deprivation of a relational content and a qualitative satisfaction of emotions. With more and more physical interactions with others being replaced by virtual form, people will complain of feeling invisible, unheard, or unsupported by others, even with all the connectivity available online. The embodied social presence changes to mediated interaction, which changes trust, empathy, and shared experience signals. Such mental changes can be minor, occurring, and they are usually not realised unless emotions come up. Importantly, perceived social isolation is not only determined by frequency of actual communication but also by expectation, subjective experiences, and contextual cues that users derive from virtual interaction(Nguyen et al., 2024). The connected yet alone paradox is a term that is used to refer to the co-occurrence of a high degree of digital connectedness and deep subjective loneliness or emotional emptiness. The virtual mediums are full of promise of universal connectivity, offering users the opportunity to engage in massive networks across time zones and geographic locations. However, studies are becoming more and more indicative of the fact that high rates of social media activity and digital interaction are associated with increased sense of isolation, poorer well-being, and reduced life satisfaction. This paradox is due to the fact that the amount of digital interaction does not imply the quality of interaction. To most of us, such brief interactions as superficial remarks, responses, and passive scrolling do not meet the more profound human urges to feel intimacy, affirmation, and an empathetic tune (Norman,2021). The design of online platforms is usually more inclined to breadth than depth: the algorithms focus more on volume, novelty, and measures of engagement, as opposed to long-term conversation and genuinely relational building. In such circumstances, hundreds or thousands of online friends and a set of a handful of people to stand by are possible which leads to the experience of social emptiness and objective connectivity via the digital. Moreover, the social comparison augmented by the edited self-presentations on social sites develops a feeling of incompetence or marginality which adds to the feeling of being out of place even though the communication is done frequently. The paradox of the loneliness connectedness is thus in the dissonance between the structural and emotional emptiness between the digital communication habits and the physical human relational needs. The paradox may be perceived by going beyond the idea of connectivity as a technical indicator to the experiences of users of their online relationships, which in the majority of the instances are to the disadvantage of face-to-face interaction (Zilka et al., 2021).The advent of online communication has changed the landscape of social interaction, which, in most instances, is not to the benefit of face-to-face interaction. Face to face communication is high in non-verbal communication, the existence of a physical body, and concurrent emotional delicacy-all of which contributes to building the trust, empathy, and depth in the relationship (Alheneidi et al., 2021). Digital substitutes are believed to be convenient and most of this embodied sense is lost and the contours of affect are leached out into text, pictures or little clips of video. The erosion of socializing face-to-face rites e.g. shared meals, spontaneous events and community participation has reduced the possibility of embodied relational strengthening. According to empirical research findings, individuals who spend more time in online contact report weaker ties that are weaker to their immediate groups and perceive less support and less sense of belonging. Virtual communication is likely to focus on performance, impression management, and identity curation rather than genuine vulnerability and emotional reciprocity. This may result in the exchange of transactional or superficial interactions as opposed to engaging in the emotional bonding that is lasting. Consequently, people can experience social exhaustion, emotional numbness, or a lack of interest in the digital and offline social worlds. The loss of face-to-face contact not only harms the well-being of each person but also impacts the social fabric, which in turn continues to add to the larger societal fragmentation and lack of collective empathy(Marinucci et al., 2022). Algorithms driven interaction can be described as personalised content feeds, recommendation engines and ranking systems based on engagement that inform the attention of users on digital platforms. Such systems give priority to content that will best increase engagement and in many cases, they increase emotionally charged or polarising content. Although this can boost the numbers of traffic and interaction, it can also increase the misleading effect on social experience by putting users in echo chambers, reinforcing their biases, and reducing the possibility of taking up another viewpoint empathetically. The experiences are filtered by algorithms to minimize the exposure to the world of different perspectives and restrict the possibility of meaningful relational reciprocity. The psychological consequences of this are far-reaching: empathy and belonging: users might experience their insatiateness to the larger social discourses and be better locked in to reduced emotional realities. Also increasing social comparison, algorithmic curation exposes the user to idealised views of the lives of other people, making them feel inadequate or excluded. In the long run, algorithm-based interactions can decrease social trust, lower the authenticity of emotions, and undermine the feelings of authentic belonging of users to social spaces. By doing so, algorithmic mediation is not only impacting what people see, but also how they feel, relate and connect with other people emotionally, making social detachment even more pronounced in highly connected spaces(Taylor et al., 2024).

THE PSYCHOLOGICAL COST OF VIRTUAL CONNECTIVITY: ANXIETY, FATIGUE AND RESILIENCE

The increased screen time has become one of the characteristics of the modern way of life, which is predetermined by the development of digital labour, distance learning, social media, and entertainment. Although digital technologies are convenient and more accessible, the prolonged use of screens has, over time, been associated with unfavourable mental health effects. Spending much time on the screen changes the daily routine, disturbs sleep patterns, and eliminates the chances to be physically active and interact with others in real life, which are essential factors in psychological well-being. Sleep disruption is one of the most common consequences of extended screen time, as the blue light exposure reduces the synthesis of melatonin and delays the circadian rhythm. Ineffective or lack of sleep, in its turn, is associated with higher degree of stress, irritability, vulnerability to situations of panic and symptoms of depression. The excessive screens used, as well as the physiological outcomes, lead to cognitive overload due to the treatment of a continuous stream of information, multitasking, and attentional change (Tang et al., 2021). This constant mental stimulation inhibits mental healing, which cultivates mental exhaustion and loss of mental clarity. Socially, the long screen time can substitute face-to-face communication with mediated communication, which will reduce emotional gratification and make a person feel lonely. The effect is not consistently the same in every form of screen use, with passive consumption of content, e.g., infinite scrolling, linked to poorer mental health outcomes than intentional or practical digital use. Significantly, the connection between screen time and mental health is not quantitative only but also qualitative, and is predetermined by the character, situation, and emotional requirements of digital communication. The psychological toll is exerted more when digital connection is not a choice but a necessity; i.e., when the work or educational process is remote. The long-term screen time is, therefore, a cumulative stressor that slowly destabilizes the emotional state, mental ability, and general state of mental well-being, which brings to the fore a necessity to engage in digital activities in moderation and mindfulness (Smith et al., 2020).There is a close linkage of virtual connectivity to various symptoms linked to psychological conditions such as anxiety, depression, emotional numbness and cognitive fatigue. The pressures of being available at any moment, being responsive, and experiencing the fear of missing out are the factors that tend to trigger anxiety, which is supported by digital platforms that are available in real time. Both notifications, messages, and algorithmic prompts generate a feeling of constant urgency, which does not allow the mind to become psychologically detached and increases stress levels. Depression, in its turn, has been associated with the over-social comparison, the lessening of the offline social support, and the sense of incompetence that are cultivated through curated online spaces. Emotional numbness is a more subtle but equally concerning consequence, characterized by a lack of emotional responsiveness and a loss of ability to experience pleasure or empathy (Lu et al., 2022). This numbness can be considered a defence mechanism against chronic emotional overstimulation and information overload. The other evident effect is cognitive fatigue due to the continuous attention demands, multi-tasking and constant access to discontinuous information. The cognitive fatigue may be defined by a statement of the inability to concentrate, loss of memories, and reduced problem-solving skills. These symptoms are even worse in virtual environments where work, social and recreation are even more difficult to separate and there is no opportunity to rest mentally. It is important to note that these psychological effects are not external to one another. Anxiety may result in cognitive fatigue and elevate emotional fatigue, as well as depressive symptoms. Such a cycle may ruin psychological strength and diminish individual and professional performance with time. The observed cumulative nature of these effects can help to emphasize that one should perceive virtual connectivity as an engine of productivity and communication and a very powerful contributor to emotional and cognitive stress when not restrained (Wang et al., 2022).Emotional regulation is the capability to control, process, and react to emotional events through adaptive means, and psychological resilience is the capability to bounce back after stress and be mentally steady during trouble. The long-term virtual connectivity has far-reaching consequences to the two processes. The digital world tends to exaggerate emotional triggers by accelerating the flow of information, providing emotional content, and providing unceasing social feedback, which puts long-term limitations on the regulatory functions of persons. Lack of natural breaks and contemplative areas decreases chances of emotional processing, making people more reactive and intolerant to stress. Negative emotions (frustration, anxiety, or disappointment) can eventually become uncontrollable by individuals, which leads to an impulsive response or emotional withdrawal. It also impacts psychological resilience because the continuous time spent on the digital level does not allow the person to get some rest to restore emotional balance (Troy et al., 2023). Individuals are always on the go, and as a result of this, stress does not have any chance to be restored, thereby undermining their adaptation strategies. Besides, in the digital platforms, validation is frequently externalised by likes, comments, and engagement indicators, so the emotional control becomes more reliant on external validation instead of inner coping mechanisms. This reliance is able to weaken the resilience by diminishing the autonomy and emotional self-efficacy of people. On the other hand, the emotional control and resilience-promoting role of intentional digital practices, which establish control and balance by recovering control and balance, has been demonstrated in terms of setting boundaries, mindful engagement, and scheduled disconnection. This realization of the influence of virtual connectivity on emotional regulation can suggest the need to develop digital spaces and practices that promote, as opposed to undermine, psychological resilience (Polizzi et al., 2021).The effect of digital fatigue is not the same on all people, but instead it is greater and more pronounced depending on the gender, age, and work conditions. Digital fatigue is associated with gender disparities that have been attributed to emotional labour differences and social expectations. An example of this is how women might be more emotionally drained by having more involvement in relational maintenance, caregiving, and affective communication within the work and social digital environment. Age also is one of the major factors, with younger people being more likely to have higher screen time and be susceptible to social comparison, anxiety, and emotional burnout, whereas older ones can develop technostress associated with the ability to adapt and digital capabilities (Dong et al., 2025). The occupational differences also contribute to the formation of digital fatigue, especially related to those occupations where a person is required to remain online continuously, to interact with others, and to think and experience emotions, i.e., education, health, corporate management, and knowledge work. Remote and hybrid work setups cause more work-related fatigue through prolonged working hours, screen addiction, and reduced boundaries between work and personal life. Long-term online education, lack of interpersonal communication, and increased mental burden pose special problems to students and teachers. These differences point to the fact that digital fatigue is relative and is determined by social roles, development stages, and work requirements. These differences are important to be aware of when developing the specific interventions, policies and support systems that help in meeting the diverse needs of the digitally immersed populations rather than placing them in the one-size-fits-all approach (Tapia-Caballero et al., 2022).

EMOTIONAL COSTS OF VIRTUAL ENGAGEMENT: INTERPERSONAL RELATIONS AND DIGITAL WORK CULTURES

The digital technologies have transformed the nature of the communicational patterns drastically in the sense that the patterns of communication have ceased to be face-to-face communication patterns, to be asynchronous and platform-dependent. The face-to-face communication was traditional (physical co-presence), non-verbal communication, and a common situational context, which helped to comprehend each other and approach each other emotionally. Digital communication, in turn, is much more focused on rapidity, briefness, and effectiveness, frequently condensing a complicated emotional expression into text, emojis, or brief audio-visual bits. Fragmented conversations, multi-tasking, and partial attention have become the norm due to the emergence of instant messaging, video conferencing, and social networking sites (De Falco, 2019). The nature of communication is becoming more and more disrupted, reactive, and multitasked, and this may potentially water down the content and personal touch of conversation. Moreover, algorithmic mediation affects a participant of the communication with whom, how frequently, and in what emotional key, slightly changing the nature of the interaction between people. On the one hand, the digital spaces allow connecting with the world beyond the spatial level, but on the other hand, they promote performative communication: people construct identities and messages to be seen and proven. This has changed the standards of courtesy, consideration, and emotional expression, which usually leaves the standards of responsiveness and connection unclear. With the move towards more transactional and efficiency-based forms of communication, there may be less room to engage in reflective conversation and emotional appeal. Thus, although online spaces are broadening the scope of communication, they are also questioning the quality, verisimilitude, and emotion of face-to-face communication (Sevignani et al., 2022).Among the most noticeable effects of the virtual interaction is the conflict between the surface level of interaction and the substantial level of connection. Likes, comments, and short messages available through digital platforms allow people to interact regularly, which gives the impression of social plenty. Such contacts are not always accompanied by sufficient layers of emotional attachment and sympathy. The emphasis of superficial interaction on visibility and responsiveness over vulnerability and emotional investment leads to interactions that are frequent but not very emotional. Not a redundant but meaningful connection, in turn, cannot occur immediately, requires attention, emotional openness, and give and take, which are absent in the hectic digital world (Heras-Saizarbitoria et al., 2022). The architecture of the social media platform stimulates the brief and emotional interaction rather than the thought-provoking or sympathetic dialogue. The individual may find himself having a huge number of friends online at the expense of the perceived intimacy and social support in the long run. Such incompatibility could cause loneliness, emotional dissatisfaction, and relational fatigue. Mediated self-presentation also makes meaningful connections even more problematic since individuals may fear to express true feelings or problems.. Digital interaction, therefore, may have an ironic effect of making people more socially active and less emotionally connected. It is vital to acknowledge this difference to comprehend the way virtual interaction redefines the quality of relationships and to come up with practices that enhance depth more than quantity in online relationships(Rachmad,2025). Relational depth is reliant on empathy and emotional expression, but their expression in virtual space is complicated and limited. The virtual empathy depends a lot on verbal expression and symbolic representations, i.e., emojis or reaction buttons, which might not be effective in expressing emotional subtext. Lack of physical contact and non-verbal communication restrains spontaneous emotional contact, and empathetic reactions become the more cognitively challenging. Although digital communication may facilitate emotional disclosure, even in a way that may even prompt people to be more open (because of the perceived anonymity), it may also result in misunderstanding and emotional detachment. The depth in relations involves long-term emotional involvement, trust and experience, that is hard to build up in the context of the incomplete or intermittent communication. Furthermore, unceasing exposure to emotional content of other people on the Internet may bring empathy fatigue, decreasing the ability of people to respond to expressive communication in a truly emotional way. Therefore, even though emotional exchange can be achieved in virtual spaces, they frequently fail to provide intimacy of depth and duration that can be sustained in relationships(Čekić,2025). Remote working and distance learning have radically transformed the professional, academic, and personal life limits. Digital mediation facilitates flexibility and makes work and learning personalized about temporal and psychological boundaries. The house becomes a space that is multifunctional and rest, productivity and social interaction are not differentiated. Such erosion of boundaries intensifies cognitive load and emotional stress as people cannot take off their work load or academic load. The lack of physical transition (commuting or classroom changes) means that there is a lack of mental restoration, which also leads to long-term stress and emotional burnout. In the long-term, this constant interaction leads to burnout, which is exhaustion, the lack of engagement, and demotivation (Johnson,2023). Digital presenteeism is defined as an unspoken rule that people have to be always available, responsive, and active on the virtual front. Emails, notifications, and messaging platforms strengthen the standards of responding directly, causing a lack of time to be unavailable. This anticipation makes emotional labour worse since one has to always control tone, responsiveness and professionalism. Digital presenteeism kills autonomy and recovery, and increases stress, anxiety, and emotional drainage. The lack of separation without an apparent penalty is a significant contributor to burnout during digitally mediated settings (Komp et al., 2022).

FINDING BACK THE BALANCE IN A DIGITAL WORLD: PERSONALITY AND COMPANY PLANS FOR WELL-BEING

Mindful technology is a behavioural pattern of careful, thoughtful, and opinionated use of digital technologies, with special focus on consciousness of cognitive, emotional, and behavioural reactions towards technology. Instead of dismissing the digital platform, mindfulness-based strategies are promoted whereby digital users are advised to be critical when, why, and how they interact with technology.

It is practiced by developing the ability to be conscious of the present moment when interacting digitally, learning how to recognise sources of emotion (anxiety, comparison, compulsive checking, etc.) and react accordingly with intentional decisions instead of automatic behaviour. Careful usage of technology encourages self-monitoring, which allows the individual to notice their overuse tendencies and emotional exhaustion (Jarrahi et al., 2023). Mindfulness restores attentional control and emotional balance by at least slowing down interaction and reducing multitasking. Empirical evidence has indicated that mindfulness-based interventions have a de-stressing, emotion-regulating, and psychologically beneficial effect in digitally saturated settings. Notably, conscious gadget utilization additionally recreates the independence that individuals can have dictated by digital customs instead of being helpless to algorithmic suggestions. By forming routines that include intentional scrolling, single-tasking, and pausing to reflect, people are able to turn digital use into a contributor of exhaustion and use it as an instrument in support of personal health (Meegasdeniya et al., 2023).Digital detoxification is a process of willingly reducing or using a digital device to regain mental clarity and emotional balance. The short-term detox could be device-free hours or screen-free days or periods of offline time where people can feel the immediate relief of information overload and attentional fragmentation. These short breaks can be used to re-focus the mind, get better sleep, and less stress. Long-term digital detoxification presupposes a long-term lifestyle change, which may be long-term. Rebuilding the platform use, less use of platforms and reconsideration of the role of technology in daily life should also be reorganized. Long-term strategies emphasize the equilibrium of assimilation of digital tools, in contrast to full lack of engagement. Relevant detoxification must be considerate thinking of what technologies are value-added and what are fatigued. Social responsibilities, career demands and the danger of being out of communication are the problems of digital detox that is why the process of implementing it should be slow and situational. Digital detoxification, in its reasonable form, may result in the improved perception of emotions, refocusing, and interpersonal presence, which is useful in the long-term welfare of the mind(Radtke et al., 2022). The strategy of setting boundaries is imperative in reducing the digital fatigue especially in an environment whereby there is unremitting connectivity. Digital boundaries entail establishing definite temporal, spatial, and psychological boundaries of technology usage, which include limiting work-related communication outside of the official work hours or establishing techno-free personal spaces. Conscious disconnection enables one to mindfully disconnect with digital pressures and recover emotionally and relieve stress. Boundary setting involves being assertive, self-aware, and in line with one own values not to mention the negotiation with colleagues and social circles. Boundary-setting is also known to lower emotional labour, improve work-life balance and guard mental health. Notably, boundaries do not imply some strict prohibitions but evolve as per the changing needs in a more adaptative manner. Awareness of when to use and when to go offline will result in people regaining control and mitigating the long-term effects of digital overload (An et al., 2025). To solve the digital fatigue issue, a constantly connected environment needs to be approached through boundary-setting. It includes developing definite boundaries of technology applications, e.g., limiting work-related communication during non-working hours and creating device-free areas. It is a disengagement, which assists people in breaking the shackles of digital demands, leading to people recovering their emotions and alleviating stress. Effective boundary-setting involves aggressiveness, self-awareness and compromise with the social and professional networks. It enhances work life balance, reduces emotional labour and protects mental health. Boundaries are considered to be a flexible practice that can be modified according to new situations, and thus one is able to decide when to go online or to disconnect, reducing the digital overload (Ibrahim et al., 2024). To succeed in digitally saturated worlds, one needs emotional stability and self-control. Emotional resilience is the ability to adjust to stress and be psychologically stable, whereas self-regulation is the ability to be able to control emotional reaction and behavior in accordance with long-term targets. The online environment poses pressures that could overstretch these abilities, so the coping strategies, including reflective journaling and stress management, need to be created. Impulse control and attentional discipline are important skills that should be used to overcome compulsive digital habits. The development of such skills helps to improve emotional resilience and mitigate burnout risk, enabling the person to be in contact with technology (Zayed,2025).

CONFERENCE

This chapter discusses the digital connectivity paradox, that is, although technologies are aimed at empowering and increasing productivity, they may result in emotional exhaustion, social isolation, and burnout. It refers to such problems as virtual environments, technostress, and social isolation and that digital strain is a systemic consequence of hyper-connected ecosystems. The loss of face-to-face communication and work-life demarcations destroy empathy and psychological strength. The chapter suggests both individual and organizational interventions, including mindful use of technology and boundaries, and sustainable technology use and ethical technology design, respectively, as a solution to enhancing digital well-being. One of the keys to harmonious purposeful relations and long-term emotional wellbeing is a change to the humanized digital cultures.

REFERENCES

Addeo, F., Punziano, G., & Mauceri, S. (2022). The Impact of Digital on Research, Socialisation, and Communication Processes. *Italian Journal of Sociology of Education, 14*(Italian Journal of Sociology of Education 14/3), 1-16.

Alheneidi, H., AlSumait, L., AlSumait, D., & Smith, A. P. (2021). Loneliness and problematic internet use during COVID-19 lock-down. *Behavioral Sciences (Basel, Switzerland), 11*(1), 5. DOI: 10.3390/bs11010005 PMID: 33418914

An, R., Qian, G., Mumtaz, A., Alotaibi, K. A., & Wang, X. (2025). Digital fatigue and academic resilience among university students with grit and flexibility as mediators. *Scientific Reports, 15*(1), 45407. DOI: 10.1038/s41598-025-29313-7 PMID: 41298778

Arnold, M., Goldschmitt, M., & Rigotti, T. (2023). Dealing with information overload: A comprehensive review. *Frontiers in Psychology, 14*, 1122200. DOI: 10.3389/fpsyg.2023.1122200 PMID: 37416535

Barykin, S. Y., Kapustina, I. V., Kirillova, T. V., Yadykin, V. K., & Konnikov, Y. A. (2020). Economics of digital ecosystems. *Journal of Open Innovation, 6*(4), 124. DOI: 10.3390/joitmc6040124

Beshley, M., Klymash, M., Beshley, H., Shkoropad, Y., & Bobalo, Y. (2024, February). Revolutionizing Digital Ecosystems with Artificial Intelligence: Challenges, Concepts, and Future Directions. In *IEEE lnternational Conference on Advanced Trends in Radioelectronics, Telecommunications and Computer Engineering* (pp. 1-21). Cham: Springer Nature Switzerland.

Bianchi, R., Schonfeld, I. S., & Laurent, E. (2019). Burnout: Moving beyond the status quo. *International Journal of Stress Management, 26*(1), 36–45. DOI: 10.1037/str0000088

Bocheliuk, V. Y., Zavatska, N. Y., Bokhonkova, Y. O., Toba, M. V., & Panov, N. S. (2020). Emotional burnout: Prevalence rate and symptoms in different socio-professional groups. *Journal of Intellectual Disability–Diagnosis and Treatment, 8*(1), 33–40. DOI: 10.6000/2292-2598.2020.08.01.5

Burström, T., Lahti, T., Parida, V., Wartiovaara, M., & Wincent, J. (2022). Software ecosystems now and in the future: A definition, systematic literature review, and integration into the business and digital ecosystem literature. *IEEE Transactions on Engineering Management, 71*, 12243–12258. DOI: 10.1109/TEM.2022.3216633

. Čekić, E. (2025). Virtual Empathy: A Systematic Review of the Impact of Digital Communication on Interpersonal Relationships and Social Dynamics.

Cimperman, S. (2023). Informal socialization in virtual work environments: Creating a digital culture of connectivity. *Global Business and Organizational Excellence, 43*(1), 53–71. DOI: 10.1002/joe.22197

Corbeanu, A., Iliescu, D., Ion, A., & Spînu, R. (2023). The link between burnout and job performance: A meta-analysis. *European Journal of Work and Organizational Psychology, 32*(4), 599–616. DOI: 10.1080/1359432X.2023.2209320

Cunneen, M. A. R. T. I. N., & Mullins, M. A. R. T. I. N. (2019). Framing risk, The new phenomenon of data surveillance and data monetisation; from an 'Always-On' culture to 'Always-On' artificial intelligence assistants. *Hybrid Worlds, 65.*

De Falco, S. (2019). Digital and urban spaces: Oxymoron or binomial? Urban transformations in the digital era. *Geography Compass, 13*(10), e12467. DOI: 10.1111/gec3.12467

Dong, Y., Wang, M., Liu, E., & Xing, L. (2025). Causes of digital fatigue among hotel employees in the digital age: Configuration study based on fsQCA. *Asia Pacific Journal of Marketing and Logistics.*

Duzbayev, N. T., Velitchenko, S. N., & Doskhozhina, Z. M. (2023). Immersive Media as a New Multimedia Experience: Prospects and Risks. In *DTESI (workshops, short papers).*

Frost, S., Kannis-Dymand, L., Schaffer, V., Millear, P., Allen, A., Stallman, H., Mason, J., Wood, A., & Atkinson-Nolte, J. (2022). Virtual immersion in nature and psychological well-being: A systematic literature review. *Journal of Environmental Psychology, 80*, 101765. DOI: 10.1016/j.jenvp.2022.101765

Heras-Saizarbitoria, I., Urbieta, L., & Boiral, O. (2022). Organizations' engagement with sustainable development goals: From cherry-picking to SDG-washing? *Corporate Social Responsibility and Environmental Management, 29*(2), 316–328. DOI: 10.1002/csr.2202

Ibrahim, R. K., Al Sabbah, S., Al-Jarrah, M., Senior, J., Almomani, J. A., Darwish, A., Albannay, F., & Al Naimat, A. (2024). The mediating effect of digital literacy and self-regulation on the relationship between emotional intelligence and academic stress among university students: A cross-sectional study. *BMC Medical Education, 24*(1), 1309. DOI: 10.1186/s12909-024-06279-0 PMID: 39543568

Jarrahi, M. H., Blyth, D. L., & Goray, C. (2023). Mindful work and mindful technology: Redressing digital distraction in knowledge work. *Digital Business, 3*(1), 100051. DOI: 10.1016/j.digbus.2022.100051

Johnson, S. M. (2023). *Work Pressure, Boundary Management, Burnout, and Toxic Work Environments for Remote Learning and Development Workers* (Doctoral dissertation, City University of Seattle).

Komp, R., Kauffeld, S., & Ianiro-Dahm, P. (2022). Student presenteeism in digital times—A mixed methods approach. *International Journal of Environmental Research and Public Health, 19*(24), 16982. DOI: 10.3390/ijerph192416982 PMID: 36554861

Lampert, B., Unterrainer, C., & Seubert, C. T. (2019). Exhausted through client interaction—Detached concern profiles as an emotional resource over time? *PLoS One, 14*(5), e0216031. DOI: 10.1371/journal.pone.0216031 PMID: 31059551

Lampropoulos, G., Barkoukis, V., Burden, K., & Anastasiadis, T. (2021). 360-degree video in education: An overview and a comparative social media data analysis of the last decade. *Smart Learning Environments, 8*(1).

Lu, Y. Y., Lu, X. M., Shao, C. Y., Wang, C. C., Xu, T. T., & Zhang, B. L. (2022). Empathetic nursing with mindful cognitive therapy for fatigue, depression, and negative emotions in leukemia patients undergoing long-term chemotherapy. *World Journal of Clinical Cases, 10*(6), 1826–1833. DOI: 10.12998/wjcc.v10.i6.1826 PMID: 35317141

Marinucci, M., Pancani, L., Aureli, N., & Riva, P. (2022). Online social connections as surrogates of face-to-face interactions: A longitudinal study under Covid-19 isolation. *Computers in Human Behavior, 128*, 107102. DOI: 10.1016/j.chb.2021.107102

Mdhluli, N. I. (2025). Perils of perpetual connectivity: Navigating the 'always-on' culture in the modern workplace. *SA Journal of Human Resource Management, 23*, 3019. DOI: 10.4102/sajhrm.v23i0.3019

Meegasdeniya, S., & Dulnath, V. (2023). Mindfulness Techniques For Digital Wellbeing. *This was a research paper our team did as research assignment we have submitted to lecturer and medium only.*

Müller, R., Schischke, D., Graf, B., & Antoni, C. H. (2023). How can we avoid information overload and techno-frustration as a virtual team? The effect of shared mental models of information and communication technology on information overload and techno-frustration. *Computers in Human Behavior, 138*, 107438. DOI: 10.1016/j.chb.2022.107438

. Nguyen, M. H., Büchi, M., & Geber, S. (2024). Everyday disconnection experiences: Exploring people's understanding of digital well-being and management of digital media use. *new media & society, 26*(6), 3657-3678.

Norman, A. (2021). *Exploring Technology's Vital Role in Digital Connectivity and Human Disconnection* (Doctoral dissertation, Northcentral University).

Oh, C., Herrera, F., & Bailenson, J. (2019). The effects of immersion and real-world distractions on virtual social interactions. *Cyberpsychology, Behavior, and Social Networking, 22*(6), 365–372. DOI: 10.1089/cyber.2018.0404 PMID: 31188686

Palmié, M., Miehé, L., Oghazi, P., Parida, V., & Wincent, J. (2022). The evolution of the digital service ecosystem and digital business model innovation in retail: The emergence of meta-ecosystems and the value of physical interactions. *Technological Forecasting and Social Change, 177*, 121496. DOI: 10.1016/j.techfore.2022.121496

Polizzi, C. P., & Lynn, S. J. (2021). Regulating emotionality to manage adversity: A systematic review of the relation between emotion regulation and psychological resilience. *Cognitive Therapy and Research, 45*(4), 577–597. DOI: 10.1007/s10608-020-10186-1

Prasetyo, A. R., Handayaningrum, W., & Rahayu, E. W. (2025, January). Digital fatigue and cognitive overload: Psychological challenges in the era of cyber education at Universitas Negeri Malang. In *Prosiding Seminar Pendidikan Seni Budaya* (Vol. 2).

Rachmad, Y. E. (2025). *The Influencer's Power: Transforming Behavior through Viral and Gimmick Strategies*. United Nations Economic and Social Council.

Radtke, T., Apel, T., Schenkel, K., Keller, J., & von Lindern, E. (2022). Digital detox: An effective solution in the smartphone era? A systematic literature review. *Mobile Media & Communication, 10*(2), 190–215. DOI: 10.1177/20501579211028647

Schulz, A. D., Schöllgen, I., Wendsche, J., Fay, D., & Wegge, J. (2021). The dynamics of social stressors and detachment: Long-term mechanisms impacting well-being. *International Journal of Stress Management, 28*(3), 207–219. DOI: 10.1037/str0000216

Sevignani, S. (2022). Digital transformations and the ideological formation of the public sphere: Hegemonic, populist, or popular communication? *Theory, Culture & Society, 39*(4), 91–109. DOI: 10.1177/02632764221103516

Sheng, N., Yang, C., Han, L., & Jou, M. (2023). Too much overload and concerns: Antecedents of social media fatigue and the mediating role of emotional exhaustion. *Computers in Human Behavior, 139*, 107500. DOI: 10.1016/j.chb.2022.107500

Smith, L., Jacob, L., Trott, M., Yakkundi, A., Butler, L., Barnett, Y., Armstrong, N. C., McDermott, D., Schuch, F., Meyer, J., López-Bueno, R., Sánchez, G. F. L., Bradley, D., & Tully, M. A. (2020). The association between screen time and mental health during COVID-19: A cross sectional study. *Psychiatry Research*, *292*, 113333. DOI: 10.1016/j.psychres.2020.113333 PMID: 32738551

Supriyadi, T., Sulistiasih, S., Rahmi, K. H., Pramono, B., & Fahrudin, A. (2025). The Impact Of Digital Fatigue On Employee Productivity And Well-Being: A Scoping Literature Review. *Environment And Social Psychology, 10*(2).

Tang, S., Werner-Seidler, A., Torok, M., Mackinnon, A. J., & Christensen, H. (2021). The relationship between screen time and mental health in young people: A systematic review of longitudinal studies. *Clinical Psychology Review*, *86*, 102021. DOI: 10.1016/j.cpr.2021.102021 PMID: 33798997

Tàpia-Caballero, P., Serrano-Fernández, M. J., Boada-Cuerva, M., Boada-Grau, J., Assens-Serra, J., & Robert-Sentís, L. (2022). Age, gender, personality, burn-out, job characteristics and job content as predictors of driver fatigue. *International Journal of Occupational Safety and Ergonomics*, *28*(4), 2396–2402. DOI: 10.1080/10803548.2021.1991672 PMID: 34633270

Taylor, S. H., & Chen, Y. A. (2024). The lonely algorithm problem: The relationship between algorithmic personalization and social connectedness on TikTok. *Journal of Computer-Mediated Communication*, *29*(5), zmae017. DOI: 10.1093/jcmc/zmae017

Troy, A. S., Willroth, E. C., Shallcross, A. J., Giuliani, N. R., Gross, J. J., & Mauss, I. B. (2023). Psychological resilience: An affect-regulation framework. *Annual Review of Psychology*, *74*(1), 547–576. DOI: 10.1146/annurev-psych-020122-041854 PMID: 36103999

Voitenko, E., Myronets, S., Osodlo, V., Kushnirenko, K., & Kalenychenko, R. (2021). Influence of Emotional Burnout on Coping Behavior in Pedagogical Activity. *International journal of organizational leadership, 10*(2).

Wang, D., Xie, X., Tian, H., Wu, T., Liu, C., Huang, K., Gong, R., Yu, Y., Luo, T., Jiao, R., & Zhang, L. (2022). Mental fatigue and negative emotion among nurses during the COVID-19 pandemic. *Current Psychology (New Brunswick, N.J.)*, *41*(11), 8123–8131. DOI: 10.1007/s12144-022-03468-2 PMID: 35854701

Zayed, A. M. (2025). The Mediating Role of Self-Regulated Learning and Digital Wisdom in the Relationship Between Digital Stress and Academic Flourishing Among Undergraduate Students. *Sohag University International Journal of Educational Research, 11*(11), 69–104. DOI: 10.21608/suijer.2025.343529.1015

Zilka, G. C. (2021). Feelings of belonging or alienation and social emotional perceptions of immigrant youths in the digital age, in comparison with native-born youths. *Education and Information Technologies*, *26*(2), 1937–1954. DOI: 10.1007/s10639-020-10333-x

Chapter 17
Exposure to Violent and Misogynistic Content With Reference to Emotional Fatigue in Recent Media

Pallavi Sengar
http://orcid.org/0009-0000-3098-5689
Lovely Professional University, India

Sukirti Priyadarshani
Lovely Professional University, India

Manish Kumar Verma
Lovely Professional University, India

ABSTRACT

The explosion of digital media has led to greater public exposure to violent and misogynistic content, on social media, in the news, and throughout the entertainment system. This chapter examines the emotional fatigue as an important psychological nutrient related to overexposure to gender-biased and violent media representations. Drawing on theories of media effects, the theorisation of feminism in relation to the media, and different models of emotional exhaustion, the chapter investigates how continued exposure to the media stimuli of distress may result in emotional exhaustion, desensitisation, decreased empathy, and disengagement. It also has shown the mediation effect of emotional exhaustion in influencing public perceptions and attitude about gender-based violence in contemporary digital media environments.

DOI: 10.4018/979-8-3373-8307-1.ch017

1. INTRODUCTION: THE MEDIA-SATURATION AND EMOTIONAL EXPERIENCES CHANGING

The character of the media environment has experienced a massive change over the last twenty years. Past types of mass communication like newspapers, broadcasts and radio were normally structured in terms of a programmed time and channels of distribution that are very limited. On the contrary, new digital media run 24/7 and are entrenched in our daily lives. Social networking sites, online news systems and smart phones enable people to get information nearly 24 hours of the day.

This move has not only led to more exposure by an individual through the media but also to an alteration in the emotional context to which this exposure happens. Digital media often places the user in the situation of being exposed to vast amounts of emotionally evoking material in a very short time frame. One of the most distinguished instances of such content would be its manifestation in the violence and the misogynistic. Domestic violence, sexual assault, harassment on social media, and gendered commentary are reports that are increasingly frequent in news media, social platforms as well as in spaces of online discussions. Due to these the gender related conflict and violence has gradually become a part of the daily media consumption.

Precedent research in media psychology mainly concerned the behavioural consequences of exposure to violent media. Powerful studies conducted on the effects of the exposure to violent representations in movies, television or video games led to the aspect of aggressive behaviour and attitudes development. An example is the social learning theory which focuses on how aggression is developed via observation. In the same vein, research on media violence has also examined how repetition could have an impact on the beliefs about appropriate social behaviour.

Emotional fatigue is one of the concepts that can aid in explaining these effects. Emotional fatigue might be seen as a psychological depletion effect caused by focusing on the repetition of emotionally demanding situations. Historically, this is an idea that has been researched in workplaces especially among those who are in the profession like a medical practitioner, counsellor, social worker who consistently deal with human ills. Nevertheless, recent research says that the same could happen when people are repeatedly subjected to distressing stories in the media worlds.

Applying the concept of emotional fatigue to the digital media environment, users can become emotionally drained when they consume information about violence, harassment, or injustice violently, without sufficient emotional rest. Emotional responses may be anger, sadness, fear, or empathy with each exposure. When this kind of reactions is persistent, a person might start to develop a psychological stress and a decreased ability to react to new facts with the same amount of emotional intensity.

The empirical studies over the recent past endorse this argument. The research on news overload and exposure to digital media shows that emotional exhaustion and disengagement are linked to repeated contact with distressing information (de Leon et al., 2021). Likewise, studies have shown that unceasing connectedness has been a factor in the numbing of emotions and withdrawal (Hoffner and Cohen, 2022).

Being exposed to such narratives can result in the development of complex moods. First of all, people could respond with shock, outrage, or empathy. But as one comes across similar stories repetitively in various mediums, these emotional reactions can start shifting. Such content might begin to seem routine or predictable instead of having a strong reaction. Such a transition does not mean that violence or misogyny is tolerated but simply the result of such a change gradually being exhausted.

This chapter focuses on how emotional fatigue contributes to the development of reactions about the violent and misogynistic media content. Special consideration is made to how emotional exhaustion can serve as a mediating variable between the exposure to media and the perception of gender-based violence.

The conversation follows a number of stages. In the following part, violent and misogynistic content types and prevalence in modern digital media will be discussed. It is then followed by a conceptual analysis of the emotional fatigue and the psychological processes involved in the emotion exhaustion to repeated exposure. Later sections look at how emotional fatigue is related to desensitisation and lower levels of empathy and what this means in terms of perceptions of relationship violence. The chapter ends with a discussion of greater societal implications and future research directions.

2. THE TYPES OF VIOLENT AND MISOGYNISTIC CONTENT AND FREQUENCY OF CONTENT ON THE DIGITAL AGE

The nature of media exposure has somewhat changed with the growth of digital communicative technologies. Unlike previous media systems that were largely centralised and under control of select few of the institutions, today's digital media exist in the network of decentralisation and participation. Social media platforms, video-sharing platforms, discussion forums and online news portals make up a media environment where the continuous creation, circulation and interpretation of content is taking place at a record pace. Within this eco-system, depictions of violence and misogyny are becoming more visible and more prevalent.

One the defining characteristics of digital media is the flow of information. News updates, user generated posts, viral videos, and commentary threads are available twenty-four hours a day, which means that a person may be exposed to emotionally-intense material multiple times throughout the day. Violent events and controversies related to gender usually go viral due to the extreme reaction of the users. Content that generates anger, shock or even moral outrage are most likely to get attention, amongst others, people will generally share them and talk about them. As a result, stories dealing with violence or gender conflict often move to an important place in terms of digital media feeds.

2.1 Transformation in Distribution of the Media

Digital platforms are not only faster than traditional broadcast media, they have different mechanisms in which the content spreads. Algorithms to assess which posts are more visible are frequently not about informational value, rather they are about engagement (comments, shares, reaction, etc.). This means that material that is capable of evoking emotional responses may get exposed more than less emotional content.

Violent events and disputes involving misogyny are likely to be the exact kind of engagement that algorithms love. When the users react to a news story relating to domestic violence or engage with conversations about sexist remarks from a public figure, the platform's system can assume that if this kind of content sparks the same kinds of interaction, similar content should be demonstrated to more users. As a consequences the people interacting with one such post may soon be exposed to others that are either posts, videos or opinion pieces that deal with the same issue.

2.2 Types of the Violent Contents in Modern Media

Violence in digital media manifests itself in a number of different but related ways. While most of the clear examples relate to direct representations of physical hurt, there are, however, a number of more representations that are added up through the course of media environments to the presence of violence in the media.

2.2.1 Direct Visual Depictions

Digital platforms have been shown to post pictures or videos of physical violence. These may be footage of assaults by bystanders, tape from domestic disputes or footage from conflict zones from the internet. Even with the attempts to control and censor the graphic contents of many of the platforms, such materials spread rapidly before the moderation measures could be applied.

Having repeated exposure to graphic imagery can have complexities to how you emotionally respond to the imagery. Initial exposure will bring forth some stronger feeling and emotions such as shock, distress, or anger. However, when you constantly come across several similar pictures throughout your digital feeds, individuals's emotional intensity could be lessened after time. In some cases, viewers may begin to knowingly scroll through such material and not actually engage with it, particularly if such exposure becomes routine.

2.2.2 Symbolic and Narrative Violence

Violence in media environment is not just in direct visual representations. Many forms of entertainment are available for a young child, from television dramas, streaming series, music videos and online storytelling platforms all include narrative elements with domination, humiliation and coercion with interpersonal relationships. These forms of symbolic violence may not be the conscious information of physical injury, but often they help to produce wider forms of understandings of acceptable behaviour within relationships in the culture.

2.2.3 News Coverage of Gender Based violence

Another form of violent content that is quite prominent comes, again, from reporting in the press. Domestic abuse, sexual assault, and intimate partner violence are stories that news organisations cover on a regular basis. Such coverage has an important role to play in informing and creating awareness of social problems among the masses of people.

2.2.4 Commentary and Online discussions

In the forums of digital media, exposure to violent situations rarely stops with the first report. Comment sections, social media threads and online forums create a huge conversation that surrounding each event. Within these spaces, users can argue about the credibility of victims and criticise perpetrators or offer broader opinions about gender relations.

While many of the discussions are an attempt to raise awareness or fight for justice, some may involve hostile or dismissive remarks. Victim-blaming narratives, conspiracy theories and misogynistic commentary emerge from these conversations sometimes. As a result, the individual following the discourses of violent incidents might not only be exposed to the original story, but to numerous interpretations and reactions.

2.3 Variations of Misogynistic Content

Misogyny in digital media does not have to manifest itself through explicit violence. It can be of several types: from open hostility towards women to subtler representations that are imbedded in the everyday communication.

2.3.1 Direct Online Harassment

One of the most evident forms of misogyny is direct harassment towards women in the digital spaces. Female journalists, activists, politicians and public figures frequently receive hostile messages and they include insults, threats, or attempts to discredit the recipients. Such harassment is common on social networking sites where people are more anonymous or distanced from one another and therefore less socially responsible.

2.3.2 Humour and Meme Culture

Another form of misogynistic content develops in meme culture and in funny posts on the Internet. Jokes that overlook the experiences of women based on gender stereotypes or that trivialise women's experiences are commonly spread due to the frame of lighthearted humour. The humorous format may hide the message it is making putting a direct challenge to such narratives.

Although many people who read these memes interpret them ironically, the continued exposure to the gender stereotypical humour may contribute to the normalisation of sexist attitudes. When misogynistic jokes feature in internet dialogues, the jokes will over time become part of the accepted language of online communication.

2.3.3 Ideological Communities

Digital media have also facilitated the creation of online communities that are focused on explicitly anti-feminist or misogynistic ideologies. There are groups in some forums and social media sites that advocate for and spread stories of women as manipulative, untrustworthy, or as responsible for social problems. These communities will tend to support each other's beliefs by discussion amongst members and spread content that summarises their world view.

2.3.4 Algorithmic Reinforcement

Algorithms that put out digital content can inadvertently serve the spread of misogynistic content. Posts that are controversial or have a strong reaction tend to get more exposure because of the high amounts of engagement. If a piece of content that espouses gender-hostile views generates a widespread discussion, this may be boosted by the recommendation system of the platform it's on.

This dynamic can, in turn, lead to feedback loops characterised by similar content continually appearing in the feeds of users. Even those who have their first contact with such material, in the contexts of criticising it, may be recommended its posts to follow.

2.4 The Role of Repetition

It is not only the nature of the content, but the frequency of it that has a psychological impact due to violent and misogynistic content. Repetition is one of the primary characteristics of digital media environment. Since stories flow on several platforms and are highly discussed by users, one can come across the said incident multiple times.

Some level of cognitive and emotional processing is required with each encounter. A user who is reading about a violent event needs to interpret the situation, assess its importance, and also to control their emotional reaction. When similar stories are experienced again and again, these processes become activated again and again. As time accumulates the requirements or burdens put on the emotional and cognitive resources can become substantial.

2.5 Circulation of Violent Narratives across the World

Digital communication technologies also enable violent incidents to reach way beyond the local context. News about gender-based violence happening in one country can be transmitted across the globe and to other regions of the world very rapidly because of online networks. While this global awareness can add to solidarity movements and advocacy campaigns, it is also creating an increase in the number of distressing information encountered by users.

2.6 Violence and Misogyny Intersection

Violence and misogyny tend to overlap while working within a digital media narrative. Stories about sexual assault, intimate partner violence or cyberstalking generally include physical harm and gender-based hostility. Discussions of the incidents, then, may be a mix of descriptions of the violent acts as well as discussions of gender roles and power dynamics.

2.7 Summary

The modern world of digital media is full of forms of violent and misogynistic content. Direct representations of violence, portrayals in the entertainment media, representation in the journalistic press and online commentary are all involved in the circulation of such. Misogyny can be manifested in explicit harassment, humorous stereotypes, ideological discourse or algorithmically amplified posts.

3. EMOTIONAL FATIGUE: DEFINITIONS, PSYCHOLOGICAL MECHANISMS

Understanding the effects of repeated exposure to violent and misogynistic media content demands the careful investigation of the psychological processes involved in an individual's response to emotionally demanding information. One concept that has been becoming more and more relevant in this context is emotional fatigue. Although the term has frequently been linked with occupational burnout, especially with professions that involve caregiving or managing a crisis, the underlying mechanisms can also apply to current media settings in which viewers are exposed to upsetting stories on a routine basis.

3.1 Understanding Concept of Emotional Fatigue

A from the point of view of psychology, a definition of emotional fatigue is the summation of the repeated emotional effort. Emotional effort is the mental and affective resources people invest when dealing with events that require them to engage in emotional interpretation. When someone is reading a news story about domestic violence, for instance, he or she may feel empathy for the victim, anger at the perpetrator, and worry about the larger issues related to social life. Each of these reactions involves the cognitive appraisal as well as the emotional involvement.

3.2 Differentiating between Emotional Fatigue and Desensitisation

In spite of that emotional fatigue is sometimes described in connection with desensitisation, the two concepts describe different psychological processes. Desensitisation is a reduction in emotional response towards a specific stimulus with repeated exposure to it. For instance, people who regularly view scenes of aggression on television and so on might get increasingly less shocked by scenes they see later.

Emotional fatigue, on the other hand, refers more to a generalised sense of psychological weariness as opposed to just a decreased sensitivity to a particular stimulus. A person suffering from emotional fatigue may not just be less emotionally sensitive to violent material but may also feel generally depleted, disengaged or mentally overloaded. In other words, desensitisation refers to a change in response to a specific type of content while emotional fatigue refers to the cumulative depletion of emotional resources.

This distinction becomes important in analysing media exposure. While Desensitisation can arise as a result of repeated exposure to specific types of violence, emotional fatigue refers to the general emotional stress that is created due to constant contact with upsetting information. In many cases, the two processes may be simultaneous: in other words, repeated exposure may contribute both to decreased sensitivity to particular stimuli and to a generalised sense of emotional exhaustion.

3.3 Emotional Fatigue/ Compassion Fatigue

Another related idea is that of compassion fatigue, which has been extensively studied in professions like healthcare, counselling and emergency services. Compassion fatigue is when someone who regularly interacts with people exposed to trauma or is regularly exposed to trauma becomes emotionally overwhelmed by whatever trauma they are witnessing. Over the years, they can lose the empathy to other people, and they may show other symptoms like emotional numbness, irritability or withdrawal.

3.4 Cognitive Processes Emotional Load

To further understand how emotional fatigue develops it is worth considering the concept of cognitive load. Cognitive load theory that proposes that people have only a certain amount of mental resources for processing information. When people have to deal with complex or emotionally challenging material, their mental resources are needed to make sense of and judge that information.

Processing stories about gender-based violence, for example, takes a number of cognitive steps. Individuals need to know the specifics of the event, the credibility of information, the actions of the participants and the larger social implications of the event. At the same time, they have to control their emotional response to the story.

3.5 Neuropsychological based perspectives

From a neuropsychological standpoint, emotional fatigue might be associated with the sequential activation of the brain systems that are engaged in the emotional processing and stress management. The amygdala, for instance, has a central role in the detection of stimuli noted as being emotionally important especially those that are linked with threat or danger. When people are exposed to upsetting images or stories, the amygdala helps to elicit an emotional response, such as fear or anger.

3.6 Emotional Fatigue like a cumulative process

One major feature of emotional fatigue is that it develops slowly. Unlike acute stress-reactions, which typically develop in response to specific situations, emotional fatigue usually develops over time the result of repeated exposure to emotionally demanding situations. Each individual encounter may be perceived as manageable but the total of many encounters may lead to exhaustion.

In the context of the media this is a highly important cumulative process. Because digital platforms promote frequent engagement with emotionally-charged content, individuals using such platforms may unknowingly accumulate emotional strain over a long period of time. The effects may not become apparent until the people start to feel persistently drained out or unconnected with issues that once evoked strong emotion in them.

3.7 Emotional Fatigue as a Mediation Device

From a theoretical standpoint, emotional fatigue can be one intermediate process between media exposure and more global, attitudinal outcomes. Rather than having a direct impact on beliefs about violence or beliefs about gender relations, repeated exposure may first create emotional fatigue. This fatigue might then affect the way that personalities perceive the information that comes afterwards.

For example, an emotionally fatigued person might be less likely to be engaging at a deeper level with stories about violence based on gender. It is possible that decreased emotional engagement towards oppressed individuals may mean that empathic behaviours with the victims are lessened, or that motivation to support policy initiative against such issues is decreased. In this way, the exhaustion may influence the public attitudes and social perceptions in a indirect way.

3.8 Summary

Emotional fatigue is a complex psychological phenomenon brought about by constant exposure to emotional heavy work. In the present digital media landscape, people are often exposed to the stories of violence, misogyny, and social conflict. Each encounter requires emotional and cognitive processing and the sum of these demands can ultimately cause a state of psychological exhaustion.

Understanding psychological fatigue as an important end consequence of digital media exposure provides an important basis for understanding its wider social implications. The following section therefore addresses the question of how media exposure contributes to emotional fatigue, more specifically how media structures, user engagement, and emotions are interrelated.

4. MECHANISMS THAT RESIDE BETWEEN MEDIA EXPOSURE AND EMOTIONAL FATIGUE

The development of emotional fatigue in media audiences cannot be explained by references to violent or misogynistic content alone. Instead, it occurs through a complex interaction of media structures and user engagement patterns with psychological processes at work in processing emotionally-charged information. Contemporary digital environments are marked by the circulation of information at an unprecedented speed, constant connectivity and the existence of algorithmic systems influencing what individuals are exposed to online. These features determine how often people interact with upsetting content as well as how distressing material can be emotionally processed over time.

4.1 Repetitive Exposure and the Effectiveness of Media

Research on media effects has for a long time focused on the role of repetition in shaping public perceptions. Cultivation theory, for example, states that people exposed to the same content over a long period of time may come to understand social reality in a particular way. When audiences are repeatedly exposed to stories about violence or an interpersonal conflict, they might begin to consider such events to be more prevalent than they actually are.

In the case of gender based violence it is the repeated media coverage that may contribute to the feeling that cases of violence of this nature are occurring frequently throughout society. While elevated awareness may be an important step in raising awareness of serious social problems, constant exposure may have unwanted psychological consequences. If people hear and view several accounts of violence over a brief period of time, there may be problems in sustaining one's emotional investment in each incident.

4.2 Emotional Appraisal and Cognitive Processing

Every act of encountering media content implies to an extent cognitive appraisal. When people read about a violent incident or see misogynistic commentary on the internet, they philtre the information based on the beliefs, social norms and experiences. This appraisal process determines the level of emotional reaction of the individual.

Stories about gender-based violence tend to have complex reactions. Readers may be sympathetic toward the victims and angry at perpetrators, and also concerned about wider societal conditions that allow such things to happen. These responses involve some emotion and some thinking. Individuals have to interpret the situation of the event, take into account the motivation of people involved, and assess the implications of the story.

4.3 Regulating Emotions in the Digital Context

Another important mechanism relating media exposure to emotional fatigue has to do with emotional regulation. Emotional regulation is the term that is used when discussing the strategies that someone uses to cope with their emotional response. When people are confronted with distressing content, they engage their means of regulating their response to help them maintain their psychological balance.

Several regulation strategies are applied in a digital context commonly. Some try cognitive reappraisal, of the events of the situation framed in such a way as to lessen the emotional disturbance. Others depend upon suppression (where one tries to predispose to minimise outward emotional responses even though one may still feel emotional discomfort inside oneself). Still others engage in avoidance; not interacting with awfully emotional content.

4.4Habituation and Depleting Emotional Response

Another mechanism that is linked to repeated exposure is habituation. Habituation is when repeated exposure to a particular stimulus of the same sort has a diminishing effect on emotional reaction to that stimulus. In terms of the media it might happen with habituation if people hear stories about violence or misogyny with too much frequency.

Habituation can also be an adaptive mechanism in that it prevents the individual from being overwhelmed by constant emotional stimulation. However, when the effects of habituation are combined with emotional fatigue, emotional numbing may result. Emotional numbing implies a more general enlargement of emotional un-reactivity, not just to violent content, but also to related social problems.

4.5 Information Overload Psychologic Withdrawal

The concept of information overload is further explained for the way how emotional fatigue develops in a digital environment. When individuals feel overwhelmed by the amount of information with which they are presented, they may use coping strategies that are designed to lessen the cognitive demands.

One of the common strategies is the use of psychological withdrawal. Individuals may avoid reading detailed news reports/avoiding discussions about controversial topics. While withdrawal may give temporary reprieve from the emotional stress, it may also decrease participation with significant social issues.

4.6 Emotional Fatigue: A Mediating Process

When considered together, these mechanisms point to the suggestion that emotional fatigue belongs to an intermediate stage between the effects of media exposure and general social consequences. Exposure to violent and misogynistic stories triggers emotional and cognitive processes that must be regulated and interpreted. As these processes are repeated over time, it is possible that emotional resources will become depleted.

Once emotional fatigue sets in, people may then start to react to new information differently. They may be less engaged with stories of violence, be less empathic about victims of violence, or be closed to the issues of gender justice in their conversations. These changes are not necessarily ideological favouritism for violence but, instead, are the psychological results of prolonged emotional strain.

4.7 Summary

Emotional fatigue is the result of interaction between media structures and psychological processes. Repetitive exposure to disturbing narrative, cognitive demands related to the processing of complex information and the effort invested in the regulation of the emotional reactions are all a source of the gradual depletion of the emotional resources. Digital platform design and algorithmic amplification make these effects even more severe by citing the frequency and congregating effect of emotionally intense content.

5. DESENSITISATION AND REDUCED EMPATHY: THE MEDIATION ROLE OF EMOTIONAL FATIGUE

The link between exposure to the media and any shift in social attitudes to violence has commonly been evaluated by the term desensitisation . Earlier research in the field of media psychology hypothesised a certain desensitisation of emotional sensitivity to aggression through repeated exposure to violent images or narratives. Over time, people exposed to such material on a frequent basis may find the violence itself to be less shocking and morally disturbing than those who are seldom exposed to such material. While this view has been influential, modern digital media settings need a more complex view of the development of emotional responses in the context of constant exposure.

In the past several years, we have seen a growing awareness among scholars that desensitisation may not be a sufficient proposition to account for the psychological effects of prolonged viewing of violent and misogynistic media material. Emotional responses to such material are not just determined by repetition but also by the additive stress on the emotional tax placed on oneself, in the repetition of exposure to distressing narratives. In this circumstance, emotional fatigue suffers become a crucial mediating factor.

5.1 Reexamining the Idea of Desensitisation

Desensitisation is the effect when the person is repeatedly exposed to a certain stimulus, he loses his emotional responsiveness. Early research on the impact of media violence was common in fictional portrayals in movies, television programmes or video games. Researchers showed that people who viewed a lot of violent media in their lives displayed lower levels of emotional arousal when watching violent screen visualisation than did people with less exposure.

In the context of contemporary media however, there has been a significant change in the nature of violent content. Digital platforms often carry information about incidents of violence in the real world such as domestic abuse, sexual assault and online harassment.

5.2 Emotional Fatigue as a Precursor for the Decline of Empathy

Empathy is one of the key elements in moral and social awareness. It allows persons to empathise with suffering of other persons, and encourages attitudes of support or protection. In response to stories of violence or injustice, empathic responses tend to involve the feelings of sadness, concern, or anger about those individuals who are responsible for causing harm.

Empirical research revealed that repeated media exposure to gender-based violence may have a significant impact on the state of empathy and attitude to victims (Ophir and Walter, 2021; Sundar and Lim, 2023).he emotional energy needed to maintain these responses charges up throughout the day.

5.3 Psychological Emotional Numbing Psychological Distance

One of the most obvious results of emotional fatigue is emotional numbing. Emotional numbing occurs when there is a decrease in the intensity of emotional responses to events that would normally be responses of significant emotional reaction. In media contexts, emotional numbing could be kind of a sense of separation that we could have had in the stories of violence or injustice.

When emotional numbing develops, people can still appreciate the fact that certain events are morally troubling. However, the sense of emotional urgency which may have attended this recognition may subside. Stories about gender-based violence may start to feel as if they begin to repeat themselves and/or become more predictable than shocking.

5.4 Being a Victim-Blaming and Lessened Perceived Severity

Research on the media's depictions of gender-based violence has found that when people are exposed to particular stories, it can impact their attitudes towards the victim. When stories focus on ambiguity or sensational elements, their audiences might focus on elements of the victim's behaviour instead of focusing on the perpetrator's actions.

Another effect is a shift in the way that people assess the seriousness of various types of violence. When audiences are exposed to visible and extreme examples of violence, more covert forms of harm (e.g. emotional manipulation or psychological abuse) might reflect it as being less severe. Emotional fatigue can therefore affect the threshold by which people consider behaviours to be an issue.

5.5 Cynicism and Social Withdrawal;

Cynicism is another possible result of emotional fatigue. When people become constantly exposed to stories of violence and do not experience any meaningful social change, questions may arise whether or not progress is even possible. This sense of pessimism can lower hours or hours of motivation to take part in social issues.

Cynicism often results in social withdrawal, especially when it comes to online settings where topics of gender issues can become highly polarised. Users who become emotionally exhausted from having the same arguments over and over again might decide to stay away from those kinds of conversations. While a state of withdrawal can make people safe from emotional strain, there are fewer opportunities for the exchange of constructive dialogue.

5.6 Normalisation of Misogyny

Repeated misogynistic discourse could over time shape one's views of what constitutes acceptable communication. When sexist jokes, harsh comments or dismissive attitudes towards women are given considerable air-time within digital spaces, they can start to become the norm.

5.7 Misperceptions of the Relationship Violence

Emotional fatigue affects the way the audience perceives incidents of relationship violence such as physical, emotional and psychological abuse in intimate partnerships. Media presentations of such incidents usually focus on dramatic or extreme cases (e.g., homicide or physical assault of a severe nature). While these stories are important in terms of bringing awareness, they can sometimes be overshadowing less visible forms of abuse.

When people are seeing severe cases repeatedly, their perception of what is violence can become skewed. Behaviours that are short of extreme violence may be considered less serious or may not be referred to as abuse at all. Emotional fatigue reinforces this pattern by decreasing the amount of attention people put into analysing the nuances of the interpersonal relationship.

5.8 Gender Differences of Emotional Fatigue

The experience of emotional fatigue may be different for different demographic groups. Women, for example, may be subject to a specific emotional burden when they are bombarded with repeated descriptions of gender-based violence, particularly if they are able to relate closely to the victim(s) in such scenarios. The repeated exposure may give rise to feelings of fear, vulnerability or frustration which may contribute to emotional exhaustion.

5.9 Consequences of the Decline in Empathy at the Group Level

When the emotional fatigue spreads widely, then the effects are not limited to individual psychology and involve collective social attitude. Empathy plays a very important part in motivating public concern, as well as policy action, with regards to social problems. If large portions of the population have attenuated levels of empathic engagement, then the social thresholds needed to do away with issues like gender-based violence may be compromised.

Public discussion can change from a sustained attention to short cycles of attention followed by rushing disinterested by short cycles of attention to disinterest. News stories can cause temporary spikes of outrage, but these responses will often fade as something else gets the attention of the public. Emotional fatigue plays a part in this trend because of depletion of emotional energy to enact long-term advocacy.

5.10 Integrative Perspective

Taken together, the evidence appears to indicate that emotional fatigue is an important sets mediating the middle between media exposure and social attitudes toward violence. Increase in the number of times retelling emotionally distressing narratives or stories recitations create activation that must be regulated and interpreted. As these demands continue to add up, the emotional resources may slowly become depleted.

5.11 Summary

Desensitisation and empathy decrease are significant effects of exposure to a pattern of violent and misogynistic media content. However, these outcomes are best understood in a larger context that includes the accumulations of demands on audiences (De Leon et al., 2021; Dhir et al., 2018). Emotional fatigue offers a useful conceptual framework to understand how long term exposure can affect changes in the way we emotionally respond and socialise toward another person.

6. REPERCUSSIONS IN PUBLIC SELF-PERCEPTIONS OF RELATIONSHIP AND GENDER VIOLENCE

Emotional fatigue is not limited to what goes on inside people's heads. Its effects are not limited to the personal emotional response and affect how society collectively renders and responds to questions of violence and gender inequality. When the audiences are repeatedly exposed to disturbing stories of domestic abuse, sexual violence, or misogynistic hostility in the media, there is a risk of the audience's emotional relevance to such stories changing over time. These changes, in turn, create public perceptions of relationship violence, affect attitudes toward victims and perpetrators of it, and impact more general cultural perceptions of gendered harm.

6.1 Changing Perceptions of Violence Through Repetition

The problem with an over-reliance on media to teach children how to behave in society is that repeated exposure to similar types of media narratives commonly leads to a gradual change in the way the audience interprets social problems. With regular reports of gender based violence appearing within the news cycles, and within social media discussion, they may begin to feel less of an exception. Instead of getting considered as uncommon or shocking events, such kind of incidents may come to be be viewed as routine aspects of contemporary society.

This shift in perception has a great deal to do with the process of normalisation. Normalisation is when after repeated exposure to a certain phenomenon, the reaction diminishes as the recognition that it is a deviation from expected social behaviour. In regard to the coverage of violence in the media, normalisation does not necessarily mean that violence is accepted; it is rather the process of a progressive adaption in the way people perceive the prevalence and importance of violence.

6.2 Changes in Emotional Thresholds Recalibration

Another effect of emotional fatigue comprises the recalibration of the emotional threshold. Emotional thresholds are the level of emotional stimulation it would take to have a strong reaction. When people are exposed to the repeated accounts of violence, their emotional response threshold may gradually rise.

In practical terms, this means that stories that he did greatly elicit emotionally may no longer stimulate the same intensity of feeling. Individuals may need more and more extreme or fantastic stories in order to feel as much emotion. As a result, some less visible, or less severe, forms of relationship violence such as emotional manipulation or coercive control, may also attract less attention from audiences.

6.3 How to Empathise and Be Credible to a Victim

Empathy is a key factor in shaping public attitude to victims of violence. When audiences develop an emotional response to victims such as empathy, they are more likely to support accountability of perpetrators in courts of law and seek policies in place for more violence than before. Empathic engagement is also linked to the way that people interpret the reliability of the testimony of victims.

This distancing may affect at least a subtle influencing of the credibility of victims. Once there is little engagement emotionally, people might end up judging stories about violence in a more sceptical fashion or with less emotional investment. Although such reactions are not necessarily a matter of the explicit disbelief, they might lead to an interpretation of the victims experiences as more detached.

6.4 Media narratives and Cultural Scripts.

Media representations contribute to the development of cultural scripts, i.e., shared frameworks for understanding social interactions and relationships by the individual. Cultural scripts about gender and relationships are influenced by common themes and stories that are developed and repeated in movies, television, news reporting, and digital discussions.

The fact is, when the stories about relationship violence are repeated in the media contexts, the stories may have effects on the way that people conceive the dynamics of intimate relationship. For instance, some portrayals may contain emphasis on jealousy, possessiveness or conflict as common features of romantic relationships. If stories of this kind seem to occur very frequently without critical context, audiences may come to accept such behaviours as disconcerting and nothing to be concerned about.

6.5 Gendered Issue of Perception

Emotional fatigue may also contribute to the way how various groups perceive gender violence. Women who are exposed repeatedly to stories of violence against women, may feel emotionally exhausted, frightened, or frustrated. For some individuals, this exposure might be the incentive to reinforce understanding of gender inequality and activism. For others, however, because of the emotional stress, withdrawal from conversations about gender violence may occur.

Men can feel emotionally fatigued in different ways, especially if they are seeing the media stories framed in terms of larger conversations on masculinity and power in relation to gender violence. Multiple exposure to accusatory or polarising discussions might cause some individuals to cheque out of the conversation entirely. This disengagement has the potential to widen the gap between groups trying to solve the problem of gender violence, and people who are experiencing a sense of disconnection from the issue.

6.6 Internalised Social Norms

Over the years, emotional fatigue may interact with existing social norms in the formation of gender and relationship analysis. Individuals are socialised in cultural contexts, which establish beliefs about how gender should be, who is in control of whom within a relationship, and what is appropriate and acceptable behaviour. When the media stories are repeated or show these norms, they may have an influence on internal beliefs.

This process underscores the importance of taking into account the emotional fatigue process not only as a psychological phenomenon but also as a phenomenon that affects the processes of reproducing social norms.

6.7 Media Trust and Scepticism of Audiences

Another result of emotional fatigue deals with how the audiences view media institutions themselves. When people are exposed to repeated reports about violent events and have not seen significant social change, they may become sceptical of the value of media in promoting social change.

Declining trust around media can have huge implications for public discourse. If the audience becomes sceptical of news reporting, they can disengage with sources of information that play an important role in raising awareness about social issues.

6.8 Implications to Bystander Behaviour

Public perceptions of violence impact ways that people respond when they come across situations where abuse is occurring in their own communities. Research on bystander intervention suggests there are more likely to intervene if they perceive the situation as a serious one and they are emotionally compelled to intervene.

This motivation can be lowered by emotional fatigue. Also, when people find themselves overwhelmed in their repeated exposure to stories of violence, they can develop a sense of helplessness about the likelihood of any meaningful intervention. This sense of helplessness may deter individuals from taking action when they observe problematic behaviour in their individual social environments.

6.9 Summary

Emotional fatigue has a great effect on the way audiences see relationship violence and gender-based harm. Through processes such as normalising, recalibrating emotional thresholds and less empathic participation, repeated exposure to violent narratives can have an impact on the emotional frameworks used to interpret these issues.

These changes have implications on public awareness, policy attitudes, and on responsibility of the collective. When emotional fatigue is too widespread, societies may not be able to maintain the emotional engagement often needed to implement social change over long periods of time.

7. DISCUSSION: THE MEDIA AND WHO IS RESPONSIBLE?

The various sections of this chapter have discussed how the repetition of violent and misogynistic content in the digital media environment plays into the building up of emotional fatigue. This fatigue occurs in the interaction between psychological activities - including cognitive overload and emotional regulation - and the structural features of modern media systems - including algorithmic amplification and constant connectivity. While emotional fatigue has an initial impact as a psychological response of an individual, consequences reach far beyond the psychological experiences of an individual. It shapes collective attitudes to violence, influences the public discourse about gender relations and raises important issues for understanding the ethics of media institutions.

7.1 Ethical Responsibilities of the Media Institutions

Traditional journalism has also been adherent to a set of ethics that have been developed for decades with the view of balancing the aggregative public's right to know with the possibility harm that may arise from some modes of reportage. In the case of gender-based violence, responsible reporting is reporting accurate information without sensationalising them or using narratives that may indirectly support the perpetuation of harmful stereotypes. Journalists have to be careful with the way stories are framed, as they can influence how audience interprets victims, perpetrators and society as a whole.

7.2 Platform Governmental And Algorithmic Responsibility

The use of digital platforms plays a growing role in influencing the way media content is delivered to audiences. Algorithms decide to show what posts are on the feed of other users, what topics are the trending discussions and what are the stories warranting popular visibility. Due to the way these systems favour metrics of engagement, such as clicks, shares and comments, the systems often favour content that will elicit strong emotional responses.

Strategies to deal with this challenge therefore demand a rethink of the principles on which to base the design of algorithms. Digital platforms increasingly get urges to take digital well-being into account in their recommendation systems. For instance, algorithms could be programmed to vary the kinds of content shown to users as opposed to repeatedly feeding them similar emotionally-dramatic stories.

7.3 Field Experiments The Commercialisation of Violence

Another critical issue is the business of violent and misogynistic narrative in digital media ecosystems. Media organisations and social platforms are frequently dependent on advertising revenue that is dependent on user engagement. Because emotionally provocative content is more likely to attract attention, stories about violent events may get an unfair amount of attention.

The commercialisation of violence opens up a set of ethical issues regarding the commodification of human suffering for the market as media content. While it is important to report incidents of violence in order to create public awareness and accountability, the way in which these stories are framed can affect whether individual audiences are engaged constructively or fatigued emotionally.

7.4 Feminist Interventions in the Media

Feminist media scholarship has long stressed the importance of taking into account the kinds of representations of gender in media systems. From this point of view, the occurrence of misogynistic narratives is not an isolated case but part of larger patterns of representation which reflect and perpetuate gender inequalities. Digital media environments offer challenges as well as possibilities for solving these problems.

7.5 Societal Effects of Emotional Fatigue

If emotional fatigue is not addressed its larger societal consequences may become more apparent. One potential consequence may be the gradual normalised ways of gender-based violence. When audiences hear stories of violence over and over again but are not engaged emotionally, those events may become taken as usual parts of social life.

Another consequence is declining participation as a citizen. Emotional fatigue can lead people to not wish to debate gender equality or encourage policy changes / activities designed to prevent violence. Without greater and sustained public attention, efforts to address the problem in a systemic way can lose momentum.

7.6 Balance between Awareness and Emotional Sustainability

One main challenge of the modern media system lies between the importance of awareness and the emotional sustainability. Raising awareness on gender based violence is crucial in bringing about social change. But if we are too much exposed to distressing narrations, it may cause disengagement rather than action.

One promising approach is through solutions-oriented journalism, which focuses not only on the problems caused by violence but is also sensitive to the efforts being made to accommodate the problem. Stories of community-driven efforts, survivor support systemic programs, and effective policy initiatives offer empathy for viewers and give audiences with the sense of agency and hope.

Such stories help offset the emotional load of being repeatedly exposed to violence. Far from traumatising or overloading, media coverage of pathways toward positive change can keep the public involved in finding solutions without adding too much to a saturation of emotion.

7.7 Summary

Emotional fatigue is a real problem in today's media systems. Although repeated exposure to violent and misogynistic narratives may make people aware of social problems, such exposure may result in psychological strain that will undermine continued engagement with social problems. Addressing this challenge involves addressing the ethical responsibilities of media institutions, designing digital platforms, and practises of media audiences.

7.8 Practical Implications

The findings of this chapter have important practical implications. Media houses ought to embrace the principle of responsible reporting that is not overly sensational and offering background insight regarding gender-based violence. Hosting companies must take into account the inclusion of user well-being into the algorithm so that they do not repeat emotionally distressing information.

Moreover, media literacy programmes can equip people with techniques that will assist them to critically access media and deal emotionally. Psychological, understanding of emotional fatigue as one of the effects of a media exposure can be used to guide an intervention strategy to enhance emotional stability.

8. CONCLUSION AND POSSIBLE FUTURE RESEARCH

The shocking change in the media environment of the contemporary world has led to the alteration of circulation of information and most importantly of the emotional state that the audiences face social issues. Digital platforms now make uniformly accessible the overflowing streams of content that flatter the borders between private c ("communication") and public c ("entertainment"), or between news reporting and public debate. Within this complicated ecosystem across all the media is themselves stories of violence and misogyny circulating in a way that had not been seen before in terms of speed and tactics for distributing content such as pictures, images, and videos.

Throughout the chapter a number of related processes have been presented with the aim of understanding the development of emotional fatigue in today's digital media environments. The first is through the structural characteristics of Digital Communication Systems. Social media platforms and algorithmic recommendation systems and constant updates from the news feed people mind a environment where we are exposed emotionally intense content with extraordinary frequency. Unlike the media systems of the past that provided intervals between exposure to the distressing information, digital media systems frequently present such content in a broken stream.

The second process is psychological demands that are associated with the interpretation of emotional charged information. When people are exposed to stories of violence, harassment or gender inequality, they practise cognitive appraisal and emotional regulation. These processes require a mental and emotional resource. When exposure is repeated, repeated, and repeated, the effort to maintain empathic engagement builds up and thus the chances of experiencing emotional fatigue rise.

The third process, which is related to the role of participatory media culture. Digital platforms do not just encourage users to consume information but also to comment and debate, and express their point of view. While this structure of participation can promote awareness and activism, this structure brings the higher emotional labour that comes with engaging with difficult social issues. Constant talk of violent incidents and gender conflicts can be psychologically wearing for so many users.

Taken together, these structural and psychological dynamics jointly create conditions in which emotional fatigue is much more seriously probable. The chapter has shown that emotional fatigue is a mediating mechanism that connects media exposure with other social effects at a wider level. Repeated experience of violent and misogynistic narratives do not directly affect an individual's attitudes but rather indirectly by gradually affecting the emotional involvement of individuals with these issues.

Guidelines for Future Research.

Although the idea of emotional fatigue is a great insight on newer media experiences, it is an emerging field of study. A number of important directions for future research can be identified.

First, empirical research is needed to analyse how emotional fatigue forms in the various types of media platforms. The digital environments are tremendously different in their organisation and the pattern of interaction. Social networking sites, video sharing sites, online news sites, and online discussion sites all present different ways of engaging and participating in content. Investigating the roles played by these environments in causing emotional fatigue in varying degrees would help in gaining an enhanced understanding of the phenomenon.

Second, in future studies, individual differences in susceptibility to emotional fatigue should be investigated. Factors such as age, gender, prior experience with violence and pattern media usage may have an impact on individual response to repeated exposure to distressing narrative.

Third, researchers should study the link between emotional exhaustion and social attitudes internalised by individuals, focusing especially on concepts of gender and violence. Emotional fatigue may interact with already existing cultural beliefs in ways which may affect attitudes towards the victims and perpetrators. Investigating exactly these interactions could offer important insights for psychology of media as well as gender studies.

Fourth, future studies should take longitudinal approaches, which focus on the change of emotional fatigue over time. Because emotional fatigue builds up slowly with repeated exposure, studies which follow changes in emotional engagement over a long period of time would be useful in providing evidence for its long-term effects.

Lastly, Interdisciplinary research involving collaboration of different perspectives by sector of psychologists, sociologists, communication studies as well as gender studies would enhance the analysis of emotional fatigue. The complexity of today's media ecosystems calls for new theoretical aid in understanding media as a variable in integration from many areas of knowledge.

Concluding Reflections

The modern world of digital media is a paradox. On the one hand, the visibility given to gender based violence has led to important conversations in the general public regarding topics of inequality, justice, and social responsibility. On the other hand, it is possible that the continuous circulation of narratives of violence and misogyny is creating emotional environments in which audiences will have difficulty engaging repeatedly with these issues.

Emotional fatigue is the major concept to be considered to explain this paradox. It elaborates how the psychological limitations of emotional engagement civilise with the structural features of digital media systems. By acknowledging emotional fatigue as an important consequence of exposure to the media, scholars and practitioners may find ways to develop more complex strategies for using the media to increase awareness while maintaining emotional viability.

Ultimately, maintaining a serious public dialogue on gender-based violence largely means accepting the feelings associated with media experience. By understanding the impact of emotional fatigue, both in shaping audience responses to news stories and media environments that are conducive to audience resilience, can research and practitioners work together to advance the idea that it is both important and possible to create media environments that foster both awareness and resilience.

REFERENCES

de Leon, E., Segura, J., & Valenzuela, S. (2021). News overload, emotional fatigue, and disengagement in the age of social media. Digital Journalism, 9(4), 491–509. https://doi.org/DOI: 10.1080/21670811.2020.1829975

Dhir, A., Yossatorn, Y., Kaur, P., & Chen, S. (2018). Online social media fatigue and psychological wellbeing. International Journal of Information Management, 40, 141–152. [](https://doi.org/)DOI: 10.1016/j.ijinfomgt.2018.01.012

Hoffner, C. A., & Cohen, E. (2022). The emotional costs of constant connectivity: Fatigue, numbness, and social withdrawal in digital life. Computers in Human Behavior, 135, 107380. [](https://doi.org/)DOI: 10.1016/j.chb.2022.107380

Ophir, Y., & Walter, N. (2021). Gender-based violence in media: Effects on perceptions, empathy, and policy attitudes. Psychology of Violence, 11(1), 87–98. [](https://doi.org/)DOI: 10.1037/vio0000358

Sundar, P., & Lim, S. (2023). Exposure to sexual and relational violence in digital media and its influence on attitudes toward victims. Journal of Interpersonal Violence, 38(1–2), 337–360. https://doi.org/DOI: 10.1177/08862605211073412

KEY TERMS AND DEFINITIONS

Algorithmic Amplification: The process by which digital platforms tend to prioritise and circularly share emotionally resonating content or even controversial pieces of information that invariably heighten the process of user exposure.

Attitudes to Relationship Violence: Individuals cognitive, emotional, and evaluative orientations towards behaviours such as physical, emotional, or psychological abuse within intimate relationships including levels of acceptance, justification or condemnation.

Cognitive Overload: A state of affairs when there is a greater volume and complexity of information than a person can process and the individual is unable to assess the information critically, resulting in an increased dependence on simplified or stereotypical judgement.

Desensitisation: A stimulus-specific decreased emotional response to repeated exposure to violent or distressing stimuli, and development of decreased shock or concern to similar future stimuli.

Emotional Fatigue: A build-up state of emotional exhaustion over period of exposure to distressing media content, and especially narratives of violence and gender hostility, leading to a reduction in the ability of individuals to sustain emotional engagement and the ability to critically reflect.

Emotional Numbing: A defensive psychological reaction, marked by a loss of emotional intensity and disengagement from the distressing problems, that arises as the result of being emotionally exhausted for an extended period of time.

Empathy Erosion: Some gradual loss of capacity to emotionally resonate with victim of violence, as a result of frequent emotional activation without renewal result in reduced prosocial concern.

Gender-Based Violence Normalised: A perceptual change in which repeated exposure to violence against women makes individual(s) regard the incidents as common, less extreme, or socially normal and not exceptional.

Internalised Misogyny: The process by which women end up unconsciously adopting and reproducing sexist beliefs, stereotypes, or negative attitudes towards their own gender, often due to the demographic's repeated exposure to media stories and cultural models of gender roles.

Media Exposure (Violent and Gendered): The frequency and intensity with which people are exposed to media depictions of violence, harassment and gender-based conflict within the digital platforms, including news, social media, and entertainment.

Misogyny: A pattern of beliefs, attitudes, and communicative practices that are de-polishing of women, objectifying them, or hostile to women. Within digital media environments the practise of misogyny runs on several levels - through both explicit abuse and subtle normalisation of gender inequality.

Victim-Blaming Tendencies: A cognitive bias whereby responsibility for this violence is in part or wholly attributed to a victim, often perpetuated by framing in the media and by stereotype and low levels of emotional engagement.

Chapter 18
Well-Being Apps and the Commodification of Emotional Care:
Psychological, Social, and Ethical Implications in the New Media Era

Nandhini S.
http://orcid.org/0009-0006-3292-7902
PES University, India

ABSTRACT

This chapter examines the expanding role of digital well-being applications in the transformation of mental health care within contemporary digital contexts. It highlights their potential to enhance accessibility and facilitate emotional self-regulation through evidence-based frameworks, including cognitive behavioural therapy and mindfulness. The analysis critically engages with algorithmic mediation, engagement-oriented design, and the commodification of emotional care within platform economies. Furthermore, it addresses key ethical and social concerns, such as data privacy, emotional surveillance, and structural inequalities in access. The chapter also considers broader psychological implications, including emotional fatigue and interpersonal disengagement, underscoring the need for a balanced and ethically grounded integration of digital technologies in emotional care.

INTRODUCTION

The rapid growth of digital technologies has significantly impacted how people seek psychological support. Today's digital support environment has seen the emer-

DOI: 10.4018/979-8-3373-8307-1.ch018

gence of well-being and mental health applications for mobile devices, enabling individuals to manage stress, emotions, mindfulness, and behavioural changes. These digital platforms are recognised worldwide as solutions that address long-standing gaps in the global mental health support system (Almuqrin et al., 2025; Gama & Laher, 2024; Shahsavar & Choudhury, 2025). The proliferation of smartphones has made well-being applications a quick and accessible form of psychological support (Diano et al., 2023; Wang et al., 2018).

The expansion of digital mental health technologies is especially evident in environments with limited access to traditional mental health services. In low- and middle-income countries, barriers such as cost, stigma, a shortage of mental health professionals, and geographical obstacles often delay essential care. In these settings, mobile health technologies are viewed as cost-effective ways to expand mental health services (Gama & Laher, 2024). Systematic reviews have shown that digital self-help tools can provide users with psychological techniques like cognitive-behavioural skills to enhance their mental well-being (Almuqrin et al., 2025; Diano et al., 2023; Shahsavar & Choudhury, 2025).

The increasing use of digital technologies for emotional support and well-being also raises important questions about how emotional support is understood and delivered in a technology-mediated context. Mental health tools utilise algorithms to manage user interactions through behavioural prompts and personalised data-driven processes (Ruckenstein, 2023). These systems can measure emotional experiences and analyse user data to suggest behavioural changes. While emotional support has traditionally been viewed as a highly personal and relational experience, it is now mediated through technological frameworks that aim to monitor and enhance psychological functioning. The integration of emotional experiences into digital infrastructure reflects changing aspects of human emotion in modern society. Such infrastructure increasingly influences emotional regulation, embedding affective engagement within a structured technological environment (Nabi & Myrick, 2023).

Online communication platforms, recommendation systems, and interactive applications shape emotional experiences in digital spaces, influencing how individuals perceive their own emotions and those of others (Nabi & Myrick, 2023; Ruckenstein, 2023). In this context, well-being applications exemplify the codification of emotional self-regulation within digital environments. A key aspect of this shift is the growing commodification of emotional care. In digital health frameworks, emotional support often becomes a marketable service within subscription models, where users' emotional experiences are integrated into economic systems based on ongoing interaction, behavioural analytics, and user retention metrics. Consequently, emotional well-being is now intertwined with technological infrastructures embedded within broader economic systems (Ruckenstein, 2023).

Emotional care is no longer solely relational but has become a commodified product in the realm of digital platforms. This commodification is closely tied to engagement-based design strategies used in many well-being apps. Research indicates that features like gamification, goal-setting, personalised reminders, and reward systems are common to foster user engagement (Wu et al., 2021). These strategies are often justified as ways to improve adherence to psychological interventions, yet they also serve the commercial interests of digital platforms, which depend on sustained engagement (Wu et al., 2021). As emotional self-care becomes embedded in these engagement-focused systems, the distinction between therapeutic support and commercial motives becomes increasingly blurred. A major concern remains whether digital platforms can truly replicate the depth of relational emotional care. Traditional psychological support involves empathy, therapeutic alliance, contextual understanding, and collaborative meaning-making, which contrasts with the standardised modules and algorithmic decision-making of mental health apps (Almuqrin et al., 2025; Shahsavar & Choudhury, 2025). There is a risk that these systems might oversimplify emotions by categorising them as behavioural responses.

Empirical evidence on the effectiveness of mental health apps reflects this complexity. Some systematic reviews suggest that mobile interventions, when rooted in evidence-based psychological methods, can offer minor improvements in anxiety, depression, and emotional regulation (Almuqrin et al., 2025; Diano et al., 2023; Shahsavar & Choudhury, 2025). Mobile technology also shows promise as an adjunct to traditional therapy, aiding in monitoring and self-management of symptoms (Diano et al., 2023; Wang et al., 2018). However, these applications often face challenges such as poor intervention quality, low engagement levels, and difficulties translating clinical evidence into digital design frameworks (Almuqrin et al., 2025; Wang et al., 2018).

The broader societal implications of digital-mediated emotional care are also under exploration by scholars, a relatively recent field of interest. Digital emotional self-management can lead individuals to feel constantly pressured to monitor, assess, and optimise their emotions, mirroring cultural trends that view self-improvement as an ongoing process requiring behavioural adjustments (Ruckenstein, 2023). Techniques like self-tracking may also increase the cognitive and emotional labour involved in maintaining psychological well-being (Ruckenstein, 2023).

Concurrently, the increased access to emotional support through digital platforms by individuals can create a potential impact on the increased use of these technological solutions in interpersonal care. The existing body of knowledge on the impact of emotional experiences in digital communication environments suggests that individuals' emotional experiences can be mediated by technology solutions. Such a potential impact can create a situation in which individuals can become emotionally detached and less engaged in interpersonal interactions (Nabi & Myrick,

2023). Hence, these new technologies can create a potential impact not only at the individual level in managing emotional experiences but also at the social norms level in interpersonal care. The relevance of these technologies can be understood in the context of the ongoing debate on emotional fatigue and interpersonal disengagement in digitally mediated societies. The continuous exposure to emotional experiences through digital platforms can create a potential impact in the form of psychological fatigue in managing one's emotional experiences.

In this regard, it is necessary to critically evaluate the importance of well-being application usage in the overall process of digital transformation in emotional care. In other words, rather than seeing these applications merely as a tool for emotional care, it is necessary to consider them part of a socio-technical system that influences emotional care in digital environments. In this regard, the overall importance of well-being application usage lies in the commodification of emotional care by converting it into quantified patterns. The overall aim of this chapter is to evaluate the psychological and social implications of well-being application usage in the overall media landscape (Almuqrin et al., 2025; Diano et al., 2023; Gama & Laher, 2024; Nabi & Myrick, 2023; Ruckenstein, 2023; Shahsavar & Choudhury, 2025; Wang et al., 2018; Wu et al., 2021).

UNDERSTANDING WELL-BEING APPS IN THE NEW MEDIA ERA

The dynamic development of digital technology has greatly impacted the way individuals access psychological resources and manage their emotional lives. An important feature in this area is the development of mobile well-being applications that are designed to assist individuals in mental health care using a smartphone platform. This application has a number of features that include a collection of resources for mental health care, which include mood monitoring, meditation, behavioural exercises, emotional management, psychoeducation, among others. This has shown a general trend in the development of digital technology for the provision of psychological resources, which is known as digital health infrastructures (Almuqrin et al., 2025; Wang et al., 2018).

Mobile well-being applications are often presented as alternatives or supplements for traditional mental health care. The increased popularity of smartphones across the world indicates that digital mental health care platforms have become an integral part of daily life, allowing individuals to access mental health resources without directly interacting with mental health care providers. This change in mental health care platforms is a part of a larger trend in health care delivery, where digital technologies are used as a means of increasing access, reducing health care costs, and self-managing health conditions (Almuqrin et al., 2025; Gama & Laher, 2024).

The proliferation of these applications can also be linked to the increased recognition of the importance of mental health issues worldwide and the lack of professional mental health resources in many countries. In low- and middle-income countries, for instance, individuals face challenges such as financial constraints and geographical inaccessibility in accessing psychological assistance. Mobile mental health applications have been promoted as a potential solution to these challenges by offering psychological assistance that can overcome these barriers (Gama & Laher, 2024). In this context, well-being applications can be regarded as a type of self-help that allows individuals to access psychological assistance in a structured manner.

Consequently, well-being applications can also be recognised as part of a broader shift in the conceptualisation and management of emotional life in digital societies. Digital technologies have increasingly become integral in shaping emotional life by incorporating emotional experiences in a technological environment that guides interactions and communication while at the same time influencing emotional expression (Nabi & Myrick, 2023). In this context, emotional self-management can be recognised as part of a digital environment that allows individuals to evaluate and manage their emotional life through structured digital practices.

Growth of Digital Mental Health Technologies

The rapid development of well-being applications indicates a change in the field of digital mental health. The development of mobile technologies, data analytics, and algorithms has made it possible for mental health care to be provided via well-being applications, which are smartphone-based platforms that offer exercises for mental health care (Almuqrin et al., 2025).

Studies on the impact of mobile mental health care technologies show that these platforms can be used for enhancing mental health outcomes. Reviews of these studies have shown that mobile mental health care platforms can be used for reducing mental health symptoms related to anxiety, depression, and emotional regulation, especially when evidence-based intervention techniques are included in these platforms (Diano et al., 2023; Shahsavar & Choudhury, 2025). These intervention techniques may include cognitive restructuring, mindfulness, behavioural activation, and stress management exercises.

Additionally, mobile-based mental health applications are increasingly being used as supplementary tools to traditional psychological interventions. This is especially true since mobile-based health applications can be used to provide tools to an individual to track their emotional states or to perform therapeutic exercises prescribed by a psychologist. This shows how mobile-based health technologies can provide psychological interventions beyond the traditional therapeutic environments. Despite all the positive developments in mobile-based health technologies, reviews have shown how the quality of the applications can vary significantly. This shows how the integration of psychological interventions into mobile-based health technologies can be a challenge. This challenge is compounded by the need to ensure that the mobile-based health technologies are not only effective but are also responsible interventions.

Accessibility and the Global Mental Health Gap

A commonly cited benefit of well-being apps is the promise they hold for increasing access to mental health resources for a variety of populations. The international health system continues to face the issue of unequal distribution of mental health resources, with many areas experiencing a significant deficit of qualified mental health professionals. In these areas, digital self-help apps may provide individuals with access to psychological resources that are otherwise unavailable (Gama & Laher, 2024).

Evidence supporting the effectiveness of mental health apps for low- and middle-income populations suggests that digital self-help tools can contribute to the improvement of mental health outcomes by addressing the contextual needs of the population. Mental health apps can alleviate issues with stigma, transportation, and cost, which may otherwise prevent individuals from engaging with mental health resources (Gama & Laher, 2024). The opportunity for individuals to access emotional resources privately through their own mobile devices may have special significance for populations experiencing stigma against mental health treatment.

Furthermore, the scalability of mobile technologies allows for the wide reach of well-being applications to large numbers of people simultaneously. This is unlike traditional therapeutic services that are restricted to the number of professionals available. The scalability of digital technologies is recognised as a major advantage of digital mental health technologies, particularly in the fight against disparities in mental health services across the world (Almuqrin et al., 2025; Gama & Laher, 2024).

However, accessibility is just the first step towards ensuring that the interventions are successful. The success of digital mental health interventions is largely dependent on the engagement of the users. A significant number of users tend to stop using mental health applications just after the download. This has been a major challenge in the use of digital self-help interventions. Therefore, the focus of recent research is on the design of applications that are successful in engaging users.

Psychological Frameworks Embedded in Well-Being Apps

A number of well-being applications have sought to incorporate some aspects of established psychological interventions by adapting these therapeutic strategies in digital formats. The most frequently integrated psychological frameworks in well-being applications include cognitive behavioural therapy, mindfulness-based stress reduction, and emotion regulation training (Almuqrin et al., 2025; Diano et al., 2023).

Cognitive behavioural therapy-based well-being applications usually offer users exercises that help them identify negative thought patterns and replace these thoughts with more adaptive cognitive processes. The applications use interactive processes that help users identify cognitive distortions and develop alternative cognitive processes for interpreting stressful life events. Another important psychological framework that has been integrated into a number of well-being applications is mindfulness-based stress reduction. The applications offer users exercises in mindfulness-based meditation that help them develop emotional awareness and reduce psychological distress. The exercises in mindfulness-based stress reduction help individuals focus their attention on the present moment and manage emotional challenges (Diano et al., 2023).

Emotion regulation training constitutes a critical psychological process that has been increasingly incorporated into contemporary well-being applications. These applications provide users with structured exercises designed to strengthen emotional regulation capacities. Through consistent practice, individuals can cultivate emotional coping strategies that enhance their ability to manage emotional challenges effectively. The acquisition of such coping skills is closely linked to improvements in both emotional resilience and psychological functioning. In essence, the development of emotional coping competencies fosters greater emotional stability and contributes to overall psychological well-being (Shahsavar & Choudhury, 2025).

However, the applications face the limitation that the processes involved in the applications do not allow users to benefit from personalised therapeutic procedures that help users cope with emotional difficulties. The procedures must be tailored to work in a computer-based system without the intervention of human beings. Well-being applications employ standardised therapeutic procedures that enable users to effectively manage emotional difficulties. In addition, these platforms integrate algorithmic processes that deliver personalised interventions, tailoring support to individual needs. This dual approach-combining structured methods with adaptive personalisation - enhances users' capacity to cope with emotional challenges and strengthens their overall psychological resilience. (Ruckenstein, 2023).

Algorithmic Systems and Emotional Self-Monitoring

A notable aspect of well-being applications is the use of algorithmic systems, which influence the processes that underpin the mechanisms of emotional regulation. The applications often require users to engage in the tracking of their emotions, either through daily check-ins, tracking, or journaling. The collected information is then analysed through the use of algorithmic systems, which create personalised recommendations, reminders, or behavioural prompts intended to aid the user in regulating their emotions (Ruckenstein, 2023).

This trend represents a paradigmatic shift with regard to the conceptualisation of emotional states within digital environments. Emotional states are translated into quantifiable metrics, which can be monitored, compared, and analysed over a period. The users' emotional states are, therefore, used as a form of input for a system that aims to optimise the users' psychological well-being through the use of constant monitoring and behavioural adaptation (Ruckenstein, 2023).

Although the applications are beneficial for the regulation of emotions, the system represents a culture that believes emotional well-being can be measured, quantified, and optimised through the use of technology. This represents a concept within digital self-tracking culture, which often considers various aspects of life, including emotions, as measurable domains that can be optimised.

Engagement-Oriented Design in Mental Health Applications

User engagement sustainability is a significant challenge associated with the design of well-being applications. Studies on the usage of mental health applications have revealed a high rate of users stopping the application shortly after the initial installation. This practice significantly reduces the therapeutic benefits of the application. This problem necessitates the incorporation of design strategies focused on encouraging user engagement. Such strategies may incorporate gamification components, progress tracking systems, achievement systems, and personalised reminders. These components are likely to enhance the motivation of the users to interact frequently with the application. Meta-analytical studies on the usage of mental health applications have revealed some significant behavioural components that enhance the engagement of the users. These components may incorporate goal-setting features, feedback features, and personalised notifications (Wu et al., 2021).

The incorporation of engagement strategies in well-being applications can be attributed to the overall commercialisation of the application. This practice ensures the sustainability of the application since the financial success of the application depends on the daily interaction of the users. This practice demonstrates the overall complexity associated with the success of well-being applications.

The development of well-being applications is a product of a larger shift in the nature of emotional care in the digital age. The technology expands the scope of psychological resources, incorporates therapeutic best practices into mobile technology, and makes it possible for users to constantly engage in emotional care practices. At the same time, it also channels emotional experiences into algorithmic systems and technology-based engagement infrastructures that alter users' understanding of their psychological states.

EMOTIONAL CARE AS A DIGITAL COMMODITY

The rising dependence on well-being apps for emotional care represents a new dimension in the evolution of emotional care infrastructures within digital settings. Traditionally, emotional care infrastructures are related to relational processes, which include family networks, peer support, and therapeutic infrastructures. Emotional care infrastructures are based on relational processes, which highlight the need for empathy, understanding, and mutual interpretation of emotional experiences. However, the development of digital mental health technologies represents a new dimension in the evolution of emotional care infrastructures. Well-being apps are based on structured psychological resources provided by mobile technology, which enables individuals to access emotional care irrespective of relational infrastructures (Almuqrin et al., 2025; Wang et al., 2018).

In the context of digital mental health technologies, emotional care infrastructures are based on the use of technology platforms to provide psychological interventions as digital services. These apps include meditation sessions, cognitive behavioural interventions, mood-tracking infrastructures, and other forms of psychological interventions provided through smartphone interfaces. These apps enable individuals to track their emotional experiences, identify their behaviours, and develop coping mechanisms to improve their psychological well-being (Diano et al., 2023; Shahsavar & Choudhury, 2025).

From a sociotechnical perspective, the evolution of emotional care infrastructures through the use of well-being applications represents a new dimension of the evolution of the infrastructures of emotional care. This new dimension of the evolution of the infrastructures of emotional care represents the process of commodification. Commodification represents the process by which social processes and human experiences become products or services produced, distributed, and consumed as part of the markets of the economy. The infrastructures of emotional care, as they exist through the use of well-being applications, become integrated into the context of digital mental health technologies. As a result, emotional regulation exercises, mindfulness programs, and other types of psychological interventions become digital services that can be downloaded, accessed, and consumed as part of the application ecosystems.

However, while the above technologies may potentially offer useful tools for emotional management, the embedding of psychological support into the digital platform economies reveals a new dynamic that fundamentally changes the architecture of emotional support. The following subsections will examine the mechanisms whereby well-being apps facilitate the commodification of emotional support.

Standardisation of Emotional Experiences

One of the main features of digital well-being platforms is the ability of such platforms to transform complex emotional experiences into an intervention framework that can be utilised by digital platforms. Emotional experiences in conventional well-being settings are explored through conversations between individuals and mental health practitioners, where emotions are considered in the broader personal, social, and cultural context in which they occur. On the other hand, digital well-being platforms include pre-designed intervention modules to help users overcome emotional challenges.

Currently, several well-being platforms include evidence-based techniques such as cognitive behavioural therapy, mindfulness, and emotional regulation (Almuqrin et al., 2025; Diano et al., 2023; Shahsavar & Choudhury, 2025). These techniques are mainly provided as interventions, reflection tools, and educational tools to help users become aware of negative thoughts, manage their emotions, and develop healthy coping mechanisms. Systematic reviews on well-being platforms show that the use of evidence-based techniques can lead to improved emotional well-being when used appropriately (Almuqrin et al., 2025; Diano et al., 2023).

The use of therapeutic techniques on digital well-being platforms may involve the standardisation or simplification of emotional experiences to facilitate their processing by digital platforms. Emotional experiences on digital well-being platforms are recorded by the use of tools such as mood tracking, emotional rating scales, and categorisation of emotions. These tools help to convert emotional experiences into quantifiable forms that can be processed by digital platforms (Wang et al., 2018). Although these tools may help understand one's emotional experiences, they standardise diverse emotional experiences by classifying them so that they can be processed by digital well-being platforms.

Algorithmic Mediation of Emotional Support

Another key factor that has contributed to the commodification of emotional support is the use of algorithmic systems to mediate emotional support on digital well-being platforms. An example of this is the use of well-being platforms that ask users to provide feedback on their emotional experiences on a daily basis. User feedback collected through these platforms is systematically analysed and processed by algorithmic systems. Based on this analysis, the applications generate and deliver tailored activities aligned with the feedback received. This feedback-driven, algorithm-mediated approach ensures that therapeutic interventions remain responsive, adaptive, and personalised to users' evolving emotional needs (Ruckenstein, 2023).

Algorithmic systems enable digital platforms to offer personalised emotional care through their ability to respond to user behaviour. For example, an app might offer relaxation techniques based on increased levels of stress reported by the user or offer motivational content based on reduced app engagement. These responses mimic the offering of emotional care through intelligent technological systems.

Algorithmic personalisation, however, is limited by the system's design architecture. The algorithms that offer emotional care are limited by the behavioural models that offer emotional experiences based on a limited number of variables. The offering of emotional care in digital platforms is thus limited by the parameters established in the app's development. Although they offer increased accessibility and efficiency, they are still limited in their ability to offer the complexity found in human relationships that account for contextual factors that influence emotional experiences (Ruckenstein, 2023).

Commercialisation of Emotional Well-Being

The commodification of emotional care is further emphasised by the economic models that various digital well-being platforms are based on. A significant portion of mental health applications is based on an economic model that relies on generating revenue from subscription-based models. Users may have access to the application for free, but they are often encouraged to purchase a membership that allows them access to various intervention modules.

The model that is followed by such applications is based on the idea that emotional well-being can be improved by continued engagement with the application. Users are often encouraged to incorporate emotional care practices that are offered by the application. While such applications may help users engage in consistent emotional regulation practices, they also promote emotional care as a function of consumer behaviour.

The implementation of an economic model in well-being applications is also related to engagement-based platform strategies. A study on mental health applications has found that developers often incorporate various behavioural techniques, such as goal-setting, progress-tracking, personalised reminders, and reward-based features, in order to engage users with the application (Wu et al., 2021). Such engagement is often based on the idea that users need to engage in consistent behaviour in order to improve emotional well-being. At the same time, such engagement is also based on the idea that user engagement is necessary for the application to generate revenue.

Emotional Data and Platform Value

Another aspect of commodification relates to the way in which emotional experiences are translated into digital data that, in turn, contributes to the operational value of well-being platforms. When an individual uses mental health applications, they are able to generate behavioural data, such as their moods, levels of task completion, and responses to certain mental health interventions. The data generated by such experiences is then analysed in an attempt to enhance the functionality of the well-being platform.

The collection and analysis of emotional data enable the developer to understand the behaviour of the users, as well as the features that are most effective in engaging users, thus enabling the application to be improved. As such, subjective emotional experiences are translated into behavioural data that is essential in informing the development and enhancement of well-being platforms.

While the insights provided by the data may improve the functionality of well-being application programs, the datafication of emotional experiences may also be seen as part of a broader transformation of emotional experiences in digital environments. Emotional experiences that have traditionally been internalised and contextualised may now be externalised as part of digital monitoring systems that transform emotional experiences into forms of data. These transformations may thus be seen as part of the broader process through which digital well-being application programs both increase access to emotional support and increasingly embed emotional experiences in technological systems that operate in platform economies.

While well-being application programs increase access to emotional support, the integration of well-being application programs in platform economies may be seen as raising questions about the authenticity of the emotional support provided by these programs. The promise of personalised emotional support may not be seen as reflecting the actual operation of well-being application programs. Therefore, it is necessary to consider the evidence regarding the effectiveness of well-being application programs as well as the limitations of these programs (Almuqrin et al., 2025; Shahsavar & Choudhury, 2025; Wang et al., 2018). The following section of the chapter discusses the effectiveness of well-being application programs and the illusion of personalised emotional support.

ENGAGEMENT MECHANISMS AND THE MARKET LOGIC OF WELL-BEING

The efficacy and sustainability of well-being applications are inextricably tied to their ability to foster consistent user engagement. This subject is particularly relevant due to the fact that mental health applications are significantly differentiated from traditional sessions in which user engagement is facilitated through structured interactions. Thus, mental health applications have adopted a range of engagement tools that aim to foster user engagement and behavioural involvement. These tools are not only psychologically complex but also deeply embedded in the commercial aspects of digital economies in which user engagement is critical for platform success (Ruckenstein, 2023; Wu et al., 2021).

In this context, user engagement tools within mental health applications should be recognised as integral components of systems that seek to reconcile psychological complexity with commercial imperatives. While such tools may effectively promote behavioural change and strengthen emotional regulation, they must also be understood as extensions of the broader digital platform economy, where sustained user engagement is a critical determinant of platform viability and success.

Gamification and Behavioural Reinforcement

One of the most prominent engagement mechanisms used in mental health applications is gamification. Gamification is defined as "the use of game design elements in non-game environments to promote user engagement." In mental health applications, gamification is used to offer the required motivation to users to participate in sessions. For example, mental health applications can offer rewards to users for participating in meditation sessions or maintaining stable mood states. This is done to offer a sense of accomplishment to users, which would help them engage with the application further, perceiving that they have reached certain milestones during their interaction with the application.

The promotion of positive behavioural patterns and sustained user motivation for continued engagement with digital platforms represents a critical dimension of mental health applications (Wu et al., 2021). From a psychological perspective, this process is closely tied to reinforcement mechanisms, whereby repetitive behaviours are strengthened through structured reward systems. Gamification, in particular, has emerged as a central strategy for fostering user motivation by embedding reward-based reinforcement into application design. However, beyond its motivational function, gamification also intersects with broader user engagement dynamics, underscoring the complex interplay between psychological mechanisms and platform interaction structures.

The utilisation of a reward system encourages further consideration of whether the intrinsic desire for emotional health is replaced by an extrinsic desire based upon the utilisation of an application. As such, engagement is somewhat constructed through platform-based feedback as opposed to solely based upon psychological objectives.

Personalised Notifications and Habit Formation

Personalised notifications and reminders are one of the most common mechanisms used by well-being applications to ensure user engagement. These notifications can prompt users to perform their daily exercises, reflect on their well-being, or interact with certain well-being modules. This would help the application ensure that users develop certain habits by integrating these notifications into their daily lives. From a behavioural point of view, these notifications serve as cues to users to perform certain actions, which could help them develop certain self-care habits. Users may develop certain habitual ways of engaging with these applications, which could be a part of their daily lives (Wu et al., 2021).

However, this also represents a broader platform-level strategy to avoid disengagement. Notifications are carefully planned to optimise engagement. This is based on the application of behavioural science and user experience. This may promote habitual engagement with the application. Nevertheless, this is also part of the larger platform-based approaches that focus on user retention as a primary performance metric.

Another prominent feature of well-being applications is the incorporation of data-driven approaches in the engagement of users. The applications collect data about the interactions of the users with the content of the app. This data may include the frequency of usage of the app and the results of the interactions with emotional tracking tools. The data collected is then used to modify the content of the app in a manner that is most relevant to the users. This creates the illusion of an app that is dynamic and changes in response to the users. However, as discussed in the previous sections, the changes in the app are within the limits of the structures that have been predetermined in the app.

The data-driven approaches in the engagement of the users also play a role in the overall incorporation of emotional care in the app. The data collected is used to refine the engagement of the users with the app and to maximise the engagement of the users with the content of the app. In this regard, the engagement of the users with the app is not only a psychological phenomenon but also a data-driven phenomenon.

Market Logic and the Prioritisation of Engagement

The engagement mechanisms in well-being applications should be viewed in the context of digital market economies. There are many mental health applications in digital app stores, and as such, they are subject to competition in the app market. This means that engagement is a key consideration in mental health applications in two ways: as a therapeutic objective and as a commercial objective.

Additionally, the economic models underlying mental health application use often promote long-term use of such applications. Some features might only be available to premium account holders, which can create a model in which engagement is rewarded through participation in a digital economy.

Therefore, mental health application design can be seen as having two components: it aims to promote mental health, but it also exists as a product of a market economy that prioritises engagement and commercial success (Ruckenstein, 2023). This point is important to this current analysis as it highlights the importance of engagement mechanisms to mental health application use.

Overall, engagement mechanisms represent a pivotal element in the design and delivery of mental health applications. By incorporating strategies such as gamification and personalisation, these mechanisms foster sustained user interaction, encourage longer engagement periods, and promote stability in behavioural patterns. At the same time, their effectiveness is shaped by broader market dynamics that influence platform development and delivery. Accordingly, this analysis underscores the dual role of engagement mechanisms: as psychological tools that reinforce user motivation and as structural components embedded within the commercial logic of the digital platform economy.

In this regard, engagement serves a dual function within mental health applications. On one hand, it ensures that users dedicate time to interacting with the platform; on the other, it facilitates exposure to emotionally oriented digital content. While this can yield psychological and social benefits, it also carries risks, particularly those related to emotional fatigue and diminished interpersonal connections. These dynamics highlight the complex implications of sustained engagement, which extend beyond platform use into broader patterns of emotional exhaustion and disengagement in relationships. The following section examines these issues in greater detail. (Nabi & Myrick, 2023).

DIGITAL MEDIATION, EMOTIONAL FATIGUE, AND SOCIAL INDIFFERENCE

This increased integration of well-being apps into daily life represents a larger trend in the mediation of emotional experiences in digital environments. Thus, as people begin to interact with emotionally oriented media in mobile applications, social media platforms, and digital communication systems, their emotional experiences become further mediated by technology. Although these platforms may be beneficial in helping people express and manage their emotions in a better manner, they are also seen to be associated with increased and prolonged engagement in emotionally oriented media. This increased engagement in digital emotional media is seen to be related to psychological fatigue and alterations in interpersonal dynamics (Nabi & Myrick, 2023; Wu et al., 2021). Thus, it is important to examine the role that technology-mediated emotional experiences play in psychological and interpersonal dynamics.

Technology-Mediated Emotional Experiences

Digital media have transformed the ways in which emotions are experienced and processed by embedding emotional expressions into technology-mediated platforms. Well-being applications, social media networks, and communication systems now enable individuals to actively monitor and reflect upon their emotional states. These systems often encourage continuous self-observation and emotional processing, thereby shaping how users engage with and interpret their emotional experiences (Nabi & Myrick, 2023).

Emotional Fatigue in Digital Environments

Emotional fatigue can also occur due to excessive exposure to emotionally related content in digital environments. Emotional fatigue can be described as a state of exhaustion caused by prolonged exposure to emotionally related content. In digitally mediated environments, it is common to come across a wide range of emotional inputs, including personal reflections, social interactions, and therapeutic content.

Although well-being applications are designed to foster emotional regulation, continuous engagement may inadvertently contribute to emotional fatigue. This aligns with broader research on digital burnout, which identifies cognitive overload and psychological exhaustion as outcomes of sustained digital interaction (Wu et al., 2021; M.A, 2025; Brown, 2025). Such findings highlight the need for balanced application design that promotes resilience without overwhelming users.

Interpersonal Disengagement and Social Indifference

The mediation of emotional experiences through digital platforms may also influence interpersonal interactions to a certain extent. However, as people become more inclined towards technology for dealing with their emotional concerns, there may be a gradual decline in the level of human interaction. Emotional well-being applications provide people with tools that can help them individually overcome their emotional concerns. Emotional interactions through digital mediation may lead people to become indifferent towards others' emotional interactions, resulting in a state of social indifference (Nabi & Myrick, 2023). This is, however, not an implication of an inability of an individual to empathise with others; it is a change in the way people conduct their emotional interactions through digital mediation. Furthermore, the availability of technology for providing emotional support may lead people towards independent emotional well-being, where an individual's emotional needs are fulfilled through independent coping mechanisms, rather than through interactions with others. This may also lead people towards a state of social indifference, as it is an aspect of human interaction.

Normalising Self-Managed Emotional Care

Well-being applications play a pivotal role in normalising self-managed emotional care by promoting individual responsibility for emotional regulation. These platforms provide users with structured exercises and personalised tools that recommend strategies for managing emotional well-being. Within the broader digital context, this trend reflects the ethos of self-optimisation, where individuals are encouraged to continuously monitor and enhance their psychological states through technology. Emotional care, therefore, becomes framed as a self-contained process, reliant on consistent engagement with digital tools. While this framing empowers individuals by positioning them as active agents in their emotional management, it simultaneously reinforces the notion that emotional well-being is primarily an individual responsibility rather than a collective or relational one (Ruckenstein, 2023).

Digitally mediated emotional environments play a critical role in shaping individual emotional experiences. Within this context, well-being applications function as essential mediators, structuring how users engage with and regulate their emotions. While these platforms provide opportunities for individuals to exercise control over their emotional states, sustained engagement within technologically mediated environments becomes a defining factor in the formation of emotional experiences. In effect, emotional life is increasingly intertwined with digital systems that guide, reinforce, and shape the ways individuals process and express emotions (Nabi & Myrick, 2023; Shukla, 2025).

The changes in the psychology of people, as well as their social behaviour, with regard to digital mediation of emotional well-being, are a matter of great ethical importance, especially with regard to well-being applications. Therefore, the next section of this paper explores the ethical and social consequences of well-being apps, especially within the context of digital mental health systems (Ruckenstein, 2023; Wang et al., 2018).

ETHICAL AND SOCIAL IMPLICATIONS

The widespread integration of well-being apps into daily emotional lives raises significant ethical and social questions. While these apps provide access to psychological support tools, they are also part of a digital landscape dominated by data collection, user engagement, and business interests. Consequently, emotional support is increasingly delivered through technological systems that influence how personal data and emotional experiences are gathered and organised. It is therefore crucial to review the ethical frameworks governing well-being apps and their societal implications (Ruckenstein, 2023; Wang et al., 2018).

Data Privacy and Emotional Surveillance

One key ethical concern with well-being apps is data privacy in relation to emotional surveillance. Users often need to share personal details such as emotional states, stress levels, behaviours, and reflections on their feelings. While this information helps tailor recommendations and improve user experiences, it also raises privacy issues. Emotional data is distinct because its collection creates the risk of ongoing emotional monitoring, where a user's emotional state is tracked and documented in digital form (Ruckenstein, 2023). Although this data can enhance user experience and intervention effectiveness, concerns remain over how the data is stored, who has access, and how it might be used beyond immediate interventions. Furthermore, since many well-being apps are part of the larger digital economy, the data collected can contribute to platform analytics and commercialisation. These processes often involve questions about informed consent and the user's awareness of how their data is used (Wang et al., 2018).

Emotional Exploitation and Commercial Interests

The financial aspect of emotional care on digital platforms can lead to emotional exploitation. Many well-being apps operate on a model where users pay for access to psychological content and resources, making emotional well-being potentially a commodity. These platforms may introduce features designed to boost engagement and prolong use, not only for therapeutic aims but also to maximise commercial gains. For example, they might offer premium content or insights accessible only through paid subscriptions, requiring users to spend money for deeper emotional support. Ethically, this creates a conflict of interest, as these apps may prioritise business objectives over genuine emotional care (Ruckenstein, 2023).

Inequality and the Digital Divide in Mental Health Access

While well-being apps extend mental health services, their availability is often uneven across different societal groups. Access to these digital services depends on factors like smartphone ownership, internet access, and financial means. This means that disadvantaged populations may be unable to benefit from these tools (Gama & Laher, 2024). Additionally, focusing on digital emotional support might overlook the need to strengthen traditional mental health systems, which continue to serve many underserved communities. Differences in cultural perceptions of emotional support may also be ignored in app development, as many are based on specific psychological models that may not suit diverse populations.

Redefining Emotional Care in Digital Societies

Embedding well-being apps into daily life influences how emotional care is understood. Traditionally linked to close relationships and professional therapy, emotional care is now being redefined through digital technology as an individualised and mediated experience. This shift encourages people to take responsibility for their emotional health via digital tools. While this may empower individuals to proactively manage their well-being, it also alters the social context of emotional support, potentially changing how emotional relationships are experienced and understood (Ruckenstein, 2023).

The integration of emotional care into digital platforms reflects broader societal trends toward the technologization of social life. As digital tools increasingly shape emotional experiences, there is a need for a critical assessment of this redefinition of emotional care. Overall, the ethical and social consequences of well-being apps extend beyond user privacy to issues of equity and the fundamental nature of emotional support in a digital age. Although these apps offer promising avenues for expanding mental health resources, they also introduce complexities that require careful exploration. The development of digital mental health tools must prioritise ethical considerations, user well-being, and inclusivity.

The ethical, psychological, and social issues discussed here reveal the complex role that well-being apps play in shaping emotional care in contemporary society.

While innovation in mental health support is valuable, it also signals changes in how emotional care is experienced and understood. This next section will synthesise the preceding analysis, highlighting how engagement mechanisms, self-managed emotional care, and digitally mediated emotional environments collectively shape the evolving role of mental health applications. It will also consider the broader implications of these trends, particularly their influence on the media landscape (Ruckenstein, 2023; Nabi & Myrick, 2023).

CONCLUSION

The proliferation of well-being applications is a clear indicator of a tremendous shift in the provision and experience of emotional care in digitally mediated societies. These applications provide a wide range of mental health care by offering users an alternative for managing their well-being. When grounded in evidence-based interventions such as cognitive-behavioural therapy and mindfulness, applications of well-being have the potential to enhance emotional well-being (Almuqrin et al., 2025; Diano et al., 2023; Shahsavar & Choudhury, 2025). Their availability makes them particularly useful in situations where traditional mental health services remain limited (Gama & Laher, 2024).

However, as this chapter has demonstrated, integrating emotional care within digitally mediated societies raises critical issues. Emotional care is being standardised, quantified, and algorithmically mediated, which shapes the way people experience their emotions (Ruckenstein, 2023). Although it may appear as if the application of technology is providing a more personal approach to care, it is, in fact, limited in terms of providing contextual and empathetic care. This is a critical issue that reflects the disconnect between the ideal of personalisation and the reality of algorithmic intervention.

The chapter also explores the role of market logic in the provision of well-being applications. For example, gamification and data adaptation are being used as mechanisms for maintaining user engagement with well-being applications, as seen in Wu et al. (2021) and Ruckenstein (2023), where the therapeutic process is aligned with economic needs in a platform-specific manner. In this sense, emotional care becomes aligned with economic imperatives that relate to user retention and monetisation.

At a broader level, it may be that sustained engagement with emotionally related digital spaces contributes to emotional exhaustion and altered interpersonal dynamics. The use and development of self-related digital tools may reduce interpersonal engagement, thereby changing the way in which individuals relate to emotional experiences in themselves and others (Nabi & Myrick, 2023).

Another set of ethical considerations further clarifies the complexities surrounding these technologies. The collection and aggregation of affective data have also raised concerns about privacy and surveillance in the context of data-driven digital ecosystems (Wang et al., 2018; Ruckenstein, 2023). Furthermore, inequalities in digital resources also highlight the limitations in solely relying on technology to address mental health challenges at large (Gama & Laher, 2024).

Therefore, well-being applications can be understood as complex interfaces situated at the intersection of psychology, technology, and market forces. While they hold tremendous potential for expanding access to emotional care, their design and delivery must be approached with balance. Only by carefully negotiating therapeutic objectives with technological innovation and commercial imperatives can digital mental health technologies provide meaningful care and foster well-being within the rapidly evolving landscape of new media.

REFERENCES

Almuqrin, A., Hammoud, R., Terbagou, I., Tognin, S., & Mechelli, A. (2025). Smartphone apps for mental health: Systematic review of the literature and five recommendations for clinical translation. *BMJ Open*, *15*(2), e093932. DOI: 10.1136/bmjopen-2024-093932 PMID: 39933815

Brown, B., PhD. (2025, November 24). How digital fatigue affects mental health: understanding "Zoom-burnout" and screen-overload. *Psyforu*.

Diano, F., Sica, L. S., & Ponticorvo, M. (2023). A systematic review of mobile apps as an adjunct to psychological interventions for emotion dysregulation. *International Journal of Environmental Research and Public Health*, *20*(2), 1431. DOI: 10.3390/ijerph20021431 PMID: 36674189

Gama, B., & Laher, S. (2024). Self-help: A systematic review of the efficacy of mental health apps for low- and middle-income communities. *Journal of Technology in Behavioral Science*, *9*(3), 428–439. DOI: 10.1007/s41347-023-00360-z

M, A. (2025). Digital Burnout: How overstimulation impacts mental health. *Dua Neuro Care*. https://duaneurocare.com/digital-burnout/

Nabi, R. L., & Myrick, J. G. (Eds.). (2023). *Emotions in the Digital World: Exploring Affective Experience and Expression in Online Interactions*. Oxford University Press. DOI: 10.1093/oso/9780197520536.001.0001

Ruckenstein, M. (2023). *The Feel of Algorithms*. University of California Press.

Shahsavar, Y., & Choudhury, A. (2025). Effectiveness of evidence-based mental health apps on user health outcome: A systematic literature review. *PLoS One*, *20*(3), e0319983. DOI: 10.1371/journal.pone.0319983 PMID: 40131942

Shukla, P. (2025). Coded emotions: Digital humanities at the crossroads of narrative design and mental spaces. *International Journal of Research and Analytical Reviews*.

Wang, K., Varma, D. S., & Prosperi, M. (2018). A systematic review of the effectiveness of mobile apps for monitoring and management of mental health symptoms or disorders. *Journal of Psychiatric Research*, *107*, 73–78. DOI: 10.1016/j.jpsychires.2018.10.006 PMID: 30347316

Wu, A., Scult, M. A., Barnes, E. D., Betancourt, J. A., Falk, A., & Gunning, F. M. (2021). Smartphone apps for depression and anxiety: A systematic review and meta-analysis of techniques to increase engagement. *NPJ Digital Medicine*, *4*(1), 20. DOI: 10.1038/s41746-021-00386-8 PMID: 33574573

Compilation of References

Abidin, C. (2021). Mapping internet celebrity on TikTok: Exploring attention economies and visibility labours. *Cultural science journal, 12*(1), 77-104.

Abidin, C. (2016). Visibility labour: Engaging with influencers' fashion brands and #OOTD advertorial campaigns on Instagram. *Media International Australia, Incorporating Culture & Policy, 161*(1), 86–100. DOI: 10.1177/1329878X16665177

Adams, J. T. (2017). *The Epic of America*. Routledge. (Original work published 1931, Little, Brown, and Company) DOI: 10.4324/9781351304122

Addeo, F., Punziano, G., & Mauceri, S. (2022). The Impact of Digital on Research, Socialisation, and Communication Processes. *Italian Journal of Sociology of Education, 14*(Italian Journal of Sociology of Education 14/3), 1-16.

Affective capitalism: Investments and investigations. (2016). [Editorial]. Ephemera: Theory & Politics in Organization, 1–13, 1–13. https://www.ephemerajournal.org

Agai, M. S. (2022). Disconnectivity synced with identity cultivation: Adolescent narratives of digital disconnection. *Journal of Computer-Mediated Communication, 27*(6), zmac025. Advance online publication. DOI: 10.1093/jcmc/zmac025

Agha, Z., Badillo-Urquiola, K., & Wisniewski, P. J. (2023). " Strike at the root": co-designing real-time social media interventions for adolescent online risk prevention. *Proceedings of the ACM on Human-Computer Interaction, 7*(CSCW1), 1-32. DOI: 10.1145/3579625

Ahluwalia, P. S. (2025). *Doomscrolling and mental fatigue: Cognitive overload in digital media environments*. Digital Psychology Review.

Ahmed, S. (2013). *The cultural politics of emotion*. routledge.

Ahmed, S. (2004). *The cultural politics of emotion*. Edinburgh University Press.

Ajewumi, O. E., Magbagbeola, V., Kalu, O. C., Ike, R. A., Folajimi, O., & Diyaolu, C. O. (2024). The impact of social media on mental health and well-being. *World Journal of Advanced Research and Reviews, 24*(1), 107–121. DOI: 10.30574/wjarr.2024.24.1.3027

Alawode, O. D. (2025). Invisible Influence: How Algorithmic News Feeds Are Reshaping Public Opinion Without Disclosure. *IOSR Journal Of Humanities and Social Science (IOSR-JHSS), 30*(8), 58-73.

Albasar, İ. D., Demiralp, S., & Parlak, F. (2025). Sosyal Medya, Bilişsel Yorgunluk ve Siyasi Apati: Dijital Dönüşümün Gençler Üzerindeki Yansımaları. *Social Review of Technology and Change, 3*(2), 103–125.

Alesina, A., Brioschi, B., & La Ferrara, E. (2016). *Violence against women: A cross-cultural analysis for Africa* (No. w21901). National Bureau of Economic Research.

Alheneidi, H., AlSumait, L., AlSumait, D., & Smith, A. P. (2021). Loneliness and problematic internet use during COVID-19 lock-down. *Behavioral Sciences (Basel, Switzerland), 11*(1), 5. DOI: 10.3390/bs11010005 PMID: 33418914

Alimour, S. A., & Alrabeei, M. (2025). Redefining psychopathology in the context of digital overload: Emerging disorders in the age of information saturation. *Frontiers in Digital Health, 7*, 1693287. DOI: 10.3389/fdgth.2025.1693287 PMID: 41312176

Alkaraki, S. M. S., Alias, N. B., & Maros, M. (2024). Exploring the impact of social media humor related to the COVID-19 pandemic: A systematic literature review on themes, coping mechanisms, critiques and linguistic devices. *Cogent Arts & Humanities, 11*(1), 2322227. DOI: 10.1080/23311983.2024.2322227

Allmer, T., Sevignani, S., & Prodnik, J. A. (2015). Mapping approaches to user participation and digital labour: A critical perspective. In *Palgrave Macmillan UK eBooks* (pp. 153–171). DOI: 10.1057/9781137478573_9

Alloway, T., & Alloway, R. (2011). Attentional control and engagement with digital technology. *Nature Precedings*. DOI: 10.1038/npre.2011.5603.1

Almuqrin, A., Hammoud, R., Terbagou, I., Tognin, S., & Mechelli, A. (2025). Smartphone apps for mental health: Systematic review of the literature and five recommendations for clinical translation. *BMJ Open, 15*(2), e093932. DOI: 10.1136/bmjopen-2024-093932 PMID: 39933815

Alptekin, H. (2023, December 2). Siyasete Yabancılaşma, Politik Apati ve Tükenmişlik Sendromu. *Türkiye Araştırmaları Vakfı*. https://www.turkiyearastirmalari.org/2023/12/02/fokus-tr/siyasete-yabancilasma-politik-apati-ve-tukenmislik-sendromu/

Alter, A. (2017). *Irresistible: The rise of addictive technology and the business of keeping us hooked*. Penguin.

Altheide, D. L. (2002). *Creating fear: News and the construction of crisis*. Aldine de Gruyter.

American Psychological Association. (2022). Stress in America 2022: Concerned for the future, beset by inflation. APA. https://www.apa.org/news/press/releases/stress/2022/concerned-future-inflation

Anand, N., Sharma, M. K., Thakur, P. C., Mondal, I., Sahu, M., Singh, P., J, A. S., Kande, J. S., Ms, N., & Singh, R. (2022). Doomsurfing and doomscrolling mediate psychological distress in COVID-19 lockdown: Implications for awareness of cognitive biases. *Perspectives in Psychiatric Care*, *58*(1), 170–172. DOI: 10.1111/ppc.12803 PMID: 33880766

Anderson, J., & Rainie, L. (2023). As AI spreads, experts predict the best and worst changes in digital life by 2035. *Pew Research Center, 21*.

Anggara, O. F., & Rahmasari, D. (2025). Enhancing digital well-being in the era of hyperconnectivity: A psychological perspective. *Journal of Positive Psychology and Digital Well Being*, *1*(1), 48–53.

Anjum, G., & Aziz, M. (2024). Advancing equity in cross-cultural psychology: Embracing diverse epistemologies and fostering collaborative practices. *Frontiers in Psychology*, *15*, 1368663. DOI: 10.3389/fpsyg.2024.1368663 PMID: 38638521

Annaki, F., Ouassou, S., & Igamane, S. (2025). Visibility and Influence in Digital Social Relations: Towards a New Symbolic Capital? arXiv preprint arXiv:2505.08797.

An, R., Qian, G., Mumtaz, A., Alotaibi, K. A., & Wang, X. (2025). Digital fatigue and academic resilience among university students with grit and flexibility as mediators. *Scientific Reports*, *15*(1), 45407. DOI: 10.1038/s41598-025-29313-7 PMID: 41298778

Antoniak, M., Mire, J., Sap, M., Ash, E., & Piper, A. (2024, August). Where do people tell stories online? story detection across online communities. In *Proceedings of the 62nd Annual Meeting of the Association for Computational Linguistics (*Volume 1*: Long Papers)* (pp. 7104-7130). DOI: 10.18653/v1/2024.acl-long.383

Arango-Kure, M., & Garz, M. (2025). Manipulation: An integrative framework of unethical influence in marketing. *Journal of Business Research*, *197*, 115476. DOI: 10.1016/j.jbusres.2025.115476

Arcy, J. (2016). Emotion work : Considering gender in digital labor. *Feminist Media Studies, 0777*(February), 365–368. Advance online publication. DOI: 10.1080/14680777.2016.1138609

Argyriadi, A., Katsarou, D., Patelarou, A., Megari, K., Patelarou, E., Kotrotsiou, S., & Argyriadis, A. (2025). Digital Stress Scale (DSS): Development and psychometric validation of a measure of stress in the digital age. *International Journal of Environmental Research and Public Health, 22*(7), 1080. DOI: 10.3390/ijerph22071080 PMID: 40724147

Arnold, M., Goldschmitt, M., & Rigotti, T. (2023). Dealing with information overload: A comprehensive review. *Frontiers in Psychology, 14*, 1122200. DOI: 10.3389/fpsyg.2023.1122200 PMID: 37416535

Arora, P. (2019). *The next billion users: Digital life beyond the West*. Harvard University Press. DOI: 10.4159/9780674238879

Ashforth, B. E., & Humphrey, R. H. (1993). Emotional labor in service roles: The influence of identity. *Academy of Management Review, 18*(1), 88–115. DOI: 10.2307/258824

Asiyah, S. N., Taufiqi, M. A. Z., Raihan, F. N., Hakiki, M. H., Putri, N. R. D., Nuzul, E., & Wahyuni, M. N. P. Emotional Exhaustion in the Digital Native Generation of Social Media Users.

Bachmann, P., & Siegert, G. (2021). How to buy, sell, and trade attention: A sociology of (digital) attention markets. In *Digital attention markets* (pp. 147–157). DOI: 10.1007/978-3-030-61619-9_10

Bakhtin, M. M. (1984). *Rabelais and his world* (Iswolsky, H., Trans.). Indiana University Press. (Original work published 1965)

Bakker, A. B., & Demerouti, E. (2017). Job demands–resources theory: Taking stock and looking forward. *Journal of Occupational Health Psychology, 22*(3), 273–285. DOI: 10.1037/ocp0000056 PMID: 27732008

Balaskas, S., Konstantakopoulou, M., Yfantidou, I., & Komis, K. (2025). Algorithmic burnout and digital well-being: Modelling young adults' resistance to personalized digital persuasion. *Societies (Basel, Switzerland), 15*(8), 232. DOI: 10.3390/soc15080232

Banaji, S., & Buckingham, D. (2013). *The civic web: Young people, the internet, and civic participation*. MIT Press. DOI: 10.7551/mitpress/8949.001.0001

Bandura, A. (2017). Moral disengagement in the perpetration of inhumanities. In *Recent developments in criminological theory* (pp. 135–152). Routledge. DOI: 10.4324/9781315089089-12

Banet-Weiser, S. (2018). *Empowered: Popular feminism and popular misogyny.* Duke University Press.

Barber, L. K., & Santuzzi, A. M. (2020). Please respond ASAP: Workplace telepressure and employee recovery. *Journal of Occupational Health Psychology, 25*(1), 1–14. PMID: 31829662

Barinkar, M. A., & Zheng, F. (2025). How digital platforms are changing the way students learn. *Preprints.org*. DOI: 10.20944/preprints202507.0332.v1

Barykin, S. Y., Kapustina, I. V., Kirillova, T. V., Yadykin, V. K., & Konnikov, Y. A. (2020). Economics of digital ecosystems. *Journal of Open Innovation, 6*(4), 124. DOI: 10.3390/joitmc6040124

Batson, C. D. (2011). *Altruism in humans.* Oxford University Press.

Batson, C. D., Fultz, J., & Schoenrade, P. A. (1987). Distress and empathy: Two qualitatively distinct vicarious emotions with different motivational consequences. *Journal of Personality, 55*(1), 19–39. DOI: 10.1111/j.1467-6494.1987.tb00426.x PMID: 3572705

Baumann, F., Arora, N., Rahwan, I., & Czaplicka, A. (2025). Dynamics of Algorithmic Content Amplification on TikTok. arXiv preprint arXiv:2503.20231.

Baumeister, R. F. (2002). Ego depletion and self-control failure: An energy model of the self's executive function. *Self and Identity, 1*(2), 129–136. DOI: 10.1080/152988602317319302

Bau, N., Nunn, N., & Voena, A. (2016). *Can Policy Crowd Out Culture?* Bride Price and Female Education.

Baurai, S., Sekhar, C., Kumar, D., & Raj, A. (2025). Digitalization and employee well-being: A fuzzy-tism approach of remote work stressors. *Journal ofManagement & Organization, 31*(6), 3004–3028. DOI: 10.1017/jmo.2025.10059

Baym, N. K. (2015). *Personal connections in the digital age.* John Wiley & Sons.

Bear, H., Fazel, M., & Skripkauskaite, S.the OxWell Study Team. (2025). Isolation despite hyper-connectivity? The association between adolescents' mental health and online behaviours in a large study of school-aged students. *Current Psychology (New Brunswick, N.J.), 44*(8), 7124–7137. DOI: 10.1007/s12144-025-07643-z

Beck, D., & Spencer, A. (2025). (Un)Funny Against All Odds: The Changing Landscape of Humour in Politics. *Alternatives, 50*(1), 3–17. DOI: 10.1177/03043754241290911

Beer, D. (2009). Power through the algorithm? Participatory web cultures and the technological unconscious. *New Media & Society, 11*(6), 985–1002. DOI: 10.1177/1461444809336551

Belaid, S., Ben Guedria, N., & Ballouk, H. (2025). Remote Work and Job Satisfaction: A Decade of Insights Through a Bibliometric Lens. *Administrative Sciences, 15*(11), 439. DOI: 10.3390/admsci15110439

Belgroun, H., Michel, F., & Gandon, F. (2025). No such thing as free brain time: For a Pigouvian tax on attention capture. In *Proceedings of the AAAI/ACM Conference on AI Ethics and Society, 8*(1), 367–378. DOI: 10.1609/aies.v8i1.36555

Benkler, Y. (2006). *The wealth of networks: How social production transforms markets and freedom*. Yale University Press.

Berger, J., Kim, Y. D., & Meyer, R. (2021). What makes content engaging? How emotional dynamics shape success. *The Journal of Consumer Research, 48*(2), 235–250. DOI: 10.1093/jcr/ucab010

Berger, J., & Milkman, K. (2012). What makes online content viral? *JMR, Journal of Marketing Research, 49*(2), 192–205. DOI: 10.1509/jmr.10.0353

Berlant, L. (2011). *Cruel optimism*. Duke University Press.

Berman, M. G., Jonides, J., & Kaplan, S. (2008). The cognitive benefits of interacting with nature. *Psychological Science, 19*(12), 1207–1212. DOI: 10.1111/j.1467-9280.2008.02225.x PMID: 19121124

Beshley, M., Klymash, M., Beshley, H., Shkoropad, Y., & Bobalo, Y. (2024, February). Revolutionizing Digital Ecosystems with Artificial Intelligence: Challenges, Concepts, and Future Directions. In *IEEE International Conference on Advanced Trends in Radioelectronics, Telecommunications and Computer Engineering* (pp. 1-21). Cham: Springer Nature Switzerland.

Bhadouria, N., Macknight, S., Francis, A., & Yadav, A. (2025). The unblinking scroll: Exploring the perceptual and cognitive impacts of continuous reel scrolling. *International Journal of Multidisciplinary Research and Analysis, 8*(9). Advance online publication. DOI: 10.47191/ijmra/v8-i09-14

Bianchi, R., Schonfeld, I. S., & Laurent, E. (2019). Burnout: Moving beyond the status quo. *International Journal of Stress Management, 26*(1), 36–45. DOI: 10.1037/str0000088

Bicalho, C. C. F., da Costa, I. T., Noce, F., & da Costa, V. T. (2020). Prevalence of burnout in soccer athletes of the under-20 category over a sports season. *Journal of Physical Education (Maringá), 31*(1), e3160. https://www.scielo.br/j/jpe/a/YBHBX49Rv5q7tCfsxYRcFJJ/?lang=en. DOI: 10.4025/jphyseduc.v31i1.3160

Bingöl, O. (2017). SİYASAL KAYITSIZLIK: APATİ. *Munzur Üniversitesi Sosyal Bilimler Dergisi, 5*(9), 44–51.

Bishop, S. (2019). Managing visibility on YouTube through algorithmic cruelty. *New Media & Society, 21*(11–12), 2586–2603.

Bishop, S. (2020). Algorithmic experts: Selling algorithmic lore on YouTube. *Social Media + Society, 6*(1), 2056305119897323. DOI: 10.1177/2056305119897323

Blanco-Moreno, S., González-Fernández, A. M., Munoz-Gallego, P. A., & Casaló, L. V. (2024). Understanding engagement with Instagram posts about tourism destinations. *Journal of Destination Marketing & Management, 34*, 100948. DOI: 10.1016/j.jdmm.2024.100948

Bloom, P. (2017). *Against empathy: The case for rational compassion.* Random House.

Bocheliuk, V. Y., Zavatska, N. Y., Bokhonkova, Y. O., Toba, M. V., & Panov, N. S. (2020). Emotional burnout: Prevalence rate and symptoms in different socio-professional groups. *Journal of Intellectual Disability–Diagnosis and Treatment, 8*(1), 33–40. DOI: 10.6000/2292-2598.2020.08.01.5

Bodle, R. (2016). A critical theory of advertising as surveillance: Algorithms, big data, and power. In *Advertising and surveillance* (pp. 148–162). DOI: 10.4324/9781315625768

Bojic, L. (2024). AI alignment: Assessing the global impact of recommender systems. *Futures, 160*, 103383. DOI: 10.1016/j.futures.2024.103383

Boltanski, L. (1999). *Distant suffering: Morality, media and politics.* Cambridge University Press. DOI: 10.1017/CBO9780511489402

Bondanini, G., Giovanelli, C., Mucci, N., & Giorgi, G. (2025). The dual impact of digital connectivity: Balancing productivity and well-being in the modern workplace. *International Journal of Environmental Research and Public Health, 22*(6), 845. DOI: 10.3390/ijerph22060845 PMID: 40566273

Bondanini, G., Sanchez-Gomez, M., Mucci, N., & Giorgi, G. (2026). Psychometric validation of the constant connectivity scale in the context of digital work in Italian organisations. *Administrative Sciences, 16*(1), 39. DOI: 10.3390/admsci16010039

Bouchaud, P. (2024). Skewed perspectives: Examining the influence of engagement maximization on content diversity in social media feeds. *Journal of Computational Social Science*, *7*(1), 721–739. DOI: 10.1007/s42001-024-00255-w

Boutros, N. (2023). Emotional numbness: Definition, causes & how to deal with it.

Brandao, B. M., & Denny, B. T. (2024). What Instagram Means to Me: Links Between Social Anxiety, Instagram Contingent Self-worth, and Automated Textual Analysis of Linguistic Authenticity. *Affective Science*, *5*(4), 449–457. DOI: 10.1007/s42761-024-00267-9 PMID: 39649457

Braun, V., & Clarke, V. (2021). *Thematic analysis: A practical guide*. SAGE Publications.

Brockmyer, J. F. (2022). Desensitization and violent video games: Mechanisms and evidence. *Child and Adolescent Psychiatric Clinics of North America*, *31*(1), 121–132. DOI: 10.1016/j.chc.2021.06.005

Brotheridge, C. M., & Grandey, A. A. (2002). Emotional labor and burnout: Comparing two perspectives of "people work.". *Journal of Vocational Behavior*, *60*(1), 17–39. DOI: 10.1006/jvbe.2001.1815

Brown, B., PhD. (2025, November 24). How digital fatigue affects mental health: understanding "Zoom-burnout" and screen-overload. *Psyforu*.

Brown, K. W., & Ryan, R. M. (2003). The benefits of being present: Mindfulness and its role in psychological well-being. *Journal of Personality and Social Psychology*, *84*(4), 822–848. DOI: 10.1037/0022-3514.84.4.822

Brown, Y., Pini, B., & Pavlidis, A. (2022). Affective design and memetic qualities: Generating affect and political engagement through bushfire TikToks. *Journal of Sociology (Melbourne, Vic.)*, *60*(1), 144078332211102. DOI: 10.1177/14407833221110267

Brumby, D. P., Janssen, C. P., & Mark, G. (2019). How do interruptions affect productivity? In *Apress eBooks* (pp. 85–107). DOI: 10.1007/978-1-4842-4221-6_9

Bryant, E. F. (2009). *The Yoga Sutras of Patanjali: A new edition, translation, and commentary*. North Point Press.

Buchanan, K., Aknin, L. B., Lotun, S., & Sandstrom, G. M. (2021). Brief exposure to social media during the COVID-19 pandemic: Doomscrolling has negative emotional consequences, but kindness-scrolling does not. *PLoS One*, *16*(10), e0257728. DOI: 10.1371/journal.pone.0257728 PMID: 34644310

Bucher, E., Fieseler, C., Lutz, C., & Newlands, G. (2016b). Shaping emotional labor practices in the sharing. In I. Maurer, J. Mair, A. Oberg (eds). *Theorizing the Sharing Economy: Variety and Trajectories of New Forms of Organizing* (pp. 55–82). DOI: 10.1108/S0733-558X20200000066004

Bucher, E., Fieseler, C., & Lutz, C. (2016a). Computers in Human Behavior What ' s mine is yours (for a nominal fee) - Exploring the spectrum of utilitarian to altruistic motives for Internet-mediated sharing. *Computers in Human Behavior, 62*, 316–326. DOI: 10.1016/j.chb.2016.04.002

Bucher, T. (2018). *If... then: Algorithmic power and politics*. Oxford University Press. DOI: 10.1093/oso/9780190493028.001.0001

Budnitsky, S. (2023). Global disengagement: Public diplomacy humor in the Russian–Ukrainian War. *Place Branding and Public Diplomacy, 19*(2), 211–217. DOI: 10.1057/s41254-022-00291-1

Burström, T., Lahti, T., Parida, V., Wartiovaara, M., & Wincent, J. (2022). Software ecosystems now and in the future: A definition, systematic literature review, and integration into the business and digital ecosystem literature. *IEEE Transactions on Engineering Management, 71*, 12243–12258. DOI: 10.1109/TEM.2022.3216633

Cameron, C. D., Hutcherson, C. A., Ferguson, A. M., Scheffer, J. A., Hadjiandreou, E., & Inzlicht, M. (2019). Empathy is hard work: People choose to avoid empathy because of its cognitive costs. *Journal of Experimental Psychology. General, 148*(6), 962–976. DOI: 10.1037/xge0000595 PMID: 30998038

Carbone, M., Soroka, S., & Dunaway, J. (2024). The Psychophysiology of News Avoidance: Does Negative Affect Drive Both Attention and In attention to News? *Journalism Studies, 25*(12), 1460–1475. DOI: 10.1080/1461670X.2024.2310672

Çarkoğlu, A., & Kalaycıoğlu, E. (2015). *Türkiye'de ve Dünya'da Vatandaşlık* [ISSP Araştırma Raporu]. https://bilimakademisi.org/turkiyede-ve-dunyada-vatandaslik-2014-issp-arastirma-raporu/

Cassilo, D., & Sanderson, J. (2019). From Social Isolation to Becoming an Advocate: Exploring Athletes' Grief Discourse About Lived Concussion Experiences in Online Forums. *Communication & Sport, 7*(5), 678–696. DOI: 10.1177/2167479518790039

Castells, M. (2010). *The rise of the network society*. Wiley-Blackwell.

Catangay, J. R. (2025). *Constructing hope in hopelessness: Playful resistances of affective publics in TikTok's #corecore #pinoycore*. Plaridel., DOI: 10.52518/2024-9ctngy

Cemiloglu, D., Naiseh, M., Catania, M., Oinas-Kukkonen, H., & Ali, R. (2021). The fine line between persuasion and digital addiction. In *Lecture Notes in Computer Science* (pp. 289–307). DOI: 10.1007/978-3-030-79460-6_23

Centre for the Study of Developing Societies (CSDS). (2022). *Media consumption and trust survey*. CSDS.

Chagas, V., Freire, F., Rios, D., & Magalhães, D. (2019). Political memes and the politics of memes: A methodological proposal for content analysis of online political memes. *First Monday*, *24*(2). Advance online publication. DOI: 10.5210/fm.v24i2.7264

Chau, C. W., Norton, C., Kruzan, K. P., & Jacobs, M. (2025, April). " All Day, Every Day, Listening to Trauma": Investigating Features of Digital Interventions for Empathy-Based Stress and Burnout. In *Proceedings of the 2025 CHI Conference on Human Factors in Computing Systems* (pp. 1-18). DOI: 10.1145/3706598.3713588

Chen, Y., Fu, Y., Chen, Z., Radesky, J., & Hiniker, A. (2024). The engagement-prolonging designs teens encounter on very large online platforms. *arXiv*. /arxiv.2411.12083DOI: 10.48550

Cheshin, A., Glikson, E., Lavee, E., & Gabriel, A. S. (2026, January). Digital emotional labor: Benefits and challenges of emotional labor in the context of text-based service. *The Journal of Applied Psychology*, *111*(1), 116–137. DOI: 10.1037/apl0001305 PMID: 40689934

Cheshin, A., Glikson, E., Lavee, E., Gabriel, A. S., Cheshin, A., Glikson, E., Lavee, E., & Gabriel, A. S. (2025). Journal of Applied Psychology Digital Emotional Labor : Bene fi ts and Challenges of Emotional Labor in the Context of Text-Based Service. *The Journal of Applied Psychology*.

Chmiel, J., & Kurpas, D. (2025). Burnout and the brain—A mechanistic review of magnetic resonance imaging (MRI) studies. *International Journal of Molecular Sciences*, *26*(17), 8379. DOI: 10.3390/ijms26178379 PMID: 40943301

Cho, H., Li, P., Ngien, A., Grace, M., & Chen, A. (2020). The bright and dark sides of social media use during COVID-19 lockdown: Contrasting social media effects through social liability vs. social support. *The Bright and Dark Sides of Social Media Use during* [*Lockdown: Contrasting Social Media Effects through Social Liability vs. Social Support, January.*]. *COVID*, •••, 19.

Choi, J., Lee, S. Y., & Ji, S. W. (2021). Engagement in emotional news on social media: Intensity and type of emotions. *Journalism & Mass Communication Quarterly*, *98*(4), 1017–1040. DOI: 10.1177/1077699020959718

Chou, H. T. G., & Edge, N. (2012). "They are happier and having better lives than I am": The impact of using Facebook on perceptions of others' lives. *Cyberpsychology, Behavior, and Social Networking*, *15*(2), 117–121. DOI: 10.1089/cyber.2011.0324 PMID: 22165917

Chouliaraki, L. (2006). The spectatorship of suffering. *Sage (Atlanta, Ga.)*.

Chouliaraki, L. (2013). *The ironic spectator: Solidarity in the age of post-humanitarianism*. Polity Press.

Chowdhury, K., & Lamacchia, D. (2019, November). Collaborative workspace for employee engagement leveraging social media architecture. In *Abu Dhabi International Petroleum Exhibition and Conference* (p. D031S093R003). SPE. DOI: 10.2118/197325-MS

Churchill, E. F., & Nichols, J. (2016). Understanding the Challenges of Designing and Developing Multi-Device Experiences. *Proceedings of the 2016 ACM Conference on Designing Interactive Systems.*, 62–72.

Chu, S. C., Deng, T., & Mundel, J. (2024). The impact of personalization on viral behavior intentions on TikTok: The role of perceived creativity, authenticity, and need for uniqueness. *Journal of Marketing Communications*, *30*(1), 1–20. DOI: 10.1080/13527266.2022.2098364

Cimperman, S. (2023). Informal socialization in virtual work environments: Creating a digital culture of connectivity. *Global Business and Organizational Excellence*, *43*(1), 53–71. DOI: 10.1002/joe.22197

Ciocîrlea, B. Z. (2025). A paradox of modern communication: The decline of physical proximity. *Buletinul Institutului Politehnic din Ia i. Seria tiin e Socio-Umane*, *71*(1–2), 119–127.

Ciolfi, L., & Lockley, E. (2018). From Work to Life and back again: Examining the digitally-mediated work/life practices of a group of knowledge workers. [CSCW]. *Computer Supported Cooperative Work*, *27*(3), 803–839. DOI: 10.1007/s10606-018-9315-3

Citton, Y. (2017). *The ecology of attention*. Polity Press.

Clemente-Suárez, V. J., Beltrán-Velasco, A. I., Herrero-Roldán, S., Rodriguez-Besteiro, S., Martínez-Guardado, I., Martín-Rodríguez, A., & Tornero-Aguilera, J. F. (2024). Digital device usage and childhood cognitive development: Exploring effects on cognitive abilities. *Children (Basel, Switzerland)*, *11*(11), 1299. DOI: 10.3390/children11111299 PMID: 39594874

Çoban, S. (2024). Emotional digital labor among young people within the context of lumpencybertariat. *Gençlik Araştırmaları Dergisi, 12*(33), 57–72.

Codagnone, C. (2016). *The Passions and the Interests : Unpacking the ' Sharing E conomy .'* DOI: 10.2791/474555

Corbeanu, A., Iliescu, D., Ion, A., & Spînu, R. (2023). The link between burnout and job performance: A meta-analysis. *European Journal of Work and Organizational Psychology, 32*(4), 599–616. DOI: 10.1080/1359432X.2023.2209320

Couldry, N., & Hepp, A. (2017). *The mediated construction of reality*. Polity Press.

Coyne, P., & Woodruff, S. J. (2023). Taking a break: The effects of partaking in a two-week social media digital detox on problematic smartphone and social media use, and other health-related outcomes among young adults. *Behavioral Sciences (Basel, Switzerland), 13*(12), 1004. DOI: 10.3390/bs13121004

Crary, J. (2013). *24/7: Late capitalism and the ends of sleep*. Verso.

Creswell, J. W., & Creswell, J. D. (2023). *Research design: Qualitative, quantitative, and mixed methods approaches* (6th ed.). SAGE Publications.

Cui, J. (2022). Respecting the old and loving the young: Emoji-based sarcasm interpretation between younger and older adults. *Frontiers in Psychology, 13*, 897153. DOI: 10.3389/fpsyg.2022.897153

Cunneen, M. A. R. T. I. N., & Mullins, M. A. R. T. I. N. (2019). Framing risk, The new phenomenon of data surveillance and data monetisation; from an 'Always-On'culture to 'Always-On'artificial intelligence assistants. *Hybrid Worlds, 65*.

Curato, N., & Niemeyer, S. (2013). Reaching Out to Overcome Political Apathy: Building Participatory Capacity through Deliberative Engagement. *Politics & Policy, 41*(3), 355–383. DOI: 10.1111/polp.12015

Damstra, A., Vliegenthart, R., Boomgaarden, H., Glüer, K., Lindgren, E., Strömbäck, J., & Tsfati, Y. (2023). Knowledge and the news: An investigation of the relation between news use, news avoidance, and the presence of (mis)beliefs. *The International Journal of Press/Politics, 28*(1), 29–48. DOI: 10.1177/19401612211031457

Darius, P. (2024, September 24). *Researcher Data Access Under the DSA: Lessons from TikTok's API Issues During the 2024 European Elections*. Tech Policy Press. https://techpolicy.press/-researcher-data-access-under-the-dsa-lessons-from-tiktoks-api-issues-during-the-2024-european-elections

Davenport, T. H., & Beck, J. C. (2001). *The attention economy*. Harvard Business School Press.

Dawkins, R. (1976). *The selfish gene*. Oxford University Press.

De Falco, S. (2019). Digital and urban spaces: Oxymoron or binomial? Urban transformations in the digital era. *Geography Compass, 13*(10), e12467. DOI: 10.1111/gec3.12467

de Leon, E., Segura, J., & Valenzuela, S. (2021). News overload, emotional fatigue, and disengagement in the age of social media. Digital Journalism, 9(4), 491–509. https://doi.org/DOI: 10.1080/21670811.2020.1829975

De Medeiros, A. S., Glatzl, L. A., & Lifschitz, S. (2024). Surveillance capitalism revealed: Tracing the hidden world of web data collection. In *Proceedings* (pp. 388–397). DOI: 10.5753/sbbd_estendido.2024.244000

de Medeiros, M. F., & Maciel, V. d'Ávila, de Medeiros, S. F., da Silva, J. C. G., de Queiros, V. S., de Almeida Neto, P. F., & Cabral, B. G. de A. T. (2025). Relationship between Social Media Induced Mental Fatigue and Sprint Performance in Young Futsal Athletes. *Interfaces Científicas-Saúde e Ambiente, 10*(1), 549–568. https://periodicos.set.edu.br/saude/article/view/12909

De Reuver, M., Sørensen, C., & Basole, R. C. (2018). The digital platform: A research agenda. *Journal of Information Technology, 33*(2), 124–135. DOI: 10.1057/s41265-016-0033-3

Dean, L., Churchill, B., Ruppanner, L., Churchill, B., & Ruppanner, L. (2022). The mental load : building a deeper theoretical understanding of how cognitive and emotional labor over load women and mothers. *The Mental Load : Building a Deeper Theoretical Understanding of How Cognitive and Emotional Labor over Load Women and Mothers*. DOI: 10.1080/13668803.2021.2002813

Decety, J., & Jackson, P. L. (2004). The functional architecture of human empathy. *Behavioral and Cognitive Neuroscience Reviews, 3*(2), 71–100. DOI: 10.1177/1534582304267187 PMID: 15537986

DeLuca, T. (1995). *The two faces of political apathy*. Temple University Press.

Demiralp, S. (2025, October 10). Arada Kalanlar: Geçişken Seçmenlerde Esneklik, Apati ve Güven Arayışı. *Global Panorama*. https://www.globalpanorama.org/2025/10/arada-kalanlar-gecisken-secmenlerde-esneklik-apati-ve-guven-arayisi/

Denegri-Knott, J., Jenkins, R., Molesworth, M., & Grigore, G. (2023). Platformised possessions and relational labour. *Marketing Theory, 24*(1), 23–44. DOI: 10.1177/14705931231201783

Dennis, M. J. (2020). Cultivating digital well-being and the rise of self-care apps. In *Philosophical Studies Series* (pp. 119–137). DOI: 10.1007/978-3-030-50585-1_6

Derks, D., & Bakker, A. B. (2014). The impact of email communication on psychological detachment, recovery, and burnout. *Work and Stress, 28*(1), 17–33. DOI: 10.1080/02678373.2013.879664

Derks, D., Bakker, A. B., & Peters, P. (2021). The psychology of digital communication at work. *Current Opinion in Psychology, 43*, 190–195.

Dhir, A., Talwar, S., Kaur, P., Budhiraja, S., & Islam, N. (2021). The dark side of social media: Stalking, online self-disclosure and problematic sleep. *International Journal of Consumer Studies, 45*(6), 1373–1391. DOI: 10.1111/ijcs.12659

Dhir, A., Yossatorn, Y., Kaur, P., & Chen, S. (2018). Online social media fatigue and psychological wellbeing—A study of compulsive use, fear of missing out, fatigue, anxiety and depression. *International Journal of Information Management, 40*, 141–152. DOI: 10.1016/j.ijinfomgt.2018.01.012

Diano, F., Sica, L. S., & Ponticorvo, M. (2023). A systematic review of mobile apps as an adjunct to psychological interventions for emotion dysregulation. *International Journal of Environmental Research and Public Health, 20*(2), 1431. DOI: 10.3390/ijerph20021431 PMID: 36674189

Diefendorff, J. M., Croyle, M. H., & Gosserand, R. H. (2005). The dimensionality and antecedents of emotional labor strategies. *Journal of Vocational Behavior, 66*(2), 339–357. DOI: 10.1016/j.jvb.2004.02.001

Dobson, A. S. (2020). The 'care crisis' in digital culture: Women, social media, and emotional labour. In Clark, J., & Sen, A. B. (Eds.), *Gender, media and digital cultures* (pp. 57–72). Routledge.

Domalewska, D. (2025). Digital entrapment. *Kultura i Spoleczenstwo, 69*(3), 151–171. DOI: 10.35757/KiS.2025.69.3.9

Domínguez-Rodríguez, A., Apprich, F., Friehs, M. A., van der Graaf, S., & Steinrücke, J. (2025). Climate change news and doomscrolling: An examination of influencing factors and psychological effects. *Acta Psychologica, 245*, 104925. DOI: 10.1016/j.actpsy.2025.104925 PMID: 40112762

Dong, Y., Wang, M., Liu, E., & Xing, L. (2025). Causes of digital fatigue among hotel employees in the digital age: Configuration study based on fsQCA. *Asia Pacific Journal of Marketing and Logistics*.

Döveling, K., Harju, A. A., & Sommer, D. (2018). From Mediatized Emotion to Digital Affect Cultures : New Technologies and Global Flows of Emotion. *Social Media + Society*, *4*(1), 2056305117743141. Advance online publication. DOI: 10.1177/2056305117743141

Drüppel, K., Dombrowski, J., & Trepte, S. (2025). Use it or lose it: The relationship between short-form video use and sustained attention. *OSF Preprints*. DOI: 10.31234/osf.io/qbxw4_v1

Duffy, B. E. (2017). *(Not) getting paid to do what you love: Gender, social media, and aspirational work*. Yale University Press. DOI: 10.12987/yale/9780300218176.001.0001

Duke, É., & Montag, C. (2017). Smartphone addiction, daily interruptions and self-reported productivity. *Addictive Behaviors Reports*, *6*, 90–95. DOI: 10.1016/j.abrep.2017.07.002 PMID: 29450241

Dunaway, J., & Graber, D. A. (2022). *Mass media and American politics* (12th ed.). CQ Press.

Dutta, D., & Mishra, S. K. (2024). "Technology is killing me!": The moderating effect of organization home-work interface on the linkage between technostress and stress at work. *Information Technology & People*, *37*(6), 2203–2222. DOI: 10.1108/ITP-03-2022-0169

Duzbayev, N. T., Velitchenko, S. N., & Doskhozhina, Z. M. (2023). Immersive Media as a New Multimedia Experience: Prospects and Risks. In *DTESI (workshops, short papers)*.

Edwards, D. J., Kaastra, L. T., Fisher, B., Chang, R., & Chen, M. (2017). Cognitive information theories of psychology and applications with visualization and HCI through crowdsourcing platforms. In *Lecture Notes in Computer Science* (pp. 139–153). DOI: 10.1007/978-3-319-66435-4_6

Ejaz, S., & Khaliq, H. M. H. (2025). Mental health in the age of hyperconnectivity: A crisis hidden in plain sight. *Pakistan Journal of Medicine and Dentistry*, *14*(3), 1–3. DOI: 10.36283//ziun-pjmd14-3/001

Elmas, T. (2023). The Impact of Data Persistence Bias on Social Media Studies. *Proceedings of the 15th ACM Web Science Conference 2023, WebSci '23*, 196–207. DOI: 10.1145/3578503.3583630

Entman, R. M. (2004). *Projections of power: Framing news, public opinion, and U.S. foreign policy*. University of Chicago Press.

Eppler, M. J., & Mengis, J. (2002). The Concept of Information Overload. *MCM Research Paper*.Figley, C. R. (1995). *Compassion fatigue*. Brunner/Mazel.

Ergas, O. (2016). Attention please: Positioning attention at the center of curriculum and pedagogy. *Journal of Curriculum Theorizing, 31*(2). Advance online publication. DOI: 10.63997/jct.v31i2.581

Ernst, A., & Schnauber-Stockmann, A. (2024). Won't stop 'til you get enough? Determinants of disengaging from mobile media apps in daily life. *OSF Preprints*. DOI: 10.31219/osf.io/atk49

Evren. (2025). A Critical Examination of Emotional Labour and Emotional Capital in Social Media Interaction. *AM Journal of Art and Media Studies, 4*(37), 57–73.

Examination, A. C. (2025). A Critical Examination of Emotional Labour and Emotional Capital in Social Media Interaction. *A Critical Examination of Emotional Labour and Emotional Capital in Social Media Interaction, 4*(37), 57–73.

Fardouly, J., & Vartanian, L. R. (2021). Social media and body image concerns: Current research and future directions. *Current Opinion in Psychology, 9*, 1–5. DOI: 10.1016/j.copsyc.2015.09.005

Ferreira, J. (2023). The challenge of hyperdistraction for design education. DOI: 10.21606/iasdr.2023.247

Figley, C. R. (1995). Compassion fatigue: Toward a new understanding of the costs of caring.

Figley, C. R. (1995). *Compassion fatigue: Coping with secondary traumatic stress disorder in those who treat the traumatized*. Brunner/Mazel.

Fish, A. (2017). Technology retreats and the politics of social media. *TripleC, 15*(1), 355–369. DOI: 10.31269/triplec.v15i1.807

Fisher, J. T., & Keene, J. R. (2020). Attention, working memory, and media multitasking. In *Cognitive perspectives on multitasking* (pp. 177–196). DOI: 10.4324/9781351235587-16

Flayelle, M., Brevers, D., King, D. L., Maurage, P., Perales, J. C., & Billieux, J. (2023). A taxonomy of technology design features that promote potentially addictive online behaviours. *Nature Reviews Psychology, 2*(3), 136–150. DOI: 10.1038/s44159-023-00153-4

Flecha Ortiz, J. A., Santos Corrada, M., Perez, S., Dones, V., & Rodriguez, L. H. (2024). Exploring the influence of uncontrolled social media use, fear of missing out, fear of better options, and fear of doing anything on consumer purchase intent. *International Journal of Consumer Studies, 48*(1), e12990. DOI: 10.1111/ijcs.12990

Folkman, S. (1997). Positive psychological states and coping with severe stress. *Social Science & Medicine, 45*(8), 1207–1221. DOI: 10.1016/S0277-9536(97)00040-3 PMID: 9381234

Fontefrancesco, M. F. (2023). Affective economy: A theoretical outline. *Encyclopedia, 3*(3), 1020–1027. DOI: 10.3390/encyclopedia3030074

Forbes. (2021, February 15). Finding brand success in the digital world. https://www.forbes.com/sites/forbesagencycouncil/2021/08/25/finding-brand-success-in-the-digital-world/

Fortes, L. S., Gantois, P., De Lima-Júnior, D., Barbosa, B. T., Ferreira, M. E. C., Nakamura, F. Y., Albuquerque, M. R., & Fonseca, F. S. (2023). Playing videogames or using social media applications on smartphones causes mental fatigue and impairs decision-making performance in amateur boxers. *Applied Neuropsychology. Adult, 30*(2), 227–238. DOI: 10.1080/23279095.2021.1927036 PMID: 34061684

Foster, J. W. (2013). *Oldenburg's great good places online: Assessing the potential for social network sites to serve as third places* [PhD Thesis, Texas Tech University]. http://hdl.handle.net/2346/58210

Foucault, M. (1977). *Discipline and punish: The birth of the prison* (Sheridan, A., Trans.). Pantheon Books. (Original work published 1975)

Fournier, C., Parent, S., & Paradis, H. (2022). The relationship between psychological violence by coaches and conformity of young athletes to the sport ethic norms. *EJSS European Journal for Sport and Society, 19*(1), 37–55. DOI: 10.1080/16138171.2021.1878436

Fournier, H., Fournel, A., Osiurak, F., Koenig, O., Pâris, F., Gaujoux, V., & Ringeval, F. (2025). Attention hijacked: How social media notifications disrupt cognitive processing. *OSF Preprints*. DOI: 10.31234/osf.io/z4ruj_v1

Frawley, D. (2000). *Ayurveda and the mind: The healing of consciousness*. Lotus Press.

Freud, S. (2003). *Jokes and their relation to the unconscious* (Crick, J., Trans.). Penguin. (Original work published 1905)

Frost, S., Kannis-Dymand, L., Schaffer, V., Millear, P., Allen, A., Stallman, H., Mason, J., Wood, A., & Atkinson-Nolte, J. (2022). Virtual immersion in nature and psychological well-being: A systematic literature review. *Journal of Environmental Psychology*, *80*, 101765. DOI: 10.1016/j.jenvp.2022.101765

Fuchs, C. (2014). Digital prosumption labour on social media in the context of the capitalist regime of time. *Time & Society*, *23*(1), 97–123. DOI: 10.1177/0961463X13502117

Fuchs, C. (2021). *Social media: A critical introduction* (3rd ed.). Sage. DOI: 10.4135/9781036232214

Funk, J. B., Baldacci, H. B., Pasold, T., & Baumgardner, J. (2004). Violence exposure in real-life, video games, television, movies, and the internet: Is there desensitization? *Journal of Adolescence*, *27*(1), 23–39. DOI: 10.1016/j.adolescence.2003.10.005

Fu, S., Li, H., Liu, Y., Pirkkalainen, H., & Salo, M. (2020). Social media overload, exhaustion, and use discontinuance: Examining the effects of information overload, system feature overload, and social overload. *Information Processing & Management*, *57*(6), 102307. DOI: 10.1016/j.ipm.2020.102307

Gabriel, A. S., Daniels, M. A., Diefendorff, J. M., & Greguras, G. J. (2020). Emotional labor actors: A latent profile analysis of emotional labor strategies. *The Journal of Applied Psychology*, *105*(1), 12–30. DOI: 10.1037/apl0000425 PMID: 25068812

Galor, O., & Sarid, A. (2017). *Geographical Origins and Economic Consequences of Language Structures*. Available. DOI: 10.2139/ssrn.2820889

Galtung, J., & Ruge, M. H. (1965). The structure of foreign news. *Journal of Peace Research*, *2*(1), 64–91. DOI: 10.1177/002234336500200104

Gama, B., & Laher, S. (2024). Self-help: A systematic review of the efficacy of mental health apps for low- and middle-income communities. *Journal of Technology in Behavioral Science*, *9*(3), 428–439. DOI: 10.1007/s41347-023-00360-z

Garcia, D., & Rimé, B. (2019). Collective Emotions and Social Resilience in the Digital Traces After a Terrorist Attack. *Psychological Science*, *1993*(4), 617–628. Advance online publication. DOI: 10.1177/0956797619831964 PMID: 30865565

Garcia-Rivadulla, S. (2016). Personalization vs. privacy. *IFLA Journal*, *42*(3), 227–238. DOI: 10.1177/0340035216662890

Gerbaudo, P. (2022). Theorizing reactive democracy. *Democratic Theory*, *9*(2), 120–138. DOI: 10.3167/dt.2022.090207

Gerbner, G., Gross, L., Morgan, M., & Signorielli, N. (1986). Living with television: The dynamics of the cultivation process. In *Perspectives on media effects*.

Ghasemi, A., & Azari Noughabi, M. (2024). Investigating the mediating role of Foreign Language Peace of mind and learning burnout in the relationship between Informal Digital Learning of English and willingness to communicate. *Computer Assisted Language Learning*, •••, 1–30. DOI: 10.1080/09588221.2024.2424321

Gillespie, T. (2014). The relevance of algorithms. *Media technologies: Essays on communication, materiality, and society, 167*(2014), 167.

Gillespie, T. (2022). *Custodians of the internet: Platforms, content moderation, and the hidden decisions that shape social media*. Yale University Press.

Gill, R., & Orgad, S. (2015). The confidence cult (ure). *Australian Feminist Studies, 30*(86), 324–344. DOI: 10.1080/08164649.2016.1148001

Gitlin, T. (2001). *Media unlimited: How the torrent of images and sounds overwhelms our lives*. Metropolitan Books.

Giuliano, P. (2017). *Gender and Cultural Perspectives*. Gender and Cultural Perspectives.

Glover, H. (1992). Emotional numbing: A possible endorphin-mediated phenomenon associated with post-traumatic stress disorders and other allied psychopathologic states. *Journal of Traumatic Stress*, *5*(4), 643–675.

Goffman, E. (1959). *The presentation of self in everyday life*. Doubleday.

Goldenberg, A., Garcia, D., Halperin, E., Gross, J. J., Goldenberg, A., Garcia, D., & Halperin, E. (2020). Collective emotions. *Current Directions in Psychological Science*, *29*(2), 154–160. DOI: 10.1177/0963721420901574

Goleman, D. (2006). *Social intelligence: The new science of human relationships*. Bantam Books.

Goodwin, G. E. (2026, January 1). Social media fuelled Mamdani's rise. Can he keep the momentum as mayor? *BBC*. https://www.bbc.com/news/articles/c4gvg46dy7vo

Google Trends. (2020). Doomscrolling search trends 2020. https://trends.google.com/trends/explore?q=doomscrolling

Google. (2025). *Google's Year in Search*. https://trends.withgoogle.com/year-in-search/2025/

Gorski, L. C. (2022). Uninterested, disenchanted, or overwhelmed? An analysis of motives behind intentional and unintentional news avoidance. *Communications*, *48*(4), 563–587. DOI: 10.1515/commun-2021-0084

Gottlieb, J., & Robinson, A. L. (2016). The Effects of Matrilineality on Gender Differences in Political Behavior across Africa. *The Effects of Matrilineality on Gender Differences in Political Behavior across. Africa*.

Government of India. (2013). *Report of the Justice Verma Committee on amendments to criminal law*. Government of India.

Govindasamy, K., Elayaraja, M., Karmakar, D., & Das, A. (2026). Ethical and practical implications of robotic exoskeletons in sports medicine. In *Robotics and Artificial Intelligence in Sports Medicine and Sports Services* (pp. 65–99). Elsevier., DOI: 10.1016/B978-0-443-21734-0.00010-X

Grandey, A. A. (2000). Emotion regulation in the workplace: A new way to conceptualize emotional labor. *Journal of Occupational Health Psychology*, *5*(1), 95–110. DOI: 10.1037/1076-8998.5.1.95 PMID: 10658889

Grandey, A. A., & Melloy, R. C. (2017). The state of the heart: Emotional labor as emotion regulation reviewed and revised. *Journal of Occupational Health Psychology*, *22*(3), 407–422. DOI: 10.1037/ocp0000067 PMID: 28150996

Gregg, M. (2013). *Work's intimacy*. John Wiley & Sons.

Gross, J. J. (1998). The emerging field of emotion regulation: An integrative review. *Review of General Psychology*, *2*(3), 271–299. DOI: 10.1037/1089-2680.2.3.271

Gross, J. J. (2015). Emotion Regulation : Current Status and Future Prospects. *Psychological Inquiry*, *26*(1), 1–26. DOI: 10.1080/1047840X.2014.940781

Group, G. S. S. (2025). *From Penthouse To Public Housing: Trump, Mamdani, And The Battle Over The American Dream* (Karoui, H., Ed.).

Gupta, T., Bodhi, R., & Salim, M. (2024). The intersection of information overload, emotional exhaustion, and social media fatigue: A comprehensive literature review. [The Intersection of Information Overload, Emotional Exhaustion, and Social Media Fatigue: A Comprehensive Literature Review]. *Academy of Marketing Studies Journal*, *28*(4), 1–6.

Gurr, G., & Metag, J. (2025). What leads to audience issue fatigue? The role of repetitive news coverage and emotional responses. *International Journal of Communication*, *17*, 5032–5053.

Guy, M. E., Newman, M. A., & Mastracci, S. H. (2022). *Emotional labor: Putting the service in public service* (Updated ed.). Routledge.

Hadi, M. A. (2025). The theme of isolation in *Robinson Crusoe*: AI treatment. *Manar Elsharq Journal for Literature and Language Studies*, *3*(4), 16–30. DOI: 10.56961/mejlls.v3i4.1129

Haktanir, A., Can, N., Seki, T., Kurnaz, M. F., & Dilmaç, B. (2022). Do we experience pandemic fatigue? current state, predictors, and prevention. *Current Psychology (New Brunswick, N.J.)*, *41*(10), 7314–7325. DOI: 10.1007/s12144-021-02397-w

Halian, I., Popovych, I., Mykhailyuk, I., Halian, A., Kononenko, A., Kruglov, K., & Hoian, I. (2025). Dispositional determinants of mental tension in future coaches. *Journal of Physical Education and Sport*, *25*(7), 1343–1352. https://www.researchgate.net/profile/Ihor-Popovych/publication/394144560_Dispositional_determinants_of_mental_tension_in_future_coaches/links/688b45e9c3cb2665f06291d5/Dispositional-determinants-of-mental-tension-in-future-coaches.pdf

Hall, E. T. (1992). *Beyond culture*. Peter Smith.

Han, B.-C. (2015). *The burnout society*. Stanford University Press.

Hans, A., Singh, N. T., Kumar, R., Kumar, A., & Choubey, A., & Suresh. (2024). The psychology behind addictive applications in technology. In *Proceedings of the conference* (pp. 669–672). DOI: 10.1109/IC2PCT60090.2024.10486603

Hardt, M., & Negri, A. (2000). *Empire*. Harvard University Press.

Hardt, M., & Negri, A. (2004). *Multitude: War and democracy in the age of empire*. Penguin Press.

Hartanto, A., Lua, V. Y. Q., Kasturiratna, K. T. A. S., Koh, P. S., Tng, G. Y. Q., Kaur, M., Quek, F. Y. X., Chia, J. L., & Majeed, N. M. (2024). The effect of mere presence of smartphone on cognitive functions: A four-level meta-analysis. *Technology, Mind, and Behavior*, *5*(1), 1–14. DOI: 10.1037/tmb0000123

Hashish, A., & Aly, E. (2025). The silent strain beyond the screen: Conceptualizing digital compassion fatigue in nursing. *BMC Nursing*, *24*(1), 1464. DOI: 10.1186/s12912-025-04143-0

Hautea, S., Parks, P., Takahashi, B., & Zeng, J. (2021). Showing They Care (Or Don't): Affective Publics and Ambivalent Climate Activism on TikTok. *Social Media + Society*, *7*(2), 20563051211012344. DOI: 10.1177/20563051211012344

Hearn, A., & Schoenhoff, S. (2016). From celebrity to influencer: Tracing the diffusion of celebrity value across the data stream. In P. D. Marshall & S. Redmond (Eds.), A companion to celebrity (pp. 194–211). Wiley-Blackwell.

Hearn, A. (2010). Structuring feeling: Web 2.0, online ranking and rating, and the digital'reputation'economy. *Ephemera*, •••, 10.

Heeris Christensen, A. B., Gyrd-Jones, R., & Beverland, M. B. (2024). Dialectical Emotional Labour in Digital Person-branding: The case of digital influencers. *Organization Studies*, *45*(4), 571–591. DOI: 10.1177/01708406231208370

Heiss, R., & Matthes, J. (2023). Social media information literacy and its relationship with information overload and news avoidance. *Computers in Human Behavior*, *140*, 107580.

Heitmayer, M. (2024). The second wave of attention economics: Attention as a universal symbolic currency on social media and beyond. *Interacting with Computers*, *37*(1), 18–29. DOI: 10.1093/iwc/iwae035

Heras-Saizarbitoria, I., Urbieta, L., & Boiral, O. (2022). Organizations' engagement with sustainable development goals: From cherry-picking to SDG-washing? *Corporate Social Responsibility and Environmental Management*, *29*(2), 316–328. DOI: 10.1002/csr.2202

Herman, E. S., & Chomsky, N. (2002). *Manufacturing consent: The political economy of the mass media*. Pantheon Books.

Heßler, P. O., Pfeiffer, J., & Hafenbrädl, S. (2022). When Self-Humanization Leads to Algorithm Aversion. *Business & Information Systems Engineering*, *64*(3), 275–292. DOI: 10.1007/s12599-022-00754-y

Hibbing, J. R., & Theiss-Morse, E. (2002). *Stealth Democracy: Americans' Beliefs About How Government Should Work*. Cambridge University Press., DOI: 10.1017/CBO9780511613722

Hillis, K., Paasonen, S., & Petit, M. (Eds.). (2015). *Networked Affect*. The MIT Press. DOI: 10.7551/mitpress/9715.001.0001

Hipfl, B. (2018). Affect in Media and Communication Studies: Potentials and Assemblages. *Media and Communication*, *6*(3), 5–14. DOI: 10.17645/mac.v6i3.1470

Hochschild, A. R. (1983). *The managed heart: Commercialization of human feeling*. University of California Press.

Hoffner, C. A., & Cohen, E. (2022). The emotional costs of constant connectivity: Fatigue, numbness, and social withdrawal in digital life. Computers in Human Behavior, 135, 107380. [](https://doi.org/)DOI: 10.1016/j.chb.2022.107380

Hofstede, G., Hofstede, G. J., & Minkov, M. (2020). *Cultures and organizations: Software of the mind* (4th ed.). McGraw-Hill.

Holman, E., Garfin, D., & Silver, R. (2014). Media's role in broadcasting acute stress following collective trauma. *Proceedings of the National Academy of Sciences of the United States of America, 111*(1), 93–98. DOI: 10.1073/pnas.1316265110 PMID: 24324161

Holz, C., Bentley, F., Church, K., & Patel, M. (2015). " I ' m just on my phone and they ' re watching TV ": Quantifying mobile device use while watching television. *Proceedings of the ACM International Conference on Interactive Experiences for TV and Online Video.*, 93–102. DOI: 10.1145/2745197.2745210

Horrigan, J. B. (2001, October 31). Part 2: The Internet, Communities, and the Virtual "Third Place." *Pew Research Center*. https://www.pewresearch.org/internet/2001/10/31/part-2-the-internet-communities-and-the-virtual-third-place/

Horton, D., & Wohl, R. (1956). Mass communication and para-social interaction: Observations on intimacy at a distance. *psychiatry, 19*(3), 215-229.

Hristova, D., Jovicic, S., Goebl, B., & Slunecko, T. (2020). The social media game: How gamification shapes our social media engagement. In *Social media and gamification* (pp. 63–94). DOI: 10.1201/9780429274596-8

Huberman, B. A., & Wu, F. (2008). The economics of attention: Maximizing user value in information-rich environments. *Advances in Complex Systems, 11*(4), 487–496. DOI: 10.1142/S0219525908001830

Hudimova, A., Popovŷch, I., Savchuk, O., Liashko, V., Pyslar, A., & Hrys, A. (2021). Research on the relationship between excessive use of social media and young athletes' physical activity. *Journal of Physical Education and Sport, 21*(6), 3364–3373. https://www.researchgate.net/profile/Ihor-Popovych/publication/357538541_Research_on_the_relationship_between_excessive_use_of_social_media_and_young_athletes'_physical_activity/links/61d34644d4500608168930b3/Research-on-the-relationship-between-excessive-use-of-social-media-and-young-athletes-physical-activity.pdf

Huff, C. (2022). Media overload is hurting our mental health. Here are ways to manage headline stress. *Monitor on Psychology, 53*, 20.

Hülsheger, U. R., & Schewe, A. F. (2021). On the costs and benefits of emotional labor: A meta-analysis of three decades of research. *Journal of Occupational Health Psychology*, *26*(2), 89–115. PMID: 21728441

Humphrey, R. H., Ashforth, B. E., & Diefendorff, J. M. (2015). The bright side of emotional labor. *Journal of Organizational Behavior*, *36*(6), 749–769. DOI: 10.1002/job.2019

Hutcheon, L. (1994). *Irony's edge: The theory and politics of irony*. Routledge.

Ibrahim, R. K., Al Sabbah, S., Al-Jarrah, M., Senior, J., Almomani, J. A., Darwish, A., Albannay, F., & Al Naimat, A. (2024). The mediating effect of digital literacy and self-regulation on the relationship between emotional intelligence and academic stress among university students: A cross-sectional study. *BMC Medical Education*, *24*(1), 1309. DOI: 10.1186/s12909-024-06279-0 PMID: 39543568

Ijaz, D., Araja, J., Walker, S., & Mahmoud, M. (2022). Understanding context collapse for social media users. In *Proceedings of the International Conference on Computational Science and Computational Intelligence* (pp. 807–812). DOI: 10.1109/CSCI58124.2022.00147

Illouz, E. (2007). *Cold intimacies: The making of emotional capitalism*. Polity Press.

Illouz, E. (2007). *Cold Intimacies: The Making of Emotional Capitalism*. Polity Press.

In, A., & Barros, L. (2025). Emotional Labor in Pediatric Palliative Care : A Scoping Review. *Nursing Reports*, •••, 1–22. PMID: 40333038

Insco, J. (2025, October 29). *Zohran Mamdani's unlikely coalition: Winning over NYC's Jewish voters*. Al Jazeera. https://www.aljazeera.com/economy/2025/10/29/zohran-mamdanis-unlikely-coalition-winning-over-nycs-jewish

Internet and Mobile Association of India. (2023). *Digital in India report*. IAMAI.

Iyengar, S., & Kinder, D. R. (2010). *News that matters: Television and American opinion*. University of Chicago Press. DOI: 10.7208/chicago/9780226388601.001.0001

Jacobs, A. (2025). *Filter fatigue: Optimization, context erosion, and attention in digital systems. Zenodo*. DOI: 10.5281/zenodo.17425040

Jacoby, J. (2002). Stimulus-organism-response reconsidered: An evolutionary step in modeling (consumer) behavior. *Journal of Consumer Psychology*, *12*(1), 51–57. DOI: 10.1207/S15327663JCP1201_05

Jaikla, P., & Piyakun, A. (2025). Teachers ' Emotional Labor : A Systematic Review. *Journal of Education and Learning*, *2000*(2), 159–171. DOI: 10.5539/jel.v14n2p159

Janáček, E. M., & Balázová, L. J. (2024). Social fatigue and the virtual self in relation to excessive online self-presentation and its impact on real-life social interactions. *Studies in Psychological Science*, *2*(4), 1–8. DOI: 10.56397/SPS.2024.12.01

Jarrahi, M. H., Blyth, D. L., & Goray, C. (2023). Mindful work and mindful technology: Redressing digital distraction in knowledge work. *Digital Business*, *3*(1), 100051. DOI: 10.1016/j.digbus.2022.100051

Jayachandran, S. (2015). The roots of gender inequality in developing countries. *Annual Review of Economics*, *7*(1), 63–88. Advance online publication. DOI: 10.1146/annurev-economics-080614-115404

Jenkins, H. (2006). *Convergence culture: Where old and new media collide*. New York University Press.

Jenkins, H., Ford, S., & Green, J. (2013). *Spreadable media: Creating value and meaning in a networked culture*. New York University Press.

Jeung, D., Kim, C., & Chang, S. (2018). Emotional Labor and Burnout : A Review of the Literature. *Emotional Labor and Burnout : A Review of the Literature, 59*(2), 187–193.

Jingtong, Z. (2023). The attention economy in the new media era: Challenges and recommendations. *International Business and Economics Studies*, *5*(3), 49–56. DOI: 10.22158/ibes.v5n3p49

Jin, M. J., Kim, J. S., Lee, H. S., Kwon, Y. J., Shim, S. H., Choi, B. S., Lee, D.-W., Paik, J.-W., Lee, B. C., Jung, S.-W., & Lee, H. Y. (2020). The impact of emotional exhaustion on psychological factors in workers with secondary traumatic experiences: A multi-group path analysis. *Psychiatry Investigation*, *17*(11), 1064–1072. DOI: 10.30773/pi.2019.0313 PMID: 33190457

Johnson, S. M. (2023). *Work Pressure, Boundary Management, Burnout, and Toxic Work Environments for Remote Learning and Development Workers* (Doctoral dissertation, City University of Seattle).

Ju, Y., & Lee, P. (2025). More Sources Create Greater Audience Engagement: An Investigation into the Relationship Between the Number of News Sources and Audience Responses. *Communication Research*, *0*(0), 00936502251324549. DOI: 10.1177/00936502251324549

Kam, C. (2024). Commentary: Accelerating the science and practice of psychology beyond WEIRD biases: Enriching the landscape through Asian psychology. *Frontiers in Psychology*, *15*, 1260468. DOI: 10.3389/fpsyg.2024.1260468 PMID: 39359965

Kamraju, M. (2025). Wired but weary: Gen Z's complex relationship with online content, digital identity, and social media burnout. *Acta Informatica Malaysia*, *9*(1), 13–21. DOI: 10.26480/aim.01.2025.17.25

Kang, H., & Lou, C. (2022). AI agency vs. human agency: Understanding human–AI interactions on TikTok and their implications for user engagement. *Journal of Computer-Mediated Communication*, *27*(5), zmac014. DOI: 10.1093/jcmc/zmac014

Kant, T. (2020). *Making it personal: Algorithmic personalization, identity, and everyday life*. Oxford University Press. DOI: 10.1093/oso/9780190905088.001.0001

Kapitan, S., van Esch, P., Soma, V., & Kietzmann, J. (2022). Influencer marketing and authenticity in content creation. *Australasian Marketing Journal*, *30*(4), 342–351. DOI: 10.1177/18393349211011171

Kaplan, R., & Kaplan, S. (1989). *The experience of nature: A psychological perspective*. Cambridge University Press.

Kaplan, S. (1995). The restorative benefits of nature: Toward an integrative framework. *Journal of Environmental Psychology*, *15*(3), 169–182. DOI: 10.1016/0272-4944(95)90001-2

Kaplan, S., & Berman, M. G. (2010). Directed attention as a common resource for executive functioning and self-regulation. *Perspectives on Psychological Science*, *5*(1), 43–57. DOI: 10.1177/1745691609356784 PMID: 26162062

Kapur, R. (2015). Gender, violence, and the law in India. *Social & Legal Studies*, *24*(3), 375–398.

Karmakar, D., Das, A., Bhutia, T. O., Govindasamy, K., & Kumar, A. (2026). Integrating Technology in Sports Education: Opportunities and Challenges for Teacher Educators. In Pelafigue, A. L. (Ed.), *Preparing Educators for Complexity and Change* (pp. 257–290). IGI Global Scientific Publishing., DOI: 10.4018/979-8-3373-9494-7.ch008

Katz, Y., & Shifman, L. (2017). Making sense? The structure and meanings of digital memetic nonsense. *Information Communication and Society*, *20*(6), 825–842. DOI: 10.1080/1369118X.2017.1291702

Kaye, D. B. V., Chen, X., & Zeng, J. (2021). The co-evolution of two Chinese mobile short video apps: Parallel platformization of Douyin and TikTok. *Mobile Media & Communication*, *9*(2), 229–253. DOI: 10.1177/2050157920952120

Kazun, A. D., & Malygina, N. (2024). Coping with negative news: Emotional experiences of doomscrolling audiences. *Russian Sociological Review*, *23*(3), 45–62. DOI: 10.19181/inter.2024.16.4.5

Kesner, L., Juríčková, V., Grygarová, D., & Horáček, J. (2025). Impact of media-induced uncertainty on mental health. *JMIR Mental Health*, *12*(1), e68640. DOI: 10.2196/68640 PMID: 40513096

Khadafi, Z. R., Pelita, D., & Gunawan, T. (2025). The Phenomenon of Digital Burnout and Social-Emotional Crisis Among Students: The Role of Counselors in Fostering Digital Balance. *Al-Wa'iyah*, *1*(2), 38–52. DOI: 10.51590/wai.v1i2.13

Khammissa, R. A., Nemutandani, S., Feller, G., Lemmer, J., & Feller, L. (2022). Burnout phenomenon: Neurophysiological factors, clinical features, and aspects of management. *The Journal of International Medical Research*, *50*(9), 03000605221106428. DOI: 10.1177/03000605221106428 PMID: 36113033

Kim, J., & Kim, M. (2022). Rise of social media influencers as a new marketing channel: Focusing on the roles of psychological well-being and perceived social responsibility among consumers. *International Journal of Environmental Research and Public Health*, *19*(4), 2362. DOI: 10.3390/ijerph19042362

Kim, M., & Beehr, T. A. (2021). Emotional labor and organizational behavior in knowledge work. *Human Relations*, *74*(9), 1393–1418. DOI: 10.1177/0018726720925098

Kline, R. B. (2023). *Principles and practice of structural equation modeling* (5th ed.). Guilford Press.

Klinger, U., & Svensson, J. (2018). The end of media logics? On algorithms and agency. *New Media & Society*, *20*(12), 4653–4670. DOI: 10.1177/1461444818779750

Komp, R., Kauffeld, S., & Ianiro-Dahm, P. (2022). Student presenteeism in digital times—A mixed methods approach. *International Journal of Environmental Research and Public Health*, *19*(24), 16982. DOI: 10.3390/ijerph192416982 PMID: 36554861

Korn, A. K. (2025). Informal Home Care in the Digital Transformation: Platform Design and Work Ethics of Care. *Social Sciences (Basel, Switzerland)*, *14*(4), 225. DOI: 10.3390/socsci14040225

Koru, S. (2025, November 3). From Istanbul to New York: How Erdoğan Defeated His "Mamdani" [Substack newsletter]. *Kültürkampf*. https://kulturkampftr.substack.com/p/from-istanbul-to-new-york-how-erdogan

Kovach, B., & Rosenstiel, T. (2021). *The elements of journalism* (4th ed.). Crown Publishing.

Kozyreva, A., Lewandowsky, S., & Hertwig, R. (2020). Citizens versus the internet: Confronting digital challenges with cognitive tools. *Psychological Science in the Public Interest*, *21*(3), 103–156. DOI: 10.1177/1529100620946707

Kusumarini, C. D., Kuncoroyakti, Y. A., & Rahella, L. K. (2024). Analysis of the Content of Tiktok Comments @Dictionarei in A DAY WITH REI PART 350/ SWISS DAY. *Review: Journal of Multidisciplinary in Social Sciences*, *1*(08), 282–302. DOI: 10.59422/rjmss.v1i08.450

Laato, S., Islam, A. N., & Laine, T. H. (2020). Did location-based games motivate players to socialize during COVID-19? *Telematics and Informatics*, *54*, 101458. DOI: 10.1016/j.tele.2020.101458 PMID: 34887611

Lampert, B., Unterrainer, C., & Seubert, C. T. (2019). Exhausted through client interaction—Detached concern profiles as an emotional resource over time? *PLoS One*, *14*(5), e0216031. DOI: 10.1371/journal.pone.0216031 PMID: 31059551

Lampropoulos, G., Barkoukis, V., Burden, K., & Anastasiadis, T. (2021). 360-degree video in education: An overview and a comparative social media data analysis of the last decade. *Smart Learning Environments, 8*(1).

Langlois, G., & Elmer, G. (2018). Impersonal subjectivation from platforms to infrastructures. *Media Culture & Society*, *41*(2), 236–251. DOI: 10.1177/0163443718818374

Laschke, M. (2023). Friction as a means of choice. *Proyecta56. Industrial Design Journal*, *3*(3). Advance online publication. DOI: 10.25267/P56-IDJ.2023.i3.08

Lazarus, R. S., & Folkman, S. (1984). *Stress, appraisal, and coping*. Springer.

Le Masurier, M. (2015). What is slow journalism? *Journalism Practice*, *9*(2), 138–152. DOI: 10.1080/17512786.2014.916471

Lee, A. R., Son, S. M., & Kim, K. K. (2016). Information and communication technology overload and social networking service fatigue: A stress perspective. *Computers in Human Behavior*, *55*, 51–61. DOI: 10.1016/j.chb.2015.08.011

Lee, Y. H., & Cho, H. (2021). The roles of different types of passion in emotional exhaustion and turnover intention among athletic coaches. *International Journal of Sports Science & Coaching*, *16*(3), 465–476. DOI: 10.1177/1747954120976955

Lehto, M. (2022). Ambivalent influencers: Feeling rules and the affective practice of anxiety in social media influencer work. *European Journal of Cultural Studies*, *25*(1), 201–216. DOI: 10.1177/1367549421988958

Lervik-Olsen, L., Andreassen, T. W., & Fennis, B. M. (2023). When enough is not enough: Behavioral and motivational paths to compulsive social media consumption. *European Journal of Marketing*, *58*(2), 519–547. DOI: 10.1108/EJM-12-2022-0898

Lesener, T., Gusy, B., & Wolter, C. (2020). The job demands–resources model: A meta-analytic review of longitudinal studies. *Work and Stress*, *34*(2), 180–205. DOI: 10.1080/02678373.2019.1678762

Lestari, D. A., Primagara, M., Sari, S. A., Meilina, A., Fauziah, S., Sugesti, A. I., & Salwi, A. D. (2024). Meme culture: A study of humor and satire in digital media. *International Journal of Advanced Multidisciplinary Research and Studies*, *4*(4), 134–140. DOI: 10.62225/2583049X.2024.4.4.3013

Li, J., & Zheng, Y. (2023). Information avoidance in the age of COVID-19: A meta-analysis of predictors and outcomes. *Information Processing & Management*, *60*(2), 103188. DOI: 10.1016/j.ipm.2022.103163

Limone, P., & Toto, G. A. (2022). Psychological and emotional effects of digital technology on digitods (14–18 years): A systematic review. *Frontiers in Psychology*, *13*, 938965. DOI: 10.3389/fpsyg.2022.938965 PMID: 35874342

Lindström, B., Bellander, M., Schultner, D. T., Chang, A., Tobler, P. N., & Amodio, D. M. (2021). A computational reward learning account of social media engagement. *Nature Communications*, *12*(1), 1311. DOI: 10.1038/s41467-020-19607-x PMID: 33637702

Litz, B. T., Litz, B. T., & Gray, M. J. (2002). Emotional numbing in posttraumatic stress disorder: Current and future research directions. *The Australian and New Zealand Journal of Psychiatry*, *36*(2), 198–204. DOI: 10.1046/j.1440-1614.2002.01002.x

Liu, X., Weng, X., Qin, H., Ma, S., & Wang, G. (2024). The successful experience of gymnastics world champion coach: An interview analysis. *Frontiers in Psychology*, *15*, 1405589. https://www.frontiersin.org/journals/psychology/articles/10.3389/fpsyg.2024.1405589/full. DOI: 10.3389/fpsyg.2024.1405589 PMID: 39091704

Liu, X., & Zheng, X. (2024). The persuasive power of social media influencers in brand credibility and purchase intention. *Humanities & Social Sciences Communications*, *11*(1), 1–12. DOI: 10.1057/s41599-023-02512-1

Liu, Y. (2024). Digital work, emotion commodification, and moral legitimacy: Transnational bloggers on Chinese social media platforms. *Youth and Globalization*, *5*(2), 271–289. DOI: 10.1163/25895745-05020004

Liu, Y., & He, J. (2021). "Why are you running away from social media?" Analysis of the factors influencing social media fatigue: An empirical data study based on Chinese youth. *Frontiers in Psychology, 12*, 674641. DOI: 10.3389/fpsyg.2021.674641

Livingstone, S., Mascheroni, G., & Staksrud, E. (2018). European research on children's internet use: Assessing the past and anticipating the future. *New Media & Society, 20*(3), 1103–1122. DOI: 10.1177/1461444816685930

Li, Y., Guan, M., Hammond, P., & Berrey, L. E. (2021). Communicating COVID-19 information on TikTok: A content analysis of TikTok videos from official accounts featured in the COVID-19 information hub. *Health Education Research, 36*(3), cyab010. Advance online publication. DOI: 10.1093/her/cyab010 PMID: 33667311

Loh, K. K., & Kanai, R. (2015). How has the internet reshaped human cognition? *The Neuroscientist, 22*(5), 506–520. DOI: 10.1177/1073858415595005 PMID: 26170005

Lorenz-Spreen, P., Mønsted, B. M., Hövel, P., & Lehmann, S. (2019). Accelerating dynamics of collective attention. *Nature Communications, 10*(1), 1759. DOI: 10.1038/s41467-019-09311-w PMID: 30988286

Lou, C. (2022). Social media influencers and followers: Theorization of a trans-parasocial relation and explication of its implications for influencer advertising. *Journal of Advertising, 51*(1), 4–21. DOI: 10.1080/00913367.2021.1880345

Lowes, S. (2016). Kinship systems, gender norms, and household bargaining: Evidence from the matrilineal belt. *JEL Classification, January.*

Lukoff, K., Lyngs, U., Zade, H., Liao, J. V., Choi, J., Fan, K., Munson, S. A., & Hiniker, A. (2021). How the design of YouTube influences user sense of agency. In *Proceedings of the CHI Conference on Human Factors in Computing Systems*. DOI: 10.1145/3411764.3445467

Lu, Y. Y., Lu, X. M., Shao, C. Y., Wang, C. C., Xu, T. T., & Zhang, B. L. (2022). Empathetic nursing with mindful cognitive therapy for fatigue, depression, and negative emotions in leukemia patients undergoing long-term chemotherapy. *World Journal of Clinical Cases, 10*(6), 1826–1833. DOI: 10.12998/wjcc.v10.i6.1826 PMID: 35317141

Lv, F. (2025). Impact of effort-reward imbalance, emotional labour, and nurse-patient relationship on physical and mental health of registered nurses in China : A structural equation modeling. *Impact of Effort-Reward Imbalance, Emotional Labour, and Nurse-Patient Relationship on Physical and Mental Health of Registered Nurses in China. Structural Equation Modeling*. PMID: 40369545

Lyon, D. (2018). *The culture of surveillance: Watching as a way of life*. Polity Press.

M, A. (2025). Digital Burnout: How overstimulation impacts mental health. *Dua Neuro Care*. https://duaneurocare.com/digital-burnout/

Malhotra, R. (2016). *Being different: An Indian challenge to western universalism*. HarperCollins India.

Mallick, M. (2025). Digital Burnout and Attention Collapse: A Review of Cross-Cultural Psychological Synthesis.

Mallick, M. K. (2025). Beyond individual agency: Rotter's locus of control reconsidered through Indian philosophical frameworks. *International Journal of Interdisciplinary Approaches in Psychology*, *3*(12), 22–35. DOI: 10.61113/ijiap.v3i12.1215

Mallick, M. K., & Mallick, A. (2025). Bridging minds: Psychoanalysis and the Indian knowledge system. *International Journal of Interdisciplinary Approaches in Psychology*, *3*(11), 12–21. DOI: 10.61113/ijiap.v3i11.1201

Maria, C., Carvalho, S., Carolina, A., & Graça, G. (2025). Does professional identity mediate the relationship between emotional labour and work engagement? A study with Portuguese police of fi cers. *International Journal of Police Science & Management*, *27*(1), 113–126. DOI: 10.1177/14613557241292959

Marinucci, M., Pancani, L., Aureli, N., & Riva, P. (2022). Online social connections as surrogates of face-to-face interactions: A longitudinal study under Covid-19 isolation. *Computers in Human Behavior*, *128*, 107102. DOI: 10.1016/j.chb.2021.107102

Mark, G., Gudith, D., & Klocke, U. (2008). The cost of interrupted work: More speed and stress. In *Proceedings of the SIGCHI Conference on Human Factors in Computing Systems* (pp. 107–110). DOI: 10.1145/1357054.1357072

Markiewicz, E. (2020). Third Places in the Era of Virtual Communities. *Studia Periegetica*, *28*(4), 9–21. DOI: 10.26349/st.per.0028.01

Márquez, B. Y., Mitre, A., Magdaleno-Palencia, J. S., & Ramirez-Ramirez, M. (2026). From connection to hyperconnection: A global cultural shift in everyday life when mobile-broadband penetration exceeds 100% (2007–2025). *Journal of Cultural Analysis and Social Change*, 318–328.

Marsh, D., O'Toole, T., & Jones, S. (2007). *Young People and Politics in the UK.*, DOI: 10.1057/9780230625631

Marwick, A. E. (2013). Status update: Celebrity, publicity, and branding in the social media age. yale university press.

Maslach, C., & Jackson, S. E. (1981). The measurement of experienced burnout. *Journal of Organizational Behavior*, *2*(2), 99–113. DOI: 10.1002/job.4030020205

Maslach, C., Jackson, S. E., & Leiter, M. P. (1996). *Maslach Burnout Inventory manual* (3rd ed.). Consulting Psychologists Press.

Maslach, C., & Leiter, M. P. (1997). *The truth about burnout: How organizations cause personal stress and what to do about it.* Jossey-Bass.

Maslach, C., & Leiter, M. P. (2016). Burnout. In Fink, G. (Ed.), *Stress: Concepts, cognition, emotion, and behavior* (pp. 351–357). Academic Press.

Maslach, C., & Leiter, M. P. (2016). *Burnout.* Springer.

Maslach, C., & Leiter, M. P. (2016). Understanding the burnout experience: Recent research and its implications for psychiatry. *World Psychiatry; Official Journal of the World Psychiatric Association (WPA), 15*(2), 103–111. DOI: 10.1002/wps.20311 PMID: 27265691

Maslach, C., & Leiter, M. P. (2022). *The burnout challenge: Managing people's relationships with their jobs.* Harvard University Press.

Massumi, B. (1995). The Autonomy of Affect. *Cultural Critique*, (31), 83–109. JSTOR. DOI: 10.2307/1354446

Massumi, B. (2002). *Parables for the virtual: Movement, affect, sensation.* Duke University Press.

Mathieu, D., & Vengerfeldt, P. P. (2020). Data loop of media and audience. *MedieKultur: Journal of Media and Communication Research, 36*(69), 116–138. DOI: 10.7146/mediekultur.v36i69.121178

Maulida, E. N., Isnaeni, H., & Suwandi, M. A. (2025). Internalisation of Islamic education values through Qur'anic *tadabbur* for emotional detox and Islamic self-healing. *Jurnal Ilmu Pendidikan dan Sains Islam Interdisipliner*, 168–176.

Mbamba, C. R., Dwumah, P., Koomson-Yalley, E., & Adaranijo, E. T. (2026). Riding the waves: Intergenerational digital storytelling to explore coastal flooding experiences. *Global Environmental Change, 97*, 103129. DOI: 10.1016/j.gloenvcha.2026.103129

McArthur, J. A., & White, A. F. (2016). Twitter Chats as Third Places: Conceptualizing a Digital Gathering Site. *Social Media + Society, 2*(3), 2056305116665857. DOI: 10.1177/2056305116665857

McCombs, M. E., & Shaw, D. L. (1972). The agenda-setting function of mass media. *Public Opinion Quarterly, 36*(2), 176–187. DOI: 10.1086/267990

McEwen, B. S. (1998). Protective and damaging effects of stress mediators. *The New England Journal of Medicine*, *338*(3), 171–179. DOI: 10.1056/NEJM199801153380307 PMID: 9428819

McEwen, B. S., & Seeman, T. (1999). Protective and damaging effects of mediators of stress: Elaborating and testing the concepts of allostasis and allostatic load. *Annals of the New York Academy of Sciences*, *896*(1), 30–47. DOI: 10.1111/j.1749-6632.1999.tb08103.x PMID: 10681886

McIntyre, K., & Gyldensted, C. (2017). Constructive journalism: An introduction and practical guide for applying positive psychology techniques to news production. *The Journal of Media Innovations*, *4*(2), 20–34. DOI: 10.5617/jomi.v4i2.2403

McStay, A. (2018). Digital advertising and adtech: Programmatic platforms, identity and moments. In *The advertising handbook* (pp. 88–100). Routledge. DOI: 10.4324/9781315558646-7

Mdhluli, N. I. (2025). Perils of perpetual connectivity: Navigating the 'always-on'culture in the modern workplace. *SA Journal of Human Resource Management*, *23*, 3019. DOI: 10.4102/sajhrm.v23i0.3019

Meegasdeniya, S., & Dulnath, V. (2023). Mindfulness Techniques For Digital Wellbeing. *This was a research paper our team did as research assignment we have submitted to lecturer and medium only.*

Mehrabian, A., & Russell, J. A. (1974). *An approach to environmental psychology*. the MIT Press.

Melimopoulos, E. (2025, November 4). *NYC mayoral election: Candidates, polls, results and what's at stake*. Al Jazeera. https://www.aljazeera.com/news/2025/11/4/nyc-mayoral-election-candidates-polls-results-and-whats-at-stake

Mesmer-Magnus, J., DeChurch, L., & Wax, A. (2022). Moving emotional labor research forward: A meta-analysis of emotional labor in digital and hybrid work. *Journal of Organizational Behavior*, *43*(5), 789–812.

Mesquita, B. (2022). *Between us: How cultures create emotions*. W. W. Norton.

Meta Platforms, Inc. (2023). Annual report 2022. https://investor.fb.com/investor-news/press-release-details/2023/Meta-Reports-Fourth-Quarter-and-Full-Year-2022-Results/

Michel, F., & Gandon, F. (2024). Pay attention: A call to regulate the attention market and prevent algorithmic emotional governance. In *Proceedings of the AAAI/ACM Conference on AI Ethics and Society, 7*, 971–983. DOI: 10.1609/aies.v7i1.31696

Microsoft. (2015). *Attention spans. Consumer insights report.* Microsoft Canada.

Milli, S., Carroll, M., Wang, Y., Pandey, S., Zhao, S., & Dragan, A. D. (2025). Engagement, user satisfaction, and the amplification of divisive content on social media. *PNAS Nexus*, *4*(3), pgaf062. Advance online publication. DOI: 10.1093/pnasnexus/pgaf062 PMID: 40070432

Mishra, B., & Chowdhury, A. (2022). Internet Memes Are Impacting Society: Perspectives from Brand Communication to World Peace Promotion. In *North-East Research Conclave* (pp. 33–48). Springer Nature Singapore.

Misra, S., & Stokols, D. (2012). Psychological and health outcomes of perceived information overload. *Environment and Behavior*, *44*(6), 737–759. DOI: 10.1177/0013916511404408

Moeller, S. D. (2002). *Compassion fatigue: How the media sell disease, famine, war and death.* Routledge. DOI: 10.4324/9780203900352

Mojumder, B., Uddin, M. J., & Dey, K. (2025). Perspectives, preparedness and challenges of the abrupt transition of emergency online learning to traditional methods in higher education of Bangladesh in the post-pandemic era. *Discover Education*, *4*(1), 33. DOI: 10.1007/s44217-025-00417-6

Momoh, E. Y., Adamu, M., & Isa, A. A. (2025). The effects of multitasking on cognitive performance and productivity: A comparative analysis. *Journal of Management Science and Entrepreneurship*. DOI: 10.70382/bejmse.v9i7.042

Montag, C., & Elhai, J. D. (2023). On social media design, (online-)time well spent and addictive behaviors in the age of surveillance capitalism. *Current Addiction Reports*, *10*(3), 610–616. DOI: 10.1007/s40429-023-00494-3

Montalvo, F. L., Miuccio, M., & Waldfogle, G. E. (2021). Ethical design of social technology. In *Advances in human and social aspects of technology* (pp. 20–47). DOI: 10.4018/978-1-7998-6453-0.ch002

Mora Pedreros, P. A., & Santiago Pajajoy, M. J. (2025). Ethical challenges of AI in Byung-Chul Han's theory. In *Proceedings of the Mexican Congress on Artificial Intelligence* (pp. 294–301). Springer Nature Switzerland.

Mühlhof, R. (2018). *Affective resonance* [Author's Manuscript]. https://docs.rainermuehlhoff.de/muehlhoff_2019_affective-resonance-key-concepts-preprint.pdf

Mukta, K. J., & Akter, S. Effect of Social Support on Mental Health: The Study of Social Networks in Times of Crisis.

Müller, R., Schischke, D., Graf, B., & Antoni, C. H. (2023). How can we avoid information overload and techno-frustration as a virtual team? The effect of shared mental models of information and communication technology on information overload and techno-frustration. *Computers in Human Behavior, 138*, 107438. DOI: 10.1016/j.chb.2022.107438

Muyidi, A. (2025). Exploring how social media usage shapes self-presentation strategies among Saudi young adults. *Frontiers in Psychology, 16*, 1562917. Advance online publication. DOI: 10.3389/fpsyg.2025.1562917 PMID: 40420990

Nabi, R. L., & Myrick, J. G. (Eds.). (2023). *Emotions in the Digital World: Exploring Affective Experience and Expression in Online Interactions*. Oxford University Press. DOI: 10.1093/oso/9780197520536.001.0001

Napoli, P. (2019). *Social media and the public interest: Media regulation in the disinformation age*. Columbia University Press. DOI: 10.7312/napo18454

Newlands, G., Lutz, C., & Fieseler, C. (2018). Collective action and provider classification in the sharing economy. *New Technology, Work and Employment, 33*(3), 1–18. DOI: 10.1111/ntwe.12119

Newman, N., Arguedas, A. R., Robertson, C. T., Nielsen, R. K., & Fletcher, R. (2025). *Digital News Report 2025 | Reuters Institute for the Study of Journalism*. Reuters Institute & University of Oxford. https://reutersinstitute.politics.ox.ac.uk/digital-news-report/2025

Newman, N., Fletcher, R., Eddy, K., Robertson, C., & Nielsen, R. (2023). *Reuters Institute digital news report 2023*. Reuters Institute for the Study of Journalism.

Newman, N., Fletcher, R., Schulz, A., Andi, S., Robertson, C., & Nielsen, R. K. (2022). *Reuters Institute digital news report 2022. Digital Journalism*. Reuters Institute for the Study of Journalism.

Newport, C. (2016). *Deep work*. Grand Central Publishing.

Newport, C. (2019). *Digital minimalism: Choosing a focused life in a noisy world*. Portfolio.

Nielsen, L. Y., Krøjer, J., & Nielsen, M. L. (2025). The entanglement of emotional labour and digital work platforms. *MedieKultur: Journal of Media and Communication Research, 40*(78). Advance online publication. DOI: 10.7146/mk.v40i78.137268

Norman, A. (2021). *Exploring Technology's Vital Role in Digital Connectivity and Human Disconnection* (Doctoral dissertation, Northcentral University).

Nor, N. F. M., Iqbal, N., & Shaari, A. H. (2025). The Role of False Self-Presentation and Social Comparison in Excessive Social Media Use. *Behavioral Sciences (Basel, Switzerland), 15*(5), 675. DOI: 10.3390/bs15050675 PMID: 40426453

Nurani, G. A., Nafis, R. Y., Ramadhani, A. N., Prastiwi, M., Hanif, N., & Ardianto, D. (2022). Online learning impacts on academic burnout: A literature review. *Journal of Digital Learning and Education*, *2*(3), 150–158. DOI: 10.52562/jdle.v2i3.433

Nye, J. S.Jr, & Keohane, R. O. (1971). Transnational Relations and World Politics: An Introduction. *International Organization*, *25*(3), 329–349. DOI: 10.1017/S0020818300026187

Odell, J. (2019). *How to do nothing: Resisting the attention economy*. Melville House.

Oh, C., Herrera, F., & Bailenson, J. (2019). The effects of immersion and real-world distractions on virtual social interactions. *Cyberpsychology, Behavior, and Social Networking*, *22*(6), 365–372. DOI: 10.1089/cyber.2018.0404 PMID: 31188686

Okhueleigbe, O. A., & Omoko, N. (2025). Technoference, technopola, and hyperconnectivity: An interpretive journalism perspective. *The Abuja Communicator*, *5*(1), 47–63.

Okonkwo, I., & Namkoisse, E. (2023). The role of influencer marketing in building authentic brand relationships online. *Journal of Digital Marketing and Communication*, *3*(2), 81–90. DOI: 10.53623/jdmc.v3i2.350

Oldenburg, R. (1999). *The great good place: Cafés, coffee shops, bookstores, bars, hair salons, and other hangouts at the heart of a community*. Marlowe ; Distributed by Publishers Group West.

Oliveira, F. B., D'Angelo, C., & Moreno, A. (2023). Emotional responses to COVID-19 news exposure and their implications for news avoidance. *Online Media and Global Communication*, *2*(1), 87–103.

Ophir, Y., & Walter, N. (2021). Gender-based violence in media: Effects on perceptions, empathy, and policy attitudes. Psychology of Violence, 11(1), 87–98. [](https://doi.org/)DOI: 10.1037/vio0000358

Orben, A., Meier, A., Dalgleish, T., & Blakemore, S. (2024). *Mechanisms linking social media use to adolescent mental health vulnerability*. Mechanisms Linking Social Media Use to Adolescent Mental Health Vulnerability. DOI: 10.1038/s44159-024-00307-y

Ou, M., Zheng, H., Kim, H. K., & Chen, X. (2023). A meta-analysis of social media fatigue: Drivers and a major consequence. *Computers in Human Behavior, 140*, 107597. DOI: 10.1016/j.chb.2022.107597

Oxenham, J. (2017). *Literacy: writing, reading and social organisation*. Routledge. DOI: 10.4324/9781351236508

Özkan, R., Akar, O. O., Uzun, R. N., İmamoğlu, O., Kımıl, K., & Yılmaz, N. H. (2026). An Examination of the Effects of Athletes' Social Media Addiction and Sports Burnout Levels on Their Emotional Commitment to Their Teams. *International Journal of Disabilities Sports & Health Sciences*, *9*(1), 11–23. https://dergipark.org.tr/en/pub/ijdshs/article/1800955. DOI: 10.33438/ijdshs.1800955

Oz, M., & Yanik, A. (2024). Fear of surveillance: Examining Turkish social media users' perception of surveillance and willingness to express opinions on social media. *Mediterranean Politics*, *29*(1), 1–25. DOI: 10.1080/13629395.2022.2046911

Paasonen, S. (2016). Fickle focus: Distraction, affect and the production of value in social media. *First Monday*. Advance online publication. DOI: 10.5210/fm.v21i10.6949

Paasonen, S. (2018). Affect, data, manipulation and price in social media. *Distinktion : Scandinavian Journal of Social Theory*, *19*(2), 214–229. DOI: 10.1080/1600910X.2018.1475289

Palmié, M., Miehé, L., Oghazi, P., Parida, V., & Wincent, J. (2022). The evolution of the digital service ecosystem and digital business model innovation in retail: The emergence of meta-ecosystems and the value of physical interactions. *Technological Forecasting and Social Change*, *177*, 121496. DOI: 10.1016/j.techfore.2022.121496

Pal, O., Goyal, A., Chandrasekharan, E., & Saha, K. (2026). The hidden toll of social media news: Causal effects on psychosocial well-being. *Computers in Human Behavior*.

Papacharissi, Z. (2011). A networked self. *A networked self: Identity, community, and culture on social network sites*, 304-318.

Papacharissi, Z. (2014). *Affective Publics: Sentiment, Technology, and Politics*. Oxford University Press., DOI: 10.1093/acprof:oso/9780199999736.001.0001

Papacharissi, Z. (2015). *Affective publics: Sentiment, technology, and politics*. Oxford University Press.

Papacharissi, Z. (2016). Affective publics and structures of storytelling: Sentiment, events and mediality. *Information Communication and Society*, *19*(3), 307–324. DOI: 10.1080/1369118X.2015.1109697

Paredes-Labra, J., Solana-Domínguez, I., Ramos-Ramiro, M., & Freitas-Cortina, A. (2025). Techno-pessimistic shock and the banning of mobile phones in secondary schools: The case of Madrid. *Social Sciences (Basel, Switzerland)*, *14*(7), 441. DOI: 10.3390/socsci14070441

Paul, S., Pruessner, L., Strakosch, A., Miano, A., Schulze, K., Barnow, S., Paul, S., Pruessner, L., Strakosch, A., Miano, A., Schulze, K., & Barnow, S. (2023). *Emotion Social Contexts Examining the Strategy-Situation Fit of Emotion Regulation in Everyday Social Contexts*. Emotions.

Pellegrino, A. (2024). Social comparison, problems of digital consumption and its implications. In *Decoding Digital Consumer Behavior: Bridging Theory and Practice* (pp. 113–131). Springer Nature Singapore. DOI: 10.1007/978-981-97-3454-2_8

Peña, A. M., Meier, L., & Nah, A. M. (2023). Exhaustion, adversity, and repression: Emotional attrition in high-risk activism. *Perspectives on Politics*, *21*(1), 27–42. DOI: 10.1017/S1537592721003273

Peng, L., Wang, J., & Zheng, N. (2024). Traversing Emotional Spaces : Social Media Affordances and Emotion Regulation in Times of Physical Isolation. *Traversing Emotional Spaces : Social Media Affordances and Emotion Regulation in Times of Physical Isolation*. DOI: 10.1177/20563051241237273

Pereira, A. D. C. (2023). *Emotional response and cognitive performance in digital environments: an exploratory study* (Doctoral dissertation).

Petersen, A. (2022). *Emotions online: Feelings and affordances of digital media*. Routledge. DOI: 10.4324/9781003147435

Pew Research Center. (2021). The state of online harassment. Pew Research Center. https://www.pewresearch.org/internet/2021/01/13/the-state-of-online-harassment/

Pew Research Center. (2022). *News consumption across social media platforms*. Pew Research Center.

Pilkington, E. (2025, November 6). How Mamdani built an 'unstoppable force' that won over New York. *The Guardian*. https://www.theguardian.com/us-news/2025/nov/06/zohran-mamdani-campaign-new-york-democrats

Poleac, G., & Ghergut-Babii, A. N. (2024). How social media algorithms influence the way users decide-perspectives of social media users and practitioners. *Technium Soc. Sci. J.*, *57*, 69–81. DOI: 10.47577/tssj.v57i1.10955

Polizzi, C. P., & Lynn, S. J. (2021). Regulating emotionality to manage adversity: A systematic review of the relation between emotion regulation and psychological resilience. *Cognitive Therapy and Research*, *45*(4), 577–597. DOI: 10.1007/s10608-020-10186-1

Porter, J., Spence, K., & Porter, J. (2025). Navigating gendered display rules : Women coaches practicing gender through emotional labour. *Sports Coaching Review*, *00*(00), 1–13. DOI: 10.1080/21640629.2025.2496864

Posner, M. I., & Rothbart, M. K. (2007). Research on attention networks as a model for the integration of psychological science. *Annual Review of Psychology*, *58*(1), 1–23. DOI: 10.1146/annurev.psych.58.110405.085516 PMID: 17029565

Prasetyo, A. R., Handayaningrum, W., & Rahayu, E. W. (2025, January). Digital fatigue and cognitive overload: Psychological challenges in the era of cyber education at Universitas Negeri Malang. In *Prosiding Seminar Pendidikan Seni Budaya* (Vol. 2).

Priego, E. (2024). Finding equilibrium in a hyperconnected world: The struggle against burnout. DOI: 10.59350/9rxbb-45j13

Prodnik, J. A. (2025). *Power asymmetries in the algorithmic formation of public opinion*. Dialogues on Digital Society., DOI: 10.1177/29768640251385702

Przybylski, A. K., Murayama, K., DeHaan, C. R., & Gladwell, V. (2013). Motivational, emotional, and behavioral correlates of fear of missing out. *Computers in Human Behavior*, *29*(4), 1841–1848. DOI: 10.1016/j.chb.2013.02.014

Putnam, R. D. (2000). *Bowling alone: The collapse and revival of American community*. Simon & Schuster.

Qin, C., Li, Y., Wang, T., Zhao, J., Tong, L., Yang, J., & Liu, Y. (2024). Too much social media? Unveiling the effects of determinants in social media fatigue. *Frontiers in Psychology*, *15*, 1277846. DOI: 10.3389/fpsyg.2024.1277846 PMID: 39108425

Quinn, C., Hillman, A., Barbosa, A., & Toms, G. (2026). Emotional Labor in Dementia Research. *Qualitative Health Research*, *36*(4-5), 319–332. DOI: 10.1177/10497323241274709 PMID: 39417805

Qureshi, I., & Bhatt, B. (2024). Social media-induced polarisation. *Information Systems Journal*, *34*(4), 1425–1431. DOI: 10.1111/isj.12525

Rachmad, Y. E. (2023). Social Media Impact Theory.

Rachmad, Y. E. (2025). *The Influencer's Power: Transforming Behavior through Viral and Gimmick Strategies*. United Nations Economic and Social Council.

Radtke, T., Apel, T., Schenkel, K., Keller, J., & von Lindern, E. (2022). Digital detox: An effective solution in the smartphone era? A systematic literature review. *Mobile Media & Communication, 10*(2), 190–215. DOI: 10.1177/20501579211028647

Ragolane, M., & Patel, S. (2025). Too much, too fast: Understanding AI fatigue in the digital acceleration era. *International Journal of Arts, Humanities &. Social Science*, *6*(8), 53–60. DOI: 10.56734/ijahss.v6n8a7

Ragu-Nathan, T. S., Tarafdar, M., Ragu-Nathan, B. S., & Tu, Q. (2008). The consequences of technostress for end users in organizations: Conceptual development and empirical validation. *Information Systems Research, 19*(4), 417–433. DOI: 10.1287/isre.1070.0165

Raichle, M. E., & Gusnard, D. A. (2002). Appraising the brain's energy budget. *Proceedings of the National Academy of Sciences of the United States of America, 99*(16), 10237–10239. DOI: 10.1073/pnas.172399499 PMID: 12149485

Rani, S., Pionera, M., Kuswandi, D., & Wedi, A. (2025). Optimization of instructional technology for attention span in the digital generation. *Pedagogika: Jurnal Pedagogika dan Dinamika Pendidikan, 13*(2), 383–393. DOI: 10.30598/pedagogika-vol13issue2page383-393

Rao, K. R., & Paranjpe, A. C. (2016). *Psychology in the Indian tradition*. Springer., DOI: 10.1007/978-81-322-2440-2

Raval, N., & Dourish, P. (2016). Standing Out from the Crowd : Emotional Labor, Body Labor, and Temporal Labor in Ridesharing. *Proceedings of the 19th ACM Conference on Computer-Supported Cooperative Work & Social Computing.*, 97–107. DOI: 10.1145/2818048.2820026

Ravindran, T., Chua, A. Y. K., & Goh, D. H. (2013). Characteristics of social network fatigue. In *Proceedings of the International Conference on Information Technology: New Generations* (pp. 431–438). DOI: 10.1109/ITNG.2013.66

Ravindran, T., Chua, A. Y. K., & Goh, D. H. (2014). Antecedents and effects of social network fatigue. *Journal of the Association for Information Science and Technology, 65*(11), 2306–2320. DOI: 10.1002/asi.23122

Rayland, A., & Andrews, J. (2023). From social network to peer support network: Opportunities to explore mechanisms of online peer support for mental health. *JMIR Mental Health, 10*, e41855. DOI: 10.2196/41855

Reckwitz, A. (2017). Practices and their affects. In *The Nexus of Practices*. Routledge.

Reddit. (2023). r/depression_memes. https://www.reddit.com/r/depression_memes/

Rheingold, H. (1993). *The virtual community: Homesteading on the electronic frontier*. Reading, Mass.: Addison-Wesley Pub. Co. http://archive.org/details/virtualcommunity00rhei

Ridanpää, J. (2009). Geopolitics of Humour: The Muhammed Cartoon Crisis and the *Kaltio* Comic Strip Episode in Finland. *Geopolitics, 14*(4), 729–749. DOI: 10.1080/14650040903141372

Rider, S. (2021). Higher education: Learning how to pay attention. In *Debating higher education: Philosophical perspectives* (pp. 81–94). DOI: 10.1007/978-3-030-69628-3_6

Ridout, B., Campbell, A., & Ellis, L. (2020). 'Off the Record': Exploring the role of social media in mental health help-seeking for young people. *JMIR Mental Health, 7*(7), e18324. DOI: 10.2196/18324

Riffe, D., Lacy, S., & Fico, F. (2006). *Analyzing Media Messages: Using Quantitative Content Analysis in Research* (2nd ed.). Routledge., DOI: 10.4324/9781410613424

Rixen, J. O., Meinhardt, L., Glöckler, M., Ziegenbein, M., Schlothauer, A., Colley, M., Rukzio, E., & Gugenheimer, J. (2023). The loop and reasons to break it: Investigating infinite scrolling behaviour in social media applications and reasons to stop. *Proceedings of the ACM on Human-Computer Interaction, 7*(MHCI), 1–22. DOI: 10.1145/3604275

Roberts, T. (2019). Feeling nothing: Numbness and emotional absence. *European Journal of Philosophy, 27*(1), 187–198. DOI: 10.1111/ejop.12375

Roemmich, K. (2023). Emotion AI at Work : Implications for Workplace Surveillance, Emotional Labor, and Emotional Privacy. In *CHI '23: ACM Conference on Human Factors in Computing Systems, April 23â•fi28, 2023,Hamburg, Germany* (Vol. 1, Issue 1). Association for Computing Machinery. DOI: 10.1145/3544548.3580950

Rofarello, A. M., Torino, P., Russis, L. De, & Torino, P. (2021). Coping with Digital Wellbeing in a Multi-Device World. *Coping with Digital Wellbeing in a Multi-Device World.*

Roffarello, M. (2018). AwareNotifications : Multi-Device Semantic Notification Handling with User-Defined Preferences. *Journal of Ambient Intelligence and Smart Environments, 10*(December), 327–343. Advance online publication. DOI: 10.3233/AIS-180492

Rogers, B. (2016). Employment Rights in the Platform Economy : Getting Back to Basics. *Employment Rights in the Platform Economy : Getting Back to Basics.*

Rooksby, J., Asadzadeh, P., Rost, M., Morrison, A., & Chalmers, M. (2016). Personal Tracking of Screen T ime on Digital Devices. *Proceedings of the 2016 CHI Conference on Human Factors in Computing Systems.* DOI: 10.1145/2858036.2858055

Rosen, L. D. (2012). *iDisorder*. Palgrave Macmillan.

Rosenblat, A., & Stark, L. (2016). Algorithmic Labor and Information Asymmetries : A Case Study of Uber ' s Drivers. *International Journal of Communication, 10*, 3758–3784.

Rosen, L. D. (2017). The distracted student mind—Enhancing its focus and attention. *Phi Delta Kappan, 99*(2), 8–14. DOI: 10.1177/0031721717734183

Rosenwein, B. H., & Cristiani, R. (2019). *Duygular Tarihi Nedir* (Özdil, K., Trans.). Islık Yayınları.

Roy, S. (2014). The Delhi gang rape: The making of a global feminist issue. *Feminist Studies*, *40*(2), 282–292.

Ruckenstein, M. (2023). *The Feel of Algorithms.* University of California Press.

Ruggieri, R. A., & Mollo, M. (2025). Connected but isolated and suddenly diagnosed: Algorithmic malaise. *Human Arenas*, 1–21.

Salehi, M., Ghasemian, A., Najar, A. V., Nazari, H., & Hooshmand, E. (2025). From compassion to burnout : Emotional labor in oncology nursing — a qualitative study. *BMC Nursing*, *24*(1), 272. DOI: 10.1186/s12912-025-02928-x PMID: 40069779

Samson, A. C., Glynn, M. A., & Gross, J. J. (2021). Humor as an emotion regulation strategy. *Psychological Science*, *32*(4), 591–602. DOI: 10.1177/0956797620969409

Sánchez-Muñoz, M., Jiménez-González, G., & Nieves-Alegre, E. (2025). Challenges and opportunities in the attention economy in the digital age. In *ECORFAN eBooks* (pp. 85–99). DOI: 10.35429/H.2025.3.85.99

Santiago-Torner, C., Corral-Marfil, J. A., & Tarrats-Pons, E. (2025). Artificial intelligence and the reconfiguration of emotional well-being (2020–2025): A critical reflection. *Societies (Basel, Switzerland)*, *16*(1), 6. DOI: 10.3390/soc16010006

Santos, L. C. O., & Alves, M. M. (2023). Social media burnout and internet addiction: The role of extroversion and social self-concept in a Brazilian sample. *Personality and Individual Differences*. Advance online publication. DOI: 10.1177/00332941231174390 PMID: 37147190

Sapolsky, R. M. (2004). *Why zebras don't get ulcers* (3rd ed.). Holt Paperbacks.

Saraswati, S. S. (2009). *Prana and Pranayama*. Yoga Publications Trust.

Satici, S. A.. (2022). Development of the doomscrolling scale and its psychological correlates. *Current Psychology (New Brunswick, N.J.)*.

Saulnier, L. (2019). *Moral Identity*. Moral Disengagement, and Online Behaviour from Adolescence to Young Adulthood.

Schneider, N., Nabben, K., Tamari, R., & Zargham, M. (2025). Online governance surfaces and attention economies. *OSF Preprints*. DOI: 10.33767/osf.io/cdrmp_v1

Schreurs, L., Meier, A., & Vandenbosch, L. (2023). Exposure to the positivity bias and adolescents' differential longitudinal links with social comparison, inspiration and envy depending on social media literacy. *Current Psychology (New Brunswick, N.J.)*, *42*(32), 28221–28241. DOI: 10.1007/s12144-022-03893-3 PMID: 36373115

Schuett, K. C. (2024). How do students and teachers respond to digital distraction in school? In *Digital education and learning* (pp. 85–94). DOI: 10.1007/978-3-031-53215-3_5

Schüll, N. D. (2004). Digital gambling: The coincidence of desire and design. *The Annals of the American Academy of Political and Social Science*, *597*(1), 65–81. DOI: 10.1177/0002716204270435

Schüll, N. D. (2012). *Addiction by design*. Princeton University Press. DOI: 10.2307/j.ctt12f4d0

Schulz, A. D., Schöllgen, I., Wendsche, J., Fay, D., & Wegge, J. (2021). The dynamics of social stressors and detachment: Long-term mechanisms impacting well-being. *International Journal of Stress Management*, *28*(3), 207–219. DOI: 10.1037/str0000216

Schumann, C.. (2022). When news topics annoy: Exploring issue fatigue and media overexposure. *Journal of Medicine*, *3*(3), 521–536.

Selimoğlu, Z. (2025). Goffman'ın Dramaturjik Yaklaşımı Bağlamında Instagram'da Benlik Sunumu: Influencer Örneği. *Journal of West European Social Sciences*, *2*(1), 149–165.

Serrano-Puche, J. (2016). Key features of digital media consumption: Implications of users' emotional dimension. In *Advances in intelligent systems and computing* (pp. 471–477). DOI: 10.1007/978-3-319-46068-0_62

Sevignani, S. (2022). Digital transformations and the ideological formation of the public sphere: Hegemonic, populist, or popular communication? *Theory, Culture & Society*, *39*(4), 91–109. DOI: 10.1177/02632764221103516

Shabahang, R.. (2024). Doomscrolling evokes existential anxiety and pessimistic worldviews. *Computers in Human Behavior Reports*.

Shafique, S. (2024). The impact of social media on political engagement: A double-edged sword. *Research Consortium Archive*, *2*(3), 141–149. DOI: 10.62019/24s60j71

Shahsavar, Y., & Choudhury, A. (2025). Effectiveness of evidence-based mental health apps on user health outcome: A systematic literature review. *PLoS One*, *20*(3), e0319983. DOI: 10.1371/journal.pone.0319983 PMID: 40131942

Shao, Y. (2025). The Impact of Digital Media on Modern Society and Culture. *Commun. Humanit. Res*, *57*(1), 117–122. DOI: 10.54254/2753-7064/2025.22829

Sharpe, A. T., Tyndall, I., Poulus, D. R., Obine, E. A., & Sharpe, B. T. (2026). The influence of doomscrolling on mental health: a scoping review. *Mental Health and Digital Technologies*, 1-53.

Shaviro, S. (2010). *Post cinematic affect*. Zero Books.

Sheng, N., & Zhang, S. (2023). Too much overload and concerns: Antecedents of social media fatigue and the mediating role of emotional exhaustion. *Computers in Human Behavior*, *139*, 107500. DOI: 10.1016/j.chb.2022.107500

Shifman, L. (2014). *Memes in digital culture*. MIT Press.

Shin, D. (2024). Misinformation, extremism, and conspiracies: Amplification and polarization by algorithms. In *Digital misinformation studies* (pp. 49–78). DOI: 10.1007/978-3-031-52569-8_3

Shin, D., & Shin, E. Y. (2025). Cascading falsehoods: Mapping the diffusion of misinformation in algorithmic environments. *AI & Society*, , 1–18.

Shin, I., Riforgiate, S. E., Godager, E. A., & Coker, M. C. (2025). Remote Worker Communication Technology Use Related to Role Clarity, Coworker Support, and Work Overload. *Sustainability (Basel)*, *17*(7), 2830. DOI: 10.3390/su17072830

Shirazi, A. S. (2015). Assessment of Notifications on Smartwatches. *Proceedings of the 17th International Conference on Human-Computer Interaction with Mobile Devices and Services*, 1111–1116. DOI: 10.1145/2786567.2794338

Shouse, E. (2005). Feeling, Emotion, Affect. *M/C Journal, 8*(6). DOI: 10.5204/mcj.2443

Shukla, P. (2025). Coded emotions: Digital humanities at the crossroads of narrative design and mental spaces. *International Journal of Research and Analytical Reviews*.

Silva, H. M. (2025). The reconfiguration of social bonds in the digital age: Virtual connections vs. face-to-face relationships. *Nature Anthropology*, *3*(1), 10003. DOI: 10.70322/natanthropol.2025.10003

Singh, P., Bala, H., Dey, B. L., & Filieri, R. (2022). Enforced remote working: The impact of digital platform-induced stress and remote working experience on technology exhaustion and subjective wellbeing. *Journal of Business Research, 151*, 269–286. DOI: 10.1016/j.jbusres.2022.07.002 PMID: 35847196

Singh, R. (2025). The algorithm effect: How social media shapes your thinking. *International Journal of Advanced Research in Science. Tongxin Jishu, 529–531*, 529–531. Advance online publication. DOI: 10.48175/IJARSCT-28066

Skovsgaard, M., & Andersen, K. (2020). Conceptualizing news avoidance. *Journalism Studies*, *21*(4), 459–476. DOI: 10.1080/1461670X.2019.1686410

Skulmowski, A., & Xu, K. M. (2022). Understanding cognitive load in digital and online learning: A new perspective on extraneous cognitive load. *Educational Psychology Review*, *34*(1), 171–196. DOI: 10.1007/s10648-021-09624-7

Smart, P. (2018). Emerging Digital Technologies. *Extended epistemology*, 266.

Smith, K., Sheridan, L., Duursma, E., Alonzo, D., Smith, K., Sheridan, L., Duursma, E., Alonzo, D., Smith, K., Sheridan, L., Duursma, E., & Alonzo, D. (2025). theory and practice Teachers ' emotional labour : The joys, demands, and constraints constraints. *Teachers and Teaching*, *31*(8), 1411–1435. DOI: 10.1080/13540602.2025.2466560

Smith, L., Jacob, L., Trott, M., Yakkundi, A., Butler, L., Barnett, Y., Armstrong, N. C., McDermott, D., Schuch, F., Meyer, J., López-Bueno, R., Sánchez, G. F. L., Bradley, D., & Tully, M. A. (2020). The association between screen time and mental health during COVID-19: A cross sectional study. *Psychiatry Research*, *292*, 113333. DOI: 10.1016/j.psychres.2020.113333 PMID: 32738551

Somani, P. P., Iyer, V., Wani, P. S., & Tambuskar, D. P. (2025). Engagement in an age of distraction. In *IGI Global eBooks* (pp. 269–302). DOI: 10.4018/979-8-3693-8089-5.ch010

Sontag, S. (2003). *Regarding the pain of others*. Farrar, Straus and Giroux. DOI: 10.3917/dio.201.0127

Sood, A., & Jones, D. T. (2013). On mind wandering, attention, brain networks, and meditation. *Explore (New York, N.Y.), 9*(3), 136–141. DOI: 10.1016/j.explore.2013.02.005 PMID: 23643368

Soraci, P., Griffiths, M. D., Bevan, N., Pisanti, R., Trovato, M., Servidio, R., D'Aleo, E., Campedelli, L., Gallo, F., & Satici, S. A. (2025). Psychometric analysis of the Italian doomscrolling scale. *Current Psychology (New Brunswick, N.J.), 44*(12), 11872–11883. DOI: 10.1007/s12144-025-07976-9

Soroka, S. (2025, December 4). *Everything everywhere all at once: How Zohran Mamdani campaigned both online and with a ground game*. The Conversation. DOI: 10.64628/AAI.ktt3ymgeu

Soror, A., Steelman, Z. R., & Turel, O. (2022). Exhaustion and dependency: A habituation–sensitization perspective on the duality of habit in social media use. *Information Technology & People, 35*(1), 67–95. DOI: 10.1108/ITP-11-2019-0603

Soroya, S. H., Farooq, A., Mahmood, K., Isoaho, J., & Zara, S. (2021). From information seeking to information avoidance: Understanding the health information behavior during a global health crisis. *Information Processing & Management, 58*(2), 102440. DOI: 10.1016/j.ipm.2020.102440 PMID: 33281273

Soukup, C. (2006). Computer-mediated communication as a virtual third place: Building Oldenburg's great good places on the world wide web. *New Media & Society, 8*(3), 421–440. DOI: 10.1177/1461444806061953

Spectrum News. (2025). *NYC Democratic Primary Debate For Mayor | Full NY1 Coverage* [Video recording]. https://www.youtube.com/watch?v=ElGfMRIox9w

Srnicek, N. (2017). *Platform capitalism*. John Wiley & Sons.

Staab, P., & Thiel, T. (2022). Social media and the digital structural transformation of the public sphere. *Theory, Culture & Society, 39*(4), 129–143. DOI: 10.1177/02632764221103527

Steinert, S., & Dennis, M. J. (2022). Emotions and digital well-being: On social media's emotional affordances. *Philosophy & Technology, 35*(2), 36. DOI: 10.1007/s13347-022-00530-6 PMID: 35450167

Steinkuehler, C., & Williams, D. (2006). Where Everybody Knows Your (Screen) Name: Online Games as "Third Places.". *Journal of Computer-Mediated Communication, 11*(4), 885–909. DOI: 10.1111/j.1083-6101.2006.00300.x

Stevens, R. E., Loudon, D. L., Yow, D. A., Bowden, W. W., & Humphrey, J. H. (2013). *Stress in college athletics: Causes, consequences, coping*. Routledge. https://api.taylorfrancis.com/content/books/mono/download?identifierName=doi&identifierValue=10.4324/9781315043593&type=googlepdf

Stewart, D. (2025, June 29). How Social Media Videos Fueled Zohran Mamdani's Success. *The New York Times*. https://www.nytimes.com/2025/06/29/nyregion/zohran-mamdani-campaign-videos.html

Stiegler, B. (2010). *For a new critique of political economy* (Ross, D., Trans.). Polity Press.

Subrahmanyam, S. (2025). Psychological Impact of AI Moderation. In Tiwari, S., & Fahrudin, A. (Eds.), *Content Moderation in the Age of AI* (pp. 191–220). IGI Global Scientific Publishing., DOI: 10.4018/979-8-3373-0335-2.ch008

Sulaiman, W. A. W., Malek, M. D. H., Yunus, A. R., Ishak, N. H., Safir, D. M., & Fahrudin, A. (2024). The impact of social media on mental health: A comprehensive review. *South Eastern European Journal of Public Health*, *XXV*, 1468–1482. DOI: 10.70135/seejph.vi.2564

Sundar, P., & Lim, S. (2023). Exposure to sexual and relational violence in digital media and its influence on attitudes toward victims. Journal of Interpersonal Violence, 38(1–2), 337–360. https://doi.org/DOI: 10.1177/08862605211073412

Sun, H., & Wu, R. (2025). Filters, algorithms, and the "imagination tax": The dilemma of aesthetic self-objectification among Chinese young women on social media. *Frontiers in Psychology*, *16*, 1651435. DOI: 10.3389/fpsyg.2025.1651435 PMID: 41488937

Sun, J., Tang, Y., Wang, W., Zhang, Y., Ji, H., & Wang, P. (2025). Multimodal neuroimaging investigation of post-stroke fatigue in middle-aged and older adults: Combining resting-state fMRI and DTI-ALPS analysis. *Frontiers in Aging Neuroscience*, *17*, 1583655. DOI: 10.3389/fnagi.2025.1583655 PMID: 40433512

Supriyadi, T., Sulistiasih, S., Rahmi, K. H., Pramono, B., & Fahrudin, A. (2025). The Impact Of Digital Fatigue On Employee Productivity And Well-Being: A Scoping Literature Review. *Environment And Social Psychology*, *10*(2).

Sustainability Directory. (2025, December 1). *Why is media literacy important for empathetic development?* Lifestyle → Sustainability Directory. https://lifestyle.sustainability-directory.com/question/why-is-media-literacy-important-for-empathetic-development/

Sweller, J. (1988). Cognitive load during problem solving: Effects on learning. *Cognitive Science*, *12*(2), 257–285. DOI: 10.1207/s15516709cog1202_4

Sweller, J. (2011). Cognitive load theory. [). Academic Press.]. *Psychology of Learning and Motivation*, *55*, 37–76. DOI: 10.1016/B978-0-12-387691-1.00002-8

Szűts, Z. (2023). Learning in an attention-based economy and society. *Opus et Educatio*, *9*(4). Advance online publication. DOI: 10.3311/ope.530

Tafesse, W., & Wood, B. P. (2023). Social media influencers' community and content strategy and follower engagement behavior in the presence of competition: An Instagram-based investigation. *Journal of Product and Brand Management*, *32*(3), 406–419. DOI: 10.1108/JPBM-02-2022-3851

Tahreem, I., & Shakeel, H. (2025). Emotional tones (anger, fear and excitement) leads to the propagation of fake news: Literature review on Covid-19 infodemic. *Journal of Media Horizons*, *6*(2), 679–684.

Tandoc, E. C.Jr, Thomas, R. J., & Bishop, L. (2022). Avoiding real news, believing in fake news? Investigating pathways from news avoidance to misinformation belief. *Journalism Studies*, *23*(10), 1256–1273.

Tang, S., Werner-Seidler, A., Torok, M., Mackinnon, A. J., & Christensen, H. (2021). The relationship between screen time and mental health in young people: A systematic review of longitudinal studies. *Clinical Psychology Review*, *86*, 102021. DOI: 10.1016/j.cpr.2021.102021 PMID: 33798997

Tang, Y. Y., Hölzel, B. K., & Posner, M. I. (2015). The neuroscience of mindfulness meditation. *Nature Reviews. Neuroscience*, *16*(4), 213–225. DOI: 10.1038/nrn3916 PMID: 25783612

Tang, Y. Y., & Posner, M. I. (2009). Attention training and attention state training. *Trends in Cognitive Sciences*, *13*(5), 222–227. DOI: 10.1016/j.tics.2009.01.009 PMID: 19375975

Tank, C. (2026, January 1). *Inside Zohran Mamdani's defiant and unruly campaign design, radiant with purpose*. Stir World. https://www.stirworld.com/see-features-inside-zohran-mamdani-s-defiant-and-unruly-campaign-design-radiant-with-purpose

Tàpia-Caballero, P., Serrano-Fernández, M. J., Boada-Cuerva, M., Boada-Grau, J., Assens-Serra, J., & Robert-Sentís, L. (2022). Age, gender, personality, burnout, job characteristics and job content as predictors of driver fatigue. *International Journal of Occupational Safety and Ergonomics*, *28*(4), 2396–2402. DOI: 10.1080/10803548.2021.1991672 PMID: 34633270

Tarafdar, M., Cooper, C. L., & Stich, J. F. (2019). The technostress trifecta-techno eustress, techno distress and design: Theoretical directions and an agenda for research. *Information Systems Journal, 29*(1), 6–42. DOI: 10.1111/isj.12169

Tarafdar, M., Tu, Q., Ragu-Nathan, B. S., & Ragu-Nathan, T. S. (2007). The impact of technostress on role stress and productivity. *Journal of Management Information Systems, 24*(1), 301–328. DOI: 10.2753/MIS0742-1222240109

Taylor, S. H., & Chen, Y. A. (2024). The lonely algorithm problem: The relationship between algorithmic personalization and social connectedness on TikTok. *Journal of Computer-Mediated Communication, 29*(5), zmae017. DOI: 10.1093/jcmc/zmae017

Tek, T., & Özsari, A. (2025). Digital literacy, phubbing, and mental well-being in the digital age: A study on young university athletes. *Frontiers in Psychiatry, 16*, 1638959. https://www.frontiersin.org/journals/psychiatry/articles/10.3389/fpsyt.2025.1638959/full. DOI: 10.3389/fpsyt.2025.1638959 PMID: 40873669

Telles, S., Singh, N., & Balkrishna, A. (2012). Managing mental health disorders resulting from trauma through yoga: A review. *Depression Research and Treatment, 401513*, 1–9. Advance online publication. DOI: 10.1155/2012/401513 PMID: 22778930

Terranova, T. (2000). Free labor: Producing culture for the information age. *Social Text, 18*(2), 33–58. DOI: 10.1215/01642472-18-2_63-33

Terranova, T. (2004). *Network culture*. Pluto Press. DOI: 10.2307/j.ctt183q5pq

Teso. (2019). THE LONG-TERM EFFECT OF DEMOGRAPHIC SHOCKS ON THE EVOLUTION OF GENDER Author (s): Edoardo Teso THE LONG-TERM EFFECT OF DEMOGRAPHIC SHOCKS ON THE EVOLUTION OF GENDER ROLES : EVIDENCE FROM THE. *Journal of the European Economic Association, 17*(2), 497–534. DOI: 10.1093/jeea/jvy010

Thakurta, P. (2015). *Media ethics and accountability in India*. Oxford University Press.

Thompson, M. J., Carlson, D. S., Kacmar, K. M., & Vogel, R. M. (2020). The cost of being ignored: Emotional exhaustion in the work and family domains. *The Journal of Applied Psychology, 105*(2), 186–195. DOI: 10.1037/apl0000433

TikTok. (2020). How TikTok recommends videos #ForYou. TikTok Newsroom. https://newsroom.tiktok.com/en-us/how-tiktok-recommends-videos-for-you

Toffler, A. (1970). *Future shock*. Random House.

Törnberg, P. (2023). Platforms as states: The rise of governance through data power. In *Bristol University Press eBooks* (pp. 42–58). DOI: 10.56687/9781529233551-006

Troy, A. S., Willroth, E. C., Shallcross, A. J., Giuliani, N. R., Gross, J. J., & Mauss, I. B. (2023). Psychological resilience: An affect-regulation framework. *Annual Review of Psychology*, *74*(1), 547–576. DOI: 10.1146/annurev-psych-020122-041854 PMID: 36103999

Tuckey, M. R., Bakker, A. B., & Dollard, M. F. (2023). Empowering leaders optimize working conditions for engagement: A multilevel study. *Journal of Occupational Health Psychology*, *28*(1), 45–59. PMID: 38059984

Tufekci, Z. (2017). *Twitter and tear gas: The power and fragility of networked protest.* Yale University Press. Twitter and Tear Gas

Tufekci, Z. (2015). Algorithmic harms beyond Facebook and Google. *Colorado Technology Law Journal*, *13*, 203–218.

Tufekci, Z. (2017). *Twitter and tear gas: The power and fragility of networked protest.* Yale University Press.

Turkle, S. (2011). *Alone together: Why we expect more from technology and less from each other*. Basic Books.

Turkle, S. (2015). *Reclaiming conversation: The power of talk in a digital age.* Penguin Press.

Turner, K. E. (2025). The Effects of TikTok Use on Mental Health and Personal Well-Being Among Undergraduate Students (Doctoral dissertation, Alliant International University).

Twenge, J. M., Haidt, J., Blake, A. B., McAllister, C., Lemon, H., & Le Roy, A. (2021). Worldwide increases in adolescent loneliness. *Journal of Adolescence*, *93*(1), 257–269. DOI: 10.1016/j.adolescence.2021.06.006 PMID: 34294429

Udupa, S. (2018). Digital media and politics in India. *International Journal of Communication*, *12*, 25–45.

Uetricht, M. (2026, January 7). *How Zohran Mamdani's Campaign Crafted a Winning Message*. Jacobin. https://jacobin.com/2026/01/zohran-mamdani-communications-strategy

Uhls, Y. T., Michikyan, M., Morris, J., Garcia, D., Small, G. W., Zgourou, E., & Greenfield, P. M. (2014). Five days at outdoor education camp without screens improves preteen skills with nonverbal emotion cues. *Computers in Human Behavior*, *39*, 387–392. DOI: 10.1016/j.chb.2014.05.036

Ulrich, R. S., Simons, R. F., Losito, B. D., Fiorito, E., Miles, M. A., & Zelson, M. (1991). Stress recovery during exposure to natural and urban environments. *Journal of Environmental Psychology, 11*(3), 201–230. DOI: 10.1016/S0272-4944(05)80184-7

United States. National Commission for the Protection of Human Subjects of Biomedical, & Behavioral Research. (1978). *The Belmont report: ethical principles and guidelines for the protection of human subjects of research* (Vol. 2). The Commission.

Usman, S.. (2025). Impact of doomscrolling on mental well-being among media users. *Journal of Arts, Humanities &. Social Sciences, 9*(1), 25–39.

Valkenburg, P. M., Meier, A., & Beyens, I. (2022). Social media use and its impact on adolescent mental health: An umbrella review of the evidence. *Current Opinion in Psychology, 44*, 58–68. DOI: 10.1016/j.copsyc.2021.08.017 PMID: 34563980

Van Dijck, J. (2013). *The culture of connectivity: A critical history of social media.* Oxford University Press. DOI: 10.1093/acprof:oso/9780199970773.001.0001

Vercellone, C., & Di Stasio, A. (2023). Free digital labor as a new form of exploitation: A critical analysis. *Science and Society, 87*(3), 334–358. DOI: 10.1521/siso.2023.87.3.334

Verduyn, P., Ybarra, O., Résibois, M., Jonides, J., & Kross, E. (2017). Do social network sites enhance or undermine subjective well-being? A critical review. *Social Issues and Policy Review, 11*(1), 274–302. DOI: 10.1111/sipr.12033

Vinney, C. (2021, November 30). *What is media psychology?* Verywell Mind. https://www.verywellmind.com/what-is-media-psychology-5210628

Vogel, E. A., Rose, J. P., Roberts, L. R., & Eckles, K. (2014). Social comparison, social media, and self-esteem. *Psychology of Popular Media Culture, 3*(4), 206–222. DOI: 10.1037/ppm0000047

Voinea, C., Marin, L., & Vică, C. (2024). Digital slot machines: Social media platforms as attentional scaffolds. *Topoi, 43*(3), 685–695. DOI: 10.1007/s11245-024-10031-0

Voinea, D. V. (2025). Reconceptualizing gatekeeping in the age of artificial intelligence: A theoretical exploration of artificial intelligence-driven news curation and automated journalism. *Journalism and Media, 6*(2), 68. DOI: 10.3390/journalmedia6020068

Voitenko, E., Myronets, S., Osodlo, V., Kushnirenko, K., & Kalenychenko, R. (2021). Influence of Emotional Burnout on Coping Behavior in Pedagogical Activity. *International journal of organizational leadership, 10*(2).

Vranken, I., Schreurs, L., Noon, E. J., & Vandenbosch, L. (2023). Understanding the relations between exposure to positive self-portrayals and mental health.... *Cyberpsychology (Brno)*, *17*(1). Advance online publication. DOI: 10.5817/CP2023-1-5

Wagh, R. K., & Packirisamy, P. (2025). Emotional labor in the digital workplace: A study of its effects on job satisfaction among remote professionals. [JRISS]. *Journal of Research in Innovative Social Sciences*, *9*(3), 4523–4529. DOI: 10.47772/IJRISS.2025.903SEDU0324

Wahl-Jorgensen, K. (2018). The emotional architecture of social media. In *Emotions, media and politics* (pp. 77–93). DOI: 10.4324/9781315193434-6

Walther, J. B. (2011). Theories of computer-mediated communication and interpersonal relations. In Knapp, M. L., & Daly, J. A. (Eds.), *The SAGE handbook of interpersonal communication* (4th ed., pp. 443–479). SAGE Publications.

Wang, B., Liu, Y., Qian, J., & Parker, S. K. (2023). Achieving effective remote working during the COVID-19 pandemic: A work design perspective. *Applied Psychology*, *72*(1), 16–59. DOI: 10.1111/apps.12290 PMID: 33230359

Wang, D., Xie, X., Tian, H., Wu, T., Liu, C., Huang, K., Gong, R., Yu, Y., Luo, T., Jiao, R., & Zhang, L. (2022). Mental fatigue and negative emotion among nurses during the COVID-19 pandemic. *Current Psychology (New Brunswick, N.J.)*, *41*(11), 8123–8131. DOI: 10.1007/s12144-022-03468-2 PMID: 35854701

Wang, H., Ding, H., & Kong, X. (2023). Understanding technostress and employee well-being in digital work: The roles of work exhaustion and workplace knowledge diversity. *International Journal of Manpower*, *44*(2), 334–353. DOI: 10.1108/IJM-08-2021-0480

Wang, K., Varma, D. S., & Prosperi, M. (2018). A systematic review of the effectiveness of mobile apps for monitoring and management of mental health symptoms or disorders. *Journal of Psychiatric Research*, *107*, 73–78. DOI: 10.1016/j.jpsychires.2018.10.006 PMID: 30347316

Ward, A. F., Duke, K., Gneezy, A., & Bos, M. W. (2017). Brain drain: The mere presence of one's own smartphone reduces available cognitive capacity. *Journal of the Association for Consumer Research*, *2*(2), 140–154. DOI: 10.1086/691462

Warren, C., Barsky, A., & McGraw, A. P. (2021). What makes things funny? An integrative review of the antecedents of laughter and amusement. *Personality and Social Psychology Review*, *25*(1), 41–65. DOI: 10.1177/1088868320961909 PMID: 33342368

Watzl, S. (2022). The ethics of attention: An argument and a framework. In *The ethics of attention* (pp. 89–112). DOI: 10.4324/9781351202114-6

Weber, D. L., Bygholm, A. K. M., & Kanstrup, A. M. (2024). Digital coping strategies of young people living with cognitive disabilities: Using emotion-focused and problem-focused coping in digital relationships. *Disability & Society*, *39*(8), 2007–2031. DOI: 10.1080/09687599.2023.2181767

Weber, D., Voit, A., Kratzer, P., & Henze, N. (2016). In-Situ Investigation of Notifications in Multi-Device Environments. *Proceedings of the 2016 ACM International Joint Conference on Pervasive and Ubiquitous Computing.*, 1259–1264. DOI: 10.1145/2971648.2971732

Webster, J. G. (2016). *The marketplace of attention: How audiences take shape in a digital age*. MIT press.

Weisser, R. A. (2024). Attention cycles, crisis coverage, and declining public engagement with conflict news. *World Development*, *176*, 106389.

Weiss, H. M., & Cropanzano, R. (1996). Affective events theory. *Research in Organizational Behavior*, *18*(1), 1–74.

Wharton, A. S. (2009). The sociology of emotional labor. *Annual Review of Sociology*, *35*(1), 147–165. DOI: 10.1146/annurev-soc-070308-115944

Williams, J. (2018). *Stand out of our light*. Cambridge University Press. DOI: 10.1017/9781108453004

Wohllebe, A. (2020). Consumer acceptance of app push notifications: Systematic review on the influence of frequency. *International Journal of Interactive Mobile Technologies*, *14*(13), 36. DOI: 10.3991/ijim.v14i13.14563

Wolfers, L. N., & Schneider, F. M. (2021). Using Media for Coping : A Scoping Review. *Communication Research*, *30–32*(8), 1210–1234. Advance online publication. DOI: 10.1177/0093650220939778

Wolfson, S., Demopoulos, A., & Niami, S. (2025, November 5). New York parties for Zohran Mamdani: 'The first time we've had hope in so long.' *The Guardian*. https://www.theguardian.com/us-news/2025/nov/05/zohran-mamdani-new-york-cheers-tears-dsa-chants

Wright, S. (2012). From "Third Place" to "Third Space": Everyday Political Talk in Non-Political Online Spaces. *Javnost - The Public*, *19*(3), 5–20. DOI: 10.1080/13183222.2012.11009088

Wu, A., Scult, M. A., Barnes, E. D., Betancourt, J. A., Falk, A., & Gunning, F. M. (2021). Smartphone apps for depression and anxiety: A systematic review and meta-analysis of techniques to increase engagement. *NPJ Digital Medicine*, *4*(1), 20. DOI: 10.1038/s41746-021-00386-8 PMID: 33574573

Wu, T. (2016). *The attention merchants*. Knopf.

Wu, T. (2016). *The attention merchants: The epic scramble to get inside our heads*. Knopf.

Xu, J., He, Z., Guo, D., & Ding, Y. (2026). Relationship between news overload and news avoidance: A meta-analysis. *Journalism*, *27*(3), 776–796. DOI: 10.1177/14648849241299667

Yang, X., & Du, J. (2024). The effect of teacher self-efficacy, online pedagogical and content knowledge, and emotion regulation on teacher digital burnout: A mediation model. *BMC Psychology*, *12*(1), 51. DOI: 10.1186/s40359-024-01540-z

Yao, L., Gao, J., Zhang, Y., & Zhang, H. (2024). Micro-breaks in focus : Mitigating emotional labour impact in the hospitality industry from a conservation of resources perspective. *Anatolia*, *00*(00), 1–15. DOI: 10.1080/13032917.2024.2363813

Yaşar, Ö. (2024). Siyasi Mizah ve Y Kuşağı. *Journal of Turkish Studies, 13*(Volume 13 Issue 18), 1389–1407. DOI: 10.7827/TurkishStudies.13844

Yıldızgörür, M. R. (2023). 'Ne Önemi Var?' Okuyucuların Haberden Kaçınma Davranışları Üzerine Nitel Bir Araştırma. *Etkileşim*, *6*(11), 266–290. DOI: 10.32739/etkilesim.2023.6.11.197

Yılmaz, Ö. (2021). Emeğin Değişen Yüzü: Dijital Emek Sömürüsü. *Simetrik İletişim Araştırmaları Dergisi*, *2*(2), 68–78.

Yin, H., Huang, S., & Wang, W. (2022). Emotional labor and burnout in knowledge-intensive professions: A systematic review. *Frontiers in Psychology*, *13*, 821233. DOI: 10.3389/fpsyg.2022.821233

Ytre-Arne, B. (2023). *Media use in digital everyday life*. Emerald Publishing. DOI: 10.1108/9781802623833

Yue, Z., Zhang, H., Kim, S., Baruh, L., & Tamul, D. (2022). COVID-19 memes and coping: A multiple-method investigation. *Computers in Human Behavior*, *128*, 107094. DOI: 10.1016/j.chb.2021.107094

Yürür, S., & Ünlü, A. G. O. (2011). Duygusal emek, duygusal tükenme ve işten ayrılma niyeti ilişkisi. ISGUC The Journal of Industrial Relations and Human Resources, 13(2).

Zanger, J. (2025, November 5). *Zohran Mamdani wins NYC mayoral election after energizing young voters with focus on affordability—CBS New York.* CBS News. https://www.cbsnews.com/newyork/news/mamdani-wins-nyc-mayoral-election-2025/

Zapf, D. (2002). Emotion work and psychological well-being: A review of the literature and some conceptual considerations. *Human Resource Management Review, 12*(2), 237–268. DOI: 10.1016/S1053-4822(02)00048-7

Zayed, A. M. (2025). The Mediating Role of Self-Regulated Learning and Digital Wisdom in the Relationship Between Digital Stress and Academic Flourishing Among Undergraduate Students. *Sohag University International Journal of Educational Research, 11*(11), 69–104. DOI: 10.21608/suijer.2025.343529.1015

Zhang, J. (2025). *The emotional economy in social media platforms: An analysis of algorithm-driven user engagement and commercial value. Highlights in Art and Design, 14*(4)

Zhang, Y., Tu, Z., Zhao, W., & He, L. (2022). Design of emotional branding communication model based on system dynamics in social media environment and its influence on new product sales. *Frontiers in Psychology, 13*, 959986. DOI: 10.3389/fpsyg.2022.959986 PMID: 35983199

Zhao, D., & Zhou, Y. (2022). Examining the psychometric properties of the controlling coach behaviors scale in Chinese elite athletes. *PLoS One, 17*(11), e0277985. https://journals.plos.org/plosone/article?id=10.1371/journal.pone.0277985. DOI: 10.1371/journal.pone.0277985 PMID: 36441802

Zhao, J., Zhou, Z., Sun, B., Zhang, X., Zhang, L., & Fu, S. (2022). Attentional bias is associated with negative emotions in problematic users of social media as measured by a dot-probe task. *International Journal of Environmental Research and Public Health, 19*(24), 16938. DOI: 10.3390/ijerph192416938 PMID: 36554818

Zhelnina, A. (2020). Apathy Syndrome: How We Are Trained Not to Care about Politics. *Social Problems, 67*(2), 358–378. DOI: 10.1093/socpro/spz019

Zhou, W., Zhang, Y., Xie, B., & Lu, Y. (2025). Balancing the Impact of Cyberbullying on Academic Performance: The Moderating Role of Sports Engagement. *SAGE Open, 15*(4), 21582440251401115. DOI: 10.1177/21582440251401115

Zilka, G. C. (2021). Feelings of belonging or alienation and social emotional perceptions of immigrant youths in the digital age, in comparison with native-born youths. *Education and Information Technologies, 26*(2), 1937–1954. DOI: 10.1007/s10639-020-10333-x

Zubair, U., Khan, M. K., & Albashari, M. (2023). Link between excessive social media use and psychiatric disorders. *Annals of Medicine and Surgery (London), 85*(4), 875–878. DOI: 10.1097/MS9.0000000000000112 PMID: 37113864

Zuboff, S. (2019). *The age of surveillance capitalism*. PublicAffairs.

Zuboff, S. (2019). *The age of surveillance capitalism: The fight for a human future at the new frontier of power, edn*. PublicAffairs.

Zuboff, S. (2019). *The age of surveillance capitalism: The fight for a human future at the new frontier of power*. PublicAffairs.

Zuboff, S. (2023). The age of surveillance capitalism. In *Social theory re-wired* (pp. 203–213). Routledge. DOI: 10.4324/9781003320609-27

Zulli, D., & Zulli, D. J. (2022). Extending the internet meme: Conceptualizing technological mimesis and imitation publics. *New Media & Society, 24*(8), 1876–1894. DOI: 10.1177/1461444820983603

About the Contributors

Ayten Bengisu Cansever Bayhan received her Ph.D. in Public Relations and Publicity from Istanbul University, where her dissertation examined the intersections of neoliberal governmentality, positive psychology, and digital media cultures. She holds a Master's degree in Interpersonal Communication and a Bachelor's degree in Communication and Sociology, both from Marmara University. In addition, she is a certified Family Counselor, bringing an interdisciplinary understanding of psychological and communicative processes into her academic work. She currently serves as a Research Assistant Doctor in the Department of Visual Communication Design at Istanbul Gelişim University, Faculty of Fine Arts. Her teaching and research focus on media psychology, communication sociology, new media, and digital game studies. Dr. Bayhan's scholarly interests revolve around how emotions, subjectivity, and power are negotiated through digital technologies. Her recent works explore algorithmic intimacy, affective governance, digital self-presentation, and the psychopolitics of media environments. Combining critical theory, affect studies, and cultural analysis, her research contributes to understanding how contemporary media ecosystems shape individual behavior, social relations, and emotional life. She has presented and published in national and international contexts, integrating empirical and theoretical perspectives to analyze the evolving relationship between media, psychology, and society.

***

Gauri Singh Bhadauria is a distinguished Assistant Professor and Researcher in Commerce, driven by a passion for knowledge advancement and academic excellence. With a robust academic foundation and extensive research experience, she has authored numerous publications in prestigious journals and presented at international conferences. As a devoted educator, Gauri empowers students through mentorship, nurturing their critical thinking and love for learning. Her writing reflects her commitment to sharing insightful perspectives and contributing to impactful discussions in the field of Commerce.

Piali Haldar earned her MBA from the Institute of Rural Management Anand and completed her PhD at Birla Institute of Technology, Mesra. Her core areas of specialization include rural marketing, rural development, branding strategy, and consumer behaviour. With over 20 years of experience in academia and research, she has published extensively in renowned journals listed in ABDC and Scopus. She has authored one textbook on Marketing and edited three academic books. Dr. Haldar has presented her research at numerous national and international conferences and has contributed more than 50 papers to reputed journals, edited volumes, and conference proceedings.

Rashid Hashmi is a distinguished TV journalist and academician with over 22 years of versatile experience in broadcast journalism and media education. Currently serving as Professor of Practice at the Sharda School of Media, Film & Entertainment, Sharda University, he blends rich industry insights with academic excellence to empower the next generation of media professionals. Prof. Hashmi's career spans key roles such as Executive Editor and Senior Anchor at India News, Editor-in-Chief at FM News, and senior editorial positions at ETV and Total News. His anchoring style and editorial acumen have earned him national acclaim, including the prestigious ENBA Best Anchor Awards for his impactful coverage of the Pakistan Political Crisis (2022) and the Sri Lanka Crisis (2023). In academia, Prof. Hashmi has significantly contributed to curriculum design, faculty mentoring, and industry-academia collaboration. At Sharda University, he leads all TV production work, mentors the Anchoring-Reporting Club, and manages the institutional media platforms Sharda TV and Sharda Samachar. He has pioneered podcasting initiatives at SSMFE and successfully organized flagship events like the Media Fusion Summit and Global Leadership Award, bringing industry leaders and influencers to campus. A Gold Medalist in Mass Communication and currently a Ph.D. scholar at IFTM University, Prof. Hashmi's research focuses on "Emergence of Digital Medium and AI: Navigating Challenges in a Changing Media Landscape." He has authored five IGI-GLOBAL book chapters, contributed to national publications, and presented research at multiple international conferences. Two of his upcoming research papers are set to be published in Scopus-indexed journals. His scholarly impact is matched by his innovation in media technology. He holds two patents: one for an AI-based system enhancing real-time decision-making in autonomous vehicles, and another for an IoT-enabled solar energy monitoring device. Prof. Hashmi is also a prolific content creator, known for his dynamic presence on YouTube and Instagram. He actively engages in knowledge dissemination through documentaries like Ayodhya Tere Kitne Ram and special reports such as Operation Meghprahar and Sarhad Ka Aakhri Gaanv. His ground-level reporting of landmark events including the 26/11 Mumbai attacks and Delhi bomb blasts underscores his frontline journalistic rigor. With a passion for bridging the gap between classroom learning and industry practice, Prof. Hashmi continues to inspire students through his teaching on anchoring, podcasting, digital media, and broadcast techniques. He remains committed to cultivating ethically grounded, tech-savvy, and industry-ready media professionals.

J.A. Jevin is an Assistant Professor in the Department of Computer Science and Engineering at Koneru Lakshmaiah Education Foundation, Andhra Pradesh. He completed his Bachelor's degree in Computer Science and Engineering from Anna University, Chennai, in 2006, and his Master's degree in Computer Science and Engineering from Anna University, Tirunelveli, in 2012. He is currently pursuing his Ph.D. in Computer Science and Engineering at SRM Institute of Science and Technology, Ramapuram Campus, Chennai. His research interests include Deep Learning and Data Science. He has been actively involved in teaching and research, contributing to academic development in his field.

Vishal Jain currently serves as a Professor and Dean of Accreditation, Statutory Compliances & Institutional Development at the School of Engineering & Technology, Vivekananda Institute of Professional Studies - Technical Campus, New Delhi. His previous roles include Professor at Sharda University, Greater Noida, and Associate Professor at Bharati Vidyapeeth's Institute of Computer Applications and Management (BVICAM), New Delhi. Dr. Jain has actively participated in various academic governance bodies, including the Faculty Board, Board of Planning and Management, Executive Council, Academic Council, Curriculum Development and Review Committee, and Academic Audit across multiple higher education institutions. He collaborates with Kuala Lumpur University of Science and Technology (KLUST), Malaysia, Lincoln University College, Malaysia and the Research Institute of IoT Cybersecurity at National Kaohsiung University of Science and Technology in Taiwan for research initiatives. He has supervised three Ph.D. candidates, with two additional scholars currently pursuing their degrees under his guidance.

Sudhanshu Joshi currently working as a Reader in Operations & Supply Chain Management Area, Doon University, INDIA. He is the Adjunct Faculty in the area of Technology Management with School of Technology, Doon University. He is into the Editorial Board of leading Technology and Operations Management Journals published by Elsevier, Springer, Emerald, Inderscience and IGI Global. His research interest anchored within Digital-Twin, Cyber Supply Chain Management with special focus on green supply chain network design, sustainable supply chain design, and coordination in humanitarian supply chain network, application of big data analytics in sustainable and humanitarian supply chains, emerging technologies (Including Industry 4.0), Circular Economy, Agriculture Supply Chain and Softcomputing Applications in Supply Chain Management. Dr. Sudhanshu Joshi is also guest editor with few Book series including Intelligent Systems Reference Library and Greening the Industry. He is member with leading Societies including CSI, IEEE, POMS, INFORMS. ORCID: http://orcid.org/0000-0003-4748-5001 SCOPUS AUTHOR ID: 56111179800

Debajit Karmakar, is a distinguished research scholar and accomplished academic in the field of Physical Education and Sports Science. Currently pursuing his Ph.D. at the prestigious Lakshmibai National Institute of Physical Education (LNIPE), Gwalior, he has established himself as a prolific researcher. Mr. Karmakar completed his educational journey with remarkable academic excellence, earning his B.A./B.Sc. (Hons) in Physical Education from Visva-Bharati University, Santiniketan, followed by his B.P.Ed. from the same institution where he topped in his class. His Master's degree in Physical Education is from LNIPE, and he subsequently qualified UGC NET-JRF & WBSET examinations, demonstrating his academic prowess. A specialist in football and sports psychology, Mr. Karmakar has made significant contributions to academic literature with extensive publications in Scopus & Web of Science indexed journals. His research focuses on mental training, performance psychology, and innovative training methodologies. He has authored multiple books on sports psychology and performance enhancement, while also serving as editor for several academic publications.

Manoj Mallick is a Senior Faculty member with a PhD in Psychology and over three decades of teaching and research experience since 1991. His academic interests span positive psychology, mental health, the Indian Knowledge System (IKS), criminal psychology, ethnic diversity, and gender equity. He has also contributed significantly to scholarship in psychological measurement theory, neurodiversity, and institutional accountability, reflecting his commitment to methodological rigor and inclusive practice. His recent publications in leading journals have examined locus of control and psychological well-being among youth in specific socio-cultural contexts, emphasizing the intersection of individual agency and structural determinants. Building on this foundation, his current research explores psychosocial learner support in under-resourced settings, systemic models of school-based counselling, and task-shifting interventions for community mental health. His broader intellectual pursuits include rural women's empowerment through digital micro-enterprises, intersectionality in education and work, resilience in cancer care, psychological safety and emotional intelligence in organizational contexts, socio-psychological implications of Green AI, algorithmic justice and workplace dignity, and the dynamics of cognitive dissonance in decision-making. He actively participates in national seminars, faculty development programs, and interdisciplinary collaborations across India, advancing scholarship that integrates cultural relevance, ethical clarity, and social impact.

Dev Kumar Mandal currently serves as an Assistant Professor in the Department of Management at Brainware University, Kolkata. Before this, he worked at ICRA Analytics Ltd and Shriram Finance Ltd. He holds an MBA in Finance and a Bachelor of Commerce degree from Vidyasagar University. Additionally, he has successfully cleared the UGC NET and WB SET examinations in Management.

Srishti Muralidharan is a UGC NET qualified postgraduate in Clinical Psychology and an Assistant Professor of Psychology in PES University, RR Nagar Bangalore. Her areas of interest include Clinical Psychology, Indian Psychology, Philosophy, Gender and Sexuality, Social Psychology and Neuropsychology. She has published a paper titled 'Mental Health Literacy for Depression and Schizophrenia among Undergraduate Students' in the International Journal of Indian Psychology. She has also co-authored several book chapters. She is a practicing psychologist and believes in making mental health care accessible to all.

Arpita Nayak is currently serving as an Assistant Professor, offering courses in management. She completed her Ph.D. in management from the KIIT School of Management. Her MBA and strong interest in Human Resource Management (HRM) led her to pursue further studies in HRM. Her passion for talent management inspired her doctoral research on "A Comparative Study on Talent Management in Private and Public Manufacturing Industries in Odisha." Dr. Nayak has presented research papers at both national and international conferences and has published articles in SCOPUS-listed journals. Over the years, she has taught a variety of subjects, including Human Resource Management, Principles of Management, Business Studies Management, Tribal Entrepreneurship, and Organizational Behaviour. In addition to her academic career, she also has several years of corporate work experience.

Rajendra Singh Negi is a media professional and academician specializing in journalism, media studies, and communication research. He began his career as a journalist, bringing a practice-oriented perspective to his teaching and scholarly work. He holds a Ph.D. in Mass Communication from HNB Garhwal University, a Central University. His academic interests include communication theory, media studies, and emerging trends in new media. He has published research papers in reputed national and international journals. Dr. Negi is actively involved in curriculum development, research supervision, and academic administration, and has mentored students at undergraduate, postgraduate, and doctoral levels. He is recognized for his contributions to media education and for promoting regional languages and culture. He currently serves as an Associate Professor at Shri Guru Ram Rai University, Dehradun.

Kumari Pallavi is currently serving as an Assistant Professor in the Department of Mass Communication, bringing with her over three years of teaching experience. She has been associated with Galgotias University since 2021 and actively contributes to academic and administrative responsibilities, including serving as the department-level IQAC coordinator. Her academic interests primarily lie in Development Communication and Intercultural Communication, along with areas such as Communication Research, Advertising, and Mass Communication Theories. Dr. Pallavi holds a Ph.D. in Mass Communication from Tezpur University, Assam, along with an M.Phil from Mahatma Gandhi Antarrashtriya Hindi Vishwavidyalaya (Wardha), an M.A. in Mass Communication from Makhanlal Chaturvedi National University of Journalism and Communication, Bhopal (where she was a Gold Medalist), and a B.A. (Hons.) in Journalism and Mass Communication from Patna Women's College, Patna University. Her research contributions include publications on green marketing, development communication among the Tharu community, media literacy, gender portrayal in media, and multiculturalism in new media. She has also enhanced her practical media skills through certification courses in audio production, video production, and photojournalism. Additionally, she has successfully qualified the UGC NET in Mass Communication and Journalism multiple times between 2013 and 2016, reflecting her strong academic foundation and commitment to excellence in teaching and research.

Shivendu Kumar Rai is working as a Head of Department in the Tecnia Institute of Advanced Studies, Rohini, New Delhi. Before that, he worked as Assistant Professor at Galgotias University, Greater Noida and as Acting Dean and assistant Professor, Faculty of Professional Studies, Department of Journalism and Mass Communication, Rama University, Kanpur (U.P.) He has done Graduation in Mass Media (2011) from Jamia Millia Islamia Central University, and Post-Graduation & M.Phil in Mass Communication (2013 & 2014) from Makhanalal Chaturvedi National University of Journalism and Communication, Bhopal.& Ph.D. (2020) in Mass Communication from Mahatma Gandhi International Hindi University, Wardha (Maharashtra). He has qualified UGC- NET examination twice in 2018 and 2019. He worked as a Doctorate Research Fellow at Indian Council of Social Science Research, New Delhi in PhD Research Topic Project "Changes In the

Communication Strategies of Political Parties: Special Reference to tribal areas of Sonbhadra". Dr. Shivendu Kumar Rai has published 35 full-length research papers in reputed UGC Listed/ Peer Review Research Journals. He has attended 55 Seminars/ Workshops/Conferences/FDP etc. His area of expertise is Communication for Development, New Media Communication Research, and Political Communication.

Nandhini S is a postgraduate student in Psychology with a growing interest in understanding human behaviour within evolving social and digital contexts. Her academic work reflects a strong inclination toward critically engaging with real-world psychological challenges, particularly in areas of emotional well-being, self-regulation, and contemporary mental health practices. She is especially interested in how individuals navigate their emotional lives in increasingly technology-mediated environments. Through her work, she aims to bridge theoretical knowledge with meaningful, context-sensitive insights that contribute to a deeper understanding of psychological experiences in modern society.

Ratan Sarkar is an Assistant Professor in the Department of Education, Tezpur University (A Central University), Assam, India. Previously, he served nearly seven years as Assistant Professor in the Department of Teachers' Training (B.Ed.), Prabhat Kumar College, Contai (Vidyasagar University), and as Guest Faculty at National Institute for Empowerment of Persons with Intellectual Disabilities, Regional Centre, Kolkata. He holds a Ph.D. in Education from Pondicherry University, an M.Ed. and M.Phil. in Special Education from Ramakrishna Mission Vivekananda Educational and Research Institute, Belur Math, and an M.A. in Education and Technology from Tata Institute of Social Sciences, Mumbai. He began his academic journey with a B.Ed. in Special Education (Jadavpur University) and a B.A. in English (Hons) from Siliguri College (University of North Bengal), Darjeeling. Dr. Sarkar has published extensively in leading journals (SAGE, Springer, Routledge, Wiley), authored books, chapters, and reviews, and led projects under the Ministry of Education, Govt. of India. His works on inclusive education, EdTech, disability studies, policy advocacy to advance equitable learning ecosystems.

Esma Nur Sezen serves as a Research Assistant at Marmara University's Faculty of Communication. She is also a PhD candidate in Media Economics and Management, within the Department of Journalism at Marmara University. She holds a Master's degree in Media Economics and Management from the same department, with a thesis examining competition among video streaming services through Porter's Five Forces Model, as well as a Bachelor's degree in Journalism from Marmara University and a Bachelor's degree in Business Administration from Istanbul University. Her scholarly interests lie at the intersection of platform studies, media economics, and the political economy of communication, focusing on platform capitalism and the evolving power dynamics between media organizations and digital platforms.

Satya Subrahmanyam is a distinguished academic leader, researcher, and institutional strategist with over 28 years of experience in higher education, business research, leadership and management. He holds two PhDs and a Postdoctoral qualification from the Polytechnic Institute of Leiria, Portugal. Currently serving as Professor and Dean (Research) at Holy Spirit University of Kaslik (USEK), Lebanon, he spearheads research initiatives that enhance academic excellence and institutional reputation. He played a pivotal role in the development of the Catholic University in Erbil, Kurdistan, where he established new departments, led research programs, and collaborated on international educational projects. As a founding member and Managing Partner of Vignan Institute of Technology and Management, India, he contributed to its transformation into a premier institution. With expertise in AI-driven business strategies, HR analytics, and leadership in technology adoption, he has published extensively, guided PhD research, and led training programs in corporate and academic settings.

Suresh Talamala Currently working as an Assistant Professor, School of Business, Aditya University, Surampalem, Kakinada. He completed his B.B.M. in 2005 and M.B.A. (HRM & Marketing) in 2008 and began his career as an Assistant Professor. He pursued additional qualifications including B.A. (Mathematics & Statistics), M. Com., PGDHRM, and M.A. (English) through distance education. He earned his Ph.D. from Andhra University in 2019 on "Stress management among medical consultants". He qualified UGC-NET twice (2012) and cleared AP SET in Commerce (2016) and Management (2012), and completed 8 NPTEL courses. His research papers published in Scopus and ABDC journals. He teaches Operations Research, Probability & Statistics, Business Research Methods, and Accounting for Managers. He has authored 5 books and 3 book chapter. He has actively participated in several seminars, conferences, workshops, and FDPs, aiming to apply academic research to real-world business challenges.

Muhammad Usman Tariq is a strategic higher education leader and scholar with more than 17 years of international experience across academia, research, and industry. He holds dual doctorates, a PhD in Artificial Intelligence and a Doctorate in Business Administration and has published extensively as the author of research articles, case studies, book chapters, and academic texts. His contributions also include several patents, reflecting his applied research in technology, business, and education. He is the Founder and CEO of TheCaseHQ.com, a global hub for professional certification programmes, narrative and video case studies, and digital learning innovation. In addition, he serves as President of the Gulf Higher Education Network (Gulf HE), an initiative dedicated to advancing academic practice, faculty development, and institutional collaboration across the region. He is a Principal Fellow of Advance HE (UK), Chartered Fellow of the CIPD (UK), Senior Fellow of SEDA (UK), and a Senior Member of IEEE, reflecting his standing as both an academic innovator and a global professional leader.

Varadharajan Bhoopathy is a Professor at Sree Rama Engineering College. He holds a Ph.D. in Information and Communication Engineering from Anna University and has over 16 years of academic experience. Specializing in wireless sensor networks and IoT, he has published numerous research papers and holds several international patents. Dr. Bhoopathy is a recipient of prestigious awards for his contributions to education and research. His commitment to academia continues to drive innovation and excellence in the field of computer science.

Manish Kumar Verma is Associate Professor in Psychology at Lovely Professional University, Phagwara. He is a doctorate from Chatrapati Sahu Ji Maharaj University, Kanpur. He has earned more than 15 years of academic and research experience in reputed institutions. He has 1 book, 22 research publications and book chapters to his credit in national and international journals other than participation in reputed conferences.

Alka Yadav is a Senior Research Fellow in Political Science with interdisciplinary training in law and media studies. She holds a Master's degree in Political Science and is UGC-NET JRF qualified (All India Rank 25). Her research engages with questions of multiculturalism, digital publics, and the politics of representation in contemporary India, with a particular focus on urban contexts such as Bengaluru. She is currently working on themes related to everyday multiculturalism, media narratives, and the intersections of identity, technology, and public policy.

Index

A

B

C

D

E

F

H

I

T

V

W

Z

www.ingramcontent.com/pod-product-compliance
Lightning Source LLC
LaVergne TN
LVHW061532290926
849162LV00004B/765